D0538529

Authorized Self-Study Guide

Designing Cisco Network Service Architectures (ARCH)

Second Edition

Keith Hutton
Mark Schofield
Diane Teare

Cisco Press

800 East 96th Street

Indianapolis, IN 46240

Authorized Self-Study Guide
Designing Cisco Network Service Architectures (ARCH), Second Edition

Keith Hutton
Mark Schofield
Diane Teare

Copyright © 2009 Cisco Systems, Inc.

Published by:
Cisco Press
800 East 96th Street
Indianapolis, IN 46240 USA

Printed in the United States of America

First Printing December 2008

Library of Congress Cataloging-in-Publication Data:

Hutton, Keith.

  Authorized self-study guide : designing Cisco network service architectures (ARCH) / Keith Hutton, Mark Schofield, Diane Teare. -- 2nd ed.
    p. cm.
  ISBN 978-1-58705-574-4 (hardcover)
  1. Computer network architectures--Examinations--Study guides. 2. Computer networks--Design--Examinations--Study guides. 3. Internetworking (Telecommunication)--Examinations--Study guides. I. Schofield,, Mark. II. Teare, Diane. III. Title. IV. Title: Designing Cisco network service architectures (ARCH).
  TK5105.52.H98 2008
  004.6'5--dc22

                        2008049128

ISBN-13: 978-1-58705-574-4

ISBN-10: 1-58705-574-0

Warning and Disclaimer

This book is designed to provide information about designing Cisco network service architectures. Every effort has been made to make this book as complete and as accurate as possible, but no warranty or fitness is implied.

The information is provided on an "as is" basis. The authors, Cisco Press, and Cisco Systems, Inc. shall have neither liability nor responsibility to any person or entity with respect to any loss or damages arising from the information contained in this book or from the use of the discs or programs that may accompany it.

The opinions expressed in this book belong to the author and are not necessarily those of Cisco Systems, Inc.

Trademark Acknowledgments

All terms mentioned in this book that are known to be trademarks or service marks have been appropriately capitalized. Cisco Press or Cisco Systems, Inc., cannot attest to the accuracy of this information. Use of a term in this book should not be regarded as affecting the validity of any trademark or service mark.

Corporate and Government Sales

The publisher offers excellent discounts on this book when ordered in quantity for bulk purchases or special sales, which may include electronic versions and/or custom covers and content particular to your business, training goals, marketing focus, and branding interests. For more information, please contact:

U.S. Corporate and Government Sales
1-800-382-3419
corpsales@pearsontechgroup.com

For sales outside the United States please contact:
International Sales
international@pearsoned.com

Feedback Information

At Cisco Press, our goal is to create in-depth technical books of the highest quality and value. Each book is crafted with care and precision, undergoing rigorous development that involves the unique expertise of members from the professional technical community.

Readers' feedback is a natural continuation of this process. If you have any comments regarding how we could improve the quality of this book, or otherwise alter it to better suit your needs, you can contact us through email at feedback@ciscopress.com. Please make sure to include the book title and ISBN in your message.

We greatly appreciate your assistance.

Publisher: Paul Boger	**Cisco Press Program Manager:** Jeff Brady
Associate Publisher: Dave Dusthimer	**Technical Editors:** Nathaly Landry, Richard Piquard
Executive Editor: Brett Bartow	**Development Editor:** Ginny Bess Munroe
Managing Editor: Patrick Kanouse	**Copy Editor:** Keith Cline
Project Editor: Seth Kerney	**Proofreader:** Paula Lowell
Editorial Assistant: Vanessa Evans	**Indexer:** Tim Wright
Book Designer: Louisa Adair	**Composition:** Mark Shirar

CISCO.

Americas Headquarters	Asia Pacific Headquarters	Europe Headquarters
Cisco Systems, Inc.	Cisco Systems, Inc.	Cisco Systems International BV
170 West Tasman Drive	168 Robinson Road	Haarlerbergpark
San Jose, CA 95134-1706	#28-01 Capital Tower	Haarlerbergweg 13-19
USA	Singapore 068912	1101 CH Amsterdam
www.cisco.com	www.cisco.com	The Netherlands
Tel: 408 526-4000	Tel: +65 6317 7777	www-europe.cisco.com
800 553-NETS (6387)	Fax: +65 6317 7799	Tel: +31 0 800 020 0791
Fax: 408 527-0883		Fax: +31 0 20 357 1100

Cisco has more than 200 offices worldwide. Addresses, phone numbers, and fax numbers are listed on the Cisco Website at **www.cisco.com/go/offices**.

About the Authors

Keith Hutton is an information technology professional with close to 20 years of experience in the industry. Over the course of his career, Keith has worked as a professional services engineer, presales engineer, third-line operational support engineer, engineering team lead, instructor, and author. Keith currently works as a professional services engineer for Bell Canada, responsible for the design and configuration of network security infrastructures. Keith has a B.A. honors degree from Queen's University, and is a certified Cisco instructor, Cisco Certified Network Professional (CCNP), Cisco Certified Design Professional (CCDP), and Cisco Certified Internetworking Professional (CCIP).

Mark Schofield has been a network architect at Bell Canada for the past six years. Working for the largest service provider in Canada, he has designed Multiprotocol Layer Switching (MPLS) virtual private networks (VPNs) with IP quality of service (QoS) for large enterprise customers. During the past five years at Bell, he has been involved in the design, implementation, and planning of large national networks for Bell Canada's federal government customers. As part of a cross-company team, he developed Bell Canada's premier MPLS VPN product. Mark has a MLIS from the University of Western Ontario and a B.A. and M.A. degrees from the University of Guelph. Industry certifications include the Cisco Certified Systems Instructor (CCIP), Cisco Certified Network Professional (CCNP), Citrix Certified Enterprise Administrator (CCEA), and Microsoft Certified Systems Engineer (MCSE).

Diane Teare is a professional in the networking, training, project management, and e-learning fields. She has more than 20 years of experience in designing, implementing, and troubleshooting network hardware and software, and has been involved in teaching, course design, and project management. She has extensive knowledge of network design and routing technologies, and is an instructor with one of the largest authorized Cisco Learning Partners. She was recently the director of e-learning for the same company, where she was responsible for planning and supporting all the company's e-learning offerings in Canada, including Cisco courses. Diane has a bachelor's degree in applied science in electrical engineering and a master's degree in applied science in management science. She is a certified Cisco instructor and currently holds her Cisco Certified Network Professional (CCNP), Cisco Certified Design Professional (CCDP), and Project Management Professional (PMP) certifications. She coauthored the Cisco Press titles *Campus Network Design Fundamentals*, the three editions of *Authorized Self-Study Guide Building Scalable Cisco Internetworks (BSCI)*, and *Building Scalable Cisco Networks*; and edited the two editions of the *Authorized Self-Study Guide Designing for Cisco Internetwork Solutions (DESGN)* and *Designing Cisco Networks*.

About the Technical Reviewers

Nathaly Landry attended the Royal Military College in Kingston, Ontario, Canada, where she graduated in 1989 with a bachelor's degree in electrical engineering. She then worked for two years in the satellite communication section before going to Ottawa University for a master's degree in electrical engineering. Upon graduation, she went back to the Department of National Defense and worked as a project manager for the implementation of the Defense Wide-Area Network, and then became the in-service support manager for the network. From 1996 to 2000, she worked as a networking consultant and instructor for Learning Tree. In May 2000, she joined Cisco, where she supported a number of federal accounts, and more recently has focused on Bell Canada as a channel systems engineer.

Richard Piquard is a senior network architect for Global Knowledge Network, Inc., one of the world's largest Cisco Learning Partners. Richard has more than eight years' experience as a certified Cisco instructor, teaching introductory and advanced routing, switching, design, and voice-related courses throughout North America and Europe. Richard has amassed a highly diverse skill set in design and implementation, of both Cisco and multivendor environments, throughout his nearly 15 years in the internetworking industry. His experience ranges from his military background as the network chief of the Marine Corps Systems Command, Quantico, Virginia, to a field engineer for the Xylan Corporation (Alcatel), Calabasas, California, to a member of a four-person, worldwide network planning and implementation team for the Household Finance Corporation in Chicago, Illinois. In addition, he has served as a technical reviewer for the Cisco Press title *Authorized Self-Study Guide Designing for Cisco Internetwork Solutions (DESGN)*, Second Edition.

Dedications

From Keith:

This book is dedicated to my parents, for teaching me how to dream.

From Mark:

This book is dedicated to Roslyn. Thank you for all your love and support in this and all my endeavors.

From Diane:

This book is dedicated to my remarkable husband, Allan Mertin, who continues to inspire me; to our charming son, Nicholas, and his amazing desire to learn everything about the world; to my parents, Syd and Beryl, for their continuous love and support; and to my friends, whose wisdom keeps me going.

Acknowledgments

We would like to thank many people for helping us put this book together:

The Cisco Press team: Brett Bartow, the executive editor, for coordinating the whole team and driving this book through the process, and for his unwavering support over the years. Vanessa Evans, for being instrumental in organizing the logistics and administration.

Ginny Bess Munroe, the development editor, has been invaluable in producing a high-quality manuscript. We would also like to thank Seth Kerney, the project editor, and Keith Cline, the copy editor, for their excellent work in steering this book through the editorial process.

The Cisco ARCH course development team: Many thanks to the members of the team who developed the latest version of the ARCH course. The team included Glenn Tapley, Dennis Masters, and Dwayne Fields from Cisco Systems; along with Dr. Peter Welcher and Carole Warner-Reece of Chesapeake Netcraftsmen.

The technical reviewers: We want to thank the technical reviewers of this book— Nathaly Landry and Richard Piquard—for their thorough, detailed review and valuable input.

Our families: Of course, this book would not have been possible without the constant understanding and patience of our families. They have always been there to motivate and inspire us. We thank you all.

Contents at a Glance

Contents

Command Syntax Conventions

The conventions used to present command syntax in this book are the same conventions used in the IOS Command Reference. The Command Reference describes these conventions as follows:

■ **Boldface** indicates commands and keywords that are entered literally as shown. In actual configuration examples and output (not general command syntax), boldface indicates commands that are manually input by the user (such as a **show** command).

■ *Italic* indicates arguments for which you supply actual values.

■ Vertical bars (|) separate alternative, mutually exclusive elements.

■ Square brackets ([ ]) indicate an optional element.

■ Braces ({ }) indicate a required choice.

■ Braces within brackets ([{ }]) indicate a required choice within an optional element.

Foreword

Cisco Certification Self-Study Guides are excellent self-study resources for networking professionals to maintain and increase internetworking skills and to prepare for Cisco Career Certification exams. Cisco Career Certifications are recognized worldwide and provide valuable, measurable rewards to networking professionals and their employers.

Cisco Press exam certification guides and preparation materials offer exceptional—and flexible—access to the knowledge and information required to stay current in one's field of expertise or to gain new skills. Whether used to increase internetworking skills or as a supplement to a formal certification preparation course, these materials offer networking professionals the information and knowledge required to perform on-the-job tasks proficiently.

Developed in conjunction with the Cisco certifications and training team, Cisco Press books are the only self-study books authorized by Cisco, and they offer students a series of exam practice tools and resource materials to help ensure that learners fully grasp the concepts and information presented.

Additional authorized Cisco instructor-led courses, e-learning, labs, and simulations are available exclusively from Cisco Learning Solutions Partners worldwide. To learn more, visit http://www.cisco.com/go/training.

I hope you will find this guide to be an essential part of your exam preparation and professional development, as well as a valuable addition to your personal library.

Drew Rosen
Manager, Learning & Development
Learning@Cisco
September 2008

Introduction

Designing Cisco Network Service Architectures (ARCH), Second Edition, covers how to perform the conceptual, intermediate, and detailed design of a network infrastructure. This design supports network solutions over intelligent network services to achieve effective performance, scalability, and availability of the network. This book enables readers, applying solid Cisco network solution models and best design practices, to provide viable and stable enterprise internetworking solutions. In addition, the book has been written to help candidates prepare for the Designing Cisco Network Service Architectures Exam (642-873 ARCH). This exam is one of the requirements for the CCDP certification. This exam tests a candidate's knowledge of the latest development in network design and technologies, including network infrastructure, intelligent network services, and converged network solutions.

Since the first edition was published in 2004, the ARCH course has changed to reflect the new exam requirements. This led to the immediate need for an update to this examination preparation text. Readers of the previous edition of *Designing Cisco Network Architectures (ARCH)* can use this text to update their knowledge and skill sets.

Goals of This Book

Upon completing this book, you will be able to meet these objectives:

- Introduce the Cisco Service-Oriented Network Architecture (SONA) framework, and explain how it addresses enterprise network needs for performance, scalability, and availability

- Describe how the Cisco Enterprise Architectures are used in the SONA framework for designing enterprise networks

- Create intermediate and detailed enterprise campus network, enterprise edge, and remote infrastructure designs that offer effective functionality, performance, scalability, and availability

- Create conceptual, intermediate, and detailed intelligent network service designs for network management, high availability, security, quality of service (QoS), and IP multicast

- Create conceptual, intermediate, and detailed virtual private network (VPN) designs

- Create conceptual, intermediate, and detailed voice over wireless network designs

Prerequisite Knowledge

Although enthusiastic readers will tackle less-familiar topics with some energy, a sound grounding in networking is advised. To gain the most from this book, you should be familiar with internetworking technologies, Cisco products, and Cisco IOS Software features. You will find knowledge about the following topics helpful for your successful understanding of the material presented in this book:

- How to design the necessary services to extend IP addresses using variable-length subnet masking (VLSM), Network Address Translation (NAT), and route summarization

- How to implement appropriate networking routing protocols, such as Open Shortest Path First (OSPF), Enhanced Interior Gateway Routing Protocol (EIGRP), and Border Gateway Protocol (BGP) on an existing internetwork

- How to redistribute routes between different routing protocols

- The required Cisco products and services that enable connectivity and traffic transport for a multilayer campus network

- The necessary services at each layer of the network to enable all users to obtain membership in multicast groups in a working enterprise network

- How to control network traffic by implementing the necessary admission policy at each layer of the network topology

- How to identify the appropriate hardware and software solutions for a given set of WAN technology requirements, including access between a central campus, branch offices, and telecommuters

- The Cisco equipment to establish appropriate WAN connections

- How to use protocols and technologies that enable traffic flow between multiple sites while minimizing the amount of overhead traffic on each connection

- QoS capabilities to ensure that mission-critical applications receive the required bandwidth within a given WAN topology

- How to implement Cisco voice solutions

- How to implement Cisco wireless solutions

- How to implement basic security steps and mitigation techniques

How This Book Is Organized

Of course, you can read the chapters in this book sequentially, but the organization also allows you to focus your reading on specific topics of interest. For example, if you want to focus on advanced routing design, you can skim Chapters 1 and 2 (which cover SONA and the elements of the enterprise campus network design), and then focus on the advanced IP addressing and routing topics in Chapter 3. Each chapter examines topics around a specific set of design issues. Specifically, the chapters in this book cover the following topics:

- Chapter 1, "Cisco SONA and the Cisco Enterprise Architecture," introduces the hierarchical model. It reviews Cisco SONA framework. This chapter also introduces the Cisco Enterprise Campus Architecture and reviews the Cisco PPDIOO network lifecycle approach.

- Chapter 2, "Enterprise Campus Network Design," reviews high-availability designs and how to implement optimal redundancy. An in-depth look at recommended practices for Layer 2 and Layer 3 design elements follows. A discussion of the Layer 2 to Layer 3 boundary designs and issues concludes with a number of considerations for supporting infrastructure services.

- Chapter 3, "Developing an Optimum Design for Layer 3," begins by reviewing the importance of IP address planning, and then covers advanced routing elements. Discussions focus on scalable EIGRP, OSPF, and BGP designs.

- Chapter 4, "Advanced WAN Services Design Considerations," covers advanced WAN service layers. This overview goes into more detail about the common WAN optical technologies of SONET, SDH, DWDM, and Resilient Packet Ring. A discussion about Metro Ethernet, VPLS, and MPLS VPN technologies follows (and includes an examination of a number of design considerations). The discussion then turns to implementing advanced WAN services.

- Chapter 5, "Enterprise Data Center Design," focuses on the enterprise data center, and covers the data center architecture model and design consideration in the data center core, aggregation, and access layers. The discussion then turns to scaling, with a look at how to scale a three-layer data center architecture.

- Chapter 6, "SAN Design Considerations," covers storage-area networks, from components and topologies to SAN technologies. SAN design factors center on port density and topology, with some discussion about extending the SAN with various protocols.

- Chapter 7, "E-Commerce Module Design," begins with an e-commerce overview and a look at the components of high availability in this module. The chapter covers common e-commerce design components, designing an integrated e-commerce architecture, and how to fine-tune e-commerce designs.

- Chapter 8, "Security Services Design," delves into designing firewall services in various scenarios. The chapter also covers network admission control services, with a review of Cisco NAC appliance fundamentals and NAS deployment options and designs. The discussion then turns to intrusion detection and prevention design.

- Chapter 9, "IPsec and SSL VPN Design," examines remote-access VPN design. Site-to-site VPN designs are covered, too. This chapter also covers IPsec VPN technologies, including Cisco Easy VPN, GRE over IPsec, and DMVPN. Recommendations for managing VPNs and considerations for scaling VPNs conclude the chapter.

- Chapter 10, "IP Multicast Design," covers IP multicast and multicast routing. Topics covered in this chapter include Protocol Independent Multicast (PIM), rendezvous points, and securing IP multicast.

- Chapter 11, "VoWLAN Design," introduces the Cisco Unified Wireless Network and examines requirements for voice over WLAN in the enterprise network. This chapter also discusses VoWLAN coverage considerations and the site survey process.

- Chapter 12, "Network Management Capabilities with Cisco IOS Software," examines Cisco network management capabilities embedded in Cisco IOS Software. This chapter also covers the syslog process, NetFlow, and NBAR, with a focus on the Cisco technologies themselves and how they enable other discovery tools, including Cisco AutoQoS. The chapter concludes with an overview of IP SLAs measurements.

This book also contains an appendix and an acronym list:

- Appendix A, "Answers to Review Questions," provides the answers to all the chapter-ending review questions.

- "Acronyms and Abbreviations," identifies abbreviations, acronyms, and initialisms used in this book.

Note: The website references in this book were accurate at the time of this writing. However, some might have changed since then. If a URL is unavailable, you can always search using the title as keywords in your favorite search engine.

After completing this chapter, you will be able to:

- Explain the Cisco Service-Oriented Network Architecture (SONA) framework

- Describe how the Cisco Enterprise Architecture is used to design enterprise networks

- Explain the Cisco six-phase network life cycle methodology: prepare, plan, design, implement, operate, and optimize (PPDIOO)

CHAPTER 1

Cisco SONA and the Cisco Enterprise Architecture

Cisco Service-Oriented Network Architecture (SONA) is a framework that enables businesses to build an intelligent enterprisewide network infrastructure. SONA accomplishes this by separating the network architecture into three modules: network infrastructure, infrastructure services, and business applications. This chapter introduces SONA and the Cisco Enterprise Architecture. It also reviews network design methodology under Cisco's six-phase network lifecycle: prepare, plan, design, implement, operate, and optimize (PPDIOO).

Reviewing Cisco SONA and the Cisco Enterprise Architecture

The rich variety of application-level business solutions available today and the need to integrate these applications has driven the establishment of a new network framework: the Cisco Service-Orientated Network Architecture (SONA). This section begins with a review of the Hierarchical Network Model and discusses how Cisco SONA enables customers to build a more intelligent network infrastructure. It reviews how the Cisco Enterprise Architectures are modules representing focused views of SONA that target each place in the network. The chapter also reviews the role of infrastructure services in an enterprise network design.

The Hierarchical Model

The foundation of the Cisco network architecture is the Hierarchical Network Model. Historically used in the design of enterprise LAN and WAN data networks, a hierarchical model also applies to the infrastructure modules of SONA and the Cisco Enterprise Architecture. Figure 1-1 shows the layers in the hierarchical model.

The Hierarchical Network Model provides a modular view of a network, making it easier to design and build a deterministic scalable infrastructure. The hierarchical network structure is composed of the access, distribution, and core layers. Each layer has its own functions, which are used to develop a hierarchical design.

The model provides a modular framework that enables flexibility in design and facilitates ease of implementation and troubleshooting. The Hierarchical Network Model divides networks into the access, distribution, and core layers, with these features:

- **Access layer:** Used to grant user access to network devices. In a network campus, the access layer generally incorporates switched LAN devices with ports that provide connectivity to workstations, IP phones, servers, and wireless access points. In the WAN environment, the access layer for teleworkers or remote sites may provide entry to the corporate network across WAN technology.

■ **Distribution layer:** Aggregates the wiring closets, using switches to segment workgroups and isolate network problems in a campus environment. Similarly, the distribution layer aggregates WAN connections at the edge of the campus and provides policy-based connectivity.

■ **Core layer (also referred to as the backbone):** A high-speed backbone, designed to switch packets as fast as possible. Because the core is critical for connectivity, it must provide a high level of availability and quickly adapt to changes. It also provides scalability and fast convergence.

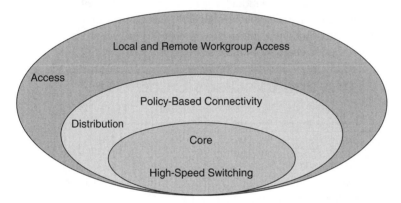

Figure 1-1   *Layers in the Hierarchical Model*

Example Hierarchical Network

Figure 1-2 shows a network mapped to the hierarchical model:

■ **Access layer:** Access layer devices control traffic by localizing service requests to the access media. Access layer devices must also provide connectivity without compromising network integrity. For example, the devices at the access layer must detect whether a user workstation is legitimate, with minimal authentication steps.

■ **Distribution layer:** Distribution layer devices control access to resources that are available at the core layer and must, therefore, make efficient use of bandwidth. In addition, a distribution layer device must address the quality of service (QoS) needs for different protocols by implementing policy-based traffic control to isolate backbone and local environments. Policy-based traffic control enables you to prioritize traffic to ensure the best performance for the most time-critical and time-dependent applications.

■ **Core layer:** Core layer devices provide services that optimize communication transport within the network. In addition, core layer devices are expected to provide maximum availability and reliability with minimum packet processing. Core layer devices

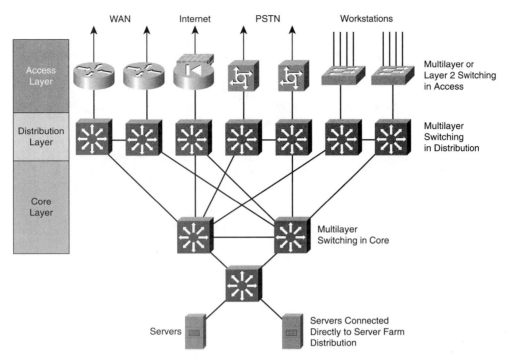

Figure 1-2 *Example Hierarchical Network*

should be able to maintain connectivity when the circuits that connect them fail. A fault-tolerant network design ensures that failures do not have a major impact on network connectivity.

Review of Cisco SONA

The intelligent networking framework defined by Cisco for the enterprise is SONA (see Figure 1-3). Cisco SONA uses the extensive product line, services, proven architectures, and experience of Cisco and its partners to help enterprises achieve their business goals.

The SONA framework illustrates the concept that the network is the common element that connects and enables all components of the IT infrastructure. SONA outlines the following three layers of intelligence in the enterprise network:

■ **The network infrastructure layer:** This layer is where all the IT resources are interconnected across a converged network foundation. The IT resources include servers, storage, and clients. The network infrastructure layer represents how these resources exist in different places in the network, including the campus, branch, data center, WAN, metropolitan-area network (MAN), and teleworker. The objective for customers in this layer is to have anywhere and anytime connectivity.

■ **The interactive services layer:** This layer enables efficient allocation of resources to applications and business processes delivered through the networked infrastructure.

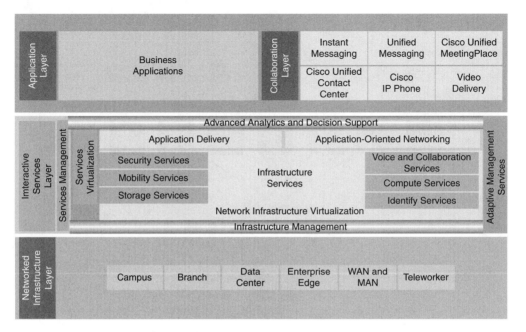

Figure 1-3   *Overview of Cisco SONA*

- **The application layer:** This includes business applications and collaboration applications. The objective for customers in this layer is to meet business requirements and achieve efficiencies by leveraging the interactive services layer.

The common thread that links the layers is that SONA embeds application-level intelligence into the network infrastructure elements so that the network itself can recognize and better support applications and services.

Benefits of Cisco SONA

SONA promotes more effective use of networked resources, and provides these benefits:

- **Functionality:** Supports the organizational requirements.

- **Scalability:** Supports growth and expansion of organizational tasks by separating functions and products into layers. This separation makes it easier to grow the network.

- **Availability:** Provides necessary services reliably anywhere, anytime.

- **Performance:** Provides desired responsiveness, throughput, and utilization on a per-application basis through the network infrastructure and services.

- **Manageability:** Provides control, performance monitoring, and fault detection.

- **Efficiency:** Through step-by-step network services growth, SONA provides network services and infrastructure with reasonable operational costs and appropriate capital investment on a migration path to a more intelligent network.

Review of the Cisco Enterprise Architecture

This section provides a review of the Cisco Enterprise Architecture modules.

The Cisco Enterprise Architecture (see Figure 1-4) consists of the following modules, representing focused views of SONA that target each place in the network:

- **Cisco Enterprise Campus Architecture:** Combines a core infrastructure of intelligent switching and routing with tightly integrated productivity-enhancing technologies; these include Cisco Unified Communications, mobility, and advanced security. The hierarchical architecture of the Cisco Enterprise Campus provides for high availability through a resilient multilayer design, redundant hardware and software features, and automatic procedures for reconfiguring network paths when failures occur. The architecture extends authentication support using standards such as 802.1x and Extensible Authentication Protocol (EAP). It also provides the flexibility to add IP Security (IPsec) and Multiprotocol Label Switching virtual private networks (MPLS VPN), identity and access management, and VLANs to compartmentalize access. Multicast provides optimized bandwidth consumption. QoS prevents oversubscription to ensure that real-time traffic, such as voice and video, or critical data is not dropped or delayed. Integrated security protects against and mitigates the impact of worms, viruses, and other attacks on the network (even at the switch port level). These additions help improve performance and security, while also decreasing costs.

- **Cisco Enterprise Edge Architecture:** Offers connectivity to voice, video, and data services outside the enterprise. This module enables the enterprise to use Internet and

Figure 1-4 *Cisco Enterprise Architecture*

partner resources, and provides resources for its customers. QoS, service levels, and security are the main issues in the enterprise edge module.

■ **Cisco Enterprise WAN and MAN Architecture:** These are part of the Cisco Enterprise Edge Architecture. This module offers the convergence of voice, video, and data services over a single Cisco Unified Communications network. It enables the enterprise to cost-effectively span large geographic areas. QoS, granular service levels, and comprehensive encryption options help ensure the secure delivery of high-quality voice, video, and data services. This enables corporate staff to work efficiently wherever they are located. Security is provided with multiservice VPNs (IPsec and MPLS) over Layer 2 and Layer 3 WANs, hub-and-spoke, or full-mesh topologies.

■ **Cisco Enterprise Data Center Architecture:** A cohesive, adaptive network architecture that supports the requirements for consolidation, business continuance, and security; while enabling service-oriented architectures, virtualization, and on-demand computing. It provides departmental staff, suppliers, or customers with secure access to applications and resources. The architecture simplifies and streamlines management and significantly reduces overhead. Redundant data centers provide backup services through synchronous and asynchronous data and application replication. The network and devices offer server and application load balancing to maximize performance. This solution enables the enterprise to scale without major changes to the infrastructure. This module can be located either at the campus as a server farm or at a remote facility.

■ **Cisco Enterprise Branch Architecture:** Allows enterprises to extend head-office applications and services to remote locations and users. An optimized branch network leverages the WAN and LAN to reduce traffic and to save bandwidth and operational expenses. The infrastructure provides secure access to voice, mission-critical data, and video applications anywhere; with features such as advanced network routing, VPNs, redundant WAN links, application content caching, and local IP telephony call processing. Cisco captures these features in the Integrated Services Router (ISR). The ISR enables enterprises to deploy new services when they are ready, without purchasing new equipment. The enterprise supports the remote configuration, monitoring, and the management of devices located at remote sites. Cisco IOS supports tools that proactively resolve congestion and bandwidth issues before they affect network performance, such as Cisco AutoQoS and the Security Device Manager (SDM).

■ **Cisco Enterprise Teleworker Architecture:** Enables enterprises to securely deliver voice and data services to small office/home office (SOHO) environments over a standard broadband access service. This provides a business-resiliency solution for the enterprise and a flexible work environment for employees. Centralized management minimizes the IT support costs, and robust integrated security mitigates the security challenges of this environment. Integrated security and Identity Based Networking Services (IBNS) enable the enterprise to extend campus security policies to the teleworker. Staff can securely log on to the network over an "always-on" VPN, and gain access to authorized applications and services from a single cost-effective platform. Their productivity can further be enhanced by adding a Cisco IP phone, providing cost-effective access to a centralized IP communications system with voice and unified messaging services.

Review of Cisco SONA Infrastructure Services

Infrastructure services add intelligence to the network by supporting application awareness. Important applications such as IP telephony require support from network services that meet enterprisewide requirements. The network must provide a common set of capabilities to ensure functionality for the most persistent application requirements, such as the following:

- **Security services:** Increase the integrity of the network by protecting network resources and users from internal and external threats.

- **Identity services:** Map resources and policies to the user and device.

- **Storage services:** Provide distributed and virtual storage across the infrastructure.

- **Compute services:** Connect and virtualize compute resources based on the application.

- **Mobility services:** Allow users to access network resources regardless of their physical location. Wireless services support mobile clients and integrate with the wired network.

- **Voice services:** Deliver the foundation by which voice can be carried across the network, such as security and high availability.

An infrastructure service may use multiple network services. For example, if the enterprise plans to implement voice services, network needs features such as QoS and security.

Network services embedded in the infrastructure services include the following:

- **Network management:** Includes LAN management for advanced management of multilayer switches; routed WAN management for monitoring, traffic management, and access control to administer the routed infrastructure of multiservice networks; service management for managing and monitoring service level agreements (SLA); and VPN and security management for optimizing VPN performance and security administration.

- **High availability:** Ensures end-to-end availability for services, clients, and sessions. Implementation includes reliable, fault-tolerant network devices (to automatically identify and overcome failures) and resilient-network technologies.

- **QoS:** Manages the delay, delay variation (jitter), bandwidth availability, and packet-loss parameters on a network to meet the diverse needs of voice, video, and data applications. QoS features provide value-added functionality such as Network-Based Application Recognition (NBAR) for classifying traffic by application type, a Cisco IOS IP Service Level Agreements (SLAs) for end-to-end QoS measurements, Resource Reservation Protocol (RSVP) signaling for admission control and reservation of resources, and a variety of configurable queue insertion and servicing disciplines.

- **IP multicasting:** Multicasting enables distribution of videoconferencing, corporate communications, distance learning, distribution of software, and other applications. Multicast packets are replicated only as necessary in the network by Cisco routers enabled with Protocol Independent Multicast (PIM) and other supporting multicast protocols, resulting in the most efficient delivery of data to multiple receivers.

Review of the Cisco SONA Application Layer

This layer includes collaborative applications that support the enterprise. Cisco has solutions to support several applications:

- **Unified messaging:** Unified communications applications provide structure and intelligence that can help organizations integrate their communications with business processes. It also ensures that information reaches recipients quickly through the most appropriate medium.

- **Cisco Unified Contact Center:** The Cisco Unified Contact Center provides intelligent contact routing, call treatment, network-to-desktop computer telephony integration (CTI), and multichannel contact management over an IP infrastructure. This application enables organizations to smoothly integrate inbound and outbound voice applications with Internet applications such as real-time chat, web collaboration, and email.

- **Cisco IP phone:** IP telephony transmits voice communications over a network using open-standards-based IP. Cisco IP phone products are a key component of the Cisco Unified Communications system, which delivers the business benefits of a converged network to organizations of all sizes.

- **Cisco Unified MeetingPlace:** This multimedia conferencing solution fully integrates voice, video, and web conferencing capabilities to give remote meetings a natural and effective, face-to-face quality for medium-size to large organizations.

- **Video delivery and conferencing:** The Cisco Unified Communications infrastructure supports video delivery. Cisco Unified videoconferencing solutions provide a reliable, versatile, and easy-to-manage network infrastructure for videoconferencing.

Reviewing the Cisco PPDIOO Approach

To design a network that meets customer needs, the organizational goals, organizational constraints, technical goals, and technical constraints must be identified. Cisco has formalized the lifecycle of a network into six phases: prepare, plan, design, implement, operate, and optimize (PPDIOO).

The section begins with a review of PPDIOO, and then discusses the design methodology under PPDIOO.

Upon completing this section, you will be able to discuss PPDIOO and its design methodology. This ability includes being able to meet these objectives:

- Describe the benefits of using the PPDIOO network lifecycle approach

- Describe the three basic steps of the design methodology under PPDIOO

PPDIOO Network Lifecycle Approach

This section reviews the PPDIOO approach for the network lifecycle (see Figure 1-5).

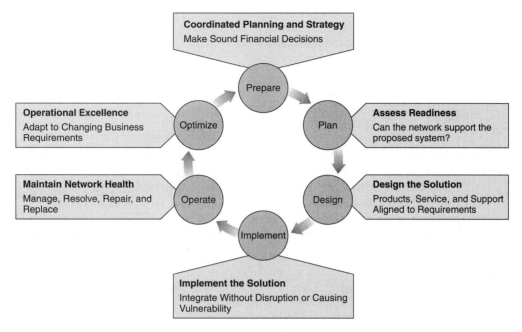

Figure 1-5   *PPDIOO Network Lifecycle Approach*

The PPDIOO network lifecycle approach reflects the lifecycle phases of a standard network. The PPDIOO phases are as follows:

- **Prepare:** The preparation phase involves establishing the organizational requirements, developing a network strategy, proposing a high-level conceptual architecture, and identifying technologies that can best support the architecture. The preparation phase can establish financial justification for network strategy by assessing the business case for the proposed architecture.

- **Plan:** The planning phase involves identifying initial network requirements based on goals, facilities, user needs, and so on. The planning phase involves characterizing sites, assessing any existing networks, and performing a gap analysis to determine whether the existing system infrastructure, sites, and operational environment can support the proposed system. A project plan facilitates management of the tasks, responsibilities, critical milestones, and resources required to implement changes to the network. The project plan should align with the scope, cost, and resource parameters established in the original business requirements.

- **Design:** The initial requirements that were derived in the planning phase drive the activities of the network design specialists. The network design specification is a comprehensive detailed design that meets current business and technical requirements and incorporates specifications to support availability, reliability, security, scalability, and performance. The design specification is the basis for the implementation activities.

- **Implement:** After the design has been approved, implementation (and verification) begins. The network or additional components are built according to the design specifications, with the goal of integrating devices without disrupting the existing network or creating points of vulnerability.

- **Operate:** Operation is the final test of the appropriateness of the design. The operate phase involves maintaining network health through day-to-day operations, including maintaining high availability and reducing expenses. The fault detection, correction, and performance monitoring that occur in daily operations provide initial data for the optimize phase.

- **Optimize:** The optimize phase involves proactive management of the network. The goal of proactive management is to identify and resolve issues before they affect the organization. Reactive fault detection and correction (troubleshooting) is needed when proactive management cannot predict and mitigate failures. In the PPDIOO process, the optimize phase may prompt a network redesign if too many network problems and errors arise, if performance does not meet expectations, or if new applications are identified to support organizational and technical requirements.

Note: Although design is listed as one of the six PPDIOO phases, some design elements may be present in all the other phases.

Benefits of the Lifecycle Approach

This section summarizes the benefits of the network lifecycle approach.

The network lifecycle approach provides four main benefits:

- Lowers the total cost of network ownership
- Increases network availability
- Improves business agility
- Speeds access to applications and services

The total cost of network ownership is lowered via these strategies:

- Identifying and validating technology requirements
- Planning for infrastructure changes and resource requirements
- Developing a sound network design aligned with technical requirements and business goals
- Accelerating successful implementation
- Improving the efficiency of your network and of the staff supporting it
- Reducing operating expenses by improving the efficiency of operation processes and tools

Network availability is increased via these strategies:

- Assessing the network's security state and its capability to support the proposed design

- Specifying the correct set of hardware and software releases and keeping them operational and current

- Producing a sound operations design and validating network operation

- Staging and testing the proposed system before deployment

- Improving staff skills

- Proactively monitoring the system and assessing availability trends and alerts

- Proactively identifying security breaches and defining remediation plans

Business agility is improved via these strategies:

- Establishing business requirements and technology strategies

- Readying sites to support the system you want to implement

- Integrating technical requirements and business goals into a detailed design and demonstrating that the network is functioning as specified

- Expertly installing, configuring, and integrating system components

- Continually enhancing performance

Access to applications and services is accelerated through these strategies:

- Assessing and improving operational preparedness to support current and planned network technologies and services

- Improving service-delivery efficiency and effectiveness by increasing availability, resource capacity, and performance

- Improving the availability, reliability, and stability of the network and the applications running on it

- Managing and resolving problems affecting your system and keeping software applications current

Note: The remainder of this book focuses on the prepare, plan, and design phases of PPDIOO.

Using the Design Methodology Under PPDIOO

The design methodology under PPDIOO consists of three basic steps:

Step 1   **Identify customer requirements.** In this step, key decision makers identify the initial requirements. Based on these requirements, a high-level conceptual architecture is proposed. This step is typically done during the PPDIOO prepare phase.

Step 2   **Characterize the existing network and sites.** The plan phase involves characterizing sites, assessing any existing networks, and performing a gap analysis to determine whether the existing system infrastructure, sites, and operational environment can support the proposed system. Characterization of the existing network and sites includes a site and network audit and network analysis. During the network audit, the existing network is thoroughly checked for integrity and quality. During the network analysis, network behavior (traffic, congestion, and so on) is analyzed. This is typically done within the PPDIOO plan phase.

Step 3   **Design the network topology and solutions.** In this step, you develop the detailed design. Decisions about network infrastructure, intelligent network services, and network solutions (VoIP, content networking, and so on) are made. You may also build a pilot or prototype network to verify the design. You also write a detailed design document.

Identifying Customer Requirements

This section reviews the process for gathering customer requirements for the enterprise network design discussed in the *Designing for Cisco Internetwork Solutions* (DESGN) course (see Figure 1-6).

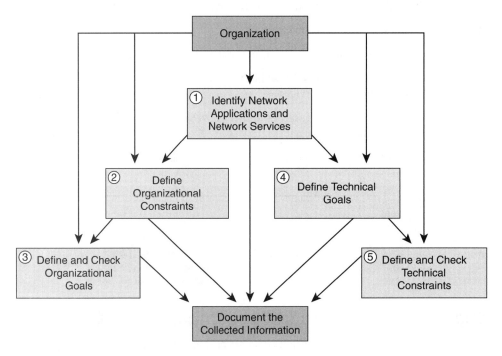

Figure 1-6   *Identifying Customer Requirements*

The design requirements gathering process includes discussions with the staff of the organization to determine and gather the necessary data and documentation.

The data-gathering steps are as follows:

Step 1   Identify network applications and network services. Define which applications have timing constraints in the traffic flows.

Step 2   Define the organizational goals.

Step 3   Define the organizational constraints.

Step 4   Define the technical goals.

Step 5   Define the technical constraints.

The process of identifying required information is not unidirectional. You might return to a step and make additional inquiries about issues as they arise during the design process.

When you complete the data-gathering process, you are ready to interpret and analyze the data and develop a design proposal.

Characterizing the Existing Network and Sites

The first step in characterizing an existing network is to gather as much information about the network as possible. Existing documentation and organizational input, site and network audits, and traffic analysis can provide the key information that you need.

Information gathering typically follows these steps:

Step 1   Gather existing documentation about the network, and query the organization to discover additional information. Organization input, a network audit, and traffic analysis provide the key information you need. (Note that existing documentation may be inaccurate.)

Step 2   Perform a network audit that adds detail to the description of the network. If possible, use traffic-analysis information to augment organizational input when you are describing the applications and protocols used in the network.

Step 3   Based on your network characterization, write a summary report that describes the health of the network. With this information, you can propose hardware and software upgrades to support the network requirements and the organizational requirements.

Note: Although this is a good idea in principle, a network audit is often too costly in terms of time and effort. Some organizations may implement expedited versions of a network audit to target specific areas.

Designing the Topology and Network Solutions

After you gather organizational requirements, and document and audit the existing network, you are ready to design a network solution, plan the implementation, and (optionally) build a network prototype.

Designing an enterprise network is a complex project. Top-down design facilitates the process by dividing it into smaller, more manageable steps. Top-down design clarifies the design goals and initiates the design from the perspective of the required applications and network solutions.

In assessing the scope of a network design, you must determine whether the design is for a new network or is a modification of the entire network, a single segment or module, a set of LANs, a WAN, or a remote-access network. The design scope may address a single function or all of the OSI model layers.

Structured top-down design practices focus on dividing the design task into related, less-complex components or modules:

■   Identify the applications that will be needed to support the customer's requirements.

■   Identify the logical connectivity requirements of the applications, with a focus on the necessary network solutions and the supporting network services. Examples of infrastructure services include voice, content networking, and storage networking, availability, management, security, QoS, and IP multicast.

■   Split the network functionally to develop the network infrastructure and hierarchy requirements. In this course, the Cisco Enterprise Architecture provides a consistent infrastructure.

■   Design each structured element separately in relation to other elements. Network infrastructure and infrastructure services design are tightly connected, because both are bound to the same logical, physical, and layered models.

When the design is completed in the PPDIOO process, the next step is to develop the implementation and migration plan in as much detail as possible. The more detailed the implementation plan documentation, the less knowledgeable the network engineer needs to be to implement the design.

After a design is complete, it often is appropriate to verify the design. You can test the design in an existing or live network (pilot), or in an isolated test network (prototype) that will not affect the existing network.

Example: Dividing the Network into Areas

Use these guidelines to create an enterprise network:

■   Divide the network into areas where the enterprise campus module includes all devices and connections within the main campus. Ensure the enterprise edge modules cover all communications with remote locations from the perspective of the enterprise campus. Finally, make certain that the remote modules include the remote branches, teleworkers, and the remote data center.

■   Define clear boundaries between the enterprise campus, the enterprise edge, and the remote modules.

Note: Depending on the network, an enterprise can have multiple campus locations. A location might be a remote branch from the perspective of a central campus location, but can locally use the Enterprise Campus Architecture.

Figure 1-7 shows an example of one step in designing an enterprise network. The network is divided into an enterprise campus area, an enterprise edge area, and some remote areas.

Summary

This chapter covered the following topics:

- The Hierarchical Network Model enables a modular approach to the design and construction of a deterministic scalable network. The hierarchical network structure is composed of the access, distribution, and core layers.

- Cisco SONA is the enterprise framework for building intelligence into the network:

  - Layer 1 is the network infrastructure layer.

  - Layer 2 is the interactive services layer (infrastructure services).

  - Layer 3 is the application layer (business applications).

- The Cisco Enterprise Architecture consists of modules representing focused views of SONA that target each place in the network. Each module has a distinct network infrastructure and services, and network applications that extend between the modules.

- Infrastructure services add intelligence to the network by supporting application awareness.

- The PPDIOO approach reflects the lifecycle phases of a standard network.

- The design methodology under PPDIOO includes the following:

  - Identifying customer requirements

  - Characterizing the existing network and sites

  - Designing the network topology and solutions

References

For more information, refer to these resources:

- Cisco Systems, Inc. "Lifecycle Services Portfolio," at http://www.cisco.com/en/US/products/ps6890/serv_category_home.html

- Cisco Systems, Inc. "Service-Oriented Network Architecture Introduction," at http://www.cisco.com/en/US/netsol/ns629/networking_solutions_market_segment_solutions_home.html

- Cisco Systems, Inc. Enterprise Architectures documentation, at http://www.cisco.com/en/US/netsol/ns517/networking_solutions_market_segment_solutions_home.html

- Cisco Systems, Inc., "Lifecycle Services Strategy Introduction," at http://www.cisco.com/en/US/products/ps6890/serv_category_home.html

Figure 1-7   *Example: Dividing the Network into Areas*

- Oppenheimer, P. *Top-Down Network Design*, Second Edition. Cisco Press; 2004.

- "Internetworking Design Basics" chapter of *Cisco Internetwork Design Guide*, at http://www.cisco.com/univercd/cc/td/doc/cisintwk/idg4/nd2002.htm

Review Questions

Answer the following questions, and then refer to Appendix A, "Answers to Review Questions," for the answers.

1. What are the layers of SONA? (Choose three.)

   a. Integrated applications layer

   b. Application layer

   c. Interactive services layer

   d. Intelligent services layer

   e. Networked infrastructure layer

   f. Integrated transport layer

2. What are the roles of the core layer in a LAN design? (Choose three.)

   a. Provides high-speed data transport

   b. Performs packet filtering

   c. Serves as a fast-convergent infrastructure with a high level of redundancy

   d. Avoids data manipulation

   e. Performs mainly policy-based decisions

   f. Provides access to the network

3. Which modules provide network infrastructure and services for remote enterprise users? (Choose three.)

   a. Enterprise Remote Database Architecture

   b. Enterprise Teleworker Architecture

   c. Enterprise Remote Branch Architecture

   d. Enterprise Branch Architecture

   e. Enterprise Data Center Architecture

4. What are the basic steps of the design methodology under PPDIOO? (Choose three.)

    a. Characterize the existing network and sites

    b. Examine conceptual architecture

    c. Design the network topology and solutions

    d. Identify customer requirements

    e. Validate the design

5. Which tasks are involved in characterizing an existing network? (Choose three.)

    a. Collecting information using the existing documentation and direct organizational input

    b. Using tools to analyze network traffic

    c. Using design tools to create a framework for the design

    d. Using tools for automated auditing of the network

    e. Identifying the business objectives of the organization

After completing this chapter, you will be able to

- Design enterprise campus network infrastructures

- Review high-availability campus design features and make recommendations

- Describe Layer 2 campus design options and make recommendations

- Describe Layer 3 campus design options and make recommendations

- Discuss options for Layer 2 to Layer 3 boundary placement in the campus

- Describe infrastructure service considerations, including IP telephony, QoS, and Cisco Catalyst Integrated Security features

CHAPTER 2

Enterprise Campus Network Design

The complexity inherent in today's campus networks necessitates a design process capable of separating solutions into basic elements. The Cisco hierarchical network model achieves this goal by dividing the network infrastructure into modular components. Each module is used to represent a functional service layer within the campus hierarchy.

Designing High Availability in the Enterprise Campus

The Cisco hierarchical network model enables the design of high-availability modular topologies. Through the use of scalable building blocks, the network can support evolving business needs. The modular approach makes the network easier to scale, troubleshoot, and understand. It also promotes the deterministic traffic patterns.

This section reviews design models, recommended practices, and methodologies for high availability in the Cisco Enterprise Campus Architecture infrastructure.

Enterprise Campus Infrastructure Review

The building blocks of the enterprise campus infrastructure are the access layer, the distribution layer, and the core layer. The principal features associated with each layer are hierarchal design and modularity. A hierarchical design avoids the need for a fully meshed network in which all nodes are interconnected. A modular design enables a component to be placed in service or taken out of service with little or no impact on the rest of the network. This methodology also facilitates troubleshooting, problem isolation, and network management.

Access Layer

The access layer is the point of entry into the network for end devices, as illustrated in Figure 2-1.

The campus access layer aggregates end users and provides uplinks to the distribution layer. The access layer can support multiple features:

- **High availability:** At the access layer, high availability is supported through various hardware and software attributes. With hardware, system-level redundancy can be provided using redundant supervisor engines and redundant power supplies. It can also be provided by default gateway redundancy using dual connections from access switches to redundant distribution layer switches. With software, high availability is supported through the use of first-hop routing protocols (FHRP), such as the Hot

Standby Router Protocol (HSRP), Virtual Router Redundancy Protocol (VRRP), and Gateway Load Balancing Protocol (GLBP).

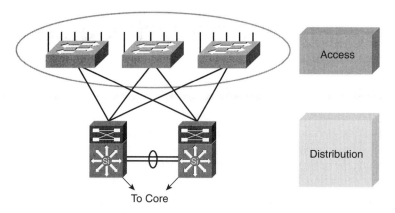

Figure 2-1   *Access Layer*

> **Note:**   Cisco offers a unique high-availability feature to its 3750 Workgroup Switch and Etherswitch Services Module called StackWise. StackWise technology enables switches to be interconnected to create a single logical unit through the use of special stack cables. The cables create a bidirectional path that behaves as a switch fabric for all the interconnected switches. The stack is managed as a single unit, eliminating the need for spanning tree and streamlining the interface to a single management session for all devices. For more information about StackWise, refer to Cisco.com.

> **Note:**   IOS Release 12.2(18) SXD extended high availability to the 6500/7600 series line of switches. It added services such as Control Plane Policing (CoPP), Nonstop Forwarding (NSF), Stateful Switchover (SSO), and Gateway Load Balancing Protocol (GLBP), which are discussed later in this chapter.

- **Convergence:** The access layer supports inline Power over Ethernet (PoE) for IP telephony and wireless access points, allowing customers to converge voice onto their data network and providing roaming wireless LAN (WLAN) access for users.

- **Security:** The access layer provides services for additional security against unauthorized access to the network through the use of tools such as IEEE 802.1x, port security, DHCP snooping, Dynamic ARP Inspection (DAI), and IP Source Guard.

- **Quality of service (QoS):** The access layer allows prioritization of mission-critical network traffic using traffic classification and queuing as close to the ingress of the network as possible. It supports the use of the QoS trust boundary.

- **IP multicast:** The access layer supports efficient network and bandwidth management using software features such as Internet Group Management Protocol (IGMP) snooping.

Distribution Layer

The distribution layer aggregates traffic from all nodes and uplinks from the access layer and provides policy-based connectivity, as illustrated in Figure 2-2.

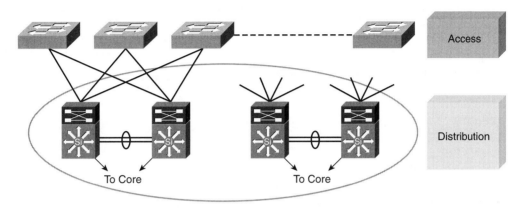

Figure 2-2 *Distribution Layer*

Availability, load balancing, QoS, and provisioning are the important considerations at this layer. High availability is typically provided through dual paths from the distribution layer to the core and from the access layer to the distribution layer. Layer 3 equal-cost load sharing allows both uplinks from the distribution to the core layer to be used.

The distribution layer is the place where routing and packet manipulation are performed and can be a routing boundary between the access and core layers. The distribution layer represents a redistribution point between routing domains or the demarcation between static and dynamic routing protocols. The distribution layer performs tasks such as controlled routing and filtering to implement policy-based connectivity and QoS. To further improve routing protocol performance, the distribution layer summarizes routes from the access layer. For some networks, the distribution layer offers a default route to access layer routers and runs dynamic routing protocols when communicating with core routers.

The distribution layer uses a combination of Layer 2 and multilayer switching to segment workgroups and isolate network problems, preventing them from impacting the core layer. The distribution layer may be used to terminate VLANs from access layer switches. The distribution layer connects network services to the access layer and implements QoS, security, traffic loading, and routing policies. The distribution layer provides default gateway redundancy using an FHRP, such as HSRP, GLBP, or VRRP, to allow for the failure or removal of one of the distribution nodes without affecting endpoint connectivity to the default gateway.

Note: Cisco has introduced the Virtual Switching System (VSS), which can reduce or eliminate the need for FHRPs at the distribution layer. For more information about VSS, visit http://www.cisco.com/go/vss.

Core Layer

The core layer provides scalability, high availability, and fast convergence to the network, as illustrated in Figure 2-3. The core layer is the backbone for campus connectivity, and is the aggregation point for the other layers and modules in the Cisco Enterprise Campus Architecture. The core provides a high level of redundancy and can adapt to changes quickly. Core devices are most reliable when they can accommodate failures by rerouting traffic and can respond quickly to changes in the network topology. The core devices implement scalable protocols and technologies, alternate paths, and load balancing. The core layer helps in scalability during future growth.

Figure 2-3   *Core Layer*

The core is a high-speed, Layer 3 switching environment using hardware-accelerated services. For fast convergence around a link or node failure, the core uses redundant point-to-point Layer 3 interconnections because this design yields the fastest and most deterministic convergence results. The core layer is designed to avoid any packet manipulation, such as checking access lists and filtering, which would slow down the switching of packets.

Not all campus implementations require a campus core. The core and distribution layer functions can be combined at the distribution layer for a smaller campus.

Without a core layer, the distribution layer switches need to be fully meshed, as illustrated in Figure 2-4. This design can be difficult to scale, and increases the cabling requirements, because each new building distribution switch needs full-mesh connectivity to all the distribution switches. The routing complexity of a full-mesh design increases as new neighbors are added.

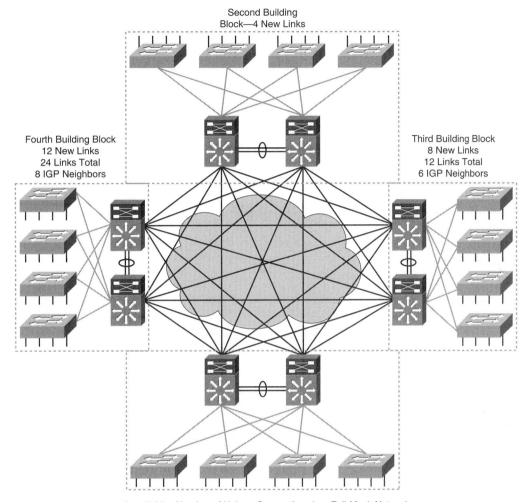

n (n − 1) / 2 = Number of Unique Connections in a Full-Mesh Network

Figure 2-4   *Is a Core Layer Needed?*

Note: Note that combining distribution and core layer functionality (collapsed core) requires a great deal of port density on the distribution layer switches. An alternative solution is a Layer 2 core with discrete VLANs on each core switch. This scenario requires only two ports per distribution layer switch—regardless of the number of buildings (switch blocks)—and so you can avoid the expense of multilayer core switches.

In Figure 2-4, a distribution module in the second building of two interconnected switches requires four additional links for full-mesh connectivity to the first module. A third distribution module to support the third building would require 8 additional links to support connections to all the distribution switches, or a total of 12 links. A fourth module supporting the fourth building would require 12 new links, for a total of 24 links between the distribution switches. Four distribution modules impose eight Interior Gateway Protocol (IGP) neighbors on each distribution switch.

As a recommended practice, deploy a dedicated campus core layer to connect three or more buildings in the enterprise campus, or four or more pairs of building distribution switches in a very large campus. The campus core helps make scaling the network easier by addressing the requirements for the following:

- Gigabit density
- Data and voice integration
- LAN, WAN, and MAN convergence

High-Availability Considerations

In the campus, high availability is concerned with minimizing link and node failures and optimizing recovery times to minimize convergence and downtime.

Implement Optimal Redundancy

The recommended design is redundant distribution layer switches and redundant connections to the core with a Layer 3 link between the distribution switches. Access switches should have redundant connections to redundant distribution switches, as illustrated in Figure 2-5.

As a recommended practice, the core and distribution layers are built with redundant switches and fully meshed links to provide maximum redundancy and optimal convergence. Access switches should have redundant connections to redundant distribution switches. The network bandwidth and capacity is engineered to withstand a switch or link failure, supporting 120 to 200 ms to converge around most events. Open Shortest Path First (OSPF) and Enhanced Interior Gateway Routing Protocol (EIGRP) timer manipulation attempt to quickly redirect the flow of traffic away from a router that has experienced a failure toward an alternate path.

In a fully redundant topology with tuned IGP timers, adding redundant supervisors with Cisco NSF and SSO may cause longer convergence times than single supervisors with tuned IGP timers. NSF attempts to maintain the flow of traffic through a router that has experienced a failure. NSF with SSO is designed to maintain a link-up Layer 3 up state during a routing convergence event. However, because an interaction occurs between the IGP timers and the NSF timers, the tuned IGP timers can cause NSF-aware neighbors to reset the neighbor relationships.

Note: Combining OSPF and EIGRP timer manipulation with Cisco NSF might not be the most common deployment environment. OSPF and EIGRP timer manipulation is designed to improve convergence time in a multiaccess network (where several IGP routing peers share a common broadcast media, such as Ethernet). The primary deployment scenario for Cisco NSF with SSO is in the enterprise network edge. Here, the data link layer generally consists of point-to-point links either to service providers or redundant Gigabit Ethernet point-to-point links to the campus infrastructure.

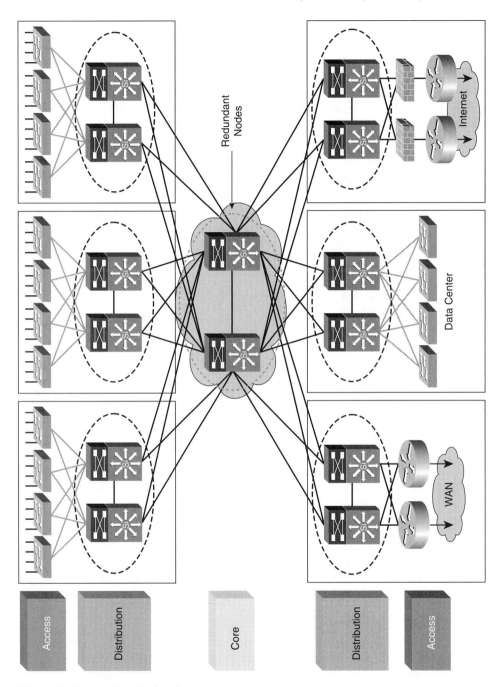

Figure 2-5   *Optimal Redundancy*

In nonredundant topologies, using Cisco NSF with SSO and redundant supervisors can provide significant resiliency improvements.

Provide Alternate Paths

The recommended distribution layer design is redundant distribution layer switches and redundant connections to the core with a Layer 3 link between the distribution switches, as illustrated in Figure 2-6.

Figure 2-6 *Provide Alternate Paths*

Although dual distribution switches connected individually to separate core switches will reduce peer relationships and port counts in the core layer, this design does not provide sufficient redundancy. In the event of a link or core switch failure, traffic will be dropped.

An additional link providing an alternate path to a second core switch from each distribution switch offers redundancy to support a single link or node failure. A link between the two distribution switches is needed to support summarization of routing information from the distribution layer to the core.

Avoid Single Points of Failure

Cisco NSF with SSO and redundant supervisors has the most impact in the campus in the access layer. An access switch failure is a single point of failure that causes outage for the end devices connected to it. You can reduce the outage to one to three seconds in this access layer, as shown in Figure 2-7, by using SSO in a Layer 2 environment or Cisco NSF with SSO in a Layer 3 environment.

Note: The SSO feature is available on the Catalyst 4500 and 6500/7600 switches.

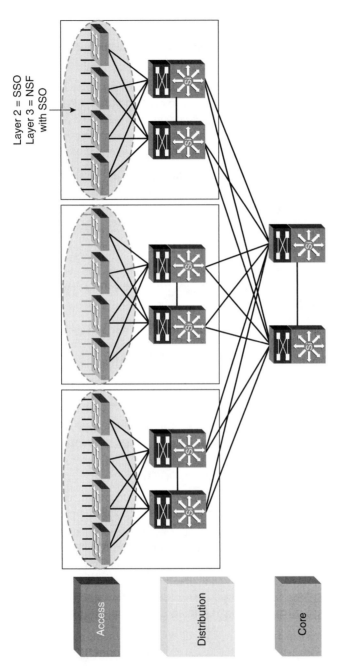

Figure 2-7 *Avoid Single Points of Failure*

Cisco NSF with SSO

Cisco NSF with SSO is a supervisor redundancy mechanism in Cisco IOS Software that allows extremely fast supervisor switchover at Layers 2 to 4.

SSO allows the standby route processor (RP) to take control of the device after a hardware or software fault on the active RP. SSO synchronizes startup configuration, startup variables, and running configuration; and dynamic runtime data, including Layer 2 protocol states for trunks and ports, hardware Layer 2 and Layer 3 tables (MAC, Forwarding Information Base [FIB], and adjacency tables) and access control lists (ACL) and QoS tables.

Cisco NSF is a Layer 3 function that works with SSO to minimize the amount of time a network is unavailable to its users following a switchover. The main objective of Cisco NSF is to continue forwarding IP packets following an RP switchover. Cisco NSF is supported by the EIGRP, OSPF, Intermediate System-to-Intermediate System (IS-IS), and Border Gateway Protocol (BGP) for routing. A router running these protocols can detect an internal switchover and take the necessary actions to continue forwarding network traffic using Cisco Express Forwarding while recovering route information from the peer devices. With Cisco NSF, peer networking devices continue to forward packets while route convergence completes and do not experience routing flaps.

Routing Protocol Requirements for Cisco NSF

Usually, when a router restarts, all its routing peers detect that routing adjacency went down and then came back up. This transition is called a *routing flap*, and the protocol state is not maintained. Routing flaps create routing instabilities, which are detrimental to overall network performance. Cisco NSF helps to suppress routing flaps.

Cisco NSF allows for the continued forwarding of data packets along known routes while the routing protocol information is being restored following a switchover. With Cisco NSF, peer Cisco NSF devices do not experience routing flaps because the interfaces remain up during a switchover and adjacencies are not reset. Data traffic is forwarded while the standby RP assumes control from the failed active RP during a switchover. User sessions established before the switchover are maintained.

The ability of the intelligent line cards to remain up through a switchover and to be kept current with the FIB on the active RP is crucial to Cisco NSF operation. While the control plane builds a new routing protocol database and restarts peering agreements, the data plane relies on pre-switchover forwarding-table synchronization to continue forwarding traffic. After the routing protocols have converged, Cisco Express Forwarding updates the FIB table and removes stale route entries, and then it updates the line cards with the refreshed FIB information.

Note: Transient routing loops or black holes may be introduced if the network topology changes before the FIB is updated.

The switchover must be completed before the Cisco NSF dead and hold timers expire; otherwise, the peers will reset the adjacency and reroute the traffic.

Cisco NSF protocol enhancements enable a Cisco NSF capable router to signal neighboring Cisco NSF-aware devices during switchover.

Note: A device is said to be Cisco NSF aware if it runs Cisco NSF-compatible software. A device is said to be Cisco NSF capable if it has been configured to support Cisco NSF. A Cisco NSF-capable device rebuilds routing information from Cisco NSF-aware or Cisco NSF-capable neighbors.

A Cisco NSF-aware neighbor is needed so that Cisco NSF-capable systems can rebuild their databases and maintain their neighbor adjacencies across a switchover.

Following a switchover, the Cisco NSF-capable device requests that the Cisco NSF-aware neighbor devices send state information to help rebuild the routing tables as a Cisco NSF reset.

The Cisco NSF protocol enhancements allow a Cisco NSF-capable router to signal neighboring Cisco NSF-aware devices. The signal asks that the neighbor relationship not be reset. As the Cisco NSF-capable router receives and communicates with other routers on the network, it can begin to rebuild its neighbor list. After neighbor relationships are reestablished, the Cisco NSF-capable router begins to resynchronize its database with all of its Cisco NSF-aware neighbors.

Based on platform and Cisco IOS Software release, Cisco NSF with SSO support is available for many routing protocols:

- EIGRP

- OSPF

- BGP

- IS-IS

Cisco IOS Software Modularity Architecture

The Cisco Catalyst 6500 series with Cisco IOS Software Modularity supports high availability in the enterprise. Figure 2-8 illustrates the key elements and components of the Cisco Software Modularity Architecture.

Figure 2-8 *Cisco IOS Software Modularity Architecture*

When Cisco IOS Software patches are needed on systems without Cisco IOS Software Modularity, the new image must be loaded on the active and redundant supervisors, and the supervisor must be reloaded or the switchover to the standby completed to load the patch.

The control plane functions (that manage routing protocol updates and management traffic) on the Catalyst 6500 series run on dedicated CPUs on the multilayer switch forwarding card complex (MSFC). A completely separate data plane is responsible for traffic forwarding. When the hardware is programmed for nonstop operation, the data plane continues forwarding traffic even if there is a disruption in the control plane. The Catalyst 6500 series switches benefit from the more resilient control plane offered by Cisco IOS Software Modularity.

Note: Catalyst switch forwarding fabrics are broken down into three planes or functional areas, as follows:

- **Control plane:** The control plane is a logical interface that connects physical chassis components and software functions into a unified logical unit. The control plane connects the system controller functionality on the RP to the service processor (SP) module used to control each card and module in the chassis.

- **Data plane:** The data plane is where packet forwarding takes place. It is the path that packets take through the routing system from the physical layer interface module (PLIM) to the modular services card (MSC) to the switch fabric. On the 6500 series platforms, this would include the policy feature card (PFC) used for high-performance packet processing, and the distributed forwarding card (DFC), which provides local packet forwarding on select line cards.

- **Management plane:** The management plane is where control/configuration of the platform takes place.

The Cisco Catalyst 6500 series with Cisco IOS Software Modularity enables several Cisco IOS control plane subsystems to run in independent processes. Cisco IOS Software Modularity boosts operational efficiency and minimizes downtime:

- It minimizes unplanned downtime through fault containment and stateful process restarts, raising the availability of converged applications.

- It simplifies software changes through subsystem in-service software upgrades (ISSU), significantly reducing code certification and deployment times and decreasing business risks.

- It enables process-level, automated policy control by integrating Cisco IOS Embedded Event Manager (EEM), offloading time-consuming tasks to the network and accelerating the resolution of network issues. EEM is a combination of processes designed to monitor key system parameters such as CPU utilization, interface counters, Simple Network Management Protocol (SNMP), and syslog events. It acts on specific events or threshold counters that are exceeded.

Note: Embedded Event Manager is discussed in more detail in Chapter 12, "Network Management Capabilities with Cisco IOS Software."

Example: Software Modularity Benefits

Cisco IOS Software Modularity on the Cisco Catalyst 6500 series provides these benefits:

- **Operational consistency:** Cisco IOS Software Modularity does not change the operational point of view. Command-line interfaces (CLI) and management interfaces such as SNMP or syslog are the same as before. New commands to EXEC and configuration mode and new **show** commands have been added to support the new functionality.

- **Protected memory:** Cisco IOS Software Modularity enables a memory architecture where processes make use of a protected address space. Each process and its associated subsystems live in an individual memory space. Using this model, memory corruption across process boundaries becomes nearly impossible.

- **Fault containment:** The benefit of protected memory space is increased availability because problems occurring in one process cannot affect other parts of the system. For example, if a less-critical system process fails or is not operating as expected, critical functions required to maintain packet forwarding are not affected.

- **Process restartability:** Building on the protected memory space and fault containment, the modular processes are now individually restartable. For test purposes or nonresponding processes, the **process restart** *process-name* command is provided to manually restart processes. Restarting a process allows fast recovery from transient errors without the need to disrupt forwarding. Integrated high-availability infrastructure constantly checks the state of processes and keeps track of how many times a process restarted in a defined time interval. If a process restart does not restore the system, the high-availability infrastructure will take more drastic actions, such as initiating a supervisor engine switchover or a system restart.

Note: Although a process restart can be initiated by the user, it should be done with caution.

- **Modularized processes:** Several control plane functions have been modularized to cover the most commonly used features. Examples of modular processes include but are not limited to these:
    - Routing process
    - Internet daemon
    - Raw IP processing
    - TCP process
    - User Datagram Protocol (UDP) process
    - Cisco Discovery Protocol process
    - Syslog daemon
    - Any EEM components

- File systems
- Media drivers
- Install manager

- **Subsystem ISSU:** Cisco IOS Software Modularity allows selective system maintenance during runtime through individual patches. By providing versioning and patch-management capabilities, Cisco IOS Software Modularity allows patches to be downloaded, verified, installed, and activated without the need to restart the system. Because data plane packet forwarding is not affected during the patch process, the network operator now has the flexibility to introduce software changes at any time through ISSU. A patch affects only the software components associated with the up-date.

Designing an Optimum Design for Layer 2

Layer 2 architectures rely on the following technologies to create a highly available, deterministic topology: Spanning Tree Protocol (STP), trunking (ISL/802.1q), Unidirectional Link Detection (UDLD), and EtherChannel.

The following section reviews design models and recommended practices for Layer 2 high availability and optimum convergence of the Cisco Enterprise Campus Infrastructure.

Recommended Practices for Spanning-Tree Configuration

For the most deterministic and highly available network topology, the requirement to support STP convergence should be avoided by design. You may need to implement STP for several reasons:

- When a VLAN spans access layer switches to support business applications.

- To protect against user-side loops. Even if the recommended design does not depend on STP to resolve link or node failure events, STP is required to protect against user-side loops. There are many ways that a loop can be introduced on the user-facing access layer ports. Wiring mistakes, misconfigured end stations, or malicious users can create a loop. STP is required to ensure a loop-free topology and to protect the rest of the network from problems created in the access layer.

- To support data center applications on a server farm.

Note: Some security personnel have recommended disabling STP at the network edge. This practice is not recommended because the risk of lost connectivity without STP is far greater than any STP information that might be revealed.

If you need to implement STP, use Rapid Per-VLAN Spanning-Tree Plus (RPVST+). You should also take advantage of the Cisco enhancements to STP known as the Cisco STP toolkit.

Cisco STP Toolkit

The Cisco enhancements to STP include the following. (Note that the enhancements marked with an * are also supported with Rapid Per-VLAN Spanning-Tree Plus [RPVST+].)

- **PortFast*:** Causes a Layer 2 LAN interface configured as an access port to enter the forwarding state immediately, bypassing the listening and learning states. Use Port-Fast only when connecting a single end station to a Layer 2 access port.

- **UplinkFast:** Provides from three to five seconds convergence after a direct link failure and achieves load balancing between redundant Layer 2 links using uplink groups.

- **BackboneFast:** Cuts convergence time by **max_age** for indirect failure. Backbone-Fast is initiated when a root port or blocked port on a network device receives inferior bridge protocol data units (BPDU) from its designated bridge.

- **Loop guard*:** Prevents an alternate or root port from becoming designated in the absence of BPDUs. Loop guard helps prevent bridging loops that could occur because of a unidirectional link failure on a point-to-point link.

- **Root guard*:** Secures the root on a specific switch by preventing external switches from becoming roots.

- **BPDU guard*:** When configured on a PortFast-enabled port, BPDU guard shuts down the port that receives a BPDU.

- **Unidirectional Link Detection (UDLD):** UDLD monitors the physical configuration of fiber-optic and copper connections and detects when a one-way connection exists. When a unidirectional link is detected, the interface is shut down and the system alerted.

Note: The STP toolkit also supports the BPDU filter option, which prevents PortFast-enabled ports from sending or receiving BPDUs. This feature effectively disables STP at the edge and can lead to STP loops. It is not recommended.

STP Standards and Features

STP enables the network to deterministically block interfaces and provide a loop-free topology in a network with redundant links. There are several varieties of STP:

- STP is the original IEEE 802.1D version (802.1D-1998) that provides a loop-free topology in a network with redundant links.

- Common Spanning Tree (CST) assumes one spanning-tree instance for the entire bridged network, regardless of the number of VLANs.

- Per VLAN Spanning Tree Plus (PVST+) is a Cisco enhancement of STP that provides a separate 802.1D spanning tree instance for each VLAN configured in the network.

The separate instance supports PortFast, UplinkFast, BackboneFast, BPDU guard, BPDU filter, root guard, and loop guard.

- The 802.1D-2004 version is an updated version of the STP standard.

- Multiple Spanning Tree (MST) is an IEEE standard inspired from the earlier Cisco proprietary Multi-Instance Spanning Tree Protocol (MISTP) implementation. MST maps multiple VLANs into the same spanning-tree instance. The Cisco implementation of MSTP is MST, which provides up to 16 instances of Rapid Spanning Tree Protocol (RSTP, 802.1w) and combines many VLANs with the same physical and logical topology into a common RSTP instance. Each instance supports PortFast, UplinkFast, BackboneFast, BPDU guard, BPDU filter, root guard, and loop guard.

- RSTP, or IEEE 802.1w, is an evolution of STP that provides faster convergence of STP.

- Rapid PVST+ (RPVST+) is a Cisco enhancement of RSTP that uses PVST+. It provides a separate instance of 802.1w per VLAN. The separate instance supports PortFast, UplinkFast, BackboneFast, BPDU guard, BPDU filter, root guard, and loop guard.

Note: When Cisco documentation and this course refer to implementing RSTP, they are referring to the Cisco RSTP implementation, or PVRST+.

STP Standards and Features

To configure a VLAN instance to become the root bridge, enter the **spanning-tree vlan** *vlan_ID* **root primary** command to modify the bridge priority from the default value (32768) to a significantly lower value. The bridge priority for the specified VLAN is set to 8192 if this value will cause the switch to become the root for the VLAN. If any bridge for the VLAN has a priority lower than 8192, the switch sets the priority to one less than the lowest bridge priority Manually placing the primary and secondary bridges along with enabling STP toolkit options enables you to support a deterministic configuration where you know which ports should be forwarding and which ports should be blocking.

Note: Defining the root bridge under MST is done using the **spanning-tree mst** *instance_id* **root primary**. When you use this command, the switch will review all bridge ID values it receives from other root bridges. If any root bridge has a bridge ID equal to or less than 24576, it will set its own bridge priority to 4096 less then the lowest bridge priority. To ensure that it will retain its position as the root bridge, you must also enable root guard.

Figure 2-9 illustrates recommended placements for STP toolkit features:

- Loop guard is implemented on the Layer 2 ports between distribution switches, and on the uplink ports from the access switches to the distribution switches.

- Root guard is configured on the distribution switch ports facing the access switches.

- UplinkFast is implemented on the uplink ports from the access switches to the distribution switches.

STP Root   LoopGuard

LoopGuard

RootGuard

UplinkFast

BPDUGuard or
RootGuard
PortFast

Figure 2-9   *Layer 2 Hardening*

Note: When you are configuring MST, UplinkFast is not required as a feature on dual-homed switches. Rapid root port failover occurs as part of the default MST protocol implementation.

- BPDU guard or root guard is configured on ports from the access switches to the end devices, as is PortFast.

- The UDLD protocol allows devices to monitor the physical configuration of the cables and detect when a unidirectional link exists. When a unidirectional link is detected, UDLD shuts down the affected LAN port. UDLD is often configured on ports linking switches.

- Depending on the security requirements of an organization, the port security feature can be used to restrict a port's ingress traffic by limiting the MAC addresses allowed to send traffic into the port.

Recommended Practices for Trunk Configuration

A trunk is a point-to-point link between two networking devices that carry the traffic of multiple VLANs. Trunks are typically deployed on the interconnection between the access and distribution layers.

The current recommended practice is to use IEEE 802.1Q trunks. Cisco extensions to 802.1Q avoid security concerns related to the 802.1Q nontagged, native VLAN. The native VLAN is assigned to an unused ID, or the tagged, native VLAN option is used to avoid VLAN hopping.

Note: *VLAN hopping* is an attack using a double 802.1Q-encapsulated packet. If the attacker has specific knowledge of the 802.1Q native VLAN, a packet could be crafted that when processed, the first or outermost tag is removed when the packet is switched onto the untagged, native VLAN. When the packet reaches the target switch, the inner or second tag is then processed, and the potentially malicious packet is switched to the target VLAN. The traffic in this attack scenario is in a single direction, and no return traffic can be switched by this mechanism. In addition, this attack cannot work unless the attacker knows the native VLAN identity.

VLAN Trunking Protocol (VTP) is a protocol that enables network managers to centrally manage the VLAN database. VTP transparent mode is now a recommended practice because it decreases the potential for operational error.

By default, Cisco switches are configured as a VTP server with no VTP domain name specified.

Therefore, it is also recommended when configuring switches along with setting the mode to Transparent, to set the VTP domain name. This is important if you are connecting your switch to other domains, such as a service provider switch. Misconfiguration of the switch as a server or client with no VTP domain name will cause it to accept the domain name of an adjacent VTP server and overwrite the local VLAN database.

As a recommended practice, when configuring switch-to-switch interconnections to carry multiple VLANs, set Dynamic Trunking Protocol (DTP) to Desirable and Desirable with Encapsulation Negotiate to support DTP negotiation.

Note: Turning DTP to On and On with Nonnegotiate could save seconds of outage when restoring a failed link or node. However, with this configuration, DTP is not actively monitoring the state of the trunk, and a misconfigured trunk is not easily identified.
One instance where you would use On with Nonnegotiate is if you are trunking between two different VTP domains. DTP includes the VTP domain name in its messages; and if the names do not match, the trunk will not come up if set to Desirable.

Another recommended practice is to manually prune unused VLANs from trunked interfaces to avoid broadcast propagation. You should avoid automatic VLAN pruning.

The final recommendation for trunk configuration is to disable trunks on host ports, because host devices will not need to negotiate trunk status. This practice speeds up Port-Fast and is also a VLAN-hopping security measure.

VLAN Trunking Protocol

VTP version 3 supports centralized VLAN administration in a switched network. VTP runs only on trunks and provides the following four modes:

- **Server:** Updates clients and servers. The VTP server switch propagates the VTP database to VTP client switches.

- **Client:** Receives updates but cannot make changes.

- **Transparent:** Does not participate in the VTP domain. Lets updates pass through.

- **Off:** Ignores VTP updates.

With VTP, when you configure a new VLAN on a switch in VTP server mode, the VLAN is distributed through all switches in the VTP domain. This redistribution reduces the need to configure the same VLAN everywhere.

With hierarchical networks that do not span VLANs across the distribution layer, there is little need for a shared common VLAN database. In the recommended campus design, the same VLAN should not appear in two access layer switches. Adding and removing VLANs is generally not a frequent network management practice. In most cases, VLANs are defined once during switch setup with few, if any, additional modifications to the VLAN database in an access layer switch. The benefits of dynamic propagation of VLAN information across the network are not worth the potential for unexpected behavior due to operational error. For these reasons, VTP transparent mode is the recommended configuration option.

Dynamic Trunking Protocol

DTP provides switch ports to negotiate the trunking method with another device and to automatically allow a link to become a trunk.

With Cisco devices, there are five Layer 2 port modes:

- **Trunk:** Puts the port into permanent trunking mode and negotiates to convert the link into a trunk link. The port becomes a trunk port even if the neighboring port does not agree to the change.

- **Desirable:** Actively attempts to form a trunk, subject to neighbor agreement. The port becomes a trunk port if the neighboring port is set to On, Desirable, or Auto mode.

- **Auto:** Makes the port willing to convert the link to a trunk link. The port becomes a trunk port if the neighboring port is set to on or desirable mode.

- **Access:** This is the access mode in Cisco IOS Software that specifies that the port never become a trunk, even if the neighbor tries. This mode puts the LAN port into permanent nontrunking mode and negotiates to convert the link into a nontrunking link.

- **Nonnegotiate:** Prevents the port from generating DTP frames. You must configure the neighboring port manually as a trunk port to establish a trunk link.

With Cisco devices, there are three Ethernet trunk encapsulation types:

- **ISL:** Uses Inter-Switch Link (ISL) encapsulation on the trunk link

- **Dot1q:** Uses 802.1Q encapsulation on the trunk link

- **Negotiate:** Specifies that the LAN port negotiate with the neighboring LAN port to become an ISL (preferred) or 802.1Q trunk, depending on the configuration and capabilities of the neighboring LAN port

The trunking mode, the trunk encapsulation type, and the hardware capabilities of the two connected LAN ports determine whether a link becomes an ISL or 802.1Q trunk.

A common practice is to configure both ends of the trunk to desirable. This has the operational benefit of providing a clear indication of a functional trunking connection with **show** commands, and is the general recommendation for DTP trunking.

An alternative practice is to set one side of the link (typically the access layer) to Auto and the other end (typically the distribution layer) to Desirable. This setting allows for automatic trunk formation, with DTP running on the interconnection to protect against some rare hardware failure scenarios and software misconfigurations.

For fastest convergence, a third configuration turns DTP to On and On with Nonnegotiate to save a few seconds of outage when restoring a failed link or node. However, DTP is not actively monitoring the state of the trunk with this configuration, and a misconfigured trunk is not easily identified. The Nonnegotiate setting can also cause loss of connectivity if the process is not performed in the correct order and there is no out-of-band connectivity to the farthest switch from where the in-band modifications are being made.

Recommended Practices for UDLD Configuration

UDLD enables devices to monitor the physical configuration of the cables and detect when a unidirectional link exists where bidirectional communication has not been established.

UDLD is typically deployed on fiber topologies where physical misconnections can occur that enable a link to appear to be up/up when there is a mismatched set of transmit/receive pairs. UDLD supports both fiber-optic and copper Ethernet cables connected to LAN ports.

Each switch port configured for UDLD will send UDLD protocol hello packets at Layer 2 containing the device and port identifications of the port, and the device and port identifications of the neighbor as seen by UDLD on that port. Neighboring ports should see their own device and port identifications in the packets received from the other side. If the port does not see its own device and port identifications in the incoming UDLD packets for a specific duration of time, the link is considered unidirectional and is shut down. The default 15-second hello timers are the same for normal and aggressive UDLD. In normal mode, UDLD will error-disable only the end where the UDLD is detected; aggressive mode will error-disable both ends of a connection after aging on a previously bidirectional link in eight seconds.

A recommended practice is to enable UDLD aggressive mode in all environments where fiber-optic interconnections are used. UDLD is enabled globally on all fiber-optic LAN ports with the Cisco IOS software **udld** {**enable** | **aggressive**} command. UDLD is enabled on individual LAN ports with the **udld** *port* [**aggressive**] interface command.

Note: You should enable UDLD in global mode so that you do not have to enable it on every individual fiber-optic interface.

Recommended Practices for EtherChannel

An EtherChannel bundles individual Ethernet links into a single logical link that provides the aggregate bandwidth of up to eight physical links.

EtherChannels are typically deployed between the distribution-to-core and core-to-core interconnections where increased availability and scaled bandwidth are required. Ether-Channel link aggregation is used to provide link redundancy and prevent a single point of failure, and to reduce peering complexity because the single logical entity reduces the number of Layer 3 neighbor relationships as compared to multiple parallel links.

Note: EtherChannel also provides an optimization to STP by enabling all member ports to be placed in the forwarding mode. STP views the EtherChannel as a single logical link.

EtherChannels create channels containing up to eight parallel links between switches. If the channels are on interfaces that are on different physical line cards, there is increased availability because the failure of a single line card does not cause a complete loss of connectivity.

There are two variants for the control mechanism for EtherChannel: the prestandard Cisco implementation that uses Port Aggregation Protocol (PAgP), and the IEEE 802.3ad standards-based implementation that uses Link Aggregation Control Protocol (LACP). PAgP and LACP do not interoperate. You can manually configure a switch with PAgP on one side and LACP on the other side in the on/on mode. When this is done, ports configured in the on mode do not negotiate, and therefore there is no negotiation traffic between the ports. This configuration results in the EtherChannel being hard-coded.

When connecting a Cisco IOS Software device to a Catalyst operating system device, make sure that the PAgP settings used for establishing EtherChannels are coordinated. The defaults are different for a Cisco IOS Software device and a Catalyst operating system device. As a recommended practice, Catalyst operating system devices should have PAgP set to Off when connecting to a Cisco IOS Software device if EtherChannels are not configured. If EtherChannel PAgP is used, set both sides of the interconnection to Desirable.

Port aggregation should be disabled when not needed. Port aggregation can most effectively be controlled by disabling it on interfaces facing end users with the set port host macro on the Catalyst operating system or the switchport host macro on Cisco ISO Software. These macros disable both trunking and EtherChannel while enabling STP PortFast.

Port Aggregation Protocol

PAgP is one of the control mechanisms for EtherChannel. PAgP has four modes related to the automatic formation of bundled, redundant switch-to-switch interconnections (see Figure 2-12):

■ **On:** Mode that forces the LAN port to channel unconditionally. In the on mode, a usable EtherChannel exists only when a LAN port group in the on mode is connected to another LAN port group in the on mode. Because ports configured in the on mode do not negotiate, no negotiation occurs traffic between the ports. You cannot configure the on mode with an EtherChannel protocol. If one end uses the on mode, the other end must also.

- **Desirable:** Places a port into an active negotiating state, in which the port starts negotiations with other ports by sending PAgP packets. This mode is not supported when the EtherChannel members are from different switches in the switch stack (cross-stack EtherChannel).

- **Auto:** Places a port into a passive negotiating state, in which the port responds to PAgP packets it receives but does not start PAgP packet negotiation. This setting minimizes the transmission of PAgP packets. This mode is not supported when the EtherChannel members are from different switches in the switch stack (cross-stack EtherChannel).

- **Off:** Do not become a member.

As with DTP, the long-standing practice for EtherChannel/PAgP has been to set one side of the interconnection (typically the access switch) to Auto and the other side (typically the distribution switch) to Desirable, or both sides to Desirable. In these configurations, an EtherChannel is established when configuration is complete, and connectivity to the remote switch is always available, even when the EtherChannel is not completely established.

Note: For Layer 2 EtherChannels, a desirable/desirable PAgP configuration is recommended so that PAgP is running across all members of the bundle, ensuring that an individual link failure will not result in a STP failure.

Link Aggregation Control Protocol

LACP is another control mechanism for EtherChannel. LACP has four modes related to the automatic formation of bundled, redundant switch-to-switch interconnections:

- **On:** Mode that forces the LAN port to channel unconditionally. In the on mode, a usable EtherChannel exists only when a LAN port group in the on mode is connected to another LAN port group in the on mode. Because ports configured in the on mode do not negotiate, no negotiation traffic occurs between the ports. You cannot configure the on mode with an EtherChannel protocol. If one end uses the on mode, the other end must also.

- **Active:** LACP mode that places a port into an active negotiating state, in which the port initiates negotiations with other ports by sending LACP packets.

- **Passive:** LACP mode that places a port into a passive negotiating state, in which the port responds to LACP packets it receives but does not initiate LACP negotiation.

- **Off:** Do not become a member.

Note: The recommended practice for EtherChannel LACP is to set one side of the interconnection (typically the access switch) to Active and the other side (typically the distribution switch) to Passive, or both sides to Active. In these configurations, a channel is established when configuration is complete, and connectivity to the remote switch is always available, even when the channel is not completely established.

Developing an Optimum Design for Layer 3

To achieve high availability and fast convergence in the Cisco enterprise campus network, the designer needs to manage multiple objectives, including the following:

■ Managing oversubscription and bandwidth

■ Supporting link load balancing

■ Routing protocol design

■ FHRPs

This section reviews design models and recommended practices for high availability and fast convergence in Layer 3 of the Cisco enterprise campus network.

Managing Oversubscription and Bandwidth

Typical campus networks are designed with oversubscription, as illustrated in Figure 2-10. The rule-of-thumb recommendation for data oversubscription is 20:1 for access ports on the access-to-distribution uplink. The recommendation is 4:1 for the distribution-to-core links. When you use these oversubscription ratios, congestion may occur infrequently on the uplinks. QoS is needed for these occasions. If congestion is frequently occurring, the design does not have sufficient uplink bandwidth.

As access layer bandwidth capacity increases to 1 Gb/s, multiples of 1 Gb/s, and even 10 Gb/s, the bandwidth aggregation on the distribution-to-core uplinks might be supported on many Gigabit Ethernet EtherChannels, on 10 Gigabit Ethernet links, and on 10 Gigabit EtherChannels.

Bandwidth Management with EtherChannel

As bandwidth from the distribution layer to the core increases, oversubscription to the access layer must be managed, and some design decisions must be made.

Just adding more uplinks between the distribution and core layers leads to more peer relationships, with an increase in associated overhead.

Figure 2-10   *Managing Oversubscription and Bandwidth*

EtherChannels can reduce the number of peers by creating single logical interface. However, you must consider some issues about how routing protocols will react to single link failure:

■ OSPF running on a Cisco IOS Software-based switch will notice a failed link, and will increase the link cost. Traffic is rerouted, and this design leads to a convergence event.

■ OSPF running on a Cisco Hybrid-based switch will not change link cost. Because it will continue to use the EtherChannel, this may lead to an overload in the remaining links in the bundle as OSPF continues to divide traffic equally across channels with different bandwidths.

■ EIGRP might not change link cost, because the protocol looks at the end-to-end cost. This design might also overload remaining links.

The EtherChannel Min-Links feature is supported on LACP EtherChannels. This feature allows you to configure the minimum number of member ports that must be in the link-up state and bundled in the EtherChannel for the port channel interface to transition to the link-up state. You can use the EtherChannel Min-Links feature to prevent low-bandwidth LACP EtherChannels from becoming active.

Bandwidth Management with 10 Gigabit Interfaces

Upgrading the uplinks between the distribution and core layers to 10 Gigabit Ethernet links is an alternative design for managing bandwidth. The 10 Gigabit Ethernet links can also support the increased bandwidth requirements.

This is a recommended design:

■ Unlike the multiple link solution, 10 Gigabit Ethernet links do not increase routing complexity. The number of routing peers is not increased.

■ Unlike the EtherChannel solution, the routing protocols will have the ability to deterministically select the best path between the distribution and core layer.

Link Load Balancing

In Figure 2-11, many equal-cost, redundant paths are provided in the recommended network topology from one access switch to the other across the distribution and core switches. From the perspective of the access layer, there are at least three sets of equal-cost, redundant links to cross to reach another building block, such as the data center.

Cisco Express Forwarding (CEF) is a deterministic algorithm. As shown in the figure, when packets traverse the network that all use the same input value to the CEF hash, a "go to the right" or "go to the left" decision is made for each redundant path. When this results in some redundant links that are ignored or underutilized, the network is said to be experiencing CEF polarization.

To avoid CEF polarization, you can tune the input into the CEF algorithm across the layers in the network. The default input hash value is Layer 3 for source and destination. If you change this input value to Layer 3 plus Layer 4, the output hash value also changes.

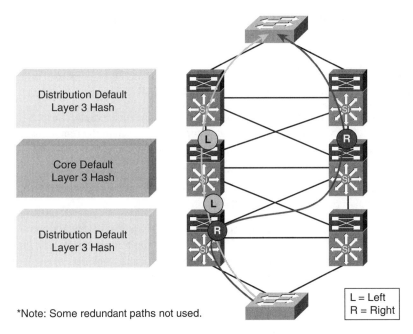

Distribution Default
Layer 3 Hash

Core Default
Layer 3 Hash

Distribution Default
Layer 3 Hash

*Note: Some redundant paths not used.

L = Left
R = Right

Figure 2-11   *CEF Load Balancing (Default Behavior)*

As a recommendation, use alternating hashes in the core and distribution layer switches:

- In the core layer, continue to use the default, which is based on only Layer 3 information.

- In the distribution layer, use the Layer 3 plus Layer 4 information as input into the CEF hashing algorithm with the command **Dist2-6500 (config)#mls ip cef load-sharing full**.

This alternating approach helps eliminate the always-right or always-left biased decisions and helps balance the traffic over equal-cost, redundant links in the network.

Link Load Balancing

EtherChannel allows load sharing of traffic among the links in the channel and redundancy in the event that one or more links in the channel fail.

You can tune the hashing algorithm used to select the specific EtherChannel link on which a packet is transmitted. You can use the default Layer 3 source and destination information, or you can add a level of load balancing to the process by adding the Layer 4 TCP/IP port information as an input to the algorithm.

Figure 2-12 illustrates some results from experiments at Cisco in a test environment using a typical IP addressing scheme of one subnet per VLAN, two VLANs per access switch, and the RFC 1918 private address space. The default Layer 3 hash algorithm provided about one-third to two-thirds utilization. When the algorithm was changed to include Layer 4 information, nearly full utilization was achieved with the same topology and traffic pattern.

Figure 2-12   *EtherChannel Load Balancing*

The recommended practice is to use Layer 3 plus Layer 4 load balancing to provide as much information as possible for input to the EtherChannel algorithm to achieve the best or most uniform utilization of EtherChannel members. The command **port-channel load-balance** is used to present the more unique values to the hashing algorithm. This can be achieved using the command **dist1-6500(config)#port-channel load-balance src-dst-port**.

To achieve the best load balancing, use two, four, or eight ports in the port channel.

Routing Protocol Design

This section reviews design recommendations for routing protocols in the enterprise campus.

Routing protocols are typically deployed across the distribution-to-core and core-to-core interconnections.

Layer 3 routing design can be used in the access layer, too, but this design is currently not as common.

Layer 3 routing protocols are used to quickly reroute around failed nodes or links while providing load balancing over redundant paths.

Build Redundant Triangles

For optimum distribution-to-core layer convergence, build redundant triangles, not squares, to take advantage of equal-cost, redundant paths for the best deterministic convergence.

The topology connecting the distribution and core switches should be built using triangles, with equal-cost paths to all redundant nodes. The triangle design is shown in Figure 2-13 Model A, and uses dual equal-cost paths to avoid timer-based, nondeterministic convergence. Instead of indirect neighbor or route-loss detection using hellos and dead timers, the triangle design failover is hardware based and relies on physical link loss to mark a path as unusable and reroute all traffic to the alternate equal-cost path. There is no need for OSPF or EIGRP to recalculate a new path.

Triangles: Link or box failure does *not* require routing protocol convergence.

Squares: Link or box failure requires routing protocol convergence.

 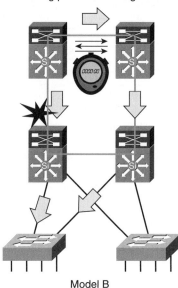

Model A   Model B

Figure 2-13   *Build Redundant Triangles*

In contrast, the square topology shown in Figure 2-14 Model B requires routing protocol convergence to fail over to an alternate path in the event of a link or node failure. It is possible to build a topology that does not rely on equal-cost, redundant paths to compensate

Figure 2-14   *Use Passive Interfaces at the Access Layer*

for limited physical fiber connectivity or to reduce cost. However, with this design, it is not possible to achieve the same deterministic convergence in the event of a link or node failure, and for this reason the design will not be optimized for high availability.

Peer Only on Transit Links

Another recommended practice is to limit unnecessary peering across the access layer by peering only on transit links.

By default, the distribution layer switches send routing updates and attempt to peer across the uplinks from the access switches to the remote distribution switches on every VLAN. This is unnecessary and wastes CPU processing time.

Figure 2-14 shows an example network where with 4 VLANs per access switch and 3 access switches, 12 unnecessary adjacencies are formed. Only the adjacency on the link between the distribution switches is needed. This redundant Layer 3 peering has no benefit from a high-availability perspective, and only adds load in terms of memory, routing protocol update overhead, and complexity. In addition, in the event of a link failure, it is possible for traffic to transit through a neighboring access layer switch, which is not desirable.

As a recommended practice, limit unnecessary routing peer adjacencies by configuring the ports toward Layer 2 access switches as passive, which will suppress the advertising of routing updates. If a distribution switch does not receive routing updates from a potential peer on a specific interface, it will not need to process these updates, and it will not form a neighbor adjacency with the potential peer across that interface.

There are two approaches to configuring passive interfaces for the access switches:

- Use the **passive-interface default** command, and selectively use the **no passive-interface** command to enable a neighboring relationship where peering is desired.

- Use the **passive-interface** command to selectively make specific interfaces passive.

  Passive interface configuration example for OSPF:
  ```
  AGG1(config)#router ospf 1
  AGG1(config-router)#passive-interface Vlan 99
  ! Or
  AGG1(config)#router ospf 1
  AGG1(config-router)#passive-interface default
  AGG1(config-router)#no passive-interface Vlan 99
  ```

  Passive interface configuration example for EIGRP:
  ```
  AGG1(config)#router EIGRP 1
  AGG1(config-router)#passive-interface Vlan 99
  ! Or
  AGG1(config)#router EIGRP 1
  AGG1(config-router)#passive-interface default
  AGG1(config-router)#no passive-interface Vlan 99
  ```

You should use whichever technique requires the fewest lines of configuration or is the easiest for you to manage.

Summarize at the Distribution Layer

A hierarchical routing design reduces routing update traffic and avoids unnecessary routing computations. Such a hierarchy is achieved through allocating IP networks in contiguous blocks that can be easily summarized by a dynamic routing protocol.

It is a recommended practice to configure route summarization at the distribution layer to advertise a single summary route to represent multiple IP networks within the building (switch block). As a result, fewer routes will be advertised through the core layer and subsequently to the distribution layer switches in other buildings (switch blocks). If the routing information is not summarized toward the core, EIGRP and OSPF require interaction with a potentially large number of peers to converge around a failed node.

Summarization at the distribution layer optimizes the rerouting process. If a link to an access layer device goes down, return traffic at the distribution layer to that device is dropped until the IGP converges. When summarization is used and the distribution nodes send summarized information toward the core, an individual distribution node does not advertise loss of connectivity to a single VLAN or subnet. This means that the core does not know that it cannot send traffic to the distribution switch where the access link has failed. Summaries limit the number of peers that an EIGRP router must query or the number of link-state advertisements (LSA) that OSPF must process, and thereby speeds the rerouting process.

Summarization should be performed at the boundary where the distribution layer of each building connects to the core. The method for configuring route summarization varies, depending on the IGP being used. Route summarization is covered in detail in Chapter 3, "Developing an Optimum Design for Layer 3." These designs require a Layer 3 link between the distribution switches, as shown in Figure 2-15, to allow the distribution node that loses connectivity to a given VLAN or subnet the ability to reroute traffic across the distribution-to-distribution link. To be effective, the address space selected for the distribution-to-distribution link must be within the address space being summarized.

Summarization relies on a solid network addressing design.

Figure 2-15   *Summarize at the Distribution Layer*

First-Hop Redundancy

First-hop redundancy or default-gateway redundancy is an important component in convergence in a highly available hierarchical network design.

First-hop redundancy allows a network to recover from the failure of the device acting as the default gateway for end nodes on a physical segment. When the access layer is Layer 2, the distribution layer switches act as the default gateway for the entire Layer 2 domain that they support, as illustrated in Figure 2-16.

First-Hop Redundancy

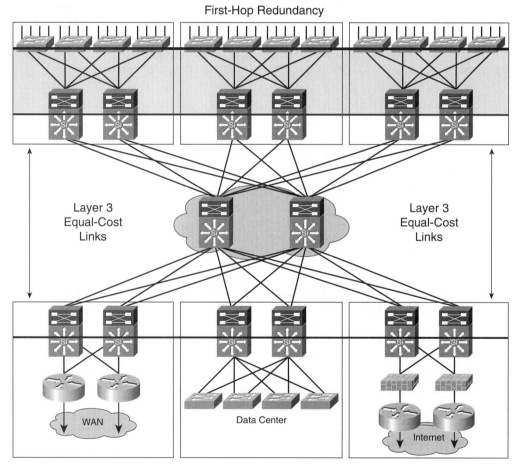

Figure 2-16   *First-Hop Redundancy*

A first-hop redundancy protocol is needed only if the design implements Layer 2 between the access switch and the distribution switch. If Layer 3 is supported to the access switch, the default gateway for end devices is at the access level.

In Cisco deployments, HSRP, developed by Cisco, is typically used as the FHRP. VRRP is an Internet Engineering Task Force (IETF) standards-based method of providing default-gateway redundancy. More deployments are starting to use GLBP, which can more easily achieve load balancing on the uplinks from the access layer to the distribution layer, and first-hop redundancy and failure protection.

HSRP and VRRP with Cisco enhancements both provide a robust method of backing up the default gateway, and can provide subsecond failover to the redundant distribution switch when tuned properly. HSRP is the recommended protocol over VRRP because it is a Cisco-owned standard, which allows for the rapid development of new features and functionality before VRRP. VRRP is the logical choice over HSRP when interoperability with other vendor devices is required.

HSRP or GLBP timers can be reliably tuned to achieve 800-ms convergence for link or node failure in the Layer 2 and Layer 3 boundary in the building distribution layer. The following configuration snippet shows how HSRP can be tuned down from its default 3-second hello timer and 10-second hold timer in a campus environment to achieve subsecond convergence on aggregation switches:

```
interface Vlan5
ip address 10.1.5.3 255.255.255.0
ip helper-address 10.5.10.20
standby 1 ip 10.1.5.1
standby 1 timers msec 200 msec 750
standby 1 priority 150
standby 1 preempt delay minimum 180
```

Preempt Delay Tuning

One important factor to take into account when tuning default gateway redundancy using HSRP or another protocol is its preemptive behavior.

Preemption causes the primary HSRP peer to re-assume the primary role when it comes back online after a failure or maintenance event. Preemption is the desired behavior because the RSTP root should be the same device as the HSRP primary for a given subnet or VLAN. However, if HSRP and RSTP are not synchronized after failure recovery, the interconnection between the distribution switches can become a transit link, and traffic takes a multihop Layer 2 path to its default gateway.

HSRP preemption needs to be aware of switch boot time and connectivity to the rest of the network. Preempt delay must be longer than the switch boot time:

- Layer 1 traffic forwarding on line cards

- Layer 2 STP convergence

- Layer 3 IGP convergence

It is possible for HSRP neighbor relationships to form and preemption to occur before the primary switch has Layer 3 connectivity to the core. If this happens, traffic from the access layer can be dropped until full connectivity is established to the core.

The recommended practice is to measure the system boot time, and set the HSRP preempt delay with the **standby preempt delay minimum** command to 50 percent greater than this value. This ensures that the HSRP primary distribution node has established full connectivity to all parts of the network before HSRP preemption is allowed to occur.

Figure 2-17 demonstrates the positive impact that proper HSRP tuning can have on network convergence.

Figure 2-17   *HSRP Preempt Delay Tuning*

Overview of Gateway Load Balancing Protocol

GLBP is a first-hop redundancy protocol designed by Cisco that allows packet load sharing between groups of redundant routers.

When HSRP or VRRP is used to provide default-gateway redundancy, the backup members of the peer relationship are idle, waiting for a failure event to occur before they take over and actively forward traffic. Methods to use uplinks with HSRP or VRRP are difficult to implement and manage. In one technique, the HSRP and STP or RSTP roots alternate between distribution node peers, with the even VLANs homed on one peer and the odd VLANs homed on the alternate. Another technique uses multiple HSRP groups on a single interface and uses DHCP to alternate between the multiple default gateways. These techniques work but are not optimal from a configuration, maintenance, or management perspective.

GLBP provides all the benefits of HSRP and includes load balancing, too. For HSRP, a single virtual MAC address is given to the endpoints when the endpoints use Address Resolution Protocol (ARP) to learn the physical MAC address of their default gateways. GLBP allows a group of routers to function as one virtual router by sharing one virtual IP address while using multiple virtual MAC addresses for traffic forwarding. Figure 2-18 shows a sample configuration supporting GLBP and its roles.

When an endpoint uses ARP for its default gateway, by default the virtual MACs are provided by the GLBP active virtual gateway (AVG) on a round-robin basis. These gateways that assume responsibility for forwarding packets sent to the virtual MAC address are known as active virtual forwarders (AVF) for their virtual MAC address. Because the traffic from a single common subnet goes through multiple redundant gateways, all the uplinks can be used.

> **Note:**   GLBP can also be configured to provide virtual MAC addresses based on a weighting value (if for example, two distribution layer devices have different capacities or utilization), or could be host based (where a particular end-station will use the same AVF MAC address every time), which would be required for tracking flows, such as Network Address Translation / Port Address Translation (NAT/PAT).

Figure 2-18   *Gateway Load Balancing Protocol*

Failover and convergence in GLBP work in a similar fashion as HSRP. A secondary virtual forwarder (SVF) takes over for traffic destined to a virtual MAC impacted by the failure and begins forwarding traffic for its failed peer. The end result is that a more equal utilization of the uplinks is achieved with minimal configuration. As a side effect, a convergence event on the uplink or on the primary distribution node affects only half as many hosts with a pair of GLBP switches, giving a convergence event an average of 50 percent less impact.

Note that using GLBP in topologies where STP has blocked one of the access layer uplinks may result in a two-hop path at Layer 2 for upstream traffic, as illustrated in Figure 2-19.

In environments where VLANs span across the distribution switches, HSRP is the preferred FHRP implementation.

In some cases, the STP environment can be tuned so that the Layer 2 link between the distribution switches is the blocking link while the uplinks from the access layer switches are in a forwarding state.

Figure 2-20 illustrates how you can tune STP by using the **spanning-tree cost interface** configuration command to change the port cost on the interface between the distribution layer switches on the STP secondary root switch. This option works if no VLANs span access switches.

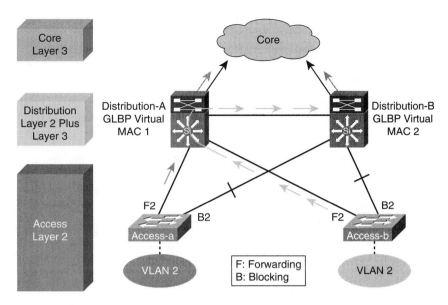

Figure 2-19   *GLBP VLAN Spanning*

Figure 2-20   *GLBP and STP Tuning*

However, if the same VLAN is on multiple access switches, you will have a looped figure-eight topology where one access layer uplink is still blocking. The preferred design is to not span VLANs across access switches.

Optimizing FHRP Convergence

HSRP can be reliably tuned to achieve 800-ms convergence for link or node failure. With HSRP, all flows from one subnet go through the active HSRP router; so the longest, shortest, and average convergence times are the same and less than a second.

VRRP can be tuned with subsecond timers, although the results of this timer tuning is not known. With VRRP, all flows from one subnet go through the same VRRP master router, so the longest, shortest, and average convergence times are the same and about a second.

GLBP can also be reliably tuned to achieve 800-ms convergence for link or node failure. With GLBP, a convergence event on an uplink or on the primary distribution node affects only half as many hosts, so a convergence event has an average of 50 percent less impact than with HSRP or VRRP if the default round-robin load-balancing algorithm is used.

GLBP is currently supported on the Cisco Catalyst 6500 series switches and the Cisco Catalyst 4500 series switches.

Figure 2-21 illustrates the difference in convergence times between each of the respective FHRP when deployed on a distribution to access link in a server farm.

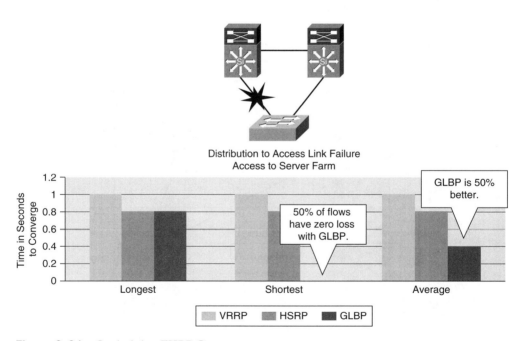

Figure 2-21   *Optimizing FHRP Convergence*

Supporting a Layer 2 to Layer 3 Boundary Design

This following section reviews design models and recommended practices for supporting the Layer 2 to Layer 3 boundary in highly available enterprise campus networks.

Layer 2 to Layer 3 Boundary Design Models

There are several design models for placement of the Layer 2 to Layer 3 boundary in the enterprise campus.

Layer 2 Distribution Switch Interconnection

If the enterprise campus requirements must support VLANs spanning multiple access layer switches, the design model uses a Layer 2 link for interconnecting the distribution switches.

The design, illustrated here in Figure 2-22, is more complex than the Layer 3 interconnection of the distribution switches. The STP convergence process will be initiated for uplink failures and recoveries.

Figure 2-22   *Layer 2 Distribution Switch Interconnection*

You can improve this suboptimal design as follows:

■   Use RSTP as the version of STP.

Note: RPVST+ is a Cisco enhancement of RSTP that uses PVST+. It provides a separate instance of 802.1w per VLAN. The separate instance supports PortFast, UplinkFast, BackboneFast, BPDU guard, BPDU filter, root guard, and loop guard. (RPVST+ is also known as PVRST+.)

■   Provide a Layer 2 trunk between the two distribution switches to avoid unexpected traffic paths and multiple convergence events.

■   If you choose to load balance VLANs across uplinks, be sure to place the HSRP primary and the STP primary on the same distribution layer switch. The HSRP and RSTP root should be collocated on the same distribution switches to avoid using the inter-distribution link for transit.

Layer 3 Distribution Switch Interconnection (HSRP)

Figure 2-23 shows the model which supports a Layer 3 interconnection between distribution switches using HSRP as the FHRP.

Figure 2-23 *Layer 3 Distribution Switch Interconnection*

In this time-proven topology, no VLANs span between access layer switches across the distribution switches. A subnet equals a VLAN, which equals an access switch. The root for each VLAN is aligned with the active HSRP instance. From a STP perspective, both access layer uplinks are forwarding, so the only convergence dependencies are the default gateway and return-path route selection across the distribution-to-distribution link.

This recommended design provides the highest availability.

With this design, a distribution-to-distribution link is required for route summarization. A recommended practice is to map the Layer 2 VLAN number to the Layer 3 subnet for ease of use and management.

Layer 3 Distribution Switch Interconnection (GLBP)

GLBP can also be used as the FHRP with the Layer 3 distribution layer interconnection model, as shown in Figure 2-24.

GLBP allows full utilization of the uplinks from the access layer. However, because the distribution of ARP responses is random, it is less deterministic than the design with HSRP. The distribution-to-distribution link is still required for route summarization. Because the VLANs do not span access switches, STP convergence is not required for uplink failure and recovery.

Layer 3 Access to Distribution Interconnection

The design extending Layer 3 to the access layer, shown here in Figure 2-25, provides the fastest network convergence.

Figure 2-24 *Layer 3 Distribution Switch Interconnection with GLBP*

Figure 2-25 *Layer 3 Access to Distribution Interconnection*

A routing protocol such as EIGRP, when properly tuned, can achieve better convergence results than designs that rely on STP to resolve convergence events. A routing protocol can even achieve better convergence results than the time-tested design placing the Layer 2 to Layer 3 boundary at the distribution layer. The design is easier to implement than configuring Layer 2 in the distribution layer because you do not need to align STP with HSRP or GLBP.

This design supports equal-cost Layer 3 load balancing on all links between the network switches. No HSRP or GLBP configuration is needed because the access switch is the default gateway for the end users. VLANs cannot span access switches in this design.

The convergence time required to reroute around a failed access-to-distribution layer uplink is reliably under 200 ms as compared to 900 ms for the design placing the Layer 2 and Layer 3 boundary at the distribution layer. Return-path traffic is also in the sub-200 ms of convergence time for an EIGRP reroute, again compared to 900 ms for the traditional Layer 2 to Layer 3 distribution layer model.

Because both EIGRP and OSPF loads share over equal-cost paths, this design provides a convergence benefit similar to GLBP. Approximately 50 percent of the hosts are not affected by a convergence event because their traffic is not flowing over the link or through the failed node.

However, some additional complexity associated with uplink IP addressing and subnetting and the loss of flexibility is associated with this design alternative.

Routing in the access layer is not as widely deployed in the enterprise environment as the Layer 2 and Layer 3 distribution layer boundary model.

Note: Deploying a layer 3 access layer may be prohibited because of conformance with the existing architecture, price of multilayer switches, application, or service requirements.

EIGRP Access Design Recommendations

When EIGRP is used as the routing protocol for a fully routed or routed access layer solution, with tuning it can achieve sub-200 ms convergence.

EIGRP to the distribution layer is similar to EIGRP in the branch, but it's optimized for fast convergence using these design rules:

■   Limit scope of queries to a single neighbor:
Summarize at the distribution layer to the core as is done in the traditional Layer 2 to Layer 3 border at the distribution layer. This confines impact of an individual access link failure to the distribution pair by stopping EIGRP queries from propagating beyond the core of the network. When the distribution layer summarizes toward the core, queries are limited to one hop from the distribution switches, which optimizes EIGRP convergence.

Configure all access switches to use EIGRP stub nodes so that the access devices are not queried by the distribution switches for routes. EIGRP stub nodes cannot act as transit nodes and do not participate in EIGRP query processing. When the distribution node learns through the EIGRP hello packets that it is talking to a stub node, it does not flood queries to that node.

■   Control route propagation to access switches using distribution lists. The access switches need only a default route to the distribution switches. An outbound distribution list applied to all interfaces facing the access layer from the distribution switch will conserve memory and optimize performance at the access layer.

■   Set hello and dead timers to 1 and 3 as a secondary mechanism to speed up convergence. The link failure or node failure should trigger convergence events. Tune EIGRP hello and dead timers to 1 and 3, respectively, to protect against a soft failure in which the physical links remain active but hello and route processing has stopped.

EIGRP optimized configuration example:
```
interface GigabitEthernet1/1 ip hello-interval eigrp 100 2 ip hold-time
  eigrp 100 6
router eigrp 100 eigrp stub connected
```

Note: An EIGRP stub is included in the base image of all Cisco multilayer Catalyst switches.

OSPF Access Design Recommendations

When OSPF is used as the routing protocol for a fully routed or routed access layer solution with tuning it can also achieve sub-200-ms convergence.

OSPF to the distribution layer is similar to OSPF in the branch, but it's optimized for fast convergence. With OSPF, summarization and limits to the diameter of OSPF LSA propagation is provided through implementation of Layer 2 to Layer 3 boundaries or Area Border Routers (ABR). It follows these design rules:

- Control the number of routes and routers in each area:
  - Configure each distribution block as a separate, totally stubby OSPF area. The distribution switches become ABRs with their core-facing interfaces in area 0, and the access layer interfaces in unique, totally stubby areas for each access layer switch. Do not extend area 0 to the access switch because the access layer is not used as a transit area in a campus environment. Each access layer switch is configured into its own unique, totally stubby area. In this configuration, LSAs are isolated to each access layer switch so that a link flap for one access layer switch is not communicated beyond the distribution pairs.
  - Tune OSPF millisecond hello, dead-interval, SPF, and LSA throttle timers as a secondary mechanism to improve convergence. Because CPU resources are not as scarce in a campus environment as they might be in a WAN environment, and the media types common in the access layer are not susceptible to the same half-up or rapid transitions as are those commonly found in the WAN, OSPF timers can safely be tuned, as shown in the configuration snippet here:

    ```
    interface GigabitEthernet1/1 ip ospf dead-interval minimal
      hello-multiplier 4
    router ospf 100 area 120 stub no-summary timers throttle spf 10 100 5000
    timers throttle lsa all 10 100 5000 timers lsa arrival 80
    ```

Note: OSPF support is not included in the base image of all Cisco multilayer Catalyst switches, but it is available with the IP Services upgrade.

Potential Design Issues

The following sections discuss potential design issues for placement of the Layer 2 to Layer 3 boundary in the enterprise campus.

Daisy Chaining Access Layer Switches

If multiple fixed-configuration switches are daisy chained in the access layer of the network, there is a danger that black holes will occur in the event of a link or node failure.

In the topology in Figure 2-26, before failures no links are blocking from a STP or RSTP perspective, so both uplinks are available to actively forward and receive traffic. Both distribution nodes can forward return-path traffic from the rest of the network toward the access layer for devices attached to all members of the stack or chain.

Two scenarios can occur if a link or node in the middle of the chain or stack fails. In the first case, the standby HSRP peer can go active as it loses connectivity to its primary peer, forwarding traffic outbound for the devices that still have connectivity to it. The primary

Figure 2-26   *Daisy Chaining Access Layer Switches*

HSRP peer remains active and also forwards outbound traffic for its half of the stack. Although this is not optimum, it is not detrimental from the perspective of outbound traffic.

The second scenario is the issue. Return-path traffic has a 50 percent chance of arriving on a distribution switch that does not have physical connectivity to the half of the stack where the traffic is destined. The traffic that arrives on the wrong distribution switch is dropped.

The solution to this issue with this design is to provide alternate connectivity across the stack in the form of a loop-back cable running from the top to the bottom of the stack. This link needs to be carefully deployed so that the appropriate STP behavior will occur in the access layer.

An alternate design uses a Layer 2 link between the distribution switches.

Cisco StackWise Technology in the Access Layer

Cisco StackWise technology can eliminate the danger that black holes occur in the access layer in the event of a link or node failure. It can eliminate the need for loop-back cables in the access layer or Layer 2 links between distribution nodes.

StackWise technology, shown in the access layer in Figure 2-27, supports the recommended practice of using a Layer 3 connection between the distribution switches without having to use a loop-back cable or perform extra configuration.

The true stack creation provided by the Cisco Catalyst 3750 series switches makes using stacks in the access layer much less complex than chains or stacks of other models. A stack of 3750 switches appears as one node from the network topology perspective.

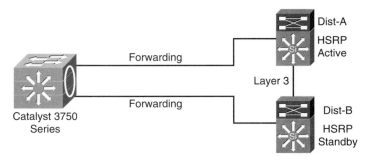

Figure 2-27   *StackWise Technology*

If you use a modular chassis switch to support ports in the aggregation layer, such as the Cisco Catalyst 4500 or Catalyst 6500 family of switches, these design considerations are not required.

Too Much Redundancy

Be aware that even if some redundancy is good, more redundancy is not necessarily better.

In Figure 2-28, a third switch is added to the distribution switches in the center. This extra switch adds unneeded complexity to the design and leads to these design questions:

■   Where should the root switch be placed? With this design, it is not easy to determine where the root switch is located.

■   What links should be in a blocking state? It is very hard to determine how many ports will be in a blocking state.

■   What are the implications of STP and RSTP convergence? The network convergence is definitely not deterministic.

Figure 2-28   *Too Much Redundancy*

■ When something goes wrong, how do you find the source of the problem? The design is much harder to troubleshoot.

Too Little Redundancy

For most designs, a link between the distribution layer switches is required for redundancy.

Figure 2-29 shows a less-than-optimal design where VLANs span multiple access layer switches. Without a Layer 2 link between the distribution switches, the design is a looped figure-eight topology. One access layer uplink will be blocking. HSRP hellos are exchanged by transiting the access switches.

Figure 2-29 *Too Little Redundancy*

Initially, traffic is forwarded from both access switches to the Distribution A switch that supports the STP root and the primary or active HSRP peer for VLAN 2. However, this design will black-hole traffic and be affected by multiple convergence events with a single network failure.

Example: Impact of an Uplink Failure

This example looks at the impact of an uplink failure on the design when there is no link between the distribution layer switches.

In Figure 2-30, when the uplink from Access A to Distribution A fails, three convergence events occur:

1. Access A sends traffic across its active uplink to Distribution B to get to its default gateway. The traffic is black-holed at Distribution B because Distribution B does not initially have a path to the primary or active HSRP peer on Distribution A because of the STP blocking. The traffic is dropped until the standby HSRP peer takes over as the default gateway after not receiving HSRP hellos from Distribution A.

Figure 2-30 *Impact of an Uplink Failure*

Note: With aggressive HSRP timers, you can minimize this period of traffic loss to approximately 900 ms.

2. The indirect link failure is eventually detected by Access B after the maximum-age (max_age) timer expires, and Access B removes blocking on the uplink to Distribution B. With standard STP, transitioning to forwarding can take as long as 50 seconds. If BackboneFast is enabled with PVST+, this time can be reduced to 30 seconds, and RSTP can reduce this interval to as little as 1 second.

3. After STP and RSTP converge, the distribution nodes reestablish their HSRP relationships and Distribution A (the primary HSRP peer) preempts. This causes yet another convergence event when Access A endpoints start forwarding traffic to the primary HSRP peer. The unexpected side effect is that Access A traffic goes through Access B to reach its default gateway. The Access B uplink to Distribution B is now a transit link for Access A traffic, and the Access B uplink to Distribution A must now carry traffic for both the originally intended Access B and for Access A.

Example: Impact on Return-Path Traffic

Because the distribution layer in Figure 2-31 is routing with equal-cost load balancing, up to 50 percent of the return-path traffic arrives at Distribution A and is forwarded to Access B. Access B drops this traffic until the uplink to Distribution B is forwarding. This indirect link-failure convergence can take as long as 50 seconds. PVST+ with UplinkFast reduces the time to three to five seconds, and RSTP further reduces the outage to one second. After the STP and RSTP convergence, the Access B uplink to Distribution B is used as a transit link for Access A return-path traffic.

Figure 2-31 *Impact on Return Path Traffic*

These significant outages could affect the performance of mission-critical applications, such as voice or video. Traffic engineering or link-capacity planning for both outbound and return-path traffic is difficult and complex, and must support the traffic for at least one additional access layer switch.

The conclusion is that if VLANs must span the access switches, a Layer 2 link is needed either between the distribution layer switches or the access switches.

Asymmetric Routing (Unicast Flooding)

When VLANs span access switches, an asymmetric routing situation can result because of equal-cost load balancing between the distribution and core layers.

Up to 50 percent of the return-path traffic with equal-cost routing arrives at the standby HSRP, VRRP, or alternate, nonforwarding GLBP peer. If the content-addressable memory (CAM) table entry ages out before the ARP entry for the end node, the peer may need to flood the traffic to all access layer switches and endpoints in the VLAN.

In Figure 2-32, the CAM table entry ages out on the standby HSRP router because the default ARP timers are four hours and the CAM aging timers are five minutes. The CAM timer expires because no traffic is sent upstream by the endpoint toward the standby HSRP peer after the endpoint initially uses ARP to determine its default gateway. When the CAM entry has aged out and is removed from the CAM table, the standby HSRP peer must forward the return-path traffic to all ports in the common VLAN. The majority of the access layer switches do not have a CAM entry for the target MAC, and they broadcast the return traffic on all ports in the common VLAN. This unicast traffic flooding can have a significant performance impact on the connected end stations because they may receive a large amount of traffic that is not intended for them.

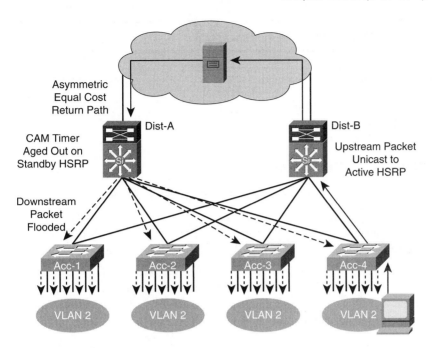

Figure 2-32   *Asymmetric Routing*

Unicast Flooding Prevention

The unicast flooding situation can be easily avoided by not spanning VLANs across access layer switches.

Unicast flooding is not an issue when VLANs are not present across multiple access layer switches because the flooding occurs only to switches supporting the VLAN where the traffic would have normally been switched. If the VLANs are local to individual access layer switches, asymmetric routing traffic is flooded on only the one VLAN interface on the distribution switch. Traffic is flooded out the same interface that would be used normally to forward to the appropriate access switch. In addition, the access layer switch receiving the flooded traffic has a CAM table entry for the host because the host is directly attached, so traffic is switched only to the intended host. As a result, no additional end stations are affected by the flooded traffic.

If you must implement a topology where VLANs span more than one access layer switch, the recommended workaround is to tune the ARP timer so that it is equal to or less than the CAM aging timer. A shorter ARP cache timer causes the standby HSRP peer to use ARP for the target IP address before the CAM entry timer expires and the MAC entry is removed. The subsequent ARP response repopulates the CAM table before the CAM entry is aged out and removed. This removes the possibility of flooding asymmetrically routed return-path traffic to all ports. You can also consider biasing the routing metrics to remove the equal cost routes.

Supporting Infrastructure Services

This section reviews considerations for supporting infrastructure services in highly available enterprise campus networks. Considerations for building a converged network to support IP telephony are discussed. QoS attributes and aspects of the Cisco Catalyst Integrated Security features are also described.

IP Telephony Considerations

IP telephony services are supported at each layer of the campus network.

High availability, redundancy, and fast convergence needed by IP telephony services are supported throughout the enterprise campus network. QoS features are implemented throughout the network. The distribution layer typically supports policy enforcement.

However, because implementing IP telephony services extends the network edge, IP telephony has the most impact at the access layer of the network. The access layer supports device attachment and phone detection, inline power for devices, and QoS features including classification, scheduling, and the trust boundary.

IP Telephony Extends the Network Edge

Because the IP phone is a three-port switch, IP telephony services actually extend the network edge, as shown in Figure 2-33.

Figure 2-33   *IP Telephony Extends the Network Edge*

The IP phone shown in Figure 2-33 contains a three-port switch that is configured in conjunction with the access switch and Cisco Unified Communications Manager:

■   Power negotiation

■   VLAN configuration

■   802.1x interoperation

■   QoS configuration

■   DHCP and Cisco Unified Communications Manager registration

When a Cisco IP phone is connected to the network, Cisco Catalyst multiservice switches detect and integrate the phone with the network. The switches can deliver Power over Ethernet (PoE) using existing copper cabling to power the IP phones. The switches place the IP phones and attached devices in the appropriate VLAN, often using 802.1x services. The switch supports the QoS configuration needed for the IP phones, and provides connection to DHCP servers and Cisco Unified Communications Manager systems for registration.

PoE is the ability for the LAN switching infrastructure to provide power over a copper Ethernet cable to an endpoint or powered device. This capability is also referred to as in-line power, and was originally developed by Cisco Systems in 2000 to support the emerging IP telephony deployments.

To support PoE delivery to power capable devices, a number of issues need to be resolved: phone detection, power delivery, power management, and cable and bandwidth management.

PoE Requirements

There are two PoE implementations available, and two ways to provide power to the IP phones:

■ Cisco line cards support prestandard PoE, IEEE 802.3af, and a mix of devices. IEEE 802.3af-only devices will not negotiate or receive power from an original Cisco PoE-only line card.

■ Cisco devices use a bidirectional Cisco Discovery Protocol (CDP) exchange to negotiate the exact power requirements. Power negotiation optimizes power consumption by allowing the switch to reserve only the power needed for the device.

The earlier Cisco prestandard PoE devices initially receive 6.3W and then optionally negotiate their power requirements using CDP. Cisco prestandard devices use a relay in the powered device to reflect a special FastLink pulse for device detection.

The devices based on the IEEE 802.3af power standard initially receive 12.95 watts of power, unless a power-sourcing equipment (PSE) device can detect a specific powered device classification. An 802.3af PSE device applies a voltage in the range of –2.8 to –10 volts on the cable and then looks for a 25K ohm signature resistor in the powered device.

IEEE 802.3af power may be delivered using a PoE-capable Ethernet port, which is referred to as an endpoint PSE, or by a midspan PSE that can be used to deliver PoE in the event an existing non-PoE-capable Ethernet switch is used. An endpoint PSE, such as a PoE-capable Ethernet switch, can use either active data wires of an Ethernet port or spare wires to a powered device. Some midspan PSEs can only implement power over spare pairs of copper cabling and cannot be used to deliver PoE over 1000BASE-T connections.

The IEEE 802.3af power standard classes are shown here in Figure 2-34.

Note: A midspan PSE takes up rack space and adds a patch point to every PoE cable, increasing cabling costs and complexity.

IEEE 802.3af Power Classes

Class	Usage	Minimum Power Levels Output at the PSE	Maximum Power Levels at the Powered Device
0	Default	15.4W	0.44 to 12.95W
1	Optional	4.0W	0.44 to 3.84W
2	Optional	7.0W	3.84 to 6.49W
3	Optional	15.4W	6.49 to 12.95W
4	Reserved for Future Use	Treat as Class 0	Reserved for Future Use: A Class 4 Signature Cannot Be Provided by a Compliant Powered Device

Figure 2-34 *PoE Power Classes*

Power Budget and Management

Power budget planning is necessary to determine what devices can be supported today and in the future.

The switches manage power by what is allocated, not by what is currently used. However, the device power consumption is not constant:

- Cisco Unified IP Phone 7960G requires 7W when the phone is ringing at maximum volume.

- Cisco Unified IP Phone 7960G requires 5W when it is on or off hook.

Delivery of PoE using the IEEE 802.3af default classification may significantly increase the power requirements on both the PSE switch and the power infrastructure. To provide PoE in a cost-effective and efficient manner, Cisco Catalyst switches support Cisco Intelligent Power Management (Cisco IPM) in addition to IEEE 802.3af classification. This enables a powered device and PSE to negotiate their respective capabilities to explicitly manage how much power is required to power the device and also how the PSE-capable switch manages the allocation of power to individual powered devices. These Cisco IPM capabilities enable a network and facilities manager to effectively and economically manage the power resources within a wiring closet and help PSE-capable switches meet the objectives of the network.

Power management is complex. Power management can have significant ramifications with respect to the power supply required to drive all the powered devices and line cards, how power is delivered within the switch, how the switch manages power allocation, and finally, for the power delivery requirements of the wiring closet. You need to plan for maximum theoretical draw that so there will be sufficient power available to be allocated to end devices and the line cards in the switch. Even if the PSE and powered device support power classification, the classification ranges are fairly broad and can lead to wasted power budget allocation. When there is insufficient power in a chassis, the power management system will deactivate line cards.

Power requirements can be estimated using the Cisco Power Calculator found at http://tools.cisco.com/cpc/launch.jsp.

The Cisco Power Calculator enables you to estimate the power supply requirements for a specific PoE and line card configuration.

The Cisco Power Calculator requires a username and password. The tool allows a series of selections for the configurable products, and provides results showing the output current, output power, and system heat dissipation for a specific configuration.

The calculator is an educational resource and a starting point in planning power requirements; it does not provide a final power recommendation from Cisco.

The Cisco Power Calculator supports the following Cisco product series: Cisco Catalyst 6500, Catalyst 4500, Catalyst 3750, and Catalyst 3560 series switches, and the Cisco 7600 series router.

The Power Consumption Summary screen shown in Figure 2-35 displays the minimum power supply required for the selected configuration and percentage of power usage. The table displays output current (amperes), output power (watts), and heat dissipation (BTUs per hour).

Power Consumption/Heat Dissipation Summary			
Slot	Line Card	Optional DFC	Power over Ethernet Capabilities
1	WS-SUP32-GE-3B	---	---
2	WS-SUP32-GE-3B	---	---
3	-- EMPTY-SLOT --	---	---
4	-- EMPTY-SLOT --	---	---
Minimum Power Supply		Percentage of Power Used	
Single/Redundant PWR-2700-DC/4 with one input		28.05%	
First Alternative Power Supply		Percentage of Power Used	
Combined PWR-2700-DC/4 with one input		16.80%	
Total Output Current	Total Output Power	Total Heat Dissipation	
8.81 Amps	370.02 Watts	1706.10 BTU/Hr	

Figure 2-35 *Power Consumption Summary*

The Cisco Power Calculator recommends the smallest power supply that meets the requirements of the configuration. The tool reports single and redundant power supply options, and also the combined power configuration mode as appropriate.

The power supply details area shown here in Figure 2-36 displays power utilization with various-sized power supplies.

The Configuration Details section of the Cisco Power Calculator output shown in Figure 2-37 displays the current, power, and heat dissipation for each component.

Multi-VLAN Access Port

The concept of an access port has been extended to a multi-VLAN access port in the enterprise campus.

Cisco Power Calculator				
Power Supply Details				
Minimum Power Supply	Percentage of Power used	Total Output Current for this PSU (A)	Total Output Current Used (A)	Total Output Current Remaining (A)
Combined WS-CAC-2500W	**68.92%**	**45.77**	**31.55**	**14.22**
Other Power Supply Options	Percentage of Power used	Total Output Current for this PSU (A)	Total Output Current Used (A)	Total Output Current Remaining (A)
Combined WS-CAC-3000W	67.87%	46.48	31.55	14.93
Single/Redundant WS-CAC-6000W with Dual 110V inputs	49.58%	63.62	31.55	32.07
Combined WS-CAC-6000W with Dual 110V inputs	35.05%	90.00	31.55	58.45

[Top]

Configuration Details				
Slot	Line Card	Output Current (A)	Output Power (W)	Heat Dissipation (BTU/Hr)
FAN2	WS-C6K-9SLOT-FAN2	0.00	0.00	546.00

Figure 2-36   *Power Supply Details*

Cisco Power Calculator				
Configuration Details				
Slot	Line Card	Output Current (A)	Output Power (W)	Heat Dissipation (BTU/Hr)
FAN2	WS-C6K-9SLOT-FAN2	0.00	0.00	546.00
1	WS-X6548-GE-45AF	3.16	132.72	566.55
2	WS-X6548-GE-45AF	3.16	132.72	566.55
3	WS-X6548-GE-45AF	3.16	132.72	566.55
4	WS-X6148A-GE-AF	2.68	112.56	480.49
5	WS-SUP720-3BXL	7.82	328.44	1402.03
6	WS-SUP720-3BXL	7.82	328.44	1402.03
7	-- EMPTY-SLOT --	0.00	0.00	0.00
8	-- EMPTY-SLOT --	0.00	0.00	0.00
9	-- EMPTY-SLOT --	0.00	0.00	0.00
	Sub Total	27.80	1167.60	5530.19
PoE Device	Quantity	Output Current (A)	Output Power (W)	Heat Dissipation (BTU/Hr)
IEEE 802.3af Device - Class 2 (7W)	20	3.75	157.30	193.39
		Output Current (A)	Output Power (W)	Heat Dissipation (BTU/Hr)
	Total	**31.55**	**1324.90**	**5723.58**

Figure 2-37   *Configuration Details*

Multiservice switches support a new parameter for IP telephony support that makes the access port a multi-VLAN access port. The new parameter is called an auxiliary VLAN. Every Ethernet 10/100/1000 port in the switch is associated with two VLANs:

- A native VLAN for data service that is identified by the port VLAN ID (PVID)

- An auxiliary VLAN for voice service that is identified by the voice VLAN ID (VVID)

- During the initial CDP exchange with the access switch, the IP phone is configured with a VVID.

- The IP phone is also supplied with a QoS configuration using CDP. Voice traffic is separated from data and supports a different trust boundary.

Data packets between the multiservice access switch and the PC or workstation are on the native VLAN. All packets going out on the native VLAN of an IEEE 802.1Q port are sent untagged by the access switch. The PC or workstation connected to the IP phone usually sends untagged packets.

Voice packets are tagged by the IP phone based on the CDP information from the access switch.

The multi-VLAN access ports are not trunk ports, even though the hardware is set to the dot1q trunk. The hardware setting is used to carry more than one VLAN, but the port is still considered an access port that is able to carry one native VLAN and the auxiliary VLAN. The **switchport host** command can be applied to a multi-VLAN access port on the access switch.

Note: The switch downloads both the data (native) VLAN and the auxiliary (voice) VLAN to the phone. The IP phone marks any traffic on the voice VLAN by modifying the priority bits in the 802.1Q/p tag to CoS 5 (binary 111), which can later be easily mapped to a Layer 3 marking (for example, DSCP 46 or EF). The trust can also be extended to any CoS markings that may have been set by the attached PC (or can mark these values up or down as desired).

QoS Considerations

Typical campus networks are built with oversubscription in mind. The network usually has multiple possible congestion points where important traffic may be dropped without QoS.

Most campus links are underutilized. Some studies have shown that 95 percent of campus access layer links are utilized at less than 5 percent of their capacity.

The rule-of-thumb recommendation for data oversubscription is 20:1 for access ports on the access-to-distribution uplink. The recommendation is 4:1 for the distribution-to-core links. When you use these oversubscription ratios, congestion may occur infrequently on the uplinks. QoS is needed for these occasions. If congestion is frequently occurring, the design does not have sufficient uplink bandwidth.

Recommended Practices for QoS

QoS helps manage oversubscription and speed-transitions in the design. The following are recommended best practices for QoS:

■ Deployed end-to-end to be effective

■ Ensures that mission-critical applications are not impacted by link or transmit queue congestion

■ Enforces QoS policies at aggregation and rate transition points

■ Uses multiple queues with configurable admission criteria, and scheduling effective QoS is deployed end-to-end with each layer supporting a role

Internet worms and denial-of-service (DoS) attacks can flood links even in a high-speed campus environment. QoS policies protect voice, video, and mission-critical data traffic while giving a lower class of service to suspect traffic.

Aggregation and rate transition points must enforce QoS policies to support preferred traffic and manage congestion. In campus networks, multiple queues with configurable admission criteria and scheduling are required on the LAN ports.

Transmit Queue Congestion

The type of congestion that is most common in a campus network is called transmit-queue (Tx-queue) starvation.

Both LANs and WANs are subject to Tx-queue congestion:

■ During a transition from LAN to WAN, a router has to make the rate transition from 10/100 Ethernet to WAN speeds. When this happens, the router must queue the packets and apply QoS to ensure that important traffic is transmitted first. Tx-queue starvation occurs when incoming packets are received faster than outgoing packets are transmitted. Packets are queued as they wait to serialize out onto the slower link.

■ In the campus, as the LAN infrastructure transitions from 10 Gb/s or 1 Gb/s uplinks in the distribution layer to 10/100 Gb/s to the desktop, packets must be queued as they wait to serialize out the 10 or 100 Mb/s link.

The difference between a WAN router and a campus switch is the number of interfaces and the amount of memory associated with each. In the campus, the amount of Tx-queue space is much smaller than the amount of memory available in a WAN router. Because of the small amount of memory, the potential for dropped traffic because of Tx-queue starvation is relatively high.

QoS Role in the Campus

QoS features are used to prioritize traffic according to its relative importance and provide preferential treatment using congestion management techniques.

Using QoS in the campus network design ensures that important traffic such as voice and video is placed in a queue that is configured so that it optimizes memory usage.

However, the network should provide an adequate level of service for all network traffic, including lower-priority, best-effort traffic under normal circumstances. For best-effort traffic, there is an implied good-faith commitment that there are at least some network resources available.

QoS is also needed to identify and potentially punish out-of-profile traffic such as potential worms, distributed denial of service (DDoS) attacks, and peer-to-peer media-sharing applications that may be placed in a scavenger class and marked with differentiated services code point (DSCP) class selector 1 (CS1). The scavenger class is intended to provide deferential services, or less-than best-effort services, to certain applications. During periods of congestion, scavenger-class traffic is the first to experience Tx-queue starvation and packet loss when the bandwidth is reserved for higher-priority traffic. As demand increases or capacity is reduced, best-effort traffic may also be affected. The minimum goal of high-availability network design is to ensure that high-priority voice, video, and mission-critical data applications are never affected by network congestion.

Campus QoS Design Considerations

Campus QoS design is primarily concerned with classification, marking, and policing, as illustrated in Figure 2-38.

Figure 2-38   *Campus QoS Design Considerations*

Queuing is enabled at any node that has the potential for congestion. The edge traffic classification scheme is mapped to the upstream queue configuration. The applications are classified and marked as close to their sources as technically and administratively feasible. Traffic flows are policed as close to their sources as possible.

Multiple queues are the only way to guarantee voice quality, protect mission-critical data, and throttle abnormal sources:

■   Voice needs to be assigned to the hardware priority queue. VoIP deployments require provisioning-explicit priority servicing for VoIP traffic and a guaranteed bandwidth service for call-signaling traffic. Strict-priority queuing is limited to 33 percent of the capacity of the link.

- At least 25 percent of the bandwidth of the link is reserved for the default best-effort class, which is the default class for data traffic. Under normal circumstances, the network should provide an adequate level of service for best-effort traffic.

- Scavenger traffic needs to be assigned its own queue with a low threshold to trigger aggressive drops. Applications assigned to this class have little or no contribution to the organizational objectives of the enterprise. Assigning a minimal bandwidth queue to scavenger traffic forces it to be squelched to virtually nothing during periods of congestion, but allows it to be available if bandwidth is not being used for business purposes, which might occur during off-peak hours.

Cisco Catalyst Integrated Security Features

The Cisco Catalyst Integrated Security capabilities provide campus security on the Cisco Catalyst switches through the use of integrated tools:

- Port security prevents MAC flooding attacks.

- DHCP snooping prevents client attacks on the DHCP server and switch.

- Dynamic ARP Inspection adds security to ARP using the DHCP snooping table to minimize the impact of ARP poisoning and spoofing attacks.

- IP Source Guard prevents IP spoofing addresses using the DHCP snooping table.

Port Security Prevents MAC-Based Attacks

Port security can be used to prevent MAC-based attacks.

A MAC-based attack occurs when an attacker sends out floods of MAC addresses to a switch to overload the CAM table. When the CAM table limit is reached, the switch can no longer keep track of legitimate addresses and starts flooding all information to all ports.

Port security enables a network administrator to restrict the MAC addresses allowed or the maximum number of MAC addresses on a per-port basis. The allowed MAC addresses on a given port can be either statically configured by the administrator or dynamically learned by the switch. A security violation occurs when either the maximum number of MAC addresses on a given port is exceeded or a frame with a nonsecure source MAC address is seen on that port. The port is then shut down, or alternatively, a Simple Network Management Protocol (SNMP) trap is generated. Aging with either inactivity or a predefined time interval can be configured with port security for the dynamic or static secure MAC addresses.

Note: When a port security violation occurs, the port will take one of three actions, depending on how the port is configured: The port will be shut down (Shutdown), frames will simply be ignored (Protect), or the frames will be ignored and the violation counter incremented (Restrict).

DHCP Snooping Protects Against Rogue and Malicious DHCP Servers

DHCP snooping can be used to protect against rogue and malicious DHCP servers.

In some cases, an intruder can attach a server to the network and have it assume the role of the DHCP server for that segment. This enables the intruder to give out false DHCP information for the default gateway and domain name servers, which points clients to the hacker's machine. This misdirection enables the hacker to become a "man in the middle" and to gain access to confidential information, such as username and password pairs, while the end user is unaware of the attack. DHCP snooping can prevent this. DHCP snooping is a per-port security mechanism used to differentiate an untrusted switch port connected to an end user from a trusted switch port connected to a DHCP server or another switch. It can be enabled on a per-VLAN basis. DHCP snooping allows only authorized DHCP servers to respond to DHCP requests and to distribute network information to clients. It also provides the ability to rate-limit DHCP request on client ports, thereby mitigating the effect of DHCP DoS attacks from an individual client or access port.

Dynamic ARP Inspection Protects Against ARP Poisoning

Dynamic ARP Inspection can provide protection against ARP poisoning.

ARP does not have any authentication. It is quite simple for a malicious user to spoof addresses by using tools such as ettercap, dsniff, and arpspoof to poison the ARP tables of other hosts on the same VLAN. In a typical attack, a malicious user can send unsolicited ARP replies (gratuitous ARP packets) to other hosts on the subnet with the attacker's MAC address and the default gateway's IP address. Frames intended for default gateways sent from hosts with poisoned ARP tables are sent to the hacker's machine (allowing the packets to be sniffed) or an unreachable host as a DoS attack. ARP poisoning leads to various man-in-the-middle attacks, posing a security threat in the network.

Dynamic ARP Inspection helps prevent the man-in-the-middle attacks by not relaying invalid or gratuitous ARP replies out to other ports in the same VLAN. Dynamic ARP Inspection intercepts all ARP requests and all replies on the untrusted ports. Each intercepted packet is verified for valid IP-to-MAC bindings, which are gathered via DHCP snooping. Denied ARP packets are either dropped or logged by the switch for auditing, so ARP poisoning attacks are stopped. Incoming ARP packets on the trusted ports are not inspected. Dynamic ARP Inspection can also rate-limit ARP requests from client ports to minimize port scanning mechanisms.

IP Source Guard Protects Against Spoofed IP Addresses

IP Source Guard is a unique Cisco IOS Software feature for Catalyst switches that helps mitigate IP spoofing.

IP Source Guard prevents a malicious host from attacking the network by hijacking its neighbor's IP address. IP Source Guard provides per-port IP traffic filtering of the assigned source IP addresses at wire speed. It dynamically maintains per-port VLAN ACLs based on IP-to-MAC-to-switch port bindings. The binding table is populated either by the DHCP snooping feature or through static configuration of entries. IP Source Guard is typically deployed for untrusted switch ports in the access layer.

Example Catalyst Integrated Security Feature Configuration

This configuration snippet shows the commands to enable the Catalyst Integrated Security features.

```
ip dhcp snooping
ip dhcp snooping vlan 2-10
ip arp inspection vlan 2-10
!c
interface fastethernet3/1
switchport port-security
switchport port-security max 3
switchport port-security violation restrict
switchport port-security aging time 2
switchport port-security aging type inactivity
ip arp inspection limit rate 100
ip dhcp snooping limit rate 100
ip verify source port-security
!
interface gigabit1/1
ip dhcp snooping trust
ip arp inspection trust
```

Summary

This chapter examined design models for high availability and fast convergence for the hierarchical layers of the Cisco Enterprise Campus Architecture. High availability in the campus minimizes convergence time after link and node failures with appropriate redundancy.

VLANs should not span access switches in the campus for predictable fast convergence. Layer 2 designs use RTSP when STP is required, define primary and secondary root switches, and use the Cisco STP toolkit to harden Layer 2. Trunks and channels are tuned for predictable fast convergence. Aggressive mode UDLD is configured on all fiber links.

Oversubscription and bandwidth are managed to minimize complexity and provide deterministic behavior. Layer 3 designs should load balance traffic over redundant equal-cost links built on triangles, not squares. Routing protocols should peer only on transit links, and summarize at the distribution layer. HSRP and GLBP support fast convergence for end devices.

The Layer 2 to Layer 3 boundary is typically at the distribution layer, but it can be placed at the access layer. Campus network designs should avoid daisy chaining access layer switches, provide appropriate redundancy, and avoid asymmetric flooding.

Infrastructure service considerations such as IP telephony and QoS impact the end-to-end network. The access layer supports device attachment, inline power for devices, and multi-VLAN access ports. End-to-end QoS helps manage oversubscriptions and network speed transitions. Tx-queue starvation is the most common campus congestion issue. Cisco Catalyst Integrated Security features provide security at the network edge.

References

For additional information, refer to these resources:

- Cisco Systems, Inc. "Designing a Campus Network for High Availability," at http://www.cisco.com/application/pdf/en/us/guest/netsol/ns432/c649/cdccont_0900aecd801a8a2d.pdf

- Cisco Systems, Inc. "Hierarchical Campus Design at a Glance," at http://www.cisco.com/application/pdf/en/us/guest/netsol/ns24/c643/cdccont_0900aecd800d8129.pdf

- Cisco Systems, Inc. "High Availability Campus Network Design—Routed Access Layer using EIGRP or OSPF" at http://www.cisco.com/application/pdf/en/us/guest/netsol/ns432/c649/ccmigration_09186a00805fccbf.pdf

- Cisco Systems, Inc. "Enterprise QoS Solution Reference Network Design Guide," at http://www.cisco.com/application/pdf/en/us/guest/netsol/ns432/c649/ccmigration_09186a008049b062.pdf

- Cisco Systems, Inc. "Cisco Nonstop Forwarding," at http://www.cisco.com/univercd/cc/td/doc/product/software/ios122s/122snwft/release/122s20/fsnsf20s.pdf

- Cisco Systems, Inc. "Cisco IOS Software Modularity on the Cisco Catalyst 6500 Series Switch," at http://www.cisco.com/application/pdf/en/us/guest/products/ps708/c1244/cdccont_0900aecd80313e09.pdf

- Cisco Systems, Inc. "Cisco Catalyst Integrated Security-Enabling the Self-Defending Network," at http://www.cisco.com/application/pdf/en/us/guest/products/ps708/c1244/cdccont_0900aecd8015f0ae.pdf

- Cisco Systems, Inc. "RST-2031: Multilayer Campus Architectures and Design Principles" Networkers 2006 presentation (accessible on a subscription basis), at http://www.networkersonline.net

- Cisco Systems, Inc. "RST-3363: Routed Fast Convergence and High Availability" Networkers 2006 presentation (accessible on a subscription basis), at http://www.networkersonline.net

- Cisco Systems, Inc. "RST-3466: Cisco IOS Software Modularity–Architecture and Deployment," Networkers 2006 presentation (accessible on a subscription basis), at http://www.networkersonline.net

Review Questions

Answer the following questions, and then refer to Appendix A, "Answers to Review Questions," for the answers.

1. Which descriptions best define the core layer? (Choose two.)

   a. It aggregates end users and supports a feature-rich environment.

   b. It provides a high-speed, Layer 3 switching environment using hardware-accelerated services.

   c. It performs high-speed routing and packet manipulations.

   d. It provides scalability and fast policy-based connectivity.

   e. It provides the backbone for campus connectivity.

2. What hardware supports Cisco IOS Software modularity? (Choose all that apply.)

   a. Cisco Catalyst 3750 series

   b. Cisco Catalyst 4500 series

   c. Cisco Catalyst 6500 series

   d. Cisco Catalyst XR series

   e. All Cisco Catalyst series switches

3. Which statements are correct descriptions of NSF?

   a. It allows the standby RP to takes control of the device after a hardware or software fault on the active RP.

   b. It is a Layer 3 function that works with SSO to minimize the amount of time a network is unavailable to its users following a switchover.

   c. It is supported by the Cisco implementation of EIGRP, OSPF, RIP, and BGP protocols.

    d. It synchronizes startup configuration, startup variables, and running configuration.

    e. The main objective of NSF is to continue forwarding IP packets following an RP switchover.

4. If you need to implement STP, which version is recommended for the enterprise campus?

    a. CST

    b. HSRP

    c. MST

    d. PVST+

    e. RSTP

5. What is the enterprise recommendation regarding UDLD?

    a. Adjust the default hello timers to three seconds for aggressive mode.

    b. Enable it to create channels containing up to eight parallel links between switches.

    c. Enable it in global mode and on every interface you need to support.

    d. Enable it in global mode to support every individual fiber-optic and Ethernet interface.

    e. Enable it in global mode to support every individual fiber-optic interface.

6. Which statements are correct descriptions of EtherChannels? (Choose two.)

    a. EtherChannels can reduce the number of peers by creating a single logical interface.

    b. EtherChannels can increase the number of peers by creating multiple logical interfaces.

    c. OSPF running on a Cisco IOS Software-based switch will not notice a failed link in a bundle.

    d. EIGRP may not change the link cost if there is a failed link in a bundle.

    e. EtherChannel Min-Links feature is supported on PAgP EtherChannels.

7. Which statements are correct descriptions of EtherChannel load balancing? (Choose three.)

    a. Load balancing using an alternate input hash can be tuned with the **cef port-channel load-balance** command.

    b. Load balancing using an alternate input hash can be tuned with the **port-channel load-balance** command.

    c. The default input hash value of Layer 3 for the source and destination does not load balance across the links.

    d. The default input hash value of Layer 3 for source and destination and Layer 4 port does load balance across the links.

    e. To achieve the best load balancing, use alternating hashes in the core and distribution layer switches.

    f. To achieve the best load balancing, use two, four, or eight ports in the port channel.

8. What are the reasons that passive interfaces should be implemented at distribution layer ports facing the access layer? (Choose two.)

    a. To limit unnecessary peering across the access layer switches when the Layer 2 to Layer 3 boundary is in the distribution layer

    b. To limit unnecessary peering across the access layer switches when the Layer 2 to Layer 3 boundary is in the access layer

    c. To provide high availability in the event of a link or node failure

    d. To support transit traffic through the access layer in the event of a link or node failure

    e. To avoid transit traffic through the access layer in the event of a link or node failure

9. What are the advantages of GLBP in the distribution layer? (Choose two.)

    a. GLBP provides all the benefits of HSRP and includes load balancing when VLANs do not span the access switches.

    b. A convergence event on the uplink affects only half as many hosts as compared to HSRP when VLANs do not span the access switches.

    c. A convergence event on the uplink affects is processed in half the time as compared to HSRP when VLANs do not span the access switches.

    d. STP can block one of the access layer uplinks, and there is at most a two-hop Layer 2 path for upstream traffic when VLANs span access switches.

    e. STP can block one of the access layer uplinks, and there is at most a two-hop Layer 3 path for upstream traffic when VLANs span access switches.

10. What is a potential issue when daisy chaining access layer switches?

    a. It is not easy to determine where the root switch is located.

    b. It is very hard to determine how many ports will be in a blocking state.

    c. The design will black-hole traffic and be affected by multiple convergence events with a single network failure.

    d. There is a danger that black holes will occur in the event of a link or node failure when the distribution interconnection is Layer 2.

    e. There is a danger that black holes will occur in the event of a link or node failure when the distribution interconnection is Layer 3.

11. What is the best mechanism to prevent unicast flooding issues?

    a. Bias the routing metrics to remove equal-cost routes.

    b. Do not span VLANs across multiple access switches.

    c. Span VLANs across multiple access switches.

    d. Tune ARP timers so they exceed CAM timers.

    e. Tune CAM timers so they exceed ARP timers.

12. What hardware is supported by the Cisco Power Calculator? (Choose all that apply.)

    a. Cisco Catalyst 3750 series

    b. Cisco Catalyst 4500 series

    c. Cisco Catalyst 6500 series

    d. Cisco Catalyst XR series

    e. All Cisco Catalyst series switches

13. What features do Cisco Catalyst Integrated Security capabilities provide? (Choose three.)

    a. DHCP snooping prevents client attacks on the DHCP server and switch.

    b. Dynamic ARP Inspection adds security to ARP to minimize the impact of ARP poisoning and spoofing attacks.

    c. DHCP snooping prevents client attacks on the DHCP server and switch using the Dynamic ARP Inspection table.

    d. IP Source Guard prevents IP spoofing using the DHCP snooping table.

    e. IP Source Guard prevents IP spoofing using the Dynamic ARP Inspection table.

After completing this chapter, you will be able to:

- Design addressing solutions to support summarization

- Design routing solutions to support summarization, route filtering, and redistribution

- Design scalable EIGRP routing solutions for the enterprise

- Design scalable OSPF routing solutions for the enterprise

- Design scalable BGP routing solutions for the enterprise

CHAPTER 3

Developing an Optimum Design for Layer 3

This chapter examines a select number of topics on both advance IP addressing and select design issues with Border Gateway Protocol (BGP), Enhanced Interior Gateway Routing Protocol (EIGRP), and Open Shortest Path First (OSPF). As one would expect, advanced IP addressing and routing protocol design encompasses a large amount of detail that has already filled a number of books on routing protocols and networking best practices. The text will parallel topics covered in the Design course.

Designing Advanced IP Addressing

Designing IP addressing at a professional level involves several advanced considerations. This section reviews the importance of IP address planning and selection and the importance of IP address summarization. It also discusses some applications of summary addressing.

IP Address Planning as a Foundation

Structured and modular cabling plant and network infrastructures are ideal for a good design with low maintenance and upgrade costs. In similar fashion, a well-planned IP addressing scheme is the foundation for greater efficiency in operating and maintaining a network. Without proper planning in advance, networks may not be able to benefit from route summarization features inherent to many routing protocols.

Route summarization is important in scaling any routing protocol. However, some existing IP addressing schemes may not support summarization. It takes time and effort to properly allocate IP subnets in blocks to facilitate summarization. The benefit of summarized addresses is reduced router workload and routing traffic. Although modern router CPUs can handle a vastly increased workload as compared to older routers, reducing load mitigates the impact of periods of intense network instability. In general, summary routes dampen out or reduce network route churn, making the network more stable. In addition, summary routes lead to faster network convergence. Summarized networks are simpler to troubleshoot because there are fewer routes in the routing table or in routing advertisements, compared to nonsummarized networks.

Just as using the right blocks of subnets enables use of more efficient routing, care with subnet assignments can also support role-based functions within the addressing scheme structure. This in turn enables efficient and easily managed access control lists (ACL) for quality of service (QoS) and security purposes.

In addition to allocating subnets in summarized blocks, it is advantageous to choose blocks of addresses within these subnets that can be easily summarized or described using wildcard masking in ACLs. With a well-chosen addressing scheme, ACLs can become much simpler to maintain in the enterprise.

Summary Address Blocks

Summary address blocks are the key to creating and using summary routes. How do you recognize a block of addresses which can be summarized? A block of IP addresses might be able to be summarized if it contains sequential numbers in one of the octets. The sequence of numbers must fit a pattern for the binary bit pattern to be appropriate for summarization. The pattern can be described without doing binary arithmetic.

For the sequential numbers to be summarized, the block must be x numbers in a row, where x is a power of 2. In addition, the first number in the sequence must be a multiple of x. The sequence will always end before the next multiple of x.

For example, any address block that matches the following is able to be summarized:

- 128 numbers in a row, starting with a multiple of 128 (0 or 128)

- 64 numbers in a row, starting with a multiple of 64 (0, 64, 128, or 192)

- 32 numbers in a row, starting with a multiple of 32

- 16 numbers in a row, starting with a multiple of 16

If you examine 172.19.160.0 through 172.19.191.0, there are $191 - 160 + 1 = 32$ numbers in a row, in sequence in the third octet. Note that 32 is 2^5, a power of 2. Note also that 160 is a multiple of 32 ($5 * 32 = 160$). Because the range meets the preceding conditions, the sequence 172.19.160.0 through 172.19.191.0 can be summarized.

Finding the correct octet for a subnet-style mask is fairly easy with summary address blocks. The formula is to subtract N from 256. For example, for 32 numbers in a row, the mask octet is $256 - 32 = 224$. Because the numbers are in the third octet, you place the 224 in the third octet, to form the mask 255.255.224.0.

A summary route expressed as either 172.19.160.0, 255.255.224.0, or as 172.169.160/19 would then describe how to reach subnets starting with 172.19.160.0 through 172.19.191.0.

Changing IP Addressing Needs

IP address redesign is needed to adapt to changes in how subnets are now being used. In some networks, IP subnets were initially assigned sequentially. Summary address blocks of subnets were then assigned to sites to enable route summarization.

However, new requirements are developing requiring additional subnets:

- **IP telephony:** Additional subnets or address ranges are needed to support voice services. In some cases, the number of subnets double when IP telephony is implemented in an organization.

- **Layer 3 switching at the edge:** Deploying Layer 3 switching to the network edge is another trend driving the need for more subnets. Edge Layer 3 switching can create the need for a rapid increase in the number of smaller subnets. In some cases, there can be insufficient address space, and readdressing is required.

■   **Network Admission Control (NAC):** NAC is also being deployed in many organizations. Some Cisco 802.1X and NAC deployments are dynamically assigning VLANs based on user logins or user roles. In these environments, ACLs control connectivity to servers and network resources based on the source subnet, which is based on the user role.

■   **Corporate requirements:** Corporate governance security initiatives are also isolating groups of servers by function, sometimes called "segmentation." Describing "production" and "development" subnets in an ACL can be painful unless they have been chosen wisely. These new subnets can make managing the network more complex. Maintaining ad hoc subnets for voice security and other reasons can be time-consuming. When it is possible, describing the permitted traffic in a few ACL statements is a highly desirable. Therefore, ACL-friendly addressing which can be summarized helps network administrators to efficiently manage their networks.

Planning Addresses

The first step in implementing ACL-friendly addressing is to recognize the need. In an environment with IP phones and NAC implemented, you will need to support IP phone subnets and NAC role subnets in ACLs. In the case of IP phones, ACLs will probably be used for both QoS and voice-security rules. For NAC role-based subnets, ACLs will most likely be used for security purposes.

Servers in medium-to-large server farms should at least be grouped so that servers with different functions or levels of criticality are in different subnets. That saves listing individual IP addresses in lengthy ACLs. If the servers are in subnets attached to different access switches, it can be useful to assign the subnets so that there is a pattern suitable for wildcarding in ACLs.

If the addressing scheme allows simple wildcard rules to be written, those simple ACL rules can be used everywhere. This avoids maintaining per-location ACLs that need to define source or destination addresses to local subnets. ACL-friendly addressing supports maintaining one or a few global ACLs, which are applied identically at various control points in the network. This would typically be done with a tool such as Cisco Security Manager.

The conclusion is that it is advantageous to build a pattern into role-based addressing and other addressing schemes so that ACL wildcards can match the pattern. This in turn supports implementing simpler ACLs.

Applications of Summary Address Blocks

Summary address blocks addressing can be used to support several network applications:

■   Separate VLANs for voice and data, and even role-based addressing

■   Bit splitting for route summarization

■   Addressing for virtual private network (VPN) clients

■   Network Address Translation (NAT)

These features are discussed in greater detail in the following sections.

Implementing Role-Based Addressing

The most obvious approach to implement role-based addressing is to use network 10. This has the virtue of simplicity. A simple scheme that can be used with Layer 3 closets is to use 10.number_for_closet.VLAN.x /24 and avoid binary arithmetic. This approach uses the second octet for closets or Layer 3 switches, the third octet for VLANs, and the fourth octet for hosts.

If you have more than 256 closets or Layer 3 switches to identify in the second octet, you might use some bits from the beginning of the third octet, because you probably do not have 256 VLANs per switch.

Another approach is to use some or all of the Class B private addressing blocks. This approach will typically involve binary arithmetic. The easiest method is to allocate bits using bit splitting. An example network is 172.0001 xxxx.xxxx xxxx.xxhh hhhh. In this case, you start out with 6 bits reserved for hosts in the fourth octet, or 62 hosts per subnet (VLAN). The x bits are to be split further.

This format initially uses decimal notation to the first octet and binary notation in the second, third, and fourth octets to minimize conversion back and forth.

If you do not need to use the bits in the second octet to identify additional closets, you end up with something like 172.16.cccc cccR.RRhh hhhh:

■   The c characters indicate that 7 bits allow for 2^7 or 128 closet or Layer 3 switches.

■   The R characters indicate 3 bits for a role-based subnet (relative to the closet block), or 8 roles per switch.

■   The h characters indicate 6 bits for the 62-host subnets specified.

This addressing plan is enough to cover a reasonably large enterprise network.

Another 4 bits are available to work with in the second octet if needed.

Using a role-aware or ACL-friendly addressing scheme, you can write a small number of global permit or deny statements for each role. This greatly simplifies edge ACL mainte-nance. It is easier to maintain one ACL for all edge VLANs or interfaces than different ACLs for every Layer 3 access or distribution switch.

Bit Splitting for Route Summarization

The previous bit-splitting technique has been around for a while. It can also be useful in coming up with summary address block for routing protocols if you cannot use simple octet boundaries. The basic idea is to start with a network prefix, such as 10.0.0.0, or a pre-fix in the range 172.16.0.0 to 172.31.0.0, 192.168.n.0, or an assigned IP address. The re-maining bits can then be thought of as available for use for the area, subnet, or host part of the address. It can be useful to write the available bits as x, then substitute a, s, or h as they are assigned. The *n* in an address indicates the network prefix portion of the address, which is not subject to change or assignment.

Generally, you know how big your average subnets need to be in buildings. (A subnet with 64 bits can be summarized and will cover most LAN switches.) That allows you to convert six *x* bits to *h* for host bits.

You can then determine how many WAN links you need and how many you are comfortable putting into one area to come up with how many *a* bits you need to assign. The leftover bits are *s* bits. Generally, one does not need all the bits, and the remaining bits (the *a* versus *s* boundary) can be assigned to allow some room for growth.

For example, suppose 172.16.0.0 is being used, with subnets of 62 hosts each. That commits the final 6 bits to host address in the fourth octet. If you need 16 or fewer areas, you might allocate 4 *a* bits for area number, which leaves 6 *s* bits for subnet. That would be 2^6 or 64 subnets per area, which is quite a few.

Example: Bit Splitting for Area 1

This example illustrates how the bit-splitting approach would support the addresses in OSPF area 1. Writing "1" as four binary bits substitutes "0001" for the *a* bits. The area 1 addresses would be those with the bit pattern 172.16.0001 ssss.sshh hhhh. This bit pattern in the third octet supports decimal numbers 16 to 31. Addresses in the range 172.16.16.0 to 172.16.31.255 would fall into area 1. If you repeat this logic, area 0 would have addresses 172.16.0.0 to 172.16.15.255, and area 2 would have addresses 172.16.32.0 to 172.16.47.255.

Subnets would consist of an appropriate third octet value for the area they are in, together with addresses in the range 0 to 63, 64 to 127, 128 to 191, or 192 to 255 in the last octet. Thus, 172.16.16.0/26, 172.16.16.64/26, 172.16.16.128/26, 172.16.16.192/26, and 172.16.17.0/26 would be the first five subnets in area 1.

One recommendation that preserves good summarization is to take the last subnet in each area and divide it up for use as /30 or /31 subnets for WAN link addressing.

Few people enjoy working in binary. Free or inexpensive subnet calculator tools can help. For those with skill writing Microsoft Excel spreadsheet formulas, you can install Excel Toolkit functions to help with decimal-to-binary or decimal-to-hexadecimal conversion. You could then build a spreadsheet that lists all area blocks, subnets, and address assignments.

Addressing for VPN Clients

Focusing some attention on IP addressing for VPN clients can also provide benefits. As role-based security is deployed, there is a need for different groupings of VPN clients. These might correspond to administrators, employees, different groups of contractors or consultants, external support organizations, guests, and so on. You can use different VPN groups for different VPN client pools.

Role-based access can be controlled via the group password mechanism for the Cisco VPN client. Each group can be assigned VPN endpoint addresses from a different pool.

Traffic from the user PC has a VPN endpoint address as its source address.

The different subnets or blocks of VPN endpoint addresses can then be used in ACLs to control access across the network to resources, as discussed earlier for NAC roles. If the pools are subnets of a summary address block, routing traffic back to clients can be done in a simple way.

NAT in the Enterprise

NAT is a powerful tool for working with IP addresses. It has the potential for being very useful in the enterprise to allow private internal addressing to map to publicly assigned addresses at the Internet connection point. However, if it is overused, it can be harmful.

NAT and Port Address Translation (PAT) are common tools for firewalls. A common approach to supporting content load-balancing devices is to perform destination NAT. A recommended approach to supporting content load-balancing devices is to perform source NAT. As long as NAT is done in a controlled, disciplined fashion, it can be useful.

Avoid using internal NAT or PAT to map private-to-private addresses internally. Internal NAT can make network troubleshooting confusing and difficult. For example, it would be difficult to determine which network 10 in an organization a user is currently connected to.

Internal NAT or PAT is sometimes required for interconnection of networks after a corporate merger or acquisition. Many organizations are now using network 10.0.0.0 internally, resulting in a "two network 10.0.0.0" problem after a merger.

It is also a recommended practice to isolate any servers reached through content devices using source NAT or destination NAT. These servers are typically isolated because the packets with NAT addresses are not useful elsewhere in the network. NAT can also be used in the data center to support small out-of-band (OOB) management VLANs on devices that cannot route or define a default gateway for the management VLAN, thereby avoiding one management VLAN that spans the entire data center.

NAT with External Partners

NAT also proves useful when a company or organization has more than a couple of external business partners. Some companies exchange dynamic routing information with external business partners. Exchanges require trust. The drawback to this approach is that a static route from a partner to your network might somehow get advertised back to you. This advertisement, if accepted, can result in part of your network becoming unreachable. One way to control this situation is to implement two-way filtering of routes to partners: Advertise only subnets that the partner needs to reach, and only accept routes to subnets or prefixes that your staff or servers need to reach at the partner.

Some organizations prefer to use static routing to reach partners in a tightly controlled way. The next hop is sometimes a virtual Hot Standby Router Protocol (HSRP) or Gateway Load Balancing Protocol (GLBP) address on a pair of routers controlled by the partner.

When the partner is huge, such as a large bank, static routing is too labor intensive. Importing thousands of external routes into the internal routing protocol for each of several large partners causes the routing table to become bloated.

Another approach is to terminate all routing from a partner at an edge router, preferably receiving only summary routes from the partner. NAT can then be used to change all partner addresses on traffic into a range of locally assigned addresses. Different NAT blocks are used for different partners. This approach converts a wide range of partner addresses into a tightly controlled set of addresses and will simplify troubleshooting. It can also avoid potential issues when multiple organizations are using the 10.0.0.0/8 network.

If the NAT blocks are chosen out of a larger block that can be summarized, a redistributed static route for the larger block easily makes all partners reachable on the enterprise network. Internal routing will then have one route that in effect says "this way to partner networks."

A partner block approach to NAT supports faster internal routing convergence by keeping partner subnets out of the enterprise routing table.

A disadvantage to this approach is that it is more difficult to trace the source of IP packets. However, if it is required, you can backtrack and get the source information through the NAT table.

Designing Advanced Routing

This section discusses elements of advanced routing solution design using route summarization and default routing. It also discusses using route filtering in advanced routing designs.

Upon mastering this section, you will be able to describe and use various concepts to perform advanced routing design. This ability includes being able to meet these objectives:

■ Describe why route summarization and default routing should be used in a routing design

■ Describe why route filtering should be used in a routing design

■ Describe why redistribution should be used in a routing design

Route Summarization and Default Routing

Route summarization procedures condense routing information. Without summarization, each router in a network must retain a route to every subnet in the network. With summarization, routers can reduce some sets of routes to a single advertisement, reducing both the load on the router and the perceived complexity of the network. The importance of route summarization increases with network size (see Figure 3-1).

Medium-to-large networks often require the use of more routing protocol features than a small network would. The bigger the network, the more important it is to have a careful design with attention to scaling the routing protocol properly. Stability, control, predictability, and security of routing are also important. And as converged networks are increasingly used to support voice, IP telephony, storage, and other drop-sensitive traffic, networks must be designed for fast routing convergence.

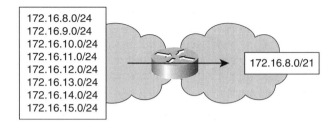

172.16.8.0/24
172.16.9.0/24
172.16.10.0/24
172.16.11.0/24
172.16.12.0/24
172.16.13.0/24
172.16.14.0/24
172.16.15.0/24

172.16.8.0/21

Figure 3-1   *Route Summarization*

Route summarization is one key network design element for supporting manageable and fast-converging routing. The Building Scalable Cisco Internetworks (BSCI) course covers configuring route summarization and the concepts of how summarization is beneficial to routing and for troubleshooting.

The design recommendations for summarizations are straightforward:

■   Use route summarization to scale routing designs.

■   Design addressing using address blocks that can be summarized.

■   Default routing can be thought of as a particularly simple form of route summarization where all other routes are summarized in the default.

Originating Default

The concept of originating default is useful for summarization in routing. Most networks use some form of default routing. It is wise to have the default route (0.0.0.0 /0) advertised dynamically into the rest of the network by the router or routers that connect to Internet service providers (ISPs). This route advertises the path to any route not found more specifically in the routing table (see Figure 3-2).

It is generally a bad idea to configure a static default route on every router, even if recursive routing is used. In recursive routing, for any route in the routing table whose next-hop IP address is not a directly connected interface of the router, the routing algorithm looks recursively into the routing table until it finds a directly connected interface to which it can forward the packets. If you configure a static default route on every router to the ISP router, the next hop is the ISP-connected router rather than a directly connected peer router. This approach can lead to black holes in the network if there is not a path to the ISP-connected router. This approach also needs to be reconfigured on every router if the exit point changes or if a second ISP connection is added.

If manually configured next hops are used, more configurations are needed. This approach can also lead to routing loops and is hard to change. If there are alternative paths, this static approach might fail to take advantage of them.

The recommended alternative is to configure each ISP-connected router with a static default route and redistribute that into the dynamic routing protocol. This needs to be done only at the network edge devices. All other routers pick up the route dynamically, and traffic out of the enterprise will use the closest exit. If the ISP-connected router loses connectivity to the ISP or fails, the default route will no longer be advertised in the organization.

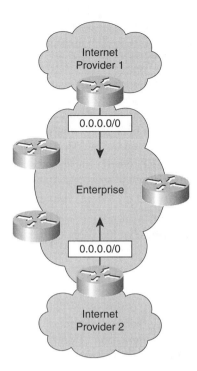

Figure 3-2 *Originating Default Routes*

You may need to use the **default-information originate** command, with options, to redistribute the default route into the dynamic routing protocol.

Note: The actual syntax of the command to inject a default route into an IGP is dependent on the IGP being used. The command in the text works for RIP, OSPF, IS-IS, and BGP. For EIGRP the ip **default-network** command is used. The reader is encouraged to consult the Cisco IP Command Reference for more in-depth study.

Stub Areas and Default Route

Explicit route summarization is not the only way to achieve the benefits of summarization. The various kinds of OSPF stub areas can be thought of as a simpler form of summarization. The point of using OSPF stub areas, totally stubby areas, not-so-stubby areas (NSSA), is to reduce the amount of routing information advertised into an area. The information that is suppressed is replaced by the default route 0.0.0.0/0 or 0/0.

OSPF cannot filter prefixes within an area. It only filters routes as they are passed between areas at an Area Border Router (ABR).

OSPF stub areas do not work to IP Security (IPsec) virtual private network (VPN) sites such as with generic routing encapsulation (GRE) over IPsec tunnels. For IPsec VPN remote sites, the 0/0 route must point to the ISP, so stub areas cannot be used. An alternative to the default route is to advertise a summary route for the organization as a "corporate default" route and filter unnecessary prefixes at the ABR. Because OSPF cannot filter routes within an area, there still will be within-area flooding of link-state advertisements (LSA).

You can use this approach with the EIGRP, too. The **ip default-network** *network-number* command is used to configure the last-resort gateway or default route. A router configured with this command considers the network listed in the command as the candidate route for computing the gateway of last resort. This network must be in the routing table either as a static route or an Interior Gateway Protocol (IGP) route before the router will announce the network as a candidate default route to other EIGRP routers. The network must be an EIGRP-derived network in the routing table or be generated by a static route, which has been redistributed into EIGRP.

EIGRP networks will typically configure the default route at ISP connection points. Filters can then be used so that only the default and any other critical prefixes are sent to remote sites.

In a site-to-site IPsec VPN network, it can be useful to also advertise a corporate summary route or corporate default route (which might be 10.0.0.0 /8) to remote sites. The advantage of doing so is that all other corporate prefixes need not be advertised to the IPsec VPN site. Even if the IPsec network uses two or three hub sites, dynamic failover will occur based on the corporate default. For the corporate default advertisement to work properly under failure conditions, all the site-specific prefixes need to be advertised between the hub sites.

Filtering the unnecessary routes out can save on the bandwidth and router CPU that is expended to provide routing information to remote sites. This increases the stability and efficiency of the network. Removing the clutter from routing tables also makes troubleshooting more effective.

Route Filtering in the Network Design

This topic discusses the appropriate use of route filtering in network design. Route filtering can be used to manage traffic flows in the network, avoid inappropriate transit traffic through remote nodes, and provide a defense against inaccurate or inappropriate routing updates. You can use different techniques to apply route filtering in various routing protocols.

Inappropriate Transit Traffic

Transit traffic is external traffic passing through a network or site (see Figure 3-3).

Remote sites generally are connected with lower bandwidth than is present in the network core. Remote sites are rarely desirable as transit networks to forward network from one place to another. Remote sites typically cannot handle the traffic volume needed to be a viable routing alternative to the core network. In general, when core connectivity fails, routing should not detour via a remote site.

172.16.8.0
172.16.9.0
172.16.10.0
172.16.11.0
172.16.12.0
172.16.13.0
172.16.14.0
172.16.15.0

172.16.8.0
172.16.9.0
172.16.10.0
172.16.11.0
172.16.12.0
172.16.13.0
172.16.14.0
172.16.15.0

Stub

172.16.8.12?
I don't know how
to get there!

Figure 3-3 *Avoid Inappropriate Transit Traffic*

In OSPF, there is little control over intra-area traffic. LSAs cannot be filtered within an area. OSPF does not allow traffic to arbitrarily route into and then out of an area. The exception is area 0, which can be used for transit when another area becomes discontiguous.

With EIGRP, it can be desirable to configure EIGRP stub networks. This informs central routers that they should not use a remote site as a transit network. In addition, the use of stub networks damps unnecessary EIGRP queries, speeding network convergence. Filtering can help manage which parts of the network are available for transit in an EIGRP network.

With BGP, the most common concern about transit traffic is when a site has two Internet connections. If there is no filtering, the connections advertise routes. This advertisement can put the site at risk of becoming a transit network. This should not be a problem with two connections to the same ISP, because the autonomous system number is present in the autonomous system path. Based on the autonomous system path, the ISP router ignores any routes advertised from the ISP to the site and then back to the ISP.

When two ISPs are involved, the site might inadvertently become a transit site. The best approach is to filter routes advertised outbound to the ISPs, and ensure that only the company or site prefixes are advertised outward. Tagging routes with a BGP community is an easy way to do this. All inbound routes received from the ISP should be filtered, too, so that you accept only the routes the ISP should be sending you.

Defensive Filtering

Route filtering can also be used defensively against inaccurate or inappropriate routing traffic (see Figure 3-4).

One common problem some organizations have is that they learn inappropriate routes from another organization, such as a business partner. Your business partner should not be

172.16.0.0/16

Business
Partner

Company A

Network 10
addresses

Why is the partner
sending me routes
for network 10?

Figure 3-4   *Defensive Filtering*

advertising your routing prefixes back to your network. Those destinations are not reached through the partner, unless you have a very odd network design. The default route should not be reached via the partner, unless the partner is providing your network with Internet connectivity.

Inappropriate partner advertisements can disrupt routing without filtering. For example, a partner may define a static route to your data center. If this route leaks into your routing process, a portion of your network might think that the data center has moved to a location behind the router of the partner.

Defensive filtering protects the network from disruptions due to incorrect advertisements of others. You configure which routing updates your routers should accept from the partner and which routing updates should be ignored. For example, you would not accept routing updates about how to get to your own prefixes or about default routing.

For security reasons, you should advertise to a partner only the prefixes that you want them to be able to reach. This provides the partner with minimum information about your network and is part of a layered security approach. It also ensures that if there is an accidental leak of another partner's routes or static routes into the dynamic routing process, the inappropriate information does not also leak to others.

The approach of blocking route advertisements is also called route hiding or route starvation. Traffic cannot get to the hidden subnets from the partner unless a summary route is also present. Packet filtering access control lists (ACL) should also be used to supplement security by route starvation.

Designing Redistribution

Redistribution is a powerful tool for manipulating and managing routing updates, particularly when two routing protocols are present in a network (see Figure 3-5).

What to Avoid:

Figure 3-5   *Designing Redistribution*

In some situations, routing redistribution is useful and even necessary. These include migration between routing protocols, corporate mergers, reorganization, and support for devices that speak only Routing Information Protocol (RIP) or OSPF.

However, redistribution should be used with planning and some degree of caution. It is very easy to create routing loops with redistribution. This is particularly true when there are multiple redistribution points, sometimes coupled with static routes, inconsistent routing summaries, or route filters.

Experience teaches that it is much better to have distinct pockets of routing protocols and redistribute than to have a random mix of routers and routing protocols with ad hoc redistribution. Therefore, running corporate EIGRP with redistribution into RIP or OSPF for a region that has routers from other vendors is viable, with due care. On the other hand, freely intermixing OSPF-speaking routers with EIGRP routers in ad hoc fashion is just asking for major problems.

When there is more than one interconnection point between two regions using different routing protocols, bidirectional redistribution is commonly considered. When running OSPF and EIGRP in two regions, it is attractive to redistribute OSPF into EIGRP, and EIGRP into OSPF.

Filtered Redistribution

When you use bidirectional redistribution, you should prevent re-advertising information back into the routing protocol region or autonomous system that it originally came from (see Figure 3-6).

Figure 3-6 *Filtered Redistribution*

For example, filters should be used so that OSPF information that was redistributed into EIGRP does not get re-advertised into OSPF. You also need to prevent information that came from EIGRP into OSPF from being re-advertised back into the EIGRP part of the network. This is sometimes called a manual split horizon. Split horizon is a routing protocol feature. The idea behind it is that it is counterproductive to advertise information back to the source of that information, because the information may be out of date or incorrect, and because the source of the information is presumed to be better informed.

If you do not do this filtering or use a manual split horizon, you will probably see strange convergence after an outage, you will probably see routing loops, and in general, there will be routing problems and instability.

Both EIGRP and OSPF support the tagging of routes. A route map can be used to add the numeric tag to specific prefixes. The tag information is then passed along in routing updates. Another router may then filter out routes that match, or do not match, the tag. This is done using a route map in a distribution list.

One typical use of tags is with redistribution. In the figure, routers A and B can apply tags to routes from IGP X when they are advertised outbound into IGP Y. This in effect marks them as routes from IGP X. When routers A and B receive routes from Y, they would then filter out routes marked as from X when received from IGP Y, because both routers learn such routes directly from IGP X. The process of filtering also applies in the opposite direction.

The point is to get routes in the most direct way, not via an indirect information path that might be passing along old information.

Migrating Between Routing Protocols

This topic discusses two common approaches for migrating between routing protocols. One approach for migrating between routing protocols is to use administrative distance (AD) to migrate the routing protocols. Another approach is to use redistribution and a moving boundary.

Migration by AD does not use redistribution. Instead, two routing protocols are run at the same time with the same routes. This assumes sufficient memory, CPU, and bandwidth are in place to support this on the routers running two routing protocols.

The first step in migration by AD is to turn on the new protocol, but make sure that it has a higher AD than the existing routing protocol so it is not preferred. This step enables the protocol and allows adjacencies or neighbors and routing databases to be checked, but does not actually rely on the new routing protocol for routing decisions.

When the new protocol is fully deployed, various checks can be done with show commands to confirm proper deployment. Then the cutover takes place. In cutover, the AD is shifted for one of the two protocols, so that the new routing protocol will now have a lower AD.

Final steps in this process include the following:

■ Check for any prefixes learned only via the old protocol.

■ Check for any strange next hops (perhaps using some form of automated comparison).

With migration by redistribution, the migration is staged as a series of smaller steps. In each step, part of the network is converted from the old to the new routing protocol. In a big network, the AD approach might be used to support this conversion. In a smaller network, an overnight cutover or simpler approach might suffice.

To provide full connectivity during migration by redistribution, the boundary routers between the two parts of the network would have to bidirectionally redistribute between protocols. Filtering via tags would be one relatively simple way to manage this. The boundary routers move as more of the region is migrated.

Designing Scalable EIGRP Designs

This section focuses on designing advanced routing solutions using Enhanced Interior Gateway Routing Protocol. It describes how to scale EIGRP designs and how to use multiple EIGRP autonomous systems in a large network. Upon mastering this lesson, you will be able to describe and use various concepts to perform advanced routing design. This ability includes being able to meet these objectives:

■ Discuss how to scale for EIGRP in a routing design

■ Discuss design options with multiple autonomous systems

Scaling EIGRP Designs

EIGRP is tolerant of arbitrary topologies for small and medium networks. This is both a strength and a weakness. It is useful to be able to deploy EIGRP without restructuring the network. As the scale of the network increases, however, the risk of instability or long convergence times becomes greater. For example, if a network has reached the point where it includes 500 routers, EIGRP may stop working well without a structured hierarchy. As the size of the network increases, more stringent design is needed for EIGRP to work well.

Note: This mechanism contrasts with OSPF, where structured design is imposed at an early stage. The counterpart to using EIGRP with an arbitrary topology would be an OSPF design that puts everything into OSPF area 0. That also may work for small-to-medium networks, up to around 200 or 300 OSPF routers.

To scale EIGRP, it is a good idea to use a structured hierarchical topology with route summarization.

One of the biggest stability and convergence issues with EIGRP is the propagation of EIGRP queries. When EIGRP does not have a feasible successor, it sends queries to its neighbors. The query tells the neighbor "I do not have a route to this destination any more; do not route through me. Let me know if you hear of a viable alternative route." The router has to wait for replies to all the queries it sends. Queries can flood through many routers in a portion of the network and increase convergence time. Summarization points and filtered routes limit EIGRP query propagation and minimize convergence time.

EIGRP Fast Convergence

Customers have been using EIGRP to achieve subsecond convergence for years. Lab testing by Cisco has shown that the key factor for EIGRP convergence is the presence or absence of a feasible successor. When there is no feasible successor, EIGRP uses queries to EIGRP peers and has to wait for responses. This slows convergence.

Proper network design is required for EIGRP to achieve fast convergence. Summarization helps limit the scope of EIGRP queries, indirectly speeding convergence. Summarization also shrinks the number of entries in the routing table, which speeds up various CPU operations. The effect of CPU operation on convergence is much less significant than the presence or absence of a feasible successor. A recommended way to ensure that a feasible successor is present is to use equal-cost routing.

EIGRP metrics can be tuned using the delay parameter. However, adjusting the delay on links consistently and tuning variance are next to impossible to do well at any scale.

In general, it is unwise to have a large number of EIGRP peers. Under worst-case conditions, router CPU or other limiting factors might delay routing protocol convergence. A somewhat conservative design is best to avoid nasty surprises.

EIGRP Fast-Convergence Metrics

This section discusses EIGRP fast-convergence metrics. Cisco tested convergence of various routing protocols in the lab (see Figure 3-7).

Figure 3-7   *EIGRP Fast Convergence*

EIGRP convergence time increases as more routes need to be processed. However, there is a much bigger impact for networks without EIGRP feasible successors than for networks with no feasible successors.

With a feasible successor present, EIGRP converges in times ranging from about 1/10 second for 1000 routes to about 1.2 seconds for 10,000 routes. Without the feasible successor, convergence times increased to 1/2 to 1 second for 1000 routes and to about 6 seconds for 10,000 routes.

Subsecond timers are not available for EIGRP. One reason is that the hello timer is not the most significant factor in EIGRP convergence time. Another is that experimentation suggests that setting the EIGRP timer below two seconds can lead to instability. The recommended EIGRP minimum timer settings are two seconds for hellos and six seconds for the dead timer. Subsecond settings are not an option.

Scaling EIGRP with Multiple Autonomous Systems

Implementing multiple EIGRP autonomous systems is sometimes used as a scaling technique. The usual rationale is to reduce the volume of EIGRP queries by limiting them to one EIGRP autonomous system. However, there can be issues with multiple EIGRP autonomous systems (see Figure 3-8).

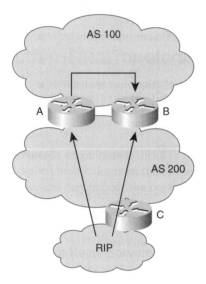

Figure 3-8 *Scaling EIGRP with Multiple Autonomous Systems*

One potential issue is with the external route redistribution. In the diagram, a route is redistributed from RIP into autonomous system 200. Router A redistributes it into autonomous system 100. Router B hears about the route prefix in advertisements from both autonomous system 200 and autonomous system 100. The AD is the same because the route is external to both autonomous systems.

The route that is installed into the EIGRP topology database first gets placed into the routing table.

Example: External Route Redistribution Issue

If router B selects the route via autonomous system 100, it then routes to the RIP autonomous system indirectly, rather than directly via autonomous system 200, illustrated in Figure 3-9.

Router B also advertises the route via autonomous system 100 back into autonomous system 200. Suppose B has a lower redistribution metric than router C does. If that is the case, A will prefer the route learned from B over the route learned from C. In this case, A will forward traffic for this route to B in autonomous system 200, and B will forward traffic back to A in autonomous system 100. This is a routing loop!

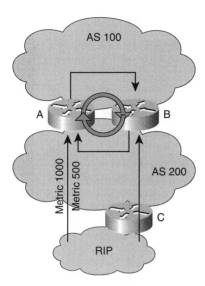

Figure 3-9 *Example: External Route Redistribution Issue*

Cisco addresses this slightly specialized situation through its bug fix CSCdm47037. Routing metrics are now also used as a tie-breaker in the situation. So, in the case where there are two routes with the same ADs, and the process type is the same, the metrics of the routes are compared, too.

The same sort of behavior may be seen with redistribution between two routing protocols, especially for routes learned from the protocol with the lower AD.

Filtering EIGRP Redistribution with Route Tags

Outbound route tags can be used to filter redistribution and support EIGRP scaling with multiple EIGRP autonomous systems (see Figure 3-10).

External routes can be configured to carry administrative tags. When the external route is redistributed into autonomous system 100 at router A or B, it can be tagged. This tag can then be used to filter the redistribution of the route back into autonomous system 200. This filtering blocks the formation of the loop, because router A will no longer receive the redistributed routes from router B through autonomous system 200.

In the configuration snippets, when routers A and B redistribute autonomous system 200 routes into autonomous system 100, they tag the routes with tag 100. Any routes tagged with tag 100 can then be prevented from being redistributed back into autonomous system 200. This will successfully prevent a routing loop from forming.

Filtering EIGRP Routing Updates with Inbound Route Tags

You can filter EIGRP routing updates with inbound route tags to support scaling with multiple EIGRP autonomous systems (see Figure 3-11).

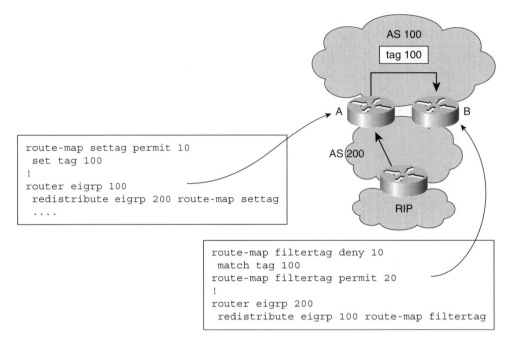

```
route-map settag permit 10
 set tag 100
!
router eigrp 100
 redistribute eigrp 200 route-map settag
 ....
```

```
route-map filtertag deny 10
 match tag 100
route-map filtertag permit 20
!
router eigrp 200
 redistribute eigrp 100 route-map filtertag
```

Figure 3-10   *Filtering EIGRP Redistribution with Route Tags*

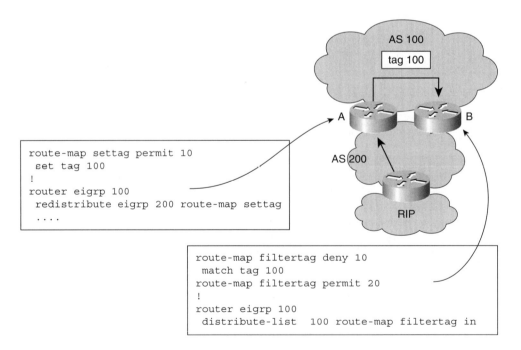

```
route-map settag permit 10
 set tag 100
!
router eigrp 100
 redistribute eigrp 200 route-map settag
 ....
```

```
route-map filtertag deny 10
 match tag 100
route-map filtertag permit 20
!
router eigrp 100
 distribute-list  100 route-map filtertag in
```

Figure 3-11   *Filtering EIGRP Routing Updates with Inbound Route Tags*

Filtering outbound tags in the previous example does not prevent router B from learning the routes from autonomous system 100. Router B could still perform suboptimal routing by accepting the redistributed route learned from autonomous system 100.

The solution is to use inbound route tag filtering. This technique prevents routers from learning such routes, in which case they also will not be redistributed or advertised outbound. The Cisco bug fix CSCdt43016 provides support for incoming route filtering based on route maps. It allows for filtering routes based on any route map condition before acceptance into the local routing protocol database. This fix works for EIGRP and OSPF, starting with the Cisco IOS Software Releases 12.2T and 12.0S.

When routes are filtered to prevent router B from learning them, you prevent suboptimal routing by router B. The syntax shifts from using a route map with a **redistribute** command to using a route map with an inbound **distribute-list** command.

Note: This example shows how filtering and administrative tags can help prevent routing loops with redistribution and suboptimal routing.

Example: Queries with Multiple EIGRP Autonomous Systems

This example looks at the query behavior with multiple EIGRP autonomous systems (see Figure 3-12).

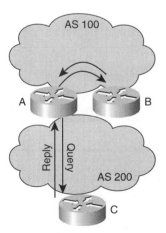

Figure 3-12   *Example: Queries with Multiple EIGRP Autonomous Systems*

If router C sends an EIGRP query to router A, router A needs to query its neighbors. Router A sends a reply to router C, because it has no other neighbors in autonomous system 200. However, router A must also query all of its autonomous system 100 neighbors for the missing route. These routers may have to query their neighbors.

In this example, the query from router C is answered promptly by router A, but router A still needs to wait for the response to its query. Having multiple autonomous systems does not stop queries; it just delays them on the way.

> **Note:** The conclusion of this example is that using multiple EIGRP autonomous systems as an EIGRP query-limiting technique does not work.

What really stops a query is general scaling methods using summarization, distribution lists, and stubs.

Reasons for Multiple EIGRP Autonomous Systems

There could be several valid reasons for having multiple EIGRP autonomous systems, including these:

- **Migration strategy after a merger or acquisition:** Although this is not a permanent solution, multiple autonomous systems are appropriate for merging two networks over time.

- **Different groups administer the different EIGRP autonomous systems:** This scenario adds complexity to the network design, but might be used for different domains of trust or administrative control.

- **Organizations with very large networks may use multiple EIGRP autonomous systems as a way to divide their networks:** Generally, this type of design approach uses summary routes at autonomous system boundaries to contain summary address blocks of prefixes in very large networks and to address the EIGRP query propagation issue.

These reasons for using multiple EIGRP autonomous systems can be appropriate, but careful attention must be paid to limiting queries.

Designing Scalable OSPF Design

The ability to scale an OSPF internetwork depends on the overall network structure and addressing scheme. As outlined in the preceding sections in this section concerning network topology and route summarization, adopting a hierarchical addressing environment and a structured address assignment are the most important factors in determining the scalability of your internetwork. Network scalability is affected by operational and technical considerations.

This section discusses designing advanced routing solutions using OSPF. It describes how to obtain scale OSPF designs and what factors can influence convergence in OSPF on a large network. Upon mastering the content, you will be able to describe and use various concepts to perform advanced routing design. This ability includes being able to meet these objectives:

- Explain how to scale OSPF routing to a large network

- Explain how to obtain fast convergence for OSPF in a routing design

Factors Influencing OSPF Scalability

Scaling is determined by the utilization of three router resources: memory, CPU, and interface bandwidth. The workload that OSPF imposes on a router depends on these factors:

- **The number of adjacent neighbors for any one router:** OSPF floods all link-state changes to all routers in an area. Routers with many neighbors have the most work to do when link-state changes occur. In general, any one router should have no more than 60 neighbors.

- **The number of adjacent routers in an area:** OSPF uses a CPU-intensive algorithm. The number of calculations that must be performed given n link-state packets is proportional to $n \log n$. As a result, the larger and more unstable the area, the greater the likelihood for performance problems associated with routing protocol recalculation. Generally, an area should have no more than 50 routers. Areas that suffer with unstable links should be smaller.

- **The number of areas supported by any one router:** A router must run the link-state algorithm for each link-state change that occurs for every area in which the router resides. Every ABR is in at least two areas (the backbone and one adjacent area). In general, to maximize stability, one router should not be in more than three areas.

- **Designated router (DR) selection:** In general, the DR and backup designated router (BDR) on a multiaccess link (for example, Ethernet) have the most OSPF work to do. It is a good idea to select routers that are not already heavily loaded with CPU-intensive activities to be the DR and BDR. In addition, it is generally not a good idea to select the same router to be the DR on many multiaccess links simultaneously.

The first and most important decision when designing an OSPF network is to determine which routers and links are to be included in the backbone area and which are to be included in each adjacent area.

Number of Adjacent Neighbors and DRs

One contribution to the OSPF workload on a router is the number of OSPF adjacent routers that it needs to communicate with.

Each OSPF adjacency represents another router whose resources are expended to support these activities:

- Exchanging hellos
- Synchronizing link-state databases
- Reliably flooding LSA changes
- Advertising the router and network LSA

Some design choices can reduce the impact of the OSPF adjacencies. Here are some recommendations:

- On LAN media, choose the most powerful routers or the router with the lightest load as the DR candidates. Set the priority of other routers to zero so they will not be DR candidates.

- When there are many branch or remote routers, spread the workload over enough peers. Practical experience suggests that IPsec VPN peers, for example, running OSPF over GRE tunnels are less stable than non-VPN peers. Volatility or amount of change and other workload need to be considered when determining how many peers a central hub router can support.

Any lab testing needs to consider typical operating conditions. Simultaneous restarts on all peers or flapping connections to all peers are the worst-case situations for OSPF.

Routing Information in the Area and Domain

The workload also depends on how much routing information there is within the area and the OSPF autonomous system. Routing information in OSPF depends on the number of routers and links to adjacent routers in an area.

There are techniques and tools to reduce this information. Stub and totally stubby areas import less information into an area about destinations outside the routing domain or the area then do normal areas. Therefore, using stub and totally stubby areas further reduces the workload on an OSPF router.

Interarea routes and costs are advertised into an area by each ABR. Totally stubby areas keep not only external routes but also this interarea information from having to be flooded into and within an area.

One way to think about Autonomous System Boundary Routers (ASBR) in OSPF is that each is in effect providing a distance vector–like list of destinations and costs. The more external prefixes and the more ASBRs there are, the more the workload for Type 5 or 7 LSAs. Stub areas keep all this information from having to be flooded within an area.

The conclusion is that area size and layout design, area types, route types, redistribution, and summarization all affect the size of the LSA database in an area.

Designing Areas

Area design can be used to reduce routing information in an area. Area design requires considering your network topology and addressing. Ideally, the network topology and addressing should be designed initially with division of areas in mind. Whereas EIGRP will tolerate more arbitrary network topologies, OSPF requires a cleaner hierarchy with a more clear backbone and area topology.

Geographic and functional boundaries should be considered in determining OSPF area placement.

As discussed previously, to improve performance minimize the routing information advertised into and out of areas. Bear in mind that anything in the LSA database must be propagated to all routers within the area. With OSPF, note that all changes to the LSA database need to be propagated; this in turn consumes bandwidth and CPU for links and routers within the area. Rapid changes or flapping only exacerbate this effect because the routers have to repeatedly propagate changes. Stub areas, totally stubby areas, and summary routes not only reduce the size of the LSA database, but they also insulate the area from external changes.

Experience shows that you should be conservative about adding routers to the backbone area 0. The first time people do an OSPF design, they end up with almost everything in area 0. Some organizations find that over time, too many routers ended up in area 0. A recommended practice is to put only the essential backbone and ABRs into area 0.

Some general advice about OSPF design is this:

- Make it simple.

- Make nonbackbone areas stub areas (or totally stubby areas).

- Make it summarized.

Area Size: How Many Routers in an Area?

Cisco experience suggests that the number of adjacent neighbors has more impact than the total number of routers in the area. In addition, the biggest consideration is the amount of information that has to be flooded within the area. Therefore, one network might have, for example, 200 WAN routers with one Fast Ethernet subnet in one area. Another might have fewer routers and more subnets.

It is a good idea to keep the OSPF router LSAs under the IP maximum transmission unit (MTU) size. When the MTU is exceeded, the result is IP fragmentation. IP fragmentation is, at best, a less-efficient way to transmit information and requires extra router processing. A large number of router LSAs also implies that there are many interfaces (and perhaps neighbors). This is an indirect indication that the area may have become too large.

Stability and redundancy are the most important criteria for the backbone. Stability is increased by keeping the size of the backbone reasonable.

Note: As a general rule, each area, including the backbone, should contain no more than 50 routers.

If link quality is high and the number of routes is small, the number of routers can be increased. Redundancy is important in the backbone to prevent partition when a link fails. Good backbones are designed so that no that single link failure can cause a partition.

Current ISP experience and Cisco testing suggest that it is unwise to have more than about 300 routers in OSPF backbone area 0, depending on all the other complexity factors that have been discussed.

Note: This number is intended as an appropriate indication that an OSPF design is getting into trouble and should be reconsidered, focusing on a smaller area 0.

OSPF Hierarchy

OSPF requires two levels of hierarchy in your network (see Figure 3-13).

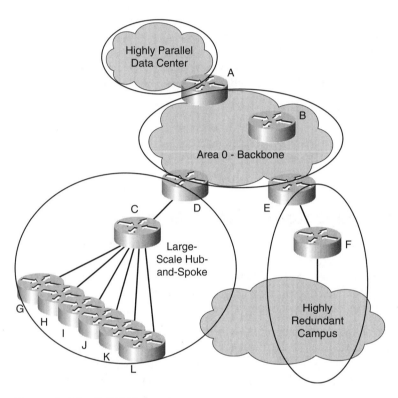

Figure 3-13   *OSPF Hierarchy*

Route summarization is extremely desirable for a reliable and scalable OSPF network. Summarization in OSPF naturally fits at area boundaries, when there is a backbone area 0 and areas off the backbone, with one or a few routers interconnecting the other areas to area 0. If you want three levels of hierarchy for a large network, BGP can be used to interconnect different OSPF routing domains.

One difficult question in OSPF design is whether distribution or core routers should be ABRs. General design advice is to separate complexity from complexity, and put complex parts of the network into separate areas. A part of the network might be considered complex when it has a lot of routing information, such as a full-mesh, a large hub-and-spoke, or a highly redundant topology such as a redundant campus or data center.

ABRs provide opportunities to support route summarization or create stub or totally stubby areas. A structured IP addressing scheme needs to align with the areas for effective route summarization. One of the simplest ways to allocate addresses in OSPF is to assign a separate network number for each area.

Stub areas cannot distinguish among ABRs for destinations external to the OSPF domain (redistributed routes). Unless the ABRs are geographically far apart, this should not matter. Totally stubby areas cannot distinguish one ABR from another, in terms of the best route to destinations outside the area. Unless the ABRs are geographically far apart, this should not matter.

Area and Domain Summarization

There are many ways to summarize routes in OSPF. The effectiveness of route summarization mechanisms depends on the addressing scheme. Summarization should be supported into and out of areas at the ABR or ASBR. To minimize route information inserted into the area, consider the following guidelines when planning your OSPF internetwork:

■ Configure the network addressing scheme so that the range of subnets assigned within an area is contiguous.

■ Create an address space that will split areas easily as the network grows. If possible, assign subnets according to simple octet boundaries.

■ Plan ahead for the addition of new routers to the OSPF environment. Ensure that new routers are inserted appropriately as area, backbone, or border routers.

Figure 3-14 shows some of the ways to summarize routes and otherwise reduce LSA database size and flooding in OSPF:

■ Area ranges per the OSPF RFCs

■ Area filtering

■ Summary address filtering

■ Originating default

■ Filtering for NSSA routes

OSPF Hub-and-Spoke Design

In an OSPF hub-and-spoke design, any change at one spoke site is passed up the link to the area hub and is then replicated to each of the other spoke sites. These actions can place a great burden on the hub router. Change flooding is the chief problem encountered in these designs.

Stub areas minimize the amount of information within the area. Totally stubby areas are better than stub areas in this regard. If a spoke site must redistribute routes into OSPF, make it a NSSA. Keep in mind that totally stubby NSSAs are also possible.

Limiting the number of spokes per area reduces the flooding at the hub. However, smaller areas allow for less summarization into the backbone. Each spoke requires either a separate interface or a subinterface on the hub router.

– Configure summarization into and out of areas at the ABR or ASBR.
– Minimize reachability information inserted into areas.

Figure 3-14   *Area and Domain Summarization*

Number of Areas in an OSPF Hub-and-Spoke Design

For a hub-and-spoke topology, the number of areas and the number of sites per area will need to be determined (see Figure 3-15).

As the number of remote sites goes up, you have to start breaking the network into multiple areas. As already noted, the number of routers per area depends on a couple of factors. If the number of remote sites is low, you can place the hub and its spokes within an area. If there are multiple remote sites, you can make the hub an ABR and split off the spokes in one or more areas.

In general, the hub should be an ABR, to allow each area to be summarized into the other areas.

The backbone area is extremely important in OSPF. The best approach is to design OSPF to have a small and highly stable area 0. For example, some large Frame Relay or ATM designs have had an area 0 consisting of just the ABRs, all within a couple of racks.

Issues with Hub-and-Spoke Design

Low-speed links and large numbers of spoke sites are the worst issues for hub-and-spoke design, as illustrated in Figure 3-16.

Low-speed links and large numbers of spokes may require multiple flooding domains or areas, which you must effectively support. You should balance the number of flooding domains on the hub against the number of spokes in each flooding domain. The link speeds and the amount of information being passed through the network determine the right balance.

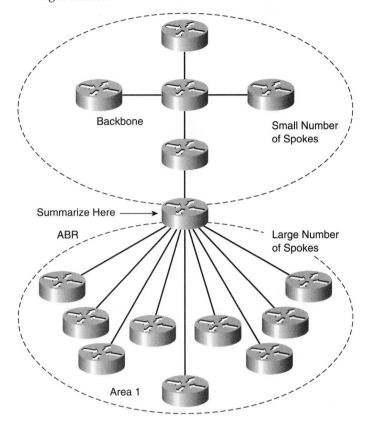

Figure 3-15 *Number of Areas in a Hub-and-Spoke Design*

Design for these situations must balance:

■ The number of areas

■ The router impact of maintaining an LSA database and doing Dijkstra calculations per area

■ The number of remote routers in each area

In situations with low bandwidth, the lack of bandwidth to flood LSAs when changes are occurring or OSPF is initializing becomes a driving factor. The number of routers per area must be strictly limited so that the bandwidth is adequate for LSA flooding under stress conditions (for example, simultaneous router startup or linkup conditions).

The extreme case of low-bandwidth links might be 9600-b/s links. Areas for a network would consist of, at most, a couple of sites. In this case, another approach to routing might be appropriate. For example, use static routes from the hub out to the spokes, with default routes back to the hub. Flooding reduction, as discussed in the "OSPF Flooding

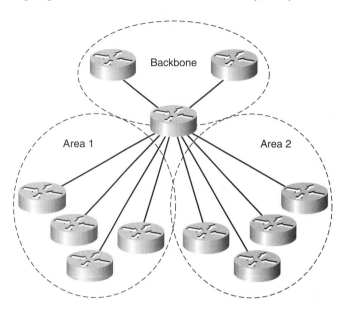

Figure 3-16   *Issues with Hub-and-Spoke Design*

Reduction" section later in this chapter might help, but would not improve bandwidth usage in a worst-case situation. The recommendation for this type of setting is lab testing under worst-case conditions to define the bandwidth requirements.

OSPF Hub-and-Spoke Network Types

When you use OSPF for hub-and-spoke networks, you have several choices for the type of network you use (see Figure 3-17).

You must use the right combination of network types for OSPF hub and spoke to work well. Generally, it is wisest to use either the point-to-multipoint OSPF network type at the hub site or configure the hub site with point-to-point subinterfaces.

Configuring point to multipoint is simple. The disadvantage of a point-to-multipoint design is that additional host routes are added to the routing table, and the default OPSF hello and dead timer interval is longer. However, point-to-multipoint implementations simplify configuration as compared to broadcast or nonbroadcast multiaccess (NBMA) implementations and conserve IP address space as compared to point-to-point implementations.

Configuring point-to-point subinterfaces takes more work initially, perhaps on the order of a few hours. Each subinterface adds a route to the routing table, making this option about equal to point-to-multipoint in terms of routing table impact. More address space gets used up, even with /30 or /31 subnetting for the point-to-point links. On the other hand, after configuration, point-to-point subinterfaces may provide the most stability, with everything including management working well in this environment.

The broadcast or NBMA network types are best avoided. Although they can be made to work with some configuration effort, they lead to less stable networks or networks where certain failure modes have odd consequences.

Network Type	Advantages	Disadvantages
Single Interface at the Hub Treated as an OSPF Broadcast or NBMA Network	• Single IP Subnet • Fewer Host Routes in Routing Table	• Manual Configuration of Each Spoke With the Correct OSPF Priority for DR/BDR • No Reachability Between Spokes or Labor-Intensive Layer 2 Configuration
Single Interface at the Hub Treated as an OSPF Point-to-Multipoint Network `ip ospf network-type point-to-multipoint`	• Single IP Subnet • No Configuration Per Spoke • Most Natural Solution	• Additional Host Routes Inserted in the Routing Table • Longer Hello and Dead Timer Intervals
Individual Point-to-Point Interface at the Hub for Each Spoke `ip ospf network-type point-to-point`	• Can Take Advantage of End-to-End Signaling for Down State • Shorter Hello and Dead Timer Intervals	• Lost IP Address Space • More Routes in the Routing Table • Overhead of Subinterfaces

Recommendation: Point-to-point or point-to-multipoint with hub-and-spoke.

Figure 3-17 *OSPF Hub-and-Spoke Network Types*

OSPF Area Border Connection Behavior

OSPF has strict rules for routing. They sometimes cause nonintuitive traffic patterns.

In Figure 3-18, dual-homed connections in hub-and-spoke networks illustrate a design challenge in OSPF, where connections are parallel to an area border. Traffic crossing the backbone must get into an area by the shortest path, and then stay in that area.

In this example, the link from D to E is in area 0. If the D-to-F link fails, traffic from D to F will go from D to G to E to F. Because D is an ABR for area 1, the traffic to F is all internal to area 1 and must remain in area 1. OSPF does not support traffic going from D to E and then to F because the D-to-E link is in area 0, not in area 1. A similar scenario applies for traffic from A to F: It must get into area 1 by the shortest path through D, and then stay in area 1.

In OSPF, traffic from area 1 to area 1 must stay in area 1 unless area 1 is partitioned, in which case the backbone area 0 can be used. Traffic from area 1 to area 2 must go from area 1 to area 0, and then into area 2. It cannot go into and out of any of the areas in other sequences.

OSPF area border connections must be considered in a thorough OSPF design. One solution to the odd transit situation just discussed is to connect ABRs with physical or virtual links for each area that both ABRs belong to. You can connect the ABRs within each area by either of two means:

■   Adding a real link between the ABRs inside area 1

■   Adding a virtual link between the ABRs inside area 0

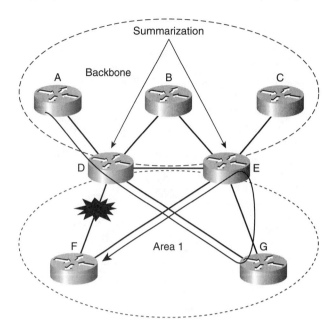

Figure 3-18 *OSPF Area Border Connection Behavior*

In general, the recommendation is to avoid virtual links when you have a good alternative. OSPF virtual links depend on area robustness and therefore are less reliable than a physical link. Virtual links add complexity and fragility; if an area has a problem, the virtual link through the area has a problem. Also, if you rely too much on virtual links, you can end up with a maze of virtual links, and possibly miss some virtual connections.

If the ABRs are Layer 3 switches or have some form of Ethernet connections, VLANs can be used to provide connections within each area common to both ABRs. With multiple logical links, whether physical, subinterfaces, or VLANs between a pair of ABRs, the following options are recommended:

■ Consider making sure that a link exists between the ABRs within each area on those ABRs.

■ Implement one physical or logical link per area as a design recommendation.

OSPF Area Filtering

This section discusses how OSPF supports filtering at ABRs. In OSPF, the link-state databases (LSDB) must be identical within an area, or there is a strong risk of a routing loop. One consequence of this is that in OSPF you cannot filter routes anywhere except at ABRs.

There are two types of OSPF filtering in Cisco OSPF:

■ Border area filtering is done via the OSPF area range command. Each range defines a single prefix and mask combination. Border area filtering allows Type 3 LSA summarization or filtering for intra-area routes advertised out of an area. This technique is defined in the base OSPF specification RFC 2328.

■ Interarea filtering uses a prefix list to filter prefixes being advertised from or to a specific area. This Cisco feature uses a prefix list to filter specific Type 3 LSA prefixes from being advertised from or to a specific area. Interarea filtering is more flexible than the area range command. It allows specification of the prefixes blocked or advertised, and the order of checking.

The generally recommended design practice is to use the **standard area range** command unless there is a strong requirement for using the **prefix list filtering** command.

Application of Interarea Filtering

This section discusses how to apply the Cisco OSPF implementation of prefix list filtering for area summarization. Figure 3-19 shows how a prefix list might be applied to an ABR for either inbound or outbound filtering.

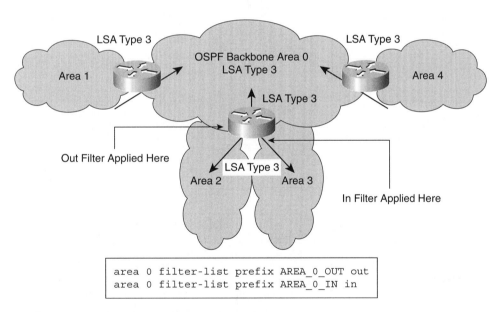

```
area 0 filter-list prefix AREA_0_OUT out
area 0 filter-list prefix AREA_0_IN in
```

Figure 3-19   *Application of Interarea Filtering*

Prefix list filtering blocks additional information from what by default would be advertised into an area. Routers within the area do not explicitly learn that certain interarea or external prefixes can be reached via a certain ABR. This is not standard OSPF behavior, but it is fully interoperable with other OSPF implementations within the affected area.

Prefix filtering allows additional information to be eliminated from LSA flooding within an area, so the routers have fewer computations to support. This reduction in routing information makes a more stable and faster-converging OSPF area.

Full-Mesh Topology and Mesh Group

This section discusses OSPF full-mesh topology issues and the use of mesh groups (see Figure 3-20).

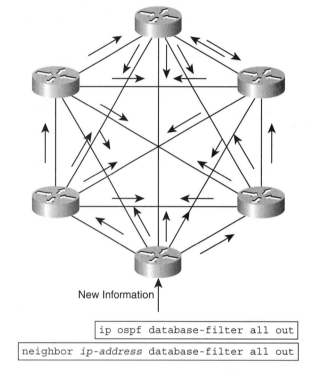

New Information

```
ip ospf database-filter all out
```

```
neighbor ip-address database-filter all out
```

Figure 3-20   *Mesh Topology and Mesh Groups*

Flooding within an OSPF full mesh is complex and does not scale well. Each router will have to talk to each of its neighbors. Each router will receive at least one copy of every new piece of information from each neighbor on the full mesh.

One technique that enables you to reduce the amount of flooding in a full-mesh network is to establish mesh groups. The mesh group is deployed by manually configuring OSPF behavior to act as if specific DRs are present by suppressing LSA flooding from all routers not designated as a DR. The specific approach is to pick at least two of the routers that will flood into the mesh, and then use filters to block flooding out of all the other routers. Flooding into all routers remains open.

Note: The OSPF mesh group concept is derived from the Intermediate System-to-Intermediate System (IS-IS) mesh group capability.

On broadcast, nonbroadcast, and point-to-point networks, use the **ip ospf database-filter all out** command in interface configuration mode to configure the routers not acting as

DRs and prevent flooding of OSPF LSAs. On point-to-multipoint networks, use the **neighbor ip-address database-filter all out** command in router configuration mode. Both of these commands are available in Cisco IOS Software Release 12.0 and later.

Note: The manually configured mesh group approach requires a fair amount of configuration effort, but leads to much better OSPF behavior in full-mesh situations.

OSPF Flooding Reduction

OSPF Flooding Reduction is a feature that you can implement when LSA flooding is having too great an impact on CPU or bandwidth. OSPF Flooding Reduction is a derivative of OSPF demand circuits, discussed in RFC 1793, based on DoNotAge (DNA) LSAs. RFC 4136 extends the nonaging behavior of demand circuits to all interface types. This feature is configured at the interface level with the **ip ospf flood-reduction** configuration command. This command is available in Cisco IOS Software Release 12.1(2)T and later.

The benefit of OSPF Flooding Reduction is that it eliminates the periodic refresh of unchanged LSAs. This means less effort for the routers doing flood reduction and less bandwidth consumed. OSPF Flooding Reduction can be particularly useful in fully meshed topologies. A periodic refresh still provides recovery from any bugs, glitches, or other LSA database inconsistencies.

However, OSPF Flooding Reduction is a tool that fixes symptoms rather than the underlying problem. If the OSPF design is such that flood reduction looks attractive or necessary, perhaps that design is not optimized.

Note: OSPF Flooding Reduction may mitigate normal flooding issues, but the underlying design may be fragile and susceptible to breakage under worst-case scenarios.

Design changes that might reduce the need for OSPF Flooding Reduction include the following:

■   Reducing the number of routers in an area

■   Reducing the number of adjacencies for stressed routers

■   Decreasing the volatility of the network, or reduce area sizes in response to volatility that is greater than expected

■   Spreading the adjacency workload across more routers

■   Using more hierarchy rather than large-scale, full-mesh topologies

Fast Convergence in OSPF

The topic looks at fast convergence for routing protocols, with an emphasis on OSPF. OSPF supports subsecond hello timers, which can help support fast convergence in these protocols. OSPF with "tuned timers" converges faster than the default OSPF operation. The OSPF routing protocol supports subsecond hello and dead timers. By comparison, subsecond timers are not available for EIGRP.

Note: Take care when tuning timers in OSPF because mismatched timers will prevent OSPF-speakers from establishing neighbor relationships.

Fast Convergence with Fast Hellos

Scaling is the major issue with fast hellos. If hello timers are set to 1/3 second for 300 interfaces, each with 10 neighbors, the router would have to generate 900 hellos per second. When the 3000 neighbors send 3 hellos per second back to the router, it has to process a total of 9900 hellos per second.

However, a good OSPF design limits the number of adjacencies. From that perspective, 300 or 3000 neighbors is too high a number.

The design conclusion is use fast hellos only in scenarios with a moderate numbers of neighbors. You can also test and observe the impact of fast hellos on a particular router CPU.

Fast Convergence with SPF

The key to OSPF fast convergence is based on a full understanding the Shortest Path First algorithm (SPF).

Understanding fast convergence in OSPF requires examining when full or partial SPF calculations are triggered and how fast SPF completes its calculations. Lab testing suggests that the SPF calculation is the biggest remaining source of delay in OSPF convergence, when a lack of hellos detects neighbor loss. Link-down conditions are generally detected more quickly, because of a loss of voltage or media keepalives.

Full SPF calculations depend on the number of nodes and links in the area, and the number of Type 3 to Type 7 LSAs in the OSPF database. The figure presents some experimental numbers for full and partial SPF convergence times on Cisco 12000 series and Cisco 7500 series routers. As expected, SPF calculation time increases for additional nodes. Partial SPF is much faster than full SPF.

Overview of OSPF Incremental SPF

A feature known as incremental SPF (iSPF) provides more rapid SPF computations. The iSPF computation uses a modified Dijkstra algorithm to recompute only the part of the path tree that has changed. The algorithm recomputes only a portion of the tree rather than the entire tree and results in faster OSPF convergence and saves CPU resources.

The performance gain of iSPF depends on how far topologically the change happens from the calculating node or how much of the SPF tree remains unchanged. If the change is far away from the node performing iSPF, the SPF tree is likely to remain mostly unchanged, in which case SPF calculation will be very fast, resulting in faster networkwide convergence. If the change is close to the iSPF node, more of the shortest path tree (SPT) will change. In that case, iSPF provides less benefit.

Lab testing indicates a router can run iSPF and update the routing table for the 1000-node network in less than 10 ms, which would improve OSPF convergence.

Topology changes cause less and less impact or computational delay the farther away a node is from where the change occurred. iSPF does not add a constant and large delay to propagating change LSAs, as full SPF does. Instead, with iSPF there is a dampening effect, where the larger the LSA propagation delay is, the less computational delay there will be in addition. This is a general observation, and specific results will vary depending on network topology.

The iSPF feature has been available since Cisco IOS Software Release 12.0(24)S, 12.3(2)T, 12.2(18)S, and 12.2(27)SBC. It is enabled with the iSPF router command under an OSPF process.

Incremental SPF Convergence Times

This section provides some experimental results from testing iSPF convergence times.

Figure 3-21 illustrates some iSPF convergence times from Cisco lab experiments. The diagram shows normal SPF and iSPF convergence times for multiples of 2000 nodes in a link flap scenario. Even for around 10,000 nodes, iSPF achieved approximately 50-ms convergence, which is extremely fast. For large networks, iSPF can provide significant savings in CPU resources and faster OSPF convergence.

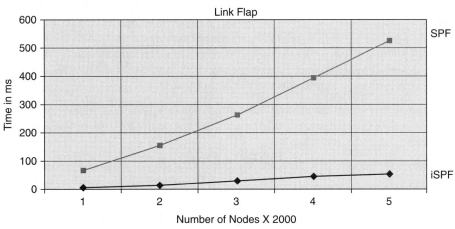

Figure 3-21 *Incremental SPF Convergence Times*

Bidirectional Forwarding Detection

Bidirectional Forwarding Detection (BFD) is another feature that helps speed up routing convergence. One of the significant factors in routing convergence is the detection of link or node failure. In the case of link failures, there is usually an electrical signal or keepalive to detect the loss of the link. BFD is a technology that uses fast Layer 2 link hellos to detect failed or one-way links, which is generally what fast hellos detect.

BFD requires routing-protocol support. BFD is available for OSPF, EIGRP, IS-IS, and BGP. BFD quickly notifies the routing protocol of link-down conditions. This can provide failure detection and response times down to around 50 ms, which is the typical SONET failure response time.

The CPU impact of BFD is less than that of fast hellos. This is because some of the processing is shifted to the data plane rather than the control plane. On nondistributed platforms, Cisco testing has shown a minor, 2 percent CPU increase above baseline when supporting 100 concurrent BFD sessions.

BFD provides a method for network administrators to configure subsecond Layer 2 failure detection between adjacent network nodes. Furthermore, administrators can configure their routing protocols to respond to BFD notifications and begin Layer 3 route convergence almost immediately.

Note: BFD is currently supported only on Cisco 6500/7600 series routers, Cisco 12000 series routers, and Cisco Carrier Routing System (CRS-1) routers.

Designing Scalable BGP Designs

Border Gateway Protocol is commonly used in sites with multiple connections to the Internet. BGP is also frequently present in medium- to large-scale networks to provide a controlled interconnection between multiple routing domains running OSPF or EIGRP. Large-scale internal BGP networks are also becoming more prevalent as large enterprises implement internal Multiprotocol Label Switching (MPLS) VPNs for security segmentation, business unit or brand isolation, and similar purposes.

This section discusses designing advanced routing solutions using BGP. It describes how to identify scaling issues in internal BGP designs and how to use techniques to alleviate these issues.

Upon mastering the content in this section, you will be able to describe and use various concepts to perform advanced routing design. This ability includes being able to meet these objectives:

■ Identify the scaling issues with internal BGP requiring a full-mesh topology

■ Describe scaling IBGP with route reflectors

■ Describe scaling IBGP with confederations

Scaling BGP Designs

This section discusses aspects of scaling in basic internal BGP (IBGP) design (see Figure 3-22).

BGP can provide a controlled interconnection between multiple routing domains running OSPF or EIGRP and support internal MPLS VPNs. IBGP requires a full mesh of BGP peers.

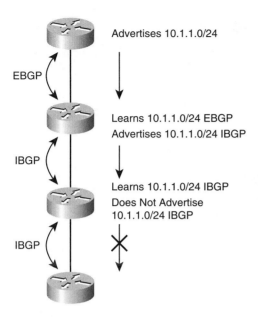

Figure 3-22   *IBGP Full-Mesh Requirement*

The full mesh of IBGP routers is needed because IBGP routers do not re-advertise routes learned via IBGP to other IBGP peers. This behavior is part of BGP protocol behavior that is used to prevent information from circulating between IBGP speaking routers in a routing information loop or cycle. External BGP (EBGP) relies on the autonomous system path to prevent loops. However, there is no way to tell whether a route advertised through several IBGP speakers is a loop. Because IBGP peers are in the same autonomous system, they do not add anything to the autonomous system path, and they do not re-advertise routes learned via IBGP.

Full-Mesh IBGP Scalability

Because IBGP requires a full mesh of peers, scaling the full mesh is a concern. In general, for N peers in an IBGP full mesh, each would have $N - 1$ peers. There are $N(N - 1) / 2$ peering relationships. This means that each peer would need the CPU, memory, and bandwidth to handle updates and peer status for all the other routers. This is not a hierarchical design, and it would not be cost-effective to scale for large networks.

There are two IBGP alternatives to scale IBGP:

■   Route reflectors

■   Confederations

The following sections explore the basic design and behavior of route reflectors and confederations and demonstrate how they can be used in a routing design.

Scaling IBGP with Route Reflectors

A BGP route reflector is an IBGP speaker that reflects or repeats routes learned from IBGP peers to some of its other IBGP peers (see Figure 3-23).

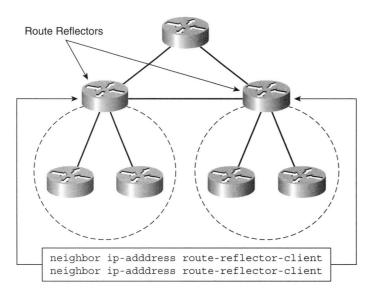

Figure 3-23 *BGP Route Reflectors*

To prevent loops, a route reflector adds an originator ID and a cluster list to routes that it reflects between IBGP speakers. These attributes act similarly to the autonomous system path attribute to prevent routing information loops.

All configuration of the route reflector is done on the route reflector itself. The configuration identifies which IBGP peers are route reflector clients.

Implementing route reflectors is fairly simple and can be done incrementally. Each client router needs to be configured as a client on the route reflector or on multiple route reflectors. Unnecessary peers can then be removed from the configuration on the client router. Often, route reflector clients peer only with the route reflectors. In a service provider network, route reflector clients might also be provider edge (PE) devices, which also peer with customers using EBGP.

To avoid a single point of failure, redundant route reflectors are typically used.

BGP Route Reflector Definitions

A route reflector client (see Figure 3-24) is an IBGP router that receives and sends routes to most other IBGP speakers via the route reflector. The route reflector client needs no special configuration, other than removing peering with some or all neighbors other than the route reflector.

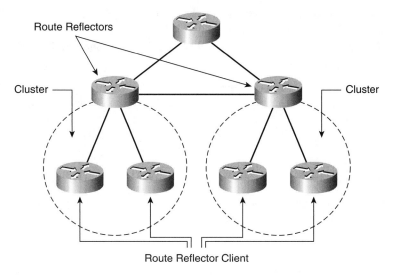

Figure 3-24 *BGP Route Reflector Definitions*

A cluster is a route reflector together with its clients. The route reflector relieves the route reflector client routers of needing to be interconnected via an IBGP full mesh.

Route reflector clusters may overlap.

A nonclient router (see Figure 3-25) is any route reflector IBGP peer that is not a route reflector client of that route reflector.

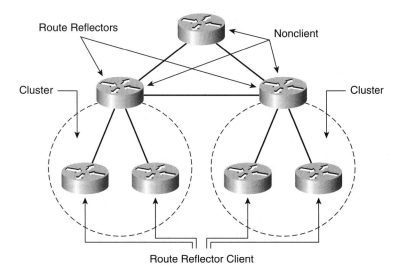

Figure 3-25 *Additional BGP Route Reflector Definitions*

Route reflectors are typically nonclients with regard to the other route reflectors in the network.

Route reflectors must still be fully IBGP meshed with nonclients. Therefore, route reflectors reduce meshing within clusters, but all mesh links outside the cluster must be maintained on the route reflector. The route reflector clients will get information from IBGP speakers outside the cluster via the route reflector.

If a route reflector receives a route from a nonclient, it reflects it to route reflector clients but not to other nonclients. The route reflector receives the routes if it has a direct peering relationship to the original nonclient. The route reflector would also send the route to EBGP peers, which is standard behavior. IBGP routes get repeated to all EBGP peers.

Route Reflector Basics

This section provides a brief look at how route advertisement works with route reflectors (see Figure 3-26).

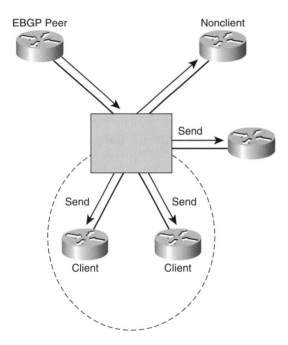

Figure 3-26 *Route Reflector Basics*

If a route reflector receives a route from an EBGP peer, it passes that route to all route reflector clients and nonclients, just as in normal IBGP peering behavior.

If the route reflector receives a route from a route reflector client, it reflects the route to the other clients within the cluster, and nonclients. It also reflects the route to EBGP peers. Another way to think of this: The route reflector takes over the communication for the route reflector clients, passing along all the messages they would normally transmit directly via a peering session.

Scaling IBGP with Confederations

BGP confederations are another way of scaling IBGP. Their behavior is defined in RFC 3065. Confederations insert information using the autonomous system path into BGP routes to prevent loops within an autonomous system. The basic idea with confederations is to divide a normal BGP autonomous system into multiple sub-autonomous systems. The outer or containing autonomous system is called the confederation autonomous system. This is all that is visible to the outside world.

Each of the inner autonomous systems is a smaller sub-autonomous system that uses a different autonomous system number, typically chosen from the private autonomous system number range of 64,512 through 65,534.

BGP Confederation Definitions

This topic defines terms used with confederations (see Figure 3-27).

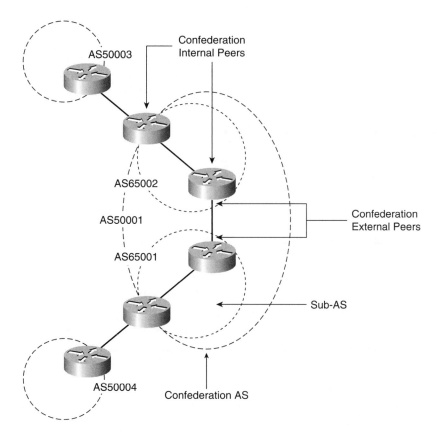

Figure 3-27   *Confederation Definitions*

Peers within the same sub-autonomous system are confederation internal peers.

IBGP peers that are in a different sub-autonomous system are confederation external peers.

As IBGP information is passed around within a confederation autonomous system, the sub-autonomous system numbers are put into a confederation sequence, which works like an autonomous system path.

Confederation Basics

Route advertisement with confederations works similarly to that of route reflectors in the following ways:

- A route learned from an EBGP peer is advertised to all confederation external and internal peers.

- A route learned from a confederation internal peer is advertised to all confederation external peers, and also to EBGP peers.

- A route learned from a confederation external peer is advertised to all confederation internal peers, and to EBGP peers.

Another way to understand this is that IBGP between sub-autonomous systems acts like EBGP. Private autonomous system numbers are used internally within the confederation autonomous system and removed from updates sent outside the confederation.

Confederations Reduce Meshing

Like route reflectors, confederations are used to reduce the amount of IBGP meshing needed. Without route reflectors or confederation, IBGP requires a full mesh of peering relationships, as illustrated in Figure 3-28.

Note: Note that the IBGP does not require peers to be directly connected.

However, confederations can reduce meshing requirements, as shown in Figure 3-29.

Routers in different sub-autonomous systems do not peer with each other, except at sub-autonomous system borders. It is generally recommended to use two or three links between sub-autonomous system borders. More links just consume CPU and memory in the border routers.

When you use sub-autonomous systems for confederations, the meshing is restricted to within the sub-autonomous systems, with some additional peering between sub-autonomous system border routers.

Route reflectors can be used within confederations to further reduce network complexity. Historically, service providers have not done this, but they are now starting to. Using route reflectors alleviates the need to fully mesh within a sub-autonomous system.

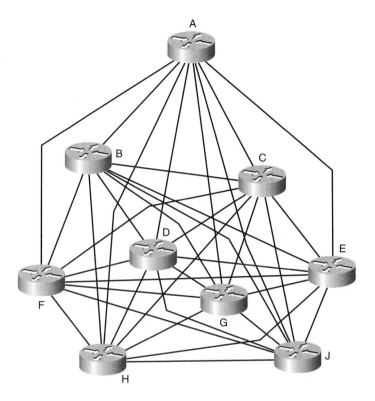

Figure 3-28   *IBGP Full-Mesh Peering*

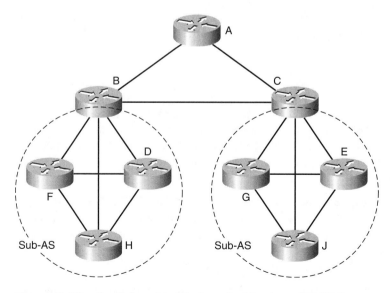

Figure 3-29   *Confederations Reduce the Number of IBGP Peers*

Deploying Confederations

In Figure 3-30, router B could be configured to set the BGP next hop to itself for advertisement to routers C and D. This is not normally done by IBGP routers. This would impose the constraint that routers C and D would need to have routes to the new next hop, router B.

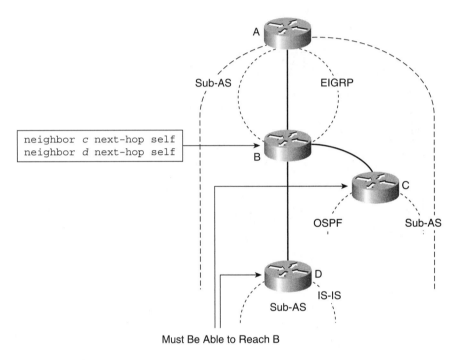

Figure 3-30   *Deploying Confederations*

Using this configuration breaks the confederation up from a next-hop perspective from both the IGP and BGP point of view. This scenario allows for more flexibility and scaling in very large networks. This deployment might make sense for very large organizations that support separate entities such as government organizations that have distinct branches or divisions.

Using confederation sub-autonomous systems has other advantages. The IBGP policies can differ internally within and between the sub-autonomous systems. In particular, multi-exit discriminator (MED) acceptance or stripping, local preference settings, route dampening, and so on can vary between sub-autonomous systems. In addition, policy controls can be used on peerings between sub-autonomous systems.

This highlights some advantages of confederations. Confederations can ease the transition in an acquisition or merger. The new network can be treated as another sub-autonomous system and keep its IGP. It can also keep its EBGP policies with its customers.

A disadvantage of confederations is that there is no graceful way to migrate from full mesh to using confederations. The migration may well require downtime.

Table 3-1 compares how confederations and route reflectors provide various IBGP scaling features.

Table 3-1   *Comparing Confederations to Route Reflectors*

	Confederation	Route Reflector
Loop prevention	AS confederation set	Originator or set cluster ID
Break up a single AS	Subautonomous systems	Clusters
Redundancy	Multiple connections between subautonomous systems	Client connects to several reflectors
External connections	Anywhere in the network	Anywhere in the network
Multilevel hierarchy	Reflectors within subautonomous systems	Clusters within clusters
Policy control	Along outside borders and outside subautonomous systems	Along outside borders
Scalability	Medium; still requires full IBGP within each sub-AS	Very high
Migration	Very difficult	Moderately easy (impossible in some situations)

In general, route reflectors are simpler to migrate to and relatively simple to use, whereas confederations are more flexible as to IGP and policy.

Summary

In summary, we've looked at elements of advanced routing design, and we also touched on the merits of a well-planned IP addressing scheme. The IP addressing scheme is the foundation for greater efficiency in operating and maintaining a network. Without proper planning in advance, networks might not be able to benefit from route summarization features inherent to many routing protocols.

The general advanced routing design discussion can be encapsulated in the following key points that were discussed previously:

- Route summarization and default routing are important in scaling routing designs.

- Route filtering can be used to manage traffic flows in the network, avoiding inappropriate transit traffic and as a defense against inappropriate routing updates.

- Redistribution can be useful for manipulating and managing routing updates, but needs to be designed properly to prevent routing loops or other problems.

EIGRP converges quickly as long as it has a feasible successor. With no feasible successor, EIGRP sends queries out to its neighbors. To limit the scope of these queries, use route summarization and filtering. By limiting EIGRP query scope, you can speed up EIGRP convergence and increase stability. In addition, large numbers of neighbors should be avoided for any one router. Multiple autonomous systems may be used with EIGRP providing that you understand that they do not directly limit EIGRP query scope. You would use them to support migration strategies, different administrative groups, or very large network design.

OSPF scaling depends on summarization and controlling how much LSA flooding is needed. Simple, stub, summarized designs scale most effectively. Several techniques speed up convergence for OSPF, including fast hellos, iSPF, and BFD.

Finally, IBGP requires a full mesh of all IBGP routers, but full-mesh peering does not scale gracefully. Route reflectors pass along routing information to and from their clients. The route reflector clients are relieved of the burden of most IBGP peering. Confederations allow an autonomous system to be divided into sub-autonomous systems, where the sub-autonomous system border routers peer with each other and then pass along routes on behalf of the other sub-autonomous system routers. Confederation sequences are used to prevent information loops. Sub-autonomous systems can have different BGP polices from each other.

Key points to remember include the following:

- IP address design allows for route summarization that supports network scaling, stability, and fast convergence.

- Route summarization, route filtering, and appropriate redistribution help minimize routing information in the network.

- EIGRP converges quickly as long as it has a feasible successor. Multiple autonomous systems with EIGRP may be used, with care, to support special situations, including migration strategies and very large network design.

- Simple, stub, summarized OSPF designs scale most effectively. Several techniques speed up convergence for OSPF, including fast hellos, iSPF, and BFD.

- IBGP designs can be scaled using route reflectors to pass routing information to and from their clients and confederations to allow an autonomous system to be divided into sub-autonomous systems.

References

- Cisco Systems, Inc. "Designing Large-Scale IP Internetworks," at http://www.cisco.com/en/US/docs/internetworking/design/guide/nd2003.html

- Cisco Systems, Inc. "Cisco IOS IP Routing Protocols Command Reference," at http://www.cisco.com/en/US/docs/ios/iproute/command/reference/irp_book.html

- The Internet Engineering Task Force. RFC 1793: Extending OSPF to Support Demand Circuits, at http://www.ietf.org/rfc/rfc1793.txt

- The Internet Engineering Task Force. RFC 2328: OSPF Version 2, at http://www.ietf.org/rfc/rfc2328.txt

- The Internet Engineering Task Force. RFC 2796: BGP Route Reflection—An Alternative to Full Mesh IBGP, at http://www.ietf.org/rfc/rfc2796.txt

- The Internet Engineering Task Force. RFC 3065: Autonomous System Confederations for BGP, at http://www.ietf.org/rfc/rfc3065.txt

- The Internet Engineering Task Force. RFC 4136: OSPF Refresh and Flooding Reduction in Stable Topologies, at http://www.ietf.org/rfc/rfc4136.txt

Review Questions

Answer the following questions, and then refer to Appendix A, "Answers to Review Questions," for the answers.

1. Which two address blocks are summarizable? (Choose two.)

   a. 172.16.20.0 to 172.16.27.0

   b. 172.16.20.0 to 172.16.23.0

   c. 10.16.0.0 to 10.31.0.0

   d. 10.16.0.0 to 10.47.0.0

   e. 10.96.0.0 to 10.159.0.0

2. Which two can bit-splitting techniques be used for? (Choose two.)

   a. OSPF area design

   b. Summarizable address blocks with convenient role-based subnets

   c. Access list convergence

   d. Detecting summarizable address blocks

   e. Manual route summarization

3. Which is the recommended design approach?

   a. Configure a static default route everywhere for predictability.

   b. Configure static default routes using recursive routing for consistency.

   c. Originate the default at the edge and redistribute it into dynamic routing.

   d. Make the OSPF backbone area 0 stubby.

   e. Do not use additional parameters with the originate default command.

4. Which two statements best describe redistribution? (Choose two.)

   a. Redistribution works poorly with an arbitrary mix of routing protocols anywhere.

   b. Redistribution seldom requires route filters.

   c. Redistribution is not useful after a merger.

   d. Redistribution works well with a limited number of redistribution points.

   e. Redistribution prevents summarization.

5. Select the best statement concerning EIGRP and OSPF routing design.

   a. Routing design needs to be done most carefully for small networks.

   b. OSPF should not be used for small networks.

   c. Routing design needs to be done most carefully for large networks.

   d. Route summarization must be used in all network designs.

   e. OSPF works best with a full mesh.

6. Which three factors are the biggest influences on OSPF scalability? (Choose three.)

   a. Flooding paths and redundancy

   b. Amount of routing information in the OSPF area or routing domain

   c. Number of routers capable of Cisco Express Forwarding

   d. Number of adjacent neighbors

   e. Other routing protocols in use

7. Which statement best describes basic IBGP?

   a. IBGP is a link-state protocol.

   b. IBGP requires a full mesh of peers because it has no other way to prevent looping of routing information.

   c. IBGP inherently handles all full-mesh scalability issues.

   d. IBGP uses split horizoning to prevent looping of routing information.

   e. IBGP uses the autonomous system path to prevent looping of routing information.

8. A route reflector reflects routes from a route reflector client to which three types of IBGP routers? (Choose three.)

   a. Nonclient routers

   b. Sub-autonomous system members

   c. Other route reflector client routers

   d. EBGP peers

   e. IBGP peers configured for EIGRP or OSPF routing

Upon completing this chapter you will be able to:

- Choose an appropriate advanced WAN technology based upon customer requirements

- Describe the optical technologies used in support of advanced WAN technologies

- Describe Metro Ethernet, VPLS, and MPLS VPN technologies

- Discuss customer requirements and SLAs as part of a WAN design

CHAPTER 4

Advanced WAN Services Design Considerations

This chapter reviews the key concepts associated with the design and selection of WAN services. The optical technologies Synchronous Optical Network (SONET), Synchronous Digital Hierarchy (SDH), coarse wavelength-division multiplexing (CWDM), dense wavelength-division multiplexing (DWDM), and Route Processor Redundancy (RPR) are considered along with their companion, Metro Ethernet services.

Advanced WAN Service Layers

Service providers are interested in providing advanced WAN services that can be supported with low impact on their existing fiber infrastructure. Managed services such as storage, content switching, web hosting, instant messaging, and security built on Ethernet allow the service provider to deliver advanced WAN services to customers that are using Ethernet user-network interfaces (UNI). Figure 4-1 shows the relationship between the different WAN services layers and customer applications.

Customers have multiple reasons for wanting advanced WAN services based on Ethernet:

■ Familiar equipment is used, so customers can use their existing devices.

■ A familiar protocol is implemented.

■ Higher bandwidth is possible than with traditional WAN links.

■ Lower bits-per-second costs can be supported.

■ The underlying optical technologies allow the service provider to provide these advanced WAN services on their existing fiber infrastructure.

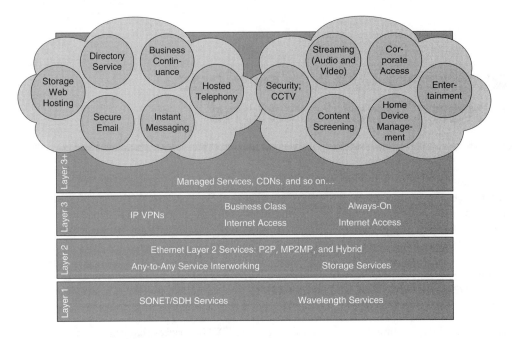

Figure 4-1   *Advanced WAN Services Layers*

Enterprise Optical Interconnections

Several common optical interconnection technologies are used to connect enterprise locations:

■ **SDH:** SONET is a North American high-speed baseband digital transport standard specifying incrementally increasing data stream rates for movement across digital optical links. SDH is the European standard for digital optical links.

■ **DWDM and CWDM:** DWDM and CWDM are technologies that increase the information-carrying capacity of existing fiber-optic infrastructure by transmitting and receiving data on different light wavelengths on a single strand of fiber.

■ **Dynamic Packet Transport (DPT) and Resilient Packet Ring (RPR):** DPT is an RPR technology designed for service providers to deliver scalable Internet service, reliable IP-aware optical transport, and simplified network operations, principally for metropolitan-area applications. DPT is based on Spatial Reuse Protocol (SRP), a Cisco-developed MAC-layer protocol for ring-based packet internetworking.

These technologies can be used directly over leased dark fiber, or used by a service provider as the transport mechanism underlying an Ethernet or other offering.

Overview of SONET and SDH

SONET is a time-division multiplexing (TDM) technique for framing voice and data onto a single wavelength on fiber. It typically uses fixed time division to allocate bandwidth between entry points on a ring. Many long-haul fiber connections are SONET, in part because SONET repeater technology is used in many service provider networks to boost signals that are carried across long distances. SONET was historically used to prevent dropped calls in a TDM environment. SONET can provide reliable transport with TDM bandwidth guarantees for TDM voice and public-safety voice and radio traffic.

The maximum distance for single-mode installations is determined by the amount of light loss in the fiber path. Good-quality single-mode fiber with very few splices can carry an OC-12c/STM-4 signal 50 miles (80 km) or more without a repeater. Good-quality multimode fiber can carry the signal up to 1640 feet (500 m).

SONET typically uses fiber rings. When the ring fails, traffic wraps the other way around the ring. One benefit of SONET is that some network equipment may not notice the 50-ms failure leading to a ring wrap, particularly if SONET access gear keeps Ethernet services on a link in an up state. One drawback to a SONET design is that it requires provisioning double the protected bandwidth. Bandwidth along SONET is committed as circuits between two points on the ring.

Not all SONET topologies are ring based. Sometimes single or double pairs of fiber are run in linear fashion from a SONET network. Physical constraints such as river crossings can narrow the two sides of the ring into more of a figure 8, which is potentially a single point of failure. Although the high reliability of SONET is often mentioned in sales presentations, it is wise to verify that the entire SONET path being used is a true ring.

SONET can be used with SONET access equipment that may statistically multiplex Ethernet (10 Mb/s, Fast Ethernet, or Gigabit Ethernet) onto a SONET circuit. This allows some degree of oversubscription of bandwidth. The actual oversubscription amount is typically not disclosed by the provider.

Optical Carrier (OC) rates are the digital hierarchies of the SONET and SDH standards. Table 4-1 shows the commonly deployed SONET and SDH rates.

Table 4-1 *Common SONET and SDH Rates*

Hierarchy	OC-x	Speed	SONET	SDH
—	OC-1	51.85 Mb/s	STS-1	STM-0
Level Zero	OC-3	155.52 Mb/s	STS-3	STM-1
Level One	OC-12	622.08 Mb/s	STS-12	STM-4
Level Two	OC-48	2.488 Gb/s	STS-48	STM-16
Level Three	OC-192	9.953 Gb/s	STS-192	STM-64
Level Four	OC-768	39.813 Gb/s	STS-768	STM-256

Note: SONET is an ANSI specification. SDH is the SONET-equivalent specification pro-posed by the ITU. European carriers use SDH widely; Asian and Pacific Rim carriers use SONET more frequently. The primary differences between the SONET and SDH specifica-tions are the basic transmission rate and some header information.

In advanced WAN designs, the designer has to balance the current and future uses of the transport and other network components, customer requirements, customer perceptions, and the costs of the various network components. Whether SONET (or SDH) is the best solution depends on the situation.

Enterprise View of SONET

From the enterprise customer perspective, SONET is the transport underlying some other form of connection. The connection might be TDM-based, such as T1 or T3, or it may be one of the various types of Ethernet services offered by a service provider. SONET may be included as part of the Ethernet service due to its robustness, and because of the service-provider-installed base in SONET infrastructure. Traditional TDM circuits may also be aggregated and then transported over SONET.

You should ask several key questions of a service provider that is offering SONET for your network transport:

- Is the service based on connecting across end-to-end SONET rings, or are there seg-ments that are linear or otherwise not geographically diverse? You need to consider whether there are single points of failure in the transport.

- What path does your service follow? If you are buying services from two providers for redundancy, it might be useful to determine whether the provider's SONET fol-lows different paths. Sometimes different providers lease fiber from the same sup-plier, or along the same rights of way such as gas pipelines, train tracks, and high-voltage electrical wire paths.

- Is there oversubscription and sharing, or is bandwidth dedicated for your use? Al-though you might not get the oversubscription details, you should know what is be-ing allocated for your use. If the service provider is managing the customer edge (CE) device, you should also be interested in the quality of service (QoS) procedures used to manage the rate transition from your site to the SONET network.

WDM Overview

A wavelength-division multiplexing (WDM) system uses a multiplexer (mux) at the trans-mitter to place multiple optical signals on a fiber, and a demultiplexer (demux) at the re-ceiver to split them off of the fiber. The signals use different wavelengths. Before being multiplexed, source signals might be converted from electrical to optical format, or from optical format to electrical format and back to optical format.

CWDM Technical Overview

CWDM is an optical technology for transmitting up to 16 channels, each in a separate wavelength or color, over the same fiber strand. The CWDM solutions help enable enterprises and service providers to increase the bandwidth of an existing Gigabit Ethernet optical infrastructure without adding new fiber strands.

Unlike DWDM, which can transmit up to 160 channels on the same fiber by tightly packing them, CWDM technology relies on wider spacing between channels. This design makes CWDM a relatively inexpensive technology for transmitting multiple Gb/s signals on a single fiber strand as compared with DWDM because it can support less-sophisticated, and therefore cheaper, transceiver designs. In the point-to-point configuration shown in Figure 4-2, two endpoints are directly connected through a fiber link. The ITU has standardized a 20-nm channel-spacing grid for use with CWDM, using the wavelengths between 1310 nm and 1610 nm. Most CWDM systems support 8 channels in the 1470-to-1610 nm range. The Cisco CWDM Gigabit Interface Converter (GBIC)/small form-factor pluggable (SFP) solution allows organizations to add or drop as many as eight channels (Gigabit Ethernet or Fibre Channel) into a pair of single-mode (SM) fiber strands. As a result, the need for additional fiber is minimized. You can create redundant point-to-point links by adding or dropping redundant channels into a second pair of SM fiber strands.

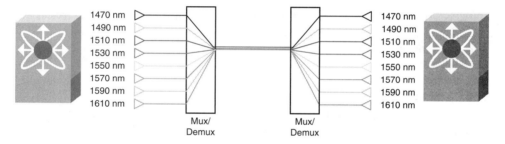

Figure 4-2   *CWDM Technical Overview*

CWDM multiplexing is achieved through special passive (nonpowered) glass devices known as filters. The filters act as prisms; directing lights from many incoming and outgoing fibers (client ports) to a common transmit and receive trunk port. Optical multiplexing in a ring with CWDM networks is supported with optical add/drop multiplexers (OADM). OADMs can drop off one or more CWDM wavelengths at a specific location and replace that signal with one or more different outbound signals.

The Cisco CWDM GBIC/SFP solution has two main components: a set of eight different pluggable transceivers (Cisco CWDM GBICs and Cisco CWDM SFPs), and a set of different Cisco CWDM passive multiplexers/demultiplexers or OADMs. Both the transceivers and the passive multiplexers are compliant with the CWDM grid defined in the ITU-T G.694.2 standards.

CWDM can be used by enterprises on leased dark fiber to increase capacity, for example from 1 to 8 or 16 Gb/s, over metro-area distances. One problem with CWDM is that the wavelengths are not compatible with erbium-doped fiber amplifier (EDFA) technology, which amplifies all light signals within their frequency range.

Note: EDFA technology is beginning to make repeaters obsolete. EDFA is a form of fiber-optical amplification that transmits a light signal through a section of erbium-doped fiber and amplifies the signal with a laser pump diode. EDFA is used in transmitter booster amplifiers, inline repeating amplifiers, and in receiver preamplifiers.

CWDM supports up to a 30-dB power budget on an SM fiber. This restricts the distances over which CWDM may be used. CWDM supports distances of about 60 miles (100 km) in a point-to-point topology, and about 25 miles (40 km) in a ring topology.

In some areas, service providers use CWDM to provide lambda or wavelength services. A lambda service is where a provider manages equipment and multiplexes customer traffic onto one or more wavelengths for a high-speed connection, typically between two or more points.

DWDM Technical Overview

DWDM is a core technology in an optical transport network. The concepts of DWDM are similar to those for CWDM. However, DWDM spaces the wavelengths more tightly, yielding up to 160 channels.

The tighter channel spacing in DWDM requires more sophisticated, precise, and therefore more expensive transceiver designs. In a service provider's backbone network, the majority of embedded fiber is standard SM fiber (G.652) with high dispersion in the 1550-nm window. DWDM supports 32 or more channels in the narrow band around 1550 nm at 100-GHz spacing or about 0.8 nm, as illustrated in Figure 4-3.

Note: Current Cisco DWDM cards can support 32 wavelengths.

Because of the EDFA compatibility of the wavelengths used, DWDM is also available over much longer distances than CDWM, and supports metropolitan-area network (MAN) and WAN applications. In practice, signals can travel for up to 75 miles (120 km) between amplifiers if fiber with EDFA is used. At distances of 375 miles (600) to 600 miles (1000 km), the signal must be regenerated.

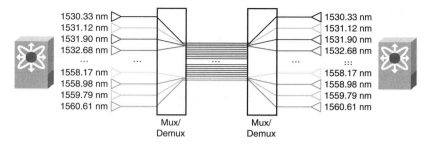

Figure 4-3 *DWDM Technical Overview*

DWDM can be used as a high-speed enterprise WAN connectivity service. Typical DWDM uses include connectivity between sites and data centers that is 1-, 2-, or 4-Gb/s fiber channel; IBM fiber connectivity (FICON) and Enterprise System Connection (ES-CON); and Gigabit and 10 Gigabit Ethernet.

Protection options include client-side protection using rerouting, an optical splitter that allows the signal to go both ways around a ring, or line-card-based protection that detects loss of signal and wraps.

DWDM Systems

DWDM typically uses a transponder, mux/demux, and an amplifier:

- **Transponder:** Receives the input optical signal (from a client-layer SONET/SDH or other signal), converts that signal into the electrical domain, and retransmits the signal using a 1550-nm band laser.

- **Multiplexer:** Takes the various 1550-nm band signals and places them onto an SM fiber. The terminal multiplexer may or may not also support a local EDFA. An OADM extracts a channel of signal, and inserts (replaces it with) an outgoing signal from a site.

- **Amplifier:** Provides power amplification of the multiwavelength optical signal.

The diagram in Figure 4-4 shows how DWDM can be used with the reconfigurable OADM (ROADM). A ROADM allows reconfiguration on-the-fly so that commands select the wavelengths to be dropped and added. Other forms of OADM are tied to specific wavelengths. Reconfiguration with older OADMs meant swapping cards to select different frequencies (wavelengths). This might require interrupting the entire set of channels.

The primary challenge with mux/demux is to minimize crosstalk and maximize channel separation so that the system can distinguish each wavelength.

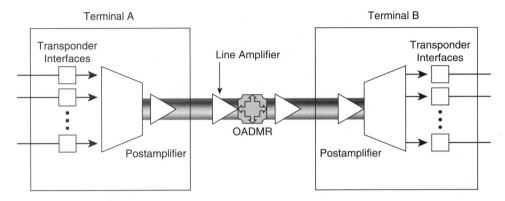

Figure 4-4   *DWDM Systems*

RPR Overview

RPR is a Layer 2 transport architecture providing packet-based transmission based on a dual counter-rotating ring topology. The June 2004 IEEE 802.17 standard defines RPR as a MAN technology supporting a ring structure using unidirectional, counter-rotating ringlets. Each ringlet is made up of links with data flow in the same direction. The use of dual fiber-optic rings provides a high level of packet survivability. If a station fails or fiber is cut, data is transmitted over the alternate ring.

RPR is similar to the older Cisco Spatial Reuse Protocol (SRP). SRP is implemented in the Cisco Dynamic Packet Transport (DPT) products. Newer Cisco DPT interfaces have been designed to include support for the 802.17 RPR protocol.

Whereas DPT and SRP use SONET/SDH as the physical medium, IEEE 802.17 RPR has been defined to use either SONET/SDH or the physical layer of Gigabit and 10 Gigabit Ethernet. DTP, SRP, and RPR can all support metro and long distance use.

RPR in the Enterprise

Figure 4-5 illustrates how the customer views RPR—as a transport ring that supports connections between their locations. RPR overcomes some limitations of SONET/SDH. Because SONET/SDH is designed to support the characteristics of voice traffic, SONET and SDH are limited in their ability to efficiently carry bursty data traffic. Voice traffic typically has consistent, well-characterized usage patterns, but data traffic bursts as large files are transferred.

Unlike point-to-point voice traffic, data traffic is characterized by the predominance of point-to-multipoint and multipoint-to-multipoint transmission and bursty traffic. RPR efficiently supports data traffic on service provider networks because RPR can take advantage of the multiple QoS and class of service (CoS) features of data traffic. RPR can also offer network efficiency by sharing or oversubscribing core bandwidth.

Figure 4-5   *RPR Customer View*

From the customer's perspective, SONET typically provides TDM bandwidth guarantees, although they do not match up precisely with typical Ethernet speeds. The guarantee holds unless the provider performs edge oversubscription, with more access bandwidth than what is available across the SONET ring.

RPR is based on a statistical multiplexing approach that behaves more like Ethernet, and does not provide TDM-style bandwidth guarantees. RPR can use QoS to protect and prioritize important traffic, but bandwidth guarantees are harder to provide. Service providers need to be prepared to use a different approach with RPR to meet service-level agreements (SLA).

Metro Ethernet Overview

A Metro Ethernet is a flexible transport architecture that uses some combination of optical, Ethernet, and IP technologies in the metropolitan area. Exactly what the mix of technologies is depends on how the service provider has designed its infrastructure.

This topic provides an overview of Metro Ethernet service models and architectures.

Metro Ethernet Service Model

Metro Ethernet leverages a service provider multiservice core.

The technology inside a Metro Ethernet network is not visible to customers; they see only the Ethernet services connection at their premises. The service provider is responsible for provisioning these services across its core network.

Metro Ethernet is a large market for the service provider, because there is an opportunity to provide services to customers with millions of existing Ethernet interfaces. Although the service provider might not want to disclose the backbone infrastructure, the more the customers know about the provider core, the more informed they can be about the quality of the services they will be receiving and the potential problems that may arise.

Note: Appropriate SLAs for the advanced WAN services are discussed in the "Implementing Advanced WAN Services" section of this chapter.

Metro Ethernet Architecture

The service provider provides Ethernet as a network infrastructure for metropolitan connectivity, possibly using various Layer 1 transport technologies. The Metro Ethernet architecture is illustrated in Figure 4-6.

The service provider may use SONET/SDH rings or point-to-point links, WDM, or RPR technology for its Metro Ethernet architecture. Edge aggregation devices or user provider edge (UPE) devices may multiplex multiple customers onto one optical circuit to the network provider edge (NPE) device. NPE devices connect to core provider (P) devices. The Ethernet service provided might include multiple services, such as LAN interconnection, IP telephony, and Internet access. It might also include varying levels of SLA and QoS for different customer needs. Edge aggregation allows the service provider to support oversubscription.

The actual implementation for the Metro Ethernet MAN service may be based on one or several of the following approaches:

- A pure Ethernet MAN uses only Layer 2 switches for all its internal structure. The switches may be in a loop-free topology and may not be running Spanning Tree Protocol (STP).

- A SONET/SDH-based Ethernet MAN is usually used as an intermediate step in the transition from a traditional, time-division based network, to a modern statistical network such as Ethernet. In this model, the existing SONET/SDH infrastructure is used to transport high-speed Ethernet connections.

- An MPLS based Metro Ethernet network uses Layer 2 MPLS VPNs in the provider network (P-network). The subscriber will get an Ethernet interface on copper or fiber, at 10-Mb/s to 1-Gb/s rates. The customer Ethernet packets are transported over Multiprotocol Layer Switching (MPLS), and the P-network may use Ethernet again as the underlying technology to transport MPLS.

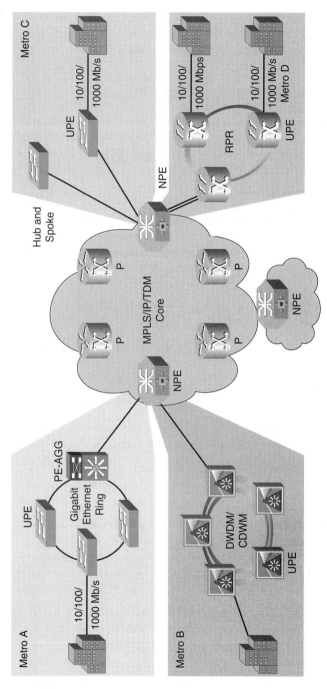

Figure 4-6   *Metro Ethernet Architecture*

Each of these approaches offers different oversubscription characteristics. Switched Ethernet and Ethernet over MPLS (EoMPLS) use statistical multiplexing (stat muxing), with no differentiation between customers or types of traffic unless QoS is provided. Ethernet over SONET implementations are not oversubscribed unless the SONET infrastructure does not go end-to-end in the provider network, in which case there may be portions of the network subject to oversubscription.

One advantage of edge aggregation is that service providers can now customize the service to customers without changing the infrastructure. For instance, with oversubscription, a provider web page might allow customers to increase their bandwidth limits.

Metro Ethernet LAN Services

Cisco offers a scalable Metro Ethernet solution over an existing SONET/SDH network, switched Ethernet network, or IP MPLS network, which provides multiple classes of service and bandwidth profiles to support critical data, voice, video, and storage applications. The Cisco Optical Metro Ethernet solution supports several Metro Ethernet Forum (MEF) service types:

- **Ethernet Private Line (EPL) service:** A port-based point-to-point Ethernet-line (E-line) service that maps Layer 2 traffic directly onto a TDM circuit

- **Ethernet Relay Service (ERS):** A point-to-point VLAN-based E-line service that is used primarily for establishing a point-to-point connection between customer routers

- **Ethernet Wire Service (EWS):** A point-to-point port-based E-line service that is used primarily to connect geographically remote LANs over a P-network

- **Ethernet Multipoint Service (EMS):** A multipoint-to-multipoint port-based emulated LAN (ELAN) service that is used for transparent LAN applications

- **Ethernet Relay Multipoint Service (ERMS):** A multipoint-to-multipoint VLAN-based ELAN service that is used primarily for establishing a multipoint-to-multipoint connection between customer routers

Metro Ethernet services are characterized by the UNI and Ethernet Virtual Circuit (EVC) attributes. EVCs can be point-to-point or point-to-multipoint services. Some UNIs can support multiple EVCs. The EPL, ERS, and EWS service types map to the E-line services defined by the MEF. The EMS and ERMS service types map to the ELAN services defined by the MEF.

Cisco Ethernet Services also include Layer 3 MPLS VPN services, which may be based on Ethernet or other underlying transport technologies. Figure 4-7 provides an illustrated overview of Cisco Ethernet-based services.

Ethernet services can be used in conjunction with Ethernet switches or with routers. For organizations with the skills and interest for managing their own routing, Layer 2 Ethernet connectivity provides routing-neutral connectivity similar to that of leased lines, Frame Relay, and ATM circuits. One potential difference of service provider Ethernet services is that using multipoint Ethernet could vastly increase the number of routing peers in the organization.

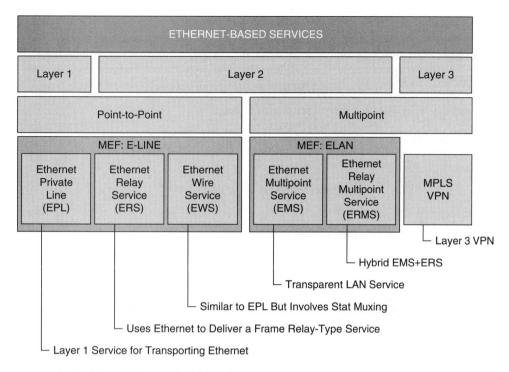

Figure 4-7   *Metro Ethernet LAN Services*

When implementing service provider Ethernet services, customers must decide whether they want to outsource routing to the service provider, or do their own routing. Outsourced routing, or routing in cooperation with the service provider, is typically done using Layer 3 MPLS VPNs.

Note: Metro Ethernet switching and large multipoint router-based architectures have design and scalability implications.

Ethernet Private Line Service

An EPL service is a dedicated point-to-point connection from one customer-specified location to another, with guaranteed bandwidth and payload transparency end to end.

EPL typically uses SONET/SDH transport. Because the bandwidth is dedicated with no oversubscription, a simple SLA concerning uptime may support all the customer requirements. SONET protection can provide high availability for EPL service.

The Cisco EPL service is ideal for transparent LAN interconnection and data center integration, for which wire-speed performance and VLAN transparency are important. Whereas TDM and Optical Carrier (OC)-based facilities have been the traditional means of providing EPL service, the Cisco EPL service also supports DWDM/CWDM, Ethernet over SONET/SDH, and dedicated Ethernet platforms interconnected via fiber.

The EPL service is typically used for the following:

- Mission-critical links

- Mainframe-to-mainframe links

- Data center or storage-area network (SAN) extension links

- Business continuity links

- Network consolidation—joining sites in MAN

Note: Organizations need to be careful of provider-managed CE devices handling the speed transitions from the customer to the P-network, because the provider-managed CE devices may impede the organization from being able to easily implement their own QoS policies.

Ethernet Relay Service

Cisco ERS is a point-to-point VLAN-based E-line service that supports service multiplexing, where multiple instances of service or EVCs can be multiplexed onto a single customer UNI.

Service multiplexing means that many connections can be provided over one link. The multiplexed UNI supports point-to-point or point-to-multipoint connections between two or more customer-specified sites, similar to a Frame Relay service. Instead of the data-link connection identifier (DLCI), the connection identifier in ERS is a VLAN tag. Each customer VLAN tag is mapped to a specific Ethernet virtual connection.

Note: ERS uses the VLAN to indicate destination. Therefore, the Ethernet service is not transparent to Layer 2 Ethernet frames—the VLAN tag dictates destination. The ERS EVC does not act like a trunk where all VLANs go from one site to one or multiple sites.

ERS uses different point-to-point VLANs to connect one site to other remote sites.

Note: If multipoint connections are available, the service is referred to as an ERMS.

Service multiplexing provides scalability for large sites, minimizing the number of Ethernet connections to the MAN or WAN Ethernet service. A router is typically the customer premise device.

ERS also provides Ethernet access through service interworking to other Layer 2 services, such as Frame Relay and ATM, so that the customers can begin using Ethernet services without replacing their existing legacy systems. With service interworking, traffic on a DLCI or virtual path identifier / virtual channel identifier (VPI/VCI) at a remote site is converted to an Ethernet frame by the provider, and arrives within a VLAN at headquarters.

The provider may offer tiers of service, based on bandwidth, CoS, and distance. A typical SLA might be based on committed information rate (CIR) or peak information rate (PIR), burst capacity, and packet-loss rate.

ERS is ideal for interconnecting routers in an enterprise network, and for connecting to Internet service providers (ISP) and other service providers for direct Internet access, VPN services, and other value-added services. Service providers can multiplex connections from many end customers onto a single Ethernet port at the service provider's point of presence (POP) for efficiency and ease of management.

Ethernet Wire Service

The Cisco EWS is a point-to-point connection between a pair of sites. Cisco EWS differs from Cisco EPLS in that it is typically provided over a shared, switched infrastructure within the service provider network that can be shared among customers. Oversubscription of the service provider network is handled using stat muxing. The benefit of EWS to the customer is that it is typically offered with a wider choice of committed bandwidth levels up to wire speed. To help ensure privacy, the service provider segregates each subscriber's traffic by applying VLAN tags on each EVC, typically using queue-in-queue (QinQ) tunneling. Customer SLA capabilities are typically based on CoS.

EWS is considered a port-based service. With EWS, the carrier network is transparent to all customer Ethernet traffic. EWS provides all-to-one bundling, where all customer packets are transmitted to the destination port transparently and the VLAN tags from the customer are preserved through the P-network. The CE device might be a router or a switch.

EWS is commonly used for point-to-point LAN extension, access to storage resources, and data center connectivity.

Ethernet Multipoint Service

EMS is a multipoint-to-multipoint service that is typically provided over a shared, switched infrastructure within the P-network.

EMS is a multipoint version of EWS, and shares the same technical access requirements and characteristics.

In EMS, the P-network acts as a virtual switch for the customer, providing the ability to connect multiple customer sites and allow for any-to-any communication. The enabling technology is Virtual Private Line Service (VPLS), implemented at the NPE. The service provider can use rate limiting to minimize the impact of a customer broadcast storm on other customers.

Oversubscription of the P-network is also handled with EMS using stat muxing. EMS is typically offered to the customer with a choice of committed bandwidth levels up to wire speed. To help ensure privacy, the service provider segregates each subscriber's traffic by applying VLAN tags on each EVC, typically using QinQ tunneling. Customer SLA capabilities are typically based on CoS.

EMS provides all-to-one bundling, where all customer packets are transmitted to the destination ports transparently and the VLAN tags from the customer are preserved through the P-network. The CE device might be a router or a switch.

For example, Verizon Transparent LAN Services (TLS) is a commercial EMS. It is based on a loop-free topology using Cisco 6500 switches and fiber-based Gigabit Ethernet links between them. TLS uses 802.1Q QinQ encapsulation to maintain customer traffic separation.

EMS is commonly used for multipoint LAN extension, LAN extension over the WAN, and disaster recovery.

Ethernet Relay Multipoint Service

ERMS is a hybrid of EMS and ERS.

ERMS offers the any-to-any connectivity characteristics of EMS, and the service multiplexing of ERS. This combination enables a single UNI to support a customer's intranet connection and one or more additional EVCs for connection to outside networks, ISPs, or content providers. Some EVCs might be point to point, and others might be multipoint. The service provider can use rate limiting to minimize the impact of a customer broadcast storm on other customers.

ERMS can be used for many applications, including branch Layer 2 VPNs, Layer 3 VPNs for intranet and extranet access, Internet access through the ISP, and disaster recovery.

End-to-End QoS

Metro Ethernet offerings should provide end-to-end QoS across the network.

A service provider can use IEEE 802.1Q tunneling to support end-to-end QoS for their customers. In Figure 4-8, the CE device is connected to the service provide UPE device using 802.1Q. The CE device adds an 802.1Q tag to all frames and supports the CoS across the network. The UPE devices add a second 802.1Q frame to support QinQ encapsulation of the customer traffic. Depending on the agreement with the service provider, the type of service (ToS) can be extended across the network. The two 802.1Q tags can be seen in the frame in the middle of the chart. The outer 802.1Q tag added by the UPE acts as a customer ID.

Switches and other devices in the service provider backbone transport the encapsulated Ethernet frame based on the outer 802.1Q tag and ToS. The outer 802.1Q tag is stripped off when the frame reaches the destination or destinations indicated in the outer tag. At the remote UPE, the Ethernet frame is transparently forwarded based on the original CE 802.1Q tag with the original CoS.

Figure 4-8   *End-to-End QoS*

The destination MAC is preserved end to end, so multicast traffic will be seen by the provider network as having a multicast destination MAC address. If the service is point to multipoint, one multicast frame sent into the provider network will be received at multiple customer sites, in accordance with multicast flooding within a VLAN.

Note: If any remote site receives a multicast stream, the stream will flood to all sites in that VLAN.

Because the service providers do not need to coordinate the customer VLANs with QinQ encapsulation, the customer VLANs can be preserved across the network, and the network supports VLAN transparency. With the QinQ encapsulation, customer VLANs can overlap.

An example of the 802.1Q encapsulation technique is a large service provider using Ethernet over MPLS to break up VLAN domains with a routed domain in the middle.

Choosing the Right Service

Figure 4-9 shows a decision tree a customer could use to help choose the appropriate Metro Ethernet service. For example, customers needing only point-to-point service can use EPL, EWS, or ERS; whereas customers needing multipoint services should use EMS or ERMS.

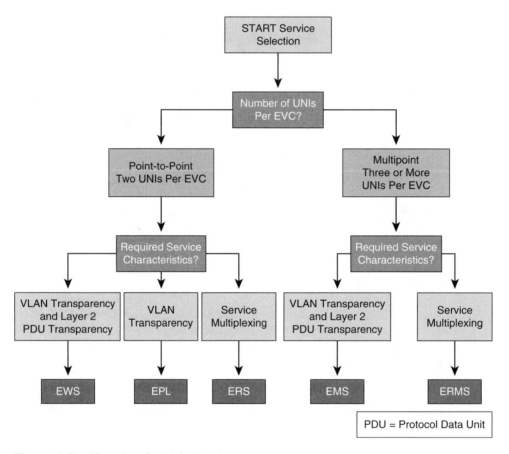

Figure 4-9   *Choosing the Right Service*

VPLS Overview

VPLS is a multipoint architecture that connects two or more customer devices using Ethernet bridging techniques over an MPLS network. In VPLS, the P-network emulates an IEEE 802.1 Ethernet bridge, with each EMS being analogous to a VLAN.

VPLS is an architecture that is still being defined. There are two RFCs that are distinct and incompatible with one another:

- **RFC 4761:** *Virtual Private LAN Service (VPLS)*. Using BGP for Auto-Discovery and Signaling is a standard proposed by Juniper.

- **RFC 4762:** *Virtual Private LAN Service (VPLS)*. Using Label Distribution Protocol (LDP) Signaling is a standard proposed by Cisco.

One of the major differences in the standard is in the VPLS provider edge (PE) discovery process, or how VPLS PE devices find each other, communicate capabilities, and perform tasks such as preprovisioning EVCs.

VPLS Architecture Model

In the VPLS architecture model, UPE devices act as IEEE 802.1D standard bridges or switches. They are interconnected in a full mesh of pseudowires (PW). In Figure 4-10, the PWs cross a routed MPLS and IP provider backbone. From the point of view of the UPEs, these PWs are just Ethernet connections to another switch.

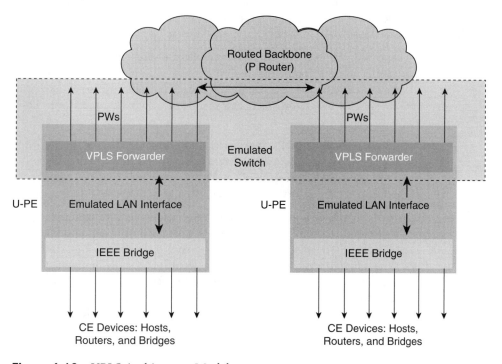

Figure 4-10   *VPLS Architecture Model*

VPLS will self-learn source MAC address to port associations, and frames are forwarded based on the destination MAC address. If the destination address is unknown, or is a broadcast or multicast address, the frame is flooded to all ports associated with the virtual bridge.

In the event of a provider outage, IP rerouting rapidly restores PW connectivity. In such a case, no MAC aging and relearning is needed.

To simplify processing, the VPLS core does not use STP. Instead, it uses split-horizon forwarding, so that Ethernet frames are not sent back out on the same PW on which they were received.

Broadcast and multicast traffic would always be flooded in VPLS.

VPLS in the Enterprise

VPLS is used as an enterprise WAN connectivity service.

VPLS looks like an Ethernet switch to the customer with the same inherent Layer 2 core issues:

- **Stability of the network as it grows:** Experience shows that purely STP-based VPLS does not scale gracefully. VPLS based on MPLS scales much better.

- **Impact of network outages:** A customer should ask about what happens to their traffic in the event of an outage, and receive enough details to justify the quoted speed of convergence.

- **Multicast and broadcast radiation between sites:** Because the VPLS network acts like a switch, customer multicasts and broadcasts sent into the VPLS cloud radiate to all sites of that customer. This can be somewhat controlled by using routers to connect to the VPLS network, but multicasts sent by the router flood to all the customer's sites.

- **Interior Gateway Protocol (IGP) peering scalability:** The VPLS network is one broadcast domain, so all attached routers would typically be routing peers. As the number of routing peers increases, the full mesh of connections becomes a scaling issue. Designs using VPLS in a hierarchical fashion should be more scalable.

- **Impact of an STP loop of another customer:** Because VPLS uses stat muxing, all customers share bandwidth. It is reasonable to ask what the impact of a customer with a spanning-tree loop would be on other customers. If the customer is attached by a Layer 2 switch, all the packets from the loop would necessarily be flooded within the links interconnecting their VPLS sites. If they connect at 1 Gb/s and the provider trunks are 20 Gb/s, this may not be so bad. If the provider links are 2 Gb/s, the impact might be far greater, particularly if EtherChannel is in use. (Deterministic assignment of traffic to channels would cause the traffic of other selected customers to share the problem customer's channels.)

A VPLS customer might also want to conduct due diligence to verify that the provider is aware of and has implemented adequate Layer 2 security measures.

Hierarchical VPLS Overview

Hierarchical VPLS (H-VPLS) provides scaling by only interconnecting the core MPLS NPE routers with a full mesh of PWs. The many UPE VPLS devices are then connected hierarchically by PWs to the NPE devices, not to each other. When there is redundancy, as shown in Figure 4-11, the software in the UPE blocks the PWs to all but the highest NPE IP address. H-VPLS partitions the network into several edge domains that are interconnected using an MPLS core.

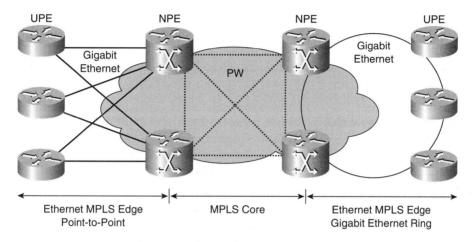

Figure 4-11   *Hierarchical VPLS Overview*

One advantage of the H-VPLS approach for the service provider is that the core of the network is an MPLS network, which may also be used for the transport of Layer 3 MPLS VPNs and other traffic. The MPLS core also serves to limit any edge spanning-tree domains, speeding up STP convergence and reducing any potential instability.

The physical topology of Ethernet Edge H-VPLS (EE H-VPLS) can comprise point-to-point Ethernet connections, or Ethernet rings using an STP to provide redundancy and loop avoidance. Other edge architectures use an aggregation layer between the UPE and NPE, or use Ethernet over SONET/SDH (EoS), or RPR as a transport between the UPE and NPE.

H-VPLS provides an extremely flexible architectural model that also enables multipoint Ethernet services (VPLS), and Ethernet point-to-point Layer 2 VPN services and Ethernet access to Layer 3 VPN services.

Scaling VPLS

A service provider VPLS design must address three major scaling factors:

■ **Scaling of the full mesh of PWs between PE devices:** As the number of PE devices scales, each edge device must form an adjacency with all other PE devices. This requires that the edge devices must have the IP address of all remote PEs in its routing table, and also requires the PE to exchange label information with all remote PE devices. That introduces an $N-1$ control plane scaling issue.

H-VPLS helps address this issue by using UPE devices to spread the edge workload across multiple, less-costly devices. The lower number of PWs between the NPE devices helps scale the network by reducing the burden on the core for frame replication and forwarding.

- **Frame replication and forwarding:** VPLS forwards Ethernet frames using Layer 2 MAC addresses. The operation of VPLS is exactly the same as that found within IEEE 802.1 bridges in that the virtual switch self-learns the source MAC address-to-port associations and forwards frames based on the destination MAC address. If the destination address is unknown, or is a broadcast or multicast address, the frame is flooded to all ports associated with the virtual bridge. H-VPLS needs a lower number of PWs, because only the NPE devices are connected in a full mesh. This helps reduce the burden on the core for frame replication and forwarding.

- **MAC address table size:** One of the biggest considerations in VPLS provider design is MAC address learning. PE devices need to be capable of handling MAC address tables for many customer devices and many customers. That number is much greater than what a typical enterprise campus switch needs to handle today.

H-VPLS allows MAC tables to be spread across multiple inexpensive devices to scale the edge. UPE devices need only learn of their local NPE devices and therefore do not need large routing table support. Core NPE devices still need to handle very large MAC address tables. Using MPLS in the core removes the MAC learning requirement from the P devices.

Note: Interconnecting only customer routers and not switches by VPLS would greatly simplify scaling MAC learning, because then only the router MAC addresses would need to be learned in VPLS devices. However, few providers are willing to limit their potential VPLS market by imposing such a requirement.

Some VPLS device vendors use proprietary MAC-in-MAC encapsulation schemes, so that the NPE devices only need learn the MAC addresses of other UPE devices. This approach may also use supporting protocols, reminiscent of ATM LAN Emulation (LANE). At the time of this writing, Cisco devices do not implement these mechanisms.

How well the provider's design handles all these factors is of interest to the customer. Poor VPLS design can lead to scaling and stability problems as the provider's network grows. While a customer should not have to be intimately familiar with VPLS designs to evaluate a provider's service, listening to a service provider's answers on these topics can provide insight into that provider's qualifications.

QoS Issues with EMS or VPLS

QoS is relatively easy to provide with point-to-point links. Oversubscription is managed by controlling what is allowed into the point-to-point link.

However, QoS for multipoint networks is harder because it requires coordination between multiple devices with unpredictable and rapidly changing traffic patterns. Careful consideration needs to be taken for interactive services such as video and IP telephony. The need for coordination implies that the service provider provide QoS, because it is not something the customer can layer on top of a connection, nor is it something the customers can just implement for their own use.

The technique of bandwidth slicing can be used by customers in an attempt to compensate for lack of provider QoS. In this approach, each CE device has a slice of the bandwidth to each remote location. Access lists then police traffic to each location, to try to ensure the remote link is not congested. The issue with this approach is that inside the VPLS cloud, Customer A traffic competes not only with Customer A traffic, but with the traffic from other customers, too. In addition, broadcast and multicast traffic fed into the VPLS cloud are received at every service provider edge site, consuming some of the bandwidth, too.

These issues illustrate that if the customer wants QoS, the service provider has to partner to provide it. Customers should expect that QoS is a premium service, and determine bandwidth levels for each QoS class to help manage QoS.

EMS or VPLS and Routing Implications

One concern when using OSPF is that the multiaccess network may not have consistent broadcast or multicast performance. If some sites experience greater packet loss levels, OSPF processing may consume more router CPU. In the extreme case, packet loss or delay might cause significant levels of OSPF instability. This is currently being seen in some large VPN networks that use generic routing encapsulation (GRE) over IP Security (IPsec) for OSPF routing.

Another concern is that retransmissions or flapping status with regard to one site might consume significant CPU resources on all its peer routers. As discussed in Chapter 3, "Developing an Optimum Design for Layer 3," it is advisable to manage the number of OSPF adjacencies in a full-mesh network, and to use designs to limit the number of adjacencies.

Note: A similar caution applies to Enhanced Interior Gateway Routing Protocol (EIGRP) routing over an EMS or VPLS service. You should avoid having high numbers of peers with EIGRP, too.

VPLS and IP Multicast

In a campus switched network, IP multicast in a VLAN floods to all ports in the VLAN, unless Internet Group Management Protocol (IGMP) snooping is in use. However, IGMP snooping is not an option with VPLS or EMS. A broadcast or multicast frame sent into the VPLS cloud ends up being sent out of the VPLS provider network to every CE device that has a port associated with the virtual switch.

Because the VPLS network has been designed for transparency by emulating a switch, the VPLS PE devices cannot provide any intelligence by delivering multicast only where it is needed. If the CE devices are routers, they will discard undesired multicast packets they receive. IP multicast traffic in MPLS can result in wasted bandwidth and router CPU utilization spent discarding unnecessary traffic.

One conclusion is that VPLS designers with customer networks that have significant amounts of multicast need to use administrative scoping to limit the propagation of multicast packets, or else allow sufficient bandwidth for unnecessary multicast traffic at the edge links.

VPLS Availability

VPLS provides some advantages in the case of P-network outages.

An advantage to using VPLS is that PWs are the underlying technology for the data plane. In the case of a failure in the P-network, traffic will automatically be routed along available backup paths in the P-network. Failover in this case will be much faster than could be achieved with STP.

There is a cost to this fast failover. If redundant PWs are used from redundant PE devices, a failure might require aging of MAC addresses followed by unicast flooding. The resulting lost packets followed by a surge of traffic would have a negative impact on customer traffic.

PW rerouting around outages prevents this potential problem.

Note: Although this section has focused primarily on VPLS, many of the same considerations apply to any Ethernet service offering. Appropriate SLAs for the advanced WAN services are discussed in the "Implementing Advanced WAN Services" lesson in this chapter.

MPLS VPN Overview

As an alternative to Metro Ethernet services, some customers are implementing MPLS VPNs. MPLS VPN services are based on MPLS label paths that are automatically formed based on IP routing. MPLS VPNs experience the same level of stability as exhibited by Layer 3 networks in general. MPLS VPNs can support either Layer 2 transport (typically a long-haul or metro-area Ethernet point-to-point service) or a Layer 3 routed service. The

characteristics of the MPLS VPNs vary depending on whether they are implemented at
Layer 3 or Layer 2:

- **Layer 3 service:** Layer 3 MPLS VPNs forward only IP packets. The CE routers become peers of MPLS VPN provider routers. In this case, routing may well be a coop-
  erative venture. Stability of the provider routing, their experience with routing, and
  speed of provider routing convergence are all valid customer considerations. Layer 3
  VPNs can support any access or backbone technology. Service providers can use
  Layer 3 VPNs as a foundation to provide advanced WAN services.

- **Layer 2 service:** Layer 2 MPLS VPNs can forward any network protocol based on
  Layer 2 frames. There is no peering with the provider. Layer 2 service allows customer
  routers to peer directly with each other without a handoff to SP router. MPLS Layer 2
  VPNs provide point-to-point service where the access technology is determined by
  the VPN type. MPLS Layer 2 VPNs may also be useful for service interworking, or
  converting Frame Relay or ATM into Ethernet for delivery on a high-bandwidth link
  at a central site or data center.

The choice of Layer 2 VPN over Layer 3 VPN will depend on how much control the enterprise wants to retain. If an enterprise has a small staff or lacks routing skills, a managed
router Layer 3 VPN service puts all CE routers in the hands of one or more providers, and
delegates all routing to the provider. Large organizations with considerable in-house routing skills may prefer Layer 2 VPNs because they can maintain control of their Layer 3
policies.

Customer Considerations with MPLS VPNs

There are several considerations for designing customer MPLS VPNs:

- **Who does the routing?** A major decision when implementing MPLS VPN is who
  will do the routing. For a simple scenario, the customer may opt to use static routing,
  where there is no dynamic interaction with the service provider routing. Another option is for the customer to use External Border Gateway Protocol (EBGP), EIGRP,
  OSPF, or Intermediate System-to-Intermediate System (IS-IS) with the provider, depending on which PE-CE routing protocol the provider supports.

  If the customer redistributes routes learned via MPLS VPN routing into their IGP,
  these routes may become external routes. In the case of OSPF or EIGRP as the PE-
  CE routing protocol, the provider may be able to redistribute them as internal routes,
  which is generally preferable from the customer's perspective.

- **Who manages the CE devices?** Depending on the size and routing experience of
  the customer, they may chose to manage their own CE devices, or buy managed services from the provider. The customer must also determine the level of redundancy
  needed, depending on whether one or two CE devices will be implemented.

- **Should one or two MPLS VPN providers be used?** Another key decision is
  whether to use one or two MPLS VPN providers. Having two providers provides better redundancy than dual-homing to one provider, because two providers are less
  likely to experience a common failure event. However, two providers can add complexity to the design. If two MPLS VPN providers are used with two CE devices per

location, the design needs to support using the appropriate default gateway with the appropriate first-hop redundancy protocol (FHRP) or other mechanism.

■   **Is QoS needed?** If QoS is available from the service provider, the customer needs to decide whether to buy an MPLS service with QoS. Using Layer 3 VPNs allows the customer to implement QoS internally.

■   **Is IP multicast supported?** With Layer 3 MPLS VPN, IP multicast may be supported. Doing IP multicast over a Layer 2 MPLS VPN requires service provider support and might cost extra. It may also require special configuration or working with the provider, particularly to support large IP multicast flows.

Routing Considerations: Backdoor Routes

Backdoor routes need to be considered when designing routing for a Layer 3 MPLS VPN WAN.

If there are internal backdoor routes—for example, a second path between locations through a GRE over IPsec tunnel or other WAN link—the internal route (even over slowed links) will be preferred over the external route. This needs to be taken into account in designing the routing to properly use the Layer 3 MPLS VPN.

In general, sites with one WAN router do not have this problem. When the PE-CE routing protocol is BGP, EBGP has a better administrative distance (AD) than the IGP in use. The potential problem with backdoor routes arises when there are several Layer 3 devices at one site, especially if the WAN routing is split across them. If the provider follows the common practice of handing off routes through EBGP, the customer may end up running EBGP at every site. In addition, the customer may have EBGP with the route reflector over the IPsec VPN.

The service provider may be able to redistribute routes as internal routes for OSPF and EIGRP. Using a separate EIGRP autonomous system for the IPsec VPN is another approach to allow simple redistribution controls and metrics.

As a recommended practice, you should minimize the locations where you implement route redistribution. Route redistribution at many locations can adversely impact network stability.

Routing Considerations: Managed Router Combined with Internal Routing

If a managed router service is purchased, it can become awkward to do your own routing.

You might find with managed routers that you still want to control your own routing, perhaps when your company purchases managed router services from one MPLS provider, and then later purchases a similar service from another organization. If not otherwise specified, both providers may choose to use static routing.

In such a setting, the lack of dynamic routing makes it hard to automate dynamic failover in response to provider failure or problems. One approach is to add another layer of routers at each site, and set up GRE tunnels between these routers, as shown in Figure 4-12. The GRE tunnels will allow an organization to control its own routing and run services such as IP multicast. The providers need to provide enough static routing to deliver packets between the added customer routers.

Several potential issues arise with this approach. The GRE tunnel adds to the cost and complexity of the network. You need another router at each site. It will be more difficult to configure the network, and there are potential performance issues related to the impact of encapsulation and possibly maximum transmission unit (MTU) sizes leading to fragmentation.

Figure 4-12   *Managed Router Combined with Internal Routing*

Routing Considerations: Managed Router From Two Service Providers

In Figure 4-13, there is a managed CE router service from two different service providers; as a result, the issue of FHRP may arise.

With two service providers providing parallel paths between your locations, you need to consider what the primary path for specific traffic types is and how to support failover. Hot Standby Router Protocol (HSRP) or another FHRP can be used, but it can be challenging to get your two providers to cooperate with each other to provide the FHRP service.

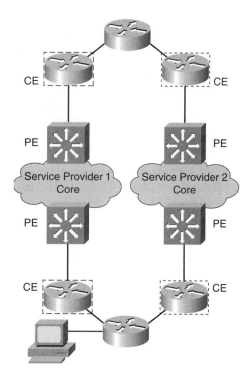

Figure 4-13   *Managed Router from Two Service Providers*

Note: If your site is large enough to use a router or Layer 3 switch in front of the service provider–managed routers, the FHRP is not an issue. However, if you are managing the Layer 3 device, you probably do not need managed router service.

You should negotiate this design with the service providers at contract time. Getting service providers to cooperate can be easier before signing contracts than after both contracts have been signed.

Implementing Advanced WAN Services

WAN service design involves a partnership between service providers and customers, where the service provider manages services for the customer on an ongoing basis. This section looks at issues that enterprise customers should consider when implementing advanced WAN services. Service providers should also understand these considerations to address customer concerns.

Advanced WAN Service Selection

It is important to know the actual characteristics of advanced WAN services. Sales presentations and marketing literature highlight the best features of a service, but probably do not cover the weak or problem areas. It is up to the customer to ask good questions and do the research. If the service is something you are already using, measure its characteristics. This information can help you, your manager, and the business make an informed decision about supporting your business applications such as IP telephony over that service. When you are considering a new service, you cannot measure its ability to support your business application. You need to make decisions based on the underlying technology, the reputation of the vendor, customer references, trade literature, and other such factors.

One way to mitigate risk with WAN services is to use two providers. When you want to deploy a new technology such as an MPLS VPN, you can implement it on one provider, and continue to use the older service with your other provider in case there are problems. Using two providers also lets you experience their technical and customer service levels. If one is providing inadequate service and not meeting your requirements, it is easier to migrate to the other provider.

In general, an advanced WAN service is a partnership between the service provider and customer. An SLA provides contractual obligations for the service provider. A good WAN contract should have an escape clause that addresses what will occur if the WAN provider consistently fails to meet the SLA or provide reasonable levels of customer service. However, most problems are better solved by working the partner relationship. You should be able to explain issues to your service provider, ask what they will do to make things better, and observe the result. If nothing changes, you have the option of considering another provider.

Business Risk Assessment

Part of a good design is to assess the business risk and base design decisions on how critical the service will be.

Any technology has associated business risks. If a WAN service deployment fails, or if the underlying technology fails, it can have a severe business impact, costing lost business or productivity and amounting to a large cost per hour.

When selecting between providers of advanced WAN services, one factor to consider is risk and the likelihood of problems. It may not be worth saving 10 percent at the risk of repeated outages, or a long outage. You need to consider the chance of such an outage happening. These are hard questions to answer, but a service provider can cite examples such as their experience, how long they have been in the business, and how long they have gone without a major outage on a particular service.

Another approach is due diligence questioning, where you conduct a survey, observe the network operations center (NOC), ask a lot of questions, and in general, try to assess the provider personnel's level of technical knowledge. There are several questions a customer can ask:

- Does the provider have several experts available for the specific technology?
- How skilled are the lower-level staff?
- How neat is the cabling?
- Are the devices and cables labeled?

- How old is the equipment?

- How big is the provider?

> **Note:**   Because the due diligence effort can be so time-consuming, it may only occur with large customers.

Obtaining more than a shallow level of information can be a challenge. Generally, providers do not like to provide these details. Patience and persistence can lead to eventually getting the information you desire.

In general, you should match risk to the purpose of the design. Noncritical internal Internet traffic might be serviced by a low-cost but riskier provider. More critical e-commerce traffic might instead be handled by a more established collocation or Internet provider.

Response to risk always involves trade-offs:

- The time and cost to get more information can be prohibitive.

- The cost of service may make due diligence questioning less practical.

- The value of the data compared to the cost of outage should be considered.

- The likelihood of an outage may not be easy to estimate.

Consultants and resellers can provide their views on risks of various technologies, but the decision of the correct risk versus cost trade-off is really up to the customer.

The scope of a possible outage is another consideration. If a network designer has seen a few Spanning Tree Protocol (STP) loops, he or she may believe that a switch and STP-based provider network is risky, because a loop can bring down the entire STP domain. Because routing outages are usually much more localized, that line of reasoning could lead to preferring an MPLS VPN–based service.

WAN Features and Requirements

Customers need to understand what WAN features are available and what they need to support their organization.

Hasty WAN purchases can result in not getting adequate information. Although it might sound obvious, it can be very useful to make sure all parties agree as to what the requirements are for the new WAN service being purchased. There are several important questions to ask:

- Will the routing work as it does currently, or will changes be required?

- Will existing VLANs be transparently supported across the service provider core?

- What QoS levels can be supported at what cost?

■   Is IP multicast available? What is the cost for multicast?

■   What level of security is provided to isolate customer traffic? Is there a cost for this service?

■   What management services and tools are available at what cost?

Defining these requirements is important because advanced WAN services are not transparent transport connections the way that leased lines, Frame Relay, and ATM are. It is important to verify that traffic fed into the provider network (P-network) will be transported appropriately across the service provider core.

It is important to define what WAN features are standard, and what features are optional upgrades:

■   In Layer 3 MPLS VPNs, the service provider's routing interacts with the customer routing in a secure way. IP multicast has to be handled differently by the provider than unicast routing, so it might not be available, or may cost extra.

■   With some Ethernet services, Cisco Discovery Protocol may not work, or may be limited to a specific VLAN.

It is necessary to get the details of any managed service. To one service provider, network management may mean occasional ping tests and some console logging, and to another service provider it means in-depth Simple Network Management Protocol (SNMP) monitoring with access to the SNMP reports. Security services that merely inform you of a threat reported by an intrusion detection system (IDS) are not as useful as an indication of what triggered that alarm and other network activity going on at the time.

In general, buying WAN services requires asking questions to get details:

■   What does "managed router" or "managed link" mean? What base services does the provider implement, such as ping testing, SNMP polling for CPU and link utilization, and other functions? What management services are optional upgrades?

■   What is the process for changes? What are the costs for changes? How fast do requested configuration changes actually happen?

■   Is the managed router cooperatively managed, or are all configuration decisions made by the provider based on some initial design?

■   Can I review the configuration of the managed router? Can I poll it via SNMP? Can I receive syslog messages and SNMP traps from it?

■   What does "QoS" mean? How many levels are supported, what sort of SLA or bandwidth guarantees are available, and how are the service levels protected and enforced?

SLA Overview

The SLA is a statement of intent from the provider.

The SLA should set customer expectations by specifying what service levels the service provider will deliver to the customer.

A good SLA covers common managed-service metrics:

■ **Mean time to repair (MTTR):** MTTR is a measure of how long it takes to repair failures.

■ **Mean time between failures (MTBF):** MTBF is a measure of how often failures occur. MTBF can be used to project how often failures are expected

Outage severity and causes vary. For many customers, it is useful to keep a log that tracks major, intermediate, and minor outages; the date and time of the outage; the time the service was restored; and the root cause of the outage. By tracking outages and noting the clarity of communication and the causes of outages, customers have concrete information to discuss at contract renewal time.

A good SLA also includes technical metrics:

■ **Packet loss:** Packet loss occurs when one or more packets traveling across a network are lost and fail to reach their destination.

■ **Latency:** Latency or delay is a measure of how much time it takes for a packet to get from one point in the network to another. Delay can be measured in either one-way or round-trip delay.

■ **Jitter:** Jitter is the variable delay that can occur between successive packets. Based on network congestion, improper queuing, or configuration errors, the delay between each packet in a data stream can vary instead of remaining constant.

■ **IP availability:** IP availability is a measure of the availability of IP services end-to-end across a network. TCP session breakage occurs after a component failure when the combination of convergence at Layer 2, Layer 3, and Layer 4 components causes a TCP session to fail.

Traffic throughput and general usefulness of a WAN link depend on very low packet loss rates (for example, 0.001 percent or lower), reasonably low latency, and low jitter. What these numbers should be depends on the type of traffic. VoIP requires good values for all. Best-effort Internet traffic is typically much more tolerant of latency and jitter. Layer 4 components such as Windows Server and Windows XP client stacks have about a nine-second tolerance for interruptions in IP availability.

Customers should avoid SLAs that average results across many devices or links. When averaging availability across enough routers, a device can be down for days and not violate some availability SLAs. Generally, customers want an SLA that covers the extreme behavior of any individual link or device.

SLA Monitoring

Customers should monitor the network status to track how well the service provider is doing at meeting the terms of the SLA.

Networks measurements let customers know what kind of service they are actually receiving. Measurements also provide a baseline for comparison when there are application issues. Measurements can help diagnose outages and performance problems, especially when it is unclear whether the problem is internal to the customer or with the service providers. Customers who receive and monitor alarms can help document the delay in notification or response from the provider after outages.

Some service providers allow their customers to view SLA performance data through a web portal. These measurements should be monitored as a way to track issues such as slow service due to congestion and to understand the health of the network. Even when service provider reports are accessible, many organizations also implement internal monitoring of key links. Internal monitoring can serve to activate an early response to a major outage, and can provide a cross-check that the service provider reports are not censoring the data shown.

Problems can arise if customers think they have been getting poor service because of violations of the SLA. Internal customer measurements can provide evidence of network issues to discuss with the service provider, especially if the service provider has not actively been measuring the service.

Summary

Underlying optical technologies such as SONET/SDH, CWDM, DWDM, and RPR enable the service provider to provide advanced WAN services such as storage, content switching, web hosting, instant messaging, and security built on an Ethernet framework.

Service providers use Metro Ethernet and MPLS VPNs as a flexible transport architecture to offer high-speed WAN Ethernet services such as transparent LAN services to support enterprise customers.

WAN service design involves a partnership between the service provider and customer, where the service provider manages services for the customer on an ongoing basis.

References

For additional information, refer to these resources:

- Cisco Systems, Inc. "Cisco MDS 9000 Family Fabric Manager Configuration Guide, Release 3.x," at http://www.cisco.com/en/US/products/ps5989/products_configuration_guide_book09186a0080667aa0.html

- Cisco Systems, Inc. "Cisco CDWM Solution at a Glance," at http://www.cisco.com/application/pdf/en/us/guest/products/ps6575/c1031/cdccont_0900aecd803a53ea.pdf

- Cisco Systems, Inc. "Cisco CDWM GBIC and SFP Solution Data Sheet," at http://www.cisco.com/application/pdf/en/us/guest/products/ps6575/c1650/ccmigration_09186a00801a557c.pdf

- Cisco Systems, Inc. Cisco ONS 15454 DWDM Engineering and Planning Guide, Release 7.x, Chapter 1, "DWDM Overview" at http://www.cisco.com/en/US/products/hw/optical/ps2006/products_technical_reference_chapter09186a0080651e3b.html

- Cisco Systems, Inc. Fundamentals of DWDM Technology, at http://www.cisco.com/univercd/cc/td/doc/product/mels/cm1500/dwdm/dwdm_ovr.htm

- Cisco Systems, Inc. "Virtual Private LAN Services (VPLS) Introduction," at http://www.cisco.com/en/US/products/ps6648/products_ios_protocol_option_home.html

- Cisco Systems, Inc. "Resilient Packet Ring Feature Guide," at http://www.cisco.com/en/US/products/sw/iosswrel/ps1829/products_feature_guide09186a008022261a.html

- IEEE 802 LAN/MAN Standards Committee. "IEEE 802.17 Resilient Packet Ring Working Group" at http://www.ieee802.org/17/

- The Internet Engineering Task Force. RFC 4761: Virtual Private LAN Service (VPLS) Using BGP for Auto-Discovery and Signaling, at http://www.ietf.org/rfc/rfc4761.txt

- The Internet Engineering Task Force. RFC 4762: Virtual Private LAN Service (VPLS) Using Label Distribution Protocol (LDP) Signaling, at http://www.ietf.org/rfc/rfc4762.txt

Review Questions

Answer the following questions, and then refer to Appendix A, "Answers to Review Questions," for the answers.

1. What technique does SONET use for framing voice and data onto a single wavelength on fiber?

   a. SHD

   b. SDH

   c. DPT

   d. TDM

   e. RPR

2. Which description best defines CWDM?

   a. A WDM system that is compatible with EDFA optical technology for transmitting up to 16 channels over multiple fiber strands

   b. A technology for transmitting multiple optical signals using less-sophisticated and less-costly transceiver designs than DWDM

   c. An optical technology for transmitting up to 32 channels over multiple fiber strands

   d. A technology for transmitting more closely packed optical signals using more sophisticated transceiver designs than DWDM

3. Which Ethernet-based services are point-to-point services? (Choose three.)

   a. EPL

   b. EPWS

   c. ERS

   d. EWS

   e. EMS

   f. ERMS

4. What definition best describes service multiplexing?

   a. Ability to multiplex services and UNIs on a single customer EVAC

   b. Ability to multiplex services and UNIs on a single customer EVC

   c. Ability to support multiple instances of services or EVACs on a single customer UNI

   d. Ability to support multiple instances of services or EVCs on a single customer UNI

   e. Ability to support multiple instances of services or UNIs on a single customer EVC

5. What are the characteristics of EMS? (Choose three.)

   a.   Service multiplexing is supported.

   b.   The P-network acts as a virtual switch for the customer.

   c.   All customer packets are transmitted to the destination ports transparently.

   d.   Oversubscription of the P-network is handled using stat muxing.

   e.   Oversubscription of the P-network is handled using time-division multiplexing.

6. What is a PW in MPLS?

   a.   A password used for MD5 authentication for the underlying IGP

   b.   A physical wire between PE routers

   c.   An Ethernet connection from the PE to the CE device

   d.   The underlying technology for the control plane

   e.   A logical PW between PE routers

7. What is a jitter?

   a.   A measure of how much time it takes for a packet to get from one point in the network to another

   b.   A measure of outage severity

   c.   A measure of packets traveling across a network that fail to reach their destination

   d.   A measure of the availability of IP services end-to-end across a network

   e.   The variation in delay in the interval between successive packets

8. Why is a business risk assessment needed?

   a.   Because the due diligence effort can be so time-consuming

   b.   To define the value of the data

   c.   As a basis for design decisions

   d.   To support due diligence questioning

   e.   To obtain more than a shallow level of service provider information

After completing this chapter, you will be able to

■   Design data center core and aggregation layer infra-
    structures

■   Design data access layer infrastructures

■   Discuss options for scaling the data center architecture

■   Describe options for scaling STP and high availabil-
    ity in the data center

CHAPTER 5

Enterprise Data Center Design

The data center is home to the computational power, storage, and applications necessary to support an enterprise business. The data center infrastructure is central to the IT architecture, from which all content is sourced or passes through. Proper planning of the data center infrastructure design is critical, and performance, resiliency, and scalability need to be carefully considered.

The data center network design is based on a proven layered approach, which has been tested and improved during the past several years in some of the largest data center implementations in the world. The layered approach is the basic foundation of the data center design that seeks to improve scalability, performance, flexibility, resiliency, and maintenance. Figure 5-1 shows the basic layered design.

The chapter discusses the three layers of the data center architecture. It also covers considerations for using modular compared to one rack unit (1RU) access switch designs. Options for scaling the data center and for high availability are also reviewed.

Designing the Core and Aggregation Layers

The data center architecture is based on a three-layer approach. The core layer provides a high-speed Layer 3 fabric for packet switching. The aggregation layer extends spanning-tree or Layer 3 routing protocols into the access layer, depending on which access layer model is used. The access later provides physical connectivity for the servers. This chapter examines the design considerations for the core and aggregation layers.

Upon mastering the content, you will be able to identify design considerations for the data center core and aggregation layers. This ability includes being able to meet these objectives:

■ Provide an overview of the data center architecture

■ Describe design considerations for the data center core layer

■ Describe design considerations for the data center aggregation layer

Data Center Architecture Overview

As mentioned in the introduction, the data center network design is based on a layered approach to improve scalability, performance, flexibility, resiliency, and maintenance. There are three layers of the data center design:

■ **Core layer:** Provides the high-speed packet switching backplane for all flows going in and out of the data center

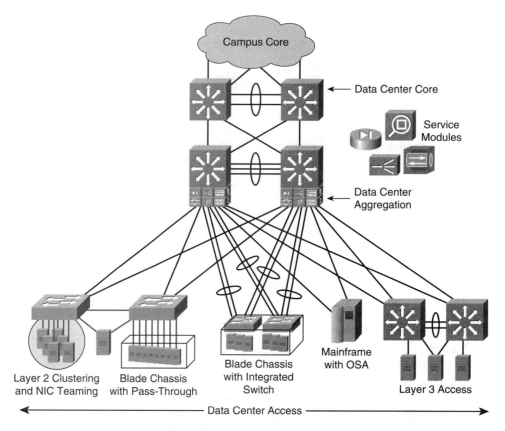

Figure 5-1 *Data Center Architectural Overview*

■ **Aggregation layer:** Provides service module integration, Layer 2 domain definitions, spanning-tree processing, default gateway redundancy, and other critical data
center functions

■ **Access layer:** Physically connects servers to the network

The multi-tier data center model is dominated by multi-tier HTTP-based applications that
support web, application, and database tiers of servers. The access layer network infrastructure can support both Layer 2 and Layer 3 topologies, and Layer 2 adjacency requirements that fulfill the various server broadcast domain or administrative requirements. The
server components can consist of single and dual attached 1RU servers, blade servers with
integral switches, blade servers with pass-through cabling, clustered servers, and mainframes with a mix of oversubscription requirements.

Multiple aggregation modules in the aggregation layer support scaling of connectivity
from the access layer. The aggregation layer supports integrated service modules that provide services such as security, load balancing, content switching, firewall, Secure Sockets
Layer (SSL) offload, intrusion detection, and network analysis.

Note: An enterprise data center network in most instances will have a three-tier design with an Ethernet access layer and an aggregation layer connected to the campus core layer. Small and medium data centers will have a two-tier design, with the Layer 3 access layer connected to the backbone database core (collapsed core and aggregation layers). Three-tier designs allow for greater scalability in the number of access ports, but a two-tier design is ideal for small server farms.

Benefits of the Three-Layer Model

There are several benefits to the three-tier model for data center design. The separation of the data center architecture into access, aggregation, and core layers permits flexibility in the following areas:

■   **Layer 2 domain sizing:** When there is a requirement to extend a VLAN from one switch to another, the domain size is determined at the aggregation layer. If the access layer is absent, the Layer 2 domain must be configured across the core for extension to occur. Extending Layer 2 through a core causes path blocking by the spanning tree, which may cause uncontrollable broadcast issues related to extending Layer 2 domains, and therefore should be avoided.

■   **Service module support:** A solution that uses the aggregation layer with the access layer and enables services to be shared across the entire access layer of switches. This lowers the total cost of ownership (TCO) and lowers complexity by reducing the number of components to configure and manage.

■   **Support for a mix of access layer models:** The three-layer approach permits a mix of both Layer 2 and Layer 3 access models with 1RU and modular platforms, permitting a more flexible solution and allowing application environments to be optimally positioned.

■   **Support for network interface card (NIC) teaming and high-availability clustering:** Supporting NIC teaming with switch fault tolerance and high-availability clustering requires Layer 2 adjacency between NICs, resulting in Layer 2 VLAN extension between switches. VLAN extension can also require extending the Layer 2 domain through the core, which is not recommended.

The three layers of hierarchy keep VLANs at or below the aggregation layer.

Data Center Core Layer Design

The data center core layer provides a fabric for high-speed packet switching between multiple aggregation modules. A data center core is not necessarily required, but is recommended when multiple aggregation modules are used for scalability. Even when a small number of aggregation modules are used, it might be appropriate to use the campus core for connecting the data center fabric. Figure 5-2 illustrates how the data center interconnects with the campus core.

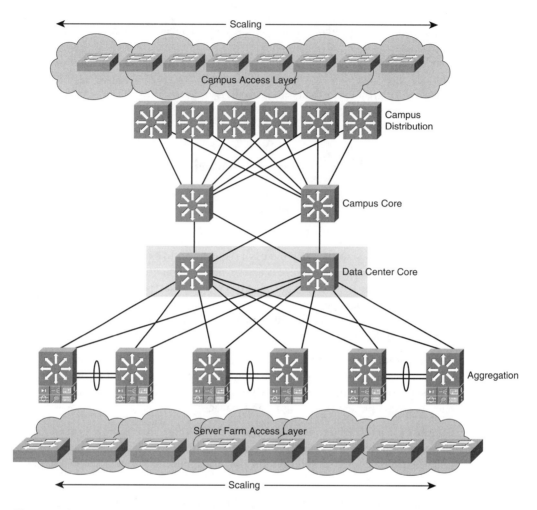

Figure 5-2   *Data Center Core Layer Overview*

When determining whether to implement a data center core, consider the following:

- **10 Gigabit Ethernet port density:** A single pair of campus core switches might not support the number of 10 Gigabit Ethernet ports required to connect the campus distribution layer and the data center aggregation layer switches.

- **Administrative domains and policies:** Separate cores help isolate campus distribution layers and data center aggregation layers in terms of administration and policies, such as quality of service (QoS), access lists, troubleshooting, and maintenance.

■ **Future growth:** The impact of implementing a separate data center core layer at a later date might make it worthwhile to implement it during the initial implementation stage.

The data center core layer is distinct from the campus core layer, with a different purpose and responsibilities. The data center core layer serves as the gateway to the campus core where other campus modules connect, including the enterprise edge and WAN modules. Links connecting the data center core are terminated at Layer 3 and use a distributed, low-latency forwarding architecture and 10 Gigabit Ethernet interfaces for a high level of throughput and performance.

Layer 3 Characteristics for the Data Center Core

When designing the enterprise data center, you should consider where in the infrastructure to place the Layer 2-to-Layer 3 boundary (see Figure 5-3).

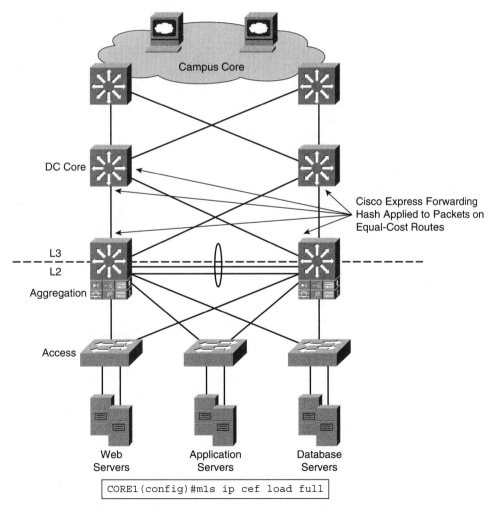

Figure 5-3 *Layer 3 Characteristics for the Data Center Core*

The recommended practice is for the core infrastructure to be implemented at Layer 3, and for the Layer 2-to-Layer 3 boundary to be implemented either within or below the aggregation layer modules. Layer 3 links allow the core to achieve bandwidth scalability and quick convergence, and to avoid path blocking or the risk of uncontrollable broadcast issues related to extending Layer 2 domains. Layer 2 should be avoided in the core because a Spanning Tree Protocol (STP) loop could cause a full data center outage.

The traffic flow in the core consists primarily of sessions traveling between the campus core and the aggregation modules. The core aggregates the aggregation module traffic flows onto optimal paths to the campus core. Server-to-server traffic typically remains within an aggregation module, but backup and replication traffic can travel between aggregation modules by way of the core.

The core layer should run an interior routing protocol such as Open Shortest Path First (OSPF) or Enhanced Interior Gateway Routing Protocol (EIGRP), and load-balance traffic between the campus core and core aggregation layers using Cisco Express Forwarding (CEF)-based hashing algorithms.

From a campus core perspective, there are at least two equal-cost routes to the server subnets, which permits the core to load balance flows to each aggregation switch in a particular module. By default, load balancing is performed using CEF-based load balancing on Layer 3 source and destination IP address hashing. An option is to use Layer 3 IP plus Layer 4 port-based CEF load-balance hashing algorithms. This usually improves load distribution because it presents more unique values to the hashing algorithm by leveraging the automatic source port randomization in the client TCP stack.

Note: To enable the Layer 3- plus-Layer 4 CEF hashing algorithm, use the **mls ip cef load full** global configuration command.

OSPF Routing Protocol Design Recommendations

The OSPF routing protocol design should be tuned for the data center core layer. Here are some recommendations on OSPF design for the data center core layer (see Figure 5-4):

■   Use a not-so-stubby area (NSSA) from the core down: It limits link-state advertisement (LSA) propagation, but permits route redistribution. You can advertise the default route into the aggregation layer, and summarize the routes coming out of the NSSA.

■   Use the **auto-cost reference-bandwidth 10000** command to set the bandwidth to a 10 Gigabit Ethernet value and allow OSPF to differentiate the cost on higher-speed links such as 10 Gigabit Ethernet trunk links. This is needed because the OSPF default reference bandwidth is 100 Mb/s.

■   Because VLANs on 10 Gigabit Ethernet trunks have an OSPF cost of 1, adjust the reference bandwidth value to reflect 10 Gigabit Ethernet for the interswitch SVI (switch virtual interface) with the **auto-cost reference-bandwidth 10000** command.

■   Use loopback interfaces for the router ID to simplify troubleshooting.

Figure 5-4 *OSPF Routing Protocol Design for the Data Center Core*

- Use the **passive-interface default** command, and advertise only on the links that need to participate in the routing process using the **no passive-interface** *interface* command.

- Use OSPF authentication for additional security and to avoid undesired adjacencies.

- Tune the OSPF timers with the **timers throttle spf** command so that OSPF can achieve subsecond convergence time.

EIGRP Routing Protocol Design Recommendations

The EIGRP routing protocol design should be tuned for the data center core layer (see Figure 5-5).

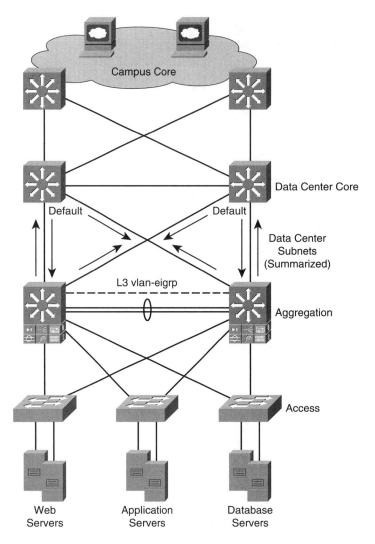

Figure 5-5   *EIGRP Routing Protocol Design for the Data Center Core*

Here are some recommendations on EIGRP design for the data center core layer:

■   Advertise a default summary route into the data center layer with the **ip summary-address eigrp** interface command into the aggregation layer.

■   If other default routes exist in the network, such as from the Internet edge, you may need to filter them using distribute lists.

■   Summarize the data center subnets with the **ip summary-address eigrp** interface command from the aggregation layer.

■ Use the **passive-interface default** command, and advertise only on the links that need to participate in the routing process using the **no passive-interface** *interface* command.

Aggregation Layer Design

The aggregation layer design is critical to the stability and scalability of the overall data center architecture. All traffic in and out of the data center not only passes through the aggregation layer but also relies on the services, path selection, and redundant architecture built in to the aggregation layer design.

The following aggregation layer design topics are discussed in this section:

■ Scaling the aggregation layer

■ STP design

■ Integrated services support

■ Service module placement considerations

■ STP, Hot Standby Router Protocol (HSRP), and service context alignment

■ Active/standby service design

■ Active/active service design

■ Establishing path preference

■ Using virtual routing and forwarding instances (VRF) in the data center

Scaling the Aggregation Layer

Multiple aggregation modules allow the data center architecture to scale as additional servers are added (see Figure 5-6).

The aggregation layer in the enterprise data center model consists of pairs of interconnected aggregation switches referred to as modules. The multiple aggregation modules are used to scale the aggregation layer:

■ **Spanning-tree scaling:** Layer 2 diameters are being pushed to scale further than ever before as Layer 2 domains continue to increase in size because of clustering, NIC teaming, and other application requirements. By using multiple aggregation modules, the Layer 2 domain size can be limited, and the failure exposure can be limited to a smaller domain.

■ **Access layer density scaling:** As the access layer demands increase in terms of bandwidth and server interface requirements, the uplinks to the aggregation layer are migrating to 10 Gigabit Ethernet. This trend can create a density challenge in existing or new aggregation layer designs. Although the long-term answer might be higher-density 10 Gigabit Ethernet line cards and larger switch fabrics, a current proven solution is the use of multiple aggregation modules. Currently, the maximum number of 10 Gigabit Ethernet ports that can be placed in the aggregation layer switch is 64 when using the WS-X6708-10G-3C line card in the Cisco Catalyst 6509 switch. Using a data center core layer and implementing multiple aggregation modules provides a higher level of 10 Gigabit Ethernet density.

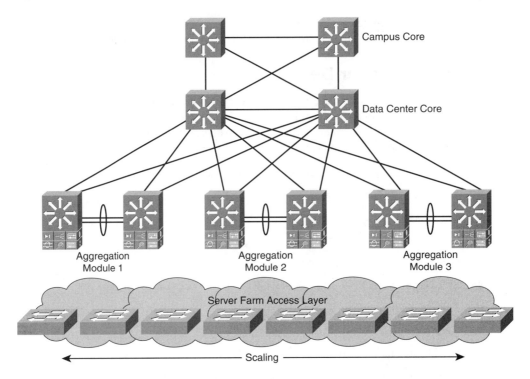

Figure 5-6   *Scaling the Aggregation Layer*

■ **HSRP scaling:** The aggregation layer provides a primary and secondary router "default gateway" address for all servers on a Layer 2 access topology across the entire
   access layer. HSRP is the most widely used protocol for default gateway redundancy
   in the enterprise data center. Based on test results on the CPU processing requirements of HSRP, Cisco recommends the maximum number of HSRP instances in an
   aggregation module to be limited to approximately 500, with recommended timers of
   a 1-second hello and a 3-second hold time.

■ **Application services scaling:** The aggregation layer supports applications on service modules across multiple access layer switches, scaling the ability of the network
   to provide application services. Some examples of supported applications are Server
   Load Balancing (SLB) and firewalls. The service modules can be deployed with virtual
   contexts, with each context behaving like an independent device with its own policies, interfaces, domains, and server.

STP Design

If you have Layer 2 in the aggregation layer, the STP design should be your first concern.
The aggregation layer carries the largest burden with Layer 2 scaling because the aggregation layer establishes the Layer 2 domain size and manages it with a spanning tree protocol such as Rapid Per-VLAN Spanning Tree (RPVST+) or Multiple Spanning Tree (MST)
(see Figure 5-7).

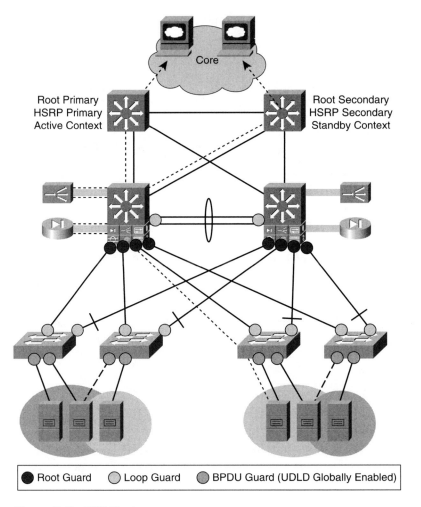

Figure 5-7   *STP Design*

The aggregation modules permit the spanning-tree domain to be distributed. For the data center environment, RSTP is recommended over MST for these reasons:

■   It has fast convergence characteristics. It already incorporates the Cisco proprietary enhancements of Per-VLAN Spanning Tree Plus (PVST+), including UplinkFast and BackboneFast.

- Access layer uplink failures are detected quickly, typically within 300 ms to 2 seconds depending on the number of VLANs.

- It is easier to implement and has more flexible design options.

- It can be combined with root guard, BPDU guard (bridge protocol data unit), loop guard, and UniDirectional Link Detection (UDLD) to achieve a stable STP environment.

Note: UDLD is globally enabled by default only on fiber ports. You must manually enable it on copper ports.

Integrated Service Modules

Integrated service modules in the aggregation layer provide services such as content switching, firewall, SSL offload, intrusion detection, and network analysis. Layer 4 through Layer 7 services such as server load balancing, firewall, and SSL offload can be integrated in modules in the Cisco Catalyst 6500 series switches.

For redundancy, the integrated services may be deployed in one of two scenarios:

- Active/standby pairs where one appliance is active and the other appliance is in standby mode. This is the traditional deployment model for the Cisco Content Switching Module (CSM) and the older Cisco Catalyst 6500 Series Firewall Services Module (FWSM) Version 2.x.

- Active/active pairs where both appliances are active and providing services. This newer deployment model can support the Cisco Application Control Engine (ACE) and Catalyst Series FWSM Version 3.1.

Integrated service modules or blades can provide flexibility and economies of scale by optimizing rack space, cabling, and management. The integrated services supported will influence many aspects of the overall design.

Service Module Placement Consideration

You might need to consider the underlying fabric when placing service modules in the Catalyst 6500 series switches.

The Cisco Catalyst 6500 series Supervisor Engine 720 integrated switch fabric provides either one or two fabric channel connections per slot based on the switch chassis configuration. In the three-, four-, and nine-slot configurations, each slot has two fabric channel connections. Single-channel fabric-attached modules include the Secure Sockets Layer Module (SSSLM), the Network Analysis Module (NAM), and the Intrusion Detection System Module (IDSM). Dual-channel fabric-attached modules include the 6700 series line cards.

Although the Cisco Catalyst 6513 switch has a 13-slot configuration, 8 of the slots provide only a single fabric channel connection. Any module that requires two fabric channel connections such as the Cisco 6748 line card will not be supported in the single fabric channel connection slots.

Cisco Catalyst 6500 Series Switch Fabric Channels

* Primary Catalyst 6500 Series Supervisor Engine 720 Placement

Figure 5-8 *Service Modules Placement Consideration*

Note: The current integrated service modules require only a single fabric channel connection.

Based on the chassis, the Catalyst 6513 switch can support more single fabric channel integrated service modules, whereas the Catalyst 6509 switch can support more dual fabric channel Gigabit and 10 Gigabit Ethernet ports.

Active STP, HSRP, and Service Context Alignment

A recommended practice is to align the active STP, HSRP, and service context in the aggregation layer to provide a more deterministic environment.

This diagram shows alignment of the STP root, the primary HSRP instance, and the active service module. The active service module is known as the service context.

Note: The primary STP root can be established using the **spanning-tree vlan** *vlan_id* **root primary** command.
The primary HSRP instance can be configured using the **standby priority** command. The active service context can be aligned by connecting the service module on the aggregation switch supporting the primary STP root and primary HSRP instance.

Active component alignment prevents session flow from entering one aggregation switch and then hopping to a second aggregation switch to reach a service context. When the traffic enters the aggregation switch that is connected to the active service context, the traffic will be forwarded to the service module directly and avoid the Inter-Switch Link

Figure 5-9   *Active STP, HSRP, and Service Content Alignment*

(ISL). This recommended model provides a more deterministic environment and offers more efficient traffic flow and simplified troubleshooting.

Active/Standby Service Module Design

The active/standby mode of operation is used by service modules that require Layer 2 adjacency with the servers.

The active/standby design typically supports the Cisco CSM, the Catalyst 6500 series FSWM 2.x, and the SSL integrated service modules.

Advantages to the active/standby design include the following:

■   It is a predictable deployment model.

■   This traditional model simplifies troubleshooting. It can be designed so that you know in the primary situation what service modules are active and where the data flows should occur.

Disadvantages to the active/standby design include the following:

■   It underutilizes the access layer uplinks because it may not use both uplinks.

■   It underutilizes service modules and switch fabrics because it does not use both modules.

This model uses the aligned spanning tree root, the primary HSRP, and the active service module.

Active/Active Service Module Design

The active/active mode of operation is used by service modules that support multiple contexts or multiple active/standby groups. This concept is illustrated in Figure 5-10.

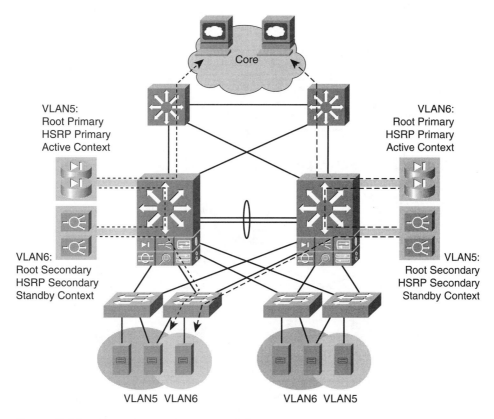

Figure 5-10   *Active/Active Service Module Design*

Newer service modules can take advantage of active/active designs. The Cisco CSM supports active/standby per context, and the Catalyst 6500 series FSWM 3.1 can implement multiple active/standby groups. In both cases, each service module in the aggregation layer is active.

Advantages to the active/active design include the following:

■   It distributes the services and processing and increases the overall service performance.

■   It supports uplink load balancing by VLAN, so that the uplinks can be used more efficiently.

Note: This model aligns the spanning-tree root, the primary HSRP, and the service module per active context on each VLAN.

Establishing Inbound Path Preference

When active/standby service module pairs are used, it becomes important to align traffic flows so that the active primary service modules are the preferred path to a particular server application (see Figure 5-11).

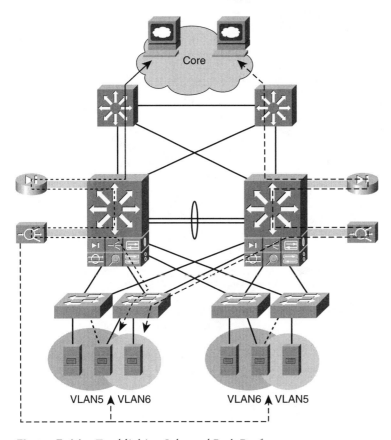

Figure 5-11   *Establishing Inbound Path Preference*

Clients connect to the Cisco CSM by directing their requests to the virtual IP address of the virtual server. When a client initiates a connection to the virtual server, the Cisco CSM chooses a real physical server in the server farm for the connection based on configured load-balancing algorithms and policies such as access rules.

The Route Health Injection (RHI) feature allows a Cisco CSM or Cisco ACE in a Catalyst 6500 series switch to install a host route in the Multilayer Switch Feature Card (MSFC) if the virtual server is in the operational state. By using RHI with specific route map attributes to set the desired metric, a /32 route for the virtual IP address is injected into the routing table. This establishes a path preference with the enterprise core so that all sessions to a particular virtual IP address go to the aggregation layer switch where the primary service module is located. If context failover occurs, the RHI and path preference point to the new active server.

Note: Inbound path preference can be established using the **advertise active** SLB virtual server command and a **set metric** route-map command applied to the appropriate virtual IP address.

RHI can support the active context on Cisco ACE, Cisco CSM, Catalyst 6500 series FWSM, and SSL service modules. This design aligns the spanning-tree root and the active service module. RHI supports a deterministic inbound session flow to a specific aggregation switch, which avoids unnecessary use of the ISL and asymmetrical flows.

Using VRFs in the Data Center

Finally, separate VRFs can be used as a virtualization and management approach in data center designs (see Figure 5-12).

Layer 3 routing virtualization can be supported using VRFs on the MSFC in the Cisco Catalyst 6500 series. VRFs enable the logical partitioning of network resources such as the MSFC, Cisco ACE, and Catalyst 6500 series FWSM.

VRFs support the provisioning of application services by context within multiple access topologies. VRFs can support path isolation from metropolitan-area network (MAN) and WAN designs, such as those that use Multiprotocol Label Switching (MPLS), down to the data center resources. VRFs could be used to map the virtualized data center to an MPLS MAN or WAN cloud. Security policy management and deployment can be implemented by user group or VRF.

Note: A Layer 3 access design that uses VRF can provide an aggregation layer service module solution, but this is beyond the scope of this book.

Designing the Access Layer

The data center access layer provides the physical-level attachment to the server resources, and operates in Layer 2 or Layer 3 modes. Either spanning-tree or Layer 3 routing protocols can be extended from the aggregation layer into the access layer, depending on which access layer model is used. This section will assist the reader to identify design considerations for the data center access layer. Successful mastery of the content includes being able to meet these objectives:

Figure 5-12   *Using VRFs in the Data Center*

- Provide an overview of the data center access layer features
- Describe design considerations using Layer 2 looped access designs
- Describe design considerations using Layer 2 loop-free access designs
- Describe design considerations using Layer 2 FlexLink access designs
- Describe design considerations using Layer 3 access designs
- Provide an overview of design considerations for blade servers in the data center

Overview of the Data Center Access Layer

The data center access layer is the first oversubscription point in the data center because it aggregates the server traffic onto Gigabit EtherChannel, 10 Gigabit Ethernet, or 10 Gigabit EtherChannel uplinks to the aggregation layer. The data center access layer provides the physical-level attachment to the server resources and can operate in Layer 2 or Layer 3 mode. The operational mode plays a critical role in meeting particular server requirements such as NIC teaming, clustering, and broadcast containment. Spanning-tree or Layer 3 routing protocols are extended from the aggregation layer into the access layer, depending on which access layer model is used. The access layer is typically one of three models:

- **Layer 2 looped:** VLANs are extended into the aggregation layer. Layer 2 services such as NIC teaming, clustering, and stateful services from the aggregation layer such as a firewall, SLB, and SSL can be provided across Layer 2 models. Layer 3 routing is first performed in the aggregation layer.

- **Layer 2 loop free:** VLANs are not extended into the aggregation layer. Layer 2 services are supported. Layer 3 routing is first performed in the aggregation layer.

- **Layer 3:** Stateful services requiring Layer 2 connectivity cannot be provisioned from the aggregation layer. Layer 3 routing is first performed in the access layer.

The access layer has deterministic traffic flows to the active service modules by leveraging the aggregation layer alignment of the primary STP, primary HSRP, and active service module.

Note: Cisco recommends that you implement access layer switches logically paired in groups to support either server redundant connections or diverse connections for production, backup, and management Ethernet interfaces.

Layer 2 Looped Designs

Access layer switches are primarily deployed in Layer 2 mode in the data center (see Figure 5-13).

A looped Layer 2 access topology provides the following benefits:

- **VLAN extension:** The Layer 2 access topology provides the flexibility to extend VLANs between switches that are connected to a common aggregation module. The Layer 3 boundary in the aggregation layer is above the trunk link that connects the aggregation switches. This simplifies the provisioning of servers to a particular subnet or VLAN and removes issues about the physical placement of the server in a particular rack or row.

- **Layer 2 adjacency requirements:** NIC teaming, high-availability clusters, and database clusters are application examples that typically require NICs to be in the same broadcast domain or VLAN. The list of applications used in a clustered environment is growing, and Layer 2 adjacency is a common requirement.

- **Custom applications:** Many developers write custom applications without considering the Layer 3 network environment, because of either a lack of skills or available tools. These custom applications can create challenges in a Layer 3 IP access topology. Customer applications that depend on Layer 2 adjacency with other servers could require rewriting code when changing IP addresses.

- **Service modules:** Layer 2 access permits services provided by service modules or appliances to be shared across the entire access layer. Examples of service modules include Cisco Catalyst 6500 series FWSM, Cisco CSM, and SSL Services Module (SSLSM). The active-standby modes of operation used by many service modules require Layer 2 adjacency with the servers that use them.

Figure 5-13 *Layer 2 Looped Design Benefits*

■ **Redundancy:** Looped designs are inherently redundant. A redundant path exists through a second path that is blocking based on STP control. VLANs may be load balanced across access layer uplinks.

Layer 2 Looped Topologies

The two Layer 2 looped topologies are the looped triangle and the looped square.

The looped triangle topology is currently the most widely implemented in the enterprise data center. This topology provides a deterministic design when the spanning-tree root, HSRP default gateway, and active service modules are aligned on the same aggregation switch. Network resiliency is achieved with dual homing and Rapid Spanning Tree Protocol (RSTP).

The looped square topology has not been as common in the enterprise data center, but is gaining more interest. This topology is similar to the triangle loop topology in terms of a deterministic design and network resilience, but differs in where the spanning-tree blocking occurs. The looped square topology uses a trunk between access switches, which increases the access layer switch density on the aggregation switches when compared to a triangle loop topology where 10 Gigabit Ethernet uplinks are used. The looped square topology optimizes the 10 Gigabit Ethernet port density on aggregation layer switches.

Figure 5-14 shows the spanning-tree blocking point on the link between the access switch pair. This topology aligns well to an active/active service module design deployed in the aggregation layer because it permits the uplinks to be load balanced without crossing the aggregation layer trunks. If active services are on only one access switch, it might be desirable to adjust the STP cost so that the uplink to the backup aggregation switch is blocking instead of the link between the access pair. This forces all traffic to the primary aggregation switch without having to traverse the aggregation layer ISL trunk.

The Layer 2 looped triangle in Figure 5-14 has the following features:

■   Supports VLAN extension/Layer 2 adjacency across the access layer.

■   Resiliency is achieved with dual-homing and RSTP.

■   Quick convergence with RSTP.

■   Supports stateful services at the aggregation layer.

■   Proven and widely used.

The Layer 2 looped square in Figure 5-14 has the following features:

■   Supports VLAN extension/Layer 2 adjacency across the access layer.

■   Resiliency is achieved with dual homing and STP.

■   Quick convergence with 802.1w and 802.1s.

■   Supports stateful services at the aggregation layer.

■   Supports more access layer switches, optimizing 10 Gigabit Ethernet aggregation layer density.

■   Active/active uplinks align well to active/active service module designs.

The disadvantages of the square loop design relate to aggregation layer ISL use, because 50 percent of access layer traffic might cross the ISL to reach the default gateway's active service module. There can also be degradation in performance in the event of an uplink failure.

Layer 2 Looped Design Issues

The main drawback to looped Layer 2 design is that if a layer 2 loop occurs, the fault has a severe impact across the entire Layer 2 domain, and the network may become unmanageable due to the infinite replication of frames.

Using RSTP with recommended STP practices helps improve stability and prevent loop conditions. However, conditions can occur that cause loops even when STP is being run. In addition to STP, these loop-prevention mechanisms should be used:

■   **BPDU guard:** Used to protect the switched network from the problems that may be caused by the receipt of bridge protocol data unit (BPDU) on ports that should not be receiving them. The receipt of unexpected BPDUs may be accidental or may be part of an unauthorized attempt to add a switch to the network. BPDU guard disables the port upon BPDU reception if PortFast is enabled on the port.

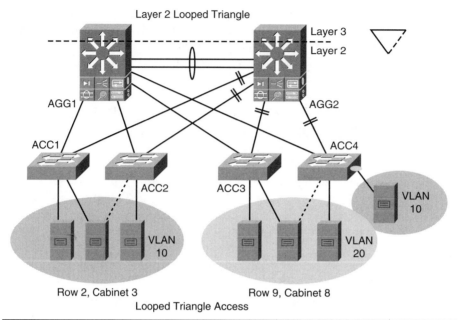

Figure 5-14   *Layer 2 Looped Topologies*

- **Root guard:** Allows a device to participate in STP so long as the device does not try to become the root. Root guard blocks the access from the device until the receipt of its superior BPDUs ceases.

- **UniDirectional Link Detection (UDLD):** Allows devices to monitor the physical configuration of the cables and detect when a unidirectional link exists. When a unidirectional link is detected, UDLD shuts down the affected port and alerts the user.

- **Loop guard:** Checks whether a root port or an alternate root port receives BPDUs. If the port is not receiving BPDUs, the loop guard feature puts the port into an inconsistent state until it starts receiving BPDUs again. Loop guard isolates the failure and lets the spanning tree converge to a stable topology without the failed link or bridge.

Layer 2 Loop-Free Designs

The loop-free Layer 2 model, as illustrated in Figure 5-15, is an alternative design model used when looped topology characteristics are undesirable but Layer 2 support is required. Some reasons for using the loop-free Layer 2 include inexperience with Layer 2 STP, a need for all uplinks to be active, or previous bad experiences related to STP implementations.

Figure 5-15 *Layer 2 Loop-Free Design*

Even with the loop-free design topology, it is still necessary to run STP as a loop-prevention tool. In the event that a cabling or configuration error creates a loop, STP prevents the loop from possibly bringing down the network.

A loop-free Layer 2 access topology has these attributes:

- **Active uplinks:** All uplinks are active, and none are blocking.

- **Layer 2 server adjacency:** Supported across a single pair of access switches with the loop-free *U* design, and across an aggregation switch pair with the loop-free inverted *U* design.

- **Stability:** Provides fewer chances for loop conditions due to misconfiguration than Layer 2 looped designs.

Loop-Free Topologies

The two Layer 2 loop-free topologies are the loop-free *U* and the loop-free inverted *U* (see Figure 5-16). The following are characteristics of loop-free U access:

- VLANs are contained in switch pairs (no extension outside of switch pairs).

- No STP blocking; all uplinks are active.

- Layer 2 service modules black-hole traffic on uplink failure.

The following are characteristics of loop-free inverted U access:

- Supports VLAN extension.

- No STP blocking; all uplinks are active.

- Access switch uplink failure black-holes single attached servers.

- ISL scaling considerations.

- Supports all service module implementations.

For both topologies, all uplinks are active with no blocking. The Layer 2-to-Layer 3 line of demarcation is different in each design. Both topologies provide a backup path in the event of an uplink failure, and permit a higher density of access switches to be supported on the aggregation module than the looped designs.

In a loop-free *U* design, a VLAN is configured on each access switch, and on the trunk between access switches and its corresponding 802.1Q uplink. Redundancy is supported through the trunk between the access layer switches. VLANs are contained on an access switch pair. The trunk between aggregation switches is Layer 3. The main disadvantages to the loop-free *U* design are that VLANs cannot be extended between aggregation switches, and that Layer 2 service modules will black-hole traffic in the event of an uplink failure.

In a loop-free inverted *U* design, a VLAN is configured on each access switch and its corresponding 802.1Q uplink, and is extended between aggregation switches but is not extended between access switches. The trunk between aggregation switches is Layer 2. This permits active/standby hellos and session-state communications from service modules to take place to support redundancy. One issue with the loop-free inverted *U* design is that access switch uplink failures can black-hole single attached servers. Redundancy can be improved using Gigabit EtherChannel or NIC teaming on servers. When an active/standby

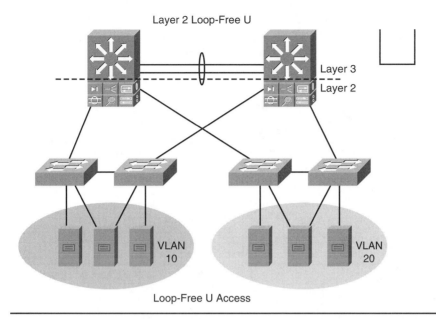

Layer 2 Loop-Free U

Layer 3
Layer 2

VLAN
10

VLAN
20

Loop-Free U Access

Layer 2 Loop-Free Inverted U

Layer 3
Layer 2

VLAN
10

VLAN
10

VLAN
20

Loop-Free Inverted U Access

Figure 5-16   *Loop-Free Topologies*

service module is being used, trunk scaling should be considered. The loop-free inverted *U*
design model supports all service module implementations.

Example: Loop-Free *U* Design and Layer 2 Service Modules

The loop-free *U* design with Layer 2 service modules can experience black-holing of traffic in the event of an uplink failure.

For example, in Figure 5-17, if the uplink connecting the access switch and the primary aggregation switch goes down, the VLAN interface on the aggregation switch MSFC goes down, too, if the uplink is the only interface in that VLAN.

Figure 5-17   *Example: Loop-Free* U *Design and Layer 2 Service Modules*

In the diagram, the switched virtual interface for VLAN 10 would go down if AGG1 loses connection to ACC1, which is supporting VLAN 10. The HSRP multicast hellos are no longer received by the AGG2 switch, which creates an active/active HSRP state for the VLAN 10 MSFC interfaces on both AGG1 and AGG2. However, the servers on ACC1 cannot reach the active service module context on AGG1 through AGG2 because there is no Layer 2 path between AGG1 and AGG2 for VLAN 10.

Note: The active/standby modes of operation used by service modules require Layer 2 adjacency with the servers that use them.

Although the service module can be configured to switch over the active/standby roles by using the interface monitoring features, this requires the entire module to switch over (all contexts) on a single uplink failure. This is not a desirable condition and is further complicated if multiple uplink failures occur, or when maintenance requires taking down an access layer switch uplink.

Note: Cisco does not recommend the use of the loop-free Layer 2 access design with active/standby Layer 2 service module implementations that do not support single context failover.

Example: Loop-Free *U* Design and Cisco ACE Service Module

The loop-free *U* design is supported with newer service modules such as Cisco ACE, which supports per context failover with autostate, or with Catalyst 6500 series FWSM 3.1, which supports an active/active service module design.

In Figure 5-18, the Cisco ACE module supports autostate on the uplinks. If the uplink between AGG1 and ACC1 fails, the active Cisco ACE service module context can fail over to AGG2 in less than one second.

Figure 5-18 *Example: Loop-Free* U *Design and ACE Service Modules*

When Catalyst 6500 series FWSM 3.1 uses the active/active service module design, it will support the loop-free *U* topology, too. If the ACC1 uplinks fail for this design, the hosts will use the active Catalyst 6500 series FWSM 3.1 on AGG2.

Layer 2 FlexLink Designs

FlexLink designs are a Layer 2 alternative to the looped access layer topology. In Figure 5-19, a pair of access switches is configured with FlexLinks.

FlexLinks provide an active/standby pair of uplinks defined on a common access layer switch. These are some of the attributes of FlexLinks:

■ FlexLinks are configured using the **switchport backup interface** *interface-id* command on the primary interface (the interface specified in the command is the port which becomes the backup for the primary interface).

■ An interface can belong to only one FlexLink.

■ The pair can be of the same or different interface types such as Gigabit Ethernet, 10 Gigabit Ethernet, or PortChannel.

Figure 5-19   *Using FlexLinks in the Data Center*

- FlexLinks automatically disable STP, so no BPDUs are propagated.

- Failover from active to standby is in the one- to two-second range, which is not as fast as with RST.

- FlexLinks operate using only a single pair of links.

- The aggregation layer switch is not aware of the FlexLink configuration. From the perspective of the aggregation switch, the links are up and STP logical and virtual ports are active and allocated.

Note: FlexLinks are currently supported on a variety of Cisco platforms as of IOS Release 12.2. Consult www.cisco.com for specific information for the platform under consideration.

FlexLink Issues and Considerations

There are some potential issues and considerations with FlexLinks. Because STP is disabled on FlexLinks, there is the possibility that a loop condition can exist in particular scenarios, such as a patch cable that is mistakenly connected between access layer switches where at least one is configured for FlexLinks.

In Figure 5-20, a new link has been added between the ACC1 and ACC2 switches. If the access switch ports have BPDU guard enabled, BPDU guard will see the loop and disable the port. The error message is in Figure 5-20.

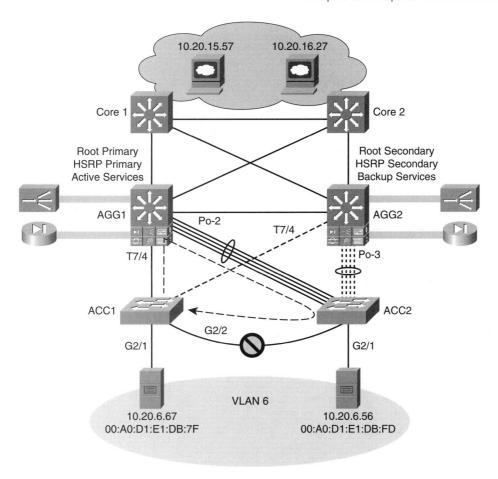

Figure 5-20   *FlexLink Considerations: Interaccess Switch Loop Issue*

Note: Without BPDU guard enabled on access ports, the aggregation switch with a loop will be subject to endless replication of broadcast or multicast frames and very high CPU usage, HSRP flapping, and other negative conditions.

There are some other considerations to take into account with FlexLink designs. You need to consider ISL bandwidth requirements under failover situations.

Another loop can occur if a second connection that is not part of the FlexLink channel group is made in parallel between the aggregation switch and an access switch.

In Figure 5-21, a new uplink has been added from the AGG1 to ACC1 G2/2. Because STP BPDUs are not passed along the FlexLink path, this parallel link creates a loop in the topology that cannot be detected by BPDU guard, and an endless replication of broadcast and multicast frames occurs, which negatively impacts the whole aggregation module.

Figure 5-21 *Example: FlexLink with Parallel Link Loop Issue*

Root guard on the aggregation switch is also ineffective in this scenario because AGG1 does not see a path to the root AGG2 through the access switch with FlexLinks enabled.

Note: FlexLink is recommended only in environments with high administrative control and limited changes.

Comparison of Layer 2 Access Designs

Table 5-1 compares the features of Layer 2 access designs.

Table 5-1 *Comparison of Layer 2 Access Designs*

	All Uplinks in Active State	VLAN Extension Supported	Service Module Black-Holing Issues[5]	Single Attached Server Black-Holing on Uplink Failure	Optimizes Access Switch Density	Must Consider ISL Scaling
Looped Triangle	No	Yes	Yes	No	No	Yes[3]
Looped Square	Yes	Yes	Yes	No	Yes	No
Loop-Free U	Yes	No	No[4]	No	Yes	Yes
Loop-Free Inverted U	Yes	Yes	Yes	Yes[1,2]	Yes	No
FlexLinks	No	Yes	Yes	No	No	Yes

[1] Use of distributed EtherChannel greatly reduces chances of black-holing condition.

[2] NIC teaming can eliminate black-holing condition.

[3] When service modules are used and active service modules are aligned to AGG1.

[4] Cisco ACE module permits Layer 2 loop-free access with per context switchover on uplink failure.

[5] Applies to when using Cisco CSM or Catalyst 6500 Series FWSM in active/standby arrangement.

The table column headings indicate whether the design provides these features:

■ **All Uplinks in Active State:** Some access layer designs can use both uplinks (active/active), whereas other designs have one link active and the other either blocked on a per-VLAN basis by spanning tree, or completely unused in a backup mode only.

■ **VLAN Extension Supported:** Some access design models permit a VLAN to be extended to all access switches that are connected to a common aggregation module.

■ **Service Module Black-Holing Issues:** Most access designs are susceptible to an uplink failure on the access layer switch breaking connectivity between the servers and the service modules.

■ **Single Attached Server Black-Holing on Uplink Failure:** If an access switch has a single uplink, it could be a large failure exposure point. Uplinks that use Distributed EtherChannel can reduce the chances of black-holing. Another technique that can be used is server load balancing to a virtual IP address that includes servers physically connected across multiple access switches. NIC teaming can also be used.

- **Optimizes Access Switch Density:** When 10 Gigabit Ethernet uplinks are used, port density at the aggregation layer can be a challenge. Some access layer designs permit a larger number of access layer switches per aggregation module than others.

- **Must Consider Trunk Scaling:** Some access layer designs send all traffic toward the primary root aggregation switch, whereas other designs send traffic toward both aggregation switches. When sending to both aggregation switches, 50 percent of the traffic typically passes over the ISL to reach the active HSRP default gateway and active service module pair. The amount of bandwidth used for the trunks becomes very important in these designs and can create scaling challenges.

Layer 3 Access Layer Designs

In a Layer 3 design, access switches connect to the aggregation switches using a Layer 3 uplink with a dedicated subnet. Layer 3 routing is first performed on the access switch. Layer 2 trunks between pairs of access switches support the Layer 2 adjacency requirements in the data center. This design limits Layer 2 adjacencies to access switch pairs, and VLAN extension across the data center is not possible (see Figure 5-22).

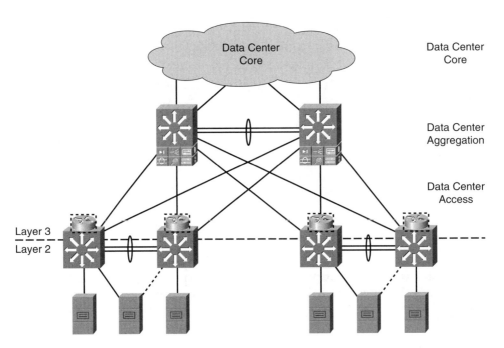

Figure 5-22   *Layer 3 Access Design Overview*

Note: When you are using a Layer 3 access model, Cisco recommends running STP as a loop-prevention tool. STP would be active only on the interswitch trunk and server ports on the access layer switches.

The Layer 3 design is typically used to limit or contain broadcast domains to a particular size. Smaller broadcast domains reduce exposure to broadcast domain issues and can shelter particular servers that could be adversely affected by a particular broadcast level. Although Layer 3 access designs are stable, they are not as common as Layer 2 designs in the data center.

With a Layer 3 access design, all uplinks are active and use CEF load balancing up to the Equal Cost Multipath (ECMP) maximum. The current ECMP maximum is eight paths. Layer 3 designs can provide convergence times faster than STP, although RSTP is close.

Multicast Source Support

Historically, Layer 3 designs have been implemented to support many multicast sources. Multicast sources on Layer 2 access works well when Internet Group Management Protocol (IGMP) snooping is available. IGMP snooping at the access switch automatically limits multicast flow to interfaces with registered clients in the VLAN (see Figure 5-23).

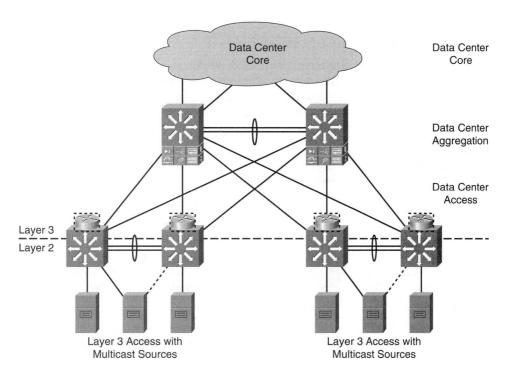

Figure 5-23 *Multicast Sources Support*

Drivers for Layer 3 designs include situations where IGMP snooping is not available at the access layer, or when particular Layer 3 administrative functions are required.

Benefits of Layer 3 Access

These are some of the benefits of Layer 3 access designs:

■ Broadcast and failure domain sizes are minimized, which leads to a higher level of network stability.

■ Server stability requirements are supported, including isolation of particular applications from multicast traffic.

■ All uplinks are available paths and are active up to the ECMP maximum.

■ Fast uplink convergence is supported for failover and fallback. The aggregation switches will not need to rebuild Address Resolution Protocol (ARP) tables. Layer 3 designs can provide convergence times faster than STP, although RSTP is close.

Drawbacks of Layer 3 Access

IP address space management is more difficult with Layer 3 access than with Layer 2 access. Migrating to a Layer 3 design usually requires re-addressing the data center devices. When trying to migrate to Layer 3 access, it can be difficult to determine all the Layer 2 adjacencies in place and which custom applications use hard-coded addresses.

Layer 2 adjacency is limited to access pairs, which will limit clustering and NIC teaming capabilities. It can also limit data center application deployments, such as with the VMware VMotion product that provides infrastructure services transferring virtual machines between servers. Service modules will need to be deployed at each access layer pair to maintain Layer 2 adjacency with servers and provide stateful failover.

Blade Server Overview

Blade servers are a technology that is often implemented in the data center access layer. A blade server is a chassis that houses many servers on a blade or module. Typically, blade servers are used to replace older server farms where increased density is a requirement, or where new applications that use clustering are being deployed. Blade servers allow the data center manager to reduce operational costs and save rack space. Blade servers are a growing portion of the server market today for many of the leading server vendors, including IBM, Hewlett-Packard, Sun Microsystems, and Dell.

Designs that use blade servers are becoming popular in the enterprise data center. Blade servers can support either integrated switches or pass-through modules for connecting servers to the network.

Blade servers present specific challenges related to designing and supporting the data center network that need to be considered:

■ **Administrative domains:** The design must define who is responsible for configuring and managing integral switches. Usually, the system administration team is responsible for the components inside of a server product, and the network team typically supports the configuration of the spanning tree and trunks. Change control and troubleshooting need to be supported, too.

■ **Interoperability:** Blade servers support many different vendor-specific switches, including Cisco, Nortel, and D-Link switches. Although many of the technologies in
  use are expected to meet interoperability standards such as spanning-tree IEEE
  802.1w, they must be verified and tested to ensure proper operation in the data center
  network.

■ **Spanning-tree scaling:** The integrated switch on the blade server is logically similar to the external rack-based server switching design. The same challenges apply relative to the increase in spanning-tree logical and virtual ports (see Figure 5-24).

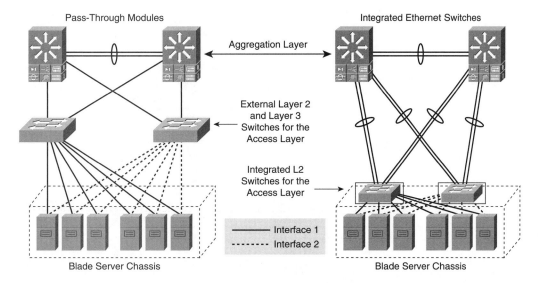

Figure 5-24 *Blade Server Overview*

■ **Pass-through cabling:** The pass-through module option on blade servers permits
  customers to use their existing external access switches for connecting the servers in
  the blade server chassis and to avoid the integrated switch option. Customers should
  examine the pass-through cabling system to make sure it can properly be supported
  in their physical cabinets.

■ **Switch trunk topologies:** Each vendor blade server implementation has unique internal and external switch trunk connectivity options. Make sure that the access
  layer topology chosen for your data center design meets requirements such as VLAN
  extension and NIC teaming while staying within the watermark values of the spanning tree.

■ **Environmental issues:** The consolidation of many servers into one enclosure requires a greater amount of cooling. This could limit the number of blade servers in a
  particular area or rack, because too much warm air can circulate around the systems.

Blade server enclosures in large data centers have been found to strain the weight limits of the data center's raised flooring and the available power.

Blade Server Connectivity Options

Blade servers connect servers to the network at the access layer. The access layer network infrastructure may need to support blade servers with integral switches or blade servers with pass-through cabling. Blade servers can support either Layer 2 or Layer 3 topologies, depending on the server broadcast domain or administrative requirements (see Figure 5-25).

Figure 5-25   *Blade Server Connectivity Options*

As previously discussed in this chapter, a Layer 2 access design supports Layer 2 capabilities, including VLAN extension and NIC teaming. A Layer 3 access design can be used to provide Layer 3 capabilities, aggregate blade server uplinks, and optimize 10 Gigabit Ethernet densities in the aggregation layer.

Stacked or dual-tier Layer 2 access designs that use the blade server integrated switches with external Layer 2 switches should be avoided. Dual Layer 2 designs are susceptible to these factors:

■ More complex STP design and blocking issues

■ Oversubscription of uplinks and trunks

■ Larger failure domain issues

The network designer may also consider implementing blade servers with integrated Cisco switches that support the trunk failover feature. Trunk failover allows rapid failover to the redundant switch in the blade enclosure if all uplinks from the primary switch fail. When the uplinks fail, the switch shuts down the ports connected to the blade servers and lets NIC teaming software direct traffic to the redundant switch.

Blade Servers with InfiniBand

An option for connecting blade servers is to use integrated InfiniBand switches (see Figure 5-26).

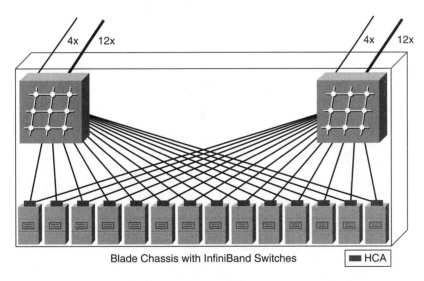

Figure 5-26 *Blade Servers with InfiniBand*

One of the key problems with server I/O is the CPU overhead associated with data movement between memory and I/O devices such as LAN and storage-area network (SAN) interfaces. InfiniBand is a standards-based protocol that provides high throughput and low-latency transport for efficient data transfer between server memory and I/O devices. InfiniBand supports computing-intensive applications with significant I/O between servers. InfiniBand uses remote direct memory access (RDMA) to offload data movement from the server CPU to the InfiniBand host channel adapter (HCA).

Note: RDMA is an extension of hardware-based direct memory access (DMA) capabilities. It allows the CPU to delegate data movement within the computer to the DMA hardware. RDMA enables data to be moved from one memory location to another, even if that memory resides on another device.

Channel adapters are used to provide an InfiniBand interface and protocol stack for communications between InfiniBand-connected devices. InfiniBand supports two types of channel adapters:

- **Host channel adapter (HCA):** Supports the full InfiniBand protocol stack and may initiate or accept connections to or from other InfiniBand-attached devices. Blade servers can use HCAs.

- **Target channel adapter (TCA):** Supports a subset of the InfiniBand protocol stack and can accept connections. InfiniBand-attached disk arrays are examples of devices that use InfiniBand TCAs.

An InfiniBand fabric may consist of a number of InfiniBand subnets that are interconnected using InfiniBand routers. Each InfiniBand subnet may consist of one or more InfiniBand switches and InfiniBand-attached devices (see Figure 5-27).

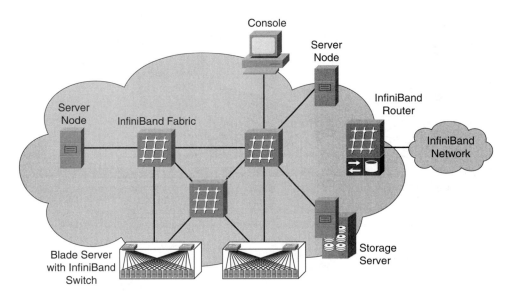

Figure 5-27   *Example: InfiniBand Fabric*

Note: InfiniBand technology is most applicable for Inter-Process Communication (IPC) networks with larger clusters and tightly coupled applications. Gigabit Ethernet is most applicable for smaller clusters with more loosely coupled applications.

InfiniBand switches and routers support unicast and multicast packet forwarding between InfiniBand-attached hosts. InfiniBand switches forward packets between hosts attached to the same InfiniBand subnet using the destination local ID within the local routing header. InfiniBand switches are also responsible for enforcing QoS and flow control within the InfiniBand network.

Blade Server Trunk Failover Feature

Layer 2 trunk failover, which is also known as link-state tracking, is a feature of blade servers that provides Layer 2 redundancy in the network when used with server NIC adapter teaming (see Figure 5-28).

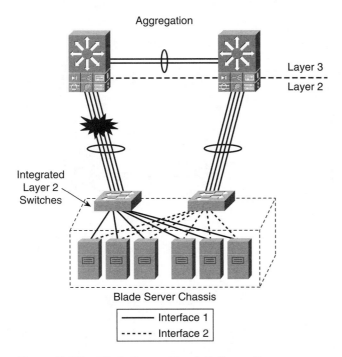

Figure 5-28 *Blade Server Trunk Failover Feature*

When you enable Layer 2 trunk failover on the integrated switch, the link state of the internal downstream ports is bound to the link state of one or more of the external upstream ports. An internal downstream port is an interface that is connected to the server. An external upstream port is an interface that is connected to the external network. When you associate a set of downstream ports to a set of upstream ports, if all the upstream ports become unavailable, trunk failover automatically puts all the associated downstream ports in an error-disabled state. This causes the server primary interface to failover to the secondary interface. This feature is dependent on the NIC feature set support for NIC teaming and failover.

When Layer 2 trunk failover is not enabled, if the upstream interfaces lose connectivity, the link states of the downstream interfaces remain unchanged. The server is not aware that external connectivity has been lost and does not failover to the secondary interface. Traffic will be black-holed.

You can distribute trunk failover groups across accesses switches to achieve maximum bandwidth utilization from the blade server chassis. Although this is a loop-free topology that does not need STP blocking, STP should be enabled for loop protection.

Layer 2 or Layer 3 Access Design?

Is there a right way to design the access layer in the data center? Both approaches have merits, as summarized in Figure 5-29. There are many trade-offs to consider when choosing between Layer 2 or Layer 3 access designs.

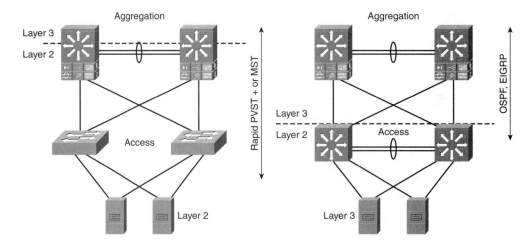

Figure 5-29   *Choosing Between Layer 2 and Layer 3 Access Designs*

A Layer 2 design has these advantages:

■   Provides NIC teaming and Layer 2 adjacency across a wider area

■   Supports high-availability clustering using Layer 2 adjacency

■   Extends VLANs to support server requirements

■   Supports custom application requirements

A Layer 3 design has these advantages:

■   Manages loops with less difficulty

■   Supports faster convergence of the network

■   Can minimize broadcast domain sizes, leading to better stability

■   Supports link utilization on all active uplinks

Depending on the organization and the network requirements, you also need to consider these factors:

■ How skilled your staff is in Layer 2 or Layer 3 technology, which will impact the time to resolve issues.

■ Oversubscription requirements for the aggregation layer switches, which impacts scaling capabilities.

■ Service module support and placement, which impacts scaling and costs.

■ The data center access layer provides physical attachment for servers using a Layer 2 or Layer 3 design.

■ Layer 2 access designs can extend VLANs between aggregation switches and support more Layer 2 adjacency options.

■ Looped designs provide a deterministic design that support network resiliency with dual-homing and RSTP.

■ Loop-free designs provide most Layer 2 features without looped topologies.

■ FlexLinks provide an active/standby pair of uplinks defined on a common access layer switch.

■ Layer 3 access designs provide fast convergence and stability, but support fewer adjacency options.

■ Blade servers increase server density and support Layer 2 or Layer 3 access.

Scaling the Data Center Architecture

As data center applications grow, the need to scale the data center also grows. The choice of access layer switch design can affect how the data center can be scaled. EtherChannel technologies and service module designs also provide options for scaling the bandwidth and density of the data center aggregation layer.

Modular Versus 1RU Designs

The access layer server components consist of 1RU servers, blade servers with integral switches, blade servers with pass-through cabling, clustered servers, and mainframes with Open Systems Adapters (OSA). The access layer network infrastructure consists of modular switches, fixed-configuration 1RU or two rack unit (2RU) switches, and blade server switches.

There are trade-offs to consider when increasing the size of the data center with either a modular or 1RU solution. These are some of the most common considerations in choosing access layer platforms:

■ **Cabling design:** Cable density in the server cabinet and under the floor can be difficult to manage and support. With a higher density of servers per rack, cable routing and management can become quite difficult to manage and maintain.

- **Cooling requirements:** Cable bulk can create cooling challenges if air passages are blocked by the number of cables at the cabinet base entry. Servers in the rack may require more cooling volume because of their higher density. The use of 1RU access switches can improve the cabling design.

- **Power requirements:** The increased density of components in the rack is driving a need for a larger power feed to the rack. Many data centers do not have the power capacity at the server rows to support this increase. Spreading out server racks in the data center can help resolve this issue.

- **Density:** Considering the density of servers along with the maximum number of interfaces used per rack and per row can help determine whether a modular or a 1RU solution is a better fit. If multiple ports per rack are used, it might take many 1RU switches in each rack to support them. Modular switches that are spaced out in the row might reduce the complexity in terms of the number of switches, and permit more flexibility in supporting varying numbers of server interfaces.

- **10 Gigabit Ethernet and 10 Gigabit EtherChannel uplink support:** It is important to determine what the oversubscription ratio is per application. When this value is known, it can be used to determine the correct amount of uplink bandwidth that is required on the access layer switch. Choosing a switch that can support 10 Gigabit Ethernet and 10 Gigabit EtherChannel might be an important option when considering current or future oversubscription ratios.

- **Resiliency features:** When servers are connected with a single NIC at the access layer, the access switch becomes a single point of failure. This makes features such as redundant power and redundant processors much more important in the access layer switch.

- **Intended use:** A development network might not require the redundancy or the software-rich features that are required by the production environment.

The right solution is usually based on business requirements and can be a hybrid implementation.

Cabinet Design with 1RU Switching

The advantage to the 1RU switching design is that it minimizes the number of cables needed from each cabinet, as diagrammed in Figure 5-30.

The access layer switch is located inside the cabinet with the servers, and the cabling from the servers to the access switch is contained in the cabinet. There are several considerations with top-of-rack designs:

- **Cooling requirements:** Although it will be easier to provide cooling volumes with less cable bulk entering the cabinet, the cooling requirements of the servers typically do not permit a full rack of servers. You could expect to see 25 to 30 1RU servers in a rack.

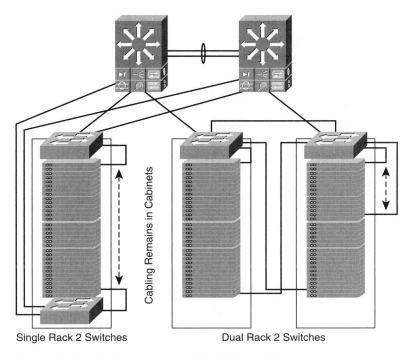

Figure 5-30 *Cabinet Design with 1RU Switching*

■ **Additional Gigabit EtherChannel (GEC) or 10 Gigabit Ethernet uplinks:** The increase in uplinks from the access layer switches requires higher GEC or 10 Gigabit Ethernet density at the aggregation layer or additional aggregation modules.

■ **Higher STP processing:** For Layer 2 looped access layer topologies, the increase in uplinks increases the STP active logical ports and the virtual port per line card instances at the aggregation layer, creating more overhead and processing requirements.

■ **More devices to manage:** The 1RU designs implement more network devices as compared to modular designs. The additional devices add to the management complexity.

■ **Number of 1RU switches required:** The port density needs to support all the servers and all the features per server planned for the cabinet. There are typically three to four interfaces connected on a server for features such as NIC teaming and out-of-band (OOB) management. Multiple 1RU switches might be needed, and they may require redundant power supplies. 1RU switches do not support redundant CPUs.

Example: Network Topology with 1RU Switching Model

This example discusses the network topology needed to support 1000 servers using 1RU switching in the access layer. In Figure 5-31, 80 switches have been provisioned to support 1000 servers based on 25 servers per cabinet, 40 cabinets, and 2 1RU switches per cabinet. The 80 switches in the topology require 2 uplinks per switch or 160 uplinks to the aggregation layer.

Figure 5-31   *Network Topology with 1RU Switching Model*

Note: Using a modular switch design with a Cisco Catalyst 6509 switch, the 1000 servers could be supported with about 8 access layer switches needing 16 uplinks to the aggregation layer.

The advantage to the 1RU switching model is efficient cabling, which supports improved cooling to the cabinet. The disadvantage of the 1RU switching model is the necessity to support an increased number of devices under network management and STP processing.

Cabinet Design with Modular Access Switches

The modular switching design minimizes the number of switches needed to support the servers and the number of uplinks needed. The access layer switches are typically located outside of the server cabinet at the ends of the row or distributed within the row. Cabling from the servers to the access switch is routed under raised floors or in overhead trays.

There are several advantages with modular designs:

- **Decreased management complexity:** There are fewer devices to manage, which makes this task less complex.

- **Decreased STP processing:** With fewer devices in the Layer 2 infrastructure and significantly fewer uplinks, there is less impact on STP processing.

- **Redundancy options:** Redundant switch power and CPUs can be supported on modular switches.

There are some disadvantages with modular designs:

- **Cable bulk:** More cabling needs to be routed and managed.

- **Cooling constraints:** The cable bulk at the cabinet floor entry can be difficult to manage and can block cool airflow.

Example: Network Topology with Modular Access Switches

In Figure 5-32, 8 Catalyst 6509 switches have been provisioned to support 1000 servers. The 8 switches in the topology require 2 uplinks per switch, or 16 uplinks to the aggregation layer.

Note: With the 1RU switch design, the 1000 servers could be supported with about 80 access layer switches needing 160 uplinks to the aggregation layer.

The advantages to the modular switching topology are fewer devices to manage and fewer uplinks to the aggregation layer. This lowers the STP processing requirements.

The disadvantage of the modular switching model is that there are challenges inherent in implementing and managing the cabling from the servers to the access switches. The cable bulk at the cabinet entry location can significantly impede cooling. One technique to help manage the cabling is to install the copper cabling in trays above the equipment racks and install the fiber cabling below the floor.

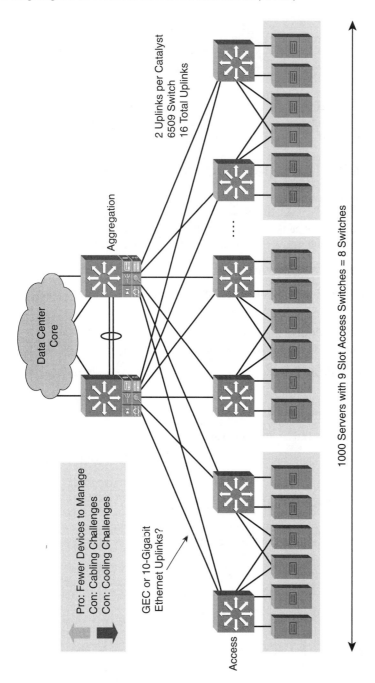

Figure 5-32   *Example: Network Topology with Modular Access Switches*

Server NIC Density

The number of NICs required per server will affect how many servers can be supported per switch. When planning for NIC support on switches, the data center designer should plan for at least three NICs per server:

■ Front-end interface for public access.

■ Storage interface on Gigabit Ethernet or Fibre Channel host bus adapter (HBA).

■ Backup interface for server backup.

■ Back-end interface for private access.

■ OOB management interface. This is a low-bandwidth application, so it can be supported on low-end switches.

NIC port density has implications on network design. It may require more than two 1RU switches per server cabinet. For example, if there are 30 servers in a rack, you could need 120 ports (30 * 4 ports = 120). This density requires three 48-port 1RU switches per cabinet. As part of the data center design, you might need to implement hard limits on servers per rack to support the cabling capacity of the access switch.

Cross-cabinet cabling should be avoided because it is difficult to manage.

Hybrid Example with a Separate OOB Switch

Figure 5-33 shows a design that has both modular and 1RU switches in the design. Both 1RU switches and modular switches are implemented in cabinets at the end of the row of server switches.

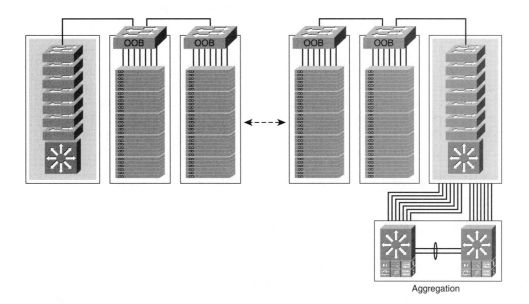

Aggregation

Figure 5-33 *Hybrid Example with Separate OOB Switches*

The design provides a lot of flexibility if you have sufficient cabling infrastructure to support the server to access switch cabling. The hybrid design provides benefits of using both 1RU switches and modular switches. The 1RU switches provide lower power consumption. The modular switches provide options for redundant CPUs and power supplies for critical applications. The design can also support NIC teaming. Low-end 1RU switches can be implemented in server cabinets to provide OOB management support.

Oversubscription and Uplinks

To define the correct amount of uplink bandwidth that is required on the access layer switch, you need to determine what the oversubscription ratio is per uplink.

The oversubscription ratio per server value can be determined by dividing the total number of server Gigabit Ethernet connections by the total aggregated uplink bandwidth on the access layer switch. For example, the ratio for a Catalyst 6509 switch with four 10 Gigabit Ethernet ECMP uplinks that supports 336 server access ports can be calculated as follows:

336 Gigabit Ethernet connections with 40-Gb uplink bandwidth = 8.4:1 oversubscription ratio

The oversubscription ratio per server is important for several reasons:

■ The ability to send a large file in a specific amount of time can be critical to cluster operation and performance.

■ Future server platform upgrade cycles will increase levels of outbound traffic.

■ The PCI-X or PCI-Express NICs provide a high-speed transfer bus speed and use large amounts of memory.

Choosing a switch that can support 10 Gigabit Ethernet and 10 Gigabit EtherChannel uplinks might be an important option when considering current or future oversubscription ratios. Depending on your future server requirements, you may want flexibility in adjusting the oversubscription ratio by upgrading to 10 Gigabit Ethernet or 10 Gigabit Ether-Channel. This ability may be better supported in modular switches than in 1RU switches. Modular switches also support the ability to upgrade the CPU and switch fabric.

Optimizing EtherChannel Utilization with Load Balancing

Test results show that EtherChannel ports configured with the default Layer 3 hash may not provide optimal utilization (see Figure 5-34).

To enable the Layer 3 IP plus Layer 4 port-based CEF hashing algorithm for EtherChannel ports, use the **port-channel load-balance** command. This command can improve load distribution for EtherChannel ports because it presents more unique values to the hashing algorithm by leveraging the automatic source-port randomization in the client TCP stack.

Figure 5-34   *Optimizing EtherChannel Utilization with Load Balancing*

Optimizing EtherChannel Utilization with Min-Links

The EtherChannel Min-Links feature allows a minimum number of available ports to be specified for a port channel to be considered a valid path (see Figure 5-35).

```
Agg1#configure terminal
Agg1 (config) # interface port-channel 1
Agg1 (config-if) # port-channel min-links 2
Agg1 (config-if) # end
```

Figure 5-35   *Optimizing EtherChannel Utilization with Min-Links*

This feature enables the user to set a minimum threshold for the number of links in an EtherChannel that must be in a link-up state, so that if fewer than the specified number of links are available, the port channel interface fails over to a standby EtherChannel. Min-Links are enabled with the **port-channel min-links** command.

The Min-Links feature is available as of Cisco IOS Software Release 12.2(18)SXF on Link Aggregation Control Protocol (LACP) EtherChannels. The Min-Links feature works at the physical interface level and is independent of spanning-tree path selection. The access layer topology can consist of looped, loop-free, or FlexLink models. This feature can be useful in making sure that a higher-bandwidth uplink path is chosen as the active path in the data center access layer. It causes LACP EtherChannels to become inactive if they have too few active member ports to supply the required minimum bandwidth.

There are some implications to using Min-Links:

- **Active/standby service modules:** If active services are primarily on the Agg1 aggregation switch, a failure that forces Min-Links to use the path to the Agg2 aggregation switch will likely cause all traffic to also traverse the ISL between the aggregation switches.

- **Dual failures:** With Min-Links, it is possible to have a situation where both uplinks would be forced down if both EtherChannels do not have the minimum required port members, which would black-hole all connected servers.

- **Looped topologies with the spanning tree:** If a looped access topology is used, it is possible to provide a similar capability by using the spanning-tree **pathcost method long** global option. This permits the spanning tree to use larger cost values when comparing the cost of different paths to root, which in turn can differentiate the cost value of various paths when a port member fails.

Scaling with Service Layer Switches

As the access layer demands increase in terms of bandwidth and server interface requirements, the uplinks to the aggregation layer are migrating beyond Gigabit Ethernet or GEC speeds and moving to 10 Gigabit Ethernet to get the full bandwidth without the hash implications.

One mechanism for scaling 10 Gigabit Ethernet port density is to move services off of the aggregation layer switches onto service layer switches that are connected via EtherChannel or GEC. The service switch is connected to both aggregation switches with GEC or 10 Gigabit Ethernet links configured as IEEE 802.1Q trunks (see Figure 5-36).

Moving classic bus-based service modules out of the aggregation layer switch increases the number of available slots and improves aggregation layer performance. Service switches are useful when a farm of classic bus-based Cisco CSMs or SSL offload modules are required.

Note: When a single classic bus module exists in the aggregation switch, all line cards that are not distributed forwarding card (DFC)-enabled must perform truncated header lookup. Performance in the aggregation layer is improved when the classic bus-based service modules are on service layer switches.

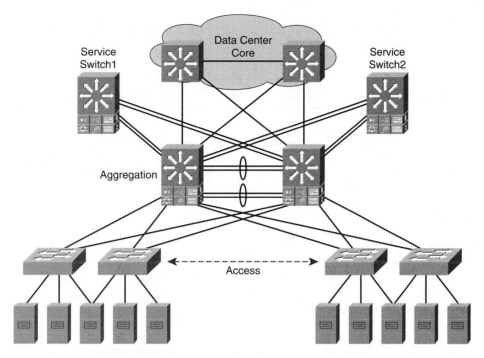

Figure 5-36 *Scaling with Service Layer Switches*

There are some implications to implementing service-level switches:

■ It might be necessary to implement QoS or separate links for fault-tolerant paths.

■ Only necessary Layer 2 VLANs should be extended to the service switches through 802.1Q trunks.

■ If a Cisco CSM in a service switch is configured for RHI, a Layer 3 link to the aggregation layer switch is necessary, because RHI knows how to insert a host route into only the routing table of the local MSFC. A Layer 3 link permits a routing protocol to redistribute the host route to the aggregation layer.

Scaling Service on Cisco ACE Modules

Another way to scale uplink port density and aggregation layer switch slots is to use Cisco ACE modules.

The Cisco ACE module can consolidate the functions of SLB, SSL acceleration, and firewall services such as protocol inspection and filtering into one service module. With the consolidation of functions, a TCP flow is terminated only once, at the Cisco ACE module, instead of at four or more places across the network. This saves time, processing power, and memory. The Cisco ACE module functions as a fabric-enabled line card and, depending on the license, can support 4 Gb/s, 8 Gb/s, or 16 Gb/s throughput.

The Cisco ACE module can support active/active service module designs.

> **Note:**   Because the Cisco ACE module is new, there may be some service module features not yet available on the current Cisco ACE software release.

Scaling Spanning Tree and High Availability

As data centers grow, the ability to scale the STP design across the data center is often necessary to meet application requirements, such as Layer 2 adjacency, and to permit a high level of flexibility in administering the servers. As more resources are deployed in the data center, there is also an increased need for high-availability solutions.

Scalability

The ability to extend VLANs across the data center is not only necessary to meet application requirements such as Layer 2 adjacency, but to permit a high level of flexibility in administering the servers. STP designs should answer several scaling questions:

- **How many VLANs can be supported in a single aggregation module?**
  Consolidating many data centers into a few is one of the drivers for larger Layer 2 domains.

- **Can a "VLAN anywhere" model be supported to avoid pruning?** Customers want to meet server installation requirements without the need to place them in the same physical proximity, and want simplified management of additions, moves, and changes.

- **How many access switches can be supported in each aggregation module?**
  Growth in data centers and 1RU access layer designs increase the number of access switches to be supported.

- **What are the maximum number of logical ports and virtual ports in STP?** STP logical and hardware restrictions can impact the data center design.

> **Note:**   STP logical ports and virtual ports are discussed in this section.

STPs in the Data Center

The STPs recommended in data center design are IEEE 802.1w, which Cisco implements as an RSTP called Rapid Per-VLAN Spanning Tree Plus (RPVST+), and IEEE 802.1s or Multiple Spanning Tree (MST). Both RSTP and MST have quick convergence characteristics but differ in flexibility and operation.

RSTP is the most common STP used in the data center today, and is the implementation recommended by Cisco for the enterprise data center. RSTP has several desirable characteristics for the enterprise data center:

- It scales to a large size (about 10,000 logical ports).

- Coupled with UDLD, loop guard, root guard, and BPDU guard, it provides a strong and stable Layer 2 design solution.

■   It is a proven solution that is easy to implement and scale.

MST is not as common in the enterprise data center because of its characteristics:

■   It permits large-scale STP implementations (about 30,000 logical ports). This is typically more useful for service providers and application service providers.

■   It isn't as flexible as RSTP.

■   It has service module implications for firewalls in transparent mode.

■   It is more commonly used with service providers and application service providers.

Note: This book focuses on the use of RSTP.

STP Scaling

Table 5-2 looks at the maximum scalability for STPs on aggregation switches in the data center.

Table 5-2   *Cisco STP Scaling Recommendations*

	MST	RPVST+ (RSTP)	PVST+
Total Active STP Logical Interfaces	50,000 Total		
	30,000 Total with Cisco IOS Software Release 12.2(17b)SXA	10,000 Total	13,000 Total
Total Virtual Ports per LineCard	6000 per Switching Module	1800 per Switching Module (6700)	1800 per Switching Module
		1200 for Earlier Modules	

In a Layer 2 looped topology design, spanning-tree processing instances are created on each interface for each active VLAN. These logical instances are used to process the spanning-tree-related packets for each VLAN. These instances are referred to as active logical ports and virtual ports.

Both active logical ports and virtual ports are important values to consider in spanning-tree designs because they affect STP convergence time and stability. Later on Figure 5-38 shows the maximum number of logical interfaces and virtual ports supported on Cisco Catalyst 6500 series switches with a Cisco Catalyst 6500 series Supervisor Engine 720 using Cisco IOS Software Release 12.2SX. These values are usually of concern only on the aggregation layer switches that have a larger number of trunks and VLANs configured than other layers in the data center topology.

When designing a large data center using extended Layer 2 VLAN topologies, it is necessary to calculate the spanning-tree logical and virtual ports to ensure that spanning tree operates with optimal convergence and stability characteristics.

STP Logical Interfaces

Active logical ports are a systemwide value that reflects the total number of spanning-tree processing instances used in the whole system.

Total active logical interfaces can be calculated by a formula:

Sum [(Each trunk on the switch) * (Active VLANs on each trunk)] + (Number of nontrunking interfaces on the switch)

In Figure 5-37, there are 10 VLANs on ACC1 and 20 VLANs on ACC2. There is an EtherChannel trunk between AGG1 and AGG2 on a pair of 10 Gigabit Ethernet links.

The total number of STP active logical interfaces on AGG1 in the figure is calculated like this:

[(10 on Te7/3) + (20 on Te7/4)] + (30 on EtherChannel Te7/1-2) = 60

Note: An STP instance for all 30 VLANs defined in the system configuration is present on each trunk unless manual VLAN pruning is performed. For example, on each trunk configuration the **switchport trunk allowed vlan x, y** command must be performed to reduce the number of spanning-tree logical interfaces being used on that port. The automatic VLAN Trunking Protocol (VTP) pruning feature does not remove STP logical instances from the port.

Figure 5-37   *STP Logical Interfaces*

You can also determine the active logical interfaces on a switch by using the **show spanning-tree summary total** command.

Virtual ports are STP instances allocated to each trunk port on a line card. Virtual ports are a per-line card value that reflects the total number of spanning-tree processing instances used on a particular line card. The number of virtual ports per line card is calculated by another formula:

> Sum (each port used as a trunk or part of a port-channel in a trunk) * (Active VLANs on each trunk)

Virtual ports are calculated per port in channel groups; so for AGG1 in the figure, they are calculated like this:

> (30 on Te7/1) + (30 on Te7/2) + (10 on Te7/3) + (20 on Te7/4) = 90 virtual ports

You can also determine the virtual ports on a switch module by using the **show vlan virtual-ports slot** command.

STP Scaling with 120 Systemwide VLANs

In Figure 5-38, the data center has a Layer 2 looped topology with 120 VLANs systemwide. No manual pruning is being performed on the trunks. This is a 1RU access switch design, and 45 access switches are connected to each aggregation switch using 4 GECs.

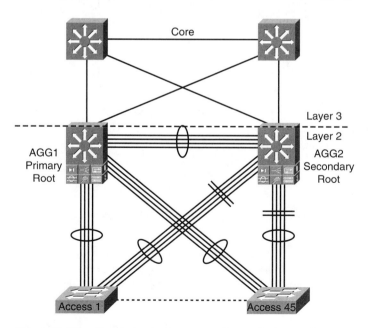

Figure 5-38   *Example: Active Logical Interfaces*

The number of active logical interfaces is calculated like this:

(120 * 45 access links) + (120 instances on link to AGG2) = 5400 + 120 = 5520

5520 is under the maximum recommendation of 10,000 active logical interfaces supported when using RSTP.

When you consider the virtual ports per line card, there are design issues with a port that uses 120 systemwide VLANs and 45 access links.

If a Cisco Catalyst 6748 Ethernet line card is used on AGG1 to terminate the access switches, it could connect 12 of the 45 access switches on 4 GECs.

The number of virtual ports is calculated like this:

(120 * 48 access links) = 5760

5750 is greater than 1800, which is the maximum number of recommended virtual ports per switching module when using RSTP.

The STP design recommendations are exceeded with 120 VLANs.

Note: The maximum number of VLANs that can be safely supported in this design is 37 (1800 divided by 48). In this case, MST should be used because it would be less than 6000, which is the maximum number of recommended virtual ports per switching module when using 802.1s/MST (Cisco Data Center Infrastructure 2.5 Design Guide, p.74, Chapter 5).

This is not a supported design, and there will be problems when convergence situations arise. This example design will experience various issues such as long convergence times and possibly degraded system-level stability.

You can expect to see a larger network impact when interfaces change between the shutdown and no shutdown states because the large number of virtual interfaces will greatly slow STP convergence times. You will also get a large number of system messages.

STP in 1RU Designs

The use of 1RU access switch designs increases the chances of a larger spanning-tree diameter and the possibility of more STP issues.

The integral switch on the blade server is logically similar to the 1RU access switch design. The same challenges apply to 1RU and blade server designs relative to the increase in spanning-tree logical and virtual ports. There are a few STP issues to consider with these designs:

■   A higher number of access-link trunks will increase STP logical port counts in the aggregation layer.

- You should determine the spanning-tree logical ports, virtual interfaces in place, and STP domain limits before extending VLANs or adding trunks.

- You can use multiple aggregation modules to scale STP and 10 Gigabit Ethernet density.

STP Scaling Design Guidelines

You have several options to choose from when scaling STP designs and reducing the total number of logical ports:

- **Add aggregation modules:** Scale the design by dividing up the STP domain using multiple aggregation modules. When multiple aggregation modules are used, it permits the spanning-tree domain to be distributed. This reduces the total port count in any one domain, which would permit STP to function within the limits of the line card or switch.

- **Limit HSRP instances:** The number of VLANs is typically tied to the number of HSRP instances. Cisco recommends a maximum of 500 HSRP instances on the Catalyst 6500 series Supervisor Engine 720 with default timers. This is somewhat dependent on other CPU-driven processes.

- **Perform manual pruning on trunks:** If the logical interfaces and virtual ports in a Layer 2 domain are near the upper limits, perform manual pruning on the trunks. Although this can be somewhat cumbersome, it dramatically reduces the total number of both active logical and virtual port instances used.

- **Use MST if it meets the requirements:** If you cannot support the STP scaling issues with RSTP, you can consider implementing MST. MST supports a large number of logical port instances and is used in some of the largest data centers in the world. The drawbacks of using MST are that it does not have as much flexibility as other STPs, such as RSTP, and it might not be supported in certain service module configurations.

High Availability in the Data Center

The common points of failure in the data center are on the path from the server to the aggregation switch. Single-attached servers connected to single-attached access switches are susceptible to failures in the server network adapter, the network media, and the access switch (see Figure 5-39).

These network failure issues can be addressed by deployment of dual-attached servers using network adapter teaming software connected to dual-attached access switches.

Common NIC teaming configurations are discussed in this section.

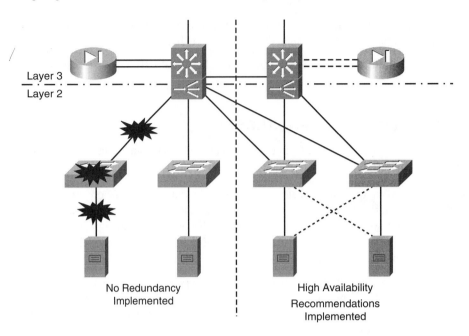

Figure 5-39   *High Availability in the Data Center*

Common NIC Teaming Configurations

Servers with a single NIC can have many single points of failure. The NIC, the cable, and the switch to which it connects are all single points of failure. NIC teaming eliminates this single point of failure by providing special drivers that allow two NICs to be connected to two different access switches or different line cards on the same access switch. If one NIC fails, the secondary NIC assumes the IP address of the server and takes over operation without disruption. The various types of NIC teaming solutions include active/standby and active/active. All NIC teaming solutions require the NICs to have Layer 2 adjacency with each other. There are three common NIC teaming configurations (see Figure 5-40):

- **Adapter fault tolerance (AFT):** With AFT designs, two NICs connect to the same switch. One adapter is active and the other standby, and they use one common IP address and MAC address.

- **Switch fault tolerance (SFT):** With SFT designs, one port is active and the other standby, and they use one common IP address and MAC address.

- **Adaptive load balancing (ALB):** With ALB designs, one port receives and all ports transmit using one IP address and multiple MAC addresses.

Note: NIC manufacturer drivers are changing and may operate differently. Also, some server operating systems have started integrating NIC teaming drivers.

Figure 5-40 *Common NIC Teaming Configurations*

Server Attachment Methods

EtherChannel is another means of providing scalable bandwidth for network servers such as large UNIX servers or PC-based web servers. Various attachments are illustrated in Figure 5-41.

Figure 5-41 *Server Attachment Methods*

In addition to single- and dual-connected servers, EtherChannel allows servers to bundle multiple links to allow higher throughputs between servers and clients, and to support redundancy.

Depending on the server, traffic from the server is distributed across the adapters in an EtherChannel based on a hash algorithm or in a round-robin fashion where packets are sent evenly across all adapters.

Incoming traffic to the server is also distributed across the adapters in the link. In addition, you can enable the Layer 3 IP plus Layer 4 port-based CEF hashing algorithm for EtherChannel ports by using the **port-channel load-balance** command. This command can improve load distribution for EtherChannel ports because it presents more unique values to the hashing algorithm by leveraging the automatic source-port randomization in the client TCP stack.

Note: Because the traffic is distributed across the adapters, it will not permit full utilization of the EtherChannel bandwidth for applications such as backups.

High Availability and Failover Times

The main objective in building a highly available data center network design is to avoid TCP session breakage while providing convergence that is unnoticeable, or as fast as possible. Figure 5-42 summarizes and compares failover times for various technologies.

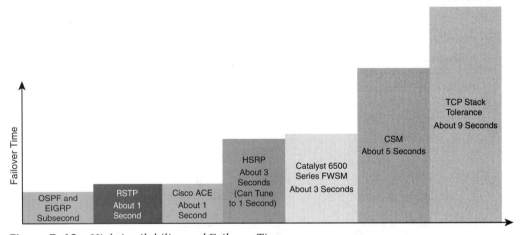

Figure 5-42   *High Availability and Failover Times*

The overall failover time in the data center is the combination of convergence at Layer 2, Layer 3, and Layer 4 components. The network components have different recovery times:

■   Tuned routing protocols can failover in less than one second. OSPF and EIGRP can both achieve subsecond convergence time with recommended timer configurations.

■   RSTP converges in about 1 second. RSTP permits subsecond convergence time for minor failures when logical ports are under watermarks, and can take 1 second to 2 seconds for major failure conditions.

■   EtherChannel can fail over in about 1 second. When a link fails, Cisco EtherChannel technology redirects traffic from the failed link to the remaining links in less than 1 second.

■   Default HSRP timers are 3 seconds for the hello time and 10 seconds for the hold time. A recommended practice is to configure the timers with a hello time of 1 second and a hold time of 3 seconds so that convergence occurs in less than 3 seconds. Convergence can be adjusted down to subsecond values, but the CPU load must be considered.

■   Stateful service modules typically fail over within 3 to 5 seconds. The convergence time for both the Cisco Catalyst 6500 series FWSM and the CSM is about 5 seconds with recommended timers. Cisco ACE can achieve failovers in about 1 second with its active/active configuration.

■   The least tolerant TCP/IP stacks are the Windows Server and Windows XP client stacks, which have about a 9-second tolerance. Each of the TCP/IP stacks that are built in to the various operating systems has a different level of tolerance for determining when a TCP session will be dropped. Other TCP/IP stacks such as those found in Linux, HP, and IBM systems are more tolerant and have a longer window before tearing down a TCP session.

High Availability and Cisco NSF with SSO

The main objective in building a highly available data center network design is to avoid TCP session breakage while providing convergence that is unnoticeable, or as fast as possible. Cisco Nonstop Forwarding (NSF) with stateful switchover (SSO) are supervisor redundancy mechanisms that provide intrachassis SSO at Layers 2 to 4.

The worst-case convergence time is the event of a supervisor failure on AGG1 (illustrated in Figure 5-43), the primary aggregation switch, which results in all the components on the switch converging to the AGG2 aggregation switch. If the CSM is in use, this failover results in a minimum convergence time of about five seconds. This convergence time will most likely be more because tables such as the content-addressable memory (CAM) and ARP have to be rebuilt, so the maximum convergence time can approach the nine-second limit of the Windows TCP/IP stack.

This convergence time and possible lost sessions can be avoided by using dual Catalyst 6500 series Supervisor Engine 720 engines and Cisco NSF with SSO on the primary aggregation switch of the data center. SSO synchronizes the Layer 2 protocol state for trunks and ports; the Layer 2 and Layer 3 MAC, Forwarding Information Base (FIB), and adjacency hardware tables; and the access control list (ACL) and QoS tables. SSO is a prerequisite of Cisco NSF.

The main objective of Cisco NSF is to continue forwarding IP packets following a route processor switchover. Cisco NSF is supported by the EIGRP, OSPF, Intermediate System-to-Intermediate System (IS-IS) Protocol, and Border Gateway Protocol (BGP). Routers running these protocols can detect a switchover and take the necessary actions to continue forwarding network traffic using CEF while recovering route information from the peer devices. With Cisco NSF, peer networking devices do not experience routing flaps.

The recommended data center design that uses service modules has a minimum convergence time of about six to seven seconds, primarily because of service modules. If Cisco NSF with SSO is implemented, the service modules do not converge in the event of a supervisor failure. Implementing dual supervisors that use Cisco NSF with SSO can achieve increased high availability in the data center network.

Figure 5-43   *High Availability and Failover Times*

With the current Cisco IOS Release 12.2(25), HSRP state is not maintained by Cisco NSF with SSO. During a switchover on AGG1 (the primary aggregation switch), the AGG2 (the backup aggregation switch) HSRP instances take over for SSO control plane recovery. Because the HSRP MAC address is statefully maintained on the Catalyst 6500 series Supervisor Engine 720 module primary switch standby, the sessions continue to flow through the primary switch, regardless of the active state that appears on the backup aggregation switch. After the control plane comes up on the primary aggregation switch, the HSRP hello messages begin to flow and preemptively move the active HSRP state back to the primary aggregation switch.

You should not set the Interior Gateway Protocol (IGP) timers so aggressively or tune them so low that Cisco NSF with SSO is defeated. The IGP process should not react to adjacent node failure before an SSO can be determined.

Summary

This chapter reviewed design models, best practices, and methodology for data centers in the Cisco Enterprise Architecture. The data center architecture is based on a three-layer approach consisting of the core, aggregation, and access layers. The core layer provides a high-speed Layer 3 fabric for packet switching. The aggregation layer extends spanning-tree or Layer 3 routing protocols into the access layer. The data center access layer provides the physical-level attachment to the server resources, and operates in Layer 2 or Layer 3 modes, often with either a modular or 1RU design. Care needs to be taken when scaling STP in the data center and managing the total number of logical interfaces and virtual ports in an STP domain. EtherChannel technologies and service module designs are options for scaling the bandwidth and density of the data center aggregation layer.

References

For additional information, refer to these resources:

- Cisco Systems, Inc. "Enterprise Data Center Introduction," at http://www.cisco.com/en/US/netsol/ns340/ns394/ns224/networking_solutions_packages_list.html

- Cisco Systems, Inc. "Cisco Application Control Engine (ACE) Module At-A-Glance," at http://www.cisco.com/en/US/prod/collateral/modules/ps2706/ps6906/prod_brochure0900aecd804585e5.pdf

- Cisco Systems, Inc. "Cisco Data Center Network Architecture and Solutions Overview," at http://www.cisco.com/en/US/solutions/collateral/ns340/ns517/ns224/ns377/net_brochure0900aecd802c9a4f.pdf

- Cisco Systems, Inc. "Configuring EtherChannels and Layer 2 Trunk Failover and Link-State Tracking," at http://www.cisco.com/en/US/products/ps6748/products_configuration_guide_chapter09186a00806c3477.html#wp1346176

- Cisco Systems, Inc. "Cisco Data Center Infrastructure 2.5 Design Guide," at http://www.cisco.com/univercd/cc/td/doc/product/lan/cat3750/12225see/scg/swethchl.pdf

- Cisco Systems, Inc. "Understanding InfiniBand," at http://www.cisco.com/en/US/prod/collateral/ps6418/ps6419/ps6421/prod_white_paper0900aecd8043ba1d.pdf

- Cisco Systems, Inc. "Advanced Services' Building Cisco Enterprise Data Center Architecture," at http://www.cisco.com/en/US/services/ps11/ps2696/ps2804/services_data_sheet0900aecd80281d85.pdf

Review Questions

Answer the following questions, and then refer to Appendix A, "Answers to Review Questions," for the answers.

1. What are the benefits of the three layer model? (Choose three.)

   a. Providing redundant Internet services

   b. Support for NIC teaming

   c. Support for Layer 2 domain sizing

   d. Support for one fixed access layer model

   e. Support for a mix of access layer models

2. What are the design recommendations for OSPF in the data center? (Choose three.)

   a. Use NSSA from the core layer down.

   b. Use NSSA from the aggregation layer down.

   c. Adjust the default bandwidth value with the **auto-cost reference-bandwidth** command.

   d. Adjust the default bandwidth value with the **auto-cost bandwidth** command.

   e. Tune the timers with the **timers throttle spf** command.

3. What are the characteristics of a Layer 2 looped design model? (Choose two.)

   a. VLANs do not extend to the aggregation layer.

   b. Layer 2 services from the aggregation layer such as NIC teaming are supported.

   c. Redundancy can be supported using a trunk between the access switches.

   d. VLANs are extended to the aggregation layer.

   e. STP is not needed for reliable operation.

   f. All uplinks are active, and none are blocking.

4. Which design is most susceptible to black-holing of service module traffic in the event of an uplink failure?

   a. Layer 2 loop-free *U*

   b. Layer 2 looped square

   c. Layer 2 looped triangle

   d. Layer 2 loop-free inverted *U*

   e. Layer 2 looped inverted triangle

5. What are the characteristics of a Layer 3 access design model? (Choose three.)

  a. VLANs do not extend to the aggregation layer.

  b. VLANs are extended to the aggregation layer.

  c. All uplinks are active, and none are blocking.

  d. Layer 2 server adjacency is supported across a single pair of access switches.

  e. Layer 2 server adjacency is not supported across access switches.

6. What are the characteristics of 1RU access switch designs as compared to modular access switch designs? (Choose three.)

  a. VLANs do not extend to the aggregation layer.

  b. Cabling from the cabinet is minimized.

  c. Uplinks to the aggregation layer are minimized.

  d. Cooling requirements are eased.

  e. STP processing requirements are minimized.

  f. The number of devices to manage increases.

7. What command is used to enable an EtherChannel hash for Layer 3 IP plus Layer 4 port-based Cisco Express Forwarding?

  a. mpls ip cef

  b. port-channel ip cef

  c. mpls ip port-channel cef

  d. port-channel load-balance

  e. mpls ip load-balance

8. Where are service layer switches typically connected in the data center architecture?

  a. At the core layer in Layer 2 access layer designs

  b. At the service layer in Layer 3 access layer designs

  c. At the access layer in Layer 2 access layer designs

  d. At the access layer in Layer 3 access layer designs

  e. At the aggregation layer in Layer 2 access layer designs

  f. At the aggregation layer in Layer 3 access layer designs

9. What are STP virtual ports?

   a.   A systemwide value that reflects the total uplinks that are not blocked

   b.   The total number of trunking interfaces on a line card

   c.   A systemwide value that reflects the total number of spanning-tree processing instances used

   d.   A per-line card value that reflects the total number of spanning-tree processing instances used on a particular line card

   e.   A per-line card value that is the sum of all ports used as trunks or part of a port-channel in a trunk

10. The integral switch on a blade server is logically similar to what design?

   a.   Layer 3 access design

   b.   1RU access switch design

   c.   Enterprisewide MST design

   d.   Modular access switch design

   e.   Multiple aggregation module design

11. What component has the largest failover time?

   a.   ACE module

   b.   FWSM

   c.   Tuned EIGRP

   d.   CSM

   e.   RSTP

   f.   HSRP

After completing this chapter, you will be able to:

- Describe SAN components and technologies
- Discuss basic SAN design and SAN extension
- Discuss SAN design using Cisco MDS 9000 series multilayer switches
- Describe SAN extension considerations

CHAPTER 6

SAN Design Considerations

The *storage-area network* (SAN) is a set of protocols and technologies that permit storage devices to have direct connections with servers over some distance. In addition, a SAN permits the storage devices to be shared among a number of servers based on select criteria. Finally, using VSAN technologies (virtual SAN), a group of discrete SANs can be connected together using a "virtual" SAN fabric.

This chapter introduces you to SAN design considerations. Beginning with the business drivers for storage-area networking, SAN components and technologies are explored. Finally, the protocols that govern SAN behavior are examined, along with references to Cisco MDS 9000 switches.

Identifying SAN Components and Technologies

SAN technology is designed to remotely attach storage devices such as disk drives to host computers. SAN technology enables a high throughput and therefore high performance. For example, an advantage of a SAN is that data access is provided at a block level via the Small Computer Systems Interface (SCSI) protocol (see Figure 6-1).

In a SAN network, the clients request files from the servers, which have knowledge of the file system structure. The servers request specific blocks of data from a storage element in the back-end storage network.

SAN technology supports shared storage that is separate from the server or servers that use it. Storage resources are easily moved or allocated with no interruption of service on the servers. Managing a SAN tends to be more complex than direct-attached storage (DAS). However, SANs provide a lower total cost of ownership (TCO) because the storage is not captive to one server and so there is a more efficient utilization of storage resources. The consolidation of multiple lower-end storage systems into centralized, higher-end systems allows for reduced administrative overhead. Backup is easier with SAN technology because it does not tie up host capacity, nor does it require a dedicated network or bandwidth on the main network. SAN technology also supports the fast implementation of high availability.

The hardware that connects servers to storage devices in a SAN is referred to as a *fabric*. The SAN fabric enables connectivity of any server to any storage device through the use of *Fibre Channel* switching technology. Fibre Channel is a standard from the T11 Technical Committee of the InterNational Committee for Information Technology Standards

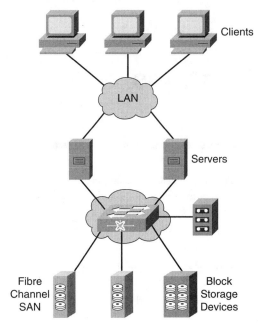

Figure 6-1   *SAN Overview*

(INCITS), an American National Standards Institute (ANSI)-accredited standards committee. The SAN fabric provides a high-speed dedicated network, with high-availability features, high throughput, and very low latency. When storage resources are consolidated
into the same fabric, organizations can more easily make use of many features, including
data replication, data sharing, and centralized backups.

The following are some of the business drivers for SAN deployments:

■   Escalating storage requirements

■   Rising storage management costs

■   Business continuity

■   Requirement to share information

■   Increasing levels of underutilized disk storage resources resulting in increased backup
    storage and backup handling costs

One disadvantage to SANs is that there is limited vendor interoperability.

SAN Components

There are three main components to a SAN: host bus adapters (HBA), data storage devices,
and storage subsystems.

An *HBA* is an I/O adapter that provides connectivity between a host server and a storage
device. The HBA is used to connect a device to a SAN using a Fibre Channel interface. In-

telligent HBAs perform many of the lower-level I/O functions to minimize the CPU impact on the host server. HBA connection methods can be either copper or fiber, similar to a typical LAN adapter.

The fundamental idea of SAN is to connect hosts to storage devices. Most data storage is done through the use of hard disk drives. Hard disk technology has been used in personal computers and servers for years. Hard disks use a number of different technologies. Interfaces on the hard disks can be one of the following:

- SCSI

- Fibre Channel

- Advanced Technology Attachment (ATA)

- Integrated Drive Electronics (IDE)

- Serial ATA (SATA)

Disk drives themselves cannot sit directly on the network. The technologies listed represent the controller intelligence that enables the drives to be used. The means needed for physical connectivity may vary. There are several methods of connecting storage devices to their host CPUs:

- **Parallel SCSI copper interconnects:** Provides historically based external server storage. Scalability tends to be a problem. Cable distances are limited.

- **Optical direct connect:** Provides much longer distance capability than SCSI copper connections.

- **Fibre Channel switch:** Provides the most scalability and complete feature set. The Fibre Channel switches are the basis for the Fibre Channel network.

Other storage devices include tape drives and CD/DVD drives.

Storage systems connect storage devices to the network. Storage organization can be supported through various subsystems from simplistic to complex with large volumes of storage and many services available. Here are some examples of storage subsystems:

- **Just a bunch of disks (JBOD):** "JBOD" refers to a simple disk array. An example of a JBOD is a server with an external cable to a cabinet that has several pluggable hard disks in it. They share the cabinet and power. It may have a Redundant Array of Independent/Inexpensive Disks (RAID) controller in it or it may not. The JBOD can be connected via SCSI technology. It can also use Fibre Channel technology. Fibre Channel–attached disks are connected to what is essentially a Fibre Channel hub.

- **Storage arrays:** Intelligent storage arrays are a group of devices that provide mass storage and other functions and services. Various internal architectures based on a bus architecture or a switched architecture are possible with storage arrays. To the SAN, the storage system internal architecture is not important. Storage arrays fundamentally include these components:
  - Connected devices (host connections) that can be supported through Fibre Channel or direct connections.

- Disk drive technologies.
- Cache that can support read-only and read-write access. Cache can be implemented with backup power sources to ensure data integrity.

- **RAID:** RAID is a technology in which disk drives are combined and configured to provide increased performance and fault tolerance.

RAID Overview

RAID is a method used to inexpensively put together a set of physical hard drives into a logical array of storage devices. RAID provides fault tolerance compared to standalone disk drives. RAID does this by mirroring data or implementing parity check operations. RAID can be performed using hardware or host-based software.

Several types of RAID can be used, including one or more of these:

- **RAID 0 (striping):** Two or more disk drives are concatenated together to form one large volume. Read and write operations can be done in parallel. RAID 0 is done for performance and increase capacity. It provides no redundancy.

- **RAID 1 (mirroring):** Data is duplicated on multiple disks. This can be done for increased reliability and availability. If Raid 1 is used on two drives, it provides twice the read transaction rate of single disks and the same write transaction rate as single disks. RAID 1 doubles the requirement for disk drives.

- **RAID 3 (error detection):** Data is striped across multiple disks, and a dedicated disk drive is used for maintaining error-correction information. This can be done for added reliability and availability. RAID 3 offers no protection for the parity disk, and therefore is rarely used.

- **RAID 5 (error correction):** Data and parity information is striped across multiple disks. This is commonly done for added reliability and availability. The error-correction information is striped on all disks. This adds a level of protection to data and parity. Redundancy with RAID 5 is better than with RAID 3, because if one drive fails the array can still function and when the drive is replaced the RAID controller will dynamically rewrite the data on the new drive. RAID 5 is one of the most commonly used implementations of RAID.

RAID technology can be used as a protection mechanism for SAN along with cache mirroring, data mirroring, and remote replication. The RAID types can also be combined, for example RAID5 arrays can be "mirrored" with another RAID5 array for an additional element of protection.

Storage Topologies

Storage topologies come in one of two main types: directly attached storage and, network-attached storage (NAS) topologies. DAS is a topology where the storage devices connect directly to the server. Storage devices that can be attached to the IP network are called NAS devices.

DAS

DAS is commonly described as captive storage. DAS is often implemented in a parallel SCSI implementation. Devices in a captive storage topology do not have direct access to the storage network and do not support efficient sharing of storage. For example, the only way to access the DAS devices in Figure 6-2 is by using the CPU of the host.

Figure 6-2 *Direct-Attached Storage*

To access data on a DAS, a user must go through a front-end network. DAS devices provide little or no mobility to other servers and little scalability. DAS devices limit file sharing, and can be complex to implement and manage.

For example, to support data backups, DAS devices require resources on the host and spare disk systems that cannot be used on other systems.

NAS

A NAS device is dedicated to file sharing. NAS devices have direct IP capabilities that allow access at a file level using a protocol such as Network File System (NFS) or Common Internet File System (CIFS) across an IP network. NAS devices provide data storage and access and the management of these functions. NAS devices support file-serving requests so that resources can be freed up on other servers. NAS servers commonly use SCSI and RAID technologies internally. An NAS device is directly connected to a front-end network. Storage devices can be shared between servers and between users (see Figure 6-3).

NAS devices respond to requests by providing portions of the file system. To retrieve a file, a NAS device has to open a directory, read it, locate the file, check permissions, and

Figure 6-3   *Network-Attached Storage*

then transfer the file. If the file is several directories deep, the NAS device needs to perform repeated operations to retrieve one file. This process can require a lot of network
traffic, although TCP can be tuned to help optimize the file transport.

Note: The block-level access operations on DAS devices are much faster than operations
requiring a search of the file or directory system on a volume.

SAN Technologies

SAN devices communicate with each other using a variety of protocols. These protocols
are introduced in the following sections. The Cisco MDS 9000 family of switches offers a
number of enhancements for SANs, and a brief overview of VSAN, IVR (Inter-VSAN
Routing), and SANTap follows.

SCSI Overview

SCSI is a parallel interface technology used by hosts to attach peripheral devices such as
hard disks and tape drives.

SCSI technology supports writing blocks of one or more files or databases to an external
disk in a SAN. The files are written using the host system attributes, including permissions, file size, and modification date. The SCSI channel used to transmit SCSI commands, data, and status is the foundation for all communications in a SAN based on SCSI
devices. Connectivity between a SCSI host and a SCSI device can be supported on either
an internal or external connection.

SCSI uses a bus technology that supports multiple devices attached to a controller and can support daisy-chaining. Through the bus connection, a host can communicate with several SCSI devices using multiple half-duplex I/O channels. SCSI communication is commonly described as being between an initiator and a target. An *initiator* is typically the host computer. A *target* is typically the storage device. In the diagram, the initiator is a SCSI adapter, and the target is a RAID array.

The parallel SCSI specification contains these elements:

- Up to 75 foot (25 meter) bus length

- Shared channel bandwidth of up to 320 MB/s

- Up to 16 devices per SCSI bus

- Half-duplex operation

Daisy-chaining slightly increases SCSI scalability. Because daisy-chained storage devices are captive behind a server, this technology still has limitation from a networking perspective.

Note: The SCSI adapter can access 7 other devices plus itself when the bus width is 8 bits. When the bus width is 16 bits, the adapter can access up to 15 other devices.

Fibre Channel Overview

Fibre Channel is a serial, data transfer architecture with a high level of scalability and a bandwidth that supports the extension of SCSI technologies.

The serial connectivity of Fibre Channel provides a mechanism for transporting SCSI information across high-speed networks. Fibre Channel provides high-speed transport for the SCSI payload but overcomes the distance and limitations that come with parallel SCSI technology.

Fibre Channel includes these features:

- Addressing for up to 16 million nodes

- Loop (shared) and fabric (switched) transport options

- Host speeds of 100 to 400 MB/s, or an effective throughput of 1 to 4 Gb/s on the fabric

- Segment distances of up to 6 miles (10 km)

- Support for multiple protocols

Fibre Channel is the integration of the best attributes of host channel and networking technologies. Fibre Channel implements attributes from channel technology in the mainframe environment, including reliability and scalability. Fibre Channel also implements attributes from networking, including connectionless services, high connectivity, and long distances.

Fibre Channel supports three topologies: point to point, arbitrated loop (similar to Token Ring), and switched fabric. Fibre Channel switching is point-to-point oriented. Both the initiator and storage target side are points. Fibre Channel has become the dominant open systems protocol for connecting servers to storage.

Fibre Channel Communications Model

Fibre Channel communications is similar to TCP in the following aspects (summarized in Figure 6-4):

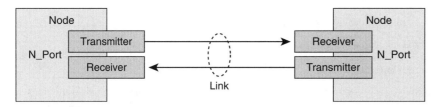

Figure 6-4   *Similarities Between Fibre Channel and TCP*

■ Fibre Channel communications are point-to-point oriented. A session is established between the two points through the device login. This session establishment is similar to TCP session establishment.

■ Fibre Channel supports a logical node connection point between node ports (N_ports). This is similar to TCP and UDP sockets.

■ Fibre Channel Protocol (FCP) supports flow control on an end-to-end basis using a buffer-to-buffer credit (BB_Credit) method. In BB_Credit flow control, the source and destination set the number of buffer credits allowed to accumulate before the source stops sending data. Each frame sent from the source must be acknowledged by the destination, and a buffer credit supports an unacknowledged frame. If an initiator wants to talk to a target, it first negotiates with the target for the number of BB_Credits allowed. During transmission, the source keeps a running count of buffer credits. If the number of credits reaches the maximum buffer credit, the source stops sending until it receives an acknowledgment from the destination. Flow control with Fibre Channel is similar to TCP flow control except that the Fibre Channel mechanism has no drops.

■ Fibre Channel supports acknowledgments for certain classes of traffic. For example, the Cisco MDS 9000 FCIP TCP stack is optimized for transporting storage traffic. It uses packet shaping to minimize the possibility of dropped packets and uses selective acknowledgment (SACK) and Fast Retransmit to recover quickly from congestion conditions. The classes are labeled 1, 2, 3, and F. For example, Class 2 uses acknowledgments for guaranteed delivery. The Fibre Channel support for acknowledgments for certain classes of traffic is similar to the TCP and UDP acknowledgment models.

■ Fibre Channel enables multiple sessions to be maintained per device. This mechanism is similar to multiple TCP and UDP sockets.

VSAN

A *virtual SAN* (VSAN), shown in Figure 6-5, is a logical SAN that provides isolation among devices that are physically connected to the same fabric.

Figure 6-5   *Virtual SANs*

A *SAN island* is a physically isolated switch or group of switches used to connect hosts to storage devices. The initial SAN deployments were more typically islands consisting of two to four switches.

The Cisco MDS 9000 SAN fabric family supports VSAN technology. VSANs provide the capability to overlay multiple virtual fabric environments within a single fabric infrastructure. This VSAN capability is sometimes called *fabric virtualization*. VSANs are a way to support independent virtual fabrics on a single switch. VSANs improve consolidation and simplify management by allowing for more efficient SAN utilization. Inter-VSAN Routing (IVR) allows a resource on any individual VSAN to be shared by users of a different VSAN without merging the fabrics.

An expansion port (E_Port) is an interface that functions as a fabric expansion port by connecting to another E_Port on another switch. E_Ports carry frames between switches for configuration and fabric management. The Cisco MDS 9000 series uses the Enhanced Inter-Switch Link (EISL) frame format to support virtual fabric trunking across trunking E_Ports (TE_Ports). Trunking enables interconnected ports to transmit and receive frames in more than one VSAN over the same physical link.

A good SAN design is required to build a large SAN and ultimately use a high number of ports. In Figure 6-5, there are several SAN islands. Instead of using different switches at each island, you can use VSANs. You can consolidate the islands into a single physical fabric but maintain logical separation. This cuts down on the physical connections needed to the various targets shared by different islands.

IVR

IVR is also known as fabric routing. IVR provides connectivity between fabrics without merging them. The connectivity is supported at Layer 3. By routing between VSANs, devices can maintain a level of separation in terms of fabric services and fabricwide events required for the highest level of availability and take advantage of data sharing across thousands of devices (see Figure 6-6).

Figure 6-6   *Inter-VSAN Routing*

IVR includes these features:

■ Sharing of centralized storage services such as tape libraries and disks across VSANs. Without IVR, you would be forced to merge the separate fabrics to share information between VSANs.

■ Enabling devices in different VSANs to communicate.

■ Enabling selective features between VSANs. One example is to enable replication across VSANs while preventing local devices from traversing the WAN.

IVR is not limited to VSANs present on a common switch. Routes that traverse one or more VSANs across multiple switches can be established, if necessary, to create proper interconnections. IVR used in conjunction with Fibre Channel over IP (FCIP) can provide efficient business continuity or disaster recovery solutions.

FSPF

Fabric Shortest Path First (FSPF) is the standard path-selection protocol used by Fibre Channel fabrics. IVR uses FSPF to calculate the best path to a remote fabric.

FSPF supports multiple paths and automatically computes an alternative path around a failed link. It provides a preferred route when two equal paths are available.

The FSPF protocol has these characteristics and features:

■ Supports multipath routing.

- Bases path status on a link state routing protocol.

- Routes hop by hop, based on only the domain ID.

- Runs on only E_Ports or TE_Ports and provides a loop-free topology.

- Runs on a per-VSAN basis. Connectivity in a given VSAN in a fabric is guaranteed only for the switches configured in that VSAN.

- Uses a topology database to keep track of the state of the links on all switches in the fabric and associates a cost with each link.

- Guarantees a fast reconvergence time in case of a topology change. FSPF uses the standard Dijkstra algorithm, but there is a static dynamic option for a more robust, efficient, and incremental Dijkstra algorithm. The reconvergence time is fast and efficient because the route computation is done on a per-VSAN basis.

Zoning

Zoning is a way to enable access between an initiator and a storage target. Zoning is a logical grouping of fabric-connected devices within a SAN or VSAN. Zoning can be used to establish access control. Devices within a zone can access each other (see Figure 6-7).

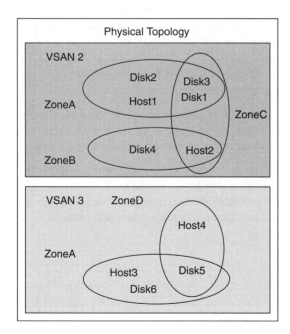

Figure 6-7   *Zoning*

Zoning provides a means of restricting visibility and connectivity between devices connected to a common Fibre Channel SAN or VSAN. Zoning increases security, because limiting access prevents unauthorized access. Zoning allows the SAN administrator to overlay a security map dictating which host devices can see which targets, thereby reducing the risk of data loss.

There are two zoning types: software based and hardware based. Software-based zoning makes use of Domain Name System (DNS) queries. Hardware-based zoning is more common and more secure. Zoning is effective at managing connectivity between end devices within a storage network. However, zoning does not offer any capability to control the path selection and flow through a storage network between zoned devices.

VSANs and zoning are two powerful tools to aid the SAN designer in building robust, secure, and manageable networking environments while optimizing the use and cost of switching hardware. VSANs are first created as isolated logical fabrics within a common physical topology; then, individual unique zone sets can be applied as necessary within each VSAN.

FICON

Fiber Connectivity (FICON) is an upper-layer protocol developed by IBM that uses the lower layers of Fibre Channel transport for connecting IBM mainframes with control units.

FICON is the next-generation replacement for the older Enterprise System Connection (ESCON) protocol, which was a 200-Mb/s unidirectional serial bit transmission protocol from IBM (see Figure 6-8). FICON is bidirectional, and runs over Fibre Channel at gigabit-per-second rates. One of the main advantages of FICON is the lack of the performance degradation over distance that is seen with ESCON. FICON can reach a distance of 60 miles (100 km) before experiencing any significant drop in data throughput.

The MDS 9000 series supports both FCP and FICON capabilities using VSAN technology for hardware-enforced, isolated environments within a single physical fabric. This provides both secure sharing of physical infrastructure and enhanced FICON mixed support.

The FICON support that the MDS 9000 series provides includes traffic and management isolation, advanced distance extension, quality of service (QoS), and scaling. Because both FICON and Fibre Channel with FCP use Fibre Channel transports, these systems can share a common network and I/O infrastructure commonly known as an intermix.

SANTap

SANTap is one of the Intelligent Storage Services features supported on the Storage Services Module (SSM) in the Cisco MDS 9500 series multilayer fabric directors and Cisco MDS 9200 multilayer fabric switches (see Figure 6-9).

The SANTap feature allows third-party data storage applications, such as long-distance replication and continuous backup, to be integrated into the SAN. SANTap enables data being written to a storage device to be duplicated at another appliance within the fabric. The appliance need not be in the primary data path. By duplicating write data to a storage target, third-party storage appliances can create either backups or replicas of primary data.

Figure 6-8 *FICON*

Figure 6-9 *SANTap*

The SANTap protocol enables transparent insertion of appliance-based storage applications. End users can take advantage of a wide range of SANTap solutions from several third-party appliance and application vendors to perform heterogeneous data migration, remote replication, snapshots, continuous data protection, and information lifecycle management through intelligent tiered storage. Cisco SANTap provides a high-performance, reliable, heterogeneous platform that integrates easily into existing environments.

A SANTap solution provides these benefits:

■ Transparent insertion and provisioning of appliance-based storage applications

■ No disruption of the primary I/O from the server to the storage array

■ On-demand storage services

■ Scalable commodity appliance-based storage applications

Designing SAN and SAN Extension

Basic SAN design using the Cisco MDS 9000 series multilayer switches is based on port counts and performance. The underlying principles of SAN design are relatively straightforward (see Figure 6-10):

■ Plan a network topology that can handle the number of ports necessary now and in the future

■ Design a network topology with a given end-to-end performance and throughput level in mind, taking into account any physical requirements of a design

■ Provide the necessary connectivity with remote data centers to handle the business requirements of continuity and disaster recovery

Port Density and Topology Requirements

The single most important factor in determining the most suitable SAN design is determining the number of end ports required both now and over the anticipated lifespan of the design. For example, the design for a SAN that will handle a network with 100 end ports will be very different from the design for a SAN that has to handle a network with 1500 end ports. You can determine the number of ports required by answering these questions:

■ How many ports are needed now?

■ How many ports will be needed in the future?

■ What is the expected life of the SAN?

A recommended practice is to design the SAN switches with the capacity to support future requirements. This does not mean that you need to install all the ports now, but you should plan for future requirements to avoid costly retrofits.

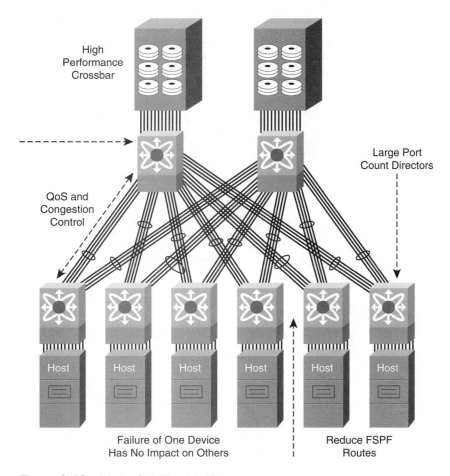

High
Performance
Crossbar

Large Port
Count Directors

QoS and
Congestion
Control

Host   Host   Host   Host   Host   Host

Failure of One Device
Has No Impact on Others

Reduce FSPF
Routes

Figure 6-10   *Major SAN Design Factors*

The SAN design should also consider topology and physical space requirements. Some questions to consider are these:

■   Is the data center located on one floor?

■   Is the data center located in one building?

■   Do you want to use an IP SAN extension for disaster recovery connectivity?

Any design should also consider increases in future port speeds, protocols, and densities that could be supported by unused module slots in switches.

Device Oversubscription

All SAN designs should have some degree of oversubscription or fan-out from storage devices to hosts. It is a common practice for storage subsystem vendors to share one port on the storage subsystem among multiple host bus adapters (HBA) on multiple servers. Most major disk subsystem vendors provide guidelines as to the recommended fan-out ratio of subsystem client-side ports to server connections in the range of 7:1 to 15:1. This ratio balances different server platforms and applications across these subsystem ports to fully utilize available bandwidth. The ratio assumes that the storage subsystem ports have access to full line-rate performance and that the Fibre Channel switching fabric is nonblocking.

Note: Some Fibre Channel switch line cards are designed to work in an oversubscribed mode. For example, on the Cisco MDS 9000 32-port Fibre Channel line card, the forwarding rate is 2.5 Gb/s, for a 3.2:1 oversubscription ratio at Fibre Channel interface speeds of 2 Gb/s or a 1.6:1 ratio at 1 Gb/s speeds.

The fan-out ratio also implies that the Fibre Channel switch ports that the server HBAs are connected to are being underused most of the time. A general principle in optimizing design fan-out is to group applications or servers that burst high I/O rates at different time slots within the daily production cycle.

Traffic Management

For some SAN designs, it makes sense to implement traffic management policies that influence traffic flow and relative traffic priorities. You should consider the answers to the following questions:

■   Do different application servers have different performance requirements?

■   Should bandwidth be reserved for specific applications?

■   Is preferential treatment and QoS necessary for some traffic?

■   Given two alternate paths for traffic between data centers, should traffic use one path in preference to the other?

Fault Isolation

Consolidation of storage into a single fabric means increased storage utilization and reduced administration overhead. The major drawback is that faults are no longer isolated. Another consideration is that SANs are more complex than simple storage, so a higher skill level is needed to manage the SAN. Technologies such as VSANs enable consolidation of storage while increasing security and stability by logically isolating devices that are physically connected to the same set of switches. Faults or mistakes in one VSAN fabric are contained and do not impact other VSAN fabrics.

Convergence and Stability

Fast convergence and stability are the primary reasons storage vendors set limits on the number of switches and devices they have certified and qualified for operation in a single fabric.

Recommended practices for supporting fast convergence and SAN stability include the following:

■   Minimize the processing required with a given SAN topology by minimizing the number of switches in a SAN and the number of parallel links in a SAN.

■   Implement appropriate levels of redundancy in the network layers and redundant hardware components within the fabric.

SAN Designs with the Cisco MDS 9000 Family

The MDS 9000 series consists of Cisco MDS 9500 series multilayer directors, Cisco MDS 9100 series and Cisco MDS 9200 series multilayer fabric switches, and the Cisco MDS 9020 series fabric switch. The product line is designed to meet requirements for storage networks of all sizes and architectures. The MDS 9000 series delivers intelligent network services such as VSANs, comprehensive security, advanced traffic management, sophisticated diagnostics, and unified SAN management. In addition, the Cisco MDS 9500 series multilayer directors and MDS 9200 series multilayer fabric switches provide multiprotocol and multitransport integration and an open platform for embedding intelligent storage services such as network-based volume management.

SAN Consolidation with VSANs

SAN consolidation refers to increasing the number of devices such as servers, storage arrays, and tape drives that have access to a SAN infrastructure while simplifying existing SAN topology layouts. If the number of devices connected to a SAN is increased, the cost and provisioning of storage resources becomes more flexible. The flexibility leads to cost reduction based on an increase in storage usage and increased management efficiencies.

Interconnecting smaller SAN islands to form larger connected fabrics or using VSANs simplifies SAN topology layouts and can lower costs by reducing physical SAN build-outs.

Comprehensive SAN Security

SAN security refers to processes and solution features that protect the integrity and availability of data stored on storage networks. There are four aspects to a comprehensive SAN security solution:

■   Secure roles-based management with centralized authentication, authorization, and logging of all changes

■   Centralized authentication of devices connected to the network to ensure that only authorized devices can be connected to the network

■   Traffic isolation and access controls to ensure that a device connected to the network can securely send and receive data and is protected from activities of other devices in the network

■   Encryption of all data leaving the storage network for business continuance, remote vaulting, and backup

Simplified SAN Management

SAN management refers to provisioning and operating a storage infrastructure while also ensuring availability, reliability, recoverability, and optimal performance.

For companies requiring large SANs, the need to simplify the management of networks has become critical. Managing multiple SAN islands with many points of management can become extremely complex. In addition, as enterprise SANs grow, end users are increasingly cautious about the lack of effective troubleshooting tools for storage networks. Many users have not had the confidence to build large SANs, in part because of the lack of troubleshooting tools and the complexity caused by the need to manage many Inter-Switch Links (ISL) across multiple SAN islands.

Large enterprise end users require management tools that are centralized, easy to use, provide significant troubleshooting capabilities to help to resolve potential problems quickly, and are standards based in an effort to integrate seamlessly with other management tools.

Storage networking solutions that incorporate Cisco Fabric Manager deliver a centralized, secure point of management with industry-leading troubleshooting and monitoring tools that help large enterprise users scale their networks. Along with the intelligent networking features built in to the MDS 9000 series, end users can easily consolidate multiple SAN islands, build SAN extension solutions for business continuance, and lower costs by moving Intelligent Fabric Applications into the network for efficient resource provisioning and utilization.

Single-Switch Collapsed-Core Design

The collapsed-core single-switch design takes a traditional core-edge topology and collapses it into a single chassis. Instead of using many small switches to provide sufficient port density, a single chassis with a high port count replaces the smaller switches. This design reduces the number of ISLs required in the network so that all available ports can be deployed for host or storage connections, leading to 100 percent port design efficiency.

In Figure 6-11, the backplane of the MDS in the collapsed-core design replaces all the ISL links. This design can also provide a lower fan-out ratio than the multiple small switches because the availability of more advanced blades for the MDS. Empty slots on the MDS can support future growth on new line cards.

The collapsed-core design on a first-generation switch has limited capabilities with regard to high availability. With later-generation Cisco MDS series switches, dual redundant crossbar switch fabrics are used on all director switches to provide low-latency, high-throughput, nonblocking, and nonoversubscribed switching capacity between line card modules. In addition, the port bandwidth reservation feature guarantees dedicated performance for those devices that require it.

Note: Second-generation MDS 9500 series director switches are fully redundant with no single point of failure with dual supervisors, crossbar switch fabrics, clock modules, or power supplies. Nonetheless, note that this design still has a single point of failure with the one chassis.

Figure 6-11 *Single-Switch Collapsed-Core Design*

Small-Scale, Dual-Fabric Collapsed-Core Design

Figure 6-12 shows a small-scale design that makes use of two Cisco MDS 9216 multilayer fabric switches. Each fabric is a storage switch and its connections. A dual fabric provides a connection from each host or storage device to each SAN fabric.

A total of 64 ports per switch are supported when the 48-port Fibre Channel blade is added to the MDS 9216 switches with 16 built-in ports. This small-scale design can support a departmental SAN.

Note: The dual physical fabric is recommended for highly redundant SAN design systems. The dual-fabric design removes the single point of failure that comes with the single-switch design.

Figure 6-12 shows a small-scale design that uses a 7:1 fan-out ratio between host devices and storage ports. Each switch has a total of 64 ports. Fifty-six ports are used for host devices, and 8 ports are used for storage per switch. The fan-out ratio is then calculated at 56:8, or simply 7:1. All available ports are deployed for host or storage connections.

MDS 9216 switches can provide VSAN support and port channels to other switches to scale the design in the future.

Medium-Scale, Dual-Fabric Collapsed-Core Design

Figure 6-13 illustrates a medium-scale collapsed-core design with dual fabric that can support up to 528 ports per switch. This solution might be useful for a medium-size enterprise. The solution makes use of a dual-fabric design so that each host and each storage

8 Storage Ports

56 User Ports

Each Fabric Switch Has:

1 x 16 Fibre Channel Port (Built-In)
1 x 48 Fibre Channel Port Modules

64 Fibre Channel Ports Per Switch

Figure 6-12   *Small Scale Dual Fabric: Collapsed Core Design*

port has connections to two fabric switches. No ISLs are needed for this design to inter-connect core and edge switches, so all the port density is used to connect hosts and stor-age devices. The only links needed will be to the hosts and storage devices. Port bandwidth reservations can be used to guarantee performance for those devices that re-quire it. The design can also provide VSAN support and port channels to other switches to scale the design in the future.

This design uses a 10:1 fan-out ratio between host ports and storage ports. This means that 480 hosts will have access to 48 storage device ports.

Note: The collapsed-core SAN design can use a large SAN device for efficiency. When the SAN port requirements outgrow the largest SAN device, the core-edge approach is needed to support the SAN.

Large-Scale, Dual-Fabric Core-Edge Design

A large-scale SAN solution requires a core-edge design to provide sufficient host and stor-age port density. Figure 6-14 shows a design capable of more than 2000 host and storage ports.

Per Director:
11 x 48-Port Modules
528 Ports Total
48 Ports for Storage
480 Ports for Hosts
10:1 Oversubscription

48 Storage
Ports

480 Host Ports

Figure 6-13   *Medium-Scale, Dual-Fabric Collapsed-Core Design*

The design makes use of both a core layer and an edge layer set of switches. Two core switches provide nonoversubscribed interconnectivity on the ISLs to the four edge layer switches. There are 128 storage ports per core switch, which are connected on 2-Gb connections. The edge switches are connected to each core switch with a 16-port port channel running at 4 Gb per port to provide 64 Gb/s to each core switch. Each core supports 4 * 64 Gb/s = 256 Gb/s from the edge switches and 2 * 128 Gb/s = 256 Gb/s to the directly connected storage devices with no oversubscription.

In this design, the Port Bandwidth Reservation feature is used to dedicate forwarding resources on edge switches for ISL connectivity from the edge to the core. The edge switches provide port density for 1984 host ports, with each edge switch supporting 496 host ports at 2 Gb/s. The fan-out between host ports to storage ports across the edge and core switches is calculated like this:

1984 * 2 Gb/s : 256 Gb/s * 2 = 7.75:1

Note: ISLs are needed between the switches. The edge-core design will scale to support much larger port densities than the collapsed-core design. A SAN of more than 2000 ports can be considered a large SAN, although SANs of more than 4000 ports can be found today.

Each Core Switch:
- 128 Storage Ports at 2 G
- 64 ISL Ports to Edge at 4 G
- 1:1 Ratio of ISLs to Storage

Each Edge Switch:
- 496 Host Ports at 2 G
- 32 ISL Ports to Core at 4 G
- 7.75:1 Ratio of Hosts to Storage

256 Storage Ports

1984 Host Ports

SAN System:
- 1984 Host Ports at 2 G
- 256 Storage Ports at 2 G
- 7.75:1 Ratio of Hosts to Storage

Figure 6-14   *Large-Scale, Dual-Fabric Core-Edge Design*

SAN Extension

SAN extension refers to transporting storage traffic over distances such as metropolitan-area networks (MAN) and WANs. Over short distances, such as within a data center, SANs are typically extended over optical links with multimode optical fiber. As the distance increases, such as within a large data center or campus, single-mode fiber or single-mode fiber with coarse wavelength-division multiplexing (CWDM) is typical. Over metropolitan distances, dense wavelength-division multiplexing (DWDM) is preferable. DWDM is also used where higher consolidation density or aggregation of Fiber Connectivity (FICON), Enterprise System Connection (ESCON), and 10 Gigabit Ethernet data center links are required. SAN extension across a MAN or WAN allows the enterprise to support applications such as distributed replication, backup, and remote storage (see Figure 6-15).

In contrast, Fibre Channel over IP (FCIP) can be used to extend a Fibre Channel SAN across any distance. FCIP can be used over metro and campus distances or over intercontinental distances where IP might be the only transport available. With a single instance of

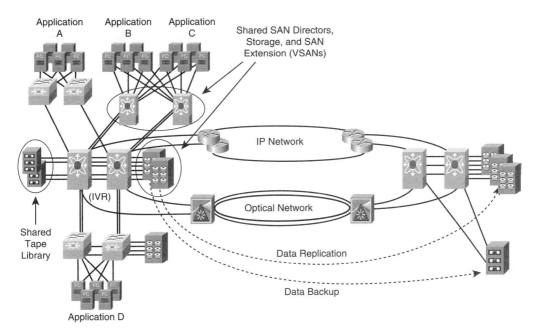

Figure 6-15 *SAN Extension*

synchronous disk replication, typically 15 to 20 MB/s of network bandwidth is required. To support this bandwidth, Optical Carrier 3 (OC-3) circuits at 155-Mb/s rates are almost a minimum requirement. However, few SAN disaster recovery designs actually require synchronous replication over the FCIP, so bandwidth at or below OC-3 rates should initially be adequate for the typical SAN extension design. QoS is highly recommended to ensure the priority of the FCIP traffic and to ensure any performance degradation resulting from network delays and congestion is kept to an absolute minimum.

The Internet Small Computer Systems Interface (iSCSI) is another protocol that can support SAN extension. iSCSI is a protocol used to carry SCSI commands, responses, and data over an IP network. With iSCSI, transport is supported over a TCP/IP network and not over a Fibre Channel network.

The primary use for iSCSI (which is also known as Internet SCSI) is for host-to-storage connectivity through an IP LAN. SCSI commands and data are encapsulated into iSCSI, adding a special header. The iSCSI data is then encapsulated directly into a TCP packet. No Fibre Channel is used at all, so this is an alternative to SAN fabric.

SAN Extension Protocols

SANs can use different protocol and transport stacks to transfer SCSI commands and data. The FCIP and iSCSI stacks support block-level storage for remote devices. Both FCIP and iSCSI are used to carry SCSI commands and status. Each uses the TCP/IP protocol suite as a transport mechanism. As a result, they support leveraging the existing network infrastructure to connect storage devices.

Although they have similarities, these protocols also differ. FCIP is Fibre Channel encapsulated in IP. Its purpose is to provide connectivity between two separate SANs over a WAN (see Figure 6-16). FCIP is a tunneling protocol. It encapsulates Fibre Channel packets and carries them within a TCP socket. The SCSI commands are encapsulated into a Fibre Channel frame. The Fibre Channel packet is encapsulated into FCIP. The FCIP protocol data unit (PDU) is then carried over TCP/IP. The result has the same effect as trunking Fibre Channel between switch fabrics over the WAN.

Figure 6-16   *FCIP*

Both FCIP and iSCSI have demanding QoS requirements. They both need high throughput with no to very few drops, low latency, and low jitter. Mixing FCIP and iSCSI traffic with other enterprise traffic can be a worst-case scenario for QoS. Often, dedicated IP connections are used to support FCIP and iSCSI.

FCIP is a standards-based protocol, outlined in RFC 3821. Before FCIP, to extend the SAN between networks you needed to extend the Fibre Channel connections from one network to another. Separate dedicated connections had to be purchased and maintained for the Fibre Channel connections. With the proper QoS mechanisms, FCIP uses the existing IP infrastructure to connect SANs.

Note: Although it is typically used for SAN extension, FCIP can also be used for host attachment.

FCIP is a means of providing a SAN extension over an IP infrastructure, enabling storage applications such as asynchronous data replication, disaster recovery, remote tape vaulting, and host initiator to remote pooled storage to be deployed, which have low sensitivity to latency and distance. FCIP tunnels Fibre Channel frames over an IP link, using TCP to provide a reliable transport stream with a guarantee of in-order delivery.

SAN extension using FCIP typically has many cost benefits over other SAN extension technologies. It is relatively common to have existing IP infrastructure between data centers that can be leveraged at no incremental cost. In addition, IP connectivity is typically available at a better price point for long-distance links compared to pricing for optical Fibre Channel transport services.

iSCSI

iSCSI is a protocol used to carry SCSI commands, responses, and data over an IP network. With iSCSI, transport is supported over a TCP/IP network and not over a Fibre Channel network. File access is at the block level.

Figure 6-17 shows a connection that uses iSCSI between the iSCSI Host and Switch B. Physical connectivity is achieved using a Gigabit Ethernet port on the switch.

Figure 6-17 *iSCSI*

Note: The new iSCSI Server Load Balancing (iSLB) feature in Cisco MDS 9000 SAN-OS Software Release 3.0 provides consolidation of Gigabit Ethernet ports and further simplifies configuration. iSLB enables multiple Gigabit Ethernet interfaces, spanning across different line cards or different Cisco MDS 9000 series switches within the same physical fabric, to act as a single iSCSI target portal. Hundreds or thousands of servers can be configured with just one target portal IP address for iSCSI storage access. The iSLB feature in the MDS 9000 series automatically assigns each server to a specific Gigabit Ethernet port. iSLB provides load balancing of iSCSI hosts within a physical fabric and a redundancy capability using Virtual Router Redundancy Protocol (VRRP).

It is recommended practice that the LAN segment used for iSCSI is its own VLAN. Diffie-Hellman Challenge Handshake Authentication Protocol (DH-CHAP) authentication should also be used to enhance security on the LAN. DH-CHAP is an authentication protocol that authenticates the devices connecting to a switch. Fibre Channel authentication allows only trusted devices to be added to a fabric, thus preventing unauthorized devices from accessing the switch. IP Security (IPsec) can also be run between the switch and host to further enhance security if desired.

> **Note:**   Encrypting gigabytes of data can get very costly.

Although it can be complex to manage, iSCSI comes with significant advantages compared to FCIP, including the following:

- Standard networking equipment can be used in the iSCSI network.

- iSCSI provides a lower overall cost of ownership when compared to building a Fibre Channel fabric.

- Like FCIP, iSCSI is a standards-based protocol, outlined in RFC 3720.

Scaling iSCSI can be done via a TCP/IP Offload Engine (TOE). *TOE* is a special network interface card (NIC) in the host computer that has some additional capabilities. The TCP/IP stack runs on the NIC rather than consuming CPU on the server for TCP/IP processing. The TOE also allows for the iSCSI device to do a network boot.

The host initiator port is an NIC. iSCSI makes the NIC look like a SCSI adapter to your host. Network portals exist on both the initiator and target. The network portal on the initiator is the IP address that the host will attach to. Hosts can have multiple portals for functions such as primary and backup use. The network portal on the target device might be a port on the IP services blade on the SAN switch. IP is stripped off at the iSCSI target and SCSI is presented to the logical units.

SAN Extension Developments

The SAN extension is becoming faster and more practical because of these new technologies (see Figure 6-18):

- **Tape acceleration:** Speeds up the I/O transactions that occur during remote backups. This reduces the latency commonly associated with backup over a WAN, and considerably reduces the time required for long-distance backups.

- **FCIP write acceleration:** Speeds up I/O transactions between servers and disk-based storage devices such as a disk array.

- **Hardware-assisted data compression over FCIP:** Achieves high data compression rates over WAN links. Through data compression, storage administrators can more efficiently use the available bandwidth and send more storage traffic between data centers.

- **Hardware-based IPsec encryption:** Ensures secure SAN extension transactions, an important consideration when transporting storage traffic outside the confines of data centers.

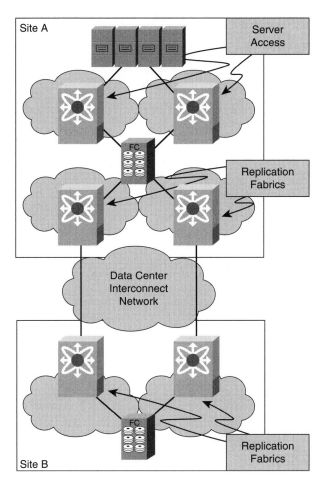

Figure 6-18   *SAN Extension Developments*

High-Availability SAN Extension

The conventional approach for a high-availability SAN extension design is achieved with dual fabrics such as a yellow VSAN and a blue VSAN. This design provides protection against failures in either fabric. It is common to augment the design with additional network protection via port channels and optical protection schemes.

In the Figure 6-19, servers are connected to storage arrays over a long distance with two replication fabrics for high availability. The use of multipath software is required by the host to utilize the dual paths.

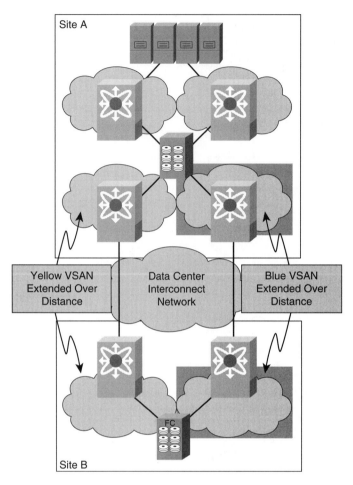

Figure 6-19 *High-Availability SAN Extension*

Summary

This chapter introduced the concept of storage area networks (SAN). Essentially, a SAN is a concept of shared storage that is separate from the servers that use it. Drilling down to the basic physical components, we find HBAs and disk drives, usually arranged in a RAID configuration. DAS and NAS topologies connect storage resources to hosts or a SAN.

Basic SAN design and SAN extension design define a network topology that can support storage requirements. It involves planning a network topology that can support current and future storage requirements. Storage technologies include SCSI, Fibre Channel, VSANs, IVR, zones, FICON, and SANTap. The iSCSI and FCIP protocols support SAN extension to transport storage traffic over a WAN or MAN and remote host attachment.

From a SAN design standpoint, the Cisco MDS 9000 family of switches offers significant SAN design flexibility, lowering the overall TCO using multiprotocol and multiservice intelligence.

References

For additional information, refer to these resources:

- Cisco Systems, Inc. "Storage Area Networking: Introduction," at http://www.cisco.com/en/US/netsol/ns893/networking_solutions_package.html

- Cisco Systems, Inc. "Cisco MDS 9000 Statement of Direction," at http://www.cisco.com/en/US/solutions/collateral/ns340/ns394/ns259/at_a_glance_c45-465839.pdf

- Cisco Systems, Inc. "Advanced SAN Design Using Cisco MDS 9500 Series Multilayer Directors," accessible with CCO account access at http://www.cisco.com/en/US/partner/products/ps5990/products_white_paper0900aecd8044c807.shtml

Review Questions

Answer the following questions, and then refer to Appendix A, "Answers to Review Questions," for the answers.

1. What are characteristics of Fibre Channel? (Choose three.)

   a. Parallel standard

   b. Full duplex

   c. Half duplex

   d. Addresses more than 16 million nodes

   e. Segment lengths of up to 6 miles (10 km)

   f. Bus lengths of up to 75 feet (25 meters)

2. What technology allows multiple logical SANs to exist in the same physical fabric?

    a. FICON

    b. IVR

    c. Zoning

    d. VSAN

    e. SANTap

3. What is a means of restricting visibility and connectivity between devices connected to a common Fibre Channel SAN or VSAN?

    a. IVR

    b. FICON

    c. Zoning

    d. SANTap

    e. VSAN

4. What are the characteristics of a large-scale SAN design? (Choose two.)

    a. Uses a collapsed core to support much larger port densities than the core-edge design FICON

    b. Uses a core-edge design to support much larger port densities than the collapsed-core design

    c. Has a lower port-density efficiency as compared to small- or medium-scale designs

    d. Has the highest port-density efficiency as compared to small- or medium-scale designs

    e. Uses oversubscribed interconnectivity on the ISLs

    f. Does not use ISLs

5. What can be a factor in SAN design? (Choose three.)

    a. Port density and topology

    b. Fast convergence and stability

    c. Fast routing protocol reservations

    d. Fault isolation using VSAN

    e. Simplified SAN management through storage captivity

    f. Network-attached file service

After completing this chapter, you will be able to

- Discuss the importance of high availability for e-commerce designs

- Discuss how firewalls, server load balancers, and multiple ISP connections are used in e-commerce designs

- Discuss how to integrate firewalls and server load balancers into functioning e-commerce designs

- Describe tuning techniques for improving the performance and availability of an e-commerce module design

CHAPTER 7

E-Commerce Module Design

The e-commerce module enables organizations to support e-commerce applications through the Internet. This chapter first describes why high availability is of particular importance for the e-commerce module. The common uses of firewalls, server load balancers (SLB), and connections to multiple Internet service providers (ISP) in e-commerce designs are introduced. How network components are integrated into e-commerce designs to provide varying levels of security is discussed, and tools and techniques for tuning e-commerce designs are described.

Designing High Availability for E-Commerce

This section discusses why high availability is so important for the e-commerce module and describes how both the technical and nontechnical components of high availability must be integrated into an e-commerce design.

E-Commerce High-Availability Requirements

E-commerce applications represent the public face of an organization; therefore, the e-commerce module has strict design requirements so that web and application responses to users are fast and downtime is minimized. E-commerce downtime is particularly harmful not only because it reflects negatively on an organization but also because lost business can cost millions of dollars per hour.

Components of High Availability

High availability aims to prevent outages, or at least to minimize downtime. Achieving high availability takes ongoing effort and usually requires iterative improvements.

High availability includes integrating the following five components:

- Redundancy
- Technology (including hardware and software features)
- People
- Processes
- Tools

The redundancy and technology components are relatively straightforward to implement because they can be purchased and deployed. A network designer expects to be involved with these two aspects of high availability.

However, no matter how much and how well redundancy and technology have been designed and deployed, high availability will not be achieved unless the people component (for example, having sufficient staff with the right skills, training, and mindset), the processes component (including managing organizational expectations, change control processes, and so on), and the tools component (including network management, good documentation, and so forth) are present. If any one of these last three high-availability components is missing, incidents will likely happen and outages will probably occur. Unfortunately, network designers might not be able to influence these areas of an organization. All too often, a consultant doing a post-outage review is the person who first discusses these components and suggests changes.

These five components are detailed in the following sections.

Redundancy

Redundancy means using additional equipment or network links to reduce or eliminate the effects of a failure.

Redundancy in designs attempts to eliminate single points of failure, where one failed device or design element causes a service to go down. The following are examples of redundancy mechanisms that may be used:

- Geographic and path diversity

- Dual devices and links

- Dual WAN providers

- Dual data centers, especially for large organizations with large e-commerce sites

- Dual facilities, dual telephone central office facilities, and dual power substations

Redundant designs must trade off costs versus benefits. For example, it takes time to plan redundancy and verify the geographic diversity of service providers, and additional links and equipment cost money to purchase and maintain. These items need to be balanced against the risk and costs of downtime and so forth. The time and money invested in redundancy design should be spent where they will have the most impact. Consequently, redundancy is most frequently found in network, data center, or e-commerce module cores, and in critical WAN links or ISP connections. Within e-commerce module designs, duplicate elements may be specified in the path between users and applications, and in the applications and back-end databases and mainframes.

Technology

The use of appropriate technologies, including Cisco technologies, can improve high availability. For example, several Cisco routing continuity capabilities, such as Cisco Nonstop Forwarding (NSF), Stateful Switchover (SSO), and graceful restart, can improve availability. These technologies allow processor failover without causing links to flap (continuously go down and up), continued forwarding of packets, and maintenance of Border Gateway Protocol (BGP) adjacencies.

> **Note:**   Cisco NSF with SSO is discussed in more detail in Chapter 2, "Enterprise Campus Network Design."

Techniques for detecting failure and triggering failover to a redundant device include service monitoring on SLBs, Enhanced Object Tracking (EOT) for Cisco IOS IP service-level agreements (SLA), and Cisco Optimized Edge Routing (OER).

> **Note:**   SLBs, EOT, IP SLAs, and OER are described in later sections of this chapter.

Other technologies that contribute to high availability include fast routing convergence and firewall stateful failover (to allow user or application sessions to be maintained across a firewall device failover).

> **Note:**   Firewall stateful failover is discussed in more detail in Chapter 8, "Security Services Design."

People

Using redundant equipment and links and advanced technologies are just the beginning of high availability. People are one of the most critical components of high availability. For example, staff work habits can impact high availability, attention to detail enhances high availability, and carelessness hurts availability.

The level of staff skills and technical training are also important. For example, staff with the proper skills can configure devices correctly and conduct appropriate testing to understand the circumstances under which failover will activate, and what failover will and will not accomplish. Thorough testing often translates into less downtime. As an example, nonstateful firewall failover may adequately pass traffic. However, understanding how a particular application behaves may result in doing other tests that shows that with nonstateful failover the application sessions lock up for an extended period of time until the application timeout causes the sessions to be reestablished. Designs that include failover must be tested to see how the entire system operates under failure conditions, not just how individual components failover.

Good communication and documentation are also important. For example, network administrators need to be able to communicate with other network, security, application, and server teams. Network documentation should indicate why things are designed the way they are, how the network is supposed to work, and expected failover behavior.

Often, if people are not given the time to do a job right, they will have to cut corners; testing and documentation are typically the first items to be eliminated. A lack of thorough testing and documentation can have long-term consequences on the ability to maintain, optimize, and troubleshoot a network.

If possible, staff teams should be aligned with services. For example, if the corporate web page and e-commerce site depends on staff who report to the Engineering or Operations department managers, the manager of the e-commerce site may be competing for staff time with these other managers. This organizational structure may cause priority conflicts and make it difficult to have routine testing or maintenance done for the e-commerce site. The owner of, or expert on, key service applications and other e-commerce components should also be identified and included in design (and redesign) efforts.

Processes

Implementing sound, repeatable processes is important to achieving high availability; continual process improvement is part of the prepare, plan, design, implement, operate, and optimize (PPDIOO) methodology. Tasks that are implemented as though they are one-time occurrences and not repeatable processes are lost opportunities for learning.

The following are some ways that organizations can build repeatable processes:

- By documenting change procedures for common changes (for example, Cisco IOS Software upgrades)
- By documenting failover planning and lab testing procedures
- By documenting a network implementation procedure, and revising and improving it each time components are deployed

Some processes are specifically related to lab testing. Labs should be used appropriately, such as in the following ways:

- By ensuring that lab equipment accurately reflects the production network
- By ensuring that failover mechanisms are tested and understood
- By ensuring that new code is systematically validated before deployment

Change control processes should be meaningful and not waste time. Examples of good change control processes include the following:

- Specifying that all changes must be tested before deployment
- Ensuring that planning includes rollback details
- Ensuring that all departments within the organization have been made aware of the proposed change (so that all repercussions of the change can be considered)

Management of operational changes is also important and includes the following:

- Ensuring that regular capacity management audits are performed
- Ensuring that Cisco IOS versions are tracked and managed
- Ensuring that design compliance is tracked, including when recommended practices change

- Ensuring that plans for disaster recovery and continuity of operations are developed

- Conducting a realistic and thorough risk analysis

Tools

Organizations should monitor service and component availability. With proper failover, services should continue operating when single components fail. Without component monitoring, if a failed redundant component is not detected and replaced, an outage may occur if the second component subsequently fails.

Performance thresholds and reporting the top N devices with specific characteristics (Top N reporting) are useful, both for noticing when capacity is depleting, and for correlating slow services with stressed network or server resources. Monitoring packet loss, latency, jitter, and drops on WAN links or ISP connections is also important. These metrics might be the first indication of an outage or of a potential SLA deterioration that could affect the delivery of services.

Good documentation is a valuable tool and includes the following:

- Network diagrams help in planning and in fixing outages more quickly. Out-of-date documentation can lead to design errors, lack of redundancy, and other undesirable consequences.

- Documentation of how and why the network is designed the way it is helps capture knowledge that can be critical when a different person needs to change the design, reexamine how failover works, or make other changes.

- Addresses, VLAN numbers, and servers should be accurately documented to aid in troubleshooting, network redesign, and so forth.

- Accurate documentation that indicates how services map to applications, how applications map to virtual servers, and how virtual servers map to physical servers can be incredibly useful when troubleshooting.

Common E-Commerce Module Designs

The e-commerce module includes routing, switching, firewall, and server content load-balancing components.

This section reviews common e-commerce designs using firewalls and SLBs and common approaches for connecting to multiple ISPs. These elements may be integrated into the more complex e-commerce module designs shown in the "Integrated E-Commerce Designs" section later in this chapter.

Common E-Commerce Firewall Designs

This section reviews common firewall designs for the e-commerce module, starting with a typical e-commerce module topology. Designs that use a server as an application gateway are described, followed by a discussion of virtualization using firewall contexts. Designs using virtual firewall layers are examined, and firewall modes are described.

Typical E-Commerce Module Topology

The e-commerce module is typically implemented in a data center facility and is connected to the Internet via one or multiple ISPs. Because there are multiple firewall layers inside the e-commerce module, this design is sometimes referred to as a "firewall sandwich." The design is illustrated in Figure 7-1. The firewall connections in the figure are either in an active or standby state. A large site might use three layers of firewalls, whereas smaller sites might use only two layers of firewalls.

As shown in Figure 7-1, a web tier—the outer demilitarized zone (DMZ) that supports the web servers—is typically protected from the Internet by a pair of firewalls. The web servers communicate with the application tier—application or middleware servers in the data center—through a second pair of firewalls. The application tier communicates with the database tier—the mainframes or databases—through the third pair of firewalls.

Although the specific connection is not shown in Figure 7-1, the e-commerce servers connect through the firewalls back to the internal network. This connectivity permits staff to update the applications and servers, and do other maintenance and monitoring. When the e-commerce module is collocated with the corporate network, the edge routers may also provide the connection back to the corporate internal network. If the e-commerce module resides within a data center, the innermost firewalls may provide the connection back to the internal network.

Note: Sites requiring high levels of security sometimes implement firewalls using different operating systems. This practice ensures that if the outer firewall is breached, the same compromise does not permit a breach of the inner firewall. This approach is more difficult to manage and support, however.

Some variations on this "firewall sandwich" design may also be used, as shown in the following sections.

Using a Server as an Application Gateway

In some architectures, all traffic between the firewall layers goes through the servers. For example, in Figure 7-2, one interface of the web servers provides web services, and a separate interface connects through another firewall to application servers. In this design, the web tier servers are acting as application-specific gateways. The outer and inner sets of interface connections on the web tier servers are on separate VLANs.

Note: Figure 7-2 shows a logical representation of the application-specific gateway design. Usually, the two web tier server interfaces connect to a switch (or four interfaces connect to two switches).

This application-specific gateway approach increases security because a hacker would have to penetrate the firewall and the web server operating system to attack the middle layer of firewalls. Using this approach may allow the network administrator to avoid operating firewalls from multiple vendors.

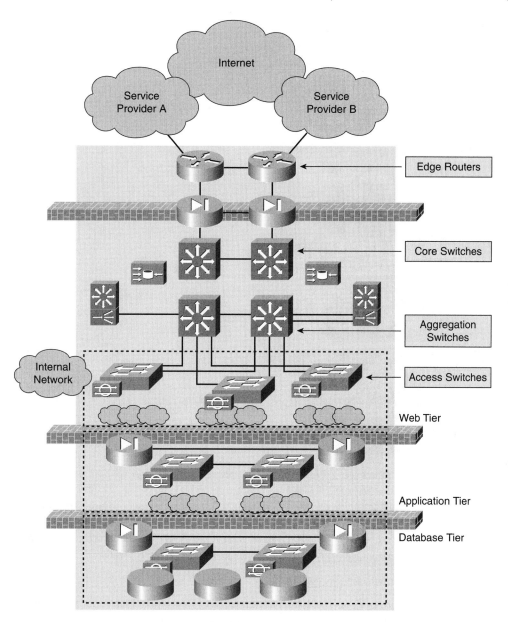

Figure 7-1 *A Typical E-Commerce Module Topology*

A variation of the application-specific gateway design has only one connection from each server to each switch, but uses a port-specific access control list (ACL) on the firewalls. The ACL on the Internet edge firewall pair allows only web and related traffic to go to the web servers. Similarly, the middle firewall allows only application traffic, from the web servers, to the application servers.

Figure 7-2   *Logical Representation of Using a Server as an Application Gateway*

If some traffic must go between firewalls, a single VLAN can connect to both firewall layers. For example, this might be needed if an application tier server needs to communicate directly with some devices on the Internet or with some devices in the internal corporate network (if the internal network is accessed via the Internet edge firewalls).

Virtualization with Firewall Contexts

A physical Cisco firewall or Cisco Application Control Engine (ACE) module can be virtualized or divided into separate *firewall contexts*. These virtual firewall contexts operate similarly to separate physical firewall devices. The physical firewall resources that each firewall context is allocated can be controlled, for example, to prevent a problem in one firewall context from affecting another.

Figure 7-3 shows a server farm connected to a firewall in which firewall contexts are used to provide virtual firewalls to different servers. The firewall contexts retain the secure separation of rules and other customer features, such as Network Address Translation (NAT), ACLs, protocols, and so forth. For example, in enterprise networks, firewall contexts can be used to separate different Internet-facing e-commerce blocks and different layers of a firewall sandwich. Firewall contexts can also be used in Cisco Catalyst 6500 series Firewall Services Modules (FWSM).

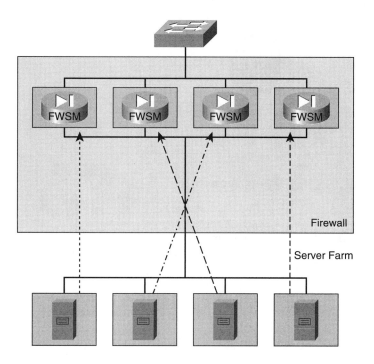

Figure 7-3   *Implementing Virtualization with Firewall Contexts*

Note: Virtual firewalls are discussed in Chapter 8.

Virtual Firewall Layers

A multitiered e-commerce module may use a single pair of firewall devices using virtual firewall layers. For example, a pair of Catalyst 6500 series FWSMs might be used rather than individual firewalls, as illustrated in the example in Figure 7-4.

The different types of lines on the left side of Figure 7-4 correspond to different layers in the logical traffic-flow diagram shown in the right side of the figure. Traffic from the Internet passes through the firewall to the web tier, passes through the firewall again to get from the web tier to the application tier, and passes once more through the firewall to get to the databases, mainframe, or internal network.

If a virtual firewall design is used, it is a good idea to provide a logical diagram showing the VLANs internal to the switch, similar to the right side of Figure 7-4. Routing and default gateway logic can also be superimposed on this diagram to indicate how packets flow, why traffic can or cannot flow from a tier directly to or from the Internet, how failover works, and so on. This design can also be documented using a firewall sandwich

Figure 7-4 *Virtual Firewall Layers Represent Logical Traffic Flows*

diagram, with notes indicating that the different firewall layers in the diagram are implemented in the same physical device.

Firewall Modes

Cisco firewall technology allows firewall designs in which the firewall operates in either transparent (bridged) mode, or in traditional routed mode, as illustrated in Figure 7-5. The mode can be established on a per-context basis, depending on licensing.

One VLAN usually corresponds to one subnet. However, in transparent mode, the firewall bridges two VLANs together, switching traffic at Layer 2 between the two VLANs, which together constitute one IP subnet. As shown on the left side of Figure 7-5, any traffic that goes through the firewall is subject to stateful IP address-based ACLs, and other firewall features. This transparent mode is sometimes described as a "bump-in-the-wire" mode.

In the traditional routed mode shown on the right side of Figure 7-5, the firewall routes traffic between VLANs (or interfaces). As traffic is routed, it passes through the firewall and is subject to stateful IP address-based ACLs, inspection, and other firewall configuration options. Most current designs use firewalls in routed mode.

Note: Firewall modes are discussed further in Chapter 8.

Figure 7-5   *A Firewall Runs in Either Transparent or Routed Mode*

An example of using a firewall in transparent mode is when there is a need to isolate a set of servers from other servers on the same VLAN. One solution to this requirement is shown in Figure 7-6. In this example, the "more secure" server ports are placed on VLAN 11. The Catalyst 6500 series FWSM is configured in transparent mode to bridge VLANs 10 and 11 together. The Multilayer Switch Feature Card (MSFC) in the Catalyst 6500 series switch routes traffic for the subnet onto the combined VLANs 10 and 11. The FWSM uses an IP ACL to control which traffic passes from VLAN 10 into VLAN 11. Recabling and readdressing are not needed to support this implementation.

Figure 7-6   *Example Use of a Firewall in Transparent Mode*

An alternative solution to this requirement is to use switch VLAN ACLs (VACL) to control traffic within a VLAN at the IP address level. Using private VLANs (PVLAN) is another way to secure the server ports.

Note: PVLANs are discussed further in Chapter 8.

Using router ACLs in the switch would require server readdressing to move some of the servers onto a different VLAN and subnet. This is difficult to do quickly and might require a lot of work from server and application staff.

Common E-Commerce Server Load Balancer Designs

This section introduces common e-commerce module design approaches using SLBs.

Functions of a Server Load Balancer

An SLB, also called a content load balancer, supports both scaling and high availability by distributing client requests for service across active servers, as shown in Figure 7-7. The SLB provides a public IP address—also called a virtual IP (VIP) address—for *each service*. Clients resolve this address through Domain Name System (DNS) requests. The SLB intelligently passes traffic to a pool of physical servers, based on the load and on configured rules. The SLB rewrites the source and destination IP or MAC addresses, depending on the mode in which it operates.

Figure 7-7   *A Server Load Balancer Represents Multiple Servers*

The SLB monitors the health and performance of the servers. For example, when a server needs to be taken down for maintenance, it is removed from the server pool, and the SLB continues providing the services using the remaining servers. Similarly, additional server capacity can be added to the pool if needed. These features contribute to enhanced availability for e-commerce modules.

Pairs of SLB devices can function in various failover configurations. Sophisticated service monitoring can be used to ensure that services fail over to the redundant device if the primary SLB device loses connectivity.

Cisco Server Load Balancer Products

Cisco has three product lines that provide content load-balancing and SLB services, and numerous other features. These products are illustrated in Figure 7-8.

Content Services Switch (CSS)		
Content Switching Module (CSM)		
Application Control Engine (ACE) Module		

Figure 7-8   *Cisco Server Load-Balancer Products*

The Cisco CSS 11500 series Content Services Switch (CSS) is a high-performance, high-availability modular device for web infrastructures. As the switch for the Cisco Web Network Services (Web NS) software, the CSS 11500 series helps businesses to build global web networks optimized for content delivery and e-commerce. By examining HTTP headers, the CSS 11500 series helps to ensure availability, optimize utilization, reduce latency, increase scalability, and enhance security for websites, server farms, cache clusters, and firewall systems. The CSS 11500 series switches monitor back-end servers and their applications to make load balancing decisions.

The Cisco Content Switching Module (CSM) adds advanced Layer 4 through Layer 7 SLB capabilities to Catalyst 6500 series switches and Cisco 7600 series routers, and provides the following features and benefits:

■   Investment protection in a high-density, scalable platform with proven reliability

■   Reduced application response times, optimized service delivery, increased application uptime and service scalability for servers, firewalls, VPN devices, and Secure Sockets Layer (SSL) protocol termination devices and caches

■   Fault-tolerant configurations for improved application uptime, using connection and sticky state redundancy for seamless failover

■   Accommodation for a wide range of common IP protocols, including TCP; User Datagram Protocol (UDP); and higher-level protocols, including HTTP, FTP, Telnet, DNS, Real Time Streaming Protocol (RTSP), and Simple Mail Transfer Protocol (SMTP)

■   Integration into an existing infrastructure, minimizing the time and resources required to deploy SLB services

The Cisco ACE module for Cisco Catalyst 6500 series switches and Cisco 7600 series routers is part of the Cisco ACE family of switches. It provides the following features and benefits:

- Centralized IT control over the deployment and management of application services while allowing individual groups to administer their own application instances. The capability to manage 250 virtual partitions, which incorporate Layer 2 through 7 services, within a single physical device, plus role-based access control, workflow management, and rollback capability help simplify management and reduce costs.

- Industry-leading application and device performance. Testing indicates a throughput of 16 gigabits per second (Gbps) and 345,000 sustained connection setups per second, providing the ability to handle large-scale operations. Unique WAN latency and bandwidth-reduction capabilities also help to provide optimal end-user response times.

- Rich levels of application and network security, including bidirectional support for content inspection, SSL encryption and decryption, and transaction logging for application security forensics.

SLB Design Models

The following are three basic design approaches used with SLB devices:

- **Router mode:** The SLB device routes between outside and inside subnets.

- **Bridge mode (inline):** The SLB device operates in transparent bridging mode.

- **One-armed or two-armed mode:** The one-armed or two-armed mode can be implemented in several ways such that replies from servers pass back through the SLB on their way to the end user. The server default gateway can be set to the SLB device, policy-based routing (PBR) can be used, or client NAT can be used.

The following redundancy options can also be included with any of the three basic design approaches:

- With active/passive redundancy, one active SLB device is backed up by the other passive SLB device.

- With active/active redundancy, one SLB device is active for some VIP addresses (representing some services), and another SLB device is active for other VIP addresses (services). The SLB devices back each other up.

There are also various configuration options for how failover is triggered.

These design approaches are detailed in the following sections.

SLB Router Mode

Using the SLB router mode is a popular SLB design approach and is illustrated in Figure 7-9.

In this approach, the SLB device routes between outside and inside subnets. The services' VIP addresses are usually in a globally routable public IP subnet. In Figure 7-9, the public

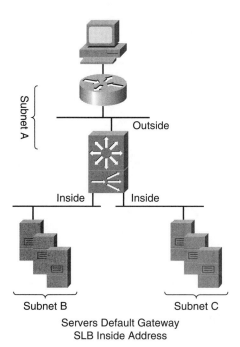

Figure 7-9   *An SLB in Router Mode Routes Between Outside and Inside Subnets*

network is subnet A. The physical servers are typically in a private IP subnet. The private subnets are subnets B and C in Figure 7-9. The SLB routes packets between the public and the private subnets.

The servers typically use the SLB inside address as their default gateway. As reply traffic from the server to the end user passes through the SLB, the SLB changes the server's IP address to the appropriate VIP address. Therefore, the end user has no way of telling that there is an SLB device in the path, nor does the end user see the IP address of the real server. Therefore, using private IP addresses for the real servers protects them from direct attacks across the Internet; would-be hackers cannot route traffic directly to the real servers.

This design is easy to deploy, works well with many server IP subnets, and is the recommended approach for the CSS 11500 series or any appliance-based content load balancer.

SLB Inline Bridge Mode

The SLB device may also be used in an inline bridge mode, as illustrated in Figure 7-10.

This mode operates much like the firewall transparent bridging mode discussed earlier. The content load balancer or SLB device acts as a "bump in the wire" or transparent bridge between the servers and the upstream firewall or Layer 3 device (a router in Figure 7-10). The servers use the IP address of the firewall or Layer 3 device as their default gateway.

In this design, the physical servers are in a globally routable IP subnet, subnet A in Figure 7-10. The VIP addresses of services can be in the same or a different IP subnet. However,

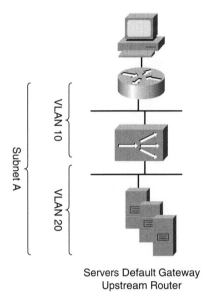

Servers Default Gateway
Upstream Router

Figure 7-10 *An SLB in Inline Bridge Mode Bridges Between VLANs in a Single Subnet*

each server farm must be in one IP subnet because the SLB changes the MAC address associated with the VIP to the specific MAC address of a physical server to direct traffic to the appropriate physical server.

This design is one suggested configuration for integrated load balancers. However, if SLB devices are deployed in a redundant configuration, spanning-tree implications must be considered in the design. Configuring and designing with SLB devices that use routed mode is typically simpler than with devices using bridged mode because troubleshooting SLB spanning-tree issues can be complicated.

SLB One-Armed Mode

The one-armed (or two-armed) mode is another popular approach for deploying SLB devices, as illustrated in Figure 7-11.

In this out-of-band approach, the SLB device is connected to a switch, typically with one or two connections; it is not directly inline with the traffic path as it is in the previous designs discussed. In the one-armed approach, the SLB VIP and the physical servers are in the same VLAN or subnet. In the two-armed approach, the SLB device routes traffic to the physical server subnet, which can be a private subnet.

Inbound end-user traffic is routed to the VIP on the SLB device. The SLB device then translates the IP destination address to a physical server IP address and forwards the traffic to the physical server, the same as it does in routed mode. The main difference is that return traffic must be forced to go to the SLB device so that the source IP address of traffic from the physical server can be translated back to the VIP that the end user device thinks it is communicating with.

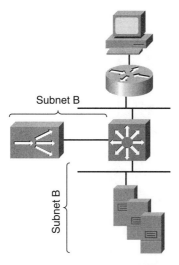

Subnet B

Subnet B

Servers Default Gateway

Figure 7-11   *An SLB in One-Armed Mode Is Not Inline with the Traffic*

The simplest way to cause return traffic to go through the SLB device is to set the server default gateway to the SLB device, rather than the router.

Another approach is to use PBR to "push" or "deflect" the appropriate outbound server traffic to the SLB device as next hop.

A third approach is to use client NAT, in which the client source address is replaced with the SLB address. The server then sends its reply back to the SLB device. The SLB changes the destination address back to the real end-user address and forwards the packet, based on a connection table in the SLB. This approach is not as popular because many organizations want to know the original end-user IP address, for logging and marketing purposes or for security audit trail purposes.

Note: Client NAT is also called "source NAT."

One advantage of the one-armed or two-armed approach is that not all inbound and outbound traffic has to go through the SLB device. For example, PBR can allow the real server to do a file transfer or backup directly, without having to burden the SLB device with processing those packets. This might be helpful in scaling the e-commerce module to support greater traffic volumes.

Another advantage is that scaling by adding SLB devices is simple. Different VIPs can be used to send traffic to different SLB devices, and PBR or client NAT can steer replies back through the correct SLB device. Server default gateways can be used to provide services using different server pools.

Misconfigured SLB One-Armed Mode Flows

Figure 7-12 shows how traffic would flow in a misconfigured network with a one-armed SLB. The steps shown in the figure are as follows:

Figure 7-12   *Traffic Flows Incorrectly in a Misconfigured Network with a One-Armed Server Load Balancer*

Step 1.   The client sends traffic to the VIP. The traffic is routed by the edge router, which uses its MAC address as the source MAC address. The router looks up the VIP in its routing table and uses the SLB MAC address as the destination MAC address.

Step 2.   The SLB device forwards the traffic, using its MAC address as the source MAC address and the selected server MAC and IP addresses as destination addresses.

Step 3.   If the server default gateway, PBR, or client NAT is not configured or is not configured correctly, the physical server reply goes directly to the client, causing a problem because the client receives traffic from a different IP address than the VIP to which its connection was established. In Figure 7-12, this problem is shown as a RESET. The problem results from no mechanism forcing replies back through the SLB device.

Properly Configured Server Load Balancer One-Armed Mode Using Client NAT

Figure 7-13 shows the same network as in Figure 7-12, but with the SLB device doing client NAT.

With client NAT, the client information is rewritten before the packet goes to the server. Note that everything about the source (MAC address, IP address, and port) is rewritten by client NAT. Therefore, when the server replies, it replies to the SLB device.

As discussed, one potential issue with client NAT is accountability; the server traffic logs will show only the IP address of the SLB, not the client's real IP address.

Source	Destination
Router MAC	SLB MAC
Client IP	VIP
Random Port	VIP Port

SLB MAC	Selected Server MAC
SLB NAT Pool IP	Selected Server IP
SLB Random Port	Specific Server Port

Figure 7-13   *Traffic Flows Correctly When the One-Armed SLB Is Configured with Client NAT*

Common E-Commerce Design Topologies for Connecting to Multiple ISPs

One of the key components for e-commerce is ISP connectivity. This section discusses common topology designs for e-commerce modules connected to multiple ISPs.

One Firewall per ISP

Figure 7-14 shows a common approach to dual-homing—connecting a site to two ISPs—using a router, a firewall, or both to connect to each ISP. This approach is commonly used in small sites because it is relatively easy to set up and administer.

> **Note:**   In Figure 7-14 and subsequent figures in this chapter, all addresses shown are private addresses. In reality, public addresses would probably be used on the ISP connections.

> **Note:**   With the Cisco IOS Firewall features, one device might be used for both routing and firewall functions. Another variation of this design uses one router to support both ISP connections.

External DNS resolves the organization's site name to an address from either ISP's external address block (172.16.1.0/24 or 172.20.1.0/24 in Figure 7-14). If DNS resolves using a round-robin approach, external users will be approximately load balanced across the two paths to the organization's web server. The traffic is routed to the outside of the relevant NAT device or firewall.

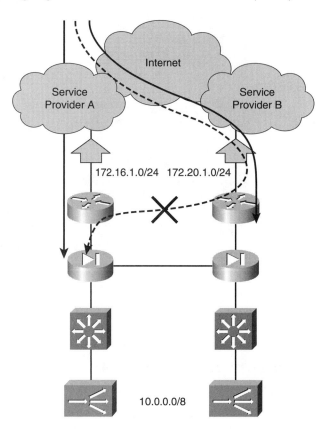

172.16.1.0/24   172.20.1.0/24

10.0.0.0/8

Figure 7-14   *Using One Firewall Per ISP*

On each edge router, NAT translates the address block provided by the ISP to the inside address of the e-commerce servers.

An issue with this design is that any failure on an edge router results in a loss of session because the failover between edge routers is not stateful. Dual routers and dual connections per ISP can be used for more robust connectivity to each ISP, but the nonstateful failover will still exist if connectivity through one ISP is lost. The external DNS would need to be aware if a site loses connectivity through one ISP so that it can stop resolving to addresses that are down.

Stateful Failover with Common External Prefix

A more sophisticated way to dual-home an e-commerce site to two ISPs uses stateful failover with a common external prefix, as illustrated in Figure 7-15.

In this case, the firewall pair and the NAT devices support some form of stateful failover. The NAT devices translate addresses to a block that both ISPs are willing to advertise for the site (172.16.1.0 /24 in the figure). This might be an address block obtained from one of the providers, or it could be a large organization's address block.

172.16.1.0/24

10.0.0.0/8

Figure 7-15 *Using Stateful Failover with a Common External Prefix*

The edge routers advertise this block via BGP to both ISPs, which advertise it to their peers.

Note: BGP configuration requires special care (for example, to prevent the site from becoming a transit link between the ISPs, and to prevent routing loops).

Note: Configuring BGP is covered in the *Authorized Self-Study Guide: Building Scalable Cisco Internetworks (BSCI)*, Third Edition, by Diane Teare and Catherine Paquet, Cisco Press, 2007 (ISBN 1-58705-223-7).

If one provider loses routing or connectivity, BGP automatically fails over to the other path to the site. The firewalls support stateful failover with an active/active design to handle a failure internal to the site's switches or links. First-hop redundancy protocols (FHRP), such as Hot Standby Router Protocol (HSRP), are used for failover in case a switch-to-router link fails.

Note: The FHRPs are HSRP, Virtual Router Redundancy Protocol (VRRP), and Gateway Load Balancing Protocol (GLBP), and are described in Chapter 2.

Distributed Data Centers

Very large e-commerce sites with critical services (such as banks) may use distributed data centers, as illustrated in Figure 7-16.

Figure 7-16   *Using Distributed Data Centers*

Just as deploying two chassis provides greater failover flexibility than deploying one chassis with dual components (such as power and supervisor modules), using two sites increases overall high availability while lessening the uptime requirements for each individual site. When e-commerce modules are implemented in well-designed distributed data centers, one site can occasionally be taken offline for maintenance without disrupting customer service. Using two e-commerce sites also protects against regional problems.

To support the distributed data center design, technology that allows active/active hot databases rather than an active database and a mirrored hot spare database is required. Technology to detect when a site is unreachable (also called "off the air") and should be failed over is also a necessity; this detection is often done external to the two sites. For example an external service provider could be used to detect that a site is down. Alternatively, Cisco Global Site Selector (GSS) technology, typically housed within a provider collocation facility, could be used to provide global server load balancing (GSLB). GSS offloads DNS servers by taking over the domain-resolution process.

> **Note:**   GLSB and GSS are discussed in the "DNS-Based Site Selection and Failover: Global Server Load Balancing with Cisco Global Site Selector" section later in this chapter.

Issues with DNS-based failover techniques may arise because DNS or browser caches retain old DNS address resolutions for a period of time, and many implementations do not use DNS Time to Live (TTL) values properly. Some implementations also incorrectly use source IP addresses to determine user locations, or reorder addresses when a DNS server or GSS provides an ordered list of addresses. Nonetheless, many large sites do use GSLB to improve their service offerings.

Another consideration at some sites is diversity of DNS, which impacts the degree of protection against distributed denial of service (DDoS) on DNS servers. Large external DNS services using anycast IP addressing are one way to protect DNS from attacks. Other possibilities include site-controlled external DNS servers or GSS devices in collocation facilities.

In some distributed e-commerce designs, the redundant sites are connected together via an internal WAN link to avoid the need for an external failover response. With this approach, DNS provides the addresses of servers at either site, using addresses from a block advertised through the ISPs of both sites. If connectivity from one site to the Internet fails, both Internet routing and internal routing redirects traffic to go through the other connection. Failover delays and the impact of any routing instability are potential drawbacks to this approach. Also, if the Internet connection failover is faster than the internal failover, instability may result.

Integrated E-Commerce Designs

This section illustrates more complex e-commerce module designs that incorporate elements from the earlier "Common E-Commerce Module Designs" section.

Base E-Commerce Module Design

This section describes a base e-commerce module design, an example of which is illustrated in Figure 7-17.

In the base design, the core layer supports the first stage of firewalls. In Figure 7-17, the core layer uses Cisco Catalyst 6509 switches with integrated FWSMs in Layer 3 routed mode. The aggregation and access layers are considered trusted zones; therefore, there is no security between the web, application, and database tiers in this base design. If one of the servers is compromised, the attacker may have full access to the other servers and to the internal network.

The aggregation layer supports connectivity to the SLB devices or firewalls, in routed mode. The default gateway for the e-commerce servers is the VIP address on these SLB devices or firewalls. In Figure 7-17, Cisco Catalyst 6513 switches with Cisco CSMs are used as SLB devices; other SLB devices such as the Cisco ACEs could be used instead. The

Figure 7-17   *Base E-Commerce Module Design*

default gateway for the Cisco CSM is an HSRP address on the MSFC on the same Catalyst 6513 switch. Because the MSFC is directly connected to the SLB device, it is possible to support host routes with route health injection (RHI).

> **Note:**   The RHI feature allows the SLB device to inject or remove host routes for its virtual servers, based on the health of the servers and applications. These routes to the virtual servers can then be propagated to the rest of the network. The RHI feature can be used to load balance a virtual server across multiple SLB devices. It can also be used as a disaster recovery mechanism; in this case, the route to a specific virtual server is propagated with a different metric for different SLB devices, either within the same data center or across data centers.

The access layer includes switches (not shown in Figure 7-17) to connect the web servers, application servers, and database servers. In more complex designs, the database servers or mainframes may be inside the main data center, isolated by firewalls from the e-commerce module.

In this design, all e-commerce traffic travels via the Cisco CSM. Additional Cisco CSM configuration is needed if direct access to the servers is required and for non-load-balanced sessions initiated by the servers.

Base Design Routing Logic

Routing in this e-commerce module design is mostly static, using VIP addresses to support failover. Figure 7-18 clarifies how the routing is intended to work.

The left side of Figure 7-18 shows how traffic is routed—using static routes to next-hop addresses—to the VIP of a service on the Cisco CSM and then to a server IP address. The right side of the figure shows how traffic is routed from servers—using default routes to next-hop addresses—to the Internet.

Inbound, the ISP uses a static or BGP route to direct traffic to the e-commerce network. The e-commerce module border router typically uses a static route with the next-hop address set to the outside IP address of the firewall. (Alternatively, Open Shortest Path First [OSPF] routing might be used.)

The firewall uses a static route with the next-hop address set to the HSRP address of the MSFC in the switch. The MSFC uses a connected route to reach the Cisco CSM (or ACE), and static routes to reach the server's actual IP addresses. If RHI is used, it provides the necessary routes to the VIPs. The server's subnets are directly connected to the Cisco CSM or ACE.

Outbound, servers use the Cisco CSM or ACE as their default gateway. From there, a default route causes traffic to go to the HSRP address on the MSFCs, and then to the firewall's inside IP address, and then to the HSRP address of the border router pair, and finally to the connected interface of the ISP router.

The VLAN connections between the aggregation layer switches are used for FHRPs and failover heartbeat detection.

Base Design Server Traffic Flows

Figure 7-19 shows representative flows going to and from a web server in this design. The left side of the figure shows a load-balanced session flow. The right side of the figure shows a server management session flow (for example, a Secure Shell [SSH] connection to a server).

In both of these flows, the firewall handles security logic and the Cisco CSM handles the SLB decision or passes management traffic directly to a specific server.

Note: Sometimes special server management addresses are used to make it easier to configure the Cisco CSM to pass management traffic directly to the server. In other cases, the actual server address is used, rather than the VIP of the service, to indicate management traffic to the SLB module.

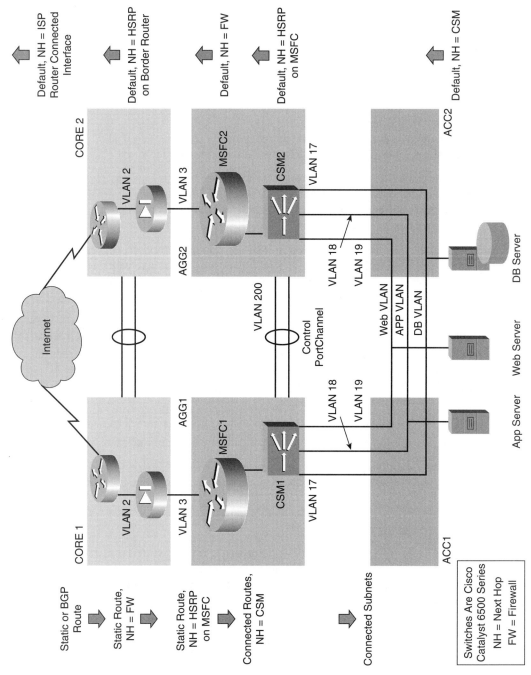

Figure 7-18 *Base E-Commerce Module Design Routing Logic*

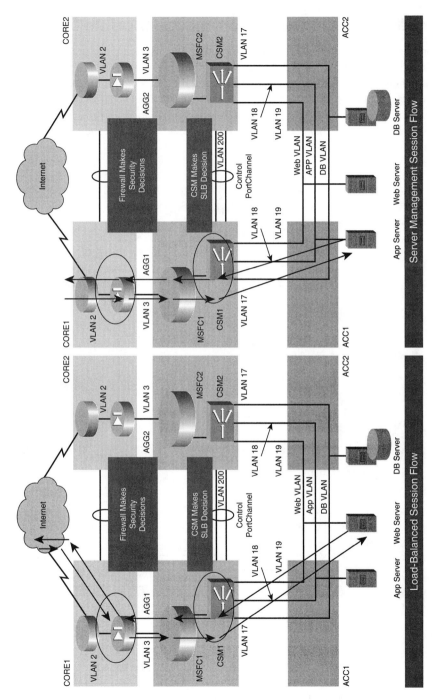

Figure 7-19   *Base E-Commerce Module Design Server Traffic Flows*

Two Firewall Layers in the E-Commerce Module Design

For more protection than in the base design, a firewall can be inserted into the aggregation layer. In the example design in Figure 7-20, FWSM modules have been added to the aggregation switches. The additional FWSM is a Layer 3 firewall with a single context. It provides security between the web, application, and database tiers. Even if the exterior-facing web servers are compromised, a high degree of protection exists for the application and database servers and any connections to the rest of the internal data center network or mainframe.

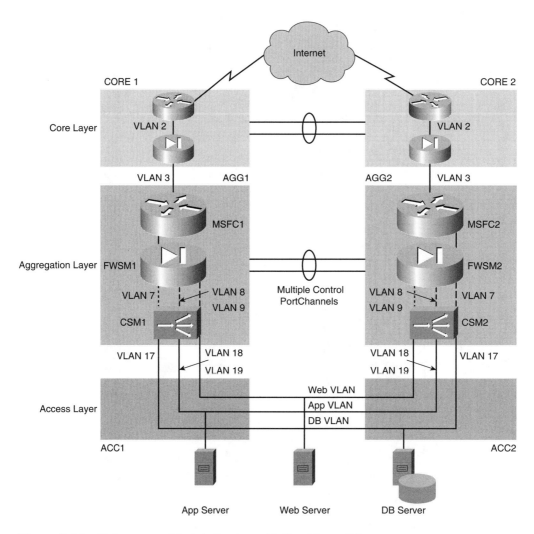

Figure 7-20   *E-Commerce Module Design with Two Firewall Layers*

With this design, the Cisco CSM can be used in routed mode, as was done in the base design, or it can be used in bridged mode to bridge between multiple VLAN pairs. Figure 7-20 illustrates a bridged approach where the default gateway for the servers is the primary FWSM interface in the aggregation switch, rather than an address on the Cisco CSM.

The aggregation switch FWSM routes traffic directly to the server subnets. This traffic is bridged through the Cisco CSM, so the traffic burden on the Cisco CSM is not reduced. However, no extra configuration is needed for direct access to the servers (for example, for deterministic testing from outside) or for non-load-balanced sessions initiated by the servers (for example, FTP downloads).

Note: The CSM default gateway is also the FWSM's primary IP address. In this scenario, because the MSFC is not directly connected to the CSM nor on the same subnet as the Cisco CSM, RHI is not possible.

The VLANs between the aggregation layer switches are used for FHRP or failover heartbeat detection.

Note: Cisco ACE modules could be used in place of the aggregation layer FWSMs, although ACEs are not full firewalls.

Traffic Flows in a Two-Firewall Layer Design

Figure 7-21 shows representative flows going to and from a web server in a design with two firewall layers.

Load-balanced user web traffic is shown in the left half of Figure 7-21. In this design, the perimeter firewall at the core still makes security decisions. The aggregation layer firewall provides an internal DMZ protecting the servers. The Cisco CSM makes the SLB decisions, as it does in the base design.

The right half of Figure 7-21 shows the traffic flow from the web server to the application server. The traffic from the web server is bridged through the Cisco CSM, to the default gateway for that subnet on the aggregation switch FWSM. The FWSM then routes the traffic to the application server subnet. The traffic from the FWSM is bridged through the Cisco CSM to the application server.

Return traffic from the application server to the web server is handled similarly. The application server subnet default gateway directs traffic to the FWSM, which routes it back onto the web server subnet.

One-Armed SLB Two-Firewall E-Commerce Module Design

Figure 7-22 illustrates an e-commerce module design using a one-armed SLB device with two firewall layers.

In a one-armed design with two firewall layers, the Cisco CSM is moved such that selected traffic to and from the servers does not go through it. The design can be scaled by adding additional Cisco FWSMs and CSM or ACE modules to the switch chassis as needed.

Figure 7-21 *E-Commerce Module Design with Two Firewall Layers Traffic Flows*

Figure 7-22 *E-Commerce Module One-Armed SLB Design with Two Firewall Layers*

The FWSM module at the aggregation layer again provides security between the web, application, and database tiers.

In this design, the default gateway of the servers is still the appropriate primary IP address on the FWSM in the aggregation switch. The default gateway of the Cisco CSM, however, is the HSRP address on the MSFCs.

Inbound traffic is routed to the Cisco CSM as a connected route to the VIP of the service on the CSM. The Cisco CSM then statically routes inbound traffic to the aggregation switch FWSM, which routes it to the connected server subnet. Traffic bound directly for a real server IP address bypasses the Cisco CSM.

The appropriate outbound traffic from the servers is directed by PBR or client NAT to the Cisco CSM. The MSFC is directly connected to the Cisco CSM, and so RHI is possible. No extra configuration is needed for direct traffic to and from the servers. All non-load-balanced traffic to and from the servers bypasses the Cisco CSM.

Traffic Flows in a One-Armed SLB Two-Firewall Layer Design

Figure 7-23 shows representative flows going to and from a web server in the one-armed SLB design with two firewall layers.

The traffic flow in the left half of Figure 7-23 is similar to the flow in Figure 7-21. The difference is that PBR or client NAT is required to direct the outbound server traffic from the MSFC to the SLB.

The right half of Figure 7-23 differs from the previous design in Figure 7-21. The traffic from the web server to the application server bypasses the Cisco CSM in this design. The FWSM routes traffic between the web server VLAN and the application server VLAN.

If server load balancing is desired for traffic from the web server to the application server, a more complex approach is required. For example, a VIP address in another subnet would allow routing of traffic from the web server to a virtual application server address, via the Cisco CSM.

Direct Server Traffic Flows in a One-Armed SLB Two-Firewall Layer Design

Figure 7-24 shows representative flows for server management traffic and direct Internet traffic going to and from a web server in the one-armed design with two firewall layers. The Cisco CSM is not in the traffic path for this type of traffic to and from the servers.

One-Armed SLB E-Commerce Module Design with Firewall Contexts

Figure 7-25 illustrates a design using a one-armed SLB with an aggregation firewall supporting multiple firewall contexts.

The aggregation FWSM is used in transparent mode, with the MSFC routing between the server VLANs.

A firewall context is also placed logically in the Layer 2 path before traffic reaches the MSFC, eliminating the need for a separate firewall in the core layer. There is firewall protection from the outside, internally, and for each DMZ. The MSFC is on a secure internal segment with protection from each connected network.

The default gateway of the servers is the HSRP primary IP address on the MSFC. No extra configuration is needed for direct access to the servers or for non-load-balanced server-initiated sessions.

The CSM default gateway is the HSRP address on the MSFC. The Cisco CSM is deployed in routed mode in a one-armed topology. With the Cisco CSM in one-armed mode,

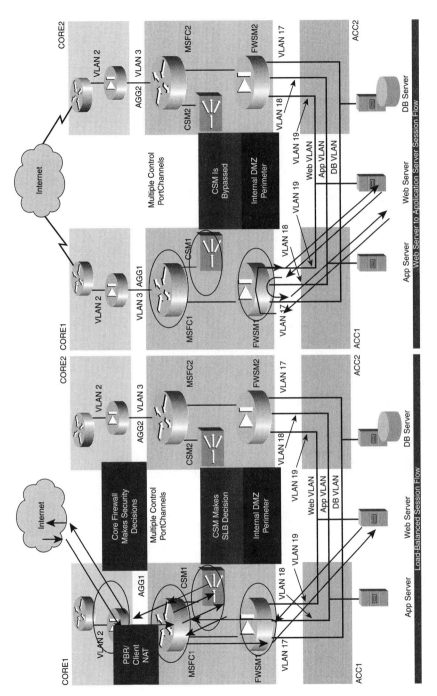

Figure 7-23 *E-Commerce Module One-Armed SLB Design with Two Firewall Layers Traffic Flows*

Figure 7-24 *Direct Server Traffic Flows in an E-Commerce Module One-Armed SLB Design with Two Firewall Layers*

non-load-balanced traffic can easily bypass the CSM. RHI is possible in this design because the MSFC is directly connected to the CSM.

Traffic Flows in a One-Armed SLB Design with Firewall Contexts

Figure 7-26 shows representative flows going to and from a web server in the one-armed SLB design with multiple firewall contexts.

Figure 7-25   *E-Commerce Module One-Armed SLB Design with Firewall Contexts*

On the left side of Figure 7-26, inbound traffic reaches the core router and is routed to the MSFC in the aggregation layer switch. To reach the MSFC, it passes through a FWSM firewall context in transparent mode for security checks and ACL filtering. The MSFC then routes inbound packets to the VIP on the Cisco CSM, which performs destination NAT processing on the packets. The Cisco CSM then routes the packets to the web server subnet. The FSWM applies ACLs and security enforcement because it is logically between the MSFC and the web server VLAN.

Note: Each subnet (web, application, and database) encompasses two VLANs that are bridged by the FWSM.

Figure 7-26   *Traffic Flows in an E-Commerce Module One-Armed SLB Design with Fire-wall Contexts*

Outbound traffic from the web server goes through the FWSM to the MSFC, is routed to the Cisco CSM via PBR, and then is routed to the core router.

The right side of Figure 7-26 shows traffic being routed by the MSFC between the web server subnet and the application server subnet. This traffic passes through the FWSM twice; the FWSM enforces ACLs and security policies both times. Return traffic also passes through the FWSM twice. All routing next-hop addresses use HSRP virtual addresses, either on the MSFCs or on the core routers.

With minimal configuration effort, traffic from the web servers to the application servers can be sent through the Cisco CSM.

Note: The trunk between the switches is necessary to support failover.

One-Armed SLB E-Commerce Module Design with CSS

Figure 7-27 illustrates a one-armed SLB design with Cisco CSS 11500 series switches.

In Figure 7-27, the FWSMs are Layer 2 firewalls with multiple security contexts. There are several DMZs, with firewall perimeters outside, inside, and at each DMZ. The aggregation layer MSFC is on a secure internal segment with protection from each connected network, including from any malicious activity on data center networks.

The external CSS 11500 series switch is used in one-armed fashion; the dual CSS devices are connected with ports in the same VLANs.

NAT is implemented on the MSFC (because the transparent firewall does not support this function). Alternatively, an additional routed context on the FWSM could support NAT.

The CSS default gateway is the HSRP address on the MSFC. The dual CSS devices are directly connected at Layer 2 to the MSFCs, so RHI is possible.

The servers' default gateway is the HSRP primary IP address on the MSFC. Non-load-balanced traffic to and from the servers bypasses the CSS devices because the CSSs are in one-armed mode.

Testing E-Commerce Module Designs

As discussed, it is important to test failover conditions within e-commerce designs as thoroughly as possible to improve high availability. This testing first requires designers to do a preliminary analysis to understand how network devices detect different types of failures and how they will failover. Testing not only confirms correct device configuration but can also help identify modes where failover does not occur. For example, applications may operate differently when packets are silently dropped (for example, because of the loss of NAT information or stateful firewall state) than when a TCP reset or ICMP unreachable message is received.

Failover testing includes simulating failures as close to the real failure conditions as possible. For example, simulating a link failure by unplugging an Ethernet connection causes

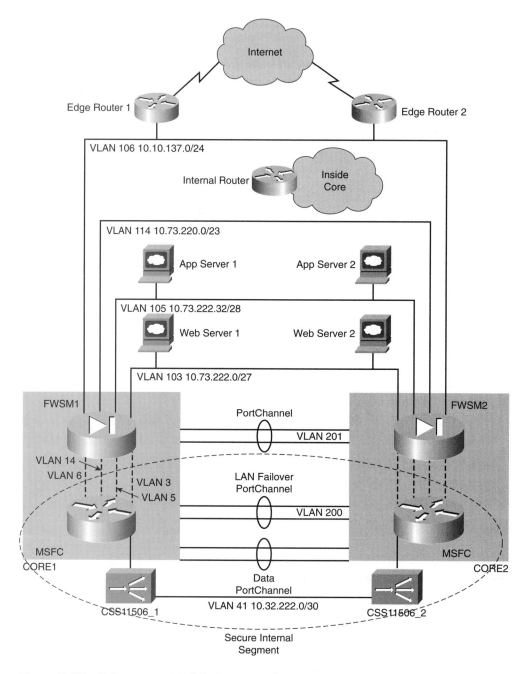

Figure 7-27   *E-Commerce Module One-Armed Design with CSS*

the switch or other device to detect the loss of the Ethernet, but this creates a relatively static condition. Silent packet drops can also be simulated.

One way that silent packet drops can be simulated is by sending traffic in a VLAN on a trunk and disallowing the VLAN at the other end of the trunk. Alternatively, some network prefixes can be routed to the NULL0 interface, causing packets to those destination prefixes to be discarded. On the other hand, implementing passive interfaces or otherwise altering routing to delete the route to a destination will not simulate a silent discard because the router normally sends "Destination network unreachable" packets back to the sender when packets are received for a prefix that is not in the routing table.

Layer 3 switches might experience a system failure (simulated by turning the power off) or a partial failure (simulated by removing one module). In the case of a partial failure, Layer 3 operations might stop functioning, but Layer 2 operations may continue. Neighboring devices would then experience loss of traffic and connectivity but not loss of Ethernet link status. This could be simulated by configuring the **no ip routing** command on the MSFC or route processor on a Layer 3 switch.

Creating testing procedure documentation aids in future troubleshooting. When an incident occurs in the production network, the test procedure documentation should be updated, reflecting lessons learned and possibly presenting alternatives to simulate the observed failure mode. Testing and the associated documentation can also be used to validate new software releases and configuration changes. For example, regression testing ensures that new software or configuration enhancements have not unnecessarily changed failover behavior.

Tuning E-Commerce Module Designs

Several technologies may be used to enhance e-commerce designs, including the following:

- BGP tuning

- EOT

- OER

- DNS-based site selection and failover, including GSLB with Cisco GSS

These techniques are explored in the following sections.

BGP Tuning

One of the main uses of BGP is for communicating to ISPs. BGP can be tuned to control packet flow by communicating the available prefixes, routing policies, and preferences between a site and its ISPs.

Network designers need to consider which traffic should enter and exit the e-commerce data center or data centers by which ISP and by which link; most sites attempt some form of load balancing. Load balancing ideally should result in traffic flows being split 50-50 across two links, but in practice this is hard to achieve. Designers should attempt to approximately balance the traffic with some simple tuning; traffic monitoring will be necessary and retuning traffic flows will require changes to BGP configurations.

With a single ISP, multi-exit discriminator (MED) or BGP communities can be used to communicate the site preferences for traffic flow from the Internet to the organization. With multiple ISPs, MED is unlikely to be advertised between providers, so BGP communities or AS prepending can be used to influence inbound traffic.

Note: The information in the following two sidebars is derived from the *Authorized Self-Study Guide: Building Scalable Cisco Internetworks (BSCI)*, Third Edition, by Diane Teare and Catherine Paquet, Cisco Press, 2007 (ISBN 1-58705-223-7), and provides background on the BGP community and MED attributes.

BGP Community Attribute

BGP communities allow routers to tag routes with an indicator (the community) and allow other routers to make decisions based on that tag. Any BGP router can tag routes in incoming and outgoing routing updates, or when doing redistribution. Any BGP router can filter routes in incoming or outgoing updates or can select preferred routes based on communities (the tag). BGP communities are used for destinations (routes) that share some common properties, and therefore share common policies; therefore, routers act on the community rather than on individual routes. Communities are not restricted to one network or one autonomous system, and they have no physical boundaries.

BGP MED Attribute

The BGP MED attribute, also called the *metric*, indicates to external (in another autonomous system) neighbors the preferred path into an autonomous system. This is a dynamic way for an autonomous system to try to influence another autonomous system as to which way it should choose to reach a certain route if there are multiple entry points into the autonomous system.

A lower metric value indicates a preferred path.

The failover behavior of BGP routing with ISPs needs to be tested and understood. Because ISPs constantly update route filters, monitoring traffic and periodic testing are necessary to ensure that the site's prefixes have not been accidentally filtered by the ISPs.

Note: RFC 1998, *An Application of the BGP Community Attribute in Multi-home Routing*, details how BGP communities are used.

Enhanced Object Tracking

EOT is a Cisco IOS capability that efficiently uses a standalone process to track the status of objects. EOT was first available in Cisco IOS Software Release 12.2(15)T.

EOT can track the following objects:

■ Line protocol.

■ IP routing state (for example, interface up, IP address known, and routing enabled).

■ Reachability of an IP route (if the route is present and accessible).

■ IP routing metric (above or below a threshold).

■ Results of IP SLAs operations (including the reachability of the target, thresholds for packet loss, latency, and jitter). This feature was first available in Cisco IOS Release 12.3(4)T and 12.2(25)S.

Note: The Cisco IOS IP SLAs feature is described in Chapter 12, "Network Management Capabilities within Cisco IOS Software."

The EOT process notifies other processes that have registered with EOT when EOT detects a problem. EOT is useful in verifying end-to-end path availability and helps identify situations where the network is sending traffic down a path that is *black-holing* packets (sending them to a place from which they will not be forwarded), has congestion, or has quality problems.

The FHRPs—HSRP, VRRP, and GLBP—can track the up or down state of a local interface on a router. If a link fails on a primary FHRP router, standby tracking causes the traffic to switch over to a standby FHRP router to ensure continued communication.

EOT adds the ability to discover nonlocal problems and react to these problems. HSRP, GLBP, and VRRP can be clients of EOT.

EOT can also track Boolean "and" and "or" combinations of conditions and weighted combinations of condition thresholds, for sophisticated failover logic.

Figure 7-28 *EOT with HSRP and IP SLAs Tracking*

HSRP and IP SLAs Tracking Example

Figure 7-28 illustrates an example of how EOT is used with HSRP and IP SLAs tracking.

In this example, a Cisco IOS IP SLAs measurement is being run from router 1 to server A across ISP 1. Local hosts reach server A via router 1 until EOT forces a failover to router 2 in response to loss of packets, latency, or jitter along the path via ISP 1.

Example 7-1 is a partial sample configuration on Router 1 in this example.

Example 7-1 *Partial Configuration of Router 1 in Figure 7-28*

```
ip sla 18
  icmp-echo {server-address}
ip sla schedule 18 start-time now life forever
track 100 rtr 18 state
interface FastEthernet0/0
  ip address 10.10.10.1 255.255.255.224
  standby 1 ip 10.10.10.10
  standby 1 priority 105
  standby 1 preempt

standby 1 track 100 decrement 10
```

The **track 100 rtr 18 state** command defines object 100 as a tracked object representing the state of IOS IP SLAs operation number 18. The **standby 1 track 100 decrement 10** command tracks object 100, and decrements the HSRP priority by 10 if the object goes down.

As this example illustrates, EOT can be used to influence the choice of exit router and the outbound path, typically done in response to conditions outside of the local network.

Injecting Routes and IP SLAs Example

The example in Figure 7-29 illustrates how the routes injected into BGP can be configured to depend on server reachability.

Figure 7-29   *Injecting Routes into BGP with IP SLAs*

Example 7-2 is a portion of the configuration on Router 1 in this example. (Router 2 is configured similarly.)

Example 7-2 *Partial Configuration of Router 1 in Figure 7-29*

```
ip sla 1
  icmp-echo {server-address}
ip sla schedule 18 start-time now life forever

track 123 rtr 1 reachability
ip route {server_network} 255.255.255.0 Null0 track 123
! (this static route is just used for BGP advertisements;
!   more specific routes will be used to forward packets)
router bgp 65505
  redistribute static
```

In this example, an IP SLAs measurement is configured from router 1 to server A. Traffic flows to the server based on a specific prefix route. The **track 123 rtr 1 reachability** command defines object 123 as a tracked object representing the reachability of IOS IP SLAs operation number 1. The **ip route** {*server_network*} **255.255.255.0 Null0 track 123** command configures a more general prefix as a static route that tracks the object 123. If server A becomes unreachable or does not respond, this static route is withdrawn.

The BGP process advertises this more general static route. If the static route is withdrawn in response to an EOT condition, BGP on Router 1 stops advertising the route to ISP 1. BGP on Router 2 advertises the alternate route to Server A to ISP2.

In this case, EOT provides a relatively simple way to track reachability through a complex network. When reachability fails, failover to another ISP link or another site is triggered.

This example illustrates how EOT controls what is advertised to a BGP peer at an ISP; the advertisement controls the path and entrance router used by inbound traffic.

Optimized Edge Routing

Cisco IOS OER is another alternative to detect and react to undesirable conditions along a path.

BGP by default determines the best outbound path based on the shortest autonomous system path, if none of the other BGP attributes are altered. OER allows the path selection to be based on policies that include measured reachability, delay, loss, jitter, synthetic Mean Opinion Score (MOS) (for voice), load, and monetary cost.

OER selects the optimal exit point, providing automatic outbound route optimization and load distribution for multiple connections. OER is an integrated Cisco IOS Software solution that allows users to monitor IP traffic flows and then define policies and rules based on prefix performance, link load distribution, link cost, and traffic type.

OER selects the best *exit* path but it does not affect routing or path selection for *inbound* traffic (from outside of the site).

To implement OER, one or more border routers (BR) are configured to communicate with a router configured as the master controller (MC). The MC makes decisions about the outbound path to use, based on the configured policy.

Figure 7-30 shows a sample network in which there are multiple paths from an enterprise or content provider to a remote office or content consumer. OER selects the best path from the enterprise to the consumer, based on configured policy.

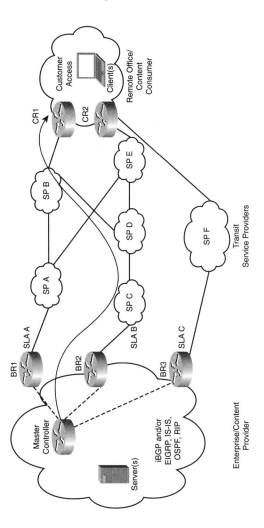

Figure 7-30   *OER Selects the Best Exit Path*

Optimized Edge Routing Operations

OER follows a cycle of learn, measure, apply policy, optimize, and verify, as illustrated in Figure 7-31 and described in the following sections.

Learn Phase

In the learn phase, OER identifies prefixes and traffic classes of interest, based on the configuration.

Measure Phase

In the measure phase, passive or active measurements are made by each BR.

OER passive monitoring is based on TCP traffic flows for IP traffic. Passive monitoring of non-TCP sessions is not supported because UDP does not readily provide delay estimates, response counts, and other traffic data.

Passive monitoring uses NetFlow data in memory. The router observes what happens when packets are sent, and records the results as internal NetFlow statistics. If no packets are being sent, there is no information or measurements. NetFlow data captures delay and throughput statistics. The delay measurements are based on TCP round-trip time (RTT) from the initial synchronization (SYN) to the following acknowledgment (ACK). OER also records packet loss (comparing the highest TCP sequence number in received packets with lower sequence numbered packets) and unreachables (SYN with no received ACK) for passive measurements.

Note: NetFlow is described in Chapter 12.

Active probing defaults to using Internet Control Message Protocol (ICMP) echo and echo reply in ping probes.

Note: Caution must be used because repeated ping probing might trigger an intrusion detection system (IDS) or intrusion prevention system (IPS) intervention on the remote site.

OER active probing can be configured to use IP SLAs measurements rather than ping, allowing OER to respond to delay or jitter in the network. Currently, OER can use ICMP, TCP connections, or UDP echo for active probing. Note that the target for the latter two must be capable of responding. If the target is a router, it must be configured with the **ip sla responder** command.

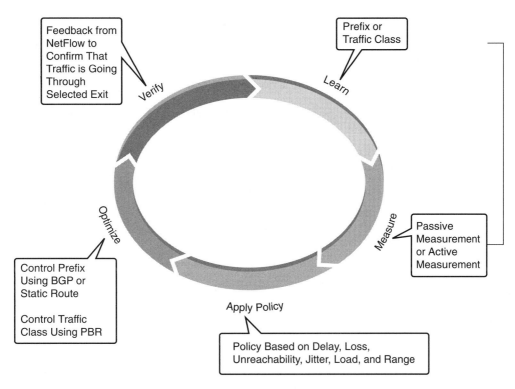

Figure 7-31 *OER Follows a Cycle of Learn, Measure, Apply Policy, Optimize, and Verify*

Note: The **ip sla responder** command is used on the destination device for IP SLAs operations to enable the sending and receiving of IP SLAs control packets, to allow the device sending IP SLAs operations to generate monitoring statistics.
(The **ip sla responder** command replaces the **ip sla monitor responder** command in Cisco IOS Release 12.4(4)T, which replaced the earlier **rtr responder** command.)

As of Cisco IOS Software Release 12.3(14)T, OER can also conduct traceroute probes. These probes collect delay, loss, and reachability information for each hop from the source address to the probe target prefix. These probes can be configured to run in three ways: continuous, policy based (running only when the prefix is outside of the policy), or on demand.

Apply Policy Phase

In the apply policy phase, the MC periodically gathers data from the BRs, and applies the configured policy to determine the best route.

Optimize Phase

In the optimize phase, controls are applied either by adding a static or BGP route, or by using PBR if traffic classes are to be controlled.

OER routing control is exerted by injecting routes into the BRs using OER command messages from the MC to the BRs, not by inserting routes on the MC.

Currently, OER influences routing in the following two ways:

- By setting the BGP local preference for a specific prefix

- By creating a temporary static route for a specific prefix

These routing changes in the BRs influence the other routers in the internal network through internal BGP peering or through BGP or static route redistribution into the Interior Gateway Protocol (IGP).

The injected BGP or static route is not advertised to external peers and has no routing impact outside of the local site.

If the BRs are close to one another (for example, if they have a high-speed LAN connection between them), default routes can be used by internal routers to get packets to the BRs, and OER can send some traffic for selected prefixes between the exit BRs. OER is used to select one BR over another. From OER's perspective, IGP routing is used to route traffic only between the BRs, or if traffic must be directed to a specific BR.

Verify Phase

In the verify phase, feedback from NetFlow confirms that traffic is using the selected exit path.

Optimized Edge Routing Topologies

Figure 7-32 illustrates some of the topologies in which OER is used.

In the first example, which could be used by a smaller site doing e-commerce, a small office/home office (SOHO) or broadband site has two exit paths, with one router connected to two ISPs or to two points of presence (POP) for a single ISP. The single edge router is configured to be both the MC and a BR, and selects between the two exit paths using OER.

In the second example, a remote office with two exit routers to two ISPs uses OER to select the best path to its headquarters office. One of the BRs is also the MC. This topology could be used by a site doing e-commerce, with two routers connected to two ISPs or to two POPs for a single ISP.

In the third example, a larger e-commerce site has an MC separate from the two BRs. OER selects the best outbound path through ISP 1 or ISP 2.

1) SOHO or Broadband

2) Remote Office

3) Headquarters Content Hosting or Data Centers

Figure 7-32 *OER Topologies*

OER is used to influence *outbound* traffic path selection. As discussed earlier, EOT with selective route advertisement is one way to influence the *inbound* traffic path.

DNS-Based Site Selection and Failover: GSLB with Cisco Global Site Selector

Another way of tuning e-commerce service delivery is to provide DNS-based selection of the best destination for each client.

Organizations that provide web and application hosting services often require network devices that can perform complex request routing to two or more redundant, geographically dispersed data centers. These network devices need to provide fast response times, disaster recovery, and failover protection.

Cisco GSS is the Cisco product that performs GSLB. As shown in the example in Figure 7-33, GSS leverages global content deployment across multiple distributed and mirrored data locations, optimizing site selection, improving DNS responsiveness, and ensuring data center availability. When a user in this example requests a connection to a website, GSS offloads the DNS servers by taking over the domain resolution process. GSS transmits the DNS requests at thousands of requests per second and complements the existing DNS infrastructure by providing centralized domain management. In this example, GSS replies to the user with the best destination address to reach the website.

GSS provides real-time global load balancing across multiple data centers and improves the global data center selection process by offering user-selectable global load-balancing algorithms, scaling to support hundreds of data centers or SLB devices.

GSS also provides traffic rerouting in case of disaster. The scalable dedicated hardware platform ensures web-based applications are always available by detecting site outages or

Figure 7-33 *GSS Offloads DNS Servers*

site congestion and rerouting content requests. The GSS traffic-management process continuously monitors the load and health of the SLB devices within each data center. This information is used in conjunction with customer-controlled load-balancing algorithms to enable the GSS to select a data center that is available and not overloaded, within user-definable load conditions in real time.

Summary

In this chapter, you learned about e-commerce module design.

High availability is important to the e-commerce module and includes the following five components:

- Redundancy, including duplicate equipment and network links to reduce the effects of a single point of failure

- Technology, including hardware and software features

- People, including staff skills and training

- Processes, including change processes and failover testing

- Tools, including proper documentation

Common e-commerce module firewall designs include the following:

- The "firewall sandwich" design that separates the web tier, the application tier, and the database tier with redundant firewall layers.

- Using servers, such as web servers, as application gateways to increase security.

- Virtualizing a physical firewall, such as an FWSM, to create firewall contexts.

- Using virtual firewall layers within physical firewalls.

- Using firewalls in routing or transparent (bridging) modes. Transparent firewalls bridge two VLANs together, switching traffic at Layer 2 between the two VLANs, which together constitute one IP subnet.

SLB devices map a VIP address for each service to a pool of real physical servers. SLB devices include the Cisco CSS 11500 series switch, the CSM, and the ACE module, and are used in router, bridge (inline), or one-armed (out-of-band) mode.

Common topologies for connecting to multiple ISPs include using one firewall per ISP with separate NAT pools, using a common external prefix advertised through BGP with a single NAT pool, and using distributed data centers with different ISPs.

The base e-commerce design includes firewalls only in the core layer. The aggregation and access layers are considered trusted zones; therefore, there is no security between the web, application, and database tiers in the base design.

A design with firewall services in the core and aggregation layers provides additional security between the web, application, and database tiers.

An SLB in one-armed mode can be used with two firewall layers to provide security. The SLB is deployed off to the side so that selected traffic to and from the servers does not go through it.

A one-armed SLB design with multiple firewall contexts can be used to provide firewall perimeters outside, inside, and at each DMZ. This design also eliminates the need for a separate firewall in the core layer. This one-armed SLB design can be further enhanced with Cisco CSS 11500 series switches.

Testing failover conditions within e-commerce module designs is important, including analyzing failure modes and doing simulations of the failure modes and their effects.

Several technologies may be used to enhance e-commerce designs, including the following:

- BGP tuning, to control packet flow by communicating the available prefixes, routing policies, and preferences between a site and its ISPs

- EOT, to track the status of remote objects and react to this status

- OER, using passive or active measurements to determine the best exit router

- DNS-based site selection and failover, including GSLB with Cisco GSS to externally load balance site selection for user traffic and respond to site outages or congestion

References

For additional information, refer to the following:

- Cisco Systems, Inc. Data Center Networking: Integrating Security, "Load Balancing, and SSL Services Using Service Modules (Solutions Reference Network Design)," at http://www.cisco.com/en/US/solutions/ns340/ns414/ns742/ns656/net_design_guidance0900aecd800f252b.pdf

- Cisco Systems, Inc. "High Availability Introduction," at http://www.cisco.com/en/US/products/ps6550/products_ios_technology_home.html

- Cisco Systems, Inc. "Data Center Networking: Internet Edge Design Architectures (Solutions Reference Network Design)," at http://www.cisco.com/en/US/solutions/ns340/ns414/ns742/ns656/net_design_guidance09186a008014ee4e.pdf

- Cisco Systems, Inc. "Configuring Secure (Router) Mode on the Content Switching Module," at http://www.cisco.com/warp/public/117/csm/csm_router.pdf

- Cisco Systems, Inc. "Configuring Single Subnet (Bridge) Mode on the CSM," at http://www.cisco.com/warp/public/117/csm/csm_bridge.pdf

- Cisco Systems, Inc. "Configuring Enhanced Object Tracking," at http://www.cisco.com/univercd/cc/td/doc/product/software/ios124/124cg/hiap_c/haipbtrk.pdf

- Cisco Systems, Inc. "Cisco IOS Optimized Edge Routing Configuration Guide, Release 12.4T," at http://www.cisco.com/en/US/docs/ios/oer/configuration/guide/12_4t/oer_12_4t_book.html

- Teare, Diane and Catherine Paquet. *Authorized Self-Study Guide: Building Scalable Cisco Internetworks (BSCI)*, Third Edition. Cisco Press, 2007.

Review Questions

Answer the following questions, and then refer to Appendix A, "Answers to Review Questions," for the answers.

1. List the five components of high availability.

2. Describe some of the ways that people affect network high availability.

3. Match the term with the definition.

   Term:
   - Web tier
   - Application tier
   - Database tier

   Definition:
   - The mainframes
   - The outer DMZ
   - Middleware servers in the data center

4. Which of the following best describes how web tier servers are connected when they act as application-specific gateways?

   a. One interface of the web servers provides web services, and a separate interface connects through another firewall to application servers.

   b. One interface of the web servers provides application services, and a separate interface connects through another firewall to web servers.

   c. The one connected interface provides web services.

   d. The one connected interface provides application services.

5. What is a firewall context?

6. Select the true statements regarding the two modes in which a Cisco firewall can operate.

   a. In transparent mode, the firewall bridges two VLANs together.

   b. In routed mode, the firewall routes between two VLANs.

   c. In transparent mode, the firewall bridges between two parts of a single VLAN.

   d. In transparent mode, two VLANs represent one IP subnet.

7. What is a virtual IP address?

8. Match each of the modes in which a Cisco SLB can operate with its best definition from the list.

Modes:
- Router mode
- Bridge mode
- One-armed or two-armed

Definitions:
- The servers typically use the SLB inside address as their default gateway.
- Return traffic must be forced to go to the SLB device so that the source IP address of traffic from the physical server can be translated back to the VIP that the end user device thinks it is communicating with.
- The SLB device acts as a "bump in the wire" between the servers and the upstream firewall or Layer 3 device.

9. You have designed an e-commerce module with an SLB in inline bridge mode. Which address will the servers typically use as their default gateway?

10. Select the true statements regarding client NAT.

a. Client NAT is used with SLB devices in router mode.

b. Client NAT is used with SLB devices in one-armed mode.

c. Client NAT replaces the source address in the packet from the client with the SLB address.

d. Client NAT replaces the destination address in the packet from the client with the SLB address.

11. You have designed an e-commerce solution using distributed data centers. How could the failover between sites be implemented?

12. What does the RHI feature on SLB devices do?

13. Describe how routing is accomplished in the base e-commerce module design.

14. Select the true statements regarding the firewalls in the two-firewall layer e-commerce module design.

a. One firewall is in the core layer, and the other is in the aggregation layer.

b. Both firewalls are in the core layer.

c. Both firewalls are in the aggregation layer.

d. One firewall provides security at the edge and the other provides security between the web, application, and database tiers.

e. One firewall provides security between the web and application tiers and the other provides security between the application and database tiers.

15. What is the advantage of using an e-commerce module design that includes a one-armed SLB device with two firewall layers?

16. In a one-armed SLB design with Cisco CSS 11500 series switches, the dual CSS devices are connected with ports in the same VLANs. The CSS default gateway is the HSRP address on the MSFC. What is the servers' default gateway?

17. Select the true statements regarding the BGP MED and community attributes.

    a. A BGP community is a tag that a router can set and upon which other routers can make decisions.

    b. BGP communities can only be used within a single autonomous system.

    c. The BGP MED indicates to neighbors within the same autonomous system the preferred path into the autonomous system.

    d. A lower BGP MED value indicates a preferred path.

18. Match the terms with the definitions.
Terms:
- EOT
- OER
- GSLB

Definitions:
- Allows the path selection to be based on policies, including measured reachability, delay, loss, and jitter
- Offloads DNS servers by taking over the domain-resolution process
- Uses a standalone process to track the status of objects, including interface up

After completing this chapter, you will be able to

■ Design security-intelligent network services for performance, scalability, and availability, given specified enterprise network needs

■ Discuss design considerations for firewall services in the enterprise

■ Describe design considerations for using network admission control services in the enterprise

■ Discuss design considerations for intrusion-detection and -prevention services in the enterprise

CHAPTER 8

Security Services Design

As enterprises continually expand their mission-critical networks with new intranet, extranet, and e-commerce applications, network security is increasingly vital to prevent corruption and intrusion, and to eliminate network security vulnerabilities. Without precautions, enterprises could experience major security breaches, resulting in serious damages or loss.

This chapter examines security design in the enterprise. It will look at design considerations for firewall services, network admission control, and intrusion-detection and -prevention services. Readers should already know how to implement firewalls and security features such as access control lists (ACL), IP security (IPsec) connections, Network Address Translation (NAT), and Port Address Translation (PAT).

Designing Firewalls

Firewalls have long provided the first line of defense in network security infrastructures. They accomplish this by comparing corporate policies about network access rights for users to the connection information surrounding each access attempt. User policies and connection information must match; otherwise, the firewall does not grant access to network resources.

This section looks at firewall design considerations. It discusses options for firewall deployment and topologies, including firewall modes, virtual firewalls, asymmetric routing using active/active topologies, scaling firewall performance, private VLANs (PVLAN), and zone-based firewalls.

Firewall Modes

A firewall can run in either routed or transparent mode (see Figure 8-1).

In the traditional routed mode, the firewall is considered to be a Layer 3 device in the network. It can perform NAT between connected networks. Routed mode supports many interfaces. Each interface is on a different subnet and requires an IP address on that subnet.

Transparent mode is a newer mode available as of Firewall Service Module (FWSM) Release 2.2 and Cisco ASA and PIX Firewall Software Version 7.0.

In transparent mode, the firewall is a Layer 2 device, not a router hop. Per context, the firewall connects the same network on its inside and outside interface in transparent mode.

Figure 8-1   *Firewall Mode: Routed or Transparent*

Firewalls can support multiple pairs of inside and outside interfaces as a bridge group. Each bridge group connects to a different network. A transparent firewall has one IP address assigned to the entire bridge group, and uses this management address as the source address for packets originating on the firewall.

Transparent mode can allow certain types of traffic in an access list that is blocked by routed mode, including unsupported protocols. Routing protocol adjacencies are supported through a transparent firewall. Open Shortest Path First (OSPF), Routing Information Protocol (RIP), Enhanced Interior Gateway Routing Protocol (EIGRP), or Border Gateway Protocol (BGP) traffic is allowed based on an extended access list. Protocols such as Hot Standby Router Protocol (HSRP), Virtual Router Redundancy Protocol (VRRP), and IP multicast can be supported through a transparent firewall. Transparent mode can also optionally use ethertype access lists to allow non-IP traffic.

Note: This section primarily uses the FWSM as the example firewall. ASA and PIX devices could be used, too. ASA or PIX operational differences are illustrated in the chapter.

The PIX, ASA, and FWSM have different ACL mechanisms for controlling traffic:

■   The PIX Firewall, by default, allows traffic to flow freely from an inside network (higher security level) to an outside network (lower security level).

■   The ASA allows IPv4 traffic through the routed or transparent firewall mode automatically from a higher security interface to a lower security interface without an access list. ARPs are allowed through the transparent firewall in both directions without an access list. For Layer 3 traffic traveling from a lower security level interface to a high security level interface, an extended access list is required.

■   The FWSM does not allow traffic to pass between interfaces unless it is explicitly permitted with an ACL. The only traffic allowed through the transparent firewall without an ACL is ARP traffic. Layer 3 traffic, such as IP traffic, cannot pass through the FWSM even though the transparent mode acts as a bridge, unless the traffic is explicitly permitted with an extended ACL.

Virtual Firewall Overview

A virtual firewall separates multiple firewall security contexts on a single firewall.

Specific VLANs are tied to a specific security context, as shown in Figure 8-2. In routed mode, up to 256 VLANs can be assigned to a context. The FWSM has an overall limit of 1000 VLAN interfaces divided among all contexts. Up to 250 contexts are supported on an FWSM depending on the software license. Each context has its own policies such as NAT, access lists, and protocol fixups.

Figure 8-2 *Virtual Firewall Overview*

The FSWM uses the administrative context for network management connectivity. Each context may also be managed individually as if they were distinct and separate firewalls. This granularity allows different groups to administer their own firewall. The system context is used to add VLANS, create contexts, and assign VLANs to contexts. With the default FWSM software, up to two security contexts (the administrative and system context) are provided.

Note: The FWSM does not include any external physical interfaces. VLAN interfaces are assigned to the FWSM in a way that is similar to how a switched virtual interface (SVI) is assigned to the Multilayer Switch Feature Card (MSFC). The FWSM includes an internal interface to the Switch Fabric Module (SFM) (if present) or to the shared bus.

Firewall Context Design Considerations

Resource classes are important to firewall operations because multiple contexts can use a resource class.

An attack or anomaly on one context can impact another context. All contexts belong to the default class if they are not assigned to another class, as illustrated in Figure 8-3. If a context belongs to a class other than the default class, those class settings always override the default class settings. However, if a class has any settings that are not defined, the member context uses the default class for those limits. By default, all security contexts have unlimited access to the resources of the FWSM or security appliance, except where maximum limits per context are enforced. If one or more contexts use too many resources, they cause other contexts to be denied connections. Resource management limits the use of resources per context.

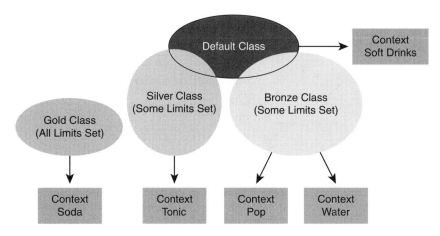

Figure 8-3   *Firewall Context Design Considerations*

Note: The FWSM does not limit the bandwidth per context; however, the switch containing the FWSM can limit the bandwidth per VLAN.

The FWSM and security appliances manage resources by assigning contexts to resource classes. Each context uses the resource limits set by the class. If some resources are oversubscribed, or are unlimited, a few contexts can use up those resources, potentially affecting service to other contexts. As a recommended practice, set limits for all resources together as a percentage of the total available for the device, and set the limit for individual resources as a percentage or as an absolute value.

The FWSM and security appliances are subject to oversubscription if more than 100 percent of the resources are assigned across all contexts. For example, if the Bronze class is set to limit connections to 20 percent per context, and 10 contexts are assigned to the class, a total of 200 percent is allocated. If contexts concurrently use more than the system limit, each context gets less than the 20 percent you intended, and some connections will be denied because the system limit is reached.

MSFC Placement

The Multilayer Switch Feature Card can be placed on the inside or the outside of the firewall depending on the VLANs assigned to the FWSM.

In Figure 8-4, the MSFC is outside of the firewall when VLAN 200 is assigned to the outside interface of the FWSM. The FWSM processes and protects all traffic to the inside VLANs 2, 4, and 6. The MSFC routes between the Internet and the switched networks. Placing the MSFC outside the FWSM makes design and management easier.

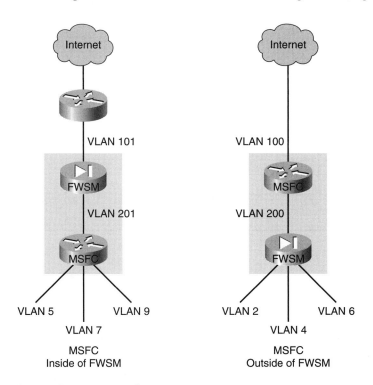

Figure 8-4 *MSFC Placement*

The MSFC is inside of the firewall when VLAN 101 is assigned to the outside interface of the FWSM. The MSFC routes between VLANs 201, 5, 7, and 9. No inside traffic goes through the FWSM unless it is destined for the Internet. The FWSM secures the MSFC.

For multiple context mode, if the MSFC is placed inside the FWSM, it should connect to only a single context. If the MSFC connects to multiple firewall contexts, the MSFC will route between the contexts, which might not be your intention.

Active/Active Firewall Topology

The active/active firewall topology uses two firewalls that are both actively providing firewall services.

When an FWSM is running in virtual firewall mode, it is possible to use active/active redundancy. In the active/active topology, the security contexts on the FWSM are divided into failover groups. A failover group is a logical group of one or more security contexts. The FWSM supports a maximum of two failover groups. The administrative context is always a member of failover group 1, and any unassigned security contexts are, by default, also members of failover group 1.

In Figure 8-5, FWSM 1 and FWSM 2 are each configured with two failover groups. FSWM 1 is active for group 1 and standby for group 2. FSWM 2 is active for group 2 and standby for group 1. The first virtual firewall is mapped to group 1, and the second virtual firewall is mapped to group 2.

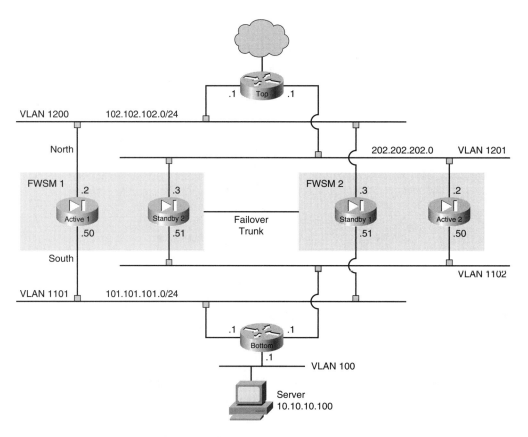

Figure 8-5   *Active/Active Firewall Topology*

Active/Active Topology Features

The active/active failover configuration requires two identical FWSMs connected to each other through a failover link associated with a dedicated VLAN and optionally a state-link VLAN using an interchassis design.

Note: The active/active failover configuration can also be supported with redundant FWSM in a single chassis. The failover link is a VLAN.

Note: All information sent over the failover and stateful failover links is sent in clear text. If FWSM is used to terminate VPN tunnels, this information includes any usernames, passwords, and preshared keys used for establishing the tunnels. Cisco recommends securing the failover communication with a failover key.

The health of the active interfaces and units is monitored to determine whether specific failover conditions are met. If those conditions are met, failover occurs. The MAC address of the primary unit is used by all interfaces in the active contexts. When an active failover group fails, it changes to the standby state and the associated standby failover group becomes active. The interfaces in the failover group that becomes active assume the MAC address and IP addresses of the interfaces in the failover group that failed.

This design supports preemption so that the FWSM with a higher priority will resume an active role after recovering from a failure condition.

Additional redundancy is supported if links from separate modules are used to form the Gigabit Ethernet EtherChannels supporting the failover trunk and state traffic VLANs.

Both devices can pass network traffic in an active/active topology; this design is capable of supporting load balancing in the network.

Asymmetric Routing with Firewalls

The FWSMs support asymmetric routing where return traffic for a session is received through a different interface than the interface from which the traffic originated.

Asymmetric routing most commonly occurs when two interfaces on a single FWSM, or two FWSMs in a failover pair, are connected to different service providers and the outbound connection does not use a NAT address. By default, the FWSM drops the return traffic because there is no connection information for the traffic received through a different interface than the interface where the traffic originated.

Asymmetric routing of the return traffic is supported by using the **asr-group** interface command. The FSWM supports up to 32 asymmetric routing (ASR) groups. Each ASR group supports a maximum of eight interfaces. Asymmetric routing is supported in the active/active failover redundancy mode, and in designs without failover redundancy in either single mode or within a virtual firewall by using ASR groups. Asymmetric routing is supported in both the routed and transparent modes of firewall operation.

Asymmetric Routing with ASR Group on a Single FWSM

Interfaces inside a common ASR group allow packets belonging to a given session to enter and leave from any interface within the ASR group, as shown in Figure 8-6.

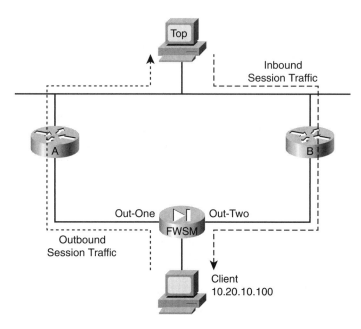

Figure 8-6   *Asymmetric Routing with ASR Groups on a Single FWSM*

When an interface configured with the **asr-group** command receives a packet for which it has no session information, it checks the session information for the other interfaces that are in the same group. If it does not find a match, the packet is dropped. If it finds a match and the incoming traffic originated on a different interface on the same unit, some or the entire Layer 2 header is rewritten and the packet is re-injected into the stream and forwarded to the intended host.

After valid synchronization (SYN) is sent out an ASR group interface, the FWSM will accept a returning synchronization-acknowledgment (SYN ACK) on another interface in the ASR group.

Asymmetric Routing with Active/Active Topology

Interfaces inside a common ASR group in an active/active topology also support asymmetric routing.

In the active/active topology, when an interface configured with the **asr-group** command receives a packet for which it has no session information, it checks the session information for the other interfaces that are in the same group. If it does not find a match, the packet is dropped. If it finds a match and the incoming traffic originated on a peer unit that was active for the context, some or all of the entire Layer 2 header is rewritten and the packet is redirected to the active peer.

Figure 8-7 shows that the traffic is forwarded though the outside interface of context A on the unit where context A is in the standby state and returns through the outside interface of context A on the unit where context A is in the active state. This redirection continues as long as the session is active.

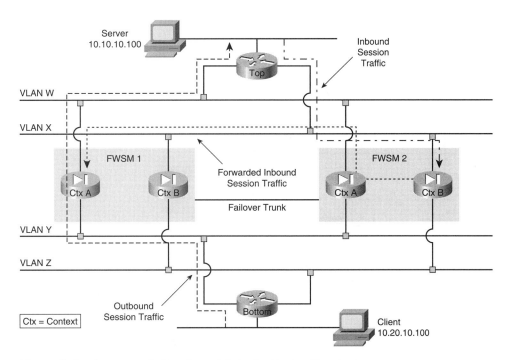

Figure 8-7   *Asymmetric Routing with Active/Active Topology*

Performance Scaling with Multiple FWSMs

For high throughput, up to four FWSMs can be installed in a single chassis using an active/active design. This section discusses two methods to load balance multiple FWSMs:

■   Traffic-engineering mechanisms, such as policy-based routing (PBR), to selectively steer traffic through multiple FWSMs

■   Routing, such as static or Equal Cost Multipath (ECMP) routing, to direct flows per FWSM

Example: Load Balancing FWSMs Using PBR

PBR is a mechanism for implementing packet forwarding and routing according to policies defined by the network administrator rather than paths selected by traditional routing methods. Instead of routing by the destination address as determined by a routing protocol, PBR uses more flexible methods such as source IP addresses or application types to match on the identity of the user and then selects the forwarding path. A redundant path could be configured in the event of a link failure or the device going down.

Figure 8-8 shows multiple FWSMs load balanced in an active/active design using PBR supported by the gateway router. A source-based selection method is used to determine the destination firewall path. This is a static load-sharing method based on class maps and route maps to divide traffic among multiple FWSMs. The route maps are configured so that if the first FWSM goes down, a backup FWSM is used.

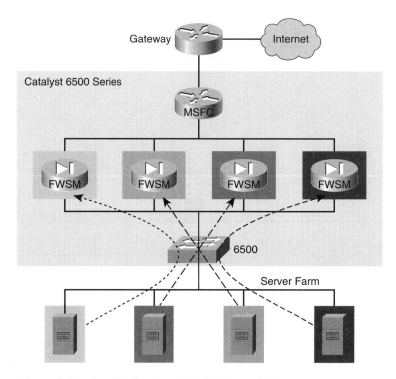

Figure 8-8   *Load Balancing FWSMs Using PBR*

Load Balancing FWSMs Using ECMP Routing

Static routing or ECMP routing can also be used to selectively route traffic through each of the FWSMs. Take care to ensure that the return path goes through the same firewall or that the FWSM supports asymmetric routing in an active/active design.

Figure 8-9 shows multiple FWSMs load balanced in an active/active design using ECMP routing. The standard destination-based selection method is used by the routing protocol to determine which FWSM to use. If an FWSM goes down, the routing protocol automatically load balances the traffic across the remaining FWSMs.

PVLAN Security

PVLANs allow Layer 2 isolation between ports within a VLAN. Figure 8-10 illustrates the PVLAN architecture and is explained in more detail in this section.

In a regular VLAN, all ports can communicate. PVLANs provide Layer 2 isolation between the ports within the same PVLAN without assigning ports to separate VLANs or

Figure 8-9   *Load Balancing FWSMs Using ECMP Routing*

Figure 8-10   *PVLAN Review*

assigning individual hosts to different Layer 3 IP networks. PVLANs provide a logical separation of the network that keeps traffic isolated.

The ports that belong to a PVLAN are associated with a primary VLAN. In addition, within the primary VLAN, ports are associated with either an isolated VLAN or a community VLAN. A PVLAN domain has one primary VLAN. Every port in a PVLAN domain is a member of the primary VLAN. Secondary VLANs provide Layer 2 isolation between ports within the same PVLAN domain. There are two types of secondary VLANs:

■ **Isolated VLANs:** Ports within an isolated VLAN cannot communicate with any other port on the switch, other than the promiscuous port.

■ **Community VLANs:** Ports within a community VLAN can communicate with each other but cannot communicate with ports in other communities or other isolated ports.

There are three types of PVLAN ports:

■ **Promiscuous:** This port communicates with all other PVLAN ports and is the port used to communicate with network devices including routers, backup servers, and administrative workstations. This port listens to the secondary VLANs, and sends traffic using the primary VLAN.

■ **Isolated:** This port has complete Layer 2 separation from the other ports within the same PVLAN with the exception of the promiscuous port. Even with static ARP entries, private ports cannot communicate with each other. Isolated ports use a secondary VLAN to send traffic out and block any traffic coming from the secondary VLAN. All the isolated ports in the system can share the same secondary VLAN.

■ **Community:** These ports communicate among themselves and with their promiscuous ports. These ports are isolated at Layer 2 from all other ports in other communities and from isolated ports. A separate secondary VLAN is allocated for each community.

Note: If a broadcast or multicast packet comes from the promiscuous port, it is sent to all the ports in the PVLAN domain, including all community and isolated ports.

FWSM in a PVLAN Environment: Isolated Ports

FWSM 3.1 supports PVLANs with Cisco IOS Release 12.2(18)SXF.

PVLANs provide an easy way to implement Layer 2 traffic segregation within a VLAN. This feature is popular in demilitarized zone (DMZ) and server farm designs.

On a Cisco Catalyst 6500 series switch, the primary and secondary VLANs are configured on the Supervisor Engine. From the perspective of the MSFC router integrated in the switch, the FWSM is sitting on a promiscuous port and sees all traffic to and from the PVLAN. Only the primary VLAN is assigned to the FWSM, but it is made aware of the primary and secondary VLAN mappings through the MSFC. The FWSM automatically supports isolation of the secondary VLAN traffic to the community and isolated VLANs. The FWSM acts as a gateway between hosts on the PVLANs and the outside world.

Figure 8-11 illustrates the use of PVLANs supporting isolated ports with the FWSM in routed mode. Isolated ports are separated at Layer 2 by the switch processor. Outbound traffic from an isolated port is sent by the FSWM to the MSFC, which routes the traffic appropriately. The FWSM will not forward traffic between isolated ports, because for a single subnet the FWSM will not route packets back out the interface they came in from.

Inbound traffic for the isolated port is sent by the MSFC to the FWSM, which sends it to the switch processor. The switch processor forwards the packets to the isolated port based on the MAC address.

Figure 8-11   *Isolated Ports on FWSM in Routed Mode*

FWSM in a PVLAN Environment: Community VLANs

Community VLANs are supported by Layer 2 functions in the switch processor.

Figure 8-12 illustrates the use of community VLANs with the FWSM in routed mode. Community ports are interconnected at Layer 2 by the switch processor. Outbound traffic from a community port is seen by all devices on the community VLAN, including the FWSM. The FSWM will forward outbound traffic to the MSFC, which routes the traffic appropriately. Inbound traffic for the community port is sent by the MSFC to the FWSM, which sends it to the community VLAN. The Layer 2 switch processor forwards it to the appropriate community port or ports based on the MAC address.

Figure 8-12   *Community Ports on FWSM in Routed Mode*

Zone-Based Policy Firewall

The zone-based policy firewall configuration model is a new design supported by the Cisco IOS Firewall feature set.

The zone-based policy firewall changes the design model from the older interface-based model to a zone-based configuration model. The zone-based policy firewall configuration model assigns interfaces to zones, and applies an inspection policy to traffic moving between the zones. Zones establish the security borders of the network. A zone defines a boundary where traffic is subjected to policy restrictions as it crosses to another region of the network.

A security zone is configured for each region of relative security within the network, so that all interfaces that are assigned to the same zone are protected with a similar level of security. For example, Figure 8-13 shows an access router with three interfaces each assigned to its own zone:

■   One interface connected to the public Internet

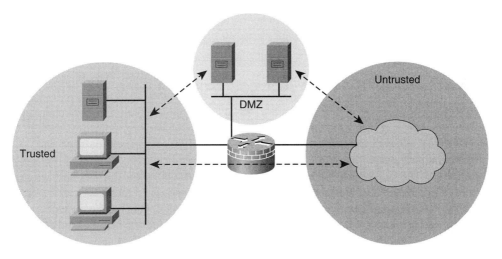

Figure 8-13   *Zone-Based Policy Firewall*

- One interface connected to a private trusted LAN that must not be accessible from the public untrusted Internet

- One interface connected to an Internet service DMZ, where a web server, Domain Name System (DNS) server, and email server must be accessible to the public Internet

In Figure 8-13, each zone holds only one interface. If an additional interface is added to the private zone, the hosts connected to the new interface in the zone can pass traffic to all hosts on the existing interface in the same zone. Traffic to hosts in other zones would be similarly affected by existing policies.

Zone-based policy firewalls allow a more flexible, more easily configured model. Firewall policy troubleshooting is based on the explicit policy on interzone traffic. The zone-based policy firewall default policy between zones is to deny all. If no policy is explicitly configured, all traffic moving between zones is blocked. This is a significant departure from statefull inspection model, in which traffic was implicitly allowed unless it was explicitly blocked with an ACL. Traffic is implicitly allowed to flow by default among interfaces that are members of the same zone.

Interzone policies offer considerable flexibility and granularity, so different inspection policies can be applied to multiple host groups connected to the same router interface. Multiple traffic classes and actions can be applied per zone pair. Zone-based policy firewalls can tie to Cisco Content Switching Module (CSM) mechanisms for ACL deployment and management.

Designing NAC Services

Network Admission Control (NAC) is a set of technologies and solutions built on an industry initiative led by Cisco. NAC uses the network infrastructure to enforce security policy compliance on all devices seeking to access network computing resources, thereby limiting damage from emerging security threats such as viruses, worms, and spyware.

Customers using NAC can allow network access to only compliant and trusted endpoint devices (PCs, servers, and personal digital assistants [PDA], for example), and can restrict the access of noncompliant devices.

Network Security with Access Control

Cisco Identity Based Networking Services (IBNS) is an integrated solution combining several Cisco products that offer authentication, access control, and user policies to secure network connectivity and resources. The Cisco IBNS solution enables greater security while simultaneously offering cost-effective management of changes throughout the organization. The Cisco IBNS framework allows enterprises to manage user mobility and reduce the overhead costs associated with granting and managing access to network resources. IEEE 802.1x authenticates clients requesting Layer 2 (data link layer) access to the network. However, with Cisco 802.1x, users and devices are authenticated and allowed admission to the network based on who or what they are, but not their condition.

NAC helps ensure that only healthy client devices, such as workstations and end-user PCs, are granted full network access. The Cisco NAC Appliance Agent (NAA) loaded on the client device queries antivirus, patch management, and personal firewall client software to assess the condition or posture of a client device before allowing that device to access the network. NAC helps ensure that a network client has an up-to-date virus signature set, the most current operating system patches, and is not infected. If the client requires an antivirus signature update or an operating system update, NAC directs the client to complete the necessary updates before allowing access to the protected network resources. If the client has been compromised or if a virus outbreak is occurring on the network, NAC places the client into a quarantined network segment. After the client has completed its update process or disinfection, the client is checked again. Clients with a healthy status are permitted normal network access.

Cisco 802.1x/IBNS/and NAC provide complementary functions: user authentication and posture validation. Both can provide per-user group VLAN assignment and access control.

NAC Comparison

Cisco supports two types of NAC, as illustrated in Figure 8-14 and in this list:

- Cisco NAC Framework is a technology standard that integrates an intelligent network infrastructure with solutions from more than 60 manufacturers of leading antivirus and other security and management software solutions to enforce security policy compliance on all devices seeking to access network computing resources. NAC Framework is embedded software within NAC-enabled products that provides ubiquitous control across all network access methods. Posture information can be gathered and access policy enforced for hosts attempting network access through routers, switches, wireless access points, and VPN concentrators. NAC Framework leverages multiple Cisco products and vendor products that support NAC.

- Cisco NAC Appliance (formerly called Cisco Clean Access) is a turnkey solution for controlling and securing networks. Cisco NAC Appliance condenses NAC capabilities into an appliance. Cisco NAC Appliance client, server, and manager products en-

Figure 8-14 *NAC Comparison*

able network administrators to authenticate, authorize, evaluate, and remediate wired, wireless, and remote users and their machines before allowing users onto the network. Cisco NAC Appliance identifies whether networked devices such as laptops, IP phones, PDAs, or printers comply with the security policies of an organization, and repairs any vulnerabilities before permitting access to the network.

Cisco NAC Appliance Fundamentals

This topic discusses fundamentals of the Cisco NAC Appliance, including components and terminology.

Cisco NAC Appliance Components

Cisco NAC Appliance provides admission control and enforces compliance.

Cisco NAC Appliance comprises four components:

- **Cisco NAC Appliance Manager (Cisco NAM):** The administration server for Cisco NAC Appliance deployment where the policies are defined. The secure web console of the Cisco NAM is the single point of management for up to 20 Cisco NAC Appliance Server (NAS) devices in a deployment (or 40 Cisco NAS devices in a super-NAM installation). Cisco NAM acts as the authentication proxy to the authentication servers that reside on the back end. For out-of-band (OOB) deployment, the Cisco NAM console allows control of switches and VLAN assignment of user ports through the use of SNMP.

■ **Cisco NAC Appliance Server (Cisco NAS):** The enforcement server between the untrusted (managed) network and the trusted network. Cisco NAS enforces the policies defined in the Cisco NAM web console, including network access privileges, authentication requirements, bandwidth restrictions, and Cisco NAC Appliance system requirements. It can be deployed in-band (always in line with user traffic) or OOB (in line with user traffic only during authentication and posture assessment). It can also be deployed in Layer 2 mode (users are adjacent to Cisco NAS) or Layer 3 mode (users are multiple hops away from the Cisco NAS).

■ **Cisco NAC Appliance Agent (Cisco NAA):** An optional read-only agent that resides on Microsoft Windows clients. Cisco NAA checks applications, files, services, or Registry keys to ensure that clients meet specified network and software requirements before gaining access to the network.

■ **Cisco NAC Appliance policy updates:** Regular updates of prepackaged policies and rules that can be used to check the up-to-date status of operating systems and antivirus, antispyware, and other client software. The Cisco NAC Appliance policy updates currently provide built-in support for 24 antivirus vendors and 17 antispyware vendors.

Cisco NAC Appliance Policy Updates

Cisco provides automatic security policy updates as part of the standard software maintenance package. These updates deliver predefined policies for the most common network access criteria, including policies that check for critical operating system updates, common antivirus software virus definition updates, and common antispyware definition updates.

The Cisco NAC Appliance is preconfigured to offer policy checks for more than 200 applications from 50 vendors.

Note: For the latest supported applications, review the "Cisco NAC Appliance (Clean Access)" release notes at http://www.cisco.com/en/US/products/ps6128/ prod_release_notes_list.html.

In addition to the preconfigured checks, the customer has full access to the Cisco NAC Appliance rules engine and can create any custom check or rule for any other third-party application.

Process Flow with the Cisco NAC Appliance

Figure 8-15 illustrates the process flow with the Cisco NAC Appliance.

Figure 8-15 *Process Flow with the NAC Appliance*

Following are the steps of the process:

Step 1.   The end user attempts to access a web page or use the Intranet.

Step 2.   The user is redirected to a login page. Cisco NAC Appliance validates the user-name and password, and performs device and network scans to assess vulnera-bilities on the device.

Step 3.   If the device is noncompliant with corporate policies or the login is incorrect, the user is denied access to the network and assigned to a quarantine role with access only to online remediation resources.

Note: After remediation, the user returns to Step 2 for validation and scanning.

Step 4.   If the login is correct and the device complies with the policies, the device is placed on the certified devices list and is granted access to network.

Cisco NAS Scaling

There are three levels of Cisco NAM for supporting Cisco NAC Appliance solutions:

■   Cisco NAC Appliance Lite Manager manages up to 3 Cisco NAS devices, supporting 100, 250, or 500 users per server.

- Cisco NAC Appliance Standard Manager manages up to 20 Cisco NAS devices supporting from 1500 to 3500 users per (NAS) depending on which model is deployed.

- Cisco NAC Appliance Super Manager manages up to 40 Cisco NAS devices supporting from 1500 to 3500 users per (NAS) depending on which model is deployed.

The number of users supported on a server is a measure of concurrent users that have been scanned for posture compliance, not network devices such as printers or IP phones.

The number of users supported per server is influenced by many factors that consume CPU and server resources:

- The number of new user authentications per second

- The number of posture assessments per second

- How many checks are in each posture assessment

- The number of agentless network scans per second

- The number of plug-ins per scan

- Rescan timer intervals

- Per-role and total online timer intervals

- Bandwidth controls

- Filters and access controls

Note: Interface bandwidth is the least important calculation for determining how many users a Cisco NAS can support.

Cisco NAS Deployment Options

This topic describes the deployment options for Cisco NAS.

There are four deployment variables with Cisco NAS deployments:

- **Virtual or real gateway mode:** Determines whether the Cisco NAS acts as a Layer 2 or Layer 3 device in the network

- **In-band or out-of-band operating mode:** Defines when traffic flows through the Cisco NAS

- **Layer 2 or Layer 3 client access mode:** Defines whether user devices are Layer 2 or Layer 3 adjacent to the Cisco NAS

- **Central or edge physical deployment:** Determines whether the Cisco NAS device is physically in line with the traffic path

Cisco NAS Gateway Modes

There are three Cisco NAS gateway modes, as shown in Figure 8-16.

Figure 8-16 *Cisco NAS Gateway Modes*

The Cisco NAS can operate as a logical Layer 2 or Layer 3 network device depending on the gateway mode configured.

- **Virtual gateway mode:** Cisco NAS operates as a standard Layer 2 Ethernet bridge, but with added functionality provided by the IP filter and IP Security (IPsec) module. This configuration is typically used when the untrusted network already has a Layer 3 gateway. It is the most common deployment option.

- **Real IP gateway mode:** Cisco NAS operates as the Layer 3 default gateway for untrusted network (managed) clients. All traffic between the untrusted and trusted network passes through Cisco NAS, which applies the IP filtering rules, access policies, and any other traffic-handling mechanisms that are configured. Cisco NAS is designated as a static route for the managed subnet and can perform DHCP services or act as a DHCP relay.

- **NAT gateway mode:** Cisco NAS functions similarly to the way it does in the real IP gateway configuration, as a Layer 3 gateway, but with added NAT services. With NAT, clients are assigned IP addresses dynamically from a private address pool. The Cisco NAS performs the translation between the private and public addresses as traffic is routed between the untrusted (managed) and external network. Cisco NAS supports standard, dynamic, and one-to-one NAT. In one-to-one NAT, a one-to-one correlation exists between public and private addresses and port numbers, and IP addresses can be mapped for translation.

> **Note:**   The NAT gateway mode is primarily intended to facilitate testing because it requires the least amount of network configuration and is easy to initially set up. However, because it is limited in the number of connections it can handle, NAT gateway mode (in-band or out-of-band) is not supported for production deployment.

The installation type and operating mode determines the services Cisco NAS will provide. For example, Cisco NAS can operate as a bridge between the untrusted and trusted network, or it can operate as a gateway for the untrusted network.

Cisco NAS Operating Modes

Cisco NAS has two traffic flow deployment models: in-band or out-of-band.

Any Cisco NAS can be configured for either method, but only one Cisco NAS method can be deployed at a time. Selection of mode is based on whether the customer wants to remove the Cisco NAS from the data path after posture assessment.

In-band traffic flow is the easiest deployment option. The Cisco NAS remains in the traffic path before and after posture assessment. In-band operation provides ongoing ACL filtering and bandwidth throttling, and role-based access control.

In out-of-band traffic flow, the Cisco NAS is in the traffic path only during the posture assessment. Out-of-band mode provides VLAN port-based and role-based access control. ACL filtering and bandwidth throttling are provided only during posture assessment.

> **Note:**   In-band traffic flow is supported with the Cisco NAS connected to any switch, hub, or access point. Out-of-band traffic flow is supported with the Cisco NAS connected to most common Cisco switches with recent software releases.

Cisco NAS Client Access Modes

The client access deployment mode selection is based on whether the client is Layer 2 adjacent to the Cisco NAS.

■ **Layer 2 mode:** The MAC address of the client device is used to uniquely identify the device. This mode supports both virtual and real IP gateway operations in both in-band and out-of-band deployments. This is the most common deployment model for LANs.

■ **Layer 3 mode:** The client device is not Layer 2 adjacent to the Cisco NAS. The IP address (and MAC address, starting with Cisco NAA Version 4.0 in Layer 3 OOB applications) of the client is used to identify the device. This mode supports both virtual and real IP gateway operations with in-band and out-of-band deployments.

Any Cisco NAS can be configured for either client access method, but only one Cisco NAS method can be configured at a time. Client access mode is configured independently from Cisco NAS operating mode.

Physical Deployment Models

The edge deployment model is the easiest physical deployment option to understand. The Cisco NAS is physically and logically in line to the traffic path. VLAN IDs are passed straight through the device when in virtual gateway mode. This deployment option can become complex when there are multiple access closets.

The central deployment model is the most common option and the easiest deployment option. In this option, the Cisco NAS is logically in line, but not physically in line. The VLAN IDs need to be mapped across the Cisco NAS when in virtual gateway mode. This deployment option is the most scalable option for large environments because each Cisco NAS can support devices from multiple access switches.

Cisco NAC Appliance Designs

This topic reviews some common Cisco NAC Appliance designs.

As a recommended practice, the Cisco NAC Appliance solutions are implemented with full redundancy. A failover bundle is either a pair of Cisco NAM devices or NAS devices. The Cisco NAM failover bundle provides management redundancy. The Cisco NAS failover bundle provides redundant Cisco NAS operations for the protected devices.

In the Figure 8-17, the network has two sets of Cisco NAS failover bundles. One Cisco NAS failover bundle supports devices on VLANs 110, 120, and 130. The other Cisco NAS failover bundle supports devices on VLANs 140, 150, and 160. All components in the design are in an active/standby state. Each failover bundle shares a virtual MAC and virtual IP address. Because of the shared MAC address, Layer 2 connectivity is required between components. The redundant distribution switches are interconnected with a Layer 2 trunk.

Note: The VLANs do not span the access layer switches in this design. The Layer 2 trunk between the distribution switches is needed only to provide Layer 2 connectivity between the Cisco NAS failover bundles.

Cisco NAM devices connect to the redundant distribution switches and support all the Cisco NAS devices in the network.

Note: Redundancy is not shown in the rest of the figures in this lesson for simplicity only. Every design that follows can, should, and would have redundancy.

Layer 2 In-Band Designs

The Layer 2 in-band topology is the most common deployment option. The Cisco NAS is logically in line with the client traffic, but is not physically in line. When the virtual gateway mode is implemented, the VLAN IDs are mapped by the Cisco NAS.

In Figure 8-18, VLAN 110 is mapped to VLAN 10 by the Cisco NAS. All client traffic passes through the Cisco NAS. The Cisco NAS securely manages all traffic after posture assessment. The MAC address of the client is used to identify the device. VLAN 90 and VLAN 91 are the management VLANs for the Cisco NAS and the NAM.

Note: Redundancy is not shown in the following examples for diagram simplicity only.

Figure 8-17   *Cisco NAC Appliance Redundancy Design*

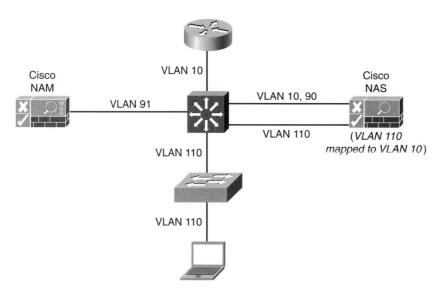

Figure 8-18   *Layer 2 In-Band Designs*

This is the most scalable design in large environments, because this design can be transparently implemented in the existing network supporting multiple access layer switches. It will support all network infrastructure equipment. The Cisco NAS supports per-user ACLs.

Example: Layer 2 In-Band Virtual Gateway

Figure 8-19 illustrates a Layer 2 in-band virtual gateway design. The Cisco NAS maps traffic from VLAN 110 to VLAN 10. VLAN 90 and VLAN 91 are the management VLANs for the Cisco NAS and NAM. The Layer 3 distribution switch has switch virtual interfaces (SVI) for the VLANs connecting to the Cisco NAM, NAS, and access switches. The distribution switch is the DHCP server and the default gateway for the access layer devices. The existing IP addressing in the network is not changed when the virtual gateway is implemented.

Figure 8-19   *Example: Layer 2 In-Band Virtual Gateway*

Example: Layer 2 In-Band Real IP Gateway

Figure 8-20 illustrates a Layer 2 in-band real IP gateway design. The Cisco NAS is now the DHCP server and the default gateway for the access layer devices. The Cisco NAS has static routes to the other subnets in the organization. The Layer 3 distribution switch has SVIs for the VLANs connecting to the Cisco NAM, NAS, and access switches. The existing IP addressing in the network changes when the real IP gateway is implemented. VLAN 90 and VLAN 91 are the management VLANs for the Cisco NAS and NAM.

Figure 8-20   *Example: Layer 2 In-Band Real IP Gateway*

Layer 2 Out-of-Band Designs

The connections of the Layer 2 out-of-band design are similar to the Layer 2 in-band design, except that the link from the access switch to the distribution switch is now a trunk supporting both the posture assessment VLAN and the network access VLAN.

The client is in line with the Cisco NAS before and during posture assessment. The user VLAN is changed and Cisco NAS is bypassed only after a successful login and assessment. The Cisco NAS securely manages traffic only during assessment. ACLs to manage users need to be applied to the user-assigned VLAN, not the Cisco NAS, because after posture assessment, user traffic does not pass through the Cisco NAS.

Note: Cisco NAM can support either dynamic VLAN assignment based on roles, or geographic VLAN assignment based on the VLANs on the switch. Only one MAC address is supported per switch port except for IP telephony devices.

This design requires use of supported out-of-band switches such as the Cisco Catalyst series 2950, 2960, 3500XL, 3550, 3560, 3750, 4500, and 6500 switches with the appropriate software image.

Note: Refer to the following link for a list of switches and versions that Cisco NAC Appliance supports: http://www.cisco.com/univercd/cc/td/doc/product/vpn/ciscosec/cca/cca40/switch.htm#wp65186.

Cisco NAM uses SNMP for traps to detect user access and perform switch configuration.

Example: Layer 2 Out-of-Band Virtual Gateway

Figure 8-21 shows addressing with a Layer 3 out-of-band virtual gateway design. Cisco NAS maps traffic from VLAN 110 to VLAN 10 during the posture assessment. The Layer 3 distribution switch has SVIs for the VLANs connecting to the Cisco NAM, NAS, and access switches. The distribution switch is the DHCP server, and the default gateway for the access layer devices. The existing IP addressing in the network is not changed when the virtual gateway is implemented.

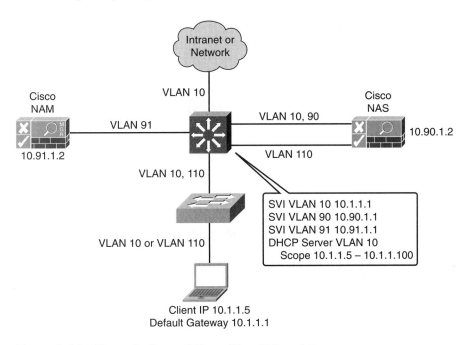

Figure 8-21   *Example: Layer 2 Out-of-Band Virtual Gateway*

Layer 3 In-Band Designs

In the Layer 3 in-band topology, the client device is not adjacent to the Cisco NAS. The IP address of the client is used to identify the device because the MAC address provided to the Cisco NAS is not from the client. This design is used to securely manage traffic from remote sites or for VPN concentrators.

Example: Layer 3 In-Band Virtual Gateway

Figure 8-22 illustrates a Layer 3 in-band virtual gateway design. The Cisco NAS maps traffic from VLAN 110 to VLAN 10. The Layer 3 distribution switch has SVIs for the VLANs connecting to the Cisco NAM, NAS, and access switches. The distribution switch is the default gateway for the access layer devices. The DHCP server is typically a remote router.

All traffic from the remote site goes through Cisco NAS.

Figure 8-22 *Example: Layer 3 In-Band Virtual Gateway*

This design also supports VPN concentrators. Instead of the remote router pair, the VPN concentrator connects to the distribution switch. Traffic from the VPN concentrator is forwarded through the Cisco NAS for posture assessment and management.

Example: Layer 3 In-Band with Multiple Remotes

Figure 8-23 illustrates a Layer 3 in-band virtual gateway design with multiple remote sites. The Cisco NAS maps traffic from VLAN 110 to VLAN 10. Traffic to centralized hosts and Internet goes through Cisco NAS.

Note: Unless additional configuration steps are taken, traffic between clients at remote sites does not go through Cisco NAS, because the campus router allows routing between the edge routers. To securely manage traffic between the remote sites, you can implement networking technologies such as policy-based routing (PBR) or virtual routing and forwarding instances to isolate the remote sites. Implementing Cisco NAS at the remote sites will also secure the traffic.

Layer 3 Out-of-Band Designs

Layer 3 support for out-of-band deployments enables administrators to deploy Cisco NAS out-of-band centrally in the core or distribution layer to support users behind Layer 3 access switches and remote users behind WAN routers in some instances. With Layer 3 out-of-band, users who are multiple Layer 3 hops away from Cisco NAS can be supported for authentication and posture assessment. After authentication and posture assessment, the client traffic no longer passes through the Cisco NAS.

Figure 8-23 *Example: Layer 3 In-Band with Multiple Remotes*

With the Layer 3 out-of-band topology, the IP address (and MAC address, starting with Cisco NAA Version 4 Layer 3 out-of-band applications) of the client is used to identify the device, because the MAC address (before the Cisco NAA Version 4 client) provided to the Cisco NAS is from the last-hop router. This design requires use of supported out-of-band switches such as the Cisco Catalyst series 2950, 2960, 3500XL, 3550, 3560, 3750, 4500, and 6500 switches with the appropriate software image. The NAM uses SNMP for traps and switch configuration. PBR is needed to direct the user traffic appropriately.

Note: Refer to the list of switches and versions that Cisco NAC Appliance supports at http://www.cisco.com/en/US/docs/security/nac/appliance/support_guide/switch_spt.html.

Example: Layer 3 OOB with Addressing

Figure 8-24 shows an example of addressing with a Layer 3 out-of-band virtual gateway design supporting remote users. Cisco NAS maps traffic from VLAN 110 to VLAN 10 during the posture assessment. The Layer 3 distribution switch has SVIs for the VLANs connecting to Cisco NAM, NAS, and access switches. The remote-site edge router is the DHCP server and the default gateway for the client devices. The remote-site edge router uses a trunk to the remote-access switch to support either the production VLAN or the posture assessment VLAN. PBR is used to direct the user traffic appropriately.

Figure 8-24   *Example: Layer 3 OOB with Addressing*

NAC Framework Overview

NAC Framework is as an architecture-based framework solution designed to take advantage of an existing base of both Cisco network technologies and existing deployments of security and management solutions from other manufacturers. Figure 8-25 illustrates the key components of the NAC Framework Architecture covered in this section.

The NAC Framework assesses the state, or posture, of a host to prevent unauthorized or vulnerable endpoints from accessing the network. The Cisco NAC posture validation process has three major architectural components.

- **Subjects:** Managed or unmanaged hosts that are accessing the network on which NAC is enforced. Typical hosts are desktop computers, laptops, and servers, but may also include IP phones, network printers, and other network-attached devices. The subjects use posture agent software to communicate with NAC devices. The Cisco Trust Agent is the Cisco implementation of the posture agent.

- **Enforcement devices:** Network devices that are acting as a NAC enforcement point. These may include Cisco access routers, VPN gateways, Cisco Catalyst Layer 2 and Layer 3 switches, and wireless access points.

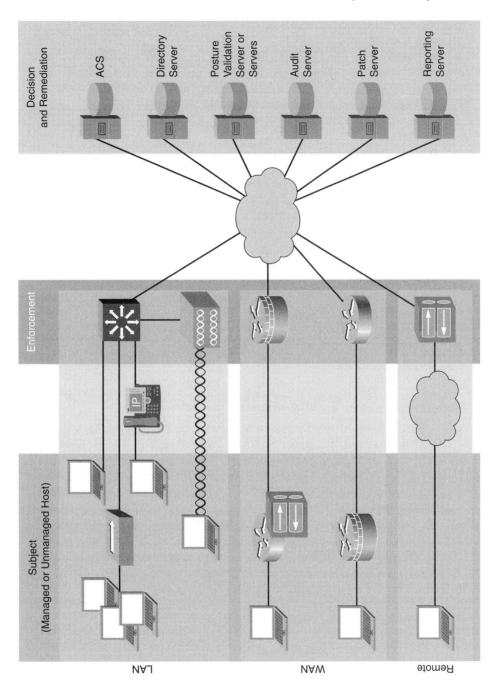

Figure 8-25 *NAC Framework*

- **Decision and remediation devices:** Many network devices support the NAC Framework Architecture:
  - **Authentication, authorization, and accounting (AAA) server:** The central policy server that aggregates one or more authentications or authorizations into a single system authorization decision and maps this decision to a network access profile for enforcement by the network access device (NAD). Cisco Secure Access Control Server (ACS) is the Cisco AAA server product that supports NAC.
  - **Directory server:** A centralized directory server for performing user or machine authentication. Possible directory services include Lightweight Directory Access Protocol (LDAP), Microsoft Active Directory, Novell Directory Services (NDS), and one-time token password (OTP) servers.
  - **Posture validation server (PVS):** A PVS from one or more third parties acts as an application-specific policy decision point in NAC for authorizing a set of posture credentials from one or more posture plug-in against a set of policy rules. Examples include antivirus servers and security application servers.
  - **Remediation server:** A management solution used to bring noncompliant hosts into compliance. This could be a specialized patch management application or as simple as a website for distributing software. The better and more efficient your host patching and remediation is, the less risk.
  - **Audit server:** A server or software that performs vulnerability assessment (VA) against a host to determine the level of compliance or risk of the host before network admission.

Router Platform Support for the NAC Framework

The NAC Layer 3 IP method uses Extensible Authentication Protocol over User Data Protocol (EAPoUDP). Routers that support the NAC Layer 3 IP method are considered NAC Release 1.0 devices. They can act as a network intrusion-prevention system (NIPS) device. NAC Layer 3 IP was first introduced as part of the initial release of NAC in mid-2004. NAC Layer 3 IP shipped in June 2004 in Cisco IOS Software Release 12.3(8)T. It is included in Cisco IOS Software T-train images with security; the same image which includes firewall, NIPS, and cryptographic support. NAC Layer 3 IP is a posture-only credential check that supports authorization capabilities, URL redirect, and downloadable ACLs. NAC Layer IP is triggered by a Layer 3 packet entering a router interface with an IP admission ACL configured. NAC Layer 3 IP is mainly positioned for aggregation deployments (WAN, VPN, WLAN, and so on). The current deployment options preclude the use of NAC Layer 3 IP in the distribution layer of a campus infrastructure because the Catalyst Layer 3 switches do not currently support NAC Layer 3 IP.

NAC agentless host (NAH) is a mechanism in NAC that allows network access to hosts that do not or cannot perform NAC or other compliance authorizations. NADs that fall into this category often include printers, scanners, photocopiers, cameras, sensors, badge readers, and specialized equipment. NAH devices may also include computers with unsupported operating systems, hardened operating systems, embedded operating systems, and personal firewalls. Static exceptions can be configured to allow hosts to bypass the posture validation process based on specified MAC or IP address. Static exceptions can be configured in ACS to allow any specified hosts to bypass the posture validation process based on MAC address. Both individual and wildcard addresses can be specified. NAH is supported in Cisco IOS Software Release 12.4(6)T. Table 8-1 illustrates which router platforms support the NAC Framework.

Table 8-1 *NAC Framework Router Platform Support*

Platform	Support?
Cisco 18xx, 28xx, 38xx	Yes
Cisco 72xx, 75xx	Yes
Cisco 37xx	Yes
Cisco 3640, 3660-ENT series	Yes
Cisco 2600XM, 2691	Yes
Cisco 1701, 1711, 1712, 1721, 1751, 1751-V, 1760	Yes
Cisco 83x	Yes
Cisco 74xx, 73xx, 71xx (S-train)	TBD
Cisco 5xxx	TBD
Cisco 3660-CO series	No
Cisco 3620	No
Cisco 2600 non-XM models	No
Cisco 1750, 1720, 1710	No

Devices that support either the NAC Layer 2 IP method that uses EAPoUDP, or the NAC Layer 2 802.1x (EAP over 802.1x) method, are NAC Release 2.0 devices. NAC Layer 2 IP is triggered by ARP or optionally DHCP traffic on a switch interface. NAC Layer 2 IP is also a posture-only credential check that supports authorization capabilities, URL redirect, and downloadable ACLs. NAC Layer 2 IP sessions are active for as long as the host responds to periodic status query messages implemented using ARP probes or until they are terminated. The ACLs that set the default policy for the switch port on the NAC Layer 2 IP switches are implemented in hardware. One of the main benefits of NAC Layer 2 IP is that it was designed to support multiple hosts per port. The network administrator needs to be aware that unlike NAC Layer 3 IP, only a limited number of hosts per port can be supported in NAC Layer 2 IP. Some network module switches for the Cisco Integrated Services Router platforms support NAC Layer 2 IP or the NAC Layer 2 802.1x.

Note: Refer to the following URL for a list of supported routers: http://www.cisco.com/en/US/docs/security/nac/framework/nac_1.0/release_notes/6276_01.html.

Switch Platform Support for the NAC Framework

Table 8-2 shows NAC Framework support in Cisco Catalyst switches. NAC performs posture validation at the Layer 2 network edge for hosts with or without 802.1x enabled. Vulnerable and noncompliant hosts can be isolated, given reduced network access, or directed to remediation servers based on organizational policy. By ensuring that every host complies with security policy, organizations can significantly reduce the damage caused by infected hosts.

Table 8-2   *NAC Framework Switch Platform Support*

Platform, Supervisor	Operating System	NAC Layer 2 802.1x	NAC Layer 2 IP	NAC Layer 3 IP	NAH
6500—Sup32, 720	Native Cisco IOS Software	Future	Yes	Future	NAC Layer 2 IP
6500—Sup2	Native Cisco IOS Software	No	No	No	No
6500—Sup2, 32, 720	Hybrid	Yes	Yes	No	NAC Layer 2 IP
6500—Sup2, 32, 720	Catalyst Operating System	Yes	Yes	No	NAC Layer 2 IP
4500 series— SupII+, II+TS, II+10GE, IV, V, V-10GE	Cisco IOS Software	Yes	Yes	Future	NAC Layer 2 IP
4900	Cisco IOS Software	Yes	Yes	Future	NAC Layer 2 IP
3550, 3560, 3750	Cisco IOS Software	Yes	Yes	No	NAC Layer 2 IP

Note: For a list of supported switches, refer to http://www.cisco.com/en/US/docs/security/nac/appliance/support_guide/switch_spt.html.

Cisco Client Security Software

Cisco has four client security software applications that support network security:

- **Cisco NAC Appliance Agent (NAA):** Is an optional client-side component of the Cisco NAC Appliance system. It is a read-only client that delivers device-based Registry scans on unmanaged environments. The agent enhances posture assessment functions and streamlines remediation. It is a free download provisioned over the Internet. Many customers who use the Cisco NAC Appliance Agent NAA often require a new download before network access is granted. It works only with Cisco NAS.

- **Cisco Security Agent:** Is security software that provides threat protection for server and desktop computing systems. The Cisco Security Agent identifies and prevents malicious behavior before it can occur, thereby removing potential known and unknown security risks that threaten enterprise networks and applications. It also provides the capability at the endpoint to apply QoS markings to application network traffic as specified by Cisco Security Agent policy rules. These markings can be used by Cisco IOS devices upstream in the enterprise network to classify the packets and apply QoS service policies such as policing and queuing. Cisco Security Agent integrates with NAC Framework and Cisco Security Monitoring, Analysis, and Response System (MARS) to support threat identification and investigation across the network. The Cisco Trust Agent client software may be installed as part of the Cisco Security Agent installation.

- **Cisco Secure Services Client (SSC):** Is client software that supports the deployment of a single authentication framework on multiple device types, for access to both wired and wireless networks. As a component of the Cisco Unified Wireless Network, the SCC performs the following functions:
    - Provides a single authentication framework for multiple device types on the basis of the 802.1x standard
    - Supports leading security standards such as Wi-Fi Protected Access (WPA), WPA2, and Extensible Authentication Protocol (EAP)
    - Supports Windows 2000 and Windows XP
    - Provides an end-to-end authentication service when combined with the Cisco Secure ACS
    - Fully integrates with the Cisco Unified Wireless Network access points and wireless LAN controllers
    - Supports third-party credential databases
    - Protects network endpoint devices
    - Enforces security policies

- **Cisco Trust Agent:** Is client software that must be installed on hosts whose host policy state requires validation prior to permitting network access under the NAC Framework. A core component of the NAC Framework, Cisco Trust Agent allows NAC to determine whether Cisco Security Agent, antivirus software, or other required third-party security or management software is installed and current. It also provides information about the operating system version and patch level. As a component of the NAC Framework, the Cisco Trust Agent performs the following functions:
    - Acts as a middleware component that takes host policy information and securely communicates the information to the AAA policy server
    - Interacts directly with "NAC-enabled" applications running on the host without user intervention
    - Can communicate at Layer 3 or Layer 2 using built-in communication components
    - Includes an 802.1x supplicant for Layer 2 communications in wired environments
    - Authenticates the requestor through encrypted communications with the AAA server

- Allows customers to build scripts for custom information gathering
- Integrates with Cisco Security Agent and can be distributed by NAC participants with their applications for simplified management and distribution
- Includes a lightweight version of the Cisco SSC client

Designing Intrusion-Detection and -Prevention Services

Cisco intrusion-detection and -prevention solutions are part of the Cisco Self-Defending Network. Designed to identify and stop worms, network viruses, and other malicious traffic, these solutions can help protect networks. Cisco provides a broad array of solutions for intrusion detection and prevention at both the network and at the endpoint.

This section provides an overview of intrusion-detection systems (IDS) and intrusion-prevention systems (IPS) used in enterprise networks.

IDS and IPS Overview

This topic provides an overview of IDS/IPS.

IPS and IDS systems can be a hardware appliance or part of the Cisco IOS Firewall software. Cisco IPS software is usually capable of both inline (IPS feature) and promiscuous (IDS feature) monitoring, whereas Cisco IDS software is capable only of promiscuous (IDS feature) monitoring.

Intrusion-Detection Systems

IDSs passively listen to network traffic, as shown in Figure 8-26. The IDS is not in the traffic path, but listens promiscuously to copies of all traffic on the network. Typically, only one promiscuous interface is required for network monitoring on an IDS. Further promiscuous interfaces could be used to monitor multiple networks. When IDS detects malicious traffic, it sends an alert to the management station. An IDS may also have the capability of sending a TCP reset to the end host to terminate any malicious TCP connections.

In promiscuous mode, packets do not flow through the sensor. The sensor analyzes a copy of the monitored traffic rather than the actual forwarded packet. The advantage of operating in promiscuous mode is that the sensor does not affect the packet flow with the forwarded traffic. The disadvantage of operating in promiscuous mode, however, is that the sensor cannot stop malicious traffic from reaching its intended target for certain types of attacks, such as atomic attacks (single-packet attacks). The response actions implemented by promiscuous sensor devices are post-event responses and often require assistance from other networking devices (for example, routers and firewalls) to respond to an attack.

Intrusion-Prevention Systems

IPSs are active devices in the traffic path, as shown in Figure 8-26. An IPS listens to inline network traffic and permits or denies flows and packets into the network. The inline interfaces have no MAC or IP address and cannot be detected directly. All traffic passes through the IPS for inspection. Traffic arrives on one IPS interface and exits on another. When an IPS detects malicious traffic, it sends an alert to the management station and can

Figure 8-26 *IDS and IPS Overview*

block the malicious traffic immediately. The original and subsequent malicious traffic is blocked as the IPS proactively prevents attacks protecting against network viruses, worms, malicious applications and vulnerability exploits. An IPS resembles a Layer 2 bridge or re-peater. By default, an IPS passes all packets unless specifically denied by a policy.

Operating in inline interface pair mode puts the IPS directly into the traffic flow and af-fects packet-forwarding rates, making them slower by adding latency. This allows the sen-sor to stop attacks by dropping malicious traffic before it reaches the intended target, thus providing a protective service. Not only is the inline device processing information on Lay-ers 3 and 4, but it is also analyzing the contents and payload of the packets for more so-phisticated embedded attacks (Layers 3 to 7). This deeper analysis lets the system identify and stop or block attacks that would normally pass through a traditional firewall device.

IDS and IPS Overview

There are two major components in an IDS or IPS solution:

- **Sensors:** Can be either host based, such as the Cisco Security Agent, or network based, such as an IPS appliance. The network-based sensors use specialized software and hardware to collect and analyze network traffic. The network-based sensors can be appliances, modules in a router, or a switch or security appliance. There are three common types of IDS/ or IPS technologies:
  - A signature-based IDS or IPS looks for specific predefined patterns or signa-tures in network traffic. Traffic patterns are compared to a database of known attacks and trigger an alarm or drop traffic if a match is found.
  - An anomaly-based IDS or IPS checks for defects or anomalies in packets or packet sequences and verifies whether there is any anomaly traffic behavior.

■   A policy-based IDS or IPS is configured based on the network security policy and detects traffic that does not match the policy.

■   **Security management and monitoring infrastructure:** Configures the sensors and serves as the collection point for alarms for security management and monitoring. The management and monitoring applications performs alert collection, aggregation, and correlation. Cisco Security Manager is used to centrally provision device configurations and security policies for Cisco firewalls, virtual private networks (VPN), and IPSs and provides some light monitoring functions. Cisco Security Monitoring, Analysis, and Response System (MARS) provides security monitoring for network security devices and host applications. Cisco IPS Device Manager (IDM) is a web-based Java application that allows configuration and management of IPS sensors. IDS Event Viewer is a Java-based application that enables network managers to view and manage alarms for up to five sensors.

Note: The Cisco IPS Device Manager has been replaced with the Cisco IPS Manager Express. The IPS Manager Express (IME) combines the IDM with the IDS Event Viewer, while adding enhanced health monitoring and the ability to manage up to five sensors. IME requires 6.1 sensor software release to provide the advanced dashboard and health monitoring features. IME is not designed to work with Cisco IOS Software sensor implementations. For more information, refer to http://www.cisco.com/en/US/products/ps9610/index.html.

Host Intrusion-Prevention Systems

Host intrusion-prevention system (HIPS) deployments include two components:

■   **Endpoint agents:** Enforces the security policy received from management server. Endpoint agents send event information to the management server, and interact with the user if necessary. The goal of an endpoint agent is to provide threat protection for the end system. Cisco Security Agent is the Cisco endpoint agent that provides threat protection for server and desktop computing systems. Cisco Security Agent consists of host-based agents that report to the Cisco Management Center for Cisco Security Agents. The Cisco Security Agent software resides between the applications and the kernel on a PC, enabling maximum application visibility with minimal impact to the stability and performance of the underlying operating system.

■   **Management server:** Deploys security policies to endpoints. The management server is responsible for configuring and maintaining the environment. The server receives and stores events information, and sends alerts to administrators. The management server may deploy software such as endpoint agent software updates. The interface to a HIPS management server is typically a GUI console that allows policy configuration and event viewing. For highly scalable environments, it is possible to have a dedicated database running where the configuration and event information is stored. The management center for Cisco Security Agents provides all management functions for Cisco Security Agent deployments.

IDS and IPS Design Considerations

The underlying security policy should be the same for an IDS or an IPS deployment. To deny traffic, an IPS solution must be deployed inline with the network, whereas an IDS sensor is connected in promiscuous mode, where packets do not flow through the sensor. The IDS sensor analyzes a copy of the monitored traffic rather than the actual forwarded packet. If your security policy does not support denying traffic, use an IDS deployment.

Note: It is common practice to deploy a sensor initially in IDS mode while baselining the network.

IDS or IPS sensors are placed in the network where they can effectively support the underlying security policy. Deployment decisions are often based on where you need to detect or stop an intrusion as soon as possible. Typical scenarios include placing the sensors at the perimeter of the network outside a firewall where the network is most exposed, internal to the network inside the firewall between boundaries between zones of trust, and at critical servers where an incident would be most costly. For example, placement outside the firewall generates many warnings that have relatively low value because no action is likely to be taken on this information.

Note: Some environments deploy an IDS outside the firewall to assist in event correlation and to determine the effectiveness of the firewall. Sensor placement depends on an organization's security policy, which is a reflection of that organization's security needs.

Traffic impact considerations are increased with inline IPS sensors over IDS deployments. A failure of the IDS means traffic monitoring has stopped. A failure of the IPS can disrupt network traffic flow unless bypass methods are implemented. An IPS deployment also impacts inline traffic. The latency through the IPS sensor should generally be under a millisecond and as low as possible. The IPS sensors have bandwidth limitations on the amount of traffic that can be supported through the device. Exceeding the performance of a sensor will result in dropped packets and a general degradation of network performance.

IDS or IPS Deployments

IDS or IPS sensors can be deployed based on the priority of targets. Internet and extranet connections are typically secured first because of their exposure. An IDS outside the firewall can detect all attacks and will generate a lot of alarms, but is useful for analyzing what kind of traffic is reaching the organization and how an attack is executed. An IDS inside the firewall can detect firewall misconfigurations by showing what kind of traffic passes through the firewall. An IPS can provide more focused application protection and firewall augmentation for extranet and DMZ resources.

Management networks and data centers are often next in priority. A layered approach for maximum protection is appropriate for the high-security areas. There might be one system installed after the firewall and a second system at the entry point to the high-security area, such as the data center. Host-specific IDS can detect attacks against a specific server. An IPS can be used to block application-specific traffic, which should not reach the server.

IPS deployments at remote and branch offices can both protect the branch from corporate incidents and protect the corporate resources from security incidents arising from branch practices. Remote-access systems need protection, too.

IPS Appliance Deployment Options

When you are placing an IPS sensor in an enterprise network, you have multiple options available depending on the infrastructure and the desired results. Figure 8-27 illustrates each of the following options:

- Two Layer 2 Devices (No Trunk)

- Two Layer 3 Devices

- Two VLANs On the Same Switch

- Two Layer 2 Devices (Trunked)

Figure 8-27   *IPS Appliance Deployment Options*

- **Two Layer 2 devices (no trunk):** Sensor placement between two Layer 2 devices without trunking is a typical campus design. In this deployment, the IPS appliance is placed between two switches. The IPS can be between the same VLAN on two different switches or between different VLANs with the same subnet on two different switches. Scenarios include placement between different security zones in a campus environment or between critical devices in a data center.

- **Two Layer 3 devices:** Sensor placement between Layer 3 devices is common in Internet, campus, and server farm designs. The two Layer 3 devices are in the same subnet. One advantage in these scenarios is the ease of configuration because the integration can take place without touching any other device.

- **Two VLANs on the same switch:** This design allows a sensor to bridge VLANs together on the same switch. The sensor brings packets in on one VLAN and out a different VLAN for traffic in the same subnet.

- **Two Layer 2 devices (trunked):** Sensor placement on a trunk port between switches is a common scenario providing protection of several VLANs from a single location.

Note: Deployments using IPS modules follow the same general guidelines as deployments for IPS appliances.

Feature: Inline VLAN Pairing

The IPS can associate VLANs in pairs on a physical interface. Packets received on one of the paired VLANs are analyzed and then forwarded to the other VLAN in the pair. The sensor brings packets in on one VLAN and out a different VLAN on the same trunk link for traffic in the same subnet. The sensor replaces the VLAN ID field in the IEEE 802.1Q header of each received packet with the ID of the egress VLAN on which the sensor forwards the packet. This design supports multiple VLAN pairs per physical interface and reduces the need to have many physical interfaces per chassis.

Note: VLAN pairs are supported on all sensors that are compatible with IPS 6.0 except Cisco IDS Network Module, Cisco ASA AIP-SSM-10, and Cisco ASA AIP-SSM-20.

IPS Deployment Challenges

Asymmetric traffic patterns and high availability are challenges for IPS deployments.

Traditional packet flows in a network are symmetrical and consist of connections that take the same path through the network in both directions. Many newer network designs do not guarantee symmetrical flows, and engineer the network to take advantage of all available links. This greatly increases the chance that traffic may use multiple paths to and from its destination.

This asymmetric traffic flow can cause problems with inline IPS devices. Because an IPS sensor inspects traffic statefully and needs to see both sides of the connection to function properly, asymmetric traffic flows may cause valid traffic to be dropped.

High availability is another deployment challenge. A failure of any redundant component in the network should not cause an interruption in network availability. This implies that existing sessions should continue to flow normally and not be dropped.

The current Cisco IPS 6.0 solutions do not support asymmetric flows or high availability natively in the product. A design workaround uses the network to mirror all traffic between two sensors in a "failover" pair. The IPS sensors in the pair see all packets traversing a point in the network. If one sensor fails for any reason, the network reroutes all traffic through the other sensor because it is the only available path. The secondary sensor has already seen all the packets and has built a complete state table for the flows, so traffic is not interrupted. Asymmetric traffic is also supported by this mirroring technique.

IDS or IPS Management Interface Deployment Options

Monitoring an IDS or IPS solution is one of the crucial elements to provide fast detection of any suspicious activity and an indication of prevented attacks. IDS or IPS management consolidates and centralizes alarms from multiple sources to provide the required view of the network.

On the network boundary, the sensors are usually installed adjacent to a firewall. The monitoring and management interfaces of an IPS sensor can therefore be connected to two different networks. This is especially critical when the outside sensor needs to communicate with the inside network.

One option is to connect the monitoring interface to the outside network, and the management interface is directly connected to the inside network. All management is done in-band over the internal network. This type of setup is simple, but provides a path around the firewall if the sensor is compromised. This design is not recommended.

A preferred design places the monitoring interface on the outside network, and the management interface on a separate inside VLAN. With this setup, the management interface is isolated by an IPS management VLAN from the rest of the inside network. If the VLAN is sufficiently trusted, this design provides good separation of the IDS or IPS sensor. A recommended practice is to use Secure Shell (SSH) or Secure Sockets Layer (SSL) protocol for management access to the IDS or IPS sensors.

Note: Using PVLANs to put all sensors on isolated ports is recommended because the sensors do not need to talk to each other except when distributed blocking is used. This prevents the compromise of a single sensor, which helps to prevent other sensors from being compromised.

In-Band Management Through Tunnels

Another option for deploying IDS or IPS uses a combination of management through an OOB network and management through secure tunnels depending on the location of the sensors.

For devices outside the perimeter firewall, the monitoring interface remains on the outside network, but the management interface is terminated on a separate DMZ. Management is supported in-band across an encrypted tunnel. The firewall protects the outside sensor from the inside devices and provides better separation compared to the previous solution. For internal devices in more secure areas, management is provided through a separate management VLAN.

IDS and IPS Monitoring and Management

Cisco Security MARS and Cisco Security Manager (CSM) are part of the Cisco Security Management Suite, which delivers policy administration and enforcement for the Cisco Self-Defending Network. Both tools should be implemented in the management VLAN in a protected place such as the server farm or data center.

Cisco Security MARS provides multivendor event correlation and proactive response, distributing IPS signatures to mitigate active threats. Cisco Security MARS proactively identifies active network threats and distributes IPS signatures to mitigate them:

- Cisco Security MARS ships with a set of predefined compliance reports that are easy to customize.

- Cisco Security MARS stores event information from every type of device. This information can be grouped in one single report.

For a small to medium-size organization, a centralized Cisco Security MARS implemented as a local controller is a typical deployment.

Note: In CS-MARS, a *local controller* is the name given to the hardware appliance that supports the features discussed in this section for monitoring, analysis, and response. The *global controller* is an appliance used to support the centralized operation and management of multiple local controllers in distributed deployments.

CSM enables organizations to manage security policies on Cisco security devices. CSM supports integrated provisioning of VPN and firewall services across Cisco IOS routers, Cisco PIX and ASA security appliances, and Cisco Catalyst 6500/Cisco 7600 service modules. It also supports IPS technologies on routers, service modules, and IPS devices. CSM supports provisioning of many platform-specific settings (for example, interfaces, routing, identity, QoS, and logging).

CSM, through its Cisco IPS Manager component, supports the management and configuration of Cisco IPS sensors (appliances, switch modules, network modules, and Security Service Modules [SSM]) and Cisco IOS IPS devices (Cisco IOS routers with IPS-enabled images and Cisco Integrated Services Routers [ISR]). You configure IPS sensors and Cisco IOS IPS devices through the use of policies, each of which defines a different part of the configuration of the sensor. Whereas CSM 3.0 allowed you to cross-launch the CiscoWorks IPS Management Center to access IPS functionality, Cisco Security Manager 3.1 provides fully integrated IPS features.

Cisco Security Manager 3.1 enables you to manage security policies on Cisco security devices. CSM supports integrated provisioning of firewall, IPS, and VPN (site to site, remote access, and SSL). It provides integrated IPS provisioning services. Starting in version 3.1, Cisco Security Manager supports Cisco IPS 5.1 and 6.0; and Cisco IOS Firewall IPS features in Cisco IOS Software Release 12.4(11)T. It provides support for the following features on IPS 6.0 devices:

- Virtual sensors

- Anomaly detection

- Passive operating system fingerprinting

- Simplified custom signature creation

- Signature update wizard, preview and tuning of new signatures

- IPS signature update license management

- External product interface (linkage of IPS sensor with Management Center for Cisco Security Agent)

Scaling Cisco Security MARS with Global Controller Deployment

The Cisco Security MARS Global controller enables network monitoring scaling, as shown in Figure 8-28.

Figure 8-28   *Scaling Cisco Security MARS with Global Controller Deployment*

If an organization is supporting multiple Cisco Security MARS local controllers, they can deploy a distributed solution using a global controller to summarize the findings of two or more local controllers and manage the local controllers.

The global controller communicates over HTTPS using certificates. Only incidents from global rules are rolled up into the global controller. The global controller can distribute updates, rules, report templates, access rules, and queries across the local controller.

Summary

In this chapter, you learned about firewalls, Network Admission Control, and intrusion-prevention and -detection systems.

Firewalls have long provided the first line of defense in network security infrastructures. They accomplish this by comparing corporate policies about network access rights for users to the connection information surrounding each access attempt. User policies and connection information must match; otherwise, the firewall does not grant access to network resources.

NAC is a set of technologies and solutions that is built on an industry initiative led by Cisco. The NAC Framework uses the network infrastructure to enforce security policy compliance on all devices seeking to access network computing resources, thereby limiting damage from emerging security threats such as viruses, worms, and spyware by using embedded software modules within NAC-enabled products. Customers using NAC can allow network access only to compliant and trusted endpoint devices (PCs, servers, and PDAs, for example) and can restrict the access of noncompliant devices. Cisco NAC Appliance condenses NAC capabilities into an appliance form where client, server, and manager products enable network administrators to authenticate, authorize, evaluate, and remediate wired, wireless, and remote users and their machines before allowing users onto the network.

Cisco intrusion-detection and -prevention solutions are part of the Cisco Self-Defending Network. Designed to identify and stop worms, network viruses, and other malicious traffic, these solutions can help protect networks. Cisco provides a broad array of solutions for intrusion detection and prevention at both the network and at the endpoint.

References

For additional information, refer to these resources:

- Cisco Systems, Inc. "Cisco Catalyst 6500 Series Firewall Services Module," at http://www.cisco.com/en/US/products/hw/modules/ps2706/ps4452/index.html

- Cisco Systems, Inc. "Network Admission Control (NAC) Framework," at http://www.cisco.com/en/US/netsol/ns617/networking_solutions_sub_solution_home.html

- Cisco Systems, Inc. "Release s for Network Admission Control, Release 2.0," at http://www.cisco.com/univercd/cc/td/doc/product/vpn/ciscosec/ntadctrl/nac20rn1.pdf

- Cisco Systems, Inc. "Cisco NAC Appliance (Clean Access) Releases," at http://www.cisco.com/en/US/products/ps6128/prod_release_s_list.html

- Cisco Systems, Inc. "Switch Support for Cisco NAC Appliance," at http://www.cisco.com/univercd/cc/td/doc/product/vpn/ciscosec/cca/cca40/switch.htm

- Cisco Systems, Inc. "Cisco NAC Appliance Data Sheet," at http://www.cisco.com/application/pdf/en/us/guest/products/ps6128/c1650/cdccont_0900aecd802da1b5.pdf

- Cisco Systems, Inc. "Cisco Intrusion Prevention System," at http://www.cisco.com/en/US/products/sw/secursw/ps2113/index.html.

- Cisco Systems, Inc. "Cisco Secure Services Client Introduction," at http://www.cisco.com/en/US/products/ps7034/index.html

- Cisco Systems, Inc. "Installing and Using Cisco Intrusion Prevention System Device Manager 6.0," at http://www.cisco.com/application/pdf/en/us/guest/products/ps4077/c2001/ccmigration_09186a00807a9287.pdf

- Cisco Systems, Inc. "Cisco Security Agent," at http://www.cisco.com/en/US/products/sw/secursw/ps5057/index.html

- Cisco Systems, Inc. "Cisco Trust Agent," at http://www.cisco.com/en/US/products/ps5923/index.html

- Cisco Systems, Inc. "Zone-Based Policy Firewall Design Guide," at http://www.cisco.com/univercd/cc/td/doc/product/software/ios124/124sup/zone_dg.pdf

Review Questions

Answer the following questions, and then refer to Appendix A, "Answers to Review Questions," for the answers.

1. What is a virtual firewall?

    a. A logical separation of multiple firewall security contexts on a single firewall

    b. A physical separation of multiple firewall security contexts in a single chassis

    c. A routed firewall mode

    d. A transparent firewall mode

    e. An administrative context for network connectivity

2. Which command provides support for asymmetric routing?

    a. **asr-active** interface command on FWSM 2.1

    b. **asr-active** interface command on FWSM 3.0

    c. **asr-group** interface command on FWSM 2.1

    d. **asr-group** interface command on FWSM 3.0

    e. **asr-redundancy** interface command on FWSM 2.1

    f. **asr-redundancy** interface command on FWSM 3.0

3. What are three components of a PVLAN? (Choose three.)

   a.   Communications VLAN

   b.   Community VLAN

   c.   Isolated VLAN

   d.   Isolation VLAN

   e.   Primary VLAN

   f.   Promiscuous VLAN

4. What are two methods to provide network security with access control?

   a.   802.1x posture alignment

   b.   802.1x posture assessment

   c.   IBNS authentication

   d.   INBS authentication

   e.   NAC posture alignment

   f.   NAC posture assessment

5. How many NAC Appliance Servers can Cisco NAC Appliance Super Manager manage?

   a.   3

   b.   5

   c.   20

   d.   40

   e.   50

6. What are two characteristics of real IP gateway mode?

   a.   The Cisco NAM has an IP address for every managed VLAN.

   b.   The Cisco NAM operates as a standard Ethernet bridge, but with added functionality.

   c.   The Cisco NAS does not operate as the default gateway for untrusted network clients.

   d.   The Cisco NAS has an IP address for every managed VLAN.

   e.   The Cisco NAS operates as a standard Ethernet bridge, but with added functionality.

   f.   The Cisco NAS operates as the default gateway for untrusted network clients.

7. What are two typical NAC agentless hosts?

    a.   Cisco Secure Services clients

    b.   Enforcement devices

    c.   Printers

    d.   Scanners

    e.   Windows 2000 devices

    f.   Windows XP devices

8. Which two of the following are characteristics of an IPS sensor?

    a.   It is an active device in the traffic path.

    b.   It passively listens to network traffic.

    c.   A permissive interface is used to monitor networks.

    d.   A promiscuous interface is used to monitor the network.

    e.   Traffic arrives on one IPS interface and exits on another.

9. What are two challenges for IPS deployments?

    a.   Supporting inline VLAN pairing

    b.   Supporting asymmetric traffic flows

    c.   Natively supporting symmetric traffic flows

    d.   Natively bridging VLANs on two switches

    e.   Supporting failover without dropping valid traffic

10. Which mechanism can be used to scale Cisco Security MARS deployments?

    a.   Inline VLAN pairing for local controllers

    b.   Symmetric traffic flows to a central controller

    c.   A global controller to summarize multiple local controllers

    d.   A central controller to summarize multiple local and global controllers

    e.   HTTPS certificates for each global controller

After completing this chapter, you will be able to:

■ Discuss design considerations for remote-access VPNs

■ Discuss design considerations for site-to-site VPNs

■ Discuss technologies for implementing VPNs

■ Discuss managing and scaling VPNs

CHAPTER 9

IPsec and SSL VPN Design

This chapter reviews virtual private network (VPN) design in the enterprise. VPNs are networks deployed on a public or private network infrastructure. VPNs are useful for telecommuters, mobile users, and remote offices, and for customers, suppliers, and partners.

For enterprises, VPNs are an alternative WAN infrastructure, replacing or augmenting existing private networks that use dedicated WANs based on leased-line, Frame Relay, ATM, or other technologies. Increasingly, enterprises are turning to their service providers for VPNs and other complete service solutions tailored to their particular business.

Designing Remote-Access VPNs

Remote-access VPNs permit secure, encrypted connections between mobile or remote users and their corporate networks through a third-party network, such as a service provider. Deploying a remote-access VPN enables enterprises to reduce communications expenses by leveraging the local packet-switching infrastructures of Internet service providers. Cisco remote-access VPN solutions deliver both IP Security (IPsec) and Secure Sockets Layer (SSL) technologies on a single platform with unified management.

Remote-Access VPN Overview

Remote-access VPNs using IPsec or SSL technologies permit secure, encrypted connections between mobile or remote users and their corporate network across public networks.

There are three remote-access VPN components:

- VPN termination device or headend supporting a high number of endpoints.
- End clients that can be mobile or fixed. The remote-access client can be built inside of operating system or application, or be installed as a Layer 3 software client such as the Cisco VPN Client.
- Technology that connects the VPN headend and the end clients. The two main protocols supporting remote-access VPNs are IPsec and SSL.
    - IPsec is used primarily for data confidentiality and device authentication, but extensions to the standard allow for user authentication and authorization to occur as part of the IPsec process.
    - The main role of SSL is to provide security for web traffic. With SSL, the browser client supports the VPN connection to a host. SSL is a default capability in leading browsers.

Both IPsec and SSL remote-access VPNs are mechanisms to provide secure communication:

■ Authenticity identifies the trusted party by asking for username and password or a credential.

■ Integrity checking verifies that packets were not altered or tampered with as they traveled across the network.

■ Confidentiality is supported using encryption to ensure communications were not read by others.

Example: Cisco Easy VPN Client IPsec Implementation

Cisco Easy VPN provides simple IPsec VPN deployments for remote offices and teleworkers.

The Cisco Easy VPN Server allows Cisco routers and security appliances to act as IPsec VPN headend devices in remote-access and site-to-site VPNs.

Note: IPsec components and features are covered in the prerequisite *Implementing Secure Converged Wide Area Networks* course.

For remote-access VPNs, the Cisco Easy VPN Server terminates VPN tunnels initiated by remote workers running the Cisco VPN Client software on PCs. This capability allows mobile and remote workers to access critical data and applications on their corporate intranet. The Cisco Easy VPN Server pushes configurations and security policies defined at the central site to the remote client device, helping to ensure that those connections have appropriate information and current policies in place before the connection is established. Cisco Easy VPN Server can pass a variety of information to the client, including IP address and mask, information on the internal Domain Name System (DNS) and Windows Internet Naming Service (WINS) server, and organization policies.

Note: Cisco Easy VPN Server is discussed in more detail in the "Using IPsec VPN Technologies" section of this chapter.

SSL VPN Overview

SSL is a protocol designed to enable secure communications on an insecure network such as the Internet.

SSL is a technology developed by Netscape to provide encryption between a web browser and a web server. SSL supports integrity of communications along with strong authentication using digital certificates:

■ Web server certificates are used to authenticate the identity of a website to visiting browsers. When a user wants to send confidential information to a web server, the browser accesses the digital certificate of the server. The certificate, which contains the public key of the web server, is used by the browser to authenticate the identity of the web server and to encrypt information for the server using SSL technology. Because the web server is the only entity with access to its private key, only the server can decrypt the information.

■ Root certificates are self-signed digital certificates that are generated during the creation of a certificate authority (CA). "Trusted" root certificates refer to CA certificates that are stored in the trust lists that are natively embedded in the leading web browsers. There are a limited number of CA certificates, which come embedded in the web browsers from Microsoft and Netscape.

SSL for VPNs can be more than a basic web page supporting secure access to the applications available as static web pages on HTTP servers:

■ SSL VPNs can fit into existing networks and application environments and provide support for complex applications such as corporate directory and calendar systems, e-commerce applications, file sharing, and remote system management.

■ SSL VPNs can support the same authentication mechanisms and often extensive application lists as those available for IPsec.

SSL VPNs have multiple access mechanisms:

■ Content rewriting and application translation using embedded clientless access and Layer 7 features. Clientless access is where a user can connect with little requirements beyond a basic web browser.

■ Port forwarding, which is known as a thin client. With a thin client, a small applet or application, generally less than 100 KB in size, provides access to a subset of resources.

■ Dynamic VPN client with full network access, which is known as a thick client. With a thick client, a larger client, generally around 500 KB, is delivered to the end user. The applications that can be reached through the thick client are similar to those available via IPsec VPNs. This client is delivered via a web page and never needs to be manually distributed or installed.

Clientless Access

The SSL VPN system supports clientless access by proxying web pages. The system connects to a web server, downloads and translates a web page, and then transfers it over an SSL connection to the browser of the end user. The SSL VPN system rewrites or translates content so that the internal addresses and names on a web page are accessible to the end users.

Only web-enabled and some client/server applications (such as intranets, applications with web interfaces, email, calendaring, and file servers) can be accessed using a clientless connection. This limited access is suitable for partners or contractors that need access to a limited set of resources on the network.

Several content-rewriting functions are involved in proxying the remote applications:

■ Translating protocol to HTTP

■ Delivering HTML user interface

■   Supporting file sharing

Clientless access for SSL VPNs does not require specialized VPN software on the user desktop, because all VPN traffic is transmitted and delivered through a standard web browser, which minimizes provisioning and support concerns.

Thin Client

Organizations that have not implemented web-based applications can often rely on the thin clients, shown here in Figure 9-1, that support port forwarding. Port forwarding requires a small application, often in the form of Java or Microsoft ActiveX that runs on the end-user system. The port forwarder acts as a local proxy server. The client application listens for connections on a port defined for an application on a local host address. It tunnels packets that arrive on this port inside of an SSL connection to the SSL VPN device, which unpacks them and forwards them to the real application server. Port forwarding maintains the native application look and feel for the end user.

Figure 9-1   *Thin Client (Port Forwarding)*

Port forwarding is an effective technique, but it also has some limitations. For port forwarding to work, the applications need to be well behaved and predictable in their network connectivity ports, patterns, and needs. Examples of applications that are not web enabled but can be addressed with port forwarding are common mail protocols, including Simple Mail Transfer Protocol (SMTP), Post Office Protocol Version 3 (POP3), Messaging Application Programming Interface (MAPI), and remote shell programs, such as Telnet. ActiveX or Java applet support may also be required on the client machine, along with the permissions in the browser to run them.

Thick Client

SSL VPN network extension connects the end-user system to the corporate network with access controls based only on network-layer information, such as destination IP address and port number. Network extension uses a thick client that provides authorized users with secure access to the entire corporate LAN.

The thick client, shown here in Figure 9-2, is automatically delivered through the web page and does not need to be manually distributed or installed. The thick client requires administrative access to the local system. The Layer 3 thick client provides a virtual adapter for the end user, typically using ActiveX and Java. The applications that can be accessed with the thick client are similar to those available through an IPsec VPN. The Cisco SSL VPN Client for WebVPN is a Cisco implementation of the thick client.

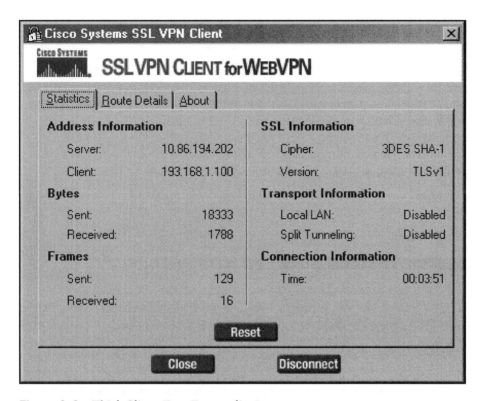

Figure 9-2 *Thick Client (Port Forwarding)*

Because the SSL VPN network extension runs on top of the SSL protocol, it is simpler to manage and has greater robustness with different network topologies such as firewalls and Network Address Translation (NAT) than the higher security of IPsec. The thick client is typically a smaller installation than the IPsec client.

Thick mode should be used when users need full application access and IT wants tighter integration with the operating system for additional security and ease of use.

Remote-Access VPN Design Considerations

When deploying remote-access VPNs, it is important to determine where to terminate the service. The decision is impacted by the originations firewall architecture, routing and addressing schema, and authentication policy. The following section examines these elements and their impact on Remote Access VPN design.

VPN Termination Device and Firewall Placement

The VPN termination device can be deployed in parallel with a firewall, inline with a firewall, or in a demilitarized zone (DMZ). For best security, the recommended practice is to place the public side of the VPN termination device in a DMZ behind a firewall.

Note: The firewall could be the VPN termination device.

The firewall policies should limit traffic coming in to the VPN termination device to IPsec and SSL. Any IPsec tunnels should terminate on the VPN appliance. For extra security, send traffic through another firewall for additional inspection after it passes through the VPN appliance.

You should also enforce endpoint security compliance on the remote system.

Routing Design Considerations

Routing design considerations are mainly a VPN headend consideration for remote-access VPNs.

For nonlocal subnet IP addresses, the most common configuration is that the internal routers use static routes for the address blocks pointing to the private interfaces of the headend device.

If a large number of networks exist behind each headend device, the configuration of static routes becomes difficult to maintain. Instead, it is recommended that you use Reverse Route Injection (RRI). RRI automatically inserts static routes into the routing table of the gateway router for those networks and hosts protected by a remote tunnel endpoint. These static routes can then be redistributed to the other routers in the network.

Note: Smaller organizations typically configure a few static routes to point to the VPN device and do not need RRI. The RRI function is usually of more benefit to larger organizations that have more complex requirements (for example, organizations that do not have a dedicated scope of DHCP addresses that are associated to a specific VPN headend).

The Firewall Services Module (FWSM) uses the administrative context for network management connectivity. Each context may also be managed individually as if they were distinct and separate firewalls. This granularity enables different groups to administer their own firewall. The system context is used to add VLANs, create contexts, and assign VLANs to contexts. With the default FWSM software, up to two security contexts are provided: the administrative and system context.

Address Assignment Considerations

For IPsec, thin, and thick clients, there are three common addressing techniques.

■   The most simple and common address assignment design is to use internal address pools per VPN headend and to implement a static route for this subnet to the VPN headend. With this approach, ACLs on an internal firewall can support group-based address pools for incoming user policies.

■ Another popular choice is to use DHCP to assign addresses. A recommended practice is to associate a dedicated scope of DHCP addresses to a specific VPN headend.

■ For situations where the remote user needs a static IP address assignment to support a specific application, organizations will need to deploy RADIUS or Lightweight Directory Access Protocol (LDAP) with an attribute to assign the user the same IP. In this case, RRI may be needed.

An IP address is not assigned for clientless end-user devices:

■ The headend device will proxy Address Resolution Protocol (ARP) on behalf of all local subnet IP addresses.

■ Because the clientless users do not receive a unique IP address, their traffic will originate from the headend interface IP. This is good for scalability, but harder to monitor.

Other Design Considerations

Two other design considerations are authentication and access control.

Authentication

Although the SSL protocol does not support client authentication methods other than digital certificates, it is possible to use other authentication methods in conjunction with SSL. The simplest approach is to use a username and password, but security-conscious organizations use stronger authentication methods, such as security tokens and one-time password (OTP).

Customers who are focused on convenience sometimes authenticate to an internal Network Termination (NT) domain controller or static RADIUS password database. Any type of static password configuration leaves the organization vulnerable to brute-force password attacks.

Access Control

Access control rules allow organizations to restrict network access. Some companies choose to maintain all access rules on an internal firewall based on the source IP of the client. This scenario supports addresses that are assigned to a specific pool based on group assignment.

Access control rules can be defined at a per-group basis on the VPN headend device. This approach is easy to deploy, but can be more difficult to maintain with large numbers of policies or across multiple devices. Access control rules can also be defined on the headend RADIUS server, although generic RADIUS has a 4-KB packet size limit. The Cisco Secure Access Control Server (ACS) offers a downloadable access control list (ACL) feature that can be used with Cisco headend devices to support large policies.

Tunnel-based VPNs (IPsec and SSL VPN clients) provide Layer 3 control at the protocol, port, and destination IP level. Clientless SSL VPNs can provide more granular Layer 7 access control, including URL-based access or file server directory-level access control.

Example: VPN Architecture

Figure 9-3 shows an example of a VPN design architecture that supports employees and partners. The employees connect across the Internet using an IPsec VPN client. The non-corporate users connect using SSL. The IPsec or SSL clients are authenticated using the authentication, authorization, and accounting (AAA) server. Both IPsec and SSL VPNs come in on the public interface of the VPN cluster and are terminated. Load balancing is used for resiliency, stateless failover, and capacity growth on the VPN cluster. The private interface of the VPN headend connects through routers to the internal corporate network. Inbound ACLs on the internal edge routers provide access control rules to permit traffic to specific internal resources.

Figure 9-3   *Example: VPN Architecture*

Users are organized into various groups with appropriate security policy profiles and user authentication and authorization information. Both Cisco IPsec VPN and SSL VPN clients are supported, as is clientless SSL VPN with an optional port-forwarding feature.

Designing Site-to-Site VPNs

Site-to-site VPNs are an alternative WAN infrastructure used to connect branch offices, home offices, or business partners to all or portions of an enterprise network. VPNs do not inherently change private WAN requirements, such as support for multiple protocols, high reliability, and extensive scalability, but instead meet these requirements more cost-effectively and with greater flexibility. Site-to-site VPNs use the most pervasive transport technologies available today, such as the public Internet or service provider IP networks, by using tunneling and encryption for data privacy and quality of service (QoS) for transport reliability.

Site-to-Site VPN Applications

Site-to-site VPNs can be used to replace costly WAN services or serve as a backup for disaster recovery purposes. Site-to-site VPNs can also help organizations meet regulatory requirements by providing encryption for sensitive data. This section examines these common uses for site-to-site IPsec VPNs.

WAN Replacement Using Site-to-Site IPsec VPNs

WAN replacement is one of the biggest reasons organizations implement IPsec VPNs.

Up to 40 percent of typical enterprise employees work in branch offices, away from the central sites that provide mission-critical applications and services required for business operations. As these services are extended to branch office employees, requirements increase for bandwidth, security, and high availability.

IPsec VPNs can provide a cost-effective replacement for a private WAN infrastructure. Often the cost of a relatively high-bandwidth IP connection, such as an Internet service provider (ISP) connection, IP VPN service provider connection, or broadband digital subscriber line (DSL) or cable access, is lower than existing or upgraded WAN circuits.

Organizations can use IPsec VPNs to connect remote branches or offices, teleworkers, and mobile users to the corporate resources as the central site. Organizations also use IPsec VPNs to provide extranet connectivity for business to business applications.

There are four key components of site-to-site VPN:

- **Headend VPN devices:** Serve as VPN headend termination devices at a central campus

- **VPN access devices:** Serve as VPN branch-end termination devices at branch office locations

- **IPsec and generic routing encapsulation (GRE) tunnels:** Interconnect the headend and branch-end devices in the VPN

- **Internet services from ISPs:** Serve as the WAN interconnection medium

WAN Backup Using Site-to-Site IPsec VPNs

Another common business application use for IPsec VPNs is for backing up an existing WAN.

When a primary network connection malfunctions, the remote branch office can rely on Internet VPN connectivity while waiting for the primary connection to be restored.

IPsec VPNs over a high-speed ISP connection or broadband cable or DSL access can provide a cost-effective secondary WAN connection for branch offices. Many customers continue to route their most critical traffic across their private WAN circuits, and route higher-bandwidth, less-critical traffic across IPsec VPNs as a secondary connection path. If a failure occurs on their primary WAN circuit, the IPsec VPN can also function as an established backup path.

Note: The Internet VPN option does not offer QoS and service level agreements (SLA), which may be necessary for applications such as IP telephony.

Regulatory Encryption Using Site-to-Site IPsec VPNs

Another common business application use for IPsec VPNs is for mandatory or regulatory encryption.

Regulations such as the Health Insurance Portability and Accountability Act (HIPAA), the Sarbanes-Oxley Act (SOX), and the Basel II agreement recommend or mandate the need for companies to implement all reasonable safeguards to protect personal, customer, and corporate information. IPsec VPNs inherently provide a high degree of data privacy through establishment of trust points between communicating devices, and data encryption with the Triple Data Encryption Standard (3DES) or Advanced Encryption Standard (AES).

Site-to-site VPNs support regulatory constraints and business policies. As network security risks increase and regulatory compliance becomes essential, organizations are using IPsec VPNs to encrypt and protect data such as medical records, corporate or personal financial data, and sensitive information such as legal, police, and academic records, whether a private WAN, IP VPN, or the Internet is used for connectivity.

Site-to-Site VPN Design Considerations

The design of site-to-site VPNS is impacted by the organization's routing and addressing schema. Other important design considerations are the size, scale, and performance expectations for the site-to-site VPN. These requirements drive the selection of and appropriate platform to provision the service. The following section examines these elements and their impact on site-to-site VPN design.

IP Addressing and Routing

An IPsec VPN is an overlay on an existing IP network.

The VPN termination devices need routable IP addresses for the outside Internet connection. Private IP addresses can be used on the inside of the VPN. Just as good IP network design supports summarization, the VPN address space needs to be designed to allow for network summarization. NAT may be needed to support overlapping address space between sites in an organization.

Most IPsec VPNs forward data across the network using IPsec tunnel mode, which encapsulates and protects an entire IP packet. Because tunnel mode encapsulates or hides the IP header of the pre-encrypted packet, a new IP header is added so that the packet can be successfully forwarded.

Many larger enterprise WANs need dynamic routing protocols such as Enhanced Interior Gateway Routing Protocol (EIGRP) and Open Shortest Path First (OSPF) to provide routing and maintain link state and path resiliency. All Interior Gateway Protocol (IGP) routing protocols use either broadcast or IP multicast as a method of transmitting routing table information. However, basic IPsec designs cannot transport IGP dynamic routing protocols or IP multicast traffic. When support for one or more of these features are required, IPsec should be used in conjunction with other technologies such as GRE.

Scaling, Sizing, and Performance

The task of scaling large IPsec VPNs while maintaining performance and high availability is challenging and requires careful planning and design. Many factors affect scalability of an IPsec VPN design, including the number of route sites, access connection speeds, routing peer limits, IPsec encryption engine throughput, features to be supported, and applications that will be transported over the IPsec VPN.

The number of remote sites is a primary factor in determining scalability of a design and affects the routing plan, high-availability design, and ultimately the overall throughput that must be aggregated by the VPN headend routers. Different routers can support different numbers of tunnels.

IPsec VPN throughput depends on several factors, including connection speeds, capacity of the crypto engine, and CPU limits of the router. An IPsec crypto engine in a Cisco IOS router is a unidirectional device that must process bidirectional packets. Outbound packets must be encrypted by the IPsec crypto engine, and inbound packets must be decrypted by the same device. For each interface having packets encrypted, it is necessary to consider the bidirectional speed of the interface. For example, a T1 connection speed is 1.544 Mb/s, but the IPsec throughput required is 3.088 Mb/s.

Cisco recommends the following practices for VPN device performance limits:

- The redundant headend device should be deployed in a configuration that results in CPU utilization less than 50 percent. The 50 percent target includes all overhead incurred by IPsec and any other enabled features such as firewall, routing, intrusion-detection system (IDS), and logging. This performance limit will allow the headend device to handle failover of the other headend device.

- Because branch devices will need to support fewer additional tunnels in a failover event, branch devices can be deployed in a configuration with less than 65 percent CPU utilization.

Cisco Router Performance with IPsec VPNs

Because IPsec VPN connections do not normally have a bandwidth associated with them, the overall physical interface connection speeds of both the headend and branch routers largely determine the maximum speeds at which the IPsec VPN must operate. Table 9-1 shows best-case scenarios with minimal features running IPsec VPNs in a lab with 1400-byte packets.

However, the packets-per-second (PPS) rate matters more than throughput bandwidth (in bits per second) for the connection speeds being terminated or aggregated. In general, routers and crypto engines have upper boundaries for processing a given number of packets per second. The size of packets used for testing and throughput evaluations can understate or overstate true performance. For example, if a device can support 20 Kb/s,

100-byte packets lead to 16 Mb/s throughput, and 1400-byte packets at the same packet rate lead to 224 Mb/s throughput. Because of such a wide variance in throughput, it is generally better to use packets per second for scalability than bits per second.

Each time a crypto engine encrypts or decrypts a packet, it performs mathematical computations on the IP packet payload using the unique crypto key for the trustpoint, agreed upon by the sender and receiver. If more than one IPsec tunnel is terminated on a router, the router has multiple trust points and therefore multiple crypto keys. When packets are to be sent to or received from a different tunnel from the last packet sent or received, the crypto engine must swap keys to use the right key matched with the trust point. This key swapping can degrade the performance of a crypto engine, depending on its architecture, and increase the router CPU utilization. For some Cisco platforms, such as Cisco 7200VXR series routers with Cisco Service Adapter VPN Acceleration Module 2+ (SA-VAM2+), as the number of tunnels increases, throughput of the IPsec crypto engine

Table 9-1 *Cisco Router Performance with IPsec VPNs*

Cisco VPN Security Router	Maximum Number of Tunnels	3DES Throughput	AES Throughput
Cisco 850 series	5	8 Mb/s	8 Mb/s
Cisco 870 series	10	30 Mb/s	30 Mb/s
Cisco 1841 Integrated Services Router with AIM-VPN/BPII	800	95 Mb/s	95 Mb/s
Cisco 2801 Integrated Services with AIM-VPN/BPII	1500	100 Mb/s	100 Mb/s
Cisco 2811 Integrated Services with AIM-VPN/EPII	1500	130 Mb/s	130 Mb/s
Cisco 2821 Integrated Services with AIM-VPN/EPII	1500	140 Mb/s	140 Mb/s
Cisco 2851 Integrated Services with AIM-VPN/EPII	1500	145 Mb/s	145 Mb/s
Cisco 3825 Integrated Services with AIM-VPN/EPII	2000	175 Mb/s	175 Mb/s
Cisco 3845 Integrated Services with AIM-VPN/EPII	2500	185 Mb/s	185 Mb/s
Cisco 7200VXR series with a Single Cisco SA-VAM2+	5000	260 Mb/s	260 Mb/s
Cisco 7301 router with Cisco SA-VAM2+	5000	370 Mb/s	370 Mb/s
Cisco Catalyst 6500/7600 router with 1 IPsec VPN SPA	8000	2.5 Gb/s	2.5 Gb/s

decreases. For other Cisco platforms, such as Cisco 7600 series routers with VPN Shared Port Adapter (SPA), performance is relatively linear, with relatively the same throughput for a single tunnel as for 1000 or even 5000 tunnels.

Cisco Router Security Performance

The Cisco Integrated Services Routers (ISR) are built with fast processors and cryptography to support high-performance security features. The Cisco IOS advanced security feature set combines a rich VPN feature set with advanced firewall, intrusion-prevention, and extensive Cisco IOS Software capabilities, including QoS, multiprotocol, multicast, and advanced routing support. The figure shows some best-case performance measures for individual security features. The VPN throughput numbers are with 1400-byte packets and Advanced Integration Module (AIM) acceleration cards installed. Figure 9-4 illustrates the performance metrics associated with the ISR series routers.

* Firewall performance is with NAT and logging enabled.
** Branch scenario when tested with optimal traffic conditions.

Figure 9-4   *Cisco Router Security Performance*

Note: The performance numbers in a production environment may differ.

Cisco ASA 5500 Series Performance

ASA 5500 series all-in-one Adaptive Security Appliances deliver enterprise-class security and VPN services to small- and medium-size businesses and large enterprise networks in a modular, purpose-built appliance. The ASA 5500 series incorporates a wide range of integrated security services, including firewall, intrusion-prevention system (IPS), and anti-X

services with SSL and IPsec VPN services in an easy-to-deploy, high-performance solution. The ASA 5500 series is the most feature-rich solution for SSL and IPsec-based remote access that Cisco offers, and it supports robust site-to-site connectivity. The series
provides higher scalability and greater throughput capabilities than the widely deployed
Cisco VPN 3000 series concentrators.

Table 9-2 shows some best-case performance measures for the ASA 5500 series.

Table 9-2   *Cisco ASA 5500 Series Performance*

Model	SSL/IPsec Scalability	Maximum VPN Throughput
Cisco ASA 5505	25 simultaneous SSL sessions 25 simultaneous VPN sessions	100 Mb/s
Cisco ASA 5510	250 simultaneous SSL sessions 250 simultaneous VPN sessions	170 Mb/s
Cisco ASA 5520	750 simultaneous SSL sessions 750 simultaneous VPN sessions	225 Mb/s
Cisco ASA 5540	2500 simultaneous SSL VPN sessions 5000 simultaneous VPN sessions	325 Mb/s
Cisco ASA 5550	5000 simultaneous SSL sessions 5000 simultaneous VPN sessions	425 Mb/s
Cisco ASA 5580	10,000 simultaneous SSL sessions 10,000 simultaneous VPN sessions	1 Gb/s

Note: The performance numbers in a production environment may differ.

Typical VPN Device Deployments

Table 9-3 shows where Cisco VPN devices are typically deployed.

Table 9-3   *Typical VPN Device Deployment*

Location	Models
Teleworkers	Cisco 850 and 870
Small office/home office (SOHO)	Cisco 850 and 870
Small business	Cisco ASA 5505
Small branch	Cisco 1800 Cisco ASA 5510

Medium branch	Cisco 2800
	Cisco ASA 5520
Enterprise branch	Cisco 3800
	Cisco ASA 5540 and 5550
Enterprise edge	Cisco 7200 and 7301
Enterprise headquarters	Catalyst 6500
Data center	Cisco 7600
	Cisco ASA 5550

The ASA 5500 series supports both IPsec VPNs and SSL-based remote-access VPN services deployments on a single integrated platform. Cisco ISRs and Cisco Catalyst switches support site-to-site IPsec VPNs of any topology, from hub-and-spoke to the more complex fully meshed VPNs on networks of all sizes, integrating security services with extensive Cisco IOS Software capabilities that include QoS, multiprotocol, multicast, and advanced routing support.

Design Topologies

A peer-to-peer IPsec VPN provides connectivity between two sites through a tunnel that secures traffic.

Typically, remote peers are connected to the central site over a shared infrastructure in a hub-and-spoke topology with tunnels from the multiple spokes to the headend hub. The hub-and-spoke topology scales well. However, a performance penalty applies because of the two encryption/decryption cycles for spoke-to-spoke traffic.

A meshed topology may be the appropriate design to use when there are multiple locations with a large amount of traffic flowing between them. To eliminate the performance penalty due to two encryption/decryption cycles for spoke-to-spoke traffic, a partial-mesh topology can be used. The partial-mesh topology is similar to a hub-and-spoke topology, but it supports some direct spoke-to-spoke connectivity.

The full-mesh topology provides direct connectivity between all locations. There are scaling issues as the number of IPsec tunnels needed grows exponentially as number of sites increases. This topology is also more difficult to provision.

Note: Design topologies are discussed in more detail in the "Using IPsec VPN Technologies" section of this chapter.

VPN Device Placement Designs

The following section provides an overview of various design options for placement of VPN devices in the network.

VPN Device Parallel to Firewall

The VPN device can be placed parallel to a firewall in the network, as shown in Figure 9-5.

Figure 9-5   *VPN Device Placement: Parallel to Firewall*

There are advantages in placing the VPN device parallel to the firewall:

■   Simplified deployment because firewall addressing does not need to change

■   High scalability because multiple VPN devices can be deployed in parallel with the firewall

There are some disadvantages to placing the VPN device parallel to the firewall:

■   IPsec decrypted traffic is not firewall inspected. This issue is a major concern if the traffic is not subject to a stateful inspection.

■   No centralized point of logging or content inspection is implemented.

VPN Device on a Firewall DMZ

The VPN device can be placed in the demilitarized zone (DMZ) on the firewall in the network, as shown here in Figure 9-6.

Figure 9-6   *VPN Device on a Firewall DMZ*

There are advantages to placing the VPN device in the DMZ of a firewall:

- The firewall can statefully inspect the decrypted VPN traffic. The design supports the layered security model and enforces firewall security policies.

- The design supports moderate-to-high scalability by adding additional VPN devices. Migration to this design is relatively straightforward with the addition of a LAN interface to firewall.

There are disadvantages to placing the VPN device in the DMZ of a firewall:

- The configuration complexity increases because additional configuration on the firewall is required to support the additional interfaces. The firewall must support policy routing to differentiate VPN versus non-VPN traffic.

- The firewall may impose bandwidth restrictions on stacks of VPN devices.

Integrated VPN and Firewall

Another option is an integrated VPN and firewall device in the network, as shown in Figure 9-7.

Figure 9-7   *Integrated VPN and Firewall*

There are advantages to integrating the VPN device and the firewall:

- The firewall can statefully inspect the decrypted VPN traffic. The design supports the layered security model and enforces firewall security policies.

- The design may be easier to manage with the same or fewer devices to support.

There are disadvantages to placing the VPN device in the DMZ of a firewall:

- Scalability can be an issue because a single device must scale to meet the performance requirements of multiple features.

- The configuration complexity increases because all the configurations are applied to one device.

Using IPsec VPN Technologies

Several types of IPsec VPNs are used to permit secure, encrypted communication between network devices.

IPsec VPN Overview

IPsec functionality provides data encryption at the IP packet level, offering a robust, standards-based security solution.

Basic IPsec provides secure point-to-point tunnels between two peers, such as two routers. These tunnels are actually sets of security associations (SA) that are established between two IPsec peers. The SAs define which protocols and algorithms should be applied to sensitive packets and specify the keying material to be used by the two peers. SAs are unidirectional and are established per security protocol, either Authentication Header (AH) or Encapsulating Security Payload (ESP).

With IPsec, the network manager can define which traffic should be protected between two IPsec peers by configuring ACLs and applying these ACLs to interfaces by way of crypto maps. The ACLs used for IPsec are used only to determine which traffic should be protected by IPsec, not which traffic should be blocked or permitted through the interface. Separate ACLs define blocking and permitting at the interface.

IPsec can support certain traffic that is receiving one combination of IPsec protection (for example, authentication only) and other traffic that is receiving a different combination of IPsec protection (for example, both authentication and encryption), by using two different crypto ACLs to define the two different types of traffic. These different ACLs are then used in different crypto map entries, which specify different IPsec policies.

Standard IPsec VPNs support only unicast traffic, which is an issue for deploying them within an enterprise.

Extensions to Basic IPsec VPNs

Several site-to-site VPN solutions extend the capabilities of basic IPsec VPNs.

Cisco provides several site-to-site VPN solutions that support routing to deliver reliable transport for complex mission-critical traffic, such as voice and client/server applications. These solutions are built on five underlying VPN technologies:

- Cisco Easy VPN
- GRE tunneling
- Dynamic Multipoint VPN (DMVPN)
- Virtual tunnel interfaces (VTIs)
- Group Encrypted Transport VPN (GET VPN)

Each technology is customized to meet specific deployment requirements.

Cisco Easy VPN

The Cisco Easy VPN solution provides simple VPN deployments for remote offices and teleworkers.

Ease of deployment is critical when technical resources are not available for VPN configuration at remote offices and for teleworkers. The Cisco Easy VPN solution centralizes VPN management across all Cisco VPN devices and reduces the management complexity of VPN deployments. The Cisco Easy VPN Remote feature and the Cisco Easy VPN Server feature offer flexibility, scalability, and ease of use for site-to-site and remote-access VPNs.

The Cisco Easy VPN Remote feature allows Cisco routers running Cisco IOS Software Release 12.2(4)YA (or later releases), Cisco PIX Firewalls, and Cisco hardware clients to act as remote VPN clients. These devices can receive predefined security policies and configuration parameters from the VPN headend at the central site, which minimizes the VPN configuration required at the remote location. Parameters such as internal IP addresses, internal subnet masks, DHCP server addresses, Microsoft WINS server addresses, and split-tunneling flags are all pushed to the remote device.

The Cisco Easy VPN Server feature, available in Cisco IOS Software Release 12.2(8)T or later releases, increases compatibility of Cisco VPN products, and allows Cisco VPN concentrators, Cisco ASA/PIX Firewalls, or Cisco routers to act as VPN headend devices in site-to-site or remote-access VPNs. With this feature, security policies defined at the headend can be pushed to the remote-office devices running the Cisco Easy VPN Remote feature.

Overview of Cisco Easy VPN Server Wizard on Cisco SDM

The Cisco Router and Security Device Manager (SDM) Easy VPN Server Wizard can configure the Cisco Easy VPN Server on Cisco routers.

The Cisco Easy VPN solution is ideal for remote offices with little IT support or for large customer deployments where it is impractical to individually configure multiple remote devices. This feature makes VPN configuration as easy as entering a password, which minimizes local IT support, increases productivity, and lowers costs. Figure 9-8 shows the starting Cisco SDM screen for the Easy VPN Server Wizard that can configure the Cisco Easy VPN Server. The Easy VPN Server Wizard guides network administrators in performing the following tasks to successfully configure a Cisco Easy VPN Server on a router:

- Selecting the interface on which the client connections will terminate
- Configuring Internet Key Exchange (IKE) policies
- Configuring the Group Policy lookup method
- Configuring user authentication
- Configuring group policies on local database, if needed
- Configuring an IPsec transform set

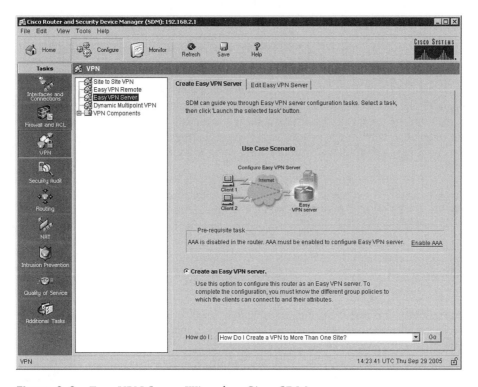

Figure 9-8 *Easy VPN Server Wizard on Cisco SDM*

Note: Cisco SDM supports VPNs with basic IPsec tunnels, GRE over IPsec tunnels, and DMVPN.

Note: The replacement for Cisco SDM is Cisco Configuration Professional (CCP). For more information about this product, refer to http://www.cisco.com/go/ciscocp.

Overview of Easy VPN Remote Wizard on Cisco SDM

The Cisco SDM Easy VPN Remote Wizard can configure the Cisco Easy VPN Remote devices. Figure 9-9 illustrates the SDM graphical configuration interface.

The Cisco SDM Easy VPN Remote Wizard can configure a remote router that will be connecting to the Cisco Easy VPN Server router. To launch the wizard in Cisco SDM, on the configuration Tasks button list on the left, click VPN. Select Easy VPN Remote in the tree hierarchy on the left. With the Create an Easy VPN Remote option selected, click the Launch the Selected Task button.

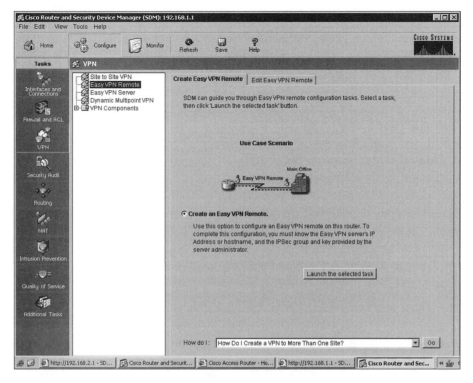

Figure 9-9   *Easy VPN Remote Wizard on Cisco SDM*

> **Note:**
> The Cisco Adaptive Security Device Manager (ASDM) can be used to configure Cisco
> Easy VPN Server or Remote operation on the Cisco ASA 5500 series Adaptive Security
> Appliances, Cisco PIX 500 series security appliances (running Cisco PIX Security Appli-
> ance Software Version 7.0 or later), and the Cisco Catalyst 6500 series Firewall Services
> Module (FWSM) Version 3.1 or later.

GRE over IPsec

Basic IPsec designs cannot transport IGP dynamic routing protocols or IP multicast traffic
because the IPsec ESP only tunnels unicast IP traffic. To support the routing or IP multicast requirements of most enterprises, IPsec should be used in conjunction with other
technologies, such as GRE.

GRE tunneling, as shown in Figure 9-10, encapsulates non-IP and IP multicast or broadcast packets into IP unicast packets. These GRE packets can be encrypted by the IPsec
tunnel. At the remote end of the IPsec tunnel, both the IPsec encapsulation and the GRE
encapsulation are removed to recover the original packet. With GRE over IPsec designs,
the hub router uses a single GRE interface for each spoke.

Figure 9-10   *Tunnels and IPsec*

GRE over IPsec Design Recommendations

A routing protocol can dynamically rebalance traffic across redundant headend routers on failover recovery. Although IPsec can typically scale to thousands of tunnels on some platforms, a routed point-to-point GRE over IPsec design is generally limited by the routing protocol being used and the number of routing peers exchanging routing information. In an aggressive design, the headend routing protocol can scale up to 500 peers:

■ Up to 500 peers for the Cisco 7200VXR series routers with Network Processing Engine-G1 (NPE-G1)

■ Up to 600 peers for the Cisco 7200VXR series with NPE-G2

■ Up to 1000 peers for the Cisco 7600 series router (or Cisco Catalyst 6500 series switches) with Supervisor Engine 720

EIGRP is recommended as the routing protocol because of its conservative use of router CPU and network bandwidth and its quick convergence times. EIGRP also provides a range of options for address summarization and default route propagation.

GRE keepalives can be used for failure detection in case of static routing on point-to-point tunnels. Beginning in Cisco IOS Software Release 12.2(8)T, the GRE keepalive feature is available for use on tunnel interfaces. This functionality allows the line protocol of the tunnel interface to track the reachability between the two tunnel endpoints. If GRE keepalives are sent and acknowledged by the remote router, the line protocol is "up." If successive GRE keepalives are not acknowledged, based on the configured interval and number of retries, the tunnel line protocol is marked "down."

Figure 9-11 shows a simple hub-and-spoke network with multiple headend devices for redundancy. Point-to-point GRE and crypto tunnels functionally coexist on the same router CPU on the headend devices. The headend supports multiple point-to-point GRE over IPsec tunnels for a prescribed number of branch-office locations. In addition to terminating the VPN tunnels at the central site, the headend can advertise branch routes using IP routing protocols such as EIGRP and Open Shortest Path First (OSPF).

To avoid asymmetric routing when routing is running over the tunnels, one of the GRE tunnels between the headend routers and each remote site must be favored. The routing metric should be consistent both upstream and downstream to prevent asymmetric routing.

There are options for configuring different paths in this design with slightly different metrics to provide preference between the tunnels:

■ Use the **delay** command under the GRE tunnel interface.

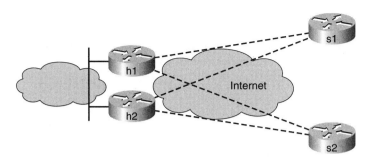

Figure 9-11   *GRE over IPsec*

■   Set the bandwidth value for the GRE interface on both ends to match the speed of
the actual link. This practice avoids unrealistic bandwidth settings that might affect
the flow control of EIGRP.

Hub-and-spoke topologies are the most common topologies in a point-to-point GRE over
IPsec design:

■   Although partial-mesh topologies are available, they are limited by both the routing
protocol and the availability of static public IP addresses for the spokes.

■   Full-mesh topologies in a point-to-point GRE over IPsec design are also available and
have the same limitations as partial-mesh topologies. With the administrative overhead involved, a full-mesh topology is not recommended in a point-to-point GRE
over IPsec design.

DMVPN

Hub-and-spoke designs do not scale well for more than 10 sites. With a traditional hub-
and-spoke topology, all spoke-to-spoke traffic is through the hub. As more nodes are
added to the topology, the configuration task becomes more complex because a separate
GRE interface is needed on the hub for every spoke and all tunnels need to be predefined.
In addition, the number of IPsec SAs grows as the number of spokes increases.

In these cases, dynamic peer discovery and on-demand tunnel creation mechanisms are
required. When there is more than 20 percent spoke-to-spoke traffic or a full-mesh VPN
topology is required, a DMVPN solution should be considered.

DMVPN Overview

DMVPN is a technology that supports IPsec VPNs with simplified configuration through
crypto profiles and dynamic discovery of tunnel endpoints.

DMVPN enables dynamic configuration and reduces the maintenance and configuration
on the hubs. DMVPN has a backbone hub-and-spoke topology, but allows direct spoke-
to-spoke functionality using tunnelling to enable the secure exchange of data between
two branch offices without traversing the head office. DMVPN is a combination of IPsec,
GRE, and Next Hop Resolution Protocol (NHRP).

DMVPN has several advantages:

- With a dynamic mesh, the number of active tunnels is much lower on each spoke than with a full-mesh design. Smaller routers can be used at the spokes.

- The configuration scales better because there is no need for static definitions for each spoke in the hub.

- It is easier to add a node to the topology because there is no need to configure the new spoke on all the other nodes.

- The spokes can have dynamic address or be behind NAT.

Note: You can use Cisco SDM to configure a router as a DMVPN hub or as a spoke router in a DMVPN network.

Example: DMVPN Topology

Figure 9-12 shows an example of a DMVPN topology. DMVPN does not alter the standards-based IPsec VPN tunnels, but it changes their configuration.

Figure 9-12   *Example: DMVPN Topology*

The hub router maintains an NHRP database of public interface addresses for each spoke. The hub uses a single multipoint GRE (mGRE) tunnel interface to support multiple IPsec tunnels.

The spokes have a permanent IPsec tunnel to the hub but not to the other spokes. The spokes register as clients of the NHRP server. The spoke learns of all private networks on the other spokes and the hub through routing updates sent by the hub. A spoke queries the NHRP database for the real address of a destination spoke when it needs to communicate to another destination. The spoke uses the real destination address to build a dynamic IPsec tunnel to the target spoke. The spoke-to-spoke tunnel is also built over an mGRE interface. After the spoke-to-spoke tunnel is built, the IP next hop for the remote spoke network is the spoke-to-spoke tunnel interface. After a programmable timeout period, the NHRP entries will age out, triggering IPsec to break down the dynamic spoke-to-spoke tunnel.

In Figure 9-12, spoke A uses the real IP address of 172.16.2.1 to bring up a tunnel to spoke B.

DMVPN Design Recommendations

Cisco recommends several practices for DMVPN with the hub-and-spoke topology:

- Use tunnel protection mode to associate a GRE tunnel with the IPsec profile on the same router. Tunnel protection specifies that IPsec encryption is performed after the GRE headers are added to the tunnel packet. Both ends of the tunnel need to be protected.

- Use IPsec in tunnel mode.

- Configure 3DES or AES for encryption of transported data.

- Use digital certificates or public key infrastructure (PKI) for scalable tunnel authentication. Typically, the CA is located on the private subnet of the hub.

- Configure EIGRP with route summarization for dynamic routing.

- Deploy hardware acceleration of IPsec to minimize router CPU overhead to support traffic with low-latency and -jitter requirements, and for the highest performance for cost.

- Use an NHRP network ID and password key to prevent unauthorized nodes from joining the VPN. Provide each mGRE tunnel interface with a unique tunnel key, NHRP network ID, and IP subnet address. The mGRE tunnel key configured on the spokes must match the hub, and it is a recommended practice that the network ID matches on both sides of the tunnel.

- Use multiple NHRP servers on multiple hubs for backup and redundancy.

Virtual Tunnel Interfaces Overview

Another mechanism for supporting VPNs is with IPsec virtual tunnel interfaces (VTI). IPsec VTIs provide a routable interface type for terminating IPsec tunnels and an easy way to define protection between sites to form an overlay network. A VTI supports native IPsec tunneling, and allows interface commands to be applied directly to the IPsec tunnels. The IPsec tunnel endpoint is associated with a virtual interface. Because there is a routable interface at the tunnel endpoint, many common interface capabilities can be applied to the IPsec tunnel.

The IPsec VTI supports QoS, multicast, and other routing functions that previously required GRE. VTIs allow for the flexibility of sending and receiving both IP unicast and multicast encrypted traffic on any physical interface, such as in the case of multiple paths. Traffic is encrypted or decrypted when it is forwarded from or to the tunnel interface and is managed by the IP routing table. Dynamic or static IP routing can be used to route the traffic to the virtual interface.

VTI simplifies VPN configuration and design. Customers can use the Cisco IOS virtual template to clone on demand new virtual access interfaces for IPsec. Using IP routing to forward the traffic to the tunnel interface simplifies the IPsec VPN configuration compared to the more complex process of using ACLs with the crypto map in native IPsec configurations. GRE or Layer 2 Tunneling Protocol (L2TP) tunnels are not needed for encapsulation. Dynamic VTIs (DVTIs) function like any other real interface, so QoS, firewall, and other security services can be applied as soon as the tunnel is active. In addition, existing management applications now can monitor separate interfaces for different sites.

The use of VTIs improves network scaling. IPsec VTIs use single SAs per site, which cover different types of traffic and enable improved scaling as compared to GRE. A major benefit associated with IPsec VTIs is that the configuration does not require a static mapping of IPsec sessions to a physical interface.

Both static VTIs (SVTI) and DVTIs are available. SVTI configurations can be used for site-to-site connectivity in which a tunnel provides always-on access between two sites. The advantage of using SVTIs as opposed to crypto map configurations is that users can enable dynamic routing protocols on the tunnel interface without the extra 4 bytes that are required for GRE headers, thus reducing the bandwidth for sending encrypted data. DVTIs can provide highly secure and scalable connectivity for remote-access VPNs. The DVTI technology replaces dynamic crypto maps and the dynamic hub-and-spoke method for establishing tunnels. DVTIs can be used for both the server and remote configuration.

Note: You can use Cisco SDM to configure Cisco Easy VPN Server and Cisco Easy VPN Remote with IPsec DVTIs.

VTIs support interoperability with standards-based IPsec installations of other vendors.

Both Cisco Easy VPN Server and Remote support DVTIs. The tunnels provide an on-demand separate virtual access interface for each Cisco Easy VPN connection. The Cisco Easy VPN with DVTI configuration provides a routable interface to selectively send traffic to different destinations, such as a Cisco Easy VPN concentrator, a different site-to-site peer, or the Internet. The IPsec DVTI configuration does not require a static mapping of IPsec sessions to a physical interface. This allows for the flexibility of sending and receiving encrypted traffic on any physical interface, such as in the case of multiple paths. Traffic is encrypted when it is forwarded from or to the tunnel interface.

Group Encrypted Transport VPN

The Cisco Group Encrypted Transport VPN (GET VPN) feature is a Cisco IOS Software solution that provides a tunnel-less technology to provide end-to-end security for voice, video, and data in a native mode for a fully meshed network. GET VPN can secure IP multicast group traffic or unicast traffic over a private WAN. It uses the ability of the core network to route and replicate the packets between various sites within the enterprise. GET VPN preserves the original source and destination addresses in the encryption header for optimal routing; hence, it is largely suited for an enterprise running a Multiprotocol Label Switching (MPLS) or IP VPN networks.

GET VPN is enabled in customer-edge routers without using tunnels. GET VPN uses Group Domain of Interpretation (GDOI) as the keying protocol with IPsec for efficiently encrypting and decrypting the data packets.

GET VPN enables the router to apply encryption to nontunneled (that is, "native") IP multicast and unicast packets and eliminates the requirement to configure tunnels to protect multicast and unicast traffic.

GET VPN is supported on Cisco IOS Software Release 12.4(11)T and on Cisco VPN acceleration modules:

- Cisco AIM-VPN/SSL module for Cisco ISRs

- Cisco VPN Acceleration Module 2+ (VAM2+) for Cisco 7200 series routers and Cisco 7301 routers

GET VPN Topology

GET VPN uses a group management model in which the GDOI protocol operates between a group member and a group controller or key server. The GET VPN architectural components are illustrated in Figure 9-13.

The key server, shown in Figure 9-13, establishes SAs among authorized group members. GDOI is protected by a Phase 1 Internet Security Association and Key Management Protocol (ISAKMP) SA.

Three traffic flows are necessary for group members to participate in a group:

- The group member registers with the key server to get the IPsec SA or SAs that are necessary to communicate with the group. The group member provides the group ID to the key server to get the respective policy and keys for this group. The key server authenticates and authorizes the group members and downloads the IPsec policy and keys that are necessary for them to encrypt and decrypt IP multicast packets. The key server is responsible for maintaining the policy and creating and maintaining the keys for the group.

- Group members exchange IP multicast packets that are encrypted using IPsec.

- Because the key server is also responsible for rekeying the group before existing keys expire, the key server pushes a rekey message to the group members. The rekey message contains new IPsec policy and keys to use when old IPsec SAs expire. Rekey

Figure 9-13   *GET VPN Topology*

messages are sent in advance of the SA expiration time to ensure that valid group keys are always available.

Managing and Scaling VPNs

The Cisco security management products and internal processes can be used for scalable VPN administration and enforcement. Scaling VPNs involves several considerations, including crypto engine performance for real traffic and routing characteristics and metrics.

Recommendations for Managing VPNs

The Cisco Security Management Suite is a framework of products and technologies designed for scalable policy administration and enforcement for the Cisco Self-Defending Network. This integrated solution can simplify and automate the tasks associated with security management operations, including configuration, monitoring, analysis, and response. Several components of this suite enable the management of VPNs:

■ **SDM:** Cisco SDM is a web-based device management tool for Cisco routers that can improve the productivity of network managers; simplify router deployments for integrated services such as dynamic routing, WAN access, wireless LANs (WLAN), firewalls, VPNs, SSL VPNs, IPSs, and QoS; and help troubleshoot complex network and VPN connectivity issues. Cisco SDM is a single device element manager that can support a wide range of Cisco IOS Software releases and is available free of charge on Cisco router models from Cisco 830 series routers to Cisco 7301 routers.

- **ASDM:** Cisco ASDM provides security management and monitoring services for the Cisco ASA 5500 series Adaptive Security Appliances, Cisco PIX 500 series security appliances (running Cisco PIX Security Appliance Software Version 7.0 or later), and the Cisco Catalyst 6500 series FWSM Version 3.1 or later through an intuitive, easy-to-use web-based management interface. Cisco ASDM is an element manager that accelerates security appliance deployment with intelligent wizards, robust administration tools, and versatile monitoring services.

Note: The replacement for Cisco SDM is Cisco Configuration Professional (CCP). For more information about this product, refer to http://www.cisco.com/go/ciscocp.

- **Cisco PIX Device Manager (PDM):** Cisco PDM security management and monitoring services for Cisco PIX security appliances (running Cisco PIX Firewall Software Version 6.3 and earlier) and the Catalyst 6500 series FWSM. PDM is an element manager that features an intuitive GUI with integrated online help and intelligent wizards to simplify setup and ongoing management. In addition, informative, real-time, and historical reports provide critical insight into usage trends, performance baselines, and security events. Administrative and device security is supported through the use of user passwords (with optional authentication via a RADIUS or TACACS server) and encrypted communications to local or remote devices.

Note: The replacement for Cisco PDM is Cisco ASDM. For more information about this product, refer to http://www.cisco.com/go/ASDM.

- **CiscoView Device Manager:** The CiscoView Device Manager for the Catalyst 6500 series switch is a device management software application that resides on a switch and manages several Layer 2 and Layer 3 features for a single chassis. A task-based tool, CiscoView Device Manager eases the initial setup and deployment of end-to-end services across modules by offering configuration templates based on recommended best practices. It further enhances the user friendliness of the Catalyst 6500 series through graphical representation of VLANs, and by providing a single launch point for multiple module managers, including the VPN service module, the SSL service module, and the WebVPN service module.

- **Cisco Security Manager:** Cisco Security Manager is a powerful but easy-to-use solution for configuring firewall, VPN, and IPS policies on multiple Cisco security appliances, firewalls, routers, and switch modules. Using a GUI, Cisco Security Manager enables you to easily configure security policies per device, per device group, or globally.

- **Cisco Security Monitoring, Analysis, and Response System (MARS):** Cisco Security MARS is an appliance-based solution that enables network and security administrators to monitor, identify, isolate, and counter security threats. Cisco Security

MARS obtains network intelligence by understanding the topology and device configurations from multiple routers, switches, NetFlow, IPS, firewalls, and other network devices and by profiling network traffic. The integrated network discovery in the system builds a topology map containing device configuration and current security policies that enables Cisco Security MARS to model packet flows through the network. Because the appliance does not operate inline and makes minimal use of existing software agents, there is minimal impact on network or system performance.

Recommendations for Managing VPNs

There are several recommended practices for managing VPNs:

- Use dedicated management interfaces if possible for out-of-band (OOB) management. If this is not possible, use a VPN for secure management and restrict access over the tunnel to management protocols only.

- Take precautions when managing a VPN device across the Internet. You should use strong authentication, integrity, and encryption practices. You should use a different username for configuration management and for troubleshooting. If you cannot use IPsec to connect to remote devices, use Secure Shell (SSH) or SSL for access.

- Use static public IP addresses at remote sites and static crypto maps at the headend to manage remote devices through a VPN tunnel. Be aware that some services such as TFTP do not always use the public IP address as the source address.

- Use the available IPsec information. IPsec information can be accessed minimally through syslog information or with the IPsec Message Information Base (MIB) via Simple Network Management Protocol (SNMP).

Considerations for Scaling VPNs

Scaling VPNs depends on many factors, but the primary issue is the offered load, in number of packets per second, from the branch routers. The rate in packets per second matters more than throughput bandwidth for the connection speeds being terminated or aggregated. In general, routers and crypto engines have upper boundaries for processing a given number of packets per second. Each time a crypto engine encrypts or decrypts a packet, it performs mathematical computations on the IP packet payload using the crypto key for the tunnel. The crypto engine performance measured in packets per second is the key for sizing the headend.

The marketing numbers for crypto performance rate performance in megabits per second, with 100 percent CPU usage, and using even maximum transmission unit (MTU)-size (approximately 1400-byte) packets to achieve the best results. This is an unrealistic traffic pattern. Internet mix (IMIX) traffic contains a mixture of frame sizes in a ratio to each other that approximates the overall makeup of frame sizes observed in real Internet traffic. Using IMIX traffic provides a better simulation of real network traffic. Converged traffic with a mix of 30 percent voice traffic at a maximum of 80 percent CPU utilization is the most realistic simulation of real network traffic for enterprise networks. Figure 9-14 compares the relative performance of three types of traffic on a router.

Figure 9-14   *Packets per Second Versus Megabits per Second*

Packets per second are a more critical metric than the number of tunnels, although the number of tunnels impacts the routing processes on the CPU. The number of tunnels also impacts crypto processing; if more than one IPsec tunnel is terminated on a router, the router has multiple crypto keys. When packets are to be sent or received to a different tunnel than the last packet sent or received, the crypto engine must swap keys. This key swapping can degrade the performance of a crypto engine, depending on its architecture, and increase the router CPU utilization.

Determining Packets per Second

The number of packets per second per connection is determined by user applications on the network. High megabit-per-second throughput in the network typically corresponds to a large byte size per packet. The presence of VoIP in network decreases the average packet size and increases the number of packets per second.

To correctly simulate network behavior, test tools must emulate real application behavior. Using packet-blasting tools for testing is a poor indicator of real-world performance.

Enterprise WAN Categories

Characterizing enterprise WANs into categories, as shown in Table 9-4, helps estimate the type of traffic to expect from the remote branches when scaling the VPN.

Table 9-4   *Enterprise WAN Categories*

	Point of Sale	Teleworker or Teleagent	Integrated Services Branch
Number of Branches	Extra Large 1000–10,000	Large 1000–3000	Medium 500–1000
VoIP Support?	No	Yes, Usually One Call	Yes, 33% Bandwidth
IP Multicast?	Generally Not	Nice to Have	Yes

Availability?	Required—Asynchronous DialBackup	Too Costly—Dial Bandwidth Insufficient for VoIP	Multiple WAN Links
Physical Interface?	Broadband or POTS	Broadband	Leased Line

Table 9-4 shows how enterprise WANs can be categorized into three groups:

- **Point-of-sale WANs:** These WANs typically support a high number of retail branches for credit card and point-of-sale applications. The number of branches here may be 2000 or more. They have low data volume and do not support VoIP or IP multicast. The WANs need availability that the routing protocol provides. The physical interface for the remote sites is typically broadband or dialup plain old telephony service (POTS).

- **Teleworker or teleagent WANs:** These WANs typically support a single user with an IP phone at the remote end. In the Cisco Enterprise Architecture, this is the "Branch of One" or "Teleworker" design. There can be large numbers of remote sites to support. Support for IP multicast is nice to have but might not be present. Backup availability is typically not provided because dial backup bandwidth is insufficient for the VoIP application. The remote sites typically connect using broadband.

- **Integrated services branch WAN:** These WANs typically connect remote enterprise branches to the central site. They also have high or bursty data volume and a relatively high number of branches, from 500 to 1000. They are likely to support converged applications, including voice, video, and IP multicast. VoIP traffic is typically 30 percent of the bandwidth. Backup availability is provided with multiple WAN links. The physical interface is typically a leased line or high-speed DSL.

Traffic Profiles per Branch Router

The major factor in headend VPN scaling is the PPS load of the hub for switching packets. Packet switching is impacted by the size of the packets. Based on field testing, the Cisco Enterprise Systems Engineering group has developed the following traffic profiles for representing real enterprise branch routers in the lab. Table 9-5 shows how the average packet size is influenced by the applications in use in the traffic profile.

- Does traffic mix include VoIP, video, or IP multicast? What VoIP codec is in use (G.711 at 4 Kb/s versus G.729 at 8 Kb/s)?

- Do the devices support changing interface MTU? Do devices use path MTU discovery? Is the router configured to adjust TCP maximum segment size (MSS)?

- What applications are in use? Is application optimization, such as HTTP pipelining, in place?

- Scaling considerations at the headend are also impacted by the number of neighbors per hub, which impacts path selection overhead.

Table 9-5 *Traffic Profiles per Branch Router*

Point of Sale	Teleworker or Teleagent	Integrated Services Branch Enterprise Mix Voice and Video-Enabled VPN
TCP, 18 HTTP Get, 300 Bytes Up, 1000 Bytes Down 2 FTP (1 Up, 1 Down, and 120K File Size)	UDP, 1 G.729 Voice Call (100 p/s), 1 DNS, 1 Post Office Protocol 3, 1 Call Setup (CS3), 1 TN3270 (Best Effort), 1 TN3270 (AF21), 1 HTTP (Best Effort), 1 HTTP (AF21), 1 FTP (1 Up 240,000 File)	UDP, 33% Bandwidth for G.729 VoIP (100 p/s per Call), 9 Calls per T1, 9 DNS, 4 POP3, 6 TN3270 (Best Effort), 6 TN3270 (AF21), 3 HTTP (Best Effort), 3 HTTP (AF21), 4 FTP (2 Up, 2 Down, 768,000 File)

Example: Enterprise Mix Packet Size

Figure 9-15 shows the average packet sizes for representative downstream and upstream traffic captured with NetFlow. The key point to notice is that the average packet size with VoIP traffic in the mix is significantly smaller than the 1400-byte packets used to describe marketing performance.

Note: Because average packet size will vary depending on the applications used, you should measure average packet size in your own environment.

Estimated PPS Based on Branch Profile

To accurately size the headend device, you need to measure the average and busy hour PPS rate of the branch routers.

The Enterprise Systems Engineering group has the following rough packets per second estimates shown in Figure 9-16 that can be starting point for VPN scaling:

■   A point-of-sale branch on a low speed link that supports only data may have only an average of 50 p/s of traffic.

Figure 9-15   *Example: Enterprise Mix Packet Size*

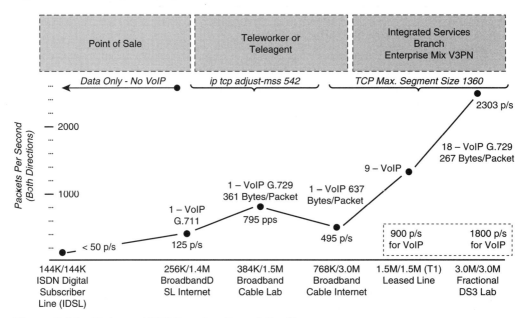

Figure 9-16   *Estimated PPS Based on Branch Profile*

- A teleworker on a higher speed link will have higher traffic requirements. The teleworker may generate 125 to 800 p/s depending on the link speed and network configuration.

- The integrated services branch may need to support multiple voice calls. If we use the general principle that 30 percent of the bandwidth is used for voice, then a T1 line could support nine voice calls of 100 or 50 p/s in both directions. The headend would need to support 900 p/s for VoIP traffic plus the data requirements of the remote site.

Determining the PPS Rate

If you are migrating an existing network, you can measure the average and busy hour PPS rate of the existing branch routers.

Measuring traffic rates at the remote branches at the busy hour will provide useful data because most network managers do not know the details of bandwidth use. Many network managers, when asked, will not have any details and may reply, "I have 500 branches and a 45-Mb/s link at the headend." Network designers need to know details of bandwidth use, not just how the network is implemented.

The measurement can be as simple as using the **show interfaces fastethernet** *number* | **include rate** command. You can also use network management tools to query SNMP or NetFlow data.

Example: Packet and Application View from NetFlow Analyzer 5

Figure 9-17 shows a view from the AdventNet ManageEngine NetFlow Analyzer 5 of the packets per hour and types of packets for a teleworker that supported a conference call, web-based data backup, and some web surfing during the day.

Figure 9-17   *Example: Packet and Application View from NetFlow Analyzer 5*

Routing Protocol Considerations for IPsec VPNs

Both EIGRP and OSPF are appropriate enterprise routing protocols that can be supported on IPsec with GRE tunnels, DMVPNs, VTIs, and GET VPNs.

The distance vector characteristics of EIGRP are typically better for the hub-and-spoke VPN topology:

■ EIGRP can summarize per interface. By summarizing to the core and to the spoke, the branch routers will have fewer routes in the routing table.

■ EIGRP is a "quiet" protocol when it is configured with stubs. There is no need to flood the topology database with EIGRP.

■ EIGRP stub eliminates queries to spokes. As a recommended practice, configure the branch routers as stubs. The stub routers receive the default route from the headend router and advertise back up the branch subnets.

There are some disadvantages to the link state characteristics of OSPF for hub-and-spoke IPsec VPNs:

■ OSPF needs to synchronize router databases periodically.

■ OSPF brings hierarchy decisions into the hub-and-spoke topology. The number of routers per area needs to be allocated. A recommended practice is to use a power of two for best summarization.

■ OSPF stubs require the use of default routes. However, the default route in OSPF typically points to the Internet, not a tunnel.

With either protocol, increasing the number of neighbors increases the amount of process switching the hub routers need to support. Buffer tuning can help maintain network stability by minimizing the number of buffer misses and failures that may equate to losing or dropping neighbors.

EIGRP Metric Component Consideration

The EIGRP metric components can impact IPsec VPNs.

EIGRP calculates delay as the cumulative network delay. It adds the delay from all the hops to the source network. EIGRP delay is based on the input interface value of the receiving router.

EIGRP uses the minimum bandwidth for all the links to a network. The default bandwidth value for a tunnel is 9000. EIGRP updates are throttled to 50 percent of bandwidth of the interface. You should consider matching tunnel bandwidth to physical link value if you send more than the default route and a summary route across a link, because the EIGRP process can be throttled by the 9000 default bandwidth value of the tunnel.

Summary

VPNs enable the secure use of cost-effective, high-speed links. VPNs also encrypt and authenticate traffic traversing the WAN to deliver true network security in an unsecure, networked world. This chapter examined the following subjects:

- Remote-access VPNs permit secure, encrypted connections between mobile or remote users and their corporate networks using IPsec and SSL technologies.

- Site-to-site VPNs are an alternative WAN infrastructure used to connect branch offices, home offices, and business partners to all or portions of an enterprise network using service provider networks.

- Several types of technologies can support IPsec VPNs, including Cisco Easy VPN, GRE over IPsec, DMVPN, VTI, and GET VPN.

- Both products and internal processes are needed for managing VPNs. Scaling VPNs involves several considerations, including crypto engine performance for real traffic and routing characteristics.

References

For additional information, refer to these resources:

- Cisco Systems, Inc. "Cisco Easy VPN," at http://www.cisco.com/warp/public/cc/so/neso/vpn/ns171/ns27/prodlit/evpnc_qa.pdf

- Cisco Systems, Inc. "IPsec VPN WAN Design Overview," at http://www.cisco.com/application/pdf/en/us/guest/netsol/ns171/c649/ccmigration_09186a008074f22f.pdf

- Cisco Systems, Inc. "Point-to-Point GRE over IPsec Design Guide," at http://www.cisco.com/application/pdf/en/us/guest/netsol/ns171/c649/ccmigration_09186a008073a0c5.pdf

- Cisco Systems, Inc. "Dynamic Multipoint VPN (DMVPN) Introduction," at http://www.cisco.com/en/US/products/ps6658/products_ios_protocol_option_home.html

- Cisco Systems, Inc. "IPsec Virtual Tunnel Interface," at http://www.cisco.com/univercd/cc/td/doc/product/software/ios124/124cg/hsec_c/part17/ch10/hipsctm.pdf

- Cisco Systems, Inc. "Virtual Tunnel Interface (VTI) Design Guide," at http://www.cisco.com/application/pdf/en/us/guest/netsol/ns171/c649/ccmigration_09186a00808255c2.pdf

- Cisco Systems, Inc. "Cisco Group Encrypted Transport VPN," at http://www.cisco.com/univercd/cc/td/doc/product/software/ios124/124newft/124t/124t11/htgetvpn.pdf

- Cisco Systems, Inc. "Cisco IPsec and SSL VPN Solutions Portfolio," at http://www.cisco.com/application/pdf/en/us/guest/products/ps7180/c1031/ccmigration_09186a00801f0a72.pdf

- AdventNet, Inc. "AdventNet ManageEngine NetFlow Analyzer User Guide," at http://manageengine.adventnet.com/products/netflow/NetFlowAnalyzer_UserGuide.pdf

Review Questions

Answer the following questions, and then refer to Appendix A, "Answers to Review Questions," for the answers.

1. What is the recommended practice for deploying the VPN termination device for best security?

    a. To terminate any IPsec tunnels on an inline firewall

    b. To place the VPN termination device in line with a firewall

    c. To place the VPN termination device parallel to a firewall

    d. To place the private side of the VPN termination device in a DMZ behind a firewall

    e. To place the public side of the VPN termination device in a DMZ behind a firewall

2. What is the most common address assignment design for remote-access VPNs?

    a. Using a dedicated scope of DHCP addresses associated with a specific VPN headend

    b. Using internal address pools per VPN headend and implementing a static route for these subnets to the VPN headend

    c. Using RRI when IPsec tunnels are terminated on an inline firewall

    d. Using static IP address assignment for end users with LDAP and RRI

    e. Using static IP address assignment for end users with RADIUS and RRI

3. Of the following, which are site-to-site VPN applications? (Choose two.)

    a. WAN replacement

    b. Content rewriting

    c. Port forwarding

    d. Data privacy through 3DES or AES

    e. Mandated or regulatory encryption

4. What is the typical IPsec deployment design?

    a. Basic IPsec tunnels transporting IP unicast and multicast traffic

    b. Full-mesh topology with direct connectivity between all locations

    c. Partial-mesh topology with direct connectivity between many locations

    d. Remote peers connected over a shared infrastructure in a spoke to-spoke topology

    e. Remote peers connected to the central site over a shared infrastructure in a hub-and-spoke topology

5. What are two characteristics of the Cisco Easy VPN solution?

    a. Use of the GDOI protocol

    b. Mesh design scalability for greater than 10 sites

    c. Reduced management complexity for VPN deployments

    d. Use of Cisco Easy VPN Remote and Easy VPN services features

    e. Centralized VPN management across all Cisco VPN devices

6. Of the following, which are advantages of implementing DMVPN tunnels? (Choose two.)

    a. IP broadcast and multicast traffic support

    b. Deterministic mesh availability with fewer active tunnels on each spoke

    c. Dynamic mesh availability with fewer active tunnels on each spoke

    d. Hub-and-spoke tunnel creation dynamically based on traffic requirements

    e. Spoke-to-spoke tunnel creation dynamically based on traffic requirements

7. Of the following, which are characteristics of GET VPN? (Choose two.)

    a. It is a set of software features that provides a tunnel-less technology for end-to-end security.

    b. It provides a routable interface type for terminating IPsec tunnels.

    c. It secures IP multicast group traffic or unicast traffic over a private WAN.

    d. It supports interoperability with standards-based IPsec installations of other vendors.

    e. It uses a NHRP network ID and password key to prevent unauthorized nodes from joining the VPN.

8. What are three recommendations for managing VPNs?

    a. Use in-band management if possible.

    b. Use dedicated management interfaces if possible.

    c. Use the same username for configuration management and for troubleshooting.

    d. Use a different username for configuration management and for troubleshooting.

    e. Use IPsec rather than SSH or SSL for access to VPN devices across the Internet.

    f. Use SSH or SSL rather than IPsec for access to VPN devices across the Internet.

9. What is the primary issue in scaling VPNs?

   a.   Crypto engine performance for large packets

   b.   Megabits-per-second capacity of a headend router

   c.   Number of routes in network

   d.   Number of tunnels terminated at a headend router

   e.   Packets-per-second capacity from remote routers

10. Which routing protocol is recommended for large-scale enterprise IPsec VPNs?

   a.   BGP

   b.   EIGRP

   c.   OSPF

   d.   RIPv2

   e.   Static routing

After completing this chapter you will be able to do the following:

- Provide an overview of IP multicast technology

- Describe design recommendations for IP multicast

- Discuss security considerations for IP multicast

CHAPTER 10

IP Multicast Design

> **Note:** Some of the information in this introduction and the first main section of this chapter is derived from the *Authorized Self-Study Guide: Building Scalable Cisco Internetworks (BSCI)*, Third Edition, by Diane Teare and Catherine Paquet, Cisco Press, 2006 (ISBN 1-58705-223-7), which provides a detailed introduction to IP multicast and its associated protocols. Some questions related to this material in the "Review Questions" section at the end of this chapter are also derived from those in this BSCI book.

Many types of data can be transferred between devices over an IP network, including document files, voice, and video. However, a traditional IP network is not efficient when sending the same data to many locations; the data is sent in unicast packets and is therefore replicated on the network for each destination. For example, if a CEO's annual video address is sent out on a company's network for all employees to watch, the same data stream must be replicated for each employee. Obviously, this would consume many resources, including precious WAN bandwidth.

> **Note:** In this chapter, the term IP refers to IP version 4 (IPv4).

IP multicast technology enables data to be sent over networks to a group of destinations in the most efficient way. The data is sent from the *source* as one stream; this single data stream travels as far as it can in the network. Devices replicate the data only if they need to send it out on multiple interfaces to reach all members of the destination group, called the *receivers*.

Multicast groups are identified by Class D IP addresses, which are in the range from 224.0.0.0 to 239.255.255.255. IP multicast involves some new protocols for network devices, including two for informing network devices which hosts require which multicast data stream—Internet Group Management Protocol (IGMP) and Cisco Group Management Protocol (CGMP)—and one for determining the best way to route multicast traffic—Protocol Independent Multicast (PIM).

This chapter first introduces IP multicast technologies, and then explores IP multicast design recommendations. The chapter concludes with a discussion of security considerations for networks with IP multicast traffic.

IP Multicast Technologies

This section provides an introduction to IP multicast, and the IGMP, CGMP, and PIM protocols.

Introduction to Multicast

This section compares multicast with unicast and introduces the concept of a multicast group. The types of applications that benefit from the use of multicasting are discussed, multicast adoption trends are reviewed, and how an application or user learns about available multicast sessions is described. The advantages and disadvantages of multicast are described, and the basics of IP and Layer 2 multicast addresses and multicast address assignment are introduced. The section concludes with an introduction to the Cisco multicast architecture.

Multicast Versus Unicast

When IP multicast is used to send data packets to multiple receivers, the packets are not duplicated for every receiver, but instead are sent in a single stream. Downstream routers replicate the packets only on links where receiving hosts exist. The sender, or source, of multicast traffic does not have to know the unicast addresses of the receivers.

In contrast, unicast transmission sends multiple copies of data packets, one copy for each receiver, addressed to the receiver's unicast address.

The unicast example at the top of Figure 10-1 shows a host transmitting three copies of a data packet, and a network forwarding each packet to three separate receivers. The host sends to only one receiver at a time; it has to create a packet with a different destination address for each receiver.

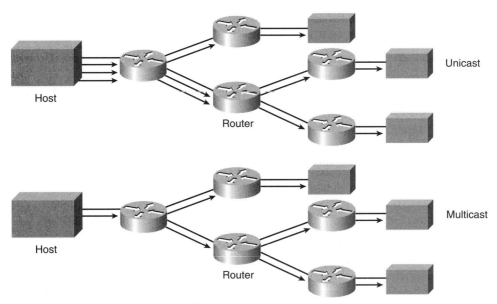

Figure 10-1   *Unicast Versus Multicast*

Unicast transmission requires a large amount of bandwidth. With unicast, the same information has to be sent multiple times, even on shared links. A large number of clients can impact the scalability of the network. If unicast is used as the means for transmitting the same data to multiple recipients, network managers must take the number of user connections and the amount of replicated unicast transmissions into consideration. If the number of user connections or the amount of data to be sent becomes large, the network, or at least parts of it, might get overloaded.

The multicast example in the lower part of Figure 10-1 shows a host transmitting one copy of a data packet and a network replicating the packet at the last possible router for each receiver.

Note that there is only a single copy of each multicast packet on any given network segment. A host sends to multiple receivers simultaneously by sending only one packet, with one multicast destination address, the multicast group address. Downstream multicast routers replicate and forward the data packet to segments where there may be receivers.

IP Multicast Group Membership

With unicast IP addresses, a packet is routed from a source address to a destination address, traversing the IP network on a hop-by-hop basis.

IP multicast relies on the concept of a group address. In IP multicast, the destination address of a packet does not represent to a single destination, but instead represents a group of devices. When a receiver joins a multicast group, packets addressed to the group address flow to that receiver. All members of the group receive the packet.

The source address for multicast packets is always a unicast source address; multicast addresses are not used as source addresses.

A device must be a member of a group to receive the group's traffic. However, any multicast source device can transmit at any time to any group, without joining that group. When a device sends multicast data to the group, all members of the group receive the data.

Figure 10-2 illustrates that packets that are sent to group addresses go to all group members, but are not delivered to nongroup members. As shown in the figure, however, nongroup members can send packets to a group.

Multicast Applications and Multicast Adoption Trends

IP multicast is used when simultaneous delivery for a group of receivers is required; hence, it is also called a *simulcast*.

There are various types of multicast applications. Two of the most common models are one to many and many to many.

In one-to-many applications, one sender sends data to many (two or more) receivers. This type of application may be used for audio or video distribution, push-media, announcements, monitoring, and so on. If a one-to-many application needs feedback from receivers, it may become a many-to-many application.

Figure 10-2 *IP Multicast Groups Define Who Receives Multicast Data*

In many-to-many applications, any number of hosts send to the same multicast group. Two or more receivers also act as senders and a host can be a sender and a receiver simultaneously. Receiving data from several sources increases the complexity of applications and creates different management challenges. Using a many-to-many multicast concept as a foundation, a whole new range of applications may be built (for example, collaboration, concurrent processing, and distributed interactive simulations).

Other models (for example, many to one or few to many) are also used, especially in financial applications. The many-to-one multicast model is when many receivers are sending data back to one sender (via unicast or multicast) and may be used for resource discovery, data collection, auctions, polling, and similar applications.

Many new multicast applications are emerging as demand for them grows. Real-time applications include live TV, radio, and corporate broadcasts; financial data delivery; whiteboard collaboration; e-learning; and videoconferencing.

Non-real-time applications include file transfer, data and file replication, and video on demand (VoD). Ghosting multiple PC images simultaneously is a common file transfer application. Some forms of e-learning are also non-real time.

Initially, multicast was adopted primarily by the research community. The first major enterprise deployments were in the financial services communities. E-learning (also called distance learning) and corporate communications were in the next wave of multicast applications. Content provisioning, multicast virtual private networks (VPN), IP Version 6 (IPv6) multicasting, and security surveillance are some of the more recent multicast applications.

Learning About Multicast Sessions

Whenever a multicast application is started on a receiver, the application has to learn about the available sessions or streams, which typically map to one or more IP multicast groups. The application may then request to join the appropriate multicast groups.

There are several possibilities for applications to learn about the sessions, including the following:

■ The application may join a well-known, predefined group to which another multicast application sends announcements about available sessions.

■ Some type of directory services may be available, and the application may contact the appropriate directory server.

■ The application may be launched from a web page on which the sessions are listed as URLs.

■ An email may be sent announcing the session; the user clicks the link in the email to join the session.

Another option is the use of the application called Session Directory (sd), which acts like a TV guide for displaying multicast content. A client application runs on a user's PC and lets the user know what content is available. This directory application uses either the Session Description Protocol (SDP) or the Session Announcement Protocol (SAP) to learn about the content. (Note that both the Session Directory application and the Session Description Protocol are sometimes called SDR or sdr, and that in Cisco documentation SDP/SAP is referred to as sdr.)

Advantages of Multicast

Multicast transmission provides many advantages over unicast transmission in a one-to-many or many-to-many environment, including the following:

■ **Enhanced efficiency:** Available network bandwidth is used more efficiently because multiple streams of data are replaced with a single transmission. Server and CPU loads are also reduced. Multicast packets do not impose as high a rate of bandwidth utilization as unicast packets, so there is a greater possibility that they will arrive almost simultaneously at the receivers.

■ **Optimized performance:** Multicast eliminates traffic redundancy because fewer copies of the data require forwarding and processing. The sender also needs much less processing power and bandwidth for the equivalent amount of multicast traffic.

■ **Support for distributed applications:** As demand and usage grows, distributed multipoint applications will not be possible with unicast transmission, because it does not scale well (traffic levels and the number of clients increase at a 1:1 rate with unicast transmission). Multicast enables a whole range of new applications that were not possible with unicast, including for example, VoD.

Disadvantages of Multicast

Most multicast applications are User Datagram Protocol (UDP)-based. This foundation results in some undesirable consequences when compared to similar unicast, TCP-based applications.

TCP supports only unicast transmissions. TCP is a connection-oriented protocol that requires a three-way handshake to establish communications. TCP enforces end-to-end reliability of packet delivery with sequence numbers and acknowledgments. TCP also supports flow control.

In contrast, UDP can support both unicast and multicast transmissions. UDP is a connectionless protocol that does not use a handshake to establish communication. UDP has no reliability mechanisms, so reliability issues have to be addressed in multicast applications if reliable data transfer is necessary.

Some of the disadvantages of multicast that need to be considered include the following:

■ UDP's best-effort delivery results in occasional packet drops. Therefore, multicast applications must not expect reliable delivery of data and should be designed accordingly; in other words, the multicast application itself must be reliable (at the application layer).

Many multicast applications that operate in real time (for example, video and audio) may be affected by these losses; requesting retransmission of the lost data at the application layer in these real-time applications is not feasible. For example, high packet-drop rates in voice applications may result in jerky, missed speech patterns that can make the content unintelligible. Moderate to heavy drops in video are sometimes tolerated by the human eye and appear as unusual "artifacts" in the picture. However, some compression algorithms may be severely affected by even low drop rates, which might cause the picture to become jerky or to freeze for several seconds while the decompression algorithm recovers.

■ UDP's lack of congestion control (due to not having a windowing or slow-start mechanism like TCP has) may result in network congestion and overall network degradation as the popularity of UDP-based multicast applications grow. If possible, multicast applications should attempt to detect and avoid congestion conditions.

■ Duplicate packets may occasionally be generated when multicast network topologies change. Multicast applications should be designed to expect occasional duplicate packets to arrive and must handle them accordingly.

■ Out-of-sequence delivery of packets to the application may also result during network topology changes or other network events that affect the flow of multicast traffic. Multicast applications must be designed to handle these packets appropriately.

■ Multicast security is still evolving. For example, the issue of how to restrict multicast traffic to only a selected group of receivers to avoid eavesdropping has not yet been sufficiently resolved.

Some commercial applications (for example, financial data delivery) will become possible only when these reliability and security issues are fully resolved.

Multicast IP Addresses

Multicast IP addresses use the Class D address space, which is indicated by the high-order 4 bits set to binary 1110. Therefore, the Class D multicast address range is 224.0.0.0 through 239.255.255.255.

The Internet Assigned Numbers Authority (IANA) assigns ranges and specific multicast addresses; a current list of assignments is available at http://www.iana.org/assignments/multicast-addresses.

Local scope addresses are addresses in the range 224.0.0.0 through 224.0.0.255 and are reserved by the IANA for network protocol use. This range of addresses is also known as the *local network control block*. Packets with multicast addresses in this range are never forwarded off the local network regardless of the Time to Live (TTL) field in the IP packet header; the TTL is usually set to 1. Examples of local scope IP multicast addresses include the following:

- **224.0.0.1:** All hosts

- **224.0.0.2:** All multicast routers

- **224.0.0.4:** All Distance Vector Multicast Routing Protocol (DVMRP) routers

- **224.0.0.5:** All Open Shortest Path First (OSPF) routers

- **224.0.0.6:** All OSPF Designated Routers (DRs)

- **224.0.0.9:** All Routing Information Protocol Version 2 (RIPv2) routers

- **224.0.0.10:** All Enhanced Interior Gateway Protocol (EIGRP) routers

Globally scoped addresses are in the range 224.0.1.0 through 238.255.255.255. Some of these addresses have been reserved through the IANA for use by multicast applications, including the range 224.0.1.0 to 224.0.1.255, and 232.0.0.0/8 and 233.0.0.0/8. The rest of the addresses in this range are transient addresses which are dynamically assigned and then returned for others to use when they are no longer needed.

Limited, or administratively, scoped addresses are in the range 239.0.0.0 through 239.255.255.255. As defined by RFC 2365, *Administratively Scoped IP Multicast*, these addresses are reserved for use inside private domains. Enterprises usually define multicast boundaries at the borders of their network so that traffic in the administratively scoped range can neither enter nor leave the enterprise network. The administratively scoped multicast address space includes the following scopes, per the IANA:

- Site-local scope (239.255.0.0/16; 239.252.0.0/16, 239.253.0.0/16, and 239.254.0.0/16 are also reserved for this purpose)

- Organization local scope (239.192.0.0 to 239.251.255.255)

The IANA has further refined these ranges, as detailed in the IANA multicast address assignment list referenced earlier.

Note: "The Guidelines for Enterprise IP Multicast Address Allocation" white paper, at http://www.cisco.com/en/US/prod/collateral/iosswrel/ps6537/ps6552/ps6592/ prod_white_paper0900aecd80310d68.pdf, provides more details.

Layer 2 Multicast Addresses

Normally, devices on a LAN segment will receive only frames destined for their own MAC address or the broadcast MAC address. For multicast to work, some means had to be devised so that multiple hosts could receive the same frame and still be capable of differentiating among multicast groups. The IEEE LAN specifications have provisions for the transmission of broadcast and multicast frames. In the IEEE 802.3 standard, bit 0 of the first octet is used to indicate a broadcast and/or multicast frame, as illustrated in Figure 10-3.

This bit indicates that the frame is destined for an arbitrary group of hosts (multicast) or all hosts on the network (broadcast); in the case of broadcast, the broadcast address is 0xFFFF.FFFF.FFFF. IP multicast makes use of this bit to transmit IP packets to a group of hostson a LAN segment.

The IANA owns a block of Ethernet MAC addresses that start with hexadecimal 01:00:5E. The lower half of this block is allocated for multicast addresses, resulting in the range of available MAC addresses of 0100.5E00.0000 through 0100.5E7F.FFFF.

The translation between IP multicast and Layer 2 multicast MAC addresses is achieved by the mapping of the low-order 23 bits of the IP (Layer 3) multicast address into the low-order 23 bits of the MAC (Layer 2) address, as shown in Figure 10-4.

Figure 10-3   *IEEE 802.3 MAC Address Format*

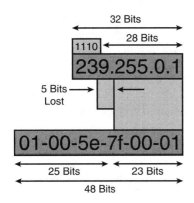

Figure 10-4   *IP Multicast to Ethernet MAC Address Mapping*

Because there are 28 bits of unique address space for an IP multicast addresses (32 minus the first 4 bits containing the 1110 Class D prefix) and there are only 23 bits mapped into the IEEE MAC address, there are five (28 − 23 = 5) bits of overlap. These 5 bits represent 2^5 = 32 addresses. Therefore, there is a 32:1 overlap of IP addresses to MAC addresses, so 32 IP multicast addresses map to the same MAC multicast address.

For example, all the IP multicast addresses in Table 10-1 map to the same Layer 2 multicast MAC address 01-00-5E-0A-00-01.

Table 10-1   *Many IP Multicast Addresses Match One MAC Address*

224.10.0.1	225.10.0.1	226.10.0.1	227.10.0.1	228.10.0.1
229.10.0.1	230.10.0.1	231.10.0.1	232.10.0.1	233.10.0.1
234.10.0.1	235.10.0.1	236.10.0.1	237.10.0.1	238.10.0.1
239.10.0.1	224.138.0.1	225.138.0.1	226.138.0.1	227.138.0.1
228.138.0.1	229.138.0.1	230.138.0.1	231.138.0.1	232.138.0.1
233.138.0.1	234.138.0.1	235.138.0.1	236.138.0.1	237.138.0.1
238.138.0.1	239.138.0.1			

Note: Organizations should avoid using IP multicast addresses that map to the 224.0.0.x or 224.0.1.x MAC addresses of 0x0100.5E00.00.xx or 0x0100.5E00.01.xx because these addresses will be flooded by the switch hardware.

Multicast Address Assignment

Layer 3 IP multicast addresses are typically assigned statically.

Aggregation and summarization of multicast group addresses are meaningless because any multicast source can send to any group address and any multicast client can receive data for any group without regard to geography. Administratively scoped, or private, address space can and should be used within the enterprise unless multicast traffic will be sourced to the Internet, requiring a unique group address. Multicast addresses can be allocated globally or locally, as follows:

■ **Enterprise internal group address assignment:** Static address allocation methods are typically used by enterprise network administrators to allocate specific addresses or address ranges from the administratively scoped address range, 239.0.0.0/8. The Multicast Address Dynamic Client Allocation Protocol (MADCAP) allows a client workstation to "lease" a multicast address from a MADCAP server in a manner similar to how a workstation can "lease" an IP address from a Dynamic Host Configuration Protocol (DHCP) server.

- **Global group address assignment:** Static multicast addresses can be assigned by
  the IANA on a permanent basis so that they are valid everywhere and in all networks.
  This technique permits applications and hardware devices to have these addresses
  hard-coded into their software or microcode. In the late 1990s, when native multicast
  was beginning to be deployed on the Internet, several content providers planned to
  begin multicasting some of their audio and video content. An experimental form of
  static address allocation was proposed by the Internet Engineering Task Force (IETF).
  This allocation methodology, called GLOP addressing, which is defined in RFC 3180,
  GLOP Addressing in 233/8, uses the multicast group range of 233.0.0.0/8.

  This block was assigned by the IANA and is an experimental, statically assigned
  range of multicast addresses intended for use by content providers, ISPs, or anyone
  wanting to source content into the global Internet. GLOP addresses have the high-order octet set to 233 (decimal). The next two octets contain the 16-bit Abstract Syntax
  Notation (ASN) of the content provider or ISP that is sourcing the multicast traffic.
  The remaining octet is used for group assignment.

Note: "GLOP" is not an acronym and does not stand for anything.

Cisco Multicast Architecture

Figure 10-5 illustrates the Cisco multicast architecture and the protocols used to support
multicast in the enterprise, in both campus multicast solutions and interdomain multicast
solutions.

For the campus, these protocols include the following:

- IGMP for host-to-router communication
- IGMP snooping on switches (or CGMP between Cisco routers and switches) for
  Layer 2 optimization
- PIM sparse mode (SM) (PIM-SM) or bidirectional PIM (bidir-PIM) for routers

For interdomain multicast, these protocols include the following:

- Multiprotocol Border Gateway Protocol (MBGP) for multicast routing across domains
- Multicast Source Discovery Protocol (MSDP) with PIM-SM for multicast source
  discovery
- PIM Source Specific Multicast (SSM) for multicast from specific sources
- Multicast Virtual Private Network (MVPN) for secure connectivity

Note: MBGP, MPVN, and MDSP are not discussed further in this book. The other protocols are discussed in the remainder of this chapter.

Figure 10-5 *Cisco Multicast Architecture*

Note: The "DR" notation in Figure 10-5 indicates designated routers, which are elected by the PIM routers and are used to avoid duplicating multicast traffic for connected hosts. The PIM router with the highest IP address on a LAN becomes the DR for that LAN.

IGMP and CGMP

This section first introduces IGMP, which has evolved through three versions (1, 2, and 3). Multicasting in Layer 2 switches is also discussed in this section; without control, Ethernet switches flood multicast packets in the same way that unknown unicast frames are flooded. IGMP snooping and CGMP are used to solve this problem and are also described in this section.

IGMP is used between hosts and their local router. Hosts use IGMP to register with the router to join (and leave) specific multicast groups; the router is then aware that it needs to forward the data stream destined to a specific multicast group to the registered hosts.

IGMP Version 1 (IGMPv1)

With IGMPv1, specified in RFC 1112, *Host Extensions for IP Multicasting*, multicast routers periodically send membership *queries* (usually every 60 to 120 seconds) to the all-hosts multicast address 224.0.0.1.

Hosts wanting to receive specific multicast group traffic send membership *reports* to the multicast address of the group they want to join. Hosts either send reports when they want to first join a group or in response to membership queries. On each subnet, only one member per group responds to a query, to save bandwidth on the subnet and minimize processing by hosts. This process is called *report suppression*.

There must be at least one active member of a multicast group on a local segment if multicast traffic is to be forwarded to that segment.

IGMPv1 does not have a mechanism defined for hosts to leave a multicast group. IGMPv1 hosts therefore leave a group silently, at any time, without any notification to the router. This is not a problem if there are multiple members on a segment, because the multicast traffic must still be delivered to the segment. However, when the last member on a segment leaves the multicast group, there will be a period when the router continues to forward the multicast traffic onto the segment needlessly. The IGMPv1 router will time out the group after several query intervals without a response. This process is inefficient, especially if there are many groups or there is a lot of traffic in the groups.

IGMP Version 2 (IGMPv2)

Because of some of the limitations discovered in IGMPv1, work was begun on IGMPv2 in an attempt to remove these restrictions. IGMPv2 is specified in RFC 2236, *Internet Group Management Protocol, Version 2*. Most of the changes between IGMPv1 and IGMPv2 deal with the issues of leave and join latencies and ambiguities in the original protocol specification. IGMPv2 is backward compatible with IGMPv1.

The following are some important changes in IGMPv2:

- Group-specific queries

- Leave Group message

- Querier election mechanism

- Query-interval response time

A group-specific query enables a router to query membership in a single group instead of in all groups, providing an optimized way to quickly find out whether any members are left in a group without asking all groups for a report. The difference between the group-specific query and the membership query is that a membership query is multicast to the all-hosts (224.0.0.1) address, whereas a group-specific query for group "G" is multicast to the group "G" multicast address.

A Leave Group message enables hosts to tell the router that they are leaving the group. This information reduces the leave latency for the group on the segment when the member who is leaving is the last member of the group. The specification includes the timing of when Leave Group messages must be sent. After receiving a Leave Group message, the router sends a group-specific query to see whether any other group members are present.

When there are two IGMP routers on the same segment (the same broadcast domain), the router with the lowest IP address is the designated querier.

The query-interval response time is used to control the "burstiness" of reports, and is specified in a query. It indicates to the members how much time they have to respond to a query by issuing a report.

IGMP Version 3 (IGMPv3)

IGMPv3 is a proposed standard, documented in RFC 3376, *Internet Group Management Protocol, Version 3*, that adds the ability to filter multicasts based on the multicast source so that hosts can indicate that they want to receive traffic only from particular sources within a multicast group. This enhancement makes the utilization of routing resources more efficient; routers need only forward traffic from specific sources from which receivers have requested traffic.

For example, as illustrated in Figure 10-6, a joining member sends an IGMPv3 report to 224.0.0.22 immediately upon joining. This report might specify a source list, which is used for source filtering. A source list is a list of multicast sources that the host will accept packets from or a list of multicast sources that the host will not accept packets from. Using a source list, a multicast router can, for example, avoid delivering multicast packets from specific sources to networks where there are no interested receivers.

Figure 10-6   *IGMPv3: Joining a Group*

Note: In IGMPv3, reports are sent to 224.0.0.22; the corresponding address used in earlier IGMP versions is 224.0.0.2. Note that in the IANA multicast addresses document referenced earlier, 224.0.0.22 is called the "IGMP" address.

Multicast with Layer 2 Switches

In a typical network, hosts are not directly connected to routers but are connected to a Layer 2 switch, which is in turn connected to a router.

IGMP is a network layer—Layer 3—protocol. Therefore, Layer 2 switches do not participate in IGMP and are not aware of which hosts attached to them might be part of a particular multicast group. By default, Layer 2 switches flood multicast frames to all ports within a virtual LAN (VLAN) (except the port from which the frame originated), which means that all multicast traffic received by a switch would be sent out on all ports within a VLAN, even if only one device on one port required the data stream.

One method Cisco Catalyst switches use to circumvent this is by allowing the administrator to configure the switch to manually associate a multicast MAC address with various ports. For example, the administrator may configure ports 5, 6, and 7 so that only those ports receive the multicast traffic destined for a specific multicast group. This method works but is not scalable because IP multicast hosts dynamically join and leave groups, using IGMP to signal to the multicast router.

To improve the behavior of the switches when they receive multicast frames, many multicast switching solutions have been developed, including IGMP snooping and CGMP.

Note: The "Multicast Catalyst Switches Support Matrix" document, available at http://www.cisco.com/en/US/tech/tk828/technologies_tech_note09186a0080122a70.shtml, includes a list of which switches support CGMP and which switches support IGMP snooping.

IGMP Snooping

With IGMP snooping, the switch eavesdrops on the IGMP messages sent between routers and hosts, and updates its MAC address table accordingly.

IGMP snooping constrains IP multicast traffic at Layer 2 by configuring the Layer 2 LAN ports dynamically to forward IP multicast traffic only to those ports that want to receive it.

As its name implies, a switch must be IGMP aware to listen in on the IGMP conversations between hosts and routers. The switch's processor must examine, or "snoop," network layer information to identify and intercept all IGMP packets flowing between routers and hosts and vice versa, including IGMP membership reports and IGMP Leave Group messages.

When the switch sees an IGMP report from a host for a particular multicast group, the switch adds the port number on which the host is attached to the associated multicast table entry. After this port association is made, any multicast traffic received by the switch destined for the particular multicast group is forwarded *only* to the ports associated with that group in the multicast table. Similarly, when the switch sees an IGMP leave group message from a host, the switch removes the associated multicast table entry. IGMP snooping is used on subnets that include end users (receiver clients) and allows a Layer 2 switch to more efficiently handle IP multicast.

A switch may have to intercept all Layer 2 multicast packets to identify IGMP packets. This processing can have a significant impact on switch performance. Therefore, switches must effectively become Layer 3 aware to maintain forwarding throughput when performing IGMP snooping. Current Cisco switches support IP multicast data packet forwarding using special hardware (Layer 3 application specific integrated circuits [ASIC]) that can distinguish IGMP information packets from other multicast packets. In addition, the Cisco Catalyst 6500 series switches and Cisco Catalyst 4500 series switches support multicast packet replication in hardware, which more efficiently copies multicast packets to the network interfaces where the multicast path flows diverge.

CGMP

CGMP is a Cisco Systems proprietary protocol that runs between a multicast router and a switch. The routers inform each of their directly connected switches of IGMP registrations that were received from hosts through the switch (in other words, from hosts accessible through the switch). The switch then forwards the multicast traffic only to ports that those requesting hosts are on rather than flooding the data to all ports.

CGMP is based on a client/server model, where the router may be considered a CGMP server, and the switch a CGMP client.

When the router sees an IGMP control message, it creates a CGMP packet that contains the request type (join or leave), the Layer 2 multicast MAC address, and the actual MAC address of the client.

This packet is sent to the well-known CGMP multicast MAC address 0x0100.0cdd.dddd to which all CGMP switches listen. The switch interprets the CGMP control message and creates the proper entries in its MAC address table (also called its forwarding table or *content-addressable memory* [CAM] table) to constrain the forwarding of multicast traffic for this group to only the appropriate ports.

Figure 10-7 illustrates the interaction of the IGMP and CGMP protocols. Hosts A and D register, using IGMP to the router, to join the multicast group to receive data from the server. The router informs both switches of these registrations, using CGMP. When the router forwards the multicast data to the hosts via the switches, the switches ensure that the data only goes out of the ports on which hosts A and D are connected. The ports on which hosts B and C are connected do not receive the multicast data.

PIM Routing Protocol

PIM is used by routers that are forwarding multicast packets. The "protocol-independent" part of the name indicates that PIM is independent of the unicast routing protocol (for example, EIGRP or OSPF) running in the network.

PIM uses the normal routing table, populated by the unicast routing protocol, in its multicast routing calculations. Unlike other routing protocols, no routing updates are sent between PIM routers.

EIGRP, OSPF, and so forth are called *unicast routing protocols* because they are used for creating and maintaining unicast routing information in the routing table. Recall, however, that unicast routing protocols use multicast packets (or broadcast packets in some protocols) to send their routing update traffic.

Note: A variant of OSPF, called multicast OSPF, supports multicast routing. Cisco routers do not support multicast OSPF.

This section explores the operation of PIM.

PIM Terminology

When a router is forwarding a unicast packet, it looks up the destination address in its routing table and forwards the packet out of the appropriate interface. However, when forwarding a multicast packet, the router might have to forward the packet out of multiple interfaces, toward all the receiving hosts.

Figure 10-7 *IGMP and CGMP Inform Network Devices About Which Hosts Want Which Multicast Data*

Multicast routing is connection oriented: Multicast traffic does not flow to the destinations until connection messages are sent toward the source to set up the flow paths for the traffic.

Multicast-enabled routers use PIM to dynamically create *distribution trees* that control the path that IP multicast traffic takes through the network to deliver traffic to all receivers. Building multicast distribution trees via connection messages is a dynamic process; when network topology changes occur, the distribution trees are rebuilt around failed links.

Distribution Trees

There are two types of distribution trees: source trees and shared trees.

A *source tree* is created for each source sending to each multicast group. The source tree has its root at the source and has branches through the network to the receivers. Source trees are also called source-routed or shortest path trees (SPT) because the tree takes a direct path—the shortest path—from source to its receivers.

A *shared tree* is a single tree that is shared between *all* sources for each multicast group. The shared tree has a single common root, called a *rendezvous point* (RP). Sources initially send their multicast packets to the RP, which in turn forwards data through a shared tree to the members of the group.

Distribution trees are further explored in the later "Multicast Distribution Trees" section.

Multicast Distribution Tree Creation

Multicast-capable routers create distribution trees that control the path that IP multicast traffic takes through the network to deliver traffic to all receivers.

Figure 10-8 illustrates an example of the creation of a multicast distribution tree, based on the source address. A host sends a request to join the multicast group 224.1.1.1 and to get the multicast data from the source 10.1.1.1. Router E selects interface E0 as the best path to the source, using its unicast routing table. Interface E0 is added to the multicast routing entry for group 224.1.1.1. The join request is forwarded to Router B. Router B selects the best path to the source, using its unicast routing table. Router B adds the interface on which it received the join request as the outgoing interface in its multicast routing table and the interface it selected as the best path to the source as the incoming interface in its multicast routing table. Router B forwards the join request to Router A. The join request is forwarded to the source and the multicast tree is built, with a forwarding state from the source to the receiver. Multicast data flows from the source down the multicast distribution tree to the receiver.

Reverse Path Forwarding

Multicast routers consider the source address and the destination address of the multicast packet, and use the distribution tree to forward the packet away from the source toward the destination.

Forwarding multicast traffic away from the source, rather than to the receiver, is called *reverse path forwarding* (RPF); this is just the opposite of unicast routing. For multicast, the source IP address denotes the known source, and the destination IP address denotes a group of unknown receivers.

To avoid routing loops, RPF uses the unicast routing table to determine the upstream (toward the source) and downstream (away from the source) neighbors and ensures that only one interface on the router, to the upstream neighbor, is considered to be an incoming interface for data from a specific source. For example, data received on one router interface and forwarded out another interface might loop around the network and come back into the same router on a different interface; RPF ensures that this data is not forwarded again.

A router will forward a multicast packet only if it is received on the upstream interface; this interface is also called the *RPF interface*.

When a multicast packet arrives at a router, the router performs the following RPF check on the packet:

■   The router looks up the source address in the unicast routing table to determine whether the packet has arrived on the interface that is on the reverse path back to the source.

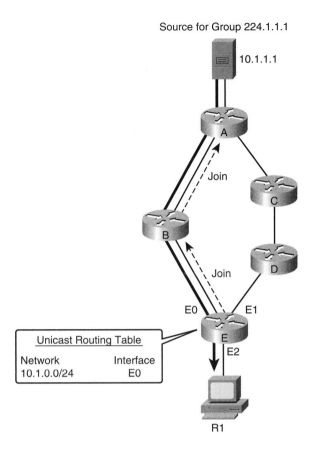

Figure 10-8 *Multicast Distribution Trees Are Created by Routers*

■   If the packet has arrived on the interface leading back to the source, the RPF check
    succeeds and the packet is forwarded.

■   If the RPF check fails, the packet is dropped.

Multicast Distribution Trees

This section further describes multicast source and shared trees.

Source Distribution Trees

Figure 10-9 illustrates a source tree between Source 1, 192.168.1.1, and Receiver 1 and Receiver 2, in group 224.1.1.1. The path between the source and receivers over Routers A, C,
and E is the path with the lowest cost. In this figure Source 1, 192.168.1.1, is forwarding to
the receivers.

Packets are forwarded according to the source and group address pair along the tree. For this reason, the forwarding state associated with the source tree is referred to by the notation (S,G) (pronounced "S comma G"), where S is the IP address of the source, and G is the multicast group address. The state for the source tree in Figure 10-9 is (192.168.1.1,224.1.1.1).

Figure 10-10 shows the same network as in Figure 10-9, but with Source 2, 192.168.2.1, active and sending multicast packets to Receiver 1 and Receiver 2. A separate source tree is built for this purpose, this time with Source 2 at the root of the tree. The state for this source tree is (192.168.2.1,224.1.1.1).

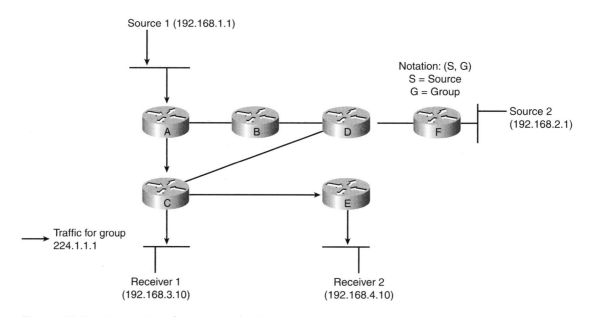

Figure 10-9 *Source Distribution Tree for Source 1*

Therefore, with source trees, a separate tree is built for every source S sending to group G.

Source trees have the advantage of creating the optimal path between the source and the receivers. This advantage guarantees the minimum amount of network latency for forwarding multicast traffic. However, this optimization comes at a cost: The routers must maintain path information for each source. In a network that has thousands of sources and thousands of groups, this overhead can quickly become a resource issue on the routers. Memory consumption due to the size of the multicast routing table is a factor that network designers must take into consideration. The multicast routing table is required to maintain current values, called state, that determine multicast routing behavior.

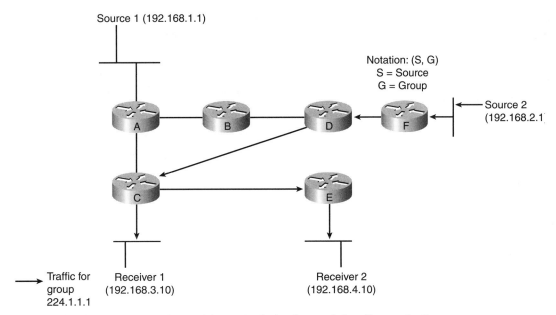

Notation: (S, G)
S = Source
G = Group

Figure 10-10 *A Separate Source Tree Is Built for Source 2 Sending to the Group*

Shared Distribution Trees

Figure 10-11 shows a shared distribution tree for group 224.2.2.2. Router D is the root of this shared tree, the RP. The tree is built from Router D to Routers C and E toward Receiver 1 and Receiver 2.

Packets are forwarded down the shared distribution tree to the receivers. The default forwarding state for the shared tree is identified by the notation (*,G) (pronounced "star comma G"), where * is a wildcard entry, meaning any source, and G is the multicast group address. The state for the shared tree in Figure 10-11 is (*,224.2.2.2).

Figure 10-12 illustrates the operation of the network in Figure 10-11. Source 1 and Source 2 are sending multicast packets toward the RP via source trees; from the RP, the multicast packets are flowing via a shared distribution tree toward Receiver 1 and Receiver 2. The shared tree is unidirectional. If a receiver is located between the source and the RP, that receiver will be serviced directly.

Shared trees have the advantage of requiring the minimum amount of state in each router. The disadvantage of shared trees is that under certain circumstances the paths between the source and receivers might not be the optimal paths, which might introduce some latency in packet delivery. For example, in Figure 10-12, the shortest path between Source 1 and Receiver 1 would be through Router A and Router C. Because Router D is being used as the root for the shared tree, the traffic must traverse Routers A, B, D, and then C.

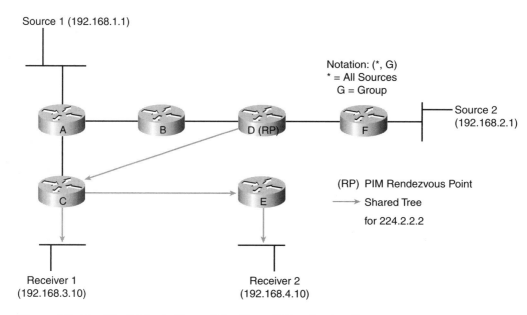

Figure 10-11 *The RP Is the Root of the Shared Distribution Tree*

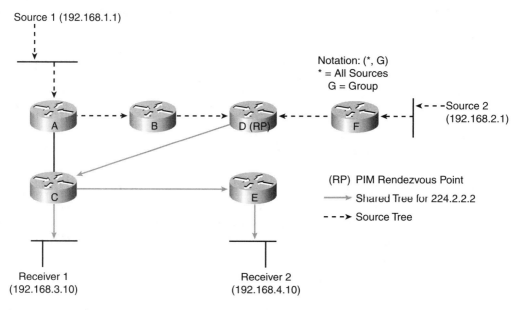

Figure 10-12 *Sources Send Toward the RP and the RP Sends to the Receivers*

Multicast Distribution Tree Notation

To summarize, the multicast forwarding entries that appear in multicast forwarding tables are read in the following way:

- **(S,G):** For the source S sending to the group G; traffic is forwarded via the shortest path from the source. These entries typically reflect a source tree, but may also appear on a shared tree.

- **(*,G):** For any source (*) sending to the group G; traffic is forwarded via an RP for this group. These entries reflect a shared tree, but are also created in Cisco routers for any existing (S,G) entry.

(S,G) source tree state entries use more router memory because there is an entry for each source and group pair. The traffic is sent over the optimal path to each receiver, therefore minimizing the delay in packet delivery.

Shared distribution tree state entries (*,G) consume less router CPU and memory, but may result in suboptimal paths from a source to receivers, thus introducing extra delay in packet delivery.

Deploying PIM and RPs

Multicast deployments require three elements: the application, the network infrastructure, and client devices. This section discusses how PIM is used in the network infrastructure and considerations for deploying RPs in multicast networks using shared trees.

PIM Deployment Models

The three main PIM deployment models used to support multicast services and applications are as follows:

- **Any Source Multicast (ASM):** ASM uses a combination of the shared and source trees and RPs. ASM is also known as PIM-SM and is described in RFC 4601, *Protocol Independent Multicast - Sparse Mode (PIM-SM): Protocol Specification (Revised)*. The majority of deployed multicast networks use this model.

- **Bidir-PIM:** Bidir-PIM exclusively uses shared trees and is recommended to support many-to-many host applications. Bidir-PIM drastically reduces the total (S,G) state information that is needed in the network.

- **SSM:** SSM exclusively uses source trees and is recommended to support one-to-many applications. SSM greatly simplifies the network and eliminates the need for RP engineering.

These deployment models are described further in the following sections.

ASM or PIM-SM

ASM, or PIM-SM, uses a "pull" model to send multicast traffic. PIM-SM forwards multicast traffic only to network segments with active receivers that have explicitly requested the data. PIM-SM distributes information about active sources by forwarding data packets on shared trees. Because PIM-SM uses shared trees at least initially, it requires the use of an RP. The RP must be administratively configured in the network.

PIM-SM Shared Tree Join

In PIM-SM, sources register with the RP. Routers along the path from active receivers that have explicitly requested to join a specific multicast group register to join that group. These routers calculate, using the unicast routing table, whether they have a better metric to the RP or to the source itself. They forward the join message to the device with which they have the better metric. Data is forwarded down the shared tree to the receivers that have joined the group. The edge routers learn about a particular source when they receive data packets on the shared tree from that source through the RP. When a receiver requests to join a group, the edge router sends PIM (S,G) join messages toward that source.

Figure 10-13 illustrates an example. In this network, an active receiver (attached to the leaf Router E at the bottom of the figure) wants to join multicast group G.

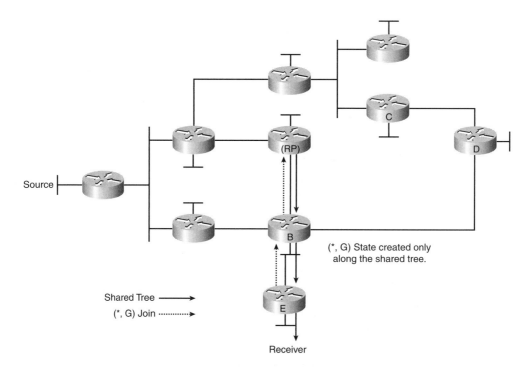

Figure 10-13   *PIM-SM Shared Tree Join*

The last-hop router (Router E in this figure) knows the IP address of the RP router for group G, and it sends a (*,G) join for this group toward the RP. This (*,G) join travels hop by hop toward the RP, building a branch of the shared tree that extends from the RP to the last-hop router (Router E) directly connected to the receiver. At this point, group G traffic can flow down the shared tree to the receiver.

PIM-SM Sender Registration

In PIM-SM, multicast sources register with the predefined RP using a sender registration.

The steps in the PM-SM sender registration process include the following, as illustrated in Figure 10-14:

Step 1.   An active source for group G sends a packet to its first-hop router, Router B.

Step 2.   The first-hop router, Router B, is responsible for registering the source with the RP (Router A) and requesting the RP to build a tree back to that router. During the sender registration process, the source router encapsulates the multicast data from the source in a special PIM-SM message called the Register message and unicasts that data to the RP.

Step 3.   When the RP receives the Register message, it de-encapsulates the multicast data packet inside of the Register message and forwards it down the shared tree to receivers in group G.

Step 4.   The RP also sends an (S,G) join message back toward the source S to create a branch of an (S,G) source tree. This results in an (S,G) state being created in all the routers along the source tree, including in the RP (Router A) and the router connected to the source (Router B).

Step 5.   The source tree is built from the source router (Router B) to the RP (Router A).

Figure 10-14 *PIM-SM Sender Registration Process*

Step 6.   Multicast traffic then begins to flow from source S to the RP.

Step 7.   When the RP begins receiving multicast data on the source tree from source S, the RP sends a Register-Stop message to the source's first-hop router (Router B) to inform it that it can stop sending the unicast Register messages.

PIM-SM SPT Switchover

PIM-SM includes the capability, known as SPT switchover, for last-hop routers (that is, routers with directly connected active receiver group members) to switch to an SPT (a source tree) and bypass the RP if the traffic rate is above a set threshold, called the SPT threshold. SPT switchover allows PIM-SM to more efficiently support multicast traffic.

The SPT threshold can be configured on Cisco routers using the **ip pim spt-threshold** {*kbps* | **infinity**} [**group-list** *access-list*] global configuration command; the default value of the SPT threshold is zero kilobits per second (kbps). With this default setting, the switch from shared to source tree happens upon the arrival of the first data packet at the last-hop router. This means that the default behavior for PIM-SM last-hop, or leaf, routers attached to active receivers is to immediately join the source tree to the source when the first packet arrives via the (*,G) shared tree.

If the **infinity** keyword is used in the command, all sources for the specified group use the shared tree, never switching to the source tree.

Figure 10-15 provides an example. The last-hop router sends an (S,G) join message toward the source to join the SPT, therefore bypassing the RP. The (S,G) join message travels hop by hop to the first-hop router (the router connected directly to the source), thereby creating another branch of the SPT. This also creates an (S,G) state in all the routers along this branch of the SPT.

Bidirectional PIM

Bidir-PIM is an enhancement of the PIM protocol that was designed for efficient many-to-many communications within an individual PIM domain. Bidir-PIM is defined in RFC 5015, *Bidirectional Protocol Independent Multicast (BIDIR-PIM)*.

The shared trees created by PIM-SM are unidirectional. Source data cannot flow *up* the shared tree to the RP. Instead, a source tree must be created to bring the data stream to the RP (the root of the shared tree) so that the data can be forwarded *down* the branches of the shared tree to the receivers.

Several multicast applications use a many-to-many model where each host is both a receiver and a sender. In a PIM-SM deployment, routers that support such hosts would need to have a source tree *to* the RP for each host, and a common shared tree *from* the RP for each group. In a PIM-SM domain supporting a large number of many-to-many hosts, (*,G) and (S,G) entries appear everywhere along the path between the hosts and the associated RP, resulting in increased memory and protocol overhead. This large number of sources can create a huge (S,G) state problem.

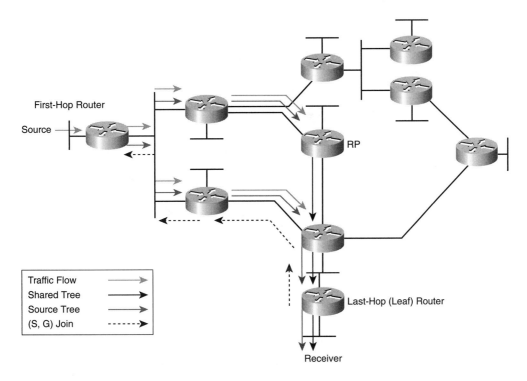

Figure 10-15 *PIM-SM Source Tree Switchover*

Bidir-PIM allows packets to be forwarded from a source to the RP using only the shared tree state. In bidirectional mode, traffic is routed through a bidirectional shared tree that is rooted at the RP for the group. Therefore, only (*,G) entries appear in multicast forwarding tables; there are no (S,G) entries and no source trees. With bidir-PIM, the path taken by packets flowing from a host (whether it is a source or receiver) to the RP and back from the RP to the host is the same.

In bidirectional mode, multicast groups can scale to include an arbitrarily large number of sources, with only a minimal amount of additional overhead.

Figure 10-16 shows a bidirectional shared tree. Data from the source flows up the shared tree (*,G) toward the RP and then down the shared tree to the receivers. There is no registration process, and no source tree (S,G) is created.

Bidir-PIM uses a designated forwarder (DF) on each link. The DF ensures that bidirectional sources can reach the RP and decides which packets need to be forwarded upstream toward the RP. Figure 10-16 shows an example where the source, Host A, is also a receiver. Traffic originating from Host A travels against the usual direction of the shared tree, breaking the rule that shared trees only accept traffic on their RPF interface. In bidir-PIM the same shared tree is used to distribute traffic both from the RP to the receivers and from the sources to the RP.

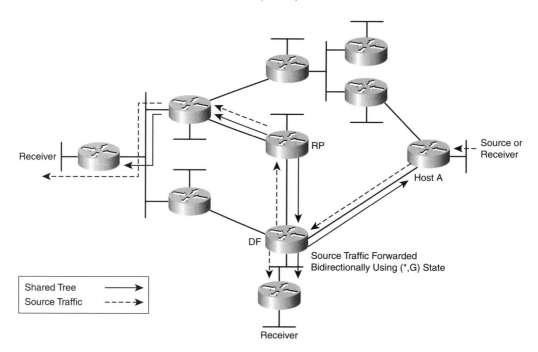

Figure 10-16   *Bidir-PIM Is Efficient for Many-to-Many Communication*

The algorithm to elect the DF is straightforward. All the PIM neighbors in a subnet advertise their unicast route to the RP, and the router with the best route is elected as the DF. This process selects the shortest path between every subnet and the RP without creating any (S,G) entries.

The RP in bidir-PIM only serves the function of getting sources and receivers to learn about each other. All routers establish a loop-free spanning-tree topology rooted in the IP address of the RP. This IP address need not be a router address but can be any unassigned IP address on a network that is reachable throughout the PIM domain. Traffic from the source is forwarded hop by hop toward the RP by the DF mechanism, and join messages from the receivers are sent to the RP.

Source Specific Multicast

SSM is an extension of the PIM protocol that allows for an efficient data delivery mechanism in one-to-many communications.

In traditional multicast implementations, source devices running multicast applications join an IP multicast group, and traffic is distributed to the entire IP multicast group. If two applications with different sources and receivers use the same IP multicast group address, receivers of both applications receive traffic from both sources, which can include unwanted network traffic.

SSM enables a receiver, after it has learned about a specific multicast source through a directory service, to receive content directly from that specific source, instead of receiving it using a shared RP. Receivers are responsible for source and group discovery and receivers select which traffic they want from a group.

SSM only uses source trees; there are no shared trees and therefore an RP is not required.

The prerequisite for SSM deployment is a mechanism that allows hosts not only to report the group they want to join but also the specific source in the group. As discussed in the earlier "IGMP Version 3 (IGMPv3)" section, this mechanism is built in to the emerging IGMPv3 standard. In an SSM-enhanced multicast network, a receiver sends a request to join a specific multicast source in a multicast group to its last-hop router (the router closest to the receiver). The receiver identifies the specific source in the group by using the IGMPv3 include mode. The last-hop router sends the request directly to the specific source rather than to a common RP, as is done in PIM-SM. The first hop router (the router closest to the source) starts forwarding the multicast traffic down the source tree to the receiver as soon as the source tree is built. This happens when the first (S,G) join request is received.

The IANA has reserved the global address range 232.0.0.0/8 for SSM applications and protocols. This assigned address range simplifies the address allocation for content and service providers. These providers can use the same group address range to deliver differing content from each source. Each (S,G) flow is unique. Routers running in SSM mode route data streams based on the full (S,G) address. Assuming that a source has a unique IP address on the Internet, any (S,G) from this source also would be unique.

The ability for SSM to explicitly include and exclude particular sources also provides limited security. Traffic from a source to a group that is not explicitly listed on the include list will not be forwarded to uninterested receivers. Only explicitly requested flows are forwarded to receivers.

Note: RFC 3569, *An Overview of Source-Specific Multicast (SSM)*, provides an outline of SSM.

SSM Join Process

Figure 10-17 illustrates an example of the SSM join process, as follows:

Step 1. A receiver determines the source address and group address for multicast data it wishes to receive, such as from a web server.

Step 2. The receiver sends a source-specific IGMPv3 join request to its closest router, the last-hop router (Router E in this example).

Step 3. The last-hop router sends a PIM (S,G) join request to the first-hop router, the router closest to the source (Router A in this example).

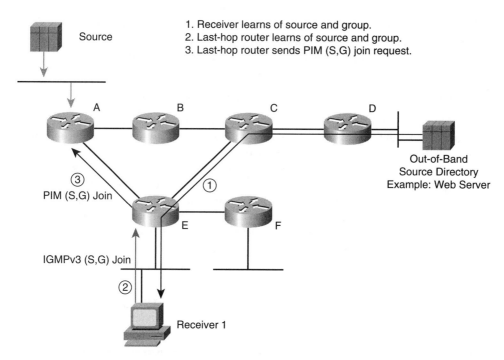

Figure 10-17   *SSM Join Process*

SSM Source Tree Creation

Figure 10-18 continues this example with the first-hop router, Router A, building the source tree to the last-hop router, Router E. The first-hop router starts forwarding the multicast traffic down the source tree to the receiver.

SSM is easy to install and provision in a network because it does not require the network to maintain which active sources are sending to which multicast groups. SSM is a recommended practice for Internet broadcast-style (one-to-many) applications.

RP Considerations

An RP is required only in networks with a shared tree. Therefore, an RP is required in networks running PIM-SM and bidir-PIM, not in networks running SSM.

This section discusses considerations for deploying RPs, including the following:

- Static RP addressing

- Anycast RP

- Auto-RP

- Bootstrap router (BSR)

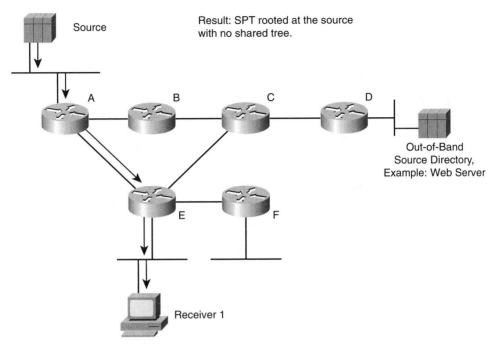

Figure 10-18   *SSM Source Path Tree Creation*

Static RP Addressing

With static RP, every router in the network is manually configured with the IP address of a single RP. However, if this RP fails, the routers cannot fail over to a standby RP.

The only case in which a static RP can fail over is if anycast RPs are used and MSDP is running between each RP in the network, as described in the next section.

Anycast RP

Anycast is an IPv6 term that refers to an address that is shared by devices performing the same function. In IPv6, a packet addressed to an anycast address is sent to the *closest* device with that anycast address, as determined by the routing table; therefore, anycast provides load-sharing capabilities.

Anycast RP is a technique for configuring a PIM-SM network to provide fault tolerance and load sharing within a single multicast domain.

IPv4 has no defined anycast addresses. However, anycast RP allows two or more RPs to share the load for source registration and to act as a hot backup for each other. To perform the anycast RP function within IPv4, a unicast host address (with a /32 mask) is assigned as an anycast address, as illustrated in the example in Figure 10-19. This address is configured on a loopback interface on *all* of the RPs, and is therefore added to the unicast routing table on the RPs. Notice in Figure 10-19 that the address 10.1.1.1/32 is assigned to *both* routers A and B.

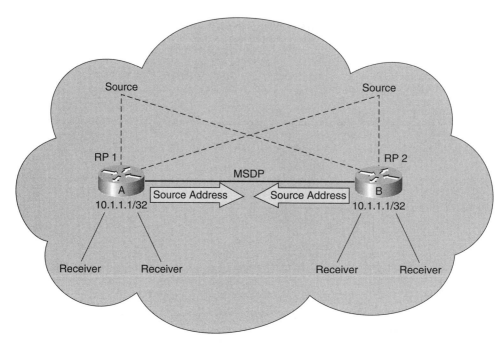

Figure 10-19   *With Anycast RP the RPs Load Share and Act as a Hot Backup for Each Other*

All the downstream routers are configured to use this anycast address as the IP address of their local RP. IP routing automatically selects the topologically closest physical RP for each source and receiver to use. Because some sources and receivers might end up using different RPs, there needs to be some way for the RPs to exchange information about active sources. This is done with MDSP. MSDP announces the source addresses of the sources sending to a group. All RPs are configured to be MSDP peers of each other so that each RP knows about the active sources in the other RPs. If any of the RPs fail, IP routing converges, and one of the remaining RPs becomes the active RP in the area of the failed RP.

Note: The RPs are used only to set up the initial connection between sources and receivers in PIM SM. After the last-hop routers join the source tree (assuming PIM-SM SPT switchover is enabled), the RP is no longer necessary.

Auto-RP

The Auto-RP protocol is a dynamic way for every router in the network to learn the RP information.

The IANA has assigned two group addresses, 224.0.1.39 and 224.0.1.40, for Auto-RP. With Auto-RP, one or more routers are designated as RP mapping agents, which receive the RP announcement messages from candidate RPs (C-RPs) and arbitrate conflicts. The network administrator configures one or more routers in the network to be the C-RPs. The C-RPs announce their willingness to serve as an RP for a particular group range by periodically multicasting Auto-RP Announce messages to the Cisco announce multicast group, 224.0.1.39, as illustrated in Figure 10-20.

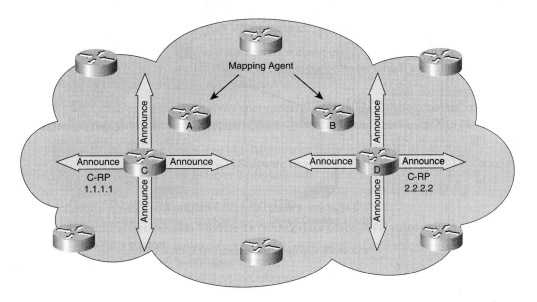

Figure 10-20   *Auto-RP Announcements Go to 224.0.1.39*

A *mapping agent* is a router that joins the Cisco RP announce group, 224.0.1.39. A mapping agent listens to all RP candidate announcements and builds a table with the information it learns. If several routers announce themselves as C-RPs for a multicast group range, the mapping agent chooses the C-RP with the highest IP address to be the RP.

The RP mapping agent sends the consistent multicast group-to-RP mappings to all other routers in an RP discovery message addressed to 224.0.1.40, in dense mode. Mapping agents send this information, as illustrated in Figure 10-21, by default every 60 seconds.

Note: PIM dense mode (DM) (PIM-DM) uses a "push" model that floods multicast traffic to the entire network. Dense mode uses source trees. In PIM-DM, routers that have no need for the data (because they are not connected to receivers that want the data or to other routers that want it) request that the tree is pruned so that they no longer receive the data.

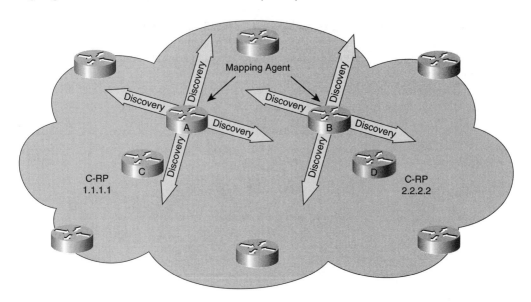

Figure 10-21 *Auto-RP Discovery Messages Go to 224.0.1.40*

All PIM-enabled routers automatically join the Cisco RP discovery group, 224.0.1.40, allowing them to receive all group-to-RP mapping information. When the network routers receive an RP discovery message, they store the information about the elected RP in their group-to-RP mapping cache, so that they know which RP to use for each group range.

Note: A C-RP and a mapping agent can be on the same router.

DM Fallback and DM Flooding

DM fallback is a condition in which the PIM mode goes from sparse mode (which requires an RP) to dense mode (which uses source trees and therefore does not use an RP). PIM-DM starts by flooding the multicast traffic, and then stops flooding on each link where it receives a Prune message. In older Cisco IOS Software releases, PIM-DM would reflood all the multicast traffic every three minutes. DM fallback occurs when RP information is lost. By default, PIM-DM fallback is enabled on Cisco routers, and a multicast group that loses its RP information will fall back to dense mode, regardless of the interface configuration.

Using earlier Cisco IOS Software versions with Auto-RP requires that all interfaces be configured in sparse-dense mode using the **ip pim sparse-dense-mode** interface configuration command. An interface configured in sparse-dense mode works in either sparse mode or dense mode of operation, depending on the mode in which the multicast group operates. If a multicast group has a known RP, the interface works in sparse mode. If a multicast group has no known RP, the interface works in dense mode and data is flooded over the interface.

Note: To configure the address of a PIM RP, use the **ip pim rp-address** [vrf *vrf-name*] **rp-address** *rp-address* [*access-list*] [**override**] [**bidir**] global configuration command. The **override** keyword permits the statically defined RP address to take precedence over Auto-RP learned group-to-RP mapping information.

Two new Cisco IOS Software configuration commands are available to prevent DM flooding and DM fallback: the **ip pim autorp listener** command and the **no ip pim dm-fallback** command.

The **ip pim autorp listener** global configuration command causes IP multicast traffic for the two Auto-RP groups, 224.0.1.39 and 224.0.1.40, to be flooded, using PIM-DM, across interfaces operating in PIM-SM. This command allows Auto-RP to operate in PIM-DM, and multicast traffic to operate in PIM-SM, bidir-PIM, or SSM mode. This command is available starting with Cisco IOS Software Releases 12.3(4)T, 12.2(28)S, and 12.2(33)SRA.

If the **ip pim autorp listener** command is not supported on the devices in your network, Cisco recommends configuring a *sink RP* for all possible multicast groups in the network, because it is possible for an unknown or unexpected source to become active. A sink RP is also known as an *RP of last* resort and is a statically configured RP that may or may not actually exist in the network, so that there is always an RP defined. If no RP is configured to limit source registration, the group reverts to dense mode operation and is flooded with data.

Configuring a sink RP does not interfere with Auto-RP operation because by default Auto-RP messages supersede static RP configurations.

The **no ip pim dm-fallback** global configuration command disables DM fallback and blocks all multicast traffic for groups not specifically configured. This command is available starting with Cisco IOS Software Releases 12.3(4)T, 12.2(28)S, and 12.2(33)SRA. When IP multicast is used in mission-critical networks, PIM-DM should be avoided. If Auto-RP is configured or a BSR (described in the next section) is used to distribute RP information, a risk exists that RP information may be lost if all RPs, Auto-RP, or the BSR for a group fails because of network congestion. This failure can lead to the network either partially or fully falling back into PIM-DM. If a network falls back into PIM-DM, DM flooding will occur. Routers that lose RP information will switch all existing states into DM, and any new states that must be created for the failed group will be created in DM.

Boot Strap Router

BSR is another dynamic RP selection protocol that also supports interoperability between vendors.

BSR performs similarly to Auto-RP in that it uses candidate routers for the RP function and for relaying the RP information for a group. The network administrator configures one or more routers in the network to serve as candidate BSRs (C-BSRs).

At network startup, all C-BSRs participate in the BSR election process by sending a PIM BSR message, containing its BSR priority, out all interfaces, as illustrated in Figure 10-22.

This information is distributed through link-local multicast messages that travel from PIM router to PIM router. These BSR messages are flooded hop by hop throughout the entire network. At the end of the BSR election interval, the BSR with the highest BSR priority is elected as the active BSR.

Figure 10-22   *To Elect an Active BSR, C-BSRs Send BSR Messages on All Interfaces*

Note: The BSR election process is similar in nature to the root-bridge election mechanism in the Spanning Tree Protocol (STP).

All routers in the network, including C-RPs, know which C-BSR has been elected as the currently active BSR. The C-RPs unicast their C-RP Announcement messages directly to the active BSR, as illustrated in Figure 10-23. The active BSR stores all incoming C-RP announcements in its group-to-RP mapping cache. The active BSR sends the entire list of C-RPs from its mapping cache in periodic BSR messages that are flooded hop by hop throughout the entire network, as also shown in Figure 10-23. As each router receives a copy of these BSR messages, it updates the information in its local group-to-RP mapping cache so that it knows the IP address of all C-RPs in the network.

Unlike Auto-RP where the mapping agent elects the active RP for a group range and announces the election results to the network, the BSR does not elect the active RP for a group. This task is left to each individual router in the network. Each router in the network elects the currently active RP for a particular group range using a well-known hashing algorithm. Because each router is running the same algorithm against the same list of C-RPs, they all elect the same RP for a particular group range.

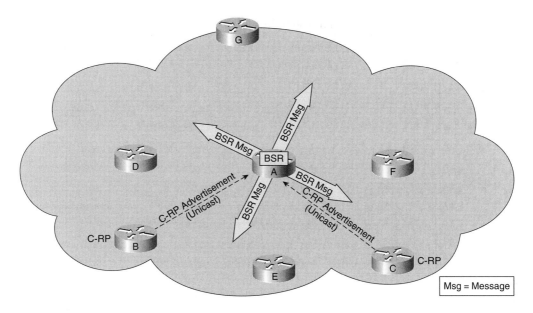

Figure 10-23   *The Active BSR Sends the Entire List of C-RPs in Periodic BSR Messages*

Securing IP Multicast

Multicast deployments have added security considerations compared to unicast routing environments. Some of the factors that distinguish multicast routing are the state information, replication process, join process, and unidirectional flows. Both multicast security considerations and access control mechanisms for multicast networks are discussed in this section.

Security Considerations for IP Multicast

This section introduces security considerations for IP multicast environments.

Security Goals for Multicast Environments

The main goal for security of multicast networks is to keep the network running even if there are configuration errors, malfunctions, or network attacks such as a denial-of-service (DoS) attack from an unknown server. Multicast security involves managing network resources and access control for multiple senders (sources) and receivers by defining what multicast traffic should be allowed in the network. Multicast security must also protect against rogue servers or RPs that should not be in the network. Network resource utilization must be managed; this includes managing multicast state information in the network and services participating in multicast activity.

You can use a wide range of tools and technologies to manage multicast security.

Control and enforcement of multicast networks includes answering the following four questions:

- **Why?** Network administrators want to control which users and servers have access to network resources, to support an organization's policies or protect access to resources and resource availability with permissions and controls.

- **How?** Control in multicast environments can include managing state creation and providing packet-level control by policing, filtering, and encryption techniques.

- **What?** Network administrators want to protect the content of the multicast service, protect the control plane of the network devices from being overloaded, and protect the data plane of the network from overloading the links between the devices.

- **Where?** Controls can be enforced in multiple locations, but most are configured locally on a router or switch. These controls may implicitly protect the service across the network. There are also protocols that can be coordinated to provide protection on a hop-by-hop basis and mechanisms that rely on policy servers to provide authentication, authorization, and accounting (AAA).

The following sections examine unicast and multicast state and replication requirements, attack traffic in unicast and multicast networks, and the use of scoped addresses.

Unicast and Multicast State Requirements

Unicast and multicast routing have different state requirements. For unicast routing, the state of the network resides in the unicast routing table. The state is relatively stable, only changing when the network topology changes. The router CPU is active after network topology changes, but end-user activity does not impact the state or the activity on the router other than the traffic through the links. The main network design constraint is the link bandwidth requirements.

For multicast routing, the state includes the unicast routing state plus the multicast state. The multicast state information increases when sources and receivers participate in multicast applications. The router CPU is active when application state changes occur and when network topology changes occur. PIM and IGMP create more periodic CPU activity than unicast protocols create. A multicast network design must take into consideration the number of multicast applications and sources to provide a robust network.

Throughput concerns are also different in unicast and multicast routing. Unicast routing is concerned with the amount of traffic received, called the *ingress* packet rate.

Multicast routing is also concerned with the amount of traffic sent, called the *egress* packet rate, and the ability to replicate outgoing packets.

Even low-input packet rates can potentially overload the capacity of the router to support the egress load because of the requirements for packet replication. Egress throughput impacts both routers and Layer 3 switches supporting IGMP snooping.

As shown in Figure 10-24, with IP multicast there is state information associated with ingress lookups per application or source. The memory requirements of the ingress state information increases with the number of applications or sources. As also shown in Figure 10-24, the egress state information is concerned with the replication of packets to multiple interfaces for supporting receiver branches in the distribution tree. The egress state information increases with the number of applications across the number of receiver branches on outgoing interfaces.

Hardware acceleration provides the optimal multicast performance, but limits apply to the amount of hardware state information permitted, based on the available chip sets on specific platforms. However, there are also limits in memory on software platforms, restricting the amount of state information permitted. These software limits are higher than the hardware limits.

Figure 10-24   *Multicast State Information Increases with the Number of Sources and Receivers*

Unicast and Multicast Replication Requirements

Multicast replication impacts where access control should be applied, as illustrated in the example in Figure 10-25.

Source X

Unicast   ------
Multicast -- -- --

R1

R2

S1

A   B

C

Figure 10-25   *Multicast Replication Impacts Where Access Control Should Be Applied*

In this example, the network engineer wants to ensure that receiver A does not receive traffic from source X. For unicast traffic, a filter can be put anywhere along the path, based on the source and receiver addresses. However, this model does not work for multicast because the receiver address is a group address.

For multicast traffic, filtering for receivers must always be placed after the last replication point to other potential receivers. In Figure 10-25, the filtering must occur on switch S1 egress, to avoid impacting receiver B. Similarly, filtering sources must happen before the first potential replication point, so that source information will be blocked throughout the network.

Attack Traffic in Unicast and Multicast Networks

This section examines how attack traffic is forwarded in unicast and multicast networks.

Attack Traffic from Rogue Sources to Receivers

First consider attack traffic from rogue sources to hosts (receivers). In unicast routing, any device can send a packet to another device. There is no implicit protection of receivers from sources. Firewalls and access control lists (ACL) can be used to protect against unwanted traffic.

In multicast routing, source devices do not send traffic to specific devices but to a multicast group. A receiver in a branch of the network needs to explicitly join a multicast group before traffic is forwarded to that branch. Therefore, multicast implicitly protects receivers against packets from unknown sources or potential attackers.

With SSM, unknown source attacks are not possible because receivers must join a specific source host in a specific multicast group. Traffic from unknown sources will only reach the first-hop router (the router closest to the source) and then be discarded; this traffic will not even create state information in the first-hop router.

With ASM (PIM-SM) and bidir-PIM, an end device will only receive traffic when it joins a group. Therefore, an attacker cannot attack a specific receiver host but can only attack against a multicast group or the entire network.

Attack Traffic from Sources to Networks Without Receivers

Another type of network attack targets network devices, using attack traffic from rogue sources to networks without receivers.

Multicast DoS attacks are often referred to as control plane attacks or state attacks. The aim of the attacker is usually to increase the multicast state information in routers above a manageable level so that the device experiences extremely slow convergence or it crashes. Multicast DoS can also be the result of misbehaving applications.

SSM networks will drop traffic from unknown sources at the first-hop router closest to the source, so will not be affected by these types of attacks. However, multicast DoS attacks can impact ASM and bidir-PIM multicast implementations.

For ASM (PIM-SM) networks, attacks from rogue sources increase the number of (S,G) states and the (*,G) states created on the first-hop router and on the RP. The first-hop router sends unicast Register messages to the RP with a (*,G) join request. The RP joins to the first-hop router with an (S,G) join if it has active receivers downstream. This state information remains for 260 seconds by default. However, for example, if an attacker is able to generate 100 IGMPv3 (S,G) joins a second for each of 10 sources, after 260 seconds there would be 260,000 state entries. One way to limit this type of attack is to limit the rate of Register messages to the RP.

If the RP does not have active receivers downstream, it sends a Register-Stop message to the first-hop router. When the first-hop router receives the Register-Stop message, it stops sending Register messages to the RP, putting the source on hold.

For bidir-PIM networks, all receiverless traffic is carried across a single route to the RP in a (*,G) route. An attack using this type of traffic is similar to a unicast traffic attack to the RP. In new Cisco IOS implementations, this will not create new (*,G) states. However, in earlier implementations, the receiverless traffic creates new (*,G) state information, except on the Cisco Catalyst 6500 series switches and the Cisco 7600 series routers.

Attack Traffic from Rogue Receivers

Receivers might also attack the network. Multicast receivers can create state attacks; there is no equivalent action in unicast networks. The following are three types of receiver attacks:

- **Attack against content:** The rogue receiver attempts to gain access to content that the receiver is not unauthorized to access.

- **Attack against bandwidth:** The receiver attempts to overload network bandwidth. This attack is typically against shared network bandwidth and is therefore actually an attack against other receivers.

- **Attack against routers and switches:** The receiver tries to create more state information than the router or switch can handle by sending multiple join requests. Processing these multiple join requests from the receiver can increase the convergence time of other states or cause the network device to reboot.

An example of a receiver attack is a user requesting many Internet TV broadcasts from the available channels.

Scoped Addresses

Scoping addresses can provide some architectural security.

Unicast addresses have two scopes: public and private. RFC 1918, *Address Allocation for Private Internets*, defines the private address ranges for IPv4.

As discussed in the "Multicast IP Addresses" section earlier in this chapter, multicast addresses have various scopes, including those defined by the IANA and as deployed within an organization. Recall that administratively, or limited, scoped addresses are in the 239.0.0.0/8 range. Although organizations can use the site-local addresses and organization-local addresses—within the administratively scoped address range—as a geographic form of access control for applications with these local addresses, there is no automatic enforcement of scopes. An example of a multicast address range allocation is illustrated in Figure 10-26.

Routers configured with ACLs can prevent multicast traffic in an address range from flowing outside an autonomous system or any user-defined domain. Within an autonomous system or domain, the administratively scoped address range can be further subdivided so that local multicast boundaries can be defined. This address subdivision is called *address scoping* and allows for address reuse between these smaller domains.

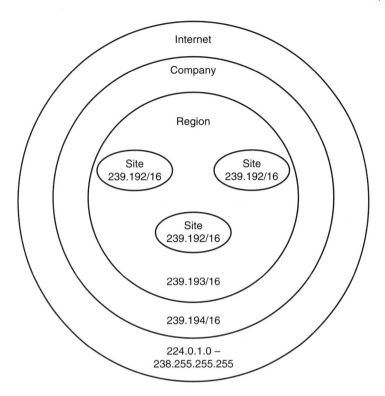

Figure 10-26   *Example Multicast Address Range Allocation*

Routers can also be configured to change the TTL threshold of multicast packets being forwarded out of an interface, using the **ip multicast ttl-threshold** *ttl* interface configuration command. This command allows only packets with a TTL value greater than the threshold specified to be forwarded out of the interface. For example, the TTL threshold on a border router interface could be set to 200, a very high value. Most multicast applications typically set the TTL value to well below 200, so no packets with a TTL lower than 200 would be forwarded out of the interface on this border router.

Multicast Access Control

This section describes access controls that can be used to secure IP multicast networks.

Packet Filter-Based Access Control

Cisco IOS Software supports packet filter–based ACLs that can help control traffic in a multicast network. These ACLs are typically implemented in hardware on most router platforms. If the packet-based ACL that filters traffic is deployed at the network ingress interface on the data plane before multicast processing, no state is created for the dropped traffic.

Figure 10-27 illustrates an example network. Example 10-1 provides the ACL configuration on the router in this network. A named ACL called *check-source* is created. This ACL permits any IP traffic from source address 10.0.0.0/8 to destination address 239.0.0.0/9 (239.0.0.0 to 239.127.255.255). Traffic to 224.0.0.0/4 is permitted and logged. All other traffic is denied and logged. This ACL is applied inbound on the router's E0 interface. As a result, the packet from the PC (10.0.0.1) to 239.10.244.1 is permitted, but the packet from the hacker (10.0.1.1) to 239.244.244.1 is denied.

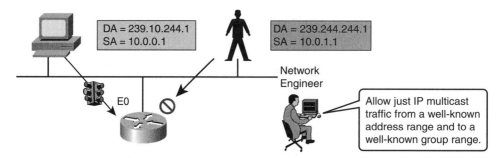

Figure 10-27   *Network for Packet Filter-Based Access Control Shown in Example 10-1*

Example 10-1   *Packet Filter-Based Access Control Configuration for Router in Figure 10-27*

```
ip access-list extended check-source
  permit ip host 10.0.0.0 0.255.255.255 239.0.0.0 0.127.255.255
  permit ip any 224.0.0.0 15.255.255.255 log
  deny ip any any log
interface ethernet0
  ip address 10.1.1.1 255.255.255.0
  ip access-group check-source in
```

The main advantage of this approach is simplicity and clarity. The disadvantages include the effort to apply an ACL to any inbound interface on which a multicast source might be, including all subnets on which users or servers reside.

Note: When using ACLs, be sure to allow appropriate unicast traffic and routing protocol multicast traffic.

Although packet filters can also be used to filter outbound traffic, *protocol* filtering is typically preferred for outbound (egress) traffic.

Host Receiver-Side Access Control

IGMP access groups can be used to provide host receiver-side access control.

The **ip igmp access-group** interface configuration command is used to filter groups in IGMP reports by using a standard access list, or to filter sources and groups in IGMPv3 reports by using an extended access list. The latter use of this command restricts receivers to join only the specific (S,G) channels permitted by the extended ACL.

When an IGMP extended access list is referenced in the **ip igmp access-group** command on an interface, the (S,G) pairs in the permit and deny statements of the extended access list are matched against the (S,G) pair of the IGMP reports received on the interface. The first part of the extended access list clause (the *source address* part) filters the source (the multicast sender); the second part of the extended access list clause (the *destination address* part) filters the multicast group.

For example, if an IGMP report with (S1,S2,...Sn,G) is received, the router first checks the group (*,G) against the access list statements. If the *group* is denied, the entire IGMP report is denied. If the group is permitted, each individual (S,G) pair is checked against the access list. Denied *sources* are taken out of the IGMP report, thereby denying any sources that match the access list from sending to the group.

Figure 10-28 illustrates an example network with two hosts. Example 10-2 provides the ACL configuration on the router. The ACL controls IGMP entries into the router. Any host is permitted to join group 225.2.2.2, and any host in network 10.0.0.0/8 is permitted to join groups in the 232.0.0.0/8 range. All other traffic is denied. The ACL is applied to the router's E0 interface. As a result, the join to group 225.2.2.2 is permitted, whereas the join to group 224.1.1.1 is denied.

Figure 10-28   *Network for Host Receiver-Based Access Control Configuration Shown in Example 10-2*

Example 10-2   *Host Receiver-Based Access Control Configuration for Router in Figure 10-28*

```
ip access-list extended allowed-multicast-igmp
  permit ip any host 225.2.2.2
  permit ip 10.0.0.0 0.255.255.255 232.0.0.0 0.255.255.255
  deny ip any any


interface ethernet 0
 ip igmp access-group allowed-multicast-igmp
```

PIM-SM Source Control

PIM-SM register messages can be filtered on a candidate RP router using the **ip pim accept-register** global configuration command.

This command prevents unauthorized sources from registering with the RP. If an unauthorized source sends a register message to the RP, the RP immediately sends back a Register-Stop message. The filter can be based on the source address using a standard ACL or based on the (S,G) pair using an extended ACL.

Figure 10-29 illustrates an example network. Example 10-3 provides the ACL configuration on the RP router. Only a source with address 192.168.1.1 is permitted to register with the RP; therefore when the source 192.168.2.2 sends a register message, the RP returns a Register-Stop message.

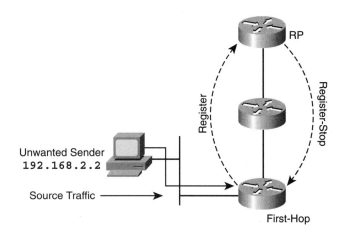

Figure 10-29   *Network for PIM-SM Source Control Configuration Shown in Example 10-3*

Example 10-3   *PIM-SM Source Control Configuration on the RP in Figure 10-29*

```
ip pim accept-register list 10

access-list 10 permit 192.168.1.1
```

This command allows for a limited form of centralized source control with PIM-SM. However, it does not inhibit (S,G) state creation on the first-hop router. Receivers that are on same first-hop router will still receive traffic from invalid sources.

An advantage of this approach is that it is configured only on the RPs, not on all the edge LAN interfaces.

Disabling Multicast Groups for IPv6

Cisco IOS Software supports disabling multicast groups by range for IPv6. The **ipv6 multicast group-range** *access-list-name* global configuration command enables a network administrator to specify an authorized IPv6 group range. If the group is denied by the referenced ACL, multicast protocol actions and traffic forwarding for unauthorized groups or channels is disabled for all interfaces. All control packets for the group are dropped, no state information is created for the group, and all data packets are dropped on hardware discarding platforms.

Note: The **ipv6 multicast group-range** command is supported in Cisco IOS Software Release 12.4(4)T for IPv6. Support for IPv4 is planned in the future.

Summary

In this chapter, you learned the basics of IP multicast, and the design and security recommendations for IP multicast networks.

With unicast transmission, multiple packets must be sent from a source to reach multiple receivers. In contrast, an IP multicast source sends a single packet; downstream routers replicate the packets only on links where receiving hosts exist.

An IP multicast group address is the destination address to which packets for the group are sent. A device must be a member of a group to receive the group's traffic.

Multicast applications can use a variety of models, including one to many or many to many. Using multicast provides advantages including enhanced efficiency and performance and support for distributed applications. However, because multicast applications are UDP based, reliability, congestion control, duplicate packets, out-of-sequence packets, and security may become issues.

Multicast addresses are in the range 224.0.0.0 through 239.255.255.255. Within this range, the multicast address scopes are shown in Table 10-2.

Table 10-2   *Multicast Address Scopes*

Range of Addresses	Description
224.0.0.0 through 224.0.0.255	Local scope addresses
224.0.1.0 through 238.255.255.255	Globally scoped addresses
239.0.0.0 through 239.255.255.255	Limited, or administratively, scoped addresses
239.255.0.0/16, 239.252.0.0/16, 239.253.0.0/16, and 239.254.0.0/16	Site-local scope addresses
239.192.0.0 to 239.251.255.255	Organization local scope addresses

IP multicast addresses are mapped to Layer 2 multicast addresses by mapping the low-order 23 bits of the IP multicast address into the low-order 23 bits of the MAC (Layer 2) address, resulting in a 32:1 overlap of IP addresses to MAC addresses.

Multicast addresses are typically statically assigned. Alternatively, MADCAP allows a client workstation to "lease" a multicast address from a MADCAP server.

IGMP is used between hosts and their local router. There are three versions of IGMP. IGMPv2 additions to IGMPv1 include leave group messages. IGMPv3 adds the ability to filter multicasts based on the multicast source so that hosts can indicate that they want to receive traffic only from particular sources within a multicast group.

With IGMP snooping, the switch eavesdrops on the IGMP messages sent between routers and hosts, and updates its MAC address table accordingly.

CGMP is a Cisco Systems proprietary protocol that runs between a multicast router and a switch; the routers inform each of their directly connected switches of IGMP registrations that were received from hosts accessible through the switch.

The PIM routing protocol is used by routers to forward multicast traffic. PIM uses the normal routing table, populated by the unicast routing protocol, in its multicast routing calculations. PIM terminology includes the following:

■ **Source tree:** A distribution tree created for each source sending to each multicast group. (S,G) multicast forwarding entries represent source S sending to the group G.

■ **Shared tree:** A single distribution tree that is shared between *all* sources for each multicast group. (*,G) multicast forwarding entries represent any source sending to the group G. Traffic is forwarded via an RP for the group.

■ **RP:** The common root of a shared tree.

■ **RPF:** Forwarding multicast traffic away from the source, rather than to the receiver.

The three main PIM deployment models are as follows:

■ ASM (PIM-SM), using a combination of shared and source trees, for general-purpose applications

■ Bidir-PIM, using only shared trees, for many-to-many applications

■ SSM, using only source trees, for one-to-many applications

Considerations for deploying an RP include the following:

■ Static RP addressing, when the RP address is manually configured. If the RP fails, routers cannot fail over to a standby RP.

■ Anycast RP to provide RP load sharing and hot backup capabilities.

■ Auto-RP, a dynamic way for routers to learn the RP information.

■ BSR, another RP dynamic selection protocol that also supports interoperability between vendors.

Multicast security considerations include unicast and multicast state and replication requirements, various types of attack traffic, and scoped addresses.

Multicast access control mechanisms include packet filter-based ACLs, IGMP access groups, and PIM-SM register message filtering. Multicast group ranges can be disabled for IPv6 multicast.

References

For additional information, refer to the following:

■ The IANA's IP multicast addressing assignments reference, at http://www.iana.org/as-signments/multicast-addresses

■ "The Internet Protocol Multicast" chapter of the Internetworking Technology Handbook, at http://www.cisco.com/en/US/docs/internetworking/technology/handbook/IP-Multi.html

■ "Multicast in a Campus Network: CGMP and IGMP Snooping," at http://www.cisco.com/en/US/products/hw/switches/ps708/products_tech_09186a00800b0871.shtml

■ Cisco Systems, Inc. "IP Multicast Technology Overview," at http://www.cisco.com/univercd/cc/td/doc/cisintwk/intsolns/mcst_sol/mcst_ovr.pdf

■ Cisco Systems, Inc. "Bidirectional PIM Deployment Guide," at http://www.cisco.com/en/US/prod/collateral/iosswrel/ps6537/ps6552/ps6592/prod_white_paper0900aecd80310db2.pdf

■ Cisco Systems, Inc. "Guidelines for Enterprise IP Multicast Address Allocation," at http://www.cisco.com/en/US/tech/tk828/technologies_white_paper 09186a00802d4643.shtml

■ Cisco Systems, Inc. "Cisco IOS IP Multicast Configuration Guide, Release 12.4," at http://www.cisco.com/en/US/docs/ios/ipmulti/configuration/guide/12_4/imc_12_4_book.html

Review Questions

Answer the following questions, and then refer to Appendix A, "Answers to Review Questions," for the answers.

1. Why is IP multicast considered more efficient than unicast?

2. Which of the following applications is a good candidate as a multicast application?

   a. Videoconferencing

   b. Software distribution

   c. Digital TV

   d. All of the above

3. Which of the following is not one of the characteristics of IP multicast?

   a. Transmission to a host group

   b. Dynamic membership

   c. Reliable transport

   d. Membership in more than one group

4. What is the range of multicast IP addresses?

5. Match the range of IP multicast addresses with its description:

Range of Addresses	Description
1: 224.0.0.0 through 224.0.0.255	**A:** Globally scoped addresses
2: 224.0.1.0 through 238.255.255.255	**B:** Organization local scope addresses
3: 239.0.0.0 through 239.255.255.255	**C:** Local scope addresses
4: 239.255.0.0/16, 239.252.0.0/16, 239.253.0.0/16, and 239.254.0.0/16	**D:** Site-local scope addresses
5: 239.192.0.0 to 239.251.255.255	**E:** Limited, or administratively, scoped addresses

6. How are IP multicast addresses translated to Layer 2 MAC multicast addresses?

7. How many IP multicast addresses map to a Layer 2 MAC multicast address?

8. Select the true statements regarding IGMP and CGMP.

   a. IGMP is used between a host and its local router.

   b. IGMP is used between routers and switches.

   c. CGMP is used between a host and its local router.

   d. CGMP is used between routers and switches.

9. Which of the following is *not* a characteristic of CGMP?

   a. Cisco-developed protocol that allows data link layer switches to leverage IGMP on Cisco routers to make data-link layer forwarding decisions

   b. Used by IPv4 hosts to communicate multicast group membership to the connected routers

   c. Provides management of group membership on switched Ethernet LANs

   d. Allows switches to forward multicast traffic to only those ports that are interested in the traffic

10. Describe the difference between how a host leaves a group when it is running IGMPv1 versus when it is running IGMPv2.

11. What is IGMP snooping?

12. Which statement best describes the interaction between the PIM protocol and a unicast routing protocol running on a network?

   a. There is no interaction between the two protocols.

   b. Only PIM or a unicast routing protocol can be run in a network; they cannot be run simultaneously.

   c. PIM uses the routing table populated by the unicast routing protocol in its multicast routing calculations.

   d. The unicast routing protocol uses the routing table populated by PIM in its multicast routing calculations.

13. Multicast forwarding is based on which of the following techniques?

   a. Destination-based forwarding

   b. Reverse path forwarding

   c. Multiprotocol Label Switching

   d. Anycast

14. Select the two true statements.

   a. A shared tree is created for each source sending to each multicast group.

   b. A source tree is created for each source sending to each multicast group.

   c. A shared tree has a single common root, called an RP.

   d. A source tree has a single common root, called an RP.

15. Which type of distribution tree does PIM-SM use?

16. What does the notation (S,G) indicate?

17. What does the notation (*,G) indicate?

18. What are the multicast addresses 224.0.1.39 and 224.0.1.40 used for?

19. What type of distribution trees are used by the following?:

   a. ASM _____

   b. Bidir-PIM _____

   c. SSM _____

20. How does a receiver join a multicast group in a PIM-SM environment?

21. What determines when a PIM-SM router will switch to a source tree from a shared tree?

22. Select the true statements regarding how data flows in a bidir-PIM environment from sources and to receivers.

    a. Data from the source flows up the source tree toward the RP.

    b. Data from the source flows down the source tree from the RP to the receivers.

    c. Data from the source flows up the source tree toward the receiver.

    d. Data from the source flows down the source tree to the receivers.

    e. Data from the source flows up the shared tree toward the RP.

    f. Data from the source flows down the shared tree from the RP to the receivers.

23. How is the DF in bidir-PIM elected?

24. How does a receiver join a multicast group in an SSM environment?

25. How is anycast RP implemented?

26. What role does a mapping agent play in Auto-RP?

27. Select the true statements regarding how auto-RP and BSR determine the active RP for a group.

    a. With Auto-RP, each individual router in the network elects the currently active RP for a particular group range.

    b. With Auto-RP, the mapping agent elects the active RP for a group range and announces the election results to the network.

    c. With BSR, each individual router in the network elects the currently active RP for a particular group range.

    d. With BSR the mapping agent elects the active RP for a group range and announces the election results to the network.

28. You want to filter multicast traffic so that a specific receiver A does not receive traffic from a specific source B. Where in the network should the filter be placed?

29. How does SSM protect receivers from attacks from unknown sources?

30. Describe the ways that rogue receivers can attack a network.

31. Which command is used to filter groups in IGMP reports?

32. Which command is used to filter PIM-SM register messages on a candidate RP?

After completing this chapter you will be able to do the following:

■ Describe the Cisco voice-ready architecture for supporting VoWLANs

■ Describe VoWLAN infrastructure considerations

■ Discuss VoWLAN coverage concerns and RF survey requirements

CHAPTER 11

VoWLAN Design

IEEE 802.11 wireless local area networks (WLAN) are rapidly becoming pervasive among enterprises. The availability of wireless voice clients, the introduction of dual-mode (wireless and cellular) smart phones, and the increased productivity realized by enabling a mobile workforce are persuading enterprises to implement Voice over WLANs (VoWLAN).

This chapter first reviews the Cisco Unified Wireless Network (UWN). The requirements for enterprise VoWLAN are then examined, followed by a discussion of infrastructure considerations for VoWLAN deployment. VoWLAN coverage considerations are examined, and the site survey process is described. The chapter concludes with a discussion of the Cisco VoWLAN Steps to Success partner program.

Cisco Unified Wireless Network Review

Note: Some of the information in this first main section of this chapter is derived from the *Authorized Self-Study Guide: Designing for Cisco Internetwork Solutions (DESGN)*, Second Edition, by Diane Teare, Cisco Press, 2007 (ISBN 1-58705-272-5) to provide a detailed review of the Cisco Unified Wireless Network. Some questions related to this material in the "Review Questions" section at the end of this chapter are also derived from those in the same DESGN book.

This section first discusses wireless radio frequency communication, antennas, and IEEE 802.11 WLAN operational standards. WLAN components, including clients and access points, are described next, followed by a discussion of WLAN operations. The Cisco UWN architecture is then introduced.

Radio Frequency Communication

A wireless communication system uses radio frequency (RF) energy to transmit data from one point to another, through the air. The term *signal* is used to refer to this RF energy. The data to be transmitted is first modulated onto a carrier and then sent; receivers demodulate the signal and process the data.

WLANs replace the Layer 1 transmission medium of a traditional wired network (usually Category 5 cable) with radio transmission over the air. WLANs can plug into a wired network and function as an overlay to wired LANs, or they can be deployed as a standalone

LAN where wired networking is not feasible. A computer with a wireless network interface card (NIC) connects to the wired LAN through an access point (AP). Other wireless endpoint devices supported include wireless phones, such as the Cisco Unified Wireless IP Phone 7921G, and software phones.

WLANs use spread-spectrum RF signals on the three unlicensed bands: 900 MHz, 2.4 GHz, and 5 GHz. The 900-MHz and 2.4-GHz bands are referred to as the *industrial, scientific, and medical bands*; and the 5-GHz band is commonly referred to as the *Unlicensed National Information Infrastructure (UNII) band*.

RF *gain* is an increase in the RF signal amplitude or strength. Two common sources of gain are amplifiers and antennas.

RF *loss* is a decrease in the RF signal strength. Losses affect WLAN design and are part of our everyday world. For example, the cables and connections between the AP and the antenna cause loss.

WLANs transmit signals just as radio stations do to reach their listeners. The transmit power levels for WLANs are in milliwatts (mW), whereas for radio stations the power levels are in megawatts (MW).

Two of the units of measure used in RF are as follows:

- **Decibel (dB):** The difference or ratio between two signal levels. Decibels are used to measure relative gains or losses in an RF system and to describe the effect of system devices on signal strength. The decibel is named after Alexander Graham Bell.

- **dB milliwatt (dBm):** A signal strength or power level. Zero dBm is defined as 1 mW of power into a terminating load such as an antenna or power meter. Small signals, those below 1 mW, are therefore negative numbers (such as −80 dBm); WLAN signals are in the range of −60 dBm to −80 dBm.

Antennas

Antennas used in WLANs come in many shapes and sizes, depending on the differing RF characteristics desired. The physical dimensions of an antenna directly relate to the frequency at which the antenna transmits or receives radio waves. As the gain increases, the coverage area becomes more focused. High-gain antennas provide longer coverage areas than low-gain antennas at the same input power level. As frequency increases, the wavelength and the antennas become smaller.

Omnidirectional antennas are the most widely used today. The radiant energy is shaped like a doughnut. Consequently, the transmitted signal is weak or absent directly under the AP (in the "hole" of the doughnut).

Directional antennas can direct and apply gain to the signal. Semidirectional antennas have radiant energy in a cowbell shape and highly directional antennas have radiant energy in a telescope shape.

IEEE 802.11 Operational Standards

Similar to wired LAN networks, IEEE 802.11 WLANs enable devices to transmit data, voice, and video, at data rates up to 54 Mbps. However, because WLANs are half duplex, the actual maximum throughput is typically 22 to 26 Mbps.

In September 1999, the IEEE ratified the IEEE 802.11a standard (5 GHz at 54 Mbps) and the IEEE 802.11b standard (2.4 GHz at 11 Mbps). In June 2003, the IEEE ratified the 802.11g standard (2.4 GHz at 54 Mbps); this standard is backward compatible with 802.11b systems, because both use the same 2.4-GHz bandwidth.

The following are the existing IEEE 802.11 standards for wireless communication:

- **802.11a:** 54 Mbps at 5 GHz, ratified in 1999

- **802.11b:** 11 Mbps 2.4 GHz, ratified in 1999

- **802.11d:** World mode, ratified in 2001

- **802.11e:** Quality of service, ratified in 2005

- **802.11F:** Inter-Access Point Protocol, withdrawn in 2006

- **802.11g:** 54 Mbps at 2.4 GHz, ratified in 2003

- **802.11h:** Dynamic frequency selection and transmit power control mechanisms, ratified in 2003

- **802.11i:** Authentication and security, ratified in 2005

- **802.11j:** Additional Japanese frequencies, ratified in 2005

- **802.11k:** Radio resource management draft, ratified in 2008

- **802.11n:** High-throughput draft, planned to be ratified in 2009

IEEE 802.11b/g Standards in the 2.4-GHz Band

The 2.4-GHz band used for 802.11b/g has multiple channels, each 22 MHz wide. In North America, 11 channels are defined, as illustrated in Figure 11-1. The top of the figure shows the channel's center frequency (which is the frequency by which the channel is known). The lower numbers show the channel's starting frequency. In North America, the 2.4-GHz band has three nonoverlapping channels: channels 1, 6, and 11.

Careful channel placement or reuse eliminates overlapping cells on the same channel so that aggregate WLAN throughput is maximized. This concept is similar to the reuse of FM radio stations throughout the country; two radio stations in the same geographic area are never on the same channel.

Therefore, three APs, using the three nonoverlapping channels, could operate in the same area without sharing the medium. For example, an AP on channel 1 does not have any frequencies in common with an AP on channel 6 or with an AP on channel 11. Therefore, there is no degradation in throughput when three APs are in the same area if they are each on a nonoverlapping channel. Figure 11-2 illustrates how 802.11b/g cells can be placed so that no adjacent channels overlap.

Different countries allow different channels and transmit power levels.

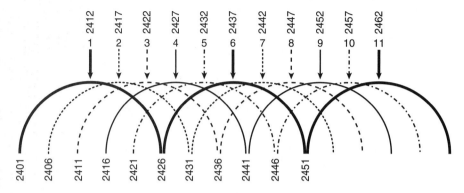

Figure 11-1 *2.4-GHz Channels in North America*

> **Note:** 802.11g is backward compatible with 802.11b. The 802.11g specification uses orthogonal frequency-division multiplexing (OFDM) modulation for 802.11g data rates and complementary code keying (CCK) modulation for 802.11b data rates. CCK is an extension of Direct Sequence Spread Spectrum (DSSS) modulation.

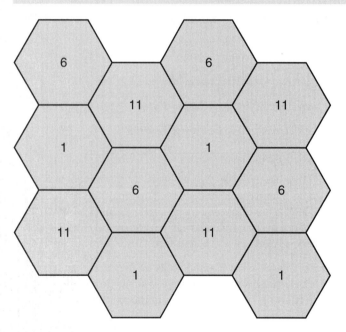

No two adjacent cells use the same channel.

Figure 11-2 *2.4-GHz Channel Reuse*

Note: Multipath interference occurs when an RF signal has more than one path between the sender and receiver. The multiple signals at the receiver might result in a distorted, low-quality signal. Multipath interference is more of an issue with 802.11b. Some Cisco APs reduce multipath interference by providing multiple antennas; this feature is called *antenna diversity*. The device selects the antenna from which the best signal is received. For example, a typical Linksys wireless router has two "rubber duck" antennas. However, only one antenna is used at a time—the one that experiences the least multipath distortion of the signal.

The 802.11g data rates are 54, 48, 36, 24, 18, 12, 9, and 6 Mbps. The 802.11b data rates are 11, 5.5, 2, and 1 Mbps.

IEEE 802.11a Standard in the 5-GHz Band

802.11a and 802.11b/g are incompatible because they use different frequencies. 802.11a requires a different radio and antenna than 802.11b/g.

The 5-GHz UNII band can be divided into multiple channels, depending on the regulations that vary by country. The United States now has three separate 100-MHz-wide bands known as the *lower, middle,* and *upper* bands. Within each of these three bands are four nonoverlapping channels. In the United States, the Federal Communications Commission (FCC) specifies that the lower band is for indoor use, the middle band is for indoor and outdoor use, and the upper band is for outdoor use. Figure 11-3 illustrates the nonoverlapping 802.11a channels.

Figure 11-3 *5-GHz 802.11a Nonoverlapping Channels*

802.11a uses the same OFDM modulation and supports the same data rates as 802.11g.

802.11a channel placement is easier to deploy than 802.11b/g, because 802.11a has 12 nonoverlapping channels that can provide a simpler channel reuse schema. However, the nonoverlapping channels for 802.11a (as shown in Figure 11-3) are close enough to each other that some clients might experience interference from adjacent channels (called *side-band* or *side-channel interference*). As a result, the recommendation for 802.11a is that neighboring cells not be placed on neighboring channels (in other words, neighboring channels are skipped) to reduce interference. Figure 11-4 illustrates an example of 802.11a channel reuse.

The 802.11a coverage area is smaller than the 802.11b/g coverage area, requiring more APs on a per-area basis.

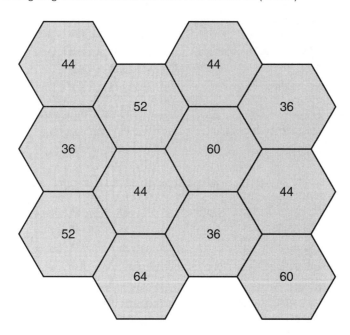

No two adjacent cells use the same channel.

Figure 11-4   *5 GHz Channel Reuse*

WLAN Components

Client devices use wireless NICs or adapters to connect to a wireless network in either ad hoc (peer-to-peer) mode, or in infrastructure mode using APs. Cisco APs can be either autonomous or lightweight.

Note: Autonomous APs used to be called thick, fat, or decentralized APs, whereas lightweight APs were called thin or centralized APs.

Note: Client devices should not be configured in ad hoc mode in the enterprise environment. Apart from the security concerns of ad hoc mode, the data sent in ad hoc mode effectively reduces the bandwidth available for other devices configured for the same channel in infrastructure mode. The remainder of this chapter focuses on infrastructure mode using APs.

These components are described in the following sections.

Cisco-Compatible WLAN Clients

The Cisco Compatible Extensions (CCX) program for WLAN client devices allows vendors of WLAN client devices or adapters to ensure interoperability with the Cisco WLAN infrastructure and take advantage of Cisco innovations. A program participant, such as a maker of a WLAN client adapter or client device, implements support for all features and then submits the product to an independent lab for rigorous testing. Passing this testing process allows the devices to be marketed as Cisco Compatible client devices. There are four versions of the Cisco Compatible specification, versions 1 through 4, as shown in Figure 11-5. Each version builds on its predecessors. With a few exceptions, every feature that must be supported in one version must also be supported in each subsequent version.

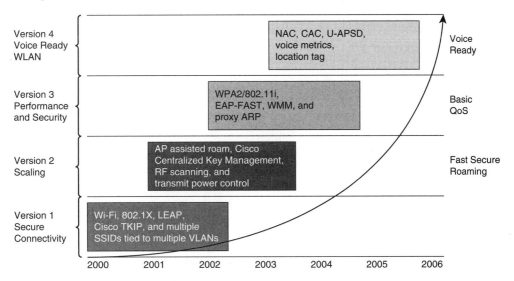

Figure 11-5 *Each Cisco Compatible Extensions Version Builds Upon Its Predecessors*

Some features of Cisco Compatible Extensions version 1 are as follows:

■ Compliance with 802.11a, b, or g, and Wi-Fi

■ Support for IEEE 802.1X and Cisco Lightweight Extensible Authentication Protocol (LEAP)

■ Support for Cisco Temporal Key Integrity Protocol (TKIP), a Cisco implementation of TKIP that includes a hashing algorithm and a message integrity check

■ Interoperability with APs that support multiple service set identifiers (SSIDs) tied to multiple VLANs, providing benefits such as flexible security schemes in a mixed client environment

Some additional features of Cisco Compatible Extensions version 2 are as follows:

■ Compliance with Wi-Fi Protected Access (WPA), including support for WPA TKIP encryption

■ Support for Protected Extensible Authentication Protocol (PEAP) with Extensible Authentication Protocol (EAP)-Generic Token Card (EAP-GTC)

■ Fast, secure, AP-assisted roaming with Cisco Centralized Key Management (CCKM) support

■ RF scanning, with scanned data sent to the AP and ultimately to CiscoWorks Wireless LAN Solution Engine (WLSE) for analysis and performance of RF management functions such as intrusion detection, assisted site survey, and detection of interference sources

■ Support for AP-specified maximum transmit power

Some additional features of Cisco Compatible Extensions version 3 are as follows:

■ Compliance with WPA version 2 (WPA2)/802.11i, including support for Advanced Encryption Standard (AES) encryption

■ Support for Extensible Authentication Protocol Flexible Authentication via Secure Tunneling (EAP-FAST)

■ Support for Wi Fi Multimedia (WMM)

■ Recognition of proxy ARP information elements in beacons to indicate whether proxy ARP is supported in an AP

Some additional features of Cisco Compatible Extensions version 4 are as follows:

■ Support for Network Admission Control (NAC), to allow network access only to compliant and trusted clients

■ Support for Call Admission Control (CAC), including addressing, VoIP stability, roaming, and other quality of service (QoS)-related issues

■ Support for a power-saving mechanism, Unscheduled Automatic Power Save Delivery (U-APSD), in QoS environments

■ VoIP metrics reporting to optimize WLAN VoIP performance

■ Ability to function as an 802.11 location tag

Note: Many of the protocols mentioned in the CCX version descriptions are described throughout this chapter.

Note: More information about the CCX program is available at the Cisco Compatible Extensions program website at http://www.cisco.com/web/partners/pr46/pr147/partners_pgm_concept_home.html.

Autonomous APs

An autonomous AP has a local configuration and requires local management, which might make consistent configurations difficult and add to the cost of network management.

Cisco's core WLAN feature set includes autonomous APs and the CiscoWorks WLSE management appliance.

CiscoWorks WLSE is a turnkey and scalable management platform for managing hundreds to thousands of Cisco Aironet autonomous APs and wireless bridges. Autonomous APs may also be configured with CiscoWorks WLSE Express, a complete WLAN management solution with an integrated authentication, authorization, and accounting (AAA) server for small to medium-sized enterprise facilities or branch offices using Cisco Aironet autonomous APs and wireless bridges.

Lightweight APs

A lightweight AP receives control and configuration from a WLAN controller (WLC) to which it is associated. This provides a single point of management and reduces the security concern of a stolen AP.

The WLCs and lightweight APs communicate over any Layer 2 (Ethernet) or Layer 3 (IP) infrastructure using the Lightweight AP Protocol (LWAPP) to support automation of numerous WLAN configuration and management functions. WLCs are responsible for centralized system-wide WLAN management functions, such as security policies, intrusion prevention, RF management, QoS, and mobility.

Note: Despite being called a *wireless* LAN controller, a WLC is connected to the *wired* LAN and to the lightweight APs by *wires*. The WLC does not have *any* wireless connections.

The Cisco advanced WLAN feature set includes lightweight APs, WLCs, and the Wireless Control System (WCS) management application. These components are the basis for the Cisco UWN.

A Cisco wireless location appliance may be added to track the location of wireless devices.

WLAN Operation

The coverage area of an AP is called the basic service set (BSS); other names for the BSS are *microcell* and *cell*. The identifier of the BSS is called the BSS identifier (BSSID).

If a single cell does not provide enough coverage, any number of cells can be added to extend the range to an extended service area (ESA). It is recommended that the ESA cells have a 10 percent to 15 percent overlap to allow remote users to roam without losing RF connections. If VoIP is implemented in the wireless network, it is recommended that the ESA cells have a 15 percent to 20 percent overlap. As discussed earlier, bordering cells should be set to different nonoverlapping channels for best performance.

An SSID is the identifier—or name—of an ESA, creating a WLAN. An SSID on an AP and on an associated client must match exactly. APs broadcast their SSIDs in a beacon, announcing their available services. Clients associate with a specific SSID or learn the available SSIDs from the beacon and choose one with which to associate.

APs can be configured not to broadcast a particular SSID, but the SSID is still sent in the header of all the packets sent and therefore is discoverable by wireless survey tools. Therefore, configuring the AP not to broadcast an SSID is not considered a strong security mechanism by itself.

Roaming occurs when a wireless client moves from being associated to one AP to another AP—from one cell to another cell—within the same SSID. Roaming is explored in the "Roaming" section later in this chapter.

The Cisco UWN Architecture

In a traditional WLAN, each AP operates as a separate autonomous node configured with SSID, RF channel, RF power settings, and so forth. Scaling to large, contiguous, coordinated WLANs and adding higher-level applications is challenging with these autonomous APs. For example, if an autonomous AP hears a nearby AP operating on the same channel, the autonomous AP has no way of determining whether the adjacent AP is part of the same network or a neighboring network. Some form of centralized coordination is needed to allow multiple APs to operate across rooms and floors.

Cisco UWN Elements

The Cisco UWN architectural elements allow a WLAN to operate as an intelligent information network and to support advanced mobility services. The Cisco UWN incorporates advanced features that elevate a wireless deployment from a means of efficient data connectivity to a secure, converged communications network for voice and data applications.

Beginning with a base of client devices, each element provides additional capabilities needed as networks evolve and grow, interconnecting with the elements above and below it to create a unified, secure, end-to-end enterprise-class WLAN solution. The five interconnected elements of the Cisco UWN architecture are as follows:

- **Client devices:** With more than 90 percent of shipping client devices certified as Cisco Compatible under the CCX program, almost any client device that is selected will support the Cisco UWN advanced features, including out-of-the-box wireless client security.

- **Lightweight APs:** Dynamically configured APs provide ubiquitous network access in all environments. Enhanced productivity is supported through "plug-and-play" with LWAPP used between the APs and the Cisco WLCs. Cisco APs are a proven platform with a large installed base and market share leadership. All Cisco lightweight APs support mobility services, such as fast secure roaming for voice, and location services for real-time network visibility.

- **Network unification:** Integration of wired and wireless networks is critical for unified network control, scalability, security, and reliability. Seamless functionality is provided through wireless integration into all major switching and routing platforms, including Cisco WLC appliances, Cisco WLC Modules (WLCM) for Integrated Services Routers (ISR), and Cisco Catalyst 6500 series Wireless Services Modules (WiSMs).

■ **Network management:** The same level of security, scalability, reliability, ease of deployment, and management for WLANs as wired LANs is provided through network management systems such as the Cisco WCS, which helps visualize and secure the airspace. The Cisco wireless location appliance provides location services.

■ **Mobility services:** Unified mobility services include advanced security threat detection and mitigation, voice services, location services, and guest access.

Benefits of the Cisco UWN architecture include ease of deployment and upgrades, reliable connectivity through dynamic RF management, optimized per-user performance through user load balancing, guest networking, Layer 2 and 3 roaming, embedded wireless intrusion detection system (IDS), location services, VoIP support, lowered total cost of ownership (TCO), and wired and wireless unification.

The Cisco WCS is an optional Windows or Linux server-based network management component that works in conjunction with Cisco lightweight APs and Cisco WLCs. With Cisco WCS, network administrators have a single solution for RF prediction, policy provisioning, network optimization, troubleshooting, user tracking, security monitoring, and WLAN systems management. The Cisco WCS includes tools for WLAN planning and design, RF management, basic location tracking, intrusion prevention systems, and WLAN systems configuration, monitoring, and management.

The Cisco wireless location appliance integrates with Cisco WCS for enhanced physical location tracking of many wireless devices to within a few meters. This appliance also records historical location information that can be used for location trending, rapid problem resolution, and RF capacity management.

An enterprise network can start with client devices, lightweight APs, and WLCs. As the enterprise's wireless networking requirements grow, additional elements, such as the Cisco WCS and the Cisco wireless location appliance, can be incorporated into the network.

Cisco UWN Lightweight AP and WLC Operation

An autonomous AP acts as an 802.1Q translational bridge and is responsible for putting the wireless client RF traffic into the appropriate local VLAN on the wired network.

In contrast, the Cisco UWN architecture centralizes WLAN configuration and control on a WLC; the APs are *lightweight*, meaning that they cannot act independently of a WLC. The lightweight APs and WLCs communicate using LWAPP, and the WLCs are responsible for putting the wireless client traffic into the appropriate VLAN. Figure 11-6 shows an example of this architecture.

It is a recommended enterprise practice that the connection between client device and APs be both authenticated and encrypted. When a WLAN client sends a packet as an RF signal, it is received by a lightweight AP, decrypted if necessary, encapsulated with an

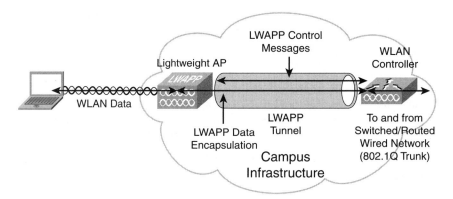

Figure 11-6   *Cisco UWN Includes Lightweight APs and WLCs*

LWAPP header, and forwarded to the WLC. From the perspective of the AP, the WLC is an LWAPP tunnel endpoint with an IP address. At the WLC, the LWAPP header is stripped off, and the frame is switched from the WLC onto the appropriate VLAN in the campus infrastructure.

In the Cisco UWN architecture, the WLC is an 802.1Q bridge that takes client traffic from the LWAPP tunnel (from the lightweight AP) and puts it on the appropriate VLAN in the wired network. Figure 11-7 illustrates this process.

Figure 11-7   *In the UWN, the WLC Bridges and Puts Traffic into VLANs*

Note: If you move a statically addressed AP to a different IP subnet, it cannot forward traffic, because it will not be able to form a LWAPP tunnel with the WLC.

When a client on the wired network sends a packet to a WLAN client, the packet first goes into the WLC, which encapsulates it with an LWAPP header and forwards it to the appropriate AP. The AP strips off the LWAPP header, encrypts the frame if necessary, and then bridges the frame onto the RF medium.

Consequently, much of the traditional WLAN functionality has moved from autonomous APs to a centralized WLC under the Cisco UWN architecture. LWAPP splits the MAC functions of an AP between the WLC and the lightweight AP. The lightweight APs handle only real-time MAC functionality, leaving the WLC to process all the non-real-time MAC functionality. This split-MAC functionality allows the APs to be deployed in a zero-touch fashion such that individual configuration of APs is not required.

Using VoWLAN in an Enterprise Network

This section identifies the drivers for using VoWLAN in the enterprise, provides an overview of the Cisco voice-ready architecture, and describes the impact of voice requirements on WLANs.

VoWLAN Drivers in the Enterprise

Because WLANs are pervasive among enterprises and because VoIP deployments offer a rich set of features, organizations are looking to combine these technologies in VoWLAN to improve productivity and reduce costs. VoWLAN deployments provide multiple benefits, including the following:

- Enabling access to enterprise unified communications, supporting one phone number and one voice mail per user

- Helping employees eliminate missed calls by providing mobility within a building or campus

- Helping organizations gain control over mobile communications costs by leveraging least-cost call routing and providing call detail recording

- Providing a consistent user experience for improved user satisfaction

These factors, coupled with the availability of wireless voice clients and the introduction of dual-mode (wireless and cellular) smart phones, are enticing enterprises to implement VoWLANs.

One alternative to VoWLAN is a cell phone solution. Cell phones can support the mobility requirements of an enterprise similar to VoWLAN. Currently, cell phone solutions have some advantages over VoWLAN solutions because of the good selection of cell phones available and the fact that multiple carriers provide cell phone service.

However, there are some disadvantages to cell phone solutions, including the following:

- There is no access to enterprise voice applications such as the corporate directory.

- Using both a cell phone and a VoIP phone results in having multiple phone numbers and multiple voice mailboxes. Productivity may decrease because users must retrieve voice mail from multiple places.

- There are access issues deep inside of some buildings.

- There may be security concerns with using mobile phones that are not managed by the organization.

Although there is currently no seamless handoff on a dual-mode phone, dual-mode smart phones will likely replace cell phones in the future.

Therefore, organizations are looking to make WLANs voice ready, for current or future use to protect the upfront investment in infrastructure and services.

Voice-Ready Architecture

Voice services place stringent performance requirements on the entire network. Because digitized voice is a sampling of an analog signal, the transmission of digitized voice is very sensitive to delays during transit. Voice requires a pervasive deployment—the network needs to have continuous coverage everywhere a client may roam to avoid any dead spots or gaps in coverage that may cause a call to drop. This pervasive coverage requirement is not as stringent in data-only networks because data applications are far more tolerant of brief network interruptions.

The end-to-end transit time of a packet is the cumulative delay for the packet to be encoded, to be put on the network by the sending client, to traverse the network, and to be received and decoded at the receiving client. For voice to work correctly over any infrastructure, the end-to-end transmit time must be less than 150 ms.

QoS for a VoIP call must be maintained, whether the call is being delivered to a wired or a wireless endpoint. Issues encountered during transit result in delays and variations in the arrival time of the received signal, known as jitter. It is critically important to minimize end-to-end delay and jitter for VoIP packets to provide optimal audio quality. To maintain QoS, voice must be a priority across the VoWLAN and the packet priority must be translated from the wireless to the wired infrastructure.

The Cisco voice-ready architecture is an end-to-end approach that builds upon the highly scalable, low-TCO Cisco UWN and addresses the convergence of VoIP and wireless networks. The voice-ready architecture is designed to support pervasive deployments that are typical of customers with mobile voice applications to flexibly extend the mobility benefits of wireless networks to their voice communications. Additional features, such as end-to-end QoS, and fast, secure roaming, backed by a portfolio of APs with enhanced radios, make the Cisco UWN voice ready.

As illustrated in Figure 11-8, the Cisco voice-ready architecture has the following four main components:

- **VoWLAN clients:** These clients can be wireless IP phones from Cisco or from vendors supporting CCX. The Cisco IP Communicator software application on a laptop can also function as a VoWLAN client.

Figure 11-8   *The Cisco Voice-Ready Architecture*

■ **The voice-ready WLAN:** The WLAN includes APs and antennas to provide optimized packet handling in the RF network.

■ **Unified wired or wireless LAN infrastructure:** This infrastructure is used to provide wired and wireless end-to-end prioritization and classification of voice. It includes management tools to control delay, roam time, and packet loss.

■ **Cisco Unified Communications and mobility applications:** These applications
support increased call capacity, higher network availability, and improved performance for all clients.

The architecture supports converged voice and data on wired and wireless networks for an
end-to-end intelligent integration.

Voice Impact on WLANs

The WLAN infrastructure is a shared medium among wireless devices. Adding voice services to a WLAN has implications in several design areas, including the following:

■ RF coverage requirements and deployment planning

■ Network infrastructure and logical subnet design

■ Wireless "over-the-air" QoS

■ Network security architecture

■ VoWLAN client requirements

These topics are discussed throughout the rest of the chapter.

VoWLAN Infrastructure Considerations

There are several voice-specific requirements to consider when you are implementing a VoWLAN, including the following:

- **Roaming:** Voice calls require network connectivity to be maintained while the client is physically moving, changing its association from one AP to another. Voice clients typically move more often than data-only clients.

- **QoS:** QoS is essential to ensure that voice traffic receives timely and reliable treatment with low delay, low jitter, and little or no packet loss on the network. QoS also includes CAC to police the call capacity on a per-AP basis.

- **Security:** Wireless IP telephony networks require a carefully planned security implementation to ensure that the telephony network operates properly and that voice traffic is secure.

- **Intelligent clients:** A voice-ready WLAN requires an intelligent client capable of supporting the voice-ready Cisco infrastructure functions for enterprise roaming, QoS, CAC, and security.

The Cisco UWN supports all these requirements through software capabilities and technological enhancements in both the infrastructure and in Cisco Compatible clients. These capabilities and enhancements are discussed in the following sections.

Roaming

Note: Some of the information in this section is derived from the *Authorized Self-Study Guide: Designing for Cisco Internetwork Solutions (DESGN)*, Second Edition, by Diane Teare, Cisco Press, 2007 (ISBN 1-58705-272-5) to provide a detailed roaming discussion.

One significant benefit of wireless networks—and a key reason they are deployed—is mobility, or roaming. This is the capability of end devices to move to new locations and remain networked without reassociation and DHCP delays. Roaming occurs when a wireless client moves its association from one AP and reassociates to another AP, within the same SSID.

A WLAN client must be able to maintain its association seamlessly from one AP to another securely and with as little latency as possible. The roaming event is triggered on signal quality, not proximity to an AP. When the signal quality for a client drops as a result of movement, the client device roams to another AP.

Mobility introduces challenges in a network implementation. Roaming must be supported when the wireless client roams from one AP to another, whether both APs are joined to the same WLC (intracontroller) or to different WLCs (intercontroller). Depending on the application, the Cisco UWN might have to support Layer 2 or Layer 3 roaming. These scenarios are described in the following sections.

When WLAN clients roam, they are always reauthenticated by the system in some way, to protect against client spoofing. CCKM is a Cisco standard (supported by Cisco Compatible clients) to provide fast, secure roaming, and is recommended for VoWLANs.

CCKM enables authenticated client devices to roam securely from one AP to another without any perceptible delay during reassociation. During the roaming process, a VoWLAN phone must scan for the nearby APs, determine which AP can provide the best service, and then reassociate with the new AP. If stronger authentication methods, such as WPA and EAP, are used, the number of information exchanges increases and causes more delay during roaming. To avoid these delays, CCKM is recommended for VoWLANs.

Note: Cisco WLCs with software release 4.0.217 or later support CCKM. The Cisco Unified Wireless IP Phone 7921G and Cisco Unified Wireless IP Phone 7920 support CCKM but cannot use Proactive Key Caching (PKC) at this time.

Note: This book discusses roaming within the enterprise framework. Handoffs or roaming for dual-mode clients between a cellular wireless network and an enterprise WLAN is not covered.

CCKM is further described in the "Security" section later in this chapter.

Intracontroller Roaming

Intracontroller roaming is roaming between APs joined to the *same* WLC.

When a wireless client associates to an AP and authenticates through a WLC, the WLC places an entry for that client in its client database. This entry includes the MAC and IP addresses of the client, security context and associations, QoS context, WLAN, and associated AP. The WLC uses this information to forward frames and manage traffic to and from the wireless client.

When the wireless client moves its association from one AP to another on the same WLC, as illustrated in Figure 11-9, the WLC simply updates the client database with the new associated AP. If necessary, new security context and associations are established, too. With intracontroller roaming, an IP address refresh is not needed.

Intercontroller Roaming at Layer 2

Intercontroller roaming occurs when a client roams from an AP joined to one WLC to an AP joined to a different WLC. Intercontroller roaming can be at Layer 2 or Layer 3.

Figure 11-10 illustrates an intercontroller Layer 2 roam.

A Layer 2 intercontroller roam occurs when the client traffic is bridged to the same IP subnet (and therefore the same VLAN) through the LAN interfaces on both WLCs.

When the client reassociates to an AP connected to a new WLC, the new WLC exchanges mobility messages with the original WLC (using a Mobility Messaging Exchange protocol), and the client database entry is *moved* to the new WLC. New security context and associations are established if necessary, and the client database entry is updated for the new AP. With Layer 2 intercontroller roaming, an IP address refresh is not needed. This process is transparent to the end user.

Figure 11-9 *Intracontroller Roaming Is Roaming Between APs on the Same WLC*

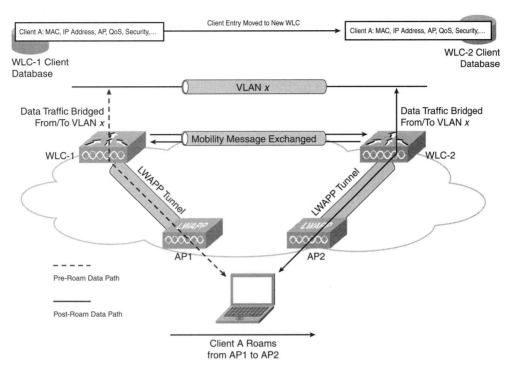

Figure 11-10 *Layer 2 Intercontroller Roaming*

Note: Both forms of intercontroller roaming require the WLCs to be in the same mobility group, as described in the upcoming "Mobility Groups" section.

Intercontroller Roaming at Layer 3

Layer 3 intercontroller roaming occurs when the client associates to an AP on a different WLC and the traffic is bridged to a different IP subnet. Layer 3 intercontroller roaming is used when Layer 2 VLANs do not extend across the entire enterprise, and therefore traffic needs to go to a different subnet.

When the client roams at Layer 3 and reassociates to an AP connected to a new WLC, the new WLC exchanges mobility messages with the original WLC, as shown in Figure 11-11.

With Layer 3 roaming, instead of *moving* the client entry to the new WLC's client database, the original WLC marks the entry for the client in its own client database with an Anchor entry and *copies* the database entry to the new WLC's client database, where it is marked with a Foreign entry.

Security credentials and context are reestablished if necessary. The roam is still transparent to the wireless client, which maintains its original IP address, even though the new WLC uses a different subnet.

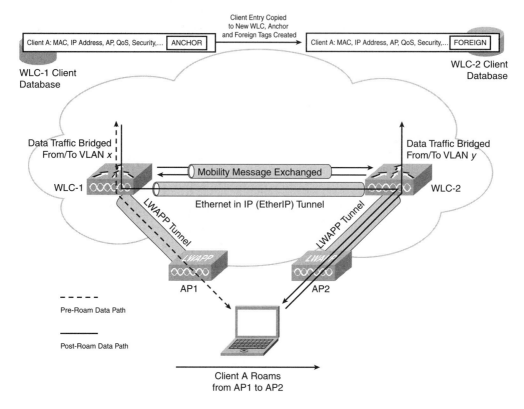

Figure 11-11   *Layer 3 Intercontroller Roaming*

After a Layer 3 roam, the data transferred to and from the wireless client might flow in an asymmetric traffic path. The Foreign WLC forwards traffic from the client to the network directly into the network. Traffic to the client arrives at the Anchor WLC, which forwards the traffic to the Foreign WLC in an Ethernet in IP (EtherIP) tunnel. The Foreign WLC then forwards the data to the client.

If a wireless client roams to a new Foreign WLC, the client database entry is moved from the original Foreign WLC to the new Foreign WLC, but the original Anchor WLC is always maintained.

Mobility Groups

A set of WLCs in a network can be configured as a mobility group, which allows them to dynamically share important information among them, including the context and state of client devices, and WLC loading information.

With this information, the network can support intercontroller roaming, AP load balancing, and WLC redundancy. A mobility group also supports forwarding of data traffic through EtherIP tunnels for Layer 3 intercontroller roaming. A mobility group does more than just define the RF connectivity of the client; it defines the infrastructure resources and their connectivity to each other. Therefore, if a client needs to seamlessly roam from one location to another across WLCs, the WLCs in those locations need to be in the same defined mobility group.

Each WLC in a mobility group is configured with a list of the other members of the mobility group. Each WLC device builds a neighbor relationship with every other member of the group.

WLCs should be placed in the same mobility group when an intercontroller roam is possible. If there is no possibility of a roaming event occurring, it might make sense to not put WLCs in the same mobility group. For example, suppose that you have deployed two separate WLCs in two buildings, with each WLC managing the APs in its building. If the buildings are separated by a large parking area with no RF coverage, a WLAN client won't roam from an AP in one building to an AP in the other building. These WLCs therefore do not need to be members of the same mobility group. In general, a single mobility group should encompass an area that covers 80 percent to 90 percent of user roaming patterns because clients cannot seamlessly roam across mobility groups. Therefore, the WLAN deployment team must have a good understanding of how users will move throughout the building and incorporate this into the mobility group creation.

A mobility group can include up to 24 WLCs. The number of APs supported in a mobility group is a maximum of 3600 and is bounded by the number of WLCs and WLC types in the mobility group.

Enhanced Neighbor Lists

VoWLAN handsets typically continually scan the APs in the neighbor list to stay associated with the best AP. With the Cisco VoWLAN solution, clients can be classified based on roaming type and participate in the roaming process based on information gathered from the infrastructure.

Examples of roaming classifications are fast roam, slow roam, and 802.11a/b/g only.

The information gathered from the network infrastructure is put in enhanced neighbor lists. The enhanced neighbor lists contain information that helps the client make association decisions between potential APs including a list of neighboring APs that have the ability to service the client based on the client classification.

The enhanced neighbor list includes information such as the following:

- Authorized APs nearby

- RF parameters of nearby APs

- RF measurements at the edge of cells

- Capacity utilization on nearby APs

Based on the information in the neighbor list, the client preemptively decides to associate with an AP that has sufficient capacity and RF parameters. If the AP can service the client, based on the client classification, the AP and the client will successfully associate.

This intelligent roaming process enables the clients to associate to the AP that will provide them the best audio quality and helps minimize or eliminate audio gaps in roams. Overall network capacity is increased through this load balancing.

QoS

QoS is essential to ensure that voice traffic receives timely and reliable treatment with low delay, low jitter, and little or no packet loss on the network.

IEEE 802.11e and Wi-Fi Multimedia

QoS on a pervasive WLAN is much more than simply prioritizing one type of packet over another.

The number of active users in any WLAN location may change dynamically and cannot be addressed through the capacity management tools used in wired networks. WLAN traffic is nondeterministic. Channel access is based on a binary back-off algorithm defined by the 802.11 standard (carrier sense multiple access with collision avoidance [CSMA/CA]) and is variable by nature, based on the number of clients accessing the network. This variability makes maintaining QoS for VoWLAN more difficult.

To improve the reliability of voice transmissions in this nondeterministic environment, the IEEE formed the 802.11e specification that adds QoS features and multimedia support to the existing 802.11b, 802.11g, and 802.11a wireless networks. Before the IEEE 802.11e was ratified, the wireless industry trade association known as the Wi-Fi Alliance accelerated the use of WLAN QoS through an early certification called WMM. The WMM includes some of the 802.11e features for wireless networks to improve the user experience for audio, video, and voice applications. WMM adds prioritization capabilities to wireless networks and optimizes performance when multiple applications, each with different latency and throughput requirements, compete for network resources.

The Cisco Unified Wireless IP Phone 7920 and 7921G devices support the 802.11e standard and are WMM certified. For the 802.11e and WMM differentiated services to provide sufficient QoS for voice packets, only a certain amount of voice bandwidth can be serviced or admitted on a channel at any one time. For example, assume that a network can handle x voice calls with its reserved bandwidth; if the number of voice calls is increased beyond this limit (to $x + 1$, for example), the quality of all calls would suffer.

Cisco WLANs support four levels of QoS over the air: Platinum (voice), Gold (video), Silver (best effort, the default), and Bronze (background). As a recommended practice, configure the voice traffic WLAN to use Platinum QoS, assign low-bandwidth WLAN traffic to use Bronze QoS, and assign all other traffic between the remaining QoS levels.

The WLAN QoS level defines a specific 802.11e user priority for over-the-air traffic. This user priority is used to derive the over-the-wire priorities for non-WMM traffic, and it also acts as the ceiling when managing WMM traffic with various levels of priorities. APs use this QoS-profile-specific user priority to derive the IP differentiated services code point (DSCP) value that is used on the wired LAN.

Note: WMM requires CCX version 3 or later.

End-to-End QoS

Separate voice and data VLANs are recommended to support different security features, to support different priorities for voice traffic so that it can be dealt with using minimal delays, and to reduce the chance of data clients crowding the voice VLAN and causing unnecessary traffic overhead and delays.

Using separate data and voice VLANs allows specific QoS settings for voice VLAN traffic, enabling end-to-end QoS for this traffic. This separation of client traffic is best continued into separate wireless RF spectrum, such as using IEEE 802.11a (5 GHz) for voice and IEEE 802.11b and IEEE 802.11g (2.4 GHz) for data. The final selection of the RF spectrum used depends on the client hardware capabilities available (for example, if the client supports only 2.4-GHz 802.11b/g or 5-GHz 802.11a, or both radios). Deploying voice in 5 GHz would also reduce the RF interference present in the crowded 2.4-GHz RF spectrum.

Note: Using separate VLANs is in addition to the RF recommendation of ensuring nonoverlapping channel frequencies to avoid interference.

As shown in the example in Figure 11-12, if the over-the-air packets from the phone or PC to the AP have trust enforced, the QoS marking from the client determines the DSCP value in the LWAPP frame. Because all WLAN traffic that passes between the AP and the WLC is LWAPP encapsulated, the LWAPP encapsulation maintains the Layer 3 marking in the original packet. When the LWAPP packet is de-encapsulated at the WLC, the original Layer 3 marking is again used by QoS mechanisms in the network infrastructure. Therefore, the edge switches of the wired network trust the QoS marking of the packets from the AP. A similar mechanism operates when packets are sent from the wired network to the wireless clients. With this capability enabled in the Cisco UWN infrastructure, the network can achieve end-to-end QoS for the voice traffic both over the air and across the wired network.

Call Admission Control

The Cisco UWN supports CAC to police the call capacity on a per-AP basis. The number of calls on a channel can be limited to a percent of the bandwidth; the remaining bandwidth can be used for data.

The Cisco Unified Communications Manager provides additional CAC features for the wired network, ensuring an end-to-end CAC implementation. Cisco requires the use of Cisco Compatible clients to enable the use of the traffic specification (TSpec) of the traffic flows for the calculation of call limits and proper WLAN load balancing. The TSpec of each voice flow allows the system to allocate bandwidth to client devices on a first-come, first-served basis and maintains a small reserve so that mobile phone clients can roam into a neighboring AP (even though the AP could otherwise be at "full capacity"). When the limit for voice bandwidth is reached, the next call is load balanced to a neighboring AP and the call is completed without affecting the quality of the existing calls on the channel.

Note: Earlier names for the Cisco Unified Communications Manager include Cisco CallManager and Cisco Unified CallManager.

Figure 11-12   *End-to-End QoS for VoWLAN Can Be Supported*

With CAC enabled and CCX devices, the Cisco UWN allows the resources to be globally managed by Cisco WLCs across all the adjacent APs. Therefore, APs will not admit the same amount of voice traffic as they could if they were operating in isolation. The number of voice calls on an RF channel is limited to a percentage of the channel bandwidth. A percentage of the bandwidth is reserved to support roaming, and the rest of the bandwidth can be made available for data. APs use measurements from clients and neighboring APs to help determine the amount of traffic on the RF channel and whether a new call should be admitted.

Security

The strict requirements for voice in terms of packet delivery time and predictability, coupled with the ability for clients to roam across APs and subnets (VLANs), presents a challenge to security architectures.

VoWLAN Authentication and Encryption Recommendations

To minimize the delay introduced by authenticating roaming clients, Cisco recommends using EAP-FAST with CCKM.

EAP-FAST is an IEEE 802.1X EAP framework for authentication that encrypts EAP transactions with a Transport Layer Security (TLS) tunnel. The EAP-FAST tunnel is established based upon strong secrets (keys) that are unique to clients. Cisco Unified Wireless IP Phone 7920 clients with firmware release 3.0 or later support EAP-FAST. All Unified Wireless IP Phone 7921G clients support EAP-FAST.

As discussed in the earlier "Roaming" section, CCKM reduces the authentication delay. The alternative is to use an AAA RADIUS server for authentication. With that method, the roaming reauthentication time to the RADIUS server can be 500 ms or more. Cisco recommends using CCKM to achieve AP-to-AP roaming latency of less than 100 ms, allowing the end-to-end latency to be less than 150 ms. CCKM permits the negotiation of a session key from a cached master key and avoids the need to go back to the RADIUS server during a roam. When the client roams, it informs the infrastructure that it has roamed, and the infrastructure forwards the keying information to the new AP.

The efficiency of EAP-FAST with CCKM helps ensure maximum protection with minimum transaction time. CCKM is available with the Unified Wireless IP Phone 7920 and 7921G clients, and any client that is compliant with CCX Version 4.

To ensure that voice traffic is secure, Cisco recommends using TKIP for encryption and using message integrity check (MIC) to ensure that encrypted packets are not being altered. TKIP encrypts both the signaling (Skinny Client Control Protocol [SCCP]) packets and voice (Real-Time Transport Protocol [RTP]) packets between the AP and the wireless IP phone and provides per-packet key ciphering and longer initialization vectors to strengthen encryption. TKIP removes the predictability of the older Wired Equivalent Privacy (WEP) protocol that allows intruders to easily decipher the WEP key.

Other Design Recommendations for VoWLAN Security

For secure voice calls, Cisco recommends creating both separate VLANs and SSIDs for voice. Associating the voice SSID with the voice VLAN creates a single, unified voice network across both the wired and wireless networks with consistent security and QoS profiles; the WLCs bridge the traffic from the voice SSIDs to the voice VLANs. The primary advantage of this physical separation of voice and data traffic is that traffic sent over the voice network is not visible to insiders or outsiders connected to the data network. The converse is also true.

Following are some of the ways that a separate voice VLAN protects the voice system from security threats:

- **Denial-of-service (DoS) attacks:** Most DoS attacks originate from a PC; PCs cannot affect IP phones and call-processing servers connected to a separate voice VLAN.

- **Eavesdropping and interception:** Hackers typically eavesdrop on conversations using a PC with special software to connect to the same VLAN as one or more parties in the conversation. If voice participants are logically separated in different VLANs, however, a hacker cannot connect to the voice VLAN with a PC.

- **Unauthorized access:** Enterprises can apply access control policies to voice VLANs, and authorize employees by their role in the organization to access these VLANs. For example, manufacturing employees may be restricted to accessing only the data segment and not be allowed to access the voice segment.

Note: In addition to these voice-specific guidelines, Cisco has published best practices for general wireless security. The paper *Five Steps to Securing Your Wireless LAN and Preventing Wireless Threats* discusses best practices for securing the network from unauthorized use through a WLAN link. These practices should be validated against the risk-management processes of each organization and complemented by a strong security implementation.

This paper is available at available at http://www.cisco.com/en/US/netsol/ns340/ns394/ns348/ns386/networking_solutions_white_paper0900aecd8042e23b.shtml.

Intelligent VoWLAN Clients

To use the voice-ready Cisco infrastructure for enterprise roaming, management, and security features, Cisco recommends the voice clients be either a Unified Wireless IP Phone 7920 or 7921G device or a voice-capable device that supports the advanced voice features through the CCX program.

Note: The CCX program is described earlier in this chapter, in the "Cisco-Compatible WLAN Clients" section.

Cisco Unified Wireless IP Phone 7921G

The Unified Wireless IP Phone 7921G, shown in Figure 11-13, is a second-generation Cisco wireless IP phone that supports dual-band 802.11a/b/g radios, and has a speakerphone and a high-resolution color display. It has dedicated volume and mute buttons, and an application button that supports push-to-talk via the Extensible Markup Language (XML). The phone is also compliant with CCX Version 4.

The 7921G supports a comprehensive list of enterprise wireless security features including EAP-FAST, TKIP, MIC, and CCKM.

Two types of batteries are available for the phone. The standard lithium-ion (Li-ion) battery provides up to 10 hours of talk time or 80 hours of standby. The extended Li-ion battery provides up to 12 hours of talk time or 100 hours of standby. The actual battery life varies based on environmental factors and the display timeout option selected.

The 7921G supports voice-quality enhancements including 802.11e, TSpec, Enhanced Distributed Channel Access (EDCA), and QoS Basic Service Set (QBSS). Because the Unified Wireless IP Phone 7921G is designed to grow with system capabilities, features will keep pace with new system enhancements.

Figure 11-13   *The Cisco Unified Wireless IP Phone 7921G*

VoWLAN Coverage Considerations

Voice clients are mobile in nature. Users expect that calls will not get dropped as they roam across a building or campus. This expectation means that the network must be deployed pervasively, with continuous coverage in areas where voice services are planned. Areas such as main lobbies; employee entrance areas; parking garages or lots; courtyards; and break, copy, supply, storage, and equipment cage rooms will need WLAN coverage when voice clients are deployed on the campus. Additional consideration should be given to providing coverage in stairwells, walkways, and elevators because users have a reasonable expectation of being able to talk on the phone in these areas. Coverage expectations have been established by the cellular network service available. Therefore, WLAN availability and coverage should be significantly more pervasive than the cellular benchmark.

The Cisco UWN provides an extensive product line that satisfies the requirements for pervasive coverage areas, ranging from just one floor of a building to complete campus coverage, for both indoors and outdoors.

A predictable service is also important. Users expect that Wi-Fi phones will, at a minimum, operate with the same quality as a cellular phone and, optimally, with the same quality as a land-line phone. This means that the WLAN will have to minimize interference to optimize call quality. Although many network administrators have already performed RF site surveys for their initial data WLAN deployments, wireless IP phones have somewhat different roaming characteristics and RF coverage requirements than data devices. Therefore, network administrators must perform another site survey for voice to prepare for the performance requirements of wireless IP phones. This additional survey gives network administrators the opportunity to tune the APs to ensure that the wireless IP phones have enough RF coverage and bandwidth to provide proper voice quality. Some of the factors to look at in the survey include signal-to-noise ratio (SNR) and nonoverlapping channel deployment, as described in the following sections.

SNR

Noise is defined as a signal that is not in an IEEE 802.11 format but is in the frequency range of the configured channel for the AP. The noise can originate from devices such as an 802.11 2.4-GHz frequency-hopping radio, a 2.4-GHz or 5-GHz wireless phone, a ham radio, a microwave oven, or a Bluetooth radio. Signals from a distant out-of-network 802.11b/g or 802.11a radio may also be seen as noise. In other words, any signal that the AP cannot decode is considered noise. Noise levels vary from site to site and also within different locations of a site. The noise level affects the ability of a radio to receive data or voice packets.

The SNR is just the ratio of the signal level to the noise level. As illustrated in Figure 11-14, because noise levels vary, increasing the signal does not always increase SNR.

Figure 11-14   *Increasing the Signal Does Not Always Increase SNR*

If the signal strength of a valid packet is higher than the AP or client radio receiver threshold, the data packet is decoded. The received signal sensitivity value is measured in dBm. Most 802.11 radios have a receiver sensitivity value of −94 to −85 dBm at a data rate of 1

Mbps (the lower the dBm value, the better the receiver sensitivity of the radio). Radio receiver sensitivity changes with data rate; for example, an AP radio might have a receiver sensitivity of –94 dBm at 1 Mbps and –84 dBm at 11 Mbps.

The AP discards random traffic, such as valid packets that can be decoded but that are not from clients associated to the AP. Random traffic can originate from shared media or from a client device that is transmitting at a data rate that the AP does not support.

A high data-rate signal needs a larger separation from noise—a larger SNR—than a lower data-rate signal. VoWLANs require higher signal strength and SNR compared to data-only WLANs. Figure 11-15 shows recommended SNR values for both data-only cells and VoWLAN cells, for 2.4-GHz WLANs.

Data Rate (Mbps)	Data Cell		VoWLAN Cell	
	Minimum Signal Strength (dBm)	Minimum SNR (dB)	Minimum Signal Strength (dBm)	Minimum SNR (dB)
54	–71	25	–56	40
36	–73	18	–58	33
24	–77	12	–62	27
11	–82	10	–67	25
6	–89	8	–74	23
2	–91	6	–76	21
1	–94	4	–79	19

Figure 11-15   *Recommended SNR Values for 2.4-GHz WLAN Cells*

When designing a VoWLAN deployment, the goal is to target a minimum data rate such as 11 Mbps to improve data throughput, reduce packet delay, and reduce the size of the RF cell. As shown in Figure 11-15, the recommended minimum signal strength of –67 dBm and minimum SNR of 25 dB will support a data rate of 11 Mbps.

Figure 11-16 shows an example of the signal strength, noise level, and SNR at a specific location within a wireless cell as measured by the Cisco Aironet Desktop Utility (ADU) and a Cisco Aironet IEEE 802.11a/b/g Wireless LAN Client Adapter. The signal strength is –74 dBm, the noise level is –95 dBm, and the SNR is 21 dB. The signal strength value of –74 dBm minus the noise value of –95 dBm equals an SNR of 21 dB as reported by the Cisco ADU.

Because the noise level reported by the Cisco ADU is –95 dBm and the Aironet IEEE 802.11a/b/g Wireless LAN Client Adapter sensitivity at 11 Mbps is –90 dBm, there is a margin of 5 dB at the receiver. The higher the SNR value, the better able the phones are to communicate with the AP.

Figure 11-16   *Example SNR Display from Cisco Aironet Site Survey Utility*

Nonoverlapping Channels

Because the wireless medium is continuous and shared, all clients that are associated with APs on the same channel share the bandwidth available in that channel, with reception power (and therefore data rates) diminishing with distance.

As mentioned, valid data packets from 802.11b, 802.11g, or 802.11a radios that are not associated to an AP are considered random data traffic. Those packets are decoded by the AP and client devices but are discarded, and therefore increase the channel utilization on the AP and limit the number of voice clients that can associate with the AP. If there are numerous clients in an area, or the supported data applications require significant bandwidth, capacity should be added to the network by using more APs on nonoverlapping channels, to minimize interference.

802.11b/g Channels

As described in the earlier "IEEE 802.11b/g Standards in the 2.4-GHz Band" section, there are 14 channels defined for 802.11b/g. Each channel is 22-MHz wide, but the channel separation is only 5 MHz. This leads to channel overlap, and signals from neighboring channels can interfere with each other. In the United States, 11 channels are usable, but only 3 nonoverlapping channels 25 MHz apart are possible: channels 1, 6, and 11. In Europe and Japan, more channels are available, and therefore different nonoverlapping channels can be used (such as 2, 7, and 12, or 1, 7, and 13).

This channel spacing governs the use and allocation of channels in a multi-AP environment, such as an office or campus. As shown earlier, APs are usually deployed in a cellular fashion within an enterprise, with adjacent APs allocated nonoverlapping channels. Alternatively, APs can be collocated using channels 1, 6, and 11; this would for example deliver

33-Mbps bandwidth to a single 802.11b area but only 11 Mbps to a single 802.11b client. A critical issue for voice services is minimizing the co-channel interference (when clients and APs in the same channel interfere with each other) and maximizing coverage and capacity.

Cell Overlap Guidelines

When communicating on one channel, wireless endpoints typically are unaware of traffic and communication occurring on other nonoverlapping channels.

AP coverage should be deployed so that minimal or no overlap occurs between APs configured with the same channel. However, proper AP deployment requires an overlap of 15 percent to 20 percent with adjoining cells (that are on nonoverlapping channels) to ensure smooth roaming for wireless voice endpoints as they move between APs and provide a near-complete redundancy. Overlap of less than 15 percent to 20 percent can result in slower roaming times and poor voice quality, and overlap of more than 15 percent to 20 percent can result in too frequent or constant roaming.

The size of a voice-ready cell is not defined in traditional measurements such as feet or meters; instead, the unit of measurement is the strength or absolute power of the signal. For an ideal voice-ready wireless cell size, the radius or size of each cell should be −67 dBm. This power level can be achieved either in very small physical areas or in cells that are quite large, depending on the RF characteristics of the environment. Separation of 19 dBm for cells on the same channel is recommended. Figure 11-17 shows the recommended cell characteristics for a typical 802.11b/g voice deployment.

In a pervasive network, maintaining this policy of nonoverlapping channels requires careful planning to ensure that the network is prepared to support voice services. In general, for office and cubical environments, a convenient guideline to use is that a single cell covers approximately 3000 square feet.

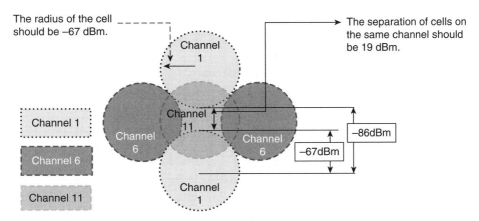

Figure 11-17   *802.11b/g Cell Overlap Guidelines*

Deploying wireless devices in a multistory building such as an office high-rise or hospital introduces a third dimension to AP and channel reuse planning. As illustrated in Figure 11-18, the 802.11b/g 2.4 GHz wave form can pass through floors, ceilings, and walls. For this reason, not only is it important to consider overlapping cells or channels on the same floor, but it is also necessary to consider channel overlap between adjacent floors. With only three channels, proper overlap can be achieved only through careful three-dimensional planning.

The RF coverage is mostly dependant on the AP transmitter power and antenna type, and its associated gain and directional beam characteristics. The example in Figure 11-18 results from omnidirectional antennas.

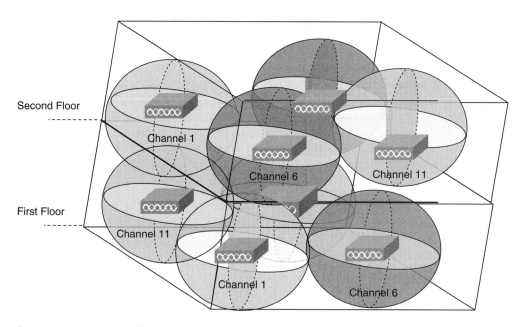

Figure 11-18   *802.11b/g Multistory Building Deployments Must Consider Channel Overlap Between Floors*

802.11a Channels

The majority of enterprises have implemented 802.11b and 802.11g for VoWLAN deployment because of their compatibility and the near ubiquity of those standards in various client devices. More recent deployments are using 802.11a because it can support 12 nonoverlapping channels, significantly more than the 3 nonoverlapping channels that 801.11b/g deployments support. These 12 nonoverlapping channels are described in the earlier "IEEE 802.11a Standard in the 5-GHz Band" section.

An 802.11a WLAN design should provide as much channel separation as possible. Recall that the recommendation is that neighboring cells *not* be placed on neighboring channels (in other words, neighboring channels are skipped) to reduce interference.

As discussed in the earlier "End-to-End QoS" section, separate VLANs for voice and data are recommended, as is keeping the voice and data on separate wireless frequencies if possible. There are notable advantages of deploying 802.11a for voice and 802.11b/g for data, including the following:

■ A significantly greater number of channels are available for higher density deployments. With more channels and a higher approximate throughput, 802.11a AP radios can support up to 14 simultaneous calls.

■ The 5-GHz spectrum does not suffer from as much interference from devices such as cordless phones and Bluetooth devices.

■ Because the range on the higher frequency radios is generally shorter, the signals will not travel through walls and floors as much as the lower frequency signals do, helping prevent floor-to-floor bleed-through of the signal.

General Recommendations for VoWLANs

This section discusses general recommendations in VoWLAN designs. A site survey is needed to measure these values; site surveys are discussed in the later "VoWLAN Site Surveys" section.

The first step in developing a VoWLAN design is to define and document the coverage areas that will be established and the number of phones to be used in the areas. The design scope should be developed with the target user community so that the appropriate network infrastructure is deployed. The number of phones that will be used in a given area helps determine the transmit power of the clients and AP. The transmit power can be decreased to create smaller coverage cells, which increases the number of APs required and the number of calls supported in a given floor space. 802.11a APs can support more calls than 802.11b and 802.11g APs.

Cisco recommends that a minimum design should use two APs on nonoverlapping channels with 15 percent to 20 percent RF coverage overlap at every location.

The Received Signal Strength Indicator (RSSI) will vary with the supported data rate, as follows:

■ For data rates of 11 Mbps, the RSSI should be greater than −67 dBm. An AP data-rate configuration of 11 Mbps minimum for VoWLAN cells is recommended.

■ For data rates of 54 Mbps, the RSSI should be greater than −56 dBm.

The channel utilization QBSS load per AP should be less than 45 percent. The QBSS load represents the percentage of time that the channel is in use by the AP. This channel utilization provides for smoother roaming and a backup AP if one of the APs suddenly becomes unavailable or busy.

The network should maintain a packet error rate (PER) of no higher than 1 percent (which means a success rate of 99 percent). TCP performance and VoIP calls can suffer substantially when the PER increases beyond a value of about 1 percent.

The same transmit power should be used on the AP and on the IP phones so that communication is the same in both directions. If the transmit power of the APs varies, set the transmit power of the phones to the highest transmit power of the APs. If enabled on the AP and supported by the WLAN device, Dynamic Transmit Power Control (DTPC) allows the AP to broadcast its transmit power so that clients can automatically configure themselves to that power while associated with that AP.

All APs should use antenna diversity to provide the best possible throughput by reducing the number of packets that are missed or retried; this is particularly important for voice. With antenna diversity, the AP samples the radio signal from two integrated antenna ports and chooses the preferred antenna. As noted earlier, antenna diversity helps reduce multipath distortion. Some WLAN phones, such as the Cisco Unified Wireless IP Phone 7921G, support antenna diversity.

The maximum number of phones supported per AP depends on the calling patterns of individual users and the AP type. Currently, the recommended call loading for 802.11b and 802.11g is seven active voice calls per AP using the G.711 voice encoding codec or eight active calls using the G.729 codec. These numbers are based on simultaneous requirements for data clients and quality voice calls with current data rates and packet sizes. Beyond the recommended number of active calls, the voice quality of all calls becomes unacceptable if excessive background data is present. In comparison, 802.11a AP radios can support 14 active voice calls using the G.711 codec.

Note: A *codec* is a device or software that encodes (and decodes) a signal into digital data stream. The G.711 codec uses the 64-kbps pulse code modulation (PCM) voice coding technique for standard uncompressed voice. The G.729 codec enables voice to be compressed into 8-kbps streams, with very good speech quality.

Channel and modulation type determine the number of concurrent calls. If more concurrent phone calls are needed in a high-usage area, more APs must be available. Using overlapping cells—APs sharing the same RF channel—reduces the number of concurrent phone calls per AP.

VoWLAN Site Surveys

An RF site survey is the first step in the design and deployment of a wireless network and is very important to ensure desired operation. When building a network designed to support voice services, the site survey and implementation steps are even more important because of the more stringent network and coverage requirements of VoIP. The goal of any site survey should be to gain a total view of the characteristics of the RF environment into which the wireless network will be deployed. Unlicensed frequencies (especially 2.4 GHz, but also 5 GHz,) can be "noisy" environments, with microwave ovens, radar systems, and Bluetooth devices vying for air time. With the advent of emerging RF technologies such as sensor networks, this trend is expected to continue.

Site Survey Process

Typical steps in an RF site survey include the following:

Step 1. Define customer requirements including the devices to support, the locations of wireless devices, and the service levels expected. Peak requirements such as support for conference rooms should also be defined.

Step 2. Based on the customer requirements, identify planned wireless coverage areas and user density. Obtain a facility diagram to identify the potential RF obstacles. Visually inspect the facility to look for potential barriers to the propagation of RF signals, such as metal racks, elevator shafts, and stairwells. Identify user areas that may be used by many people simultaneously, such as conference rooms, and areas that may only be used for voice, such as stairwells.

Step 3. Determine preliminary AP locations. These locations must include power and wired network access, and must consider cell coverage and overlap, channel selection, antenna, and mounting locations.

Step 4. Perform the actual RF site survey to verify the AP locations. Make sure to use the same AP model for the survey that is in use or that will be used in production. While the survey is being performed, relocate APs as needed and retest.

Step 5. Document the findings, including recording the AP locations and log signal readings and the data rates at outer boundaries.

The site survey should identify areas within the deployment that may require additional capacity because of a concentration of users or the likelihood of co-channel interference.

The site survey should be conducted using the same frequencies as intended for the actual deployment. This provides a more accurate estimate of how a particular channel at a particular location will react to interference and multipath distortion. The site survey should also use the voice client that will be deployed. Each client has a unique RF performance, so different clients will yield different results. The same is true for the radios and external or internal antennas in the infrastructure. In summary, AP and client selection should be finalized before the site survey. As new client devices are added, periodically updating the site survey proactively ensures that the RF network is optimized.

It is also advisable to conduct several site surveys, varying the times and days to ensure that a comprehensive view of the RF domain is obtained. RF activity can vary and depends on many factors, including employee activity. The site survey should identify sources of RF interference and variability in RF patterns due to physical building changes (for example, movement of machinery, and elevators moving in elevator shafts) and employee movements (for example, weekly staff meetings in a conference room).

Spectrum Analysis Tool

The site survey should provide an accurate view of any other RF activity that is present, to help mitigate potential sources of interference. A spectrum analysis tool such as Cognio Spectrum Expert can provide analysis to classify the interference, determine the impact of the interference on the Wi-Fi network, and enable the administrator to physically locate the source of interference, so that appropriate action can be taken. Example output from this tool is provided in Figure 11-19.

Figure 11-19 *Example Cognio Spectrum Expert Report Regarding 802.11 and Non-802.11 Devices*

WCS Planning Tool

The Cisco UWN integrates Radio Resource Management (RRM) software, which works with the integrated network planning and design features in the Cisco WCS.

Cisco WCS provides integrated RF prediction tools that can be used to create a detailed WLAN design, including AP placement, configuration, and performance or coverage estimates. IT staff can import real floor plans into Cisco WCS and assign RF characteristics to building components to increase the accuracy of the design. The resulting map can help provide a starting point for the location of APs during the site survey and initial estimates on the quantity of APs; an example is provided in Figure 11-20. During the final site survey, the actual number and location of APs and associated antennas should be adjusted.

The WCS deployment planning tool is ideal for general open space office environments. For challenging RF environments, such as those found in hospitals and manufacturing plants, Cisco recommends specialized survey services. In addition, for manual verification of the wireless network, the Cisco Unified Wireless IP Phone 7920 and the Wireless IP Phone 7921G integrate site survey tools that can display a list of APs that are within range. These tools are useful for validating and troubleshooting specific problem areas.

Figure 11-20 *Preliminary AP Locations Can Be Predicted Based on the Floor Plan*

AP Locations

The location of the APs is the most important characteristic of a voice-ready network.

Traditional Large Cell Deployment

The traditional method of AP deployments recommends deploying APs for greatest range to support data, as illustrated in Figure 11-21. However, this approach limits the number of voice calls that can be supported or the data bandwidth per user. Another issue with large cell coverage areas is the lower data rate on VoWLAN clients when users reach the outer edge of a cell. Even though the VoWLAN traffic might have been designed for high data rates, the actual call will receive far less throughput because of the weaker signal, causing a down shift in data rate. An increased cell coverage area also increases the chance of RF interference between the APs and their associated clients.

Small Cell Deployment for VoWLANs

The voice-services-ready approach to WLANs recommends deploying smaller cell sizes with as many APs as possible to cover a given area without creating excessive interference. An example deployment is illustrated in Figure 11-22.

Smaller, overlapping cells increase average capacity and provide higher availability in the event of an AP failure. The cell size is estimated based on the requirements for VoWLAN phone call capacities. In dense deployments with many APs, the transmit power of each AP is lowered to limit co-channel interference with neighboring APs. The design should specify the antennas needed and the transmit power required for each of the APs within the site.

Figure 11-21   *Traditional Larger Cells Support Fewer Calls*

Note: It is a good idea to keep the transmit power of the AP and the phone at the same level to avoid one-way audio occurrences, which are a result of a mismatch in the reach of the signal.

As a guideline and starting point for site surveys in a voice-ready WLAN, APs should be deployed approximately every 3000 square feet, versus the recommended AP every 5000 square feet for data-only networks. This AP density helps ensure that voice services have the necessary RF coverage redundancy and throughput required to provide optimal service capacity. The site survey should be conducted to maximize coverage and minimize interference.

Alternative Cell Deployment

An alternative deployment model, shown in Figure 11-23, has APs with directional antennas placed around the perimeter of the floor, and APs with omnidirectional antennas staggered in the center of the floor for more complete coverage and greater redundancy, facilitating location tracking and VoWLAN deployment.

Figure 11-22 *Smaller Cells Support More Calls*

This deployment design requires specific placement of APs during the site survey. As a goal, a device at each location on the floor should be able to associate with at least three APs.

This alternative AP deployment facilitates location tracking when combined with the Cisco Wireless Location Appliance along with Cisco WCS for visual maps and reports. The Cisco Wireless Location Appliance performs location computations based on the RSSI information received from the Cisco WLCs. After site floor plans and APs are added to the appliance, RF predictions and heat maps can be generated to graphically display the location of devices on site floor plans. Cisco WCS displays the location information visually, providing an immediate location service for customers who want to enhance their RF capacity management, utilize location-based security, and have asset visibility for WLAN devices.

Conducting a Site Survey

After the requirements are defined, the coverage areas are identified, and the preliminary VoWLAN AP locations are defined, the next step is to conduct the actual RF survey.

When surveying with an existing WLAN or VoWLAN, you should expect that there will be areas to be filled in and changes to be made to existing data rate and transmit power settings, and possibly to the antenna types.

Note: Uses directional antennas at wall. RF extending outside walls is not shown.

Figure 11-23   *Alternative Design Includes Perimeter APs with Directional Antennas and Center APs with Omnidirectional Antennas*

At a multifloor site, the coverage survey should also include measurements on the floor above and below the current floor. When doing a manual survey, record the cell edges of the current floor, and then use your survey tool on other floors to measure and record the signal levels. When doing an automated survey, be sure to include the AP on the floors above and below.

When surveying a site without an existing 802.11 network, plan to use two or three APs to measure cell coverage and cell overlap. For example, the cell edge for the Cisco Unified Wireless IP Phone 7920 at an 11-Mbps data rate is –67 dBm. The signal strength at the edge of the cell needs to be 19 dB stronger than the signal from the next cell on the same channel. That means at the –67 dBm edge of the cell, the next cell on the same channel should measure –86 dBm.

Site Survey Documentation

After completing the RF survey, document the plan for the VoWLAN infrastructure.

The survey documentation should include the following information:

■   Antenna placement and type information for final implementation.

■   Coverage patterns and heat maps for baseline data.

- Coverage verification information based on at least a two-voice conversation walk-around of all areas. The test should be conducted with known interference sources operational. Document the call results from an analytical tool if available.

- Coverage area call-capacity test results, for baseline data. For example, you could have seven users make phone calls in a given area and then move apart while placing new calls. Voice quality should be verified during this process.

After conducting an RF site survey and configuring the APs and the phones, it is crucial to conduct verification tests to ensure that everything works as desired. These tests should be performed throughout the VoWLAN coverage area at various times during the day. Tests may include verifying phone association with the appropriate AP and verifying that calls can be placed successfully from the VoWLAN IP phone with acceptable voice quality.

VoWLAN Steps to Success Partner Program

VoWLAN coverage and capacity can vary by deployment because of factors such as physical AP placement, building materials, antenna selection, and the type of clients used. In addition, environmental factors such as microwave ovens and cordless phones can also cause interference that may impact VoWLAN performance.

VoWLAN deployments are supported by the Cisco partner Steps to Success program. Cisco partners need both the Cisco Advanced Unified Communications and Advanced Wireless LAN specializations to be authorized to resell Cisco VoWLAN phones. The Steps to Success program provides important templates and tools to assist partners in the proper planning and implementation of WLAN and VoWLAN installations. The following documents are among those accessible with Cisco partner login at the Partner Central Steps to Success home page (at http://www.cisco.com/go/stepstosuccess):

- **Cisco VoWLAN Site Survey Deliverable:** This document provides a template to ensure the proper recording of the survey results of the Cisco VoWLAN site survey. It provides a checklist of all items that need to be considered before a network implementation.

- **VoWLAN Configuration Checklist:** This document provides instructions to help partners apply pertinent configuration information regarding a VoWLAN solution.

- **VoWLAN Design Checklist:** This document provides a checklist template to help partners apply pertinent design information regarding a VoWLAN solution.

- **Voice over Wireless LAN High-Level Design for the Cisco VoWLAN Phone:** This document provides required specifications for availability, capacity, and security that will meet the defined service requirements.

These documents help minimize the chance of an improperly or insufficiently designed VoWLAN. As part of the program, the assessment-to-quality VoWLAN team reviews each order to ensure that the proposed solution and partner meet the published and current Cisco VoWLAN standards. The team may also help identify potential problem areas and suggest solutions as appropriate.

Summary

In this chapter, you learned about the Cisco UWN, and the requirements, infrastructure considerations, and coverage considerations for enterprise VoWLAN deployments.

WLAN signals are in the range of −60 dBm to −80 dBm and are transmitted using antennas. Omnidirectional antennas, with radiant energy shaped like a doughnut, are the most widely used today.

The IEEE 802.11a, b, and g WLAN standards are half-duplex connections, using the CSMA/CA algorithm. 802.11a operates at 5 GHz with a maximum speed of 54 Mbps; 802.11b operates at 2.4 GHz with a maximum speed of 11 Mbps; 802.11g operates at 2.4 GHz with a maximum speed of 54 Mbps. 802.11e adds QoS to WLANs.

In North America, the 2.4 GHz band has three nonoverlapping channels: channels 1, 6, and 11. Adjacent cells should use nonoverlapping channels.

802.11a has 12 nonoverlapping channels. The recommendation for 802.11a is that neighboring cells not be placed on neighboring channels (in other words, neighboring channels are skipped) to reduce interference.

A computer with a wireless NIC and other wireless devices, such as VoWLAN phones, connect to the wired LAN through an AP. CCX-compliant clients are compatible with Cisco APs. Cisco APs can be either autonomous or lightweight.

An autonomous AP has a local configuration and requires local management.

A lightweight AP receives control and configuration from a WLC to which it is associated. The WLCs and lightweight APs communicate over a wired network using the LWAPP. The WLCs are responsible for putting the wireless client traffic into the appropriate VLAN.

The Cisco UWN elements are CCX WLAN clients, lightweight APs, network unification, network management, and mobility services.

VoWLAN deployment requires a network with continuous coverage, an end-to-end transmit time of less than 150 ms, and QoS to reduce delay and jitter. The Cisco voice-ready architecture includes VoWLAN clients, a voice-ready WLAN, a unified wired or wireless LAN infrastructure, and Cisco Unified Communications and mobility applications.

Voice implications for WLANs include the following:

- RF coverage requirements and deployment planning

- Network infrastructure and logical subnet design, including roaming, QoS, security, and the use of intelligent clients

- Wireless "over-the-air" QoS

- Network security architecture

- VoWLAN client requirements

An SSID is the identifier—or name—of an ESA, creating a WLAN. *Roaming* occurs when a wireless client moves from being associated to one AP to another AP within the same SSID.

Intracontroller roaming is roaming between APs joined to the *same* WLC. The WLC just updates the client database with the new associated AP.

Intercontroller roaming occurs when a client roams from an AP joined to one WLC to an AP joined to a different WLC. The WLCs must be in the same mobility group. Layer 2 intercontroller roaming occurs when the client traffic is bridged to the same IP subnet. The client database entry is *moved* to the new WLC. Layer 3 intercontroller roaming occurs when the client associates to an AP on a different WLC and the traffic is bridged to a different IP subnet. The original WLC marks the entry for the client in its own client database with an Anchor entry, and *copies* the database entry to the new WLC's client database, where it is marked with a Foreign entry.

The Cisco UWN supports CAC to police the call capacity on a per-AP basis.

Recommendations for VoWLAN deployment include the following:

- Using the EAP-FAST with CCKM for authentication.

- Using TKIP for encryption and using MIC to ensure that encrypted packets are not being altered.

- Using separate voice and data VLANs and keeping the voice and data on separate wireless frequencies if possible. For secure voice calls, Cisco recommends creating both separate VLANs and SSIDs for voice.

- An overlap of 15 percent to 20 percent between adjoining cells (that are on nonoverlapping channels).

- A cell radius of −67 dBm, with a separation of 19 dBm for cells on the same channel.

- A channel utilization QBSS load per AP of less than 45 percent.

- A PER of no higher than 1 percent on the network.

- Using the same transmit power on the AP and the IP phones.

- Using antenna diversity on all APs.

- Having a maximum of 7 active voice calls per AP using the G.711 voice encoding codec or 8 active calls using the G.729 codec for 802.11b/g, and having a maximum of 14 active voice calls using the G.711 codec for 802.11a.

Typical steps in an RF site survey process include the following:

Step 1. Define customer requirements.

Step 2. Identify coverage areas and user density.

Step 3. Determine preliminary AP locations.

Step 4. Perform the actual RF site survey.

Step 5. Document the findings.

A possible deployment model for VoWLANs has APs with directional antennas placed around the perimeter of a floor, and APs with omnidirectional antennas staggered in the center of the floor.

The Cisco partner Steps to Success program provides templates and tools to assist partners in the proper planning and implementation of WLAN and VoWLAN installations.

References

For additional information, refer to the following:

- Cisco Systems, Inc., Cisco UWN home page, at http://www.cisco.com/go/unifiedwireless/

- Cisco Systems, Inc. "Design Principles for Voice Over WLAN," at http://www.cisco.com/en/US/solutions/collateral/ns340/ns394/ns348/net_implementation_white_paper0900aecd804f1a46.html

- Cisco Systems, Inc. "Cisco Unified Wireless IP Phone 7920 Design and Deployment Guide," at http://www.cisco.com/en/US/docs/voice_ip_comm/cuipph/7920/5_0/english/design/guide/7920ddg.html

- Cisco Systems, Inc. "Five Steps to Securing Your Wireless LAN and Preventing Wireless Threats," at http://www.cisco.com/en/US/netsol/ns340/ns394/ns348/ns386/networking_solutions_white_paper0900aecd8042e23b.shtml

- Cisco Systems, Inc. Cisco Compatible Extensions program website, at http://www.cisco.com/web/partners/pr46/pr147/partners_pgm_concept_home.html

- Cisco Systems, Inc., "Cisco Compatible Client Devices," at http://www.cisco.com/web/partners/pr46/pr147/partners_pgm_partners_0900aecd800a7907.html

- Cisco Systems, Inc. Cisco Wireless Control System home page, at http://www.cisco.com/en/US/products/ps6305/index.html

Review Questions

Answer the following questions, and then refer to Appendix A, "Answers to Review Questions," for the answers.

1. Select the device through which a client with a wireless NIC connects to the wired network.

   a.   WLC

   b.   AP

   c.   Switch

   d.   WCS

2. Match the standards with the frequency at which they operate.

   Standard:
   - 802.11a
   - 802.11b
   - 802.11g

Frequency:

- 2.4 GHz
- 2.4 GHz
- 5 GHz

3. Which of the following are the nonoverlapping 2.4-GHz channels used in North America?

   a. 1

   b. 2

   c. 4

   d. 5

   e. 6

   f. 10

   g. 11

   h. 12

4. What is the recommendation for reuse of 802.11a cells?

5. For a given area, select the true statement regarding the number of APs required by 802.11a versus 802.11b/g to provide the same coverage.

   a. 802.11a requires less APs on a per-area basis than 802.11b/g.

   b. 802.11a requires more APs on a per-area basis than 802.11b/g.

   c. 802.11a requires the same number of APs on a per-area basis as 802.11b/g.

6. What is the difference between an autonomous AP and a lightweight AP?

7. What is CCX?

8. What is an SSID?

9. Which of the following are elements of the Cisco UWN?

   a. client devices

   b. lightweight APs

   c. autonomous APs

   d. network management

   e. mobility services

10. In the Cisco UWN, which device is responsible for putting the wireless client traffic into the appropriate VLAN?

11. How is a WLC connected to an AP?

    a.   Via an 802.11a connection

    b.   Via an 802.11b/g connection

    c.   Via a wired connection

    d.   Via an IPsec tunnel

12. What are some of the advantages of VoWLAN deployments?

13. What are some of the requirements that voice adds to a WLAN deployment?

14. Name the four main components of the Cisco voice-ready architecture.

15. Select the true statements regarding roaming.

    a.   Roaming occurs when a wireless client re-associates to different AP, within the same SSID.

    b.   Roaming occurs when a wireless client re-associates to different AP, using a different SSID.

    c.   Intracontroller roaming is roaming between APs associated to different WLCs.

    d.   Intracontroller roaming is roaming between APs associated to the same WLC.

    e.   Intercontroller roaming is roaming between APs associated to different WLCs.

    f.   Intercontroller roaming is roaming between APs associated to the same WLC.

16. What does a WLC do with the client entries in its client database for Layer 3 and Layer 2 intercontroller roaming?

17. Which IEEE standard adds QoS features to WLANs?

    a.   802.11a

    b.   802.11d

    c.   802.11e

    d.   802.11i

    e.   802.11j

18. True or false: Separate voice and data VLANs are recommended when using WLANs.

19. What does CAC do?

20. Which protocols are recommended for authentication and encryption when using VoWLAN?

    a.   EAP-FAST with CCKM

    b.   AAA RADIUS

    c.   TKIP and MIC

    d.   WEP

21. What is the recommended signal strength and SNR for a 2.4-GHz WLAN at 11 Mbps?

    a. Signal strength 40 dB and SNR –56 dBm

    b. Signal strength –56 dBm and SNR 40 dB

    c. Signal strength –67 dBm and SNR 25 dB

    d. Signal strength 25 dB and SNR –67 dBm

    e. Signal strength –79 dBm and SNR 19 dB

    f. Signal strength 19 dB and SNR –79 dBm

22. What is the recommended cell overlap for VoWLAN deployments?

    a. 5 percent to 10 percent

    b. 10 percent to 15 percent

    c. 15 percent to 20 percent

    d. 20 percent to 25 percent

23. What is the recommended size of a voice-ready 802.11b/g wireless cell? What is the recommended separation for cells on the same channel?

24. Select the recommended maximum number of active voice calls per AP on an 802.11b/g WLAN.

    a. 3 per AP when using G.711

    b. 4 per AP when using G.729

    c. 7 per AP when using G.711

    d. 8 per AP when using G.729

    e. 10 per AP when using G.711

    f. 15 per AP when using G.729

25. List the five typical steps in an RF site survey process.

After completing this chapter, you will be able to

■   Identify the rationale for using embedded manage-
    ment functionality in network infrastructure devices

■   Discuss design considerations for NetFlow

■   Discuss design considerations for NBAR

■   Discuss design considerations for IP SLAs

CHAPTER 12

Network Management Capabilities Within Cisco IOS Software

The Cisco IOS Software includes embedded management functionality that enables network engineers to achieve efficient network performance, scalability, and availability. These management tools provide critical data for establishing baselines, capacity planning, and determining network bottlenecks. This chapter discusses the importance, requirements, and considerations for implementing the embedded Cisco IOS Software management tools in an enterprise design.

Cisco IOS Embedded Management Tools

Network management includes a broad range of policies, procedures, and purpose-built hardware and software tools used to manage networks. Network management affects the performance, reliability, and security of the entire network.

Network administrators use network management to verify that the network is working well and behaving in the planned manner. Network management is also used to characterize the performance of the network, to reveal how much traffic is flowing and where it is flowing in the network, and when troubleshooting a network.

Embedded management software subsystems in Cisco IOS Software help manage, monitor, and automate actions within a router or switch, enabling devices to automatically collect data and take action.

Network Management Support in Cisco IOS Software

Managed equipment provides a variety of information such as the equipment type deployed and how it is connected, the version of software it is running, its status, and so forth. Cisco IOS Software provides extensive management capabilities, including the following:

- A broad range of **show** commands provide network information for both in-band and out-of-band (OOB) management.

- Many Simple Network Management Protocol (SNMP) Management Information Bases (MIB) provide access to vast amounts of information.

- Device management applications such as the Cisco Router and Security Device Manager (SDM) and the Cisco Adaptive Security Device Manager (ASDM) provide web-based tools for managing single devices.

- The following embedded management software subsystems in Cisco IOS Software help manage, monitor, and automate network management:
  - Cisco IOS syslog
  - NetFlow
  - Network-Based Application Recognition (NBAR)
  - Cisco IOS IP service level agreements (IP SLAs)

Application Optimization and Cisco IOS Technologies

Traditional network management processes focus on managing WAN links because of their scarce bandwidth and susceptibility to issues, including the following:

- The expense of WAN connections, sometimes resulting in organizations implementing lower-speed, lower-cost links.

- Speed mismatches between LAN and WAN links, leading to congestion, packet loss, and degraded application performance.

- Different types of application traffic with different delivery requirements using the same WAN links. Real-time applications such as voice and video are especially sensitive to congestion and suffer from degraded performance due to delay, jitter, and packet loss. (Jitter is the variance of delay.)

However, there is increasing interest in extending network management to support application optimization at the data center and throughout the enterprise. The embedded Cisco IOS technologies provide network management support for application optimization in the network, as illustrated in Figure 12-1.

Figure 12-1   *Cisco IOS Technologies Support Application Optimization*

The phases in the application optimization cycle shown in Figure 12-1 are as follows:

- **Baseline application traffic:** In the first phase, a baseline is developed that measures network data so that the network manager can understand the basic traffic and application flows and the default network performance. Cisco IOS software technologies that support this phase include NetFlow, NBAR Protocol Discovery, and IP SLAs.

- **Optimize to meet objectives:** After establishing the baseline, the network manager can apply policies and prioritize traffic so that each application has an optimal portion of network resources. Resources are allocated based on their value to the organization. Quality of service (QoS) is used to reduce congestion, prioritize specific traffic, and optimize end-to-end performance of critical applications. Cisco IOS Software technologies that support this phase include QoS, NBAR, Cisco AutoQoS VoIP, and Cisco AutoQoS for the Enterprise.

Note: The Cisco AutoQoS features are described later in the "NBAR and Cisco AutoQoS" section of this chapter.

- **Measure, adjust, and verify:** In the third phase of the application optimization cycle, the network manager uses ongoing measurements and proactive adjustments to verify that the optimization techniques and QoS provide the network resources needed to meet the service objectives of the applications. This information is also used to resolve network issues that may occur. Several Cisco IOS Software features help measure network performance, including NetFlow, NBAR Protocol Discovery, IP SLAs, and syslog.

- **Deploy new applications:** In this phase, network engineers determine the service objectives for new applications, estimate the network resources that will be needed to support these objectives, and allocate resources for new applications. Network management tools and processes enable the network manager to have the confidence to deploy new applications based on an understanding of the existing applications. NBAR and NetFlow are common Cisco IOS technologies used to support this phase.

Figure 12-2 highlights where Cisco IOS technologies are commonly deployed in the enterprise environment. Syslog should be deployed on every device; NetFlow, NBAR, and IP SLAs monitoring are deployed at selected locations in the network.

A recommended practice is to use a predefined template to structure network management configuration and reporting information.

The remainder of this chapter details the four Cisco IOS embedded network management features: syslog, NetFlow, NBAR, and IP SLAs.

Syslog

The Cisco IOS system message logging (syslog) process enables a device to report and save important error and notification messages; the messages can be saved either locally or to a remote logging server. Syslog messages can be sent to local console connections, terminal monitor connections (vty and tty), the system buffer, or to remote syslog servers, as illustrated in Figure 12-3. Syslog sends text messages to a syslog server using UDP port 514.

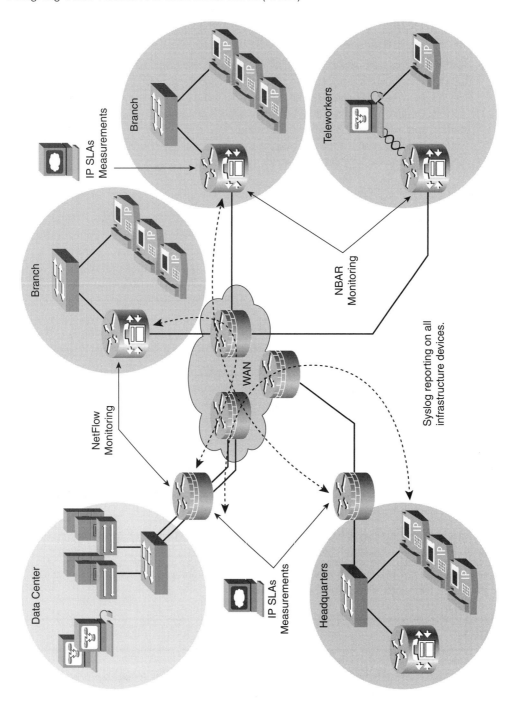

Figure 12-2   *Using Cisco IOS Technologies in the Enterprise*

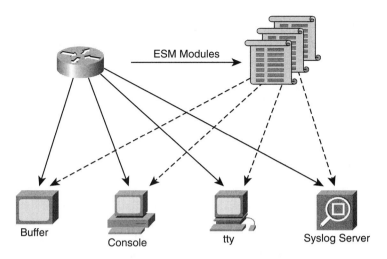

Figure 12-3 *Syslog Messages Can Be Sent to Many Destinations*

Syslog provides a comprehensive reporting mechanism that logs system messages in plain English text. The syslog messages include both messages in a standardized format (called system logging messages, system error messages, or simply system messages) and output from **debug** commands. The messages are generated during network operation to assist with identifying the type and severity of a problem, or to aid users in monitoring device activity such as configuration changes.

The Cisco IOS Embedded Syslog Manager (ESM) feature provides a programmable framework that allows a network manager to filter, escalate, correlate, route, and customize system logging messages before delivery by the Cisco IOS system message logger. ESM is available in Cisco IOS Software Release 12.3(2)T and later versions. ESM also allows system messages to be logged independently as standard messages, Extensible Markup Language (XML)-formatted messages, or ESM-filtered messages. These outputs can be sent to any of the traditional syslog targets. For example, a network manager could enable standard logging to the console connection, XML-formatted message logging to the buffer, and ESM-filtered message logging to a monitor connection. Similarly, each type of output could be sent to different remote hosts. Separate logging processes ensure that even if there is some problem with one of the formats or filtering, messages from the other processes will be unaffected.

Cisco IOS Syslog Message Standard

Note: Some of the information in this section is derived from *Authorized Self-Study Guide: Designing for Cisco Internetwork Solutions (DESGN)*, Second Edition, by Diane Teare, Cisco Press, 2007 (ISBN 1-58705-272-5).

Syslog messages contain up to 80 characters; a percent sign (%) follows the optional sequence number or timestamp information if configured. Syslog messages are structured as follows:

```
seq no:timestamp: %facility-severity-MNEMONIC:description
```

The following parameters are used in the syslog messages:

- A sequence number appears on the syslog message if the **service sequence-numbers** global configuration command is configured.

- The timestamp shows the date and time of the message or event if the **service time-stamps log [datetime | log]** global configuration command is configured. The time-stamp can be have one of three formats:
  - *mm/dd hh:mm:ss*
  - *hh:mm:ss* (for short uptimes)
  - *d h* (for long uptimes)

- **Facility:** A code consisting of two or more uppercase letters that indicate the facility to which the message refers. Syslog facilities are service identifiers used to identify and categorize system state data for error and event message reporting. A facility can be a hardware device, a protocol, or a module of the system software. Cisco IOS Software has more than 500 different facilities. The following are some common facilities:
  - IP
  - OSPF (Open Shortest Path First Protocol)
  - SYS (operating system)
  - IPsec (IP Security)
  - RSP (route switch processor)
  - IF (interface)
  - LINK (data link messages)

  Other facilities include Cisco Discovery Protocol (CDP), QoS, RADIUS, multicast (MCAST), multilayer switching (MLS), Transmission Control Protocol (TCP), virtual local-area network (VLAN) trunking protocol (VTP), Telnet, and Trivial File Transfer Protocol (TFTP).

- **Severity:** A single-digit code (from 0 to 7) that reflects the severity of the condition; the lower the number, the more serious the situation. Syslog defines the following severity levels:
  - Emergency (level 0, which is the highest level)
  - Alert (level 1)
  - Critical (level 2)
  - Error (level 3)
  - Warning (level 4)
  - Notice (level 5)
  - Informational (level 6)
  - Debugging (level 7)

- **Mnemonic:** A code that uniquely identifies the error message.

- **Description:** A text string that describes the condition. This portion of the message sometimes contains detailed information about the event, including port numbers, network addresses, or addresses that correspond to locations in the system memory address space.

Note: For more syslog information, refer to http://www.cisco.com/univercd/cc/td/doc/
product/software/ios124/124sup/124sms/index.htm.

Example 12-1 shows a typical message that indicates that the operating system (facility =
SYS) is providing a notification (severity = 5) that it has been configured (mnemonic =
CONFIG). The message text indicates that a user on vty 0 at address 192.168.64.25 per-
formed this configuration.

Example 12-1   *Example Syslog Message*

```
%SYS-5- CONFIG I: Configured from console by cwr2000 on vty0 (192.168.64.25)
```

Note: The documentation for each Cisco IOS Software release, such as the "Cisco IOS
Release 12.4T System Message Guide," found at http://www.cisco.com/en/US/products/
ps6441/products_system_message_guide_book09186a00806f9890.html, explains the
meaning of these messages.

Syslog Issues

This section describes some of the issues with syslog.

The syslog message severity is not used consistently across the different Cisco platforms and
Cisco IOS versions. For example, the environmental monitor shutdown event is level 0 in Cisco
IOS Release 12.0 and level 1 in Cisco IOS Release 11.2. Therefore, documentation for each
Cisco IOS Software release must be read to understand the meaning of the syslog messages.
This inconsistency can be problematic if different software releases are running on devices and
you want to filter syslog messages to extract information at specific levels of severity.

Another issue with syslog is that it can be verbose and may provide a mixture of many informational messages interspersed with messages that are useful for analyzing a specific
problem or condition. Network managers can use filters or scripts to isolate important
messages. Third-party tools, including syslog-ng and Kiwi Syslog Daemon, can also be
used to help manage syslog messages.

The syslog delivery communication mechanism is based on UDP and is therefore not sent
over a reliable mechanism. However, this is typically not a problem for a monitoring and
alerting tool. RFC 3195, *Reliable Delivery for Syslog*, is a specification for a reliable delivery mechanism for syslog. Cisco IOS Software Release 12.4(11)T provides support for
the Reliable Delivery for Syslog over Blocks Extensible Exchange Protocol (BEEP) feature
that enables reliable and secure syslog message delivery. BEEP also allows multiple sessions to a single logging host, independent of the underlying transport method, and provides a filtering mechanism called a message discriminator.

Syslog is not a secure mechanism. Therefore, secure practices, such as establishing access
control lists (ACL), to allow receipt of syslog packets only from internal resources, should
be used.

NetFlow

NetFlow is an important embedded Cisco IOS Software technology that provides visibility into network behavior and how network assets are being used. This section describes how both traditional and Flexible NetFlow can help the network manager understand the behavior of traffic in the network.

NetFlow Overview

Note: Some of the information in this section is derived from *Authorized Self-Study Guide: Designing for Cisco Internetwork Solutions (DESGN)*, Second Edition, by Diane Teare, Cisco Press, 2007 (ISBN 1-58705-272-5).

In 1996, Cisco developed and patented the Cisco IOS NetFlow measurement technology for measuring flows passing through Cisco devices. A *network flow* is a unidirectional sequence of packets between source and destination endpoints.

Note: NetFlow was originally implemented only on larger devices; it is now available on other devices, including Integrated Services Routers (ISR).

NetFlow answers the questions of what, when, where, and how traffic is flowing in the network.

NetFlow data can be exported to network management applications for further processing of the collected information. Cisco IOS NetFlow-collected data is the basis for a key set of IP application services, including network traffic accounting, usage-based network billing, network planning, security, denial-of-service (DoS) monitoring capabilities, and network monitoring. NetFlow provides valuable information about network users and applications, peak usage times, and traffic routing. NetFlow also provides the measurement base for QoS applications: It captures the traffic classification (or precedence) associated with each flow, thereby enabling differentiated charging based on QoS.

There are a variety of formats for exporting packets, called *export versions*. The most common is version 5, but version 9 is the latest format.

The focus of NetFlow used to be on IP flow information. This is changing with the Cisco implementation of NetFlow Version 9, a generic export transport format. NetFlow Version 9 is a flexible and extensible export format that is now on the Internet Engineering Task Force (IETF) standards track in the IP Flow Information Export (IPFIX) working group. IPFIX export is a new generic data transport capability within Cisco routers. It can be used to transport a variety of performance information from a router or switch, including Layer 2 information, security detection and identification information, IP Version 6 (IPv6), multicast, Multiprotocol Label Switching (MPLS), and Border Gateway Protocol (BGP) information, and so forth.

Note: Export versions are detailed in the "NetFlow Export Versions" section later in this chapter.

Organizations use NetFlow in different ways, depending on the focus of the organization. Both service providers and enterprises use NetFlow to analyze new applications and their impact on the network. Understanding who is using the network and the endpoints of traffic flows is important for service providers for network planning and traffic engineering, and important to enterprises for monitoring network resources, users, and applications. For example, NetFlow data can be used to determine application ports for ACLs.

While a service provider is concerned about customer accounting and billing, enterprises may be concerned about charge-back billing for their departments. In addition, NetFlow can help organizations avoid costly bandwidth upgrades by identifying the applications causing congestion and thus help reduce peak WAN traffic.

Both types of organizations use NetFlow for security monitoring and troubleshooting the network. NetFlow can help in diagnosing slow network performance, determining bandwidth hogs, and providing bandwidth utilization in real time, and can be used to confirm that appropriate bandwidth has been allocated to each class of service (CoS). NetFlow can help detect unauthorized WAN traffic and support anomaly detection and worm diagnosis.

NetFlow Flows

Each packet forwarded within a router or switch is part of a flow. Flows are very granular; a flow is identified as the combination of the following seven key fields:

- **Source IP address:** The address of the originator of the traffic

- **Destination IP address:** The address of the intended recipient of the traffic

- **Source port number:** The source application port number

- **Destination port number:** The destination application port number

- **Layer 3 protocol field:** The protocol field in the Layer 3 packet, indicating the Layer 4 protocol

- **Type of service (ToS) byte:** The CoS, defined as IP precedence or differentiated services code point (DSCP)

- **Input interface:** The interface through which the traffic is flowing

These seven key fields define a unique flow. Two packets in which only one of these key fields is different belong to different flows. NetFlow is scalable because it uses key attributes to determine a flow and therefore condenses large amounts of network information. NetFlow may also keep other fields, and keeps track of the number of packets and bytes per flow.

Cisco IOS Flexible NetFlow is the next-generation in NetFlow technology. Flexible NetFlow supports additional flexibility, scalability, and aggregation of flow data beyond traditional NetFlow. Flexible NetFlow is described in the "Flexible NetFlow" section later in this chapter.

Traditional NetFlow IP Flows

Note: Some of the information in this section is derived from *Authorized Self-Study Guide: Designing for Cisco Internetwork Solutions (DESGN)*, Second Edition, by Diane Teare, Cisco Press, 2007 (ISBN 1-58705-272-5).

Key components of NetFlow are the NetFlow cache that stores IP flow information and the NetFlow export or transport mechanism that sends NetFlow data to a network management collector. NetFlow information can be accessed using either Cisco IOS **show** commands or by viewing the exported information on the NetFlow collector server.

Switching of packets is handled differently on NetFlow-enabled devices. Non-NetFlow-enabled switching handles incoming packets independently, with separate serial tasks for switching, security services (ACLs), and traffic measurements that are applied to each packet. In contrast, the NetFlow cache on NetFlow-enabled devices contains a flow record for all active flows and is built by processing only the first packet of a flow through the standard switching path. Subsequent packets in the flow are handled via a single, streamlined task that handles switching, security services, and data collection concurrently.

Each flow record in the NetFlow cache contains key fields that can be later used for exporting data to a collection device. NetFlow export, unlike SNMP polling, pushes information periodically to the NetFlow reporting collector. The NetFlow cache constantly fills with flows. Software in the router or switch searches the cache for flows that have terminated or expired and exports these flow records to the NetFlow management collector server. Figure 12-4 shows this process.

The flow cache information is also exported to a flow collector server periodically based on flow timers. The collector therefore contains a history of flow information switched within the Cisco device. Depending on the network topology and the location of the collector server, NetFlow may utilize noticeable bandwidth, but it is relatively efficient: approximately 1.5 percent of switched traffic volume is exported to the collector server.

NetFlow can be configured to only provide NetFlow data for a specific subset of traffic (using filters) or for only a sampling of traffic. (Note, however, that not all reporting tools support these options.) When these features are not configured, NetFlow provides information for every packet, resulting in a highly condensed and detailed view of all network traffic that entered the router or switch.

NetFlow Flow Record Creation

When packets arrive at a NetFlow-enabled router, the router inspects the seven key field values of the packets and compares the results to existing flows in the NetFlow cache. If the values are unique, NetFlow creates a new flow record in the cache. In both traditional and Flexible NetFlow, additional information defined in the nonkey fields, such as the outbound interface, is added to the NetFlow cache. These nonkey fields can also be exported but are not used to create or characterize the flows. Only the first packet of the flow is typically used to populate the nonkey fields.

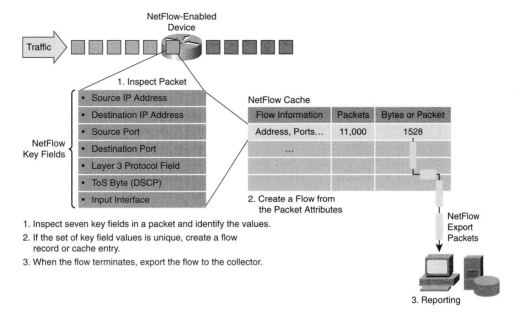

Figure 12-4 *Traditional NetFlow Handling of IP Flows*

In Figure 12-5, two unique flows are created in the NetFlow cache because the two input packets have different values in the source IP address key field.

As an example, Figure 12-6 illustrates a few of the flows in the NetFlow cache on a router. The ToS field in all of these flows is zero because QoS is not yet implemented in this network. The highlighted line in the figure shows the one traffic flow between a specific source and destination pair of devices, 172.16.21.2 and 10.0.227.12.

Note: The abbreviations used in Figure 12-6, Figure 12-7, and Figure 12-8 are as follows:

- **SrcIf:** Source interface

- **SrcIPadd:** Source IP address

- **DstIf:** Destination interface

- **DstIPadd:** Destination IP address

- **ToS:** Type of service

- **Pkts:** Number of packets

- **Src Port:** Source port number (in hexadecimal)

- **Dst Port:** Destination port number (in hexadecimal)

- **NextHop:** IP address of next hop device

- **Bytes/Pkt:** Bytes per packet

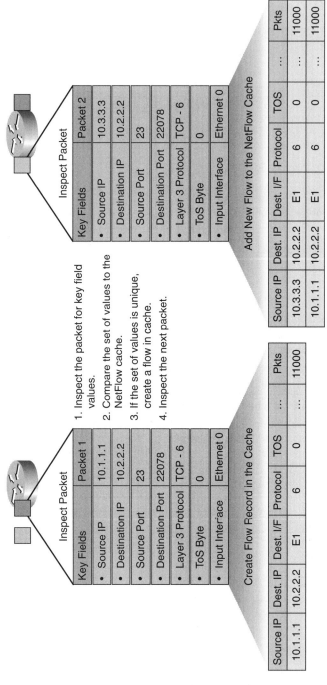

1. Inspect the packet for key field values.
2. Compare the set of values to the NetFlow cache.
3. If the set of values is unique, create a flow in cache.
4. Inspect the next packet.

Inspect Packet

Key Fields	Packet 2
• Source IP	10.3.3.3
• Destination IP	10.2.2.2
• Source Port	23
• Destination Port	22078
• Layer 3 Protocol	TCP - 6
• ToS Byte	0
• Input Interface	Ethernet 0

Add New Flow to the NetFlow Cache

Source IP	Dest. IP	Dest. I/F	Protocol	TOS	...	Pkts
10.3.3.3	10.2.2.2	E1	6	0	...	11000
10.1.1.1	10.2.2.2	E1	6	0	...	11000

Inspect Packet

Key Fields	Packet 1
• Source IP	10.1.1.1
• Destination IP	10.2.2.2
• Source Port	23
• Destination Port	22078
• Layer 3 Protocol	TCP - 6
• ToS Byte	0
• Input Interface	Ethernet 0

Create Flow Record in the Cache

Source IP	Dest. IP	Dest. I/F	Protocol	TOS	...	Pkts
10.1.1.1	10.2.2.2	E1	6	0	...	11000

Figure 12-5 *A New Flow Record Is Created When a Packet Has Unique Values for Any of the Seven Key Fields*

Srclf	SrcIPadd	Dstlf	DstIPadd	ToS	Pkts	Src Port	Dst Port	NextHop	Bytes/ Pkt	Start Time	End Time
Fa1/0	172.16.21.2	Fa0/0	10.0.227.12	0	11,000	00A2	00A2	10.0.23.2	1,528	..	..
Fa1/0	172.16.3.2	Fa0/0	10.0.227.12	0	2,491	0015	0015	10.0.23.2	740	..	..
Fa1/0	172.16.20.2	Fa0/0	10.0.227.12	0	10,000	00A1	00A1	10.0.23.2	1,428	..	..
Fa1/0	172.16.6.2	Fa0/0	10.0.227.12	0	2,210	0019	0019	10.0.23.2	1,040	..	..

Figure 12-6   *Flow Records Before QoS Is Deployed*

Note: Using **show** commands allows the cache to be examined in real time; collection and reporting tools provide better visibility into historical and trend information. The **show ip cache verbose flow** command displays a detailed summary of the NetFlow accounting data, including the ToS settings, in addition to the fields that are displayed with the **show ip cache flow** command.

Figure 12-7 shows the NetFlow cache on the same device after QoS is implemented in the network. The highlighted lines show the multiple flows resulting because of the multiple ToS values between the specific source and destination pair 172.16.21.2 and 10.0.227.12; traffic is distributed per class.

Srclf	SrcIPadd	Dstlf	DstIPadd	ToS	Pkts	Src Port	Dst Port	NextHop	Bytes/ Pkt	Start Time	End Time
Fa1/0	172.16.21.2	Fa0/0	10.0.227.12	EF	3,020	00A2	00A2	10.0.23.2	1,528	..	..
Fa1/0	172.16.21.2	Fa0/0	10.0.227.12	CS5	2,212	00A2	00A2	10.0.23.2	1,528	..	..
Fa1/0	172.16.21.2	Fa0/0	10.0.227.12	AF41	4,000	00A2	00A2	10.0.23.2	501	..	..
Fa1/0	172.16.21.2	Fa0/0	10.0.227.12	CS4	3,333	00A2	00A2	10.0.23.2	93	..	..
Fa1/0	172.16.21.2	Fa0/0	10.0.227.12	CS3	7,474	00A2	00A2	10.0.23.2	82	..	..
Fa1/0	172.16.21.2	Fa0/0	10.0.227.12	AF21	2,828	00A2	00A2	10.0.23.2	111	..	..
Fa1/0	172.16.21.2	Fa0/0	10.0.227.12	CS2	993	00A2	00A2	10.0.23.2	256	..	..
Fa1/0	172.16.21.2	Fa0/0	10.0.227.12	AF11	1,404	00A2	00A2	10.0.23.2	64	..	..
Fa1/0	172.16.21.2	Fa0/0	10.0.227.12	CS1	500	00A2	00A2	10.0.23.2	98	..	..
Fa1/0	172.16.21.2	Fa0/0	10.0.227.12	0	11,000	00A2	00A2	10.0.23.2	98	..	..
Fa1/0	172.16.3.2	Fa0/0	10.0.227.12	0	2,491	0015	0015	10.0.23.2	740	..	..
Fa1/0	172.16.20.2	Fa0/0	10.0.227.12	0	10,000	00A1	00A1	10.0.23.2	1,428	..	..
Fa1/0	172.16.6.2	Fa0/0	10.0.227.12	0	2,210	0019	0019	10.0.23.2	1,040	..	..

Figure 12-7   *Flow Records After QoS Is Deployed*

Analyzing traffic based on ToS can be useful for verifying that a QoS configuration is working and that bandwidth levels are set appropriately for the volume of traffic in each class.

NetFlow Cache Management

The key to NetFlow-enabled switching scalability and performance is highly intelligent flow cache management.

The NetFlow cache management software contains a highly sophisticated set of algorithms for efficiently determining whether a packet is part of an existing flow or should generate a new flow cache entry. The algorithms are also capable of dynamically updating the per-flow accounting measurements residing in the NetFlow cache and determining cache aging and flow expiration.

Figure 12-8 shows an example of NetFlow cache management.

Rules for expiring NetFlow cache entries include the following:

- Flows that have been idle for a specified time (15 seconds by default) are expired and removed from the cache.

- Long-lived flows are expired and removed from the cache. (Flows are not allowed to live more than 30 minutes—1800 seconds—by default; the underlying packet conversation remains undisturbed.)

- As the cache becomes full, a number of heuristics are applied to aggressively age groups of flows simultaneously; the oldest flows are expired first.

- TCP connections that have reached the end-of-byte stream (FIN) or that have been reset (RST) are expired.

Expired flows are grouped together into NetFlow export datagrams for export from the NetFlow-enabled device. NetFlow export datagrams may consist of up to 30 flow records for NetFlow Version 5 or 9 flow export.

1. Create and Update Flows in NetFlow Cache

SrcIf	*SrcIPadd	DstIf	*DstIPadd	*Protocol	*ToS	Flgs	Pkts	*Src Port	Src Msk	Src AS	*Dst Port	Dst Msk	Dst AS	NextHop	Bytes/Pkt	Active	Idle
Fa1/0	172.16.21.2	Fa0/0	10.0.227.12	11	80	10	11,000	00A2	/24	5	00A2	/24	15	10.0.23.2	1,528	1,745	4
Fa1/0	172.16.3.2	Fa0/0	10.0.227.12	6	40	0	2,491	0015	/26	196	0015	/24	15	10.0.23.2	740	41.5	1
Fa1/0	172.16.20.2	Fa0/0	10.0.227.12	11	80	10	10,000	00A1	/24	180	00A1	/24	15	10.0.23.2	1,428	1,145.5	3
Fa1/0	172.16.6.2	Fa0/0	10.0.227.12	6	40	0	2,210	0019	/30	180	0019	/24	15	10.0.23.2	1,040	24.5	14

* Key Fields

2. Expire Timers

SrcIf	*SrcIPadd	DstIf	*DstIPadd	*Protocol	*ToS	Flgs	Pkts	*Src Port	Src Msk	Src AS	*Dst Port	Dst Msk	Dst AS	NextHop	Bytes/Pkt	Active	Idle
Fa1/0	172.16.21.2	Fa0/0	10.0.227.12	11	80	10	11,000	00A2	/24	5	00A2	/24	15	10.0.23.2	1,528	1,800	4

3. Package Flows in Export Packet

Non-Aggregated Flows—Export Version 5 or 9
Aggregated Flows—Export Version 8 or 9

4. Transport Flows to Reporting Server

30 Flows Per 1500-Byte Export Packet for Version 5 or 9

Export Packet: Header | Payload (Flows)

Figure 12-8 *NetFlow Cache Management Expires Flows as Necessary*

NetFlow Export Versions

As mentioned earlier, there are various versions of NetFlow export formats.

The early versions of NetFlow export support statically defined fields, as follows:

- Version 1 is the original export version.

- Version 5 is the most common and adds BGP autonomous system data and flow sequencing information to the NetFlow data export (NDE) packets. NetFlow Version 5 is used with traditional NetFlow and is a fixed export format that exports a limited set of information.

- Version 7 is supported on Cisco Catalyst 6500 series switches with a Multilayer Switch Feature Card (MSFC) running the Catalyst Operating System (CatOS) version 5.5(7) and later.

- Version 8 supports on-router aggregation of NetFlow cache information and includes a choice of 11 aggregation schemes.

The latest generation of NetFlow export, version 9, supports dynamically defined fields without requiring a new NDE version. NetFlow version 9 is template based; routers send out a template with field IDs and lengths that define the subsequent NDE packets.

Although the most common format used is NetFlow export version 5, version 9 has some key technology advantages, such as security, traffic analysis, and multicast. However, some reporting tools may prefer the nonaggregated version 5 to version 9 because version 9 requires more complicated processing.

Flexible NetFlow

Cisco IOS Flexible NetFlow is the next-generation flow technology from Cisco.

Flexible NetFlow is an important technology available in Cisco devices to help with visibility into the network behavior and how network assets are being used. Flexible NetFlow is an improved NetFlow, bringing better scalability, aggregation of data, and user customization. Flexible NetFlow enhances the ability to detect security incidents and understand the behavior of traffic in the network beyond what is possible in other flow-based technologies.

Flexible NetFlow Overview

Fields in a flow record that are not key fields are called nonkey fields. Nonkey fields are added to the flow record in the NetFlow cache and exported. With Flexible NetFlow, these nonkey fields are user configurable. Examples of nonkey fields include flow timestamps, BGP next-hop addresses, and IP address subnet masks.

Flexible NetFlow uses the flexible and extensible NetFlow Version 9 export format, illustrated in Figure 12-9, to provide enhanced optimization of the network infrastructure, and improved capacity planning and security detection. A NetFlow Version 9 template is periodically sent to the NetFlow collector telling it what data to expect from the router or switch. The data records are then sent to the collector for analysis. Matching ID numbers are used to help associate templates to the data records.

The NetFlow Version 9 record format consists of a packet header followed by at least one or more *FlowSets*. A FlowSet is a generic term for a collection of records that follow the packet header in an export packet. There are both template and data FlowSets in NetFlow Version 9. An export packet contains one or more FlowSets, and both template and data FlowSets can be mixed within the same export packet. A template FlowSet provides a description of the fields that will be present in future data FlowSets that may occur later within the same export packet or in subsequent export packets.

Because NetFlow Version 9 is configurable and customizable, any data available in the device can theoretically be sent in NetFlow Version 9 format. The network manager can configure the key and nonkey fields that define flows.

Flexible NetFlow Advantages

The Flexible NetFlow model has several advantages over traditional NetFlow.

By flexibly targeting specific information, Flexible NetFlow reduces the amount of information and the number of flows being exported, allowing enhanced scalability and aggregation of data beyond traditional NetFlow.

Flexible NetFlow can monitor a wider range of packet information, allowing the tracking of information at Layer 2 for switching environments, at Layer 3 and 4 for IP information, and up to Layer 7 with deep packet inspection for application monitoring.

In Flexible NetFlow, nonkey fields are configurable by the user, and the user can select which key and nonkey fields define flows, providing customization and flexibility beyond traditional NetFlow.

Flexible NetFlow provides an architecture that can track multiple NetFlow applications simultaneously by using different *flow monitors*. A flow monitor describes the NetFlow cache—information stored in the cache—and contains the flow records—key and nonkey fields within the cache. The flow monitor also contains the flow exporter, which includes information about the export of NetFlow information, including the destination address of the NetFlow collector. The flow monitor includes various cache characteristics, including the timers for exporting, the size of the cache, and if required, the packet sampling rate. Users can create simultaneous separate flow monitors for security analysis and for traffic analysis.

Flexible NetFlow provides enhanced security detection and network troubleshooting by allowing customization of flow information. For example, a user can create a specific flow monitor to analyze a particular network issue or incident. Flexible NetFlow allows a customizable active timer (to track long-lasting flows, such as a download) for the cache that can be set as low as 1 second, compared to the traditional NetFlow minimum value of 60 seconds. This customizable timer aids in tracking security incidents where open or partial flows might be recorded (for example, a SYN flood attack), and provides real-time monitoring with immediate flow cache capabilities and long-term or permanent tracking of flow data.

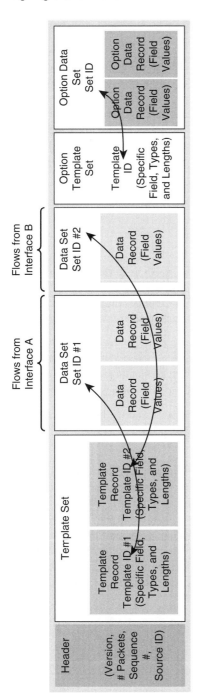

Figure 12-9   *NetFlow Version 9 Export Packet*

NetFlow Collectors

A large number of NetFlow collectors are available—including Cisco, freeware, and third-party commercial products—to report and use NetFlow data. Many solutions are available for both Microsoft Windows and Linux operating systems.

Some reporting systems offer a two-tier architecture where collectors are placed near key sites in the network and aggregate and forward the data to a main reporting server. Other solutions use multiple distributed collectors, a central database, a management server, and a reporting server. Smaller deployments may have a single server for reporting and collection.

Note: For a list of Cisco partners and freeware NetFlow reporting tools, refer to the Cisco white paper "Introduction to Cisco IOS NetFlow—A Technical Overview," at http:/ /www.cisco.com/en/US/products/ps6601/products_white_paper0900aecd80406232.shtml. Links to Cisco NetFlow partners are also available on the "Cisco IOS NetFlow Introduction" page, at http://www.cisco.com/en/US/products/ps6601/products_ios_protocol_group_home.html.

NetFlow Deployment

The key to managing the NetFlow data volume is careful planning. NetFlow should be deployed incrementally (for example, interface by interface) and strategically (on well-chosen routers) instead of pervasively on every interface on every router in the network. The network designer should determine key routers and key interfaces where NetFlow should be activated, based on the customer traffic flow patterns, the network topology and architecture, and the data required for planning, monitoring, and accounting applications.

NetFlow is typically deployed at a central site to characterize all traffic from remote sites.

The location where NetFlow is deployed depends on the location of the reporting solution and the topology of the network. If the reporting collection server is centrally located, implementing NetFlow close to the reporting collector server is optimal. NetFlow can also be enabled at remote-branch locations. In this case, a two-tier architecture solution may be appropriate, allowing remote aggregation of exported data to minimize WAN bandwidth utilization. NetFlow collection and export should be enabled on carefully selected interfaces to ensure that flows are not double-counted.

NetFlow is in general an *ingress* measurement technology and therefore should be deployed on appropriate interfaces on edge, aggregation, or WAN access routers to gain a comprehensive view of originating and terminating traffic to meet customer needs for accounting, monitoring, or network planning data.

Egress NetFlow accounting is available in newer releases of the Cisco IOS Software, including Release 12.3(11)T and later.

NBAR

Enterprise applications require different levels of service based on business requirements. These requirements can be translated into network policies. NBAR is an important embedded Cisco IOS Software technology that provides visibility into how network assets are being used by applications.

NBAR Overview

Traffic classification can help organizations answer many questions about network resources, such as the following:

- Which applications run on the network?

- What is the application resource utilization?

- Are users following application usage policies?

- How much bandwidth should be assigned to different QoS classes?

- How should applications (for example, VoIP) be allocated and deployed most efficiently?

NBAR is an embedded Cisco IOS Software classification engine that recognizes and classifies a wide variety of protocols and applications. NBAR provides full packet stateful inspection that identifies applications, including protocols that use dynamic TCP and UDP port assignments.

NBAR includes an optional feature called NBAR Protocol Discovery that analyzes application traffic patterns in real time and discovers which traffic is running on the network. NBAR develops statistics on protocol traffic on interfaces.

NBAR supports the business requirements of an organization by allowing multiple network applications to be classified to deliver more granular identification and control. NBAR can be used as the foundation for applying QoS policies to traffic flows in the network by enabling network administrators to see the variety of protocols and the amount of traffic generated by each protocol. After gathering this information, NBAR enables the network administrator to organize traffic into classes. The network can then be configured to apply the appropriate QoS to these traffic classes, providing different levels of service for specific applications and protocols. NBAR therefore allows better network management by enabling the appropriate level of network resources to be provided for each type of network traffic.

NBAR Packet Inspection

As illustrated in Figure 12-10, NBAR uses the following five elements, from Layers 3 through 7, to identify an NBAR flow on each interface:

- Source IP address

Figure 12-10 *NBAR Inspects Many Fields in a Packet*

- Destination IP address
- Source port
- Destination port
- Layer 3 protocol field

Note: Recall that traditional NetFlow uses these same identifiers, plus the ToS and incoming interface.

NBAR supports several classification methods to identify more than 90 applications and protocols, including the following:

- **Statically assigned TCP and UDP port numbers:** NBAR can classify application traffic by looking at statically assigned TCP and UDP port numbers. Although ACLs can also be used for classifying static ports, NBAR is easier to configure and provides classification statistics that are not available in ACLs.

- **Dynamically assigned TCP and UDP port numbers:** NBAR can also classify dynamically assigned TCP and UDP port numbers by using stateful protocol inspection across multiple packets during packet classification. NBAR uses approximately 150 bytes of DRAM for each traffic flow that requires stateful inspection.

- **Subport and deep-packet inspection:** NBAR looks beyond the port numbers of a packet by looking into the payload itself and classifying packets based on content within the payload, such as the transaction identifier, message type, or other similar data.

  For example, if a packet is classified as HTTP traffic, it may be further classified by URL, host, Multipurpose Internet Mail Extensions (MIME) type, and so forth. NBAR classifies HTTP traffic using text within the URL or host fields of a request using regular expression matching. HTTP URL matching in NBAR supports most HTTP request methods such as GET, PUT, HEAD, POST, DELETE, and TRACE. NBAR converts the specified match string into a regular expression.

- **Native and nonnative Packet Description Language Modules (PDLM):** NBAR can monitor only applications that it recognizes. However, application-recognition modules, known as PDLMs, can be added to provide support for additional applications. A non-native PDLM is a separate downloadable file available at Cisco.com used to add support for a protocol that is not available as part of the native PDLM currently embedded in the Cisco IOS Software release.

NBAR also provides custom protocol support for static port-based protocols and applications that are not currently supported in NBAR. There are 10 custom applications that can be assigned using NBAR, and each custom application can have up to 16 TCP and 16 UDP ports each mapped to the individual custom protocol. The real-time statistics of each custom protocol can be monitored using NBAR Protocol Discovery.

Note: NBAR is enabled by default when class maps with a **match protocol** option are applied to an interface.

NBAR Protocol Discovery

NBAR Protocol Discovery discovers any protocol traffic supported by NBAR and gathers real-time statistics associated with that protocol. NBAR Protocol Discovery maintains the following per-protocol statistics for each enabled interface:

- Total number of input packets and bytes

- Total number of output packets and bytes

- Input bit rates

- Output bit rates

These statistics can be used to define traffic classes, and traffic policies for each traffic class. The traffic policies or policy maps are used to apply specific QoS features and functionality to the traffic classes.

Note: NBAR Protocol Discovery is configured with the **ip nbar protocol-discovery** interface configuration command.

NBAR and NetFlow

NetFlow and NBAR are complementary technologies, as illustrated in Figure 12-11.

Recall that the main objective of NetFlow is to provide visibility into the network behavior and how network assets are being used. In traditional NetFlow, flows are defined by a set of seven key characteristics that define who is using which part of the network for what purposes at what times. NetFlow is a passive technology that monitors network activity, typically from OSI Layers 2 through 4. NetFlow data export allows trending of network records.

Flexible NetFlow can monitor packet information from Layer 2 for switching environments, Layer 3 and 4 for IP information, and up to Layer 7 with deep-packet inspection for application monitoring.

In contrast, the main objective of NBAR is to identify and classify traffic based on payload attributes and protocol characteristics. NBAR flows are defined by a set of five key characteristics for each interface. NBAR can support static and stateful dynamic inspections and QoS mechanisms can be applied to the classified packets to support optimization of application performance. NBAR is an active technology that can be used to

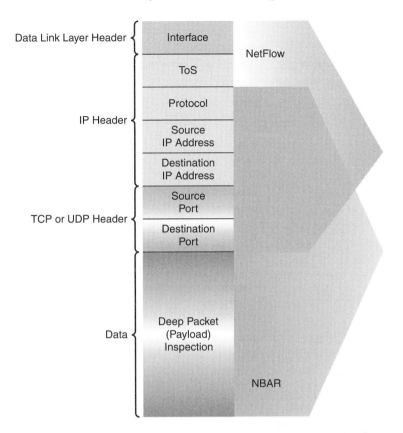

Figure 12-11 *NetFlow and NBAR are Complementary Technologies*

validate or reclassify ToS marking based on packet inspection in Layers 3 through 7.
NBAR Protocol Discovery provides an easy way to discover the application protocols that
are operating on an interface.

Examining NBAR Protocol Discovery Statistics

NBAR Protocol Discovery statistics can be viewed from the Cisco IOS Software command-line interface (CLI) or through third-party vendor applications.

Example 12-2 shows a portion of the output from the **show ip nbar protocol-discovery**
command for the Fast Ethernet 6/0 interface on a Cisco router. (If the interface is not specified, this command displays statistics for all interfaces on which NBAR Protocol Discovery is enabled.) The default output from this command includes the protocol name and the
input and output packet count, byte count, and bit rate (in bits per second [bps]).

Example 12-2 *NBAR Protocol Discovery Statistics*

```
router# show ip nbar protocol-discovery interface FastEthernet 6/0
  FastEthernet6/0
               Input                          Output
```

```
Protocol      Packet Count              Packet Count
              Byte Count                Byte Count
              5 minute bit rate (bps)   5 minute bit rate (bps)
----          ----------------          ----------------
http          316773                    0
              26340105                  0
              3000                      0
pop3          4437                      7367
              2301891                   339213
              3000                      0
snmp          279538                    14644
              319106191                 673624
              0                         0
. . .
Total         17203819                  151684936
              19161397327               50967034611
              4179000                   6620000
```

An optional keyword on this command is **top-n** *number*, used to show the most active NBAR-supported protocols, where *number* is the number of protocols to be displayed. For example, if **top-n 3** is specified, the three most active NBAR supported protocols are displayed.

NBAR Protocol Discovery can be used to monitor both input and output traffic and may be applied with or without a service policy enabled.

NBAR Protocol Discovery gathers statistics for packets switched to output interfaces. These statistics are not necessarily for packets that exited the router on the output interfaces because packets may have been dropped after switching for various reasons, including policing at the output interface, ACLs, or queue drops.

Figure 12-12 shows a screen shot from the AdventNet ManageEngine NetFlow Analyzer application that uses the NBAR Discovery Protocol information. The information displayed includes the application's traffic speed and percent of total traffic.

Figure 12-13 shows a screen shot from the CA eHealth application that shows the top protocol distribution from the NBAR Discovery Protocol statistics.

Figure 12-14 shows a screen shot from the InfoVista VistaView application, displaying interface speed, traffic, utilization; and inbound and outbound traffic by application.

Figure 12-15 provides a screen shot from the IBM Tivoli IT Netcool/Provisio application, showing the Top N protocol statistics. This information enables the network manager to identify the traffic mix on a specific link and understand which applications are consuming bandwidth.

Figure 12-16 shows an example screen shot using the Multi Router Traffic Grapher (MRTG) freeware application to graph NBAR Protocol Discovery statistics. The MRTG

Figure 12-12   *AdventNet ManageEngine NetFlow Analyzer*

tool uses the Vermeer add-on to report on NBAR data collected through SNMP from routers.

NBAR and Cisco AutoQoS

The Cisco IOS Software includes two features to automate the deployment of QoS in the network: AutoQoS VoIP and AutoQoS for the Enterprise. Both of these features use the NBAR traffic-classification functionality.

The Cisco AutoQoS features on routers and switches provide a simple, automatic way to enable QoS configurations in conformance with Cisco best-practice recommendations. The router or switch creates configuration commands to perform such things as classifying and marking VoIP traffic and then applying a low-latency queuing (LLQ) strategy on WAN links for that traffic. The configuration created by AutoQoS becomes part of the normal configuration file and can therefore be edited if required.

Figure 12-13 *CA eHealth Protocol Distribution*

Figure 12-14 *InfoVista VistaView Traffic Monitoring*

Figure 12-15 *IBM Tivoli IT Netcool/Provisio Top N Protocol Statistics*

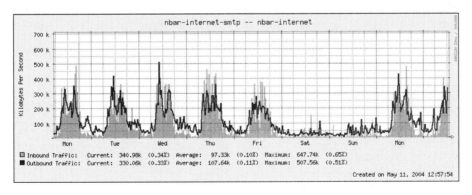

Figure 12-16 *MRTG Graphs NBAR Protocol Discovery Statistics*

Cisco AutoQoS VoIP

The Cisco AutoQoS VoIP feature is available with Cisco IOS Software Release 12.2(15)T and later releases and provides a way to simplify the implementation and provisioning of QoS for VoIP traffic.

Cisco AutoQoS for the Enterprise

The Cisco AutoQoS for the Enterprise feature is available with Cisco IOS Software Release 12.3(11)T and later releases and helps automate the deployment of QoS in a general business environment, particularly for midsize companies and branch offices of larger companies. It expands on the functionality in the Cisco AutoQoS VoIP with support for QoS features required for voice, video, and data traffic.

This feature uses NBAR Protocol Discovery to gather traffic statistics, and then creates class maps and policy maps based on the detected traffic; suggested bandwidth settings per class are based on Cisco best practice recommendations.

The Cisco AutoQoS for the Enterprise feature consists of a two-phase configuration process.

In the first phase, Auto Discovery collects data and evaluates traffic in the network. The Auto Discovery phase is started by using the **auto discovery qos [trust]** interface configuration command.

In untrusted mode (without the **trust** keyword), NBAR Protocol Discovery is used to detect and classify the applications on the network and perform statistical analysis on the network traffic.

In trusted mode (with the **trust** keyword), packets are classified based on DSCP values in the IP header. NBAR Protocol Discovery statistics are used to calculate the bandwidth and average or peak rate, which is passed to the template module.

The data should be collected over a period of time (for several days to a week), to ensure a realistic traffic analysis.

The **show auto discovery qos** command displays the results of the data collected during the Auto Discovery phase. Example 12-3 shows an example output from the **show auto discovery qos** command, illustrating the results of the Cisco AutoQoS Discovery process.

Example 12-3   *AutoQoS Discovery Process*

```
router# show auto discovery qos
AutoQoS Discovery enabled for applications
 Discovery up time: 2 days, 55 minutes
 AutoQoS Class information:
 Class VoIP:
 Recommended Minimum Bandwidth: 517 Kbps/50% (PeakRate)
 Detected applications and data:
 Application/    AverageRate    PeakRate    Total
 Protocol        (kbps/%)       (kbps/%)    (bytes)
 rtp audio       76/7           517/50      703104
 Class Interactive Video:
 Recommended Minimum Bandwidth: 24 Kbps/2% (AverageRate)
 Detected applications and data:
 Application/    AverageRate    PeakRate    Total
```

```
Protocol          (kbps/%)          (kbps/%)    (bytes)
rtp video          24/2             5337/52     704574
Class Transactional:
Recommended Minimum Bandwidth: 0 Kbps/0% (AverageRate)
Detected applications and data:
Application/    AverageRate      PeakRate    Total
Protocol        (kbps/%)         (kbps/%)    (bytes)
citrix           36/3             74/7        30212
sqlnet           12/1             7/<1        1540
```

In the second phase, the Cisco AutoQoS template generation and installation process generates templates from the data collected during the Auto Discovery phase and installs the templates on the configured interface. These templates are used as the basis for creating the class maps and policy maps for the network, with values for bandwidth and scheduling parameters based on the Auto Discovery statistics. The maps are then installed on the interface.

The Cisco AutoQoS template generation phase is started by using the **auto qos** interface configuration command. The generated class maps and policy maps should be reviewed by using the **show auto qos** command, and customized as necessary.

By default, the NBAR mechanisms do not show unclassified traffic. As illustrated in Example 12-4, the **show ip nbar unclassified-port-stats** command returns an error message if the feature to analyze unclassified traffic is not enabled.

Example 12-4 *Attempting to View Statistics for Unclassified Traffic*

```
router1# show ip nbar unclassified-port-stats
Port statistics for unclassified packets is not turned on.
```

The **debug ip nbar unclassified-port-stats** command can be used to configure the router to begin tracking the ports on which packets arrive. The **show ip nbar unclassified-port-stats** command can then be used to verify the collected information; the output will display a histogram of the most commonly used ports.

Note: Like all **debug** commands, the **debug ip nbar** command should be used with caution. Using NetFlow to look at the unclassified traffic is typically a better practice than using the **debug ip nbar** command because it has less potential for overloading the router CPU.

Example 12-5 shows example partial output of the **show auto qos** command, illustrating a suggested policy from the Cisco AutoQoS template-generation process.

Example 12-5 *Suggested Policy from Cisco AutoQoS*

```
router1# show auto qos
<output omitted>
 !
```

```
 class-map match-any AutoQoS-Voice-Et3/1
 match protocol rtp audio
 !
 class-map match-any AutoQoS-Inter-Video-Et3/1
 match protocol rtp video
 !
 class-map match-any AutoQoS-Signaling-Et3/1
 match protocol sip
 match protocol rtcp
 !
 class-map match-any AutoQoS-Transactional-Et3/1
 match protocol citrix
 !
 class-map match-any AutoQoS-Bulk-Et3/1
 match protocol exchange

policy-map AutoQoS-Policy-Et3/1
 class AutoQoS-Voice-Et3/1
 priority percent 1
 set dscp ef
 class AutoQoS-Inter-Video-Et3/1
 bandwidth remaining percent 1
 set dscp af41
 class AutoQoS-Signaling-Et3/1
 bandwidth remaining percent 1
 set dscp cs3
```

IP SLAs

Enterprises are under increasing pressure to offer SLAs to their internal customers or other departments and to verify and measure SLAs of outsourced services. The embedded Cisco IOS IP SLAs measurement capability allows network managers to validate network performance, proactively identify network issues, and verify service guarantees by using active monitoring to generate probe traffic in a continuous, reliable, and predictable manner.

IP SLAs Overview

The network has become increasingly critical for customers, and any downtime or degradation can adversely impact revenue. Therefore, companies need some form of predictability with IP services.

SLAs

An SLA is a contract between a network provider and its customers, or between a network department and internal corporate customers, that specifies connectivity and performance agreements for an end-user service. It provides a form of guarantee to customers about the level of user experience.

An SLA typically outlines the minimum and expected level of service. For example, an IT department can use SLAs to verify that the service provider is meeting its own SLAs or to define service levels for critical business applications. An SLA can also be used as the basis for planning budgets and justifying network expenditures. SLAs also support problem isolation, allowing administrators to reduce the mean time to repair (MTTR). Network configurations and other changes can be planned based on optimized performance metrics from SLAs.

Typically, the technical components of an SLA contain a guarantee level for network availability, network performance in terms of round-trip time (RTT), and network response in terms of latency, jitter, and packet loss. The specifics of an SLA vary depending on the applications an organization is supporting in the network.

For example, converged IP networks must be optimized for performance levels, including delay, packet loss, jitter, packet sequencing, and connectivity to gauge the QoS experienced by an end user.

Table 12-1 shows typical multimedia service requirements, which are more stringent than data-only requirements.

Table 12-1 *Multimedia Service Requirements*

Traffic Type	Maximum Packet Loss	Maximum One-Way Latency (Delay)	Maximum Jitter (Variation in Delay)
VoIP	1%	150 ms	30 ms
Video conferencing	1%	150 ms	30 ms
Streaming video	2%	5 sec	(not applicable)

Note: One-way delay is the difference between the time a packet leaves the sender and the time the packet arrives at the receiver.

IP SLAs Measurements

The embedded IOS IP SLAs measurement capability helps create a network that is "performance aware." Using IP SLAs measurements, Cisco network equipment can verify service guarantees, validate network performance, improve network reliability, proactively identify network issues, and react to performance metrics with changes to the configuration and network.

Note: IP SLAs measurement has evolved from technologies called the Cisco IOS Service Assurance Agent (SAA) and the Response Time Reporter (RTR).

The Cisco IOS IP SLAs feature allows performance measurements to be taken within and between Cisco devices, or between a Cisco device and a host, providing data about service levels for IP applications and services.

IP SLAs measurements perform active monitoring by generating and analyzing traffic to measure performance between Cisco IOS Software devices or between a Cisco IOS device and a host, such as a network application server. With the IP SLAs feature enabled, a router sends synthetic traffic to the other device, as illustrated in Figure 12-17.

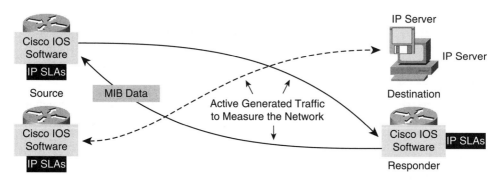

Figure 12-17 *IP SLAs Takes Measurements Between a Cisco Device and Another Cisco Device or a Host*

Figure 12-18 illustrates example IP SLAs goals in various parts of a network.

Common uses for IP SLAs measurement data include the following:

- Edge-to-edge network availability monitoring

- Network performance monitoring and network performance visibility

- VoIP, video, and virtual private network (VPN) monitoring

- SLA monitoring

- IP service network health readiness or assessment

- MPLS network monitoring

- Troubleshooting network operations

IP SLAs measurement uses a variety of operations and actively generated traffic probes to gather many types of measurement statistics, including the following:

- Network latency and response times

- Packet-loss statistics

- Network jitter and voice quality scores

- Statistical end-to-end matrix of performance information

- End-to-end network connectivity

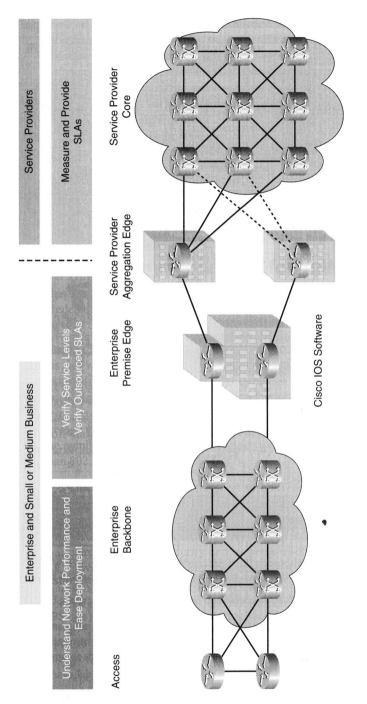

Figure 12-18   *IP SLAs Measurements Support a Variety of Goals Throughout a Network*

Multiple IP SLAs measurements can be running in a network simultaneously. Reporting tools use SNMP to extract the data into a database and allow the user to examine and analyze the data.

IP SLAs Capability Support

The IP SLAs measurement capability has comprehensive hardware support. Most Cisco devices that run Cisco IOS Software support IP SLAs measurements. IP SLAs measurement data collection and reporting support is included in several third-party partner performance management products.

Because IP SLAs measurements are embedded within Cisco IOS Software, no additional devices need be deployed, learned, or managed. Therefore, IP SLAs measurements provide a scalable, cost-effective solution for network performance measurement.

IP SLAs Functions

This section describes IP SLAs terminology and operations.

IP SLAs Source and Responder

All the IP SLAs measurement probe operations are configured on the IP SLAs *source*, either by the CLI or through an SNMP tool that supports IP SLAs operation. The **ip sla** global configuration command enters IP SLAs configuration mode to begin configuring an IP SLAs operation. (The **ip sla** command replaces the **ip sla monitor** command in Cisco IOS Release 12.4(4)T.)

The source sends probe packets to the *target*.

There are two types of IP SLAs operations: those in which the target device is running the IP SLAs *responder* component, and those in which the target device is not running the IP SLAs responder component (such as when the target is a web server or IP host).

A Cisco IOS device is configured as an IP SLAs responder with the **ip sla responder** global configuration command and does not require any complex or per-operation configuration. (The **ip sla responder** command replaces the **ip sla monitor responder** command in Cisco IOS release 12.4(4)T.)

The IP SLAs measurement accuracy is improved when the target is an IP SLAs responder, as described in the upcoming "IP SLAs Operation with Responder" section.

IP SLAs Operations

An *IP SLAs operation* is a measurement that includes protocol, frequency, traps, and thresholds.

The network manager configures the IP SLAs source with the target device address, protocol, and UDP or TCP port number, for each operation. When the operation is finished and the response is received, the results are stored in the IP SLAs MIB on the source, and are retrieved using SNMP.

IP SLAs operations are specific to target devices. Operations such as Domain Name System (DNS) or HTTP can be sent to any suitable computer. However, for operations such as testing the port used by a database, there may be risks associated with unexpected effects on actual database servers, and therefore IP SLAs responder functionality on a router can be configured to respond in place of the actual database server.

IP SLAs Operation with Responder

Using an IP SLAs responder provides enhanced measurement accuracy—without the need for dedicated third-party external probe devices—and additional statistics that are not otherwise available via standard Internet Control Message Protocol (ICMP)-based measurements.

When a network manager configures an IP SLAs operation on the IP SLAs source, reaction conditions can also be defined, and the operation can be scheduled to be run for a period of time to gather statistics. The source uses the IP SLAs control protocol to communicate with the responder before sending test packets. To increase security of IP SLAs control messages, message digest 5 (MD5) authentication can be used to secure the control protocol exchange.

The following sequence of events occurs for each IP SLAs operation that requires a responder on the target, as illustrated in Figure 12-19:

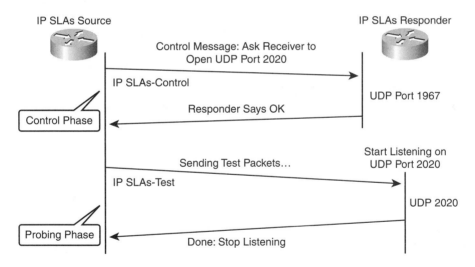

Figure 12-19 *IP SLAs Operation with a Responder*

1. At the start of the control phase, the IP SLAs source sends a control message with the configured IP SLAs operation information to IP SLAs control port UDP 1967 on the target router (the responder). The control message includes the protocol, port number, and duration of the operation. In Figure 12-19, UDP port 2020 is used for the IP SLAs test packets.

If MD5 authentication is enabled, the MD5 checksum is sent with the control message.If MD5 authentication is enabled, the responder verifies the MD5 checksum; if the authentication fails, the responder returns an authentication failure message.

2. If the responder processes the control message, it sends an OK message to the source and listens on the port specified in the control message for a specified duration. If the responder cannot process the control message, it returns an error. If the IP SLAs source does not receive a response from the responder, it tries to retransmit the control message; it will eventually time out if it does not receive a response.

> **Note:**   The responder is capable of responding to multiple IP SLAs measurement operations that try to connect to the same port number.

3. If an OK message is returned, the IP SLAs operation on the source moves to the probing phase in which it sends one or more test packets to the responder to compute response times. (The control message return code can be seen in the output of the **show ip sla statistics** command.) In Figure 12-19, the test messages are sent on UDP port 2020.

4. The responder accepts the test packets and responds. Based on the type of operation, the responder may add an "in" timestamp and an "out" timestamp in the response packet payload to account for the CPU time spent measuring unidirectional packet loss, latency, and jitter. These timestamps are described in the next section and help the IP SLAs source make accurate assessments of one-way delay and processing time in target routers. The responder disables the user-specified port after it responds to the IP SLAs measurements packet or when the specified time expires.

IP SLAs with Responder Timestamps

Figure 12-20 illustrates the use of timestamps in round-trip calculations in an operation using an IP SLAs responder. The IP SLA source uses four timestamps for the RTT calculation.

Figure 12-20   *Timestamps in an IP SLAs Operation with a Responder*

The IP SLAs source sends a test packet at time T1.

Because of other high-priority processes, routers might take tens of milliseconds to process incoming packets. For example, the reply to a test packet might be sitting in a queue waiting to be processed. To account for this delay, the IP SLAs responder includes both the receipt time (T2) and the transmitted time (T3) in the response packet; the time-stamps are accurate to submilliseconds.

The IP SLAs source subtracts T2 from T3 to determine the delta value—the time spent processing the test packet in the IP SLAs responder. The delta value is subtracted from the overall RTT.

The same principle is applied by IP SLAs source; the incoming timestamp (T4) is taken at the interrupt level to allow for greater accuracy in the RTT calculation. The T4 time-stamp, rather than the T5 timestamp—when the packet is processed—is used in the RTT calculation.

The two timestamps taken in the IP SLAs responder also allow one-way delay, jitter, and directional packet loss to be tracked. These statistics are critical for understanding asyn-chronous network behavior. To calculate these one-way delay measurements, the source and target need to be synchronized to the same clock source, requiring the Network Time Protocol (NTP) to be configured on both.

IP SLAs SNMP Features

Compared to NetFlow, which passively monitors the network, IP SLAs measurements ac-tively send data across the network to measure performance between multiple network lo-cations on a hop-by-hop basis or across end-to-end network paths. The IP SLAs measurements are accessible through SNMP.

The Cisco Round-Trip Time Monitor (RTTMON) MIB is used with IP SLAs measure-ments; the data from the IP SLAs operations is stored within the RTTMON MIB. Network management applications can retrieve network performance statistics from this MIB, as il-lustrated in Figure 12-21, and network managers can build custom equations to monitor specific statistics.

Figure 12-21 *IP SLAs Information Can Be Retrieved with SNMP*

The RTTMON MIB can store measurements over a period of time. IP SLAs operations can also be configured to measure traffic with different classes of services over the same link using the DSCP in the ToS byte. The **tos** *number* command configures these bits; this command is configured in an IP SLAs configuration submode. The *number* specifies the ToS (DSCP) value. This command is supported by all IP SLAs operations.

IP SLAs measurements can proactively notify network managers about conditions by using an SNMP trap. Each measurement operation can monitor against a preset performance threshold and generate an SNMP trap to alert management applications if this threshold is crossed. Available thresholds include RTT, average jitter, one-way latency, jitter, packet loss, mean opinion score (MOS), and connectivity tests. IP SLAs measurements can also be configured to run a new SNMP operation automatically when a threshold is crossed after a configurable number of times. For example, if the latency threshold is exceeded three times, a secondary operation could measure hop-by-hop latencies to help isolate the problem area in the network.

Deploying IP SLAs Measurements

The first step in IP SLAs deployment is determining exactly what needs to be monitored. Table 12-2 shows the requirements and resulting common IP SLAs measurements for several network profiles.

Table 12-2   *IP SLAs Deployment Profiles*

	Data-Only Traffic	VoIP	SLA Verification	Availability	Streaming Video
Requirement	Minimize delay and packet loss Verify QoS	Minimize delay, packet loss, and jitter	Measure delay, packet loss, and jitter One way	Connectivity testing	Minimize delay and packet loss
IP SLAs Measurement	Jitter Packet loss Latency	Jitter Packet loss Latency MOS voice-quality score	Jitter Packet loss Latency One way Enhanced accuracy NTP	Connectivity tests to IP devices	Jitter Packet loss Latency

A variety of IP SLAs operations support different deployment profiles. The most common operation used is the *UDP jitter operation*, which measures IP performance for UDP performance-sensitive applications. The UDP jitter operation measurements include round-trip delay, one-way jitter, one-way packet loss, and connectivity testing. Other operations include ICMP path jitter—for measuring hop-by-hop jitter, packet loss, and delay—and UDP jitter for VoIP—with all the features of the UDP jitter operation, plus codec simulation and voice-quality scoring capabilities.

As noted in Table 12-2, data-only deployments typically seek to minimize delay and packet loss. Appropriate IP SLAs measurements for these scenarios are jitter, packer loss, and latency measurements using the UDP jitter operation.

With the addition of real-time traffic such as VoIP, delays, jitter, and packet loss are still very important. For VoIP traffic, packet loss is manageable to some extent, but frequent losses impair communication. The UDP jitter for VoIP operation provides packet loss, jitter, and latency measurements, including unidirectional measurements, plus MOS voice-quality scores.

Impact of QoS Deployment on IP SLAs Statistics

The highlighted line in the example in Figure 12-22 shows the IP SLAs statistics for a particular flow before QoS is deployed in the network. Notice that the ToS field is 0.

SrcIPadd	DstIPadd	ToS	SD Latency	DS Latency	SD Packet Loss	DS Packet Loss	SD Jitter	DS Jitter
172.16.21.2	10.0.227.12	0	55	45	5	0	28	22
172.16.3.2	10.0.227.12	0	42	35	105	30	23	8
172.16.20.2	10.0.227.12	0	66	70	144	28	34	22
172.16.6.2	10.0.227.12	0	73	69	20	10	11	9

Figure 12-22 *Example IP SLAs Data Before QoS Is Deployed*

Note: The abbreviations used in Figure 12-22 and Figure 12-23 are as follows:

■ **SrcIPadd:** Source IP address

■ **DstIPadd:** Destination IP address

■ **ToS:** Type of service

■ **SD:** Source to destination

■ **DS:** Destination to source

Figure 12-23 shows the IP SLAs statistics from the same operation spread across multiple flows after QoS has been deployed in the network. In this case, a measurement is taken for each ToS value monitored. The varied results per ToS show that the QoS performance per class is working end-to-end through the network.

SrcIPadd	DstIPadd	ToS	SD Latency	DS Latency	SD Packet Loss	DS Packet Loss	SD Jitter	DS Jitter
172.16.21.2	10.0.227.12	EF	15	32	0	0	5	3
172.16.21.2	10.0.227.12	CS5	55	45	20	0	22	21
172.16.21.2	10.0.227.12	AF41	45	48	0	0	32	30
172.16.21.2	10.0.227.12	CS4	48	74	0	0	25	33
172.16.21.2	10.0.227.12	CS3	39	45	0	0	25	28
172.16.21.2	10.0.227.12	AF21	45	75	22	20	41	35
172.16.21.2	10.0.227.12	CS2	99	75	100	45	28	35
172.16.21.2	10.0.227.12	AF11	99	75	75	100	46	35
172.16.21.2	10.0.227.12	CS1	99	75	99	45	33	35
172.16.21.2	10.0.227.12	0	99	75	100	190	51	64
172.16.3.2	10.0.227.12	0	42	35	105	30	23	8
172.16.20.2	10.0.227.12	0	66	70	144	28	34	22
172.16.6.2	10.0.227.12	0	73	69	20	10	11	9

Figure 12-23   *Example IP SLAs Data After QoS Has Been Deployed*

QoS is used for providing preferential treatment for certain traffic classes. Therefore, if you have QoS configured and IP SLAs shows that all your traffic is getting the same treatment, either the network is not congested or your QoS configuration is not working properly.

Scaling IP SLAs Deployments

The processing requirements for IP SLAs operations may be a concern when there is a large amount of switching traffic passing through an IP SLAs source. In these cases, it is necessary to reduce the frequency of the sampling interval or use a dedicated IP SLAs router to perform the IP SLAs measurement operations.

A dedicated router for sourcing IP SLAs measurement operations—called a shadow router—is used when there is a large number of operations (hundreds or thousands) needed on an IP SLAs source. Dedicated routers are often deployed in large hub-and-spoke topologies, with the dedicated router at the hub site and the spokes as IP SLAs responders.

Advantages of deploying a dedicated router include the following:

■   The dedicated router focuses on IP SLAs operations, and therefore its separate memory and CPU are not in the switching path.

■   The Cisco IOS Software release on the dedicated router can be upgraded without affecting production devices or traffic.

- Management and deployment is flexible; dedicated routers can be deployed at a hub site or at regional aggregation locations.

- The solution is scalable to a large number of endpoints; a dedicated router allows polling a central source location.

Hierarchical Monitoring with IP SLAs Measurements

If the number of sites is extremely large, the number of IP SLAs measurements required to test every remote site may be prohibitive for even a dedicated router. An option in this case is to use multiple dedicated routers, with a mesh of IP SLAs measurements taken at multiple points in the network.

Another option is to use a series of measurements in a hierarchical design, as illustrated in Figure 12-24.

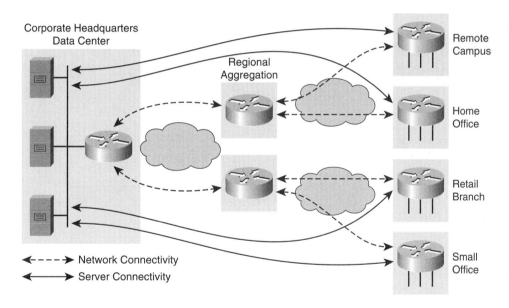

Figure 12-24   *Hierarchical Monitoring with IP SLAs*

This hierarchical approach allows regional aggregation routers to be the source of IP SLAs measurement traffic for the access routers in each region, and a centralized router to be the source of IP SLAs measurement traffic for the regional aggregation routers. Resulting RTTs can be summed to give an approximate end-to-end measurement. When using a hierarchical deployment, the network manager may need to examine individual measurements if the reporting tools do not correlate end-to-end times. However, threshold violations on single links may be all that are needed to detect a problem.

Network Management Applications Using IP SLAs Measurements

IP SLAs are supported by both Cisco applications and a wide range of vendor partners' network management applications that report and use IP SLAs data.

Cisco solutions include Cisco Unified Service Monitor for telephony monitoring and CiscoWorks Internetwork Performance Monitor (IPM) for enterprise performance measurements.

CiscoWorks IPM Application Example

Figure 12-25 shows some images from the CiscoWorks IPM application. CiscoWorks IPM is a network response-time and availability troubleshooting application that measures network performance based on the traffic-generation technology within IP SLAs. CiscoWorks IPM facilitates performance measurement of differentiated services (for example, voice, video, and data) in an enterprise network.

Figure 12-25   *CiscoWorks IPM Measurements*

CiscoWorks IPM allows the network response times to be proactively monitored and can notify the network engineer if the response time degrades or a monitored link becomes unavailable, helping pinpoint the link causing the problem.

CiscoWorks IPM enables the network manager to define a collector consisting of one or many IP SLAs sources, many IP SLAs responders, and many IP SLAs operations.

IP SLAs Network Management Application Considerations

Several design considerations are involved in selecting a network management application to use with IP SLAs measurements.

One consideration is how the network management application supports provisioning IP SLAs operations. For example, consider whether the network management tool provisions IP SLAs easily, or if manual configuration using the CLI is needed for every IP SLAs source and responder. Manual configuration of every device should be avoided for large deployments.

The effort involved in enabling IP SLAs measurements should also be investigated. The ease of setting up and maintaining the application is also important and will help promote the use of the application.

Another consideration is the reporting supported by the network management application. A variety of predefined and customizable reports help provide quick views of results. Hierarchical reporting is becoming an important consideration. If you use hierarchical measurements, you want a tool that supports aggregation of these measurements.

Summary

In this chapter, you learned about the embedded network management tools in the Cisco IOS Software to support application optimization, performance measurement, and SLA verification.

Syslog is a Cisco IOS Software process that enables a device to report and save important error and notification messages. The messages can be saved either locally or to a remote logging server. Syslog messages include both messages in a standardized format and output from **debug** commands. Syslog messages contain up to 80 characters. Some issues with syslog include the severity level is not used consistently, the messages can be verbose, the standard UDP communication mechanism used, and syslog is not a secure mechanism.

The Cisco IOS NetFlow measurement technology measures flows passing through Cisco devices. A NetFlow network flow is a unidirectional sequence of packets between source and destination endpoints and is identified as the combination of seven key fields: source and destination IP address, source and destination port number, layer 3 protocol field, ToS byte, and input interface.

The NetFlow cache stores IP flow information. The NetFlow export or transport mechanism sends NetFlow data to a network management collector. There are a variety of formats for exporting packets, called export versions. The most common is version 5, but version 9 is the latest format.

Fields in a flow record that are not key fields are called nonkey fields. Nonkey fields are added to the flow record in the NetFlow cache and exported. Examples of nonkey fields include flow timestamps, BGP next-hop addresses, and IP address subnet masks. With Cisco IOS Flexible NetFlow, the next-generation in NetFlow technology, these nonkey fields are user configurable. A large number of NetFlow collectors are available—including Cisco, freeware, and third-party commercial products—to report and use NetFlow data.

NBAR is an embedded Cisco IOS Software classification engine that provides full packet stateful inspection to identify and classify a wide variety of protocols and applications, including those that use dynamic TCP and UDP port assignments. NBAR Protocol Discovery analyzes application traffic patterns in real time to discover which traffic is running on the network. NBAR develops statistics on protocol traffic on interfaces that can be used to apply specific QoS functionality to traffic classes. Application-recognition modules, known as PDLMs, can be added to provide support for additional applications.

An NBAR flow on an interface is identified by five elements: source and destination IP address, source and destination port, and Layer 3 protocol field. NBAR Protocol Discovery statistics can be viewed from the Cisco IOS CLI or through third-party vendor applications.

The Cisco AutoQoS VoIP and AutoQoS for the Enterprise features both use NBAR traffic classification functions to provide a simple, automatic way to enable QoS configurations in conformance with Cisco best-practice recommendations. The two-phase configuration process for the Cisco AutoQoS for the Enterprise feature uses data collected from NBAR to create templates on the configured interface. These templates are used as the basis for creating the class maps and policy maps for the network.

An SLA is a contract between a network provider and its customers, or between a network department and internal corporate customers, that specifies connectivity and performance agreements for an end-user service. The embedded Cisco IOS IP SLAs measurement capability provides end-to-end performance measurements by generating and analyzing traffic to measure performance between Cisco IOS Software devices or between a Cisco IOS device and a host, such as a network application server. Jitter, packet loss, and latency are key measurements.

All the IP SLAs measurement probe operations are configured on the IP SLAs source. The source sends probe packets to the target, which may be a device is running the IP SLAs responder component; the IP SLAs measurement accuracy is improved when the target is an IP SLAs responder. An IP SLAs operation is a measurement that includes protocol, frequency, traps, and thresholds. The most common operation used is the UDP jitter operation, which measures IP performance for UDP performance-sensitive applications.

The IP SLAs measurements are accessible through SNMP. Both Cisco and a wide range of vendor partners' network management applications report and use IP SLAs data.

References

For additional information, refer to the following:

- Cisco Systems, Inc. "Cisco IOS Software Releases 12.4 Mainline Error and System Messages," at http://www.cisco.com/en/US/products/ps6350/products_system_message_guides_list.html

- Cisco Systems, Inc. "Cisco IOS Software Releases 12.3T Embedded Syslog Manager (ESM)," at http://www.cisco.com/en/US/products/sw/iosswrel/ps5207/products_feature_guide09186a00801a8516.html

- Cisco Systems, Inc. "Cisco IOS NetFlow Introduction," at http://www.cisco.com/go/netflow

- Cisco Systems, Inc. "Cisco NetFlow Collection Engine NetFlow Services Solutions Guide," at http://www.cisco.com/en/US/products/sw/netmgtsw/ps1964/products_implementation_design_guide09186a00800d6a11.html

- Cisco Systems, Inc. "Introduction to Cisco IOS NetFlow - A Technical Overview," at http://www.cisco.com/en/US/products/ps6601/products_white_paper0900aecd80406232.shtml

- Cisco Systems, Inc. "Cisco IOS IP Service Level Agreements (SLAs) Introduction," at http://www.cisco.com/go/ipsla

- Cisco Systems, Inc. "Network Based Application Recognition (NBAR) Introduction," at http://www.cisco.com/go/nbar

- Cisco Systems, Inc. User Guide for Internetwork Performance Monitor 2.6 (With LMS 2.5.1)," at http://www.cisco.com/en/US/products/sw/cscowork/ps1008/products_user_guide_book09186a0080366cf7.html

- Cisco Systems, Inc. "Cisco IOS Release 12.4 T System Message Guide," at http://www.cisco.com/en/US/products/ps6441/products_system_message_guide_book09186a00806f9890.html

- The Internet Engineering Task Force. RFC 3195: *Reliable Delivery for syslog*, at http://www.ietf.org/rfc/rfc3195.txt

Review Questions

Answer the following questions, and then refer to Appendix A, "Answers to Review Questions," for the answers.

1. Which embedded Cisco IOS network management tools support each of the four phases in the application optimization cycle: baseline application traffic; optimize to meet objectives; measure, adjust, and verify; deploy new applications?

2. What is the Cisco IOS Embedded Syslog Manager?

3. Put the numeric severity level for syslog messages next to the appropriate severity-level description.

    ____Warning

    ____Emergency

    ____Alert

    ____Error

    ____Critical

    ____Informational

    ____Notice

4. Which NetFlow export format allows IPv6 information to be exported?

    a. Version 1

    b. Version 2

    c. Version 5

    d. Version 9

    e. All of the above

    f. None of the above

5. Which fields are used to identify a NetFlow flow? (Choose five.)

   a. Source IP address

   b. Destination IP address

   c. Layer 2 protocol field

   d. Layer 3 protocol field

   e. Destination port number

   f. ToS byte

   g. IP subnet mask

6. When are NetFlow flows exported? (Choose four.)

   a. If the TCP connection completes

   b. If they are idle for 90 seconds by default

   c. If they expire, after 1800 seconds by default

   d. If they are idle for 15 seconds by default

   e. If they expire, after 300 seconds by default

   f. As the cache becomes full

7. What is the difference between traditional NetFlow and Flexible NetFlow?

8. Which of the following fields are used to identify an NBAR flow? (Choose four.)

   a. Source IP address

   b. Destination IP address

   c. Layer 2 protocol field

   d. Layer 3 protocol field

   e. Destination port number

   f. ToS byte

   g. IP subnet mask

9. What are NBAR PDLMs?

10. Which statistics does NBAR Protocol Discovery keep for each protocol on an enabled interface? (Choose four.)

   a. Input bit rate

   b. Output bit rate

   c. Total number of input packets

   d. Input packet rate

   e. Output packet rate

   f. Total number of output bytes

   g. Input byte rate

   h. Output byte rate

11. Which command displays NBAR statistics for an interface?

   a. show nbar statistics

   b. show ip nbar statistics

   c. show ip nbar protocol-discovery

   d. show ip nbar protocol-discovery statistics

12. Which command enables the Cisco AutoQoS template generation phase on an interface?

   a. auto discovery qos

   b. auto qos

   c. auto qos template

   d. auto qos generate

13. What is an SLA?

14. What are typical maximum requirements for one-way latency, packet-loss percentage, and jitter for VoIP traffic?

15. Select three true statements about IP SLAs.

   a. Operations are configured on the IP SLAs source.

   b. Operations are configured on the IP SLAs responder.

   c. A Cisco IOS device can be an IP SLAs responder.

   d. A Cisco IOS device can be an IP SLAs source.

   e. A web server can be an IP SLAs source.

16. Select the four timestamps that are used to calculate RTT in operations with an IP SLAs responder.

    a.   When the IP SLAs source sends the test packet

    b.   When the IP SLAs responder receives the test packet

    c.   When the IP SLAs responder sends the test packet

    d.   When the IP SLAs source receives the test packet

    e.   When the IP SLAs source processes the test packet

17. What is an IP SLAs shadow router?

Answers to Review Questions

Chapter 1

1. B, C, E.
2. A, C, D.
3. B, D, E.
4. A, C, D.
5. A, B, D.

Chapter 2

1. B, E.
2. C.
3. B, E.
4. E.
5. E.
6. A, D.
7. B, C, E.
8. A, E.
9. A, B.
10. E.
11. B.
12. B, C.
13. A, B, D.

Chapter 3

1. B, C.
2. A, B.
3. C.
4. A, D.
5. C.
6. A, B, D.
7. B.
8. A, C, D.

Chapter 4

1. D.
2. B.
3. A, C, D.
4. D.
5. B, C, D.
6. A, D.
7. E.
8. C.

Chapter 5

1. B, C, E.
2. A, C, E.
3. C, D.
4. A.
5. A, C, D.
6. B, D, F.
7. D.
8. E.
9. D.
10. B.
11. D.

Chapter 6

1. B, D, E.

2. D.

3. C.

4. B, C.

5. A, B, D.

Chapter 7

1. High availability includes integrating the following five components:

   - Redundancy

   - Technology (including hardware and software features)

   - People

   - Processes

   - Tools

2. Some of the ways that people affect high availability include the following:

   - Staff work habits

   - Level of staff skills and technical training

   - Communication skills

   - Documentation created

   - Organizational structure alignment with services

3. - **Web tier:** The outer DMZ

   - **Application tier:** Middleware servers in the data center

   - **Database tier:** The mainframes

4. A.

5. A physical Cisco firewall or Cisco ACE module can be virtualized, or divided into separate firewall contexts. These virtual firewall contexts operate similar to separate physical firewall devices, retaining the secure separation of rules and other customer features, such as NAT, ACLs, protocols, and so forth. The physical firewall resources that each firewall context is allocated can be controlled, for example, to prevent a problem in one firewall context from affecting another.

6. A, B, D.

7. A virtual IP (VIP) address is a public IP address provided by an SLB for *each service* provided by servers. Clients resolve this address through DNS requests. The SLB intelligently passes traffic to a pool of physical servers, based on the load and on configured rules. The SLB rewrites the source and destination IP or MAC addresses, depending on the mode in which it is operating.

8. ■ **Router mode:** The servers typically use the SLB inside address as their default gateway.

   ■ **Bridge mode:** The SLB device acts as a "bump in the wire" between the servers and the upstream firewall or Layer 3 device.

   ■ **One-armed or two-armed:** Return traffic must be forced to go to the SLB device so that the source IP address of traffic from the physical server can be translated back to the VIP that the end user device thinks it is communicating with.

9. In this design, the servers use the IP address of the firewall or Layer 3 device as their default gateway.

10. B, C.

11. Technology to detect when a site is unreachable (also called "off the air") and should be failed over is a necessity; this detection is often done external to the two sites. For example an external service provider could be used to detect that a site is down. Alternatively, Cisco GSS technology, typically housed within a provider collocation facility, could be used to provide GSLB. GSS offloads DNS servers by taking over the domain resolution process.

12. The RHI feature allows the SLB device to inject or remove host routes for its virtual servers, based on the health of the servers and applications. These routes to the virtual servers can then be propagated to the rest of the network. The RHI feature can be used to load balance a virtual server across multiple SLB devices. It can also be used as a disaster recovery mechanism; in this case, the route to a specific virtual server is propagated with a different metric for different SLB devices, either within the same data center or across data centers.

13. In the base e-commerce module design, inbound traffic is routed first by a static or BGP route into the e-commerce network. A series of static routes to next-hop addresses in turn route to the server IP address. Outbound traffic is routed from the servers, using default routes to next-hop addresses, to the Internet.

14. A, D.

15. In a one-armed design with two firewall layers, the Cisco CSM is moved from being inline such that selected traffic to and from the servers does not go through it. The design can be scaled by adding additional Cisco FWSMs and CSM or ACE modules to the switch chassis as needed. All non-load-balanced traffic to and from the servers bypasses the Cisco CSM.

16. The servers' default gateway is the HSRP primary IP address on the MSFC. Because the CSS devices are in one-armed mode, non-load-balanced traffic to and from the servers bypasses the CSS devices.

17. A, D.

18. ■ **EOT:** Uses a standalone process to track the status of objects, including interface up.

   ■ **OER:** Allows the path selection to be based on policies, including measured reachability, delay, loss, and jitter.

   ■ **GSLB:** Offloads DNS servers by taking over the domain-resolution process.

Chapter 8

1. B.

2. D.

3. B, C, E.

4. C, F.

5. D.

6. D, F.

7. C, D.

8. A, E.

9. B, E.

10. C.

Chapter 9

1. E.

2. B.

3. A, E.

4. E.

5. C, E.

6. C, E.

7. A, C.

8. B, D, E.

9. E.

10. B.

Chapter 10

1. Multicast data is sent from the source as one stream; this single data stream travels as far as it can in the network. Devices only replicate the data if they need to send it out on multiple interfaces to reach all members of the destination multicast group.

2. D.

3. C.

4. The Class D multicast address range is 224.0.0.0 through 239.255.255.255.

5. 1—C
2—A
3—E
4—D
5—B

6. The translation between IP multicast and layer 2 multicast MAC address is achieved by the mapping of the low-order 23 bits of the IP (Layer 3) multicast address into the low-order 23 bits of the MAC (Layer 2) address.

7. Because there are 28 bits of unique address space for an IP multicast address (32 minus the first 4 bits containing the 1110 Class D prefix), and there are only 23 bits mapped into the MAC address, there are five (28 − 23 = 5) bits of overlap. These 5 bits represent 2^5 = 32 addresses. Therefore, there is a 32:1 overlap of IP addresses to MAC addresses, so 32 IP multicast addresses map to the same MAC multicast address.

8. A, D.

9. B.

10. IGMPv1 does not have a mechanism defined for hosts to leave a multicast group. IGMPv1 hosts therefore leave a group silently at any time, without any notification to the router. An IGMPv2 Leave Group message allows hosts to tell the router they are leaving the group.

11. With IGMP snooping, a switch eavesdrops on the IGMP messages sent between routers and hosts, and updates its MAC address table accordingly. The switch must be IGMP aware to listen in on the IGMP conversations between hosts and routers.

12. C.

13. B.

14. B, C.

15. PIM-SM uses a shared tree and therefore requires an RP to be defined.

16. The notation (S,G) (pronounced "S comma G") is the forwarding state associated with a source tree, where S is the IP address of the source, and G is the multicast group address.

17. The notation (*,G) (pronounced "star comma G") is the default forwarding state for a shared tree, where * is a wildcard entry, meaning any source, and G is the multicast group address.

18. An RP router sends an auto-RP message to 224.0.1.39, announcing itself as a candidate RP. An RP-mapping agent router listens to the 224.0.1.39 address and sends a RP-to-group mapping message to 224.0.1.40. Other PIM routers listen to 224.0.1.40 to automatically discover the RP.

19. ASM uses a combination of the shared and source trees. Bidir-PIM uses shared trees. SSM uses source trees.

20. In PIM-SM, sources register with the RP. Routers along the path from active receivers that have explicitly requested to join a specific multicast group register to join that group. These routers calculate, using the unicast routing table, whether they have a better metric to the RP or to the source itself; they forward the join message to the device with which they have the better metric. Data is forwarded down the shared tree to the receivers that have joined the group. The edge routers learn about a particular source when they receive data packets on the shared tree from that source through the RP. When a receiver requests to join a group, the edge router sends PIM (S,G) join messages toward that source.

21. A PIM-SM last-hop router (that is, a router with directly connected active receiver group members) will switch to a source tree and therefore bypass the shared tree's RP if the traffic rate is above a set threshold, called the SPT threshold.

22. E, F.

23. Bidir-PIM uses a DF on each link so that bidirectional sources can reach the RP. All the PIM neighbors in a subnet advertise their unicast route to the RP, and the router with the best route is elected as the DF. This process selects the shortest path between every subnet and the RP without creating any (S,G) entries.

24. In an SSM network, a receiver sends a request to join a specific multicast source in a multicast group to its last-hop router (the router closest to the receiver), identifying the specific source in the group by using the IGMPv3 include mode. The last-hop router sends the request directly to the specific source rather than to a common RP, as is done in PIM-SM. The first hop router (the router closest to the source) starts forwarding the multicast traffic down the source tree to the receiver as soon as the source tree is built; this happens when the first (S,G) join request is received.

25. There are no defined anycast addresses in IPv4 as there are in IPv6. To implement the anycast RP, a unicast host address (with a /32 mask) is assigned as an anycast address. This same address is configured on a loopback interface on all of the RPs and is therefore added to the unicast routing table on the RPs. All the downstream routers are configured to use this anycast address as the IP address of their local RP. IP routing automatically selects the topologically closest physical RP for each source and receiver to use. Because some sources and receivers might end up using different RPs, the RPs use MDSP to exchange information about active sources. MSDP announces the source addresses of the sources sending to a group. All RPs are configured to be MSDP peers of each other so that each RP knows about the active sources in the other RPs. If any of the RPs fail, IP routing converges, and one of the remaining RPs becomes the active RP in the area of the failed RP.

26. With Auto-RP, one or more routers are designated as RP mapping agents, which receive the RP announcement messages from candidate RPs (C-RPs) and arbitrate conflicts. The C-RPs announce their willingness to serve as an RP for a particular group range by periodically multicasting Auto-RP Announce messages to the Cisco announce multicast group, 224.0.1.39. The mapping agent listens to these announcements and builds a table with the information it learns. If several routers announce themselves as C-RPs for a multicast group range, the mapping agent chooses the C-RP with the highest IP address to be the RP. The mapping agent sends the consistent multicast group-to-RP mappings to all other routers in an RP discovery message addressed to 224.0.1.40, in dense mode, every 60 seconds by default.

27. B, C.

28. For multicast traffic, filtering for receivers must always be placed after the last replication point to other potential receivers, so that the other receivers can still receive the traffic.

29. With SSM, unknown source attacks are not possible because receivers must join a specific source host in a specific multicast group. Traffic from unknown sources will only reach the first-hop router (the router closest to the source) and then be discarded; this traffic will not even create state information in the first-hop router.

30. Multicast receivers can create state attacks; there is no equivalent action in unicast networks. The following are three types of receiver attacks:

- **Attack against content:** The rogue receiver attempts to gain access to content that the receiver is not unauthorized to access.

- **Attack against bandwidth:** The receiver attempts to overload network bandwidth. This attack is typically against shared network bandwidth and is therefore actually an attack against other receivers.

- **Attack against routers and switches:** The receiver tries to create more state information than the router or switch can handle by sending multiple join requests. Processing these multiple join requests from the receiver can increase the convergence time of other states or cause the network device to reboot.

31. The **ip igmp access-group** interface configuration command is used to filter groups in IGMP reports by using a standard access list, or to filter sources and groups in IGMPv3 reports by using an extended access list.

32. PIM-SM register messages can be filtered on a candidate RP router using the **ip pim accept-register** global configuration command.

Chapter 11

1. B.

2. ■ 802.11a: 5 GHz

- 802.11b: 2.4 GHz

- 802.11g: 2.4 GHz

3. A, E, G.

4. The recommendation for 802.11a is that neighboring cells not be placed on neighboring channels (in other words, neighboring channels are skipped) to reduce interference.

5. B.

6. An autonomous AP has a local configuration and requires local management, whereas a lightweight AP receives control and configuration from a WLC to which it is associated.

7. The CCX program for WLAN client devices allows vendors of WLAN client devices or adapters to ensure interoperability with the Cisco WLAN infrastructure and take advantage of Cisco innovations. A program participant, such as a maker of a WLAN client adapter or client device, implements support for all features and then submits the product to an independent lab for rigorous testing; passing this testing process allows the devices to be marketed as Cisco Compatible client devices. There are four versions of the Cisco Compatible specification, versions 1 through 4. Each version builds on its predecessors; with a few exceptions, every feature that must be supported in one version must also be supported in each subsequent version.

8. An SSID is the identifier—or name—of an ESA, creating a WLAN.

9. A, B, D, E.

10. The WLCs are responsible for putting the wireless client traffic into the appropriate VLAN.

11. C.

12. Some of the advantages of VoWLAN deployments are as follows:

- Enabling access to enterprise unified communications, supporting one phone number and one voice mail per user

- Helping employees eliminate missed calls by providing mobility within a building or campus

- Helping organizations gain control over mobile communications costs by leveraging least-cost call routing and providing call detail recording

- Providing a consistent user experience for improved user satisfaction

13. Some of the requirements that voice adds to a WLAN include the following:

- The network needs to have continuous coverage everywhere a client may roam.

- The end-to-end transmit time must be less than 150 ms.

- The QoS of the VoIP call must be maintained: The end-to-end delay and jitter must be minimized.

- The network must be secure.

14. The four main components of the Cisco voice-ready architecture are as follows:

- VoWLAN clients

- The voice-ready WLAN

- Unified wired or wireless LAN infrastructure

- Cisco Unified Communications and mobility applications

15. A, D, E.

16. When a client re-associates to an AP connected to a new WLC with a Layer 2 roam, the new WLC exchanges mobility messages with the original WLC and the client database entry is *moved* to the new WLC.

With Layer 3 roaming, instead of *moving* the client entry to the new WLC's client database, the original WLC marks the entry for the client in its own client database with an Anchor entry, and *copies* the database entry to the new WLC's client database where it is marked with a Foreign entry.

17. C.

18. True. Separate voice and data VLANs are recommended to support different security features, to support different priorities for voice traffic so that it can be dealt with using minimal delays, and to reduce the chance of data clients crowding the voice VLAN and causing unnecessary traffic overhead and delays.

19. CAC polices the call capacity and allows the number of calls on a channel to be limited to a specified percentage of the bandwidth.

20. A, C.

21. C.

22. C.

23. The radius or size of each voice-ready wireless cell should be −67 dBm. This power level can be achieved either in very small physical areas or in cells that are quite large, depending on the RF characteristics of the environment. Separation of 19 dBm for cells on the same channel is recommended.

24. C, D.

25. Typical steps in an RF site survey process include the following:

Step 1. Define customer requirements.
Step 2. Identify coverage areas and user density.
Step 3. Determine preliminary AP locations.
Step 4. Perform the actual RF site survey.
Step 5. Document the findings.

Chapter 12

1. The embedded Cisco IOS network management tools that support each of the four phases in the application optimization cycle are as follows:

- **Baseline application traffic (measure network data):** NetFlow, NBAR Protocol Discovery, and IP SLAs

- **Optimize to meet objectives (apply policies and prioritize traffic):** QoS, NBAR, Cisco AutoQoS VoIP, and Cisco AutoQoS for the Enterprise

- **Measure, adjust, and verify (use ongoing measurements and proactive adjustments):** NetFlow, NBAR Protocol Discovery, IP SLAs, and syslog

- **Deploy new applications (allocate resources for new applications):** NBAR and NetFlow

2. The Cisco IOS ESM feature provides a programmable framework that allows a network manager to filter, escalate, correlate, route, and customize system logging messages before delivery by the Cisco IOS system message logger.

3. __4__ Warning
  __0__ Emergency
  __1__ Alert
  __3__ Error
  __2__ Critical
  __6__ Informational
  __5__ Notice

4. D.

5. A, B, D, E, F.

6. A, C, D, F.

7. Fields in a flow record that are not key fields are called nonkey fields. Nonkey fields are added to the flow record in the NetFlow cache and exported. With Flexible NetFlow, these nonkey fields are user configurable. Examples of nonkey fields include flow timestamps, BGP next-hop addresses, and IP address subnet masks.

Flexible NetFlow uses the NetFlow 9 export format.

8. A, B, D, E.

9. NBAR PDLMs are application-recognition modules that can be downloaded to add support for a protocol that is not available as part of the native PDLM currently embedded in the Cisco IOS Software release.

10. A, B, C, F.

11. C.

12. B.

13. An SLA is a contract between a network provider and its customers, or between a network department and internal corporate customers, that specifies connectivity and performance agreements for an end-user service. It provides a form of guarantee to customers about the level of user experience.

14. For VoIP traffic, typical maximum one-way latency is 150 ms, packet loss is 1 percent, and jitter is 30 ms.

15. A, C, D.

16. A, B, C, D.

17. An IP SLAs shadow router is a dedicated router for sourcing IP SLAs measurement operations, used when there is a large number of operations (hundreds or thousands) needed on an IP SLAs source.

ACRONYMS AND ABBREVIATIONS

This element identifies abbreviations, acronyms, and initialisms used in this book and in the internetworking industry.

Many of these acronyms and other terms are also described in the Cisco Internetworking Terms and Acronyms resource, available at http://www.cisco.com/en/US/docs/internetworking/terms_acronyms/ita.html.

Acronym	Expanded Term
1RU	one rack unit
2RU	two rack units
AAA	authentication, authorization, and accounting
ABR	Area Border Router
ACE	Application Control Engine
ACK	acknowledgment
ACL	access control list
ACS	access control server
AD	administrative distance
ADU	Aironet Desktop Utility
AES	Advanced Encryption Standard
AH	Authentication Header
ALG	application-level gateway
ANSI	American National Standards Institute
AP	access point
ARCH	Designing Cisco Network Service Architectures
ARP	Address Resolution Protocol
AS	autonomous system
ASA	Adaptive Security Appliance

ASBR   Autonomous System Boundary Router

ASDM   Adaptive Security Device Manager

ASM   Any Source Multicast

ASN   Abstract Syntax Notation

ASR   asymmetric routing

ATA   Advanced Technology Attachment

ATM   Asynchronous Transport Mode

BEEP   Blocks Extensible Exchange Protocol

BASc   Bachelor's degree in applied science

BCMSN   Building Cisco Multilayer Switched Networks

BDR   backup designated router

BFD   bidirectional forwarding detection

BGP   Border Gateway Protocol

bidir-PIM   bidirectional PIM

BPDU   bridge protocol data unit

bps   bits per second

BR   border router

BSCI   Building Scalable Cisco Internetworks

BSR   bootstrap router

BSS   basic service set

BSSID   basic service set identifier

CA   certificate authority

CAC   call admission control

CAM   content-addressable memory

CatOS   Catalyst Operating System

C-BSR   candidate BSR

CCDA   Cisco Certified Design Associate

CCDP   Cisco Certified Design Professional

CCK   Complementary Code Keying

CCKM   Cisco Centralized Key Management

CCIP   Cisco Certified Internetworking Professional

CCNA   Cisco Certified Network Associate

CCNP   Cisco Certified Network Professional

CCSI   Cisco Certified Systems Instructor

CCX   Cisco Compatible Extensions

CDP   Cisco Discovery Protocol

CE   customer edge

CEF   Cisco Express Forwarding

CGMP   Cisco Group Management Protocol

CIFS   Common Internet File System

CLI   command-line interface

CoS   class of service

CPU   central processing unit

C-RP   candidate RP

CS1   Class Selector 1

CSA   Cisco Security Agent

CSM   **1.** Cisco Security Manager
            2. Content Switching Module

CSMA/CA   carrier sense multiple access collision avoidance

CSS   Content Services Switch

CWDM   coarse wavelength-division multiplexing

DAI   Dynamic ARP Inspection

DAS   direct-attached storage

dB   decibel

dBm   dB milliwatt

DDoS   distributed denial of service

DES   Data Encryption Standard

DESGN   Designing for Cisco Internetwork Solutions

DF   designated forwarder

DFC   distributed forwarding card

DH-CHAP   Diffie-Hellman Challenge Handshake Authentication Protocol

DHCP   Dynamic Host Configuration Protocol

DLCI   data-link connection identifier

DM   dense mode

DMA   direct memory access

DMVPN   Dynamic Multipoint VPN

DMZ   demilitarized zone

DNA   Do Not Age

DNS   Domain Name Service or Domain Name System

DoS   denial of service

DR   designated router

DSCP   differentiated services code point

DSSS   Direct Sequence Spread Spectrum

DTCP   dynamic transmit power control

DTP   Dynamic Trunk Protocol

DVMRP   Distance Vector Multicast Routing Protocol

DWDM   dense wavelength-division multiplexing

EAP   Extensible Authentication Protocol

EAP-FAST   Cisco EAP-Flexible Authentication via Secure Tunneling

EAP-GTC   EAP-Generic Token Card

EBGP   Exterior Border Gateway Protocol

ECMP   Equal Cost Multipath

EDCA   Enhanced Distributed Channel Access

EF   expedited forwarding

EIGRP   Enhanced Interior Gateway Routing Protocol

EMS   Ethernet Multipoint Service

EoMPLS   Ethernet over MPLS

EOT   Enhanced Object Tracking

EPL   Ethernet Private Line

ERMS   Ethernet Relay Multipoint Service

ERS   Ethernet Relay Service

ESA   extended service area

ESCON   Enterprise System Connection

ESM   Embedded Syslog Manager

ESP   Encapsulation Security Protocol

EtherIP   Ethernet in IP

EVC   Ethernet virtual circuit

EWS   Ethernet Wire Service

FCIP   Fibre Channel over IP

FCP   Fibre Channel Protocol

FHRP   first-hop redundancy protocol

FIB   Forwarding Information Base

FICON   fiber connectivity

FSPF   Fabric Shortest Path First

FTP   File Transfer Protocol

FWSM   Firewall Services Module

GBIC   gigabit interface converter

GDOI   Group Domain of Interpretation

GE   Gigabit Ethernet

GEC   Gigabit EtherChannel

GET VPN   Group Encrypted Transport VPN

GLBP   Gateway Load Balancing Protocol

GRE   generic routing encapsulation

GSLB   global server load balancing

GSS   Global Site Selector

HBA   host bus adapter

HCA   host channel adapter

HSRP   Hot Standby Router Protocol

HTTP   Hypertext Transfer Protocol

H-VPLS   Hierarchical VPLS

IANA   Internet Assigned Numbers Authority

IBGP   Internal Border Gateway Protocol

IBNS   Identity Based Networking Services

ICMP   Internet Control Message Protocol

IDE   Integrated Drive Electronics

IDS   intrusion detection system

IETF   Internet Engineering Task Force

IGMP   Internet Group Management Protocol

IGMPv1   IGMP Version 1

IGMPv2   IGMP Version 2

IGMPv3   IGMP Version 3

IGP   Interior Gateway Protocol

IKE   Internet Key Exchange

INCITS   InterNational Committee for Information Technology Standards

IOS   Internetwork Operating System

IP   Internet Protocol

IPFIX   IP Flow Information Export

IPM   Internetwork Performance Monitor

IPS   intrusion prevention system

IPsec   IP Security

IP SLA   IP service level agreement

IPv4   IP Version 4

IPv6   IP Version 6

iSCSI   Internet Small Computer Systems Interface

IS-IS   Intermediate System-to-Intermediate System Protocol

ISL   Inter-Switch Link

iSLB   iSCSI Server Load Balancing

ISP   Internet service provider

iSPF   Incremental Shortest-Path First

ISR   Integrated Services Router

ISSU   In-Service Software Update

IVR   Inter-VSAN Routing

JBOD   just a bunch of disks

LACP   Link Aggregation Control Protocol

LAN   local-area network

LANE   LAN Emulation

LDAP   Lightweight Directory Access Protocol

LEAP   Cisco Lightweight Extensible Authentication Protocol

Li-ion   lithium-ion

LSA   link-state advertisement

LSDB   link-state database

LWAPP   Lightweight AP Protocol

MAC   Media Access Control

MADCAP   Multicast Address Dynamic Client Allocation Protocol

MAN   metropolitan area network

MARS   Monitoring, Analysis, and Response System

MASc   Master's degree in applied science

MBGP   Multiprotocol Border Gateway Protocol

MC   multipoint controller

MD5   message digest 5

MDSP   Multicast Source Discovery Protocol

MED   multi-exit discriminator

MIB   Management Information Base

MIC   Message Integrity Check

MIME   Multipurpose Internet Mail Extensions

MISTP   Multiple Instances Spanning Tree Protocol

MLS   multilayer switching

MPLS   Multiprotocol Label Switching

MRTG   Multi Router Traffic Grapher

MSFC   Multilayer Switch Feature Card

MST   Multiple Spanning Tree

MTBF   mean time between failure

MTTR   mean time to repair

MTU   maximum transmission unit

MVPN   Multicast Virtual Private Network

mW   milliwatt

MW   megawatt

NAA   NAC Appliance Agent

NAC   Network Admission Control

NAM   NAC Appliance Manager

NAS   **1.** NAC Appliance Server
2. network-attached storage

NAT   Network Address Translation

NBAR   Network-Based Application Recognition

NBMA   nonbroadcast multiaccess

NDE   NetFlow data export

NDS   Novell Directory Service

NHRP   Next Hop Resolution Protocol

NIC   network interface card

NIPS   network intrusion prevention system

NSSA   not-so-stubby area

NSF   nonstop forwarding

NTP   Network Time Protocol

OADM   optical add/drop multiplexer

OC   Optical Carrier

OER   Optimized Edge Routing

OFDM   orthogonal frequency division multiplexing

OOB   out-of-band

OSA   Open Systems Adapters

OSI   Open Systems Interconnection

OSPF   Open Shortest Path First

OTP   one-time password

PAgP   Port Aggregation Protocol

PAT   Port Address Translation

PBR   policy-based routing

PDLM   Packet Description Language Module

PDM   PIX Device Manager

PE   provider edge

PEAP   Protected Extensible Authentication Protocol

PER   packet error rate

PIM   Protocol Independent Multicast

PIM-DM   PIM dense mode

PIM-SM   PIM sparse mode

PIX   Private Internet Exchange

PKC   Proactive Key Caching

PKI   public key infrastructure

PMP   Project Management Professional

PoE   Power over Ethernet

POP   **1.** point of presence
2. Post Office Protocol

POTS   plain old telephone service/system

PPDIOO   prepare, plan, design, implement, operate, optimize

PSE   power sourcing equipment

PVLAN   private VLAN

PBRST   Per-VLAN Rapid Spanning Tree

PVS   posture validation server

PVST+   Per-VLAN Spanning Tree Plus

QBSS   QoS basic service set

QoS   quality of service

RAID   Redundant Array of Independent/Inexpensive Disks

RDMA   remote direct memory access

RF   radio frequency

RFC   Request For Comments

RHI   Route Health Injection

RIP   Routing Information Protocol

RIPv2   Routing Information Protocol Version 2

ROADM   reconfigurable OADM

RP   rendezvous point

RPF   Reverse Path Forwarding

RPR   Resilient Packet Ring

RPVST   Rapid Per-VLAN Spanning Tree

RRM   radio resource management

RSSI   received signal strength indicator

RTP   Real-Time Transport Protocol

RTR   Response Time Reporter

RTSP   Real Time Streaming Protocol

RTT   round-trip time

RTTMON   Round-Trip Time Monitor

SA   security association

SAA   service assurance agent

SAN   storage-area network

SAP   Session Announcement Protocol

SATA   Serial ATA

SCCP   Skinny Client Control Protocol

SCSI   Small Computer Systems Interface

sd   Session Directory

SDH   Synchronous Digital Hierarchy

SDM   Security Device Manager

SDP   Session Description Protocol

SFP   Small Form-Factor Pluggable

SLA   service level agreement

SLB   server load balancer

SM   single mode

SMTP   Simple Mail Transfer Protocol

SNMP   Simple Network Management Protocol

SNR   signal-to-noise ratio

SOHO   small office/home office

SONA   Service-Oriented Network Architecture

SONET   Synchronous Optical Network

SPA   shared port adapter

SPF   shortest path first algorithm

SPT   shortest path tree

SRP   Spatial Reuse Protocol

SSC   Secure Services Client

SSH   Secure Shell

SSID   service set identifier

SSL   Secure Sockets Layer

SSLM   Secure Sockets Layer Module

SSM   **1.** Source Specific Multicast
2. Storage Services Module

SSO   stateful switchover

STP   Spanning Tree Protocol

SVF   secondary virtual forwarder

TCA   target channel adapter

TCO   total cost of ownership

TCP   Transmission Control Protocol

TDM   time-division multiplexing

TFTP   Trivial File Transfer Protocol

TKIP   Temporal Key Integrity Protocol

TLS   Transport Layer Security

ToS   type of service

Tspec   traffic specification

TTL   Time To Live

UAPSD   Unscheduled Automatic Power Save Delivery

UDLD   UniDirectional Link Detection

UDP   User Datagram Protocol

UNII   Unlicensed National Information Infrastructure

URL   Uniform Resource Locator

UWN   Unified Wireless Network

VACL   VLAN ACL

VAM   VPN Acceleration Module

VIP   virtual IP

VLAN   virtual local-area network

VLSM   variable-length subnet mask

VoD   video on demand

VoIP   Voice over IP

VoWLAN   Voice over WLAN

VPLS   Virtual Private LAN Service

VPN   virtual private network

VRF   virtual routing and forwarding

VRRP   Virtual Router Redundancy Protocol

VSAN   virtual storage-area network

VTI   virtual tunnel interface

VTP   VLAN Trunking Protocol

WAN   wide-area network

WCS   Wireless Control System

Web NS   Web Network Services

WEP   Wired Equivalent Privacy

WINS   Windows Internet Naming Service

WiSM   Wireless Services Module

WLAN   wireless LAN

WLC   WLAN controller

WLCM   WLC Module

WLSE   Wireless LAN Solutions Engine

WMM   Wi-Fi Multimedia

WPA   WiFi Protected Access

WPA2   WPA Version 2

WWW   World Wide Web

XML   Extensible Markup Language

Index

FREE Online Edition

Your purchase of **Designing Cisco Network Service Architectures (ARCH)** includes access to a free online edition for 45 days through the Safari Books Online subscription service. Nearly every CIsco Press book is available online through Safari Books Online, along with more than 5,000 other technical books and videos from publishers such as Addison-Wesley Professional, Exam Cram, IBM Press, O'Reilly, Prentice Hall, Que, and Sams.

SAFARI BOOKS ONLINE allows you to search for a specific answer, cut and paste code, download chapters, and stay current with emerging technologies.

Activate your FREE Online Edition at www.informit.com/safarifree

> **STEP 1:** Enter the coupon code: ILMSLZG.

> **STEP 2:** New Safari users, complete the brief registration form.
> Safari subscribers, just log in.

If you have difficulty registering on Safari or accessing the online edition, please e-mail customer-service@safaribooksonline.com

Addison Wesley · Adobe Press · ALPHA · Cisco Press · FT Press · IBM Press · lynda.com · Microsoft Press · New Riders

O'REILLY · Peachpit Press · PRENTICE HALL · QUE · Redbooks · SAMS · SAS Publishing · Sun Microsystems · Wharton School Publishing · WILEY